By the same author

MAX HASTINGS

Finest Years

Churchill as Warlord 1940–45

Harper
Press

HarperPress
An imprint of HarperCollins*Publishers*
77–85 Fulham Palace Road,
Hammersmith, London W6 8JB
www.harpercollins.com

Published by HarperPress in 2009

2

A catalogue record for this book
is available from the British Library

ISBN 978 0 00 733774 3 (TPB)
ISBN 978 0 00 726367 7 (HB)

Set in Minion by Palimpsest Book Production Limited,
Grangemouth, Stirlingshire

Printed and bound in Great Britain by
Clays Ltd, St Ives plc

Mixed Sources

Product group from well-managed
forests and other controlled sources
www.fsc.org Cert no. SW-COC-1806
© 1996 Forest Stewardship Council

FSC is a non-profit international organization established to promote the
responsible management of the world's forests. Products carrying the
FSC label are independently certified to assure consumers that they come from
forests that are managed to meet the social, economic and ecological needs
of present and future generations.

Find out more about HarperCollins and the environment at
www.harpercollins.co.uk/green

In memory of Roy Jenkins,
and our Indian summer friendship

CONTENTS

ILLUSTRATIONS

Churchill in Whitehall with Halifax in March 1938. *(Getty Images)*
Churchill outside Downing Street in May 1940. *(Getty Images)*
German columns advancing through France in May 1940. *(Imperial War Museum RML193)*
Churchill in Paris on 31 May 1940 with Dill, Attlee and Reynaud. *(Getty Images)*
British troops awaiting evacuation from Dunkirk. *(Imperial War Museum NYP68075)*
Dead British soldier at Dunkirk. *(ECPAD, France)*
Churchill inspecting a roadblock. *(Imperial War Museum H2653)*
The Mid-Devon Hunt patrol Dartmoor.
French warships blaze at Mers-el-Kebir under British bombardment, 3 July 1940. *(Musée National de Marine)*
The Battle of Britain: Hurricane pilots scramble. *(Time & Life Pictures/Getty Images)*
The filter room at RAF Fighter Command, Bentley Priory. *(MoD Air Historical Branch)*
A Luftwaffe Heinkel over the London docks in September 1940. *(Imperial War Museum C5422)*
The blitz: a street scene repeated a thousand times across the cities of Britain. *(Popperfoto/Getty Images)*
Churchill portrayed by Cecil Beaton in the Cabinet Room at 10 Downing Street on 20 November 1940. *(Courtesy of the Cecil Beaton Studio Archive at Sotheby's)*
Blazing shore facilities on Crete in May 1941. *(Imperial War Museum E3104E)*
A Russian soldier surrenders to the Wehrmacht during the first year of Operation *Barbarossa. (BA-MA Koblenz)*
Harry Hopkins and Churchill outside Downing Street on 10 January 1941. *(Getty Images)*

Roosevelt and Churchill at Placentia Bay on 10 August 1941. *(Imperial War Museum H12739)*

British troops advance through a minefield in North Africa. *(Imperial War Museum E18542)*

Some of the tens of thousands of Italian prisoners who fell into British hands during Wavell's Operation *Compass*. *(Imperial War Museum E1591)*

George King. *(Courtesy of Judith Avery)*

Vere Hodgson.

Sir John Kennedy. *(National Portrait Gallery, London)*

Sir Alexander Cadogan. *(Press Association Images)*

Harold Nicolson. *(Getty Images)*

Charles Wilson, Lord Moran. *(National Portrait Gallery, London)*

Hugh Dalton. *(National Portrait Gallery, London)*

Leo Amery. *(Getty Images)*

Cuthbert Headlam. *(Press Association Images)*

Oliver Harvey. *(Press Association Images)*

Lt.Gen. Sir Henry Pownall. *(Imperial War Museum FE556)*

Churchill working on his train. *(Imperial War Museum H10874)*

Churchill viewing new aircraft with Lindemann, Portal and Pound. *(Imperial War Museum H10306)*

Jock Colville's September 1941 farewell to Downing Street. *(Harriet Bowes-Lyon)*

Churchill at the controls of the Boeing Clipper which brought him home from Washington in January 1942. *(Imperial War Museum H16645)*

One of the many Second Front rallies held in Britain in 1942–43. *(Imperial War Museum D4593)*

The Cairo conference, August 1942. *(AP/Press Association Images)*

Harriman and Churchill with Molotov on their arrival in Moscow. *(Imperial War Museum MoI FLM115)*

Dieppe after the disastrous August 1942 raid. *(Imperial War Museum HU1904)*

Soviet troops advance towards Stalingrad. *(The Archive of the Panoramic Museum of the Battle of Stalingrad)*

The British advance at El Alamein, November 1942. *(Imperial War Museum E18807)*

American war leaders at Casablanca, January 1943. *(© Bettmann/Corbis)*

Aneurin Bevan. *(Getty Images)*

Stafford Cripps. *(Getty Images)*

Clement Attlee. *(Getty Images)*

Ernest Bevin. *(Getty Images)*

Lord Beaverbrook. *(Getty Images)*

Churchill with General Anderson at the Roman amphitheatre at Carthage, May 1943. *(Imperial War Museum NA3253)*

US troops advance through Italy. *(NARA)*

Beaufighters attack German shipping off Kos on 3 October 1943. *(Hansjürgen Weissenborn/Anthony Rogers Collection)*

German troops land on Kos. *(Imperial War Museum HU67424)*

Algiers, June 1943. *(Imperial War Museum NA3286)*

Churchill with Clementine in the saloon of his special train in Canada in August 1943. *(Imperial War Museum H32954)*

The 'Big Three' at Tehran on 30 November 1943. *(Imperial War Museum E26640)*

The Anzio landing, January 1944. *(Time & Life Pictures/Getty Images)*

Instructing French *maquisards* on the use of the sten sub-machine gun. *(Getty Images)*

An SOE mission in occupied Yugoslavia. *(Imperial War Museum HU67565)*

American troops approaching the Normandy beaches, 6 June 1944. *(Imperial War Museum EA25641)*

Operation *Overlord*, 6 June 1944. *(Imperial War Museum EA29655)*

Churchill with Alexander in Italy, 26 August 1944. *(Imperial War Museum NA18041)*

Churchill with De Gaulle in Paris on Armistice Day, 11 November 1944. *(Imperial War Museum BU1294)*

Churchill meeting the warring Greek factions in Athens on 26 December 1944. *(Imperial War Museum NAM163)*

King, Brooke, Ismay and Marshall at Yalta in February 1945. *(Liddell Hart Centre for Military Archives)*

Victorious Russian soldiers in Sofia, the Bulgarian capital. *(Courtesy of the Central Museum of the Armed Forces, Moscow)*

Churchill overlooks the Rhine with Brooke and Montgomery in March 1945. *(Liddell Hart Centre for Military Archives)*

On the balcony of Buckingham Palace with the royal family on VE-Day. *(Imperial War Museum MH21835)*

Churchill broadcasts from Downing Street. *(Imperial War Museum H41846)*

Churchill with Truman and Stalin at Potsdam on 17 July 1945. *(Getty Images)*

MAPS

It may well be that the most glorious chapters of our history have yet to be written. Indeed, the very problems and dangers that encompass us and our country ought to make English men and women of this generation glad to be here at such a time. We ought to rejoice at the responsibilities with which destiny has honoured us, and be proud that we are guardians of our country in an age when her life is at stake.

WSC, April 1933

History with its flickering lamp stumbles along the trail of the past, trying to reconstruct its scenes, to revive its echoes, and kindle with pale gleams the passion of former days.

WSC, November 1940

INTRODUCTION

Winston Churchill was the greatest Englishman and one of the greatest human beings of the twentieth century, indeed of all time. Yet beyond that bald assertion there are infinite nuances in considering his conduct of Britain's war between 1940 and 1945, which is the theme of this book. It originated nine years ago, when Roy Jenkins was writing his biography of Churchill. Roy flattered me by inviting my comments on the typescript, chapter by chapter. Some of my suggestions he accepted, many he sensibly ignored. When we reached the Second World War, his patience expired. Exasperated by the profusion of my strictures, he said: 'You're trying to get me to do something which you should write yourself, if you want to!' By that time, his health was failing. He was impatient to finish his own book, which achieved triumphant success.

In the years that followed I thought much about Churchill and the war, mindful of some Boswellian lines about Samuel Johnson: 'He had once conceived the thought of writing The Life Of Oliver Cromwell ... He at length laid aside his scheme, on discovering that all that can be told of him is already in print; and that it is impracticable to procure any authentick information in addition to what the world is already possessed of.' Among the vast Churchillian bibliography, I was especially apprehensive about venturing anywhere near the tracks of David Reynolds's extraordinarily original and penetrating *In Command of History* (2004). The author dissected successive drafts of Churchill's war memoirs, exposing contrasts between judgements on people and events which the old statesman initially proposed to make, and those which he finally deemed it prudent to publish. Andrew Roberts has painted a striking portrait of wartime Anglo–American relations, and especially of the great summit meetings, in *Masters and Commanders* (2008). We have been told more about Winston Churchill than any other human being. Tens of thousands of people of many nations have recorded even the most trifling encounters, noting every word they heard him utter. The most vivid wartime memory of one soldier of Britain's Eighth Army derived from a day in 1942 when he found the prime minister his neighbour in a North African desert latrine. Churchill's speeches and writings fill many volumes.

Yet much remains opaque, because he wished it thus. Always mindful of his role as a stellar performer upon the stage of history, he became supremely so after 10 May 1940. He kept no diary because, he observed, to do so would be to expose his follies and inconsistencies to posterity. Within months of his ascent to the premiership, however, he told his staff that he had already schemed the chapters of the book which he would write as soon as the war was over. The outcome was a ruthlessly partial six-volume work which is poor history, if sometimes peerless prose. We shall never know with complete confidence what he thought about many personalities – for instance Roosevelt, Eisenhower, Alanbrooke, King George VI, his cabinet colleagues – because he took good care not to tell us.

Churchill's wartime relationship with the British people was much more complex than is often acknowledged. Few denied his claims upon the premiership. But between the end of the Battle of Britain in 1940 and the Second Battle of El Alamein in November 1942, not only many ordinary citizens, but also some of his closest colleagues, wanted operational control of the war machine to be removed from his hands, and some other figure appointed to his role as Minister of Defence. It is hard to overstate the embarrassment and even shame of British people as they perceived the Russians playing a heroic part in the struggle against Nazism, while their own army seemed incapable of winning a battle. To understand Britain's wartime experience, it appears essential to recognise, as some narratives do not, the sense of humiliation which afflicted Britain amid the failures of its soldiers, contrasted – albeit often on the basis of wildly false information – with the achievement of Stalin's.

Churchill was dismayed by the performance of the British Army, even after victories began to come at the end of 1942. Himself a hero, he expected others likewise to show themselves heroes. In 1940, the people of Britain, together with their navy and air force, wonderfully fulfilled his hopes. Thereafter, however, much of the story of Britain's part in the war seems to me that of the prime minister seeking more from his own nation and its warriors than they could deliver. The failure of the army to match the prime minister's aspirations is among the central themes of this book.

Much discussion of Britain's military effort in World War II focuses upon Churchill's relationship with his generals. In my view, this preoccupation is overdone. The difficulties of fighting the Germans and Japanese went much deeper than could be solved by changes of commander. The British were beaten again and again between 1940 and 1942, and continued to suffer battlefield difficulties thereafter, in consequence of failures of tactics, weapons, equipment and culture even more significant than lack of mass or inspired leadership. The gulf between Churchillian aspiration and reality extended to the peoples of occupied Europe, hence his faith in 'setting Europe ablaze' through the agency of Special Operations Executive, which had malign consequences that he failed to anticipate. SOE armed many occupied peoples to fight more energetically against each other in 1944–45 than they had done earlier against the Germans.

It is a common mistake, to suppose that those who bestrode the stage during momentous times were giants, set apart from the personalities of our own humdrum society. I have argued in earlier books that we should instead see 1939–45 as a period when men and women not much different from ourselves strove to grapple with stresses and responsibilities which stretched their powers to the limit. Churchill was one of a tiny number of actors who proved worthy of the role in which destiny cast him. Those who worked for the prime minister, indeed the British people at war, served as a supporting cast, seeking honourably but sometimes inadequately to play their own parts in the wake of a titan.

Sir Edward Bridges, then Cabinet Secretary, wrote of Churchill between 1940 and 1942: 'Everything depended upon him and him alone. Only he had the power to make the nation believe that it could win.' This remains the view of most of the world, almost seventy years later. Yet there is also no shortage of iconoclasts. In a recent biography Cambridge lecturer Nigel Knight writes contemptuously of Churchill: 'He was not mad or simple; his misguided decisions were a product of his personality – a mixture of arrogance, emotion, self-indulgence, stubbornness and a blind faith in his own ability.' Another modern biographer, Chris Wrigley, suggests that Sir Edward Bridges' tribute to Churchill 'may over-state his indispensability'.

Such strictures seem otiose to those of us convinced that, in his absence, Britain would have made terms with Hitler after Dunkirk. Thereafter, beyond his domestic achievement as war leader, he performed a diplomatic role of which only he was capable: as suitor of the United States on behalf of the British nation. To fulfil this, he was obliged to overcome intense prejudices on both sides of the Atlantic. So extravagant was Churchill's – and Roosevelt's – wartime rhetoric about the Anglo–American alliance, that even today the extent of mutual suspicion and indeed dislike between the two peoples is often under-estimated. The British ruling class, in particular, condescended amazingly towards Americans.

In 1940–41, Winston Churchill perceived with a clarity which eluded some of his fellow countrymen that only American belliger-ence might open a path to victory. Pearl Harbor, and not the prime minister's powers of seduction, eventually brought Roosevelt's nation into the war. But no other statesman could have conducted British policy towards the United States with such consummate skill, nor have achieved such personal influence upon the American people. This persisted until 1944, when his standing in the US declined precipi-tously, to revive only when the onset of the Cold War caused many Americans to hail Churchill as a prophet. His greatness, which had come to seem too large for his own impoverished country, then became perceived as a shared Anglo-American treasure.

From June 1941 onwards, Churchill saw much more clearly than most British soldiers and politicians that Russia must be embraced as an ally. But it seems important to strip away legends about aid to the Soviet Union, and to acknowledge how small this was in the decisive 1941–42 period. Stalin's nation saved itself with little help from the Western Allies. Only from 1943 onwards did supplies to Russia gain critical mass, and Anglo-American ground operations absorb a significant part of the Wehrmacht's attention. The huge popularity of the Soviet Union in wartime Britain was a source of dismay, indeed exasperation, to the small number of people at the top who knew the truth about the barbarity of Stalin's regime, its hostility to the West, and its imperialistic designs on Eastern Europe.

The divide between the sentiments of the public and those of the prime minister towards the Soviet Union became a chasm in May 1945. One of Churchill's most astonishing acts, in the last weeks of his premiership, was to order the Joint Planning Staff to produce a draft for Operation *Unthinkable*. The resulting document considered the practicability of launching an Anglo-American offensive against the USSR, with forty-seven divisions reinforced by the remains of Hitler's Wehrmacht, to restore the freedom of Poland. Though Churchill recognised this as a remote contingency, it is remarkable that he caused the chiefs of staff to address it at all.

I am surprised how few historians seem to notice that many things which the British and Americans believed they were concealing from the Soviets – for instance, Bletchley Park's penetration of Axis ciphers and Anglo–American arguments about launching a Second Front – were well known to Stalin, through the good offices of communist sympathisers and traitors in Whitehall and Washington. The Soviets knew much more about their allies' secret policy-making than did the British and Americans about that of the Russians.

It is fascinating to study public mood swings through wartime British, American and Russian newspapers, and the diaries of ordinary citizens. These often give a very different picture from that of historians, with their privileged knowledge of how the story ended. As for sentiment at the top, some men who were indifferent politicians or commanders contributed much more as contemporary chroniclers. The diaries of such figures as Hugh Dalton, Leo Amery and Lt.Gen. Henry Pownall make them more valuable to us as eye-witnesses and eavesdroppers than they seemed to their contemporaries as players in the drama.

Maj.Gen. John Kennedy, for much of the war the British Army's Director of Military Operations, kept a diary which arguably ranks second only to that of Gen. Sir Alan Brooke for its insights into the British military high command. On 26 January 1941, in the darkest days of the conflict, Kennedy expressed a fear that selective use of accounts of the meetings of Britain's leaders might mislead posterity:

It would be easy by a cunning or biased selection of evidence to give the impression for instance that the P.M.'s strategic policy was nearly always at fault, & that it was only by terrific efforts that he is kept on the right lines – and it would be easy to do likewise with all the chiefs of staff. The historian who has to deal with the voluminous records of this war will have a frightful task. I suppose no war has been so well documented. Yet the records do not often reveal individual views. It is essentially a government of committees . . . Winston is of course the dominating personality & he has in his entourage and among his immediate advisers no really strong personality. Yet Winston's views do not often prevail if they are contrary to the general trend of opinion among the service staffs. Minutes flutter continually from Winston's typewriter on every conceivable subject. His strategic imagination is inexhaustible and many of his ideas are wild and unsound and impracticable . . . but in the end they are killed if they are not acceptable.

These observations, made in the heat of events, deserve respect from every historian of the period. Another banal and yet critical point is that circumstances and attitudes shifted. The prime minister often changed his mind, and deserves more credit than he sometimes receives for his willingness to do so. Meanwhile, others vacillated in their views of him. Some who revered Churchill in the first months of his premiership later became bitterly sceptical, and vice versa. After Dunkirk, Britain's middle classes were considerably more staunch than some members of its traditional ruling caste, partly because they knew less about the full horror of the country's predicament. History perceives as pivotal Britain's survival through 1940, so that the weariness and cynicism that pervaded the country by 1942, amid continuing defeats, are often underrated. Industrial unrest, manifested in strikes especially in the coalfields, and in the aircraft and ship-building industries, revealed fissures in the fabric of national unity which are surprisingly seldom acknowledged.

This book does not seek to retell the full story of Churchill at war, but rather to present a portrait of his leadership from the day on which he became prime minister, 10 May 1940, set in the context of Britain's national experience. It is weighted towards the first half of the conflict, partly because Churchill's contribution was then much greater than it became later, and partly because I have sought to emphasise issues and events about which there seem new things to be said. There is relatively little in this book about the strategic air offensive. I addressed this earlier in *Bomber Command* and *Armageddon*. I have here confined myself to discussion of the prime minister's personal role in key bombing decisions. I have not described land and naval campaigns in detail, but instead considered the institutional cultures which influenced the performance of the British Army, Royal Navy and RAF, and the three services' relationships with the prime minister.

To maintain coherence, it is necessary to address some themes and episodes which are familiar, though specific aspects deserve reconsideration. There was, for instance, what I have called the second Dunkirk, no less miraculous than the first. Churchill's biggest misjudgement of 1940 was his decision to send more troops to France in June after the rescue of the BEF from the beaches. Only the stubborn insistence of their commander, Lt.Gen. Sir Alan Brooke, made it possible to overcome the rash impulses of the prime minister and evacuate almost 200,000 men who would otherwise have been lost.

The narrative examines some subordinate issues and events in which the prime minister's role was crucial, such as the strategic contribution of SOE – as distinct from romantic tales of its agents' derring-do – the Dodecanese campaign and Churchill's Athens adventure in December 1944. I have attempted little original research in his own papers. Instead, I have explored the impression he made upon others – generals, soldiers, citizens, Americans and Russians. Moscow's closure of key archives to foreign researchers has curtailed the wonderful bonanza of the post-Cold War period. But much important material was published in Russian documentary collections.

It seems mistaken to stint on quotation from Alan Brooke, John Colville and Charles Wilson (Lord Moran), merely because their records have been long in the public domain. Recent research on Moran's manuscript suggests that, rather than being a true contemporary record, much of it was written up afterwards. Yet most of his anecdotes and observations appear credible. The diaries of Churchill's military chief, junior private secretary and doctor provide, for all their various limitations, the most intimate testimony we shall ever have about Churchill's wartime existence.

He himself, of course, bestrides the tale in all his joyous splendour. Even at the blackest periods, when his spirits sagged, flashes of exuberance broke through, which cheered his colleagues and contemporaries, but caused some people to recoil from him. They were dismayed, even disgusted, that he so conspicuously thrilled to his own part in the greatest conflict in human history. 'Why do we regard history as of the past and forget we are making it?' he exulted to Australian prime minister Robert Menzies in 1941. It was this glee which caused such a man as the aesthete and diarist James Lees-Milne to write fastidiously after it was all over: 'Churchill so evidently enjoyed the war that I could never like him. I merely acknowledge him, like Genghis Khan, to have been great.'

Lees-Milne and like-minded critics missed an important aspect of Churchill's attitude to conflict in general, and to the Second World

War in particular. He thrilled to the cannon's roar, and rejoiced in its proximity to himself. Yet never for a moment did he lose his sense of dismay about the death and destruction that war visited upon the innocent. 'Ah, horrible war, amazing medley of the glorious and the squalid, the pitiful and the sublime,' he wrote as a correspondent in South Africa in January 1900. 'If modern men of light and leading saw your face closer simple folk would see it hardly ever.' Hitler was indifferent to the sufferings his policies imposed upon mankind. Churchill never flinched from the necessity to pay in blood for the defeat of Nazi tyranny. But his sole purpose was to enable the guns to be silenced, the peoples of the world restored to their peaceful lives.

Appetite for the fray was among Churchill's most convincing credentials for national leadership in May 1940. Neville Chamberlain had many weaknesses as prime minister, but foremost among them was a revulsion from the conflict to which his country was committed, shared by many members of his government. One of them, Rob Bernays, said: 'I wish I were twenty. I cannot bear this responsibility.' A nation which found itself committed to a life-and-death struggle against one of the most ruthless tyrannies in history was surely wise to entrust its leadership to a man eager to embrace the role, rather than one who shrank from it. This book discusses Churchill's follies and misjudgements, which were many and various. But these are as pimples upon the mountain of his achievement. It is sometimes said that the British and American peoples are still today, in the twenty-first century, indecently obsessed with the Second World War. The reason is not far to seek. We know that here was something which our parents and grandparents did well, in a noble cause that will forever be identified with the person of Winston Churchill, warlord extraordinary.

Max Hastings
Chilton Foliat, Berkshire
May 2009

ONE

The Battle of France

For seven months after the Second World War began in September 1939, many British people deluded themselves that it might gutter out before there was a bloodbath in the West. On 5 April 1940, while the armed but passive confrontation which had persisted since the fall of Poland still prevailed on the Franco–German border, prime minister Neville Chamberlain told a Conservative Party meeting: 'Hitler has missed the bus.' Less than five weeks later, however, on 7 May, he addressed the House of Commons to explain the disastrous outcome of Britain's campaign to frustrate the German occupation of Norway. Beginning with a tribute to British troops who had 'carried out their task with magnificent gallantry', in halting tones he continued:

> I hope that we shall not exaggerate the extent or the importance of the check we have received. The withdrawal from southern Norway is not comparable to the withdrawal from Gallipoli ... There were no large forces involved. Not much more than a single division ... Still, I am quite aware ... that some discouragement has been caused to our friends, and that our enemies are crowing ... I want to ask hon. Members not to form any hasty opinions on the result of the Norwegian campaign so far as it has gone ... A minister who shows any sign of confidence is always called complacent. If he fails to do so, he is labelled defeatist. For my part I try to steer a middle course – [Interruption] – neither raising undue expectations [Hon. Members: 'Hitler missed the bus'] which are unlikely to be fulfilled, nor making

people's flesh creep by painting pictures of unmitigated gloom. A great many times some hon. Members have repeated the phrase 'Hitler missed the bus' – [Hon. Members: 'You said it'] . . . While I retain my complete confidence on our ultimate victory, I do not think that the people of this country yet realise the extent or the imminence of the threat which is impending against us [An Hon. Member: 'We said that five years ago'].

When the debate ended the following night, thirty-three Tories voted against their own party on the Adjournment Motion, and a further sixty abstained. Though Chamberlain retained a parliamentary majority, it was plain that his Conservative government had lost the nation's confidence. This was not merely the consequence of the Norway campaign, but because through eight fumbling months it had exposed its lack of stomach for war. An all-party coalition was indispensable. Labour would not serve under Chamberlain. Winston Churchill became Britain's prime minister following a meeting between himself, Chamberlain, Foreign Secretary Lord Halifax and Tory chief whip David Margesson on the afternoon of 9 May 1940, at which Halifax declared his own unsuitability for the post, as a member of the House of Lords who would be obliged to delegate direction of the war to Churchill in the Commons. In truth, some expedient could have been adopted to allow the Foreign Secretary to return to the Commons. But Halifax possessed sufficient self-knowledge to recognise that no more than Neville Chamberlain did he possess the stuff of a war leader.

While much of the ruling class disliked and mistrusted the new premier, he was the overwhelming choice of the British people. With remarkably sure instinct, they perceived that if they must wage war, the leadership of a warrior was needed. David Reynolds has observed that when the Gallipoli campaign failed in 1915, many people wished to blame Churchill – then, as in 1940, First Lord of the Admiralty – while after Norway nobody did. 'It was a marvel,' Churchill wrote in an unpublished draft of his war memoirs, 'I really do not know how – I survived and maintained my position in public esteem while all the blame was thrown on poor Mr Chamberlain.' He may also have perceived his own good fortune that he had not achieved the highest office in earlier years, or even in the earlier months of the war. Had he done so, it is likely that by May 1940 his country would have tired of the excesses which he would surely have committed, while being no more capable than Chamberlain of stemming the tide of fate on the Continent. Back in 1935, Stanley Baldwin explained to a friend his unwillingness to appoint Churchill to his own cabinet: 'If there is going to be a war – and who can say there is not – we must keep him fresh to be our war Prime Minister.' Baldwin's tone was jocular and patronising, yet there proved to be something in what he said.

In May 1940 only generals and admirals knew the extent of Churchill's responsibility for Britain's ill-starred Scandinavian deployments. Nonetheless the familiar view, that he was sole architect of disaster, seems overstated. Had British troops been better trained, motivated and led, they would have made a better showing against Hitler's forces, which repeatedly worsted them in Norway while often inferior in numbers. The British Army's failure reflected decades of neglect, together with institutional weaknesses that would influence the fortunes of British arms through the years which followed. These were symbolically attested by a colonel who noticed among officers' baggage being landed at Namsos on the central Norwegian coast 'several fishing rods and many sporting guns'. No German officer would have gone to war with such frivolous accoutrements.

Now Halifax wrote disdainfully to a friend: 'I don't think WSC will be a very good PM though . . . the country will think he gives them a fillip.' The Foreign Secretary told his junior minister R.A. Butler, when they discussed his own refusal to offer himself for the premiership: 'It's all a great pity. You know my reasons, it's no use discussing that – but the gangsters will shortly be in complete control.' Humbler folk disagreed. Lancashire housewife Nella Last wrote in her diary on 11 May: 'If I had to spend my whole life with a man, I'd choose Mr Chamberlain, but I think I would sooner have Mr Churchill if there was a storm and I was shipwrecked. He has a funny face, like a bulldog living in our street who has done more to drive out unwanted dogs and cats ... than all the complaints of householders.' London correspondent Mollie Panter-Downes told *New Yorker* readers: 'Events are moving so fast that England acquired a new Premier almost absent-mindedly ... It's paradoxical but true that the British, for all their suspicious dislike of brilliance, are beginning to think they'd be safer with a bit of dynamite around.' National Labour MP Harold Nicolson, a poor politician but a fine journalist and diarist, wrote in the *Spectator* of Churchill's 'Elizabethan zest for life ... His wit ... rises high in the air like some strong fountain, flashing in every sunbeam, and renewing itself with ever-increasing jets and gusts of image and association.'

Though Churchill's appointment was made by the King on the advice of Chamberlain, rather than following any elective process, popular acclaim bore him to the premiership – and to the role as Minister of Defence which he also appropriated. Tory MP Leo Amery was among those sceptical that Churchill could play so many parts: 'How Winston thinks that he can be Prime Minister, co-ordinator of defence and leader of the House all at once, is puzzling, and confirms my belief that he really means the present arrangement to be temporary. Certainly no one can coordinate defence properly who is not prepared to be active head of the three Chiefs of Staff and in fact directly responsible for plans.' Critics were still expressing dismay about Churchill's joint role as national leader and defence minister three years later. Yet this was prompted not by mere personal conceit, but by dismay at the shocking lack of coordination between the services which characterised the Norway campaign. And posterity perceives, as did he himself at the time, that beyond his own eagerness to run Britain's war machine, there was no other political or military figure to whom delegation of such power would have been appropriate.

In one of the most famous and moving passages of his memoirs, Churchill declared himself on 10 May 'conscious of a profound sense of relief. At last I had the authority to give directions over the whole scene. I felt as if I were walking with destiny, and that all my past life had been but a preparation for this hour and this trial.' He thrilled to his own ascent to Britain's leadership. Perhaps he allowed himself a twitch of satisfaction that he could at last with impunity smoke cigars through cabinet meetings, a habit that had annoyed his predecessor. If, however, he cherished a belief that it would be in his gift to shape strategy, events immediately disabused him.

At dawn on 10 May, a few hours before Churchill was summoned to Buckingham Palace, Hitler's armies stormed across the frontiers of neutral Holland, Belgium and Luxembourg. Captain David Strangeways, serving with the British Expeditionary Force near Lille just inside the French border, bridled at the impertinence of an orderly room clerk who rushed into the quarters where he lay abed shouting: 'David, sir, David!' Then the officer realised that the clerk was passing the order for Operation *David*, the BEF's advance from the fortified line which it had held since the previous autumn, deep into Belgium to meet the advancing Germans. Though the Belgians had declared themselves neutrals since 1936, Allied war planning felt obliged to anticipate an imperative requirement to offer them aid if Germany violated their territory.

David perfectly fulfilled Hitler's predictions and wishes. On 10 May the British, together with the French First and Seventh Armies, hastened to abandon laboriously prepared defensive positions. They mounted their trucks and armoured vehicles, then set off in long columns eastward towards the proffered 'matador's cloak', in Liddell Hart's phrase, which the Germans flourished before them in Belgium. Further south in the Ardennes forest, Panzer columns thrashed forward to launch one of the war's great surprises, a thrust at the centre of the Allied line, left inexcusably weak by the deployments of the Allied supreme commander, France's General Maurice Gamelin. Guderian's and Reinhardt's tanks, racing for the Meuse, easily brushed aside French cavalry posturing in their path. Luftwaffe paratroops and glider-borne forces burst upon the Dutch and Belgian frontier fortresses. Stukas and Messerschmitts poured bombs and machine-gun fire upon bewildered formations of four armies.

May 1940 deployments

No more than his nation did the prime minister grasp the speed of approaching catastrophe. The Allied leaders supposed themselves at the beginning of a long campaign. The war was already eight months old, but thus far neither side had displayed impatience for a decisive confrontation. The German descent on Scandinavia was a sideshow. Hitler's assault on France promised the French and British armies the opportunity, so they supposed, to confront his legions on level terms. The paper strengths of the two sides in the west were similar – about 140 divisions apiece, of which just ten were British. Allied commanders and governments believed that weeks, if not months, would elapse before the critical clash came. Churchill retired to bed on the night of 10 May knowing that the Allies' strategic predicament was grave, but bursting with thoughts and plans, and believing that he had time to implement them.

Events which tower in the perception of posterity must at the time compete for attention with trifles. The BBC radio announcer who told the nation of the German invasion of Belgium and Holland followed this by reporting: 'British troops have landed in Iceland,' as if the second news item atoned for the first. *The Times* of 11 May 1940 reported the issue of an arrest warrant at Brighton bankruptcy court for a playwright named Walter Hackett, said to have fled to America. An army court martial was described, at which a colonel was charged with 'undue familiarity' with a sergeant in his searchlight unit. What would soldiers think, demanded the prosecutor, on hearing a commanding officer address a sergeant as 'Eric'? Advertisements for Player's cigarettes exhorted smokers: 'When cheerfulness is in danger of disturbance, light a Player . . . with a few puffs put trouble in its proper place.' The Irish Tourist Association promised: 'Ireland will welcome you.' On the front page, a blue Persian cat was offered for sale at £2.10s: 'house-trained: grandsire Ch. Laughton Laurel; age 7 weeks – Bachelor, Grove Place, Aldenham'. Among Business Offers, a 'Gentleman with extensive experience wishes join established business, Town or Country, capital available.' A golf report on the sports page was headed: 'What the public want.' There was a poem by Walter de la Mare:

'O lovely England, whose ancient peace/War's woful dangers strain and fret.'

The German blitzkrieg was reported under a double-column headline: 'Hitler strikes at the Low Countries'. Commentaries variously asserted: 'Belgians confident of victory; ten times as strong as in 1914'; 'The side of Holland's economic life of greatest interest to Hitler is doubtless her agricultural and allied activities'; 'The Military Outlook: No Surprise This Time'. *The Times*'s editorial column declared: 'It may be taken as certain that every detail has been prepared for an instant strategic reply . . . The Grand Alliance of our time for the destruction of the forces of treachery and oppression is being steadily marshalled.'

A single column at the right of the main news, on page six, proclaimed: 'New prime minister. Mr Churchill accepts'. The newspaper's correspondence was dominated by discussion of Parliament's Norway debate three days earlier, which had precipitated the fall of Chamberlain. Mr Geoffrey Vickers urged that Lord Halifax was by far the best-qualified minister to lead a national government, assisted by a Labour leader of the Commons. Mr Quintin Hogg, Tory MP for Oxford, noted that many of those who had voted against the government were serving officers. Mr Henry Morris-Jones, Liberal MP for Denbigh, deplored the vote that had taken place, observing complacently that he himself had abstained. The news from France was mocked by a beautiful spring day, with bluebells and primroses everywhere in flower.

'Chips' Channon, millionaire Tory MP, diarist and consummate ass, wrote on 10 May: 'Perhaps the darkest day in English history . . . We were all sad, angry and felt cheated and out-witted.' His distress was inspired by the fall of Chamberlain, not the blitzkrieg in France. Churchill himself knew better than any man how grudgingly he had been offered the premiership, and how tenuous was his grasp on power. Much of the Conservative Party hated him, not least because he had twice in his life 'ratted' – changed sides in the House of Commons. He was remembered as architect of the disastrous 1915 Gallipoli campaign, 1919 sponsor of war against the Bolsheviks in

Russia, 1933–34 opponent of Indian self-government, 1936 supporter of King Edward VIII in the Abdication crisis, savage backbench critic of both Baldwin and Chamberlain, Tory prime ministers through his own 'wilderness years'.

In May 1940, while few influential figures questioned Churchill's brilliance or oratorical genius, they perceived his career as wreathed in misjudgements. Robert Rhodes-James subtitled his 1970 biography of Churchill before he ascended to the premiership *A Study in Failure*. As early as 1914, the historian A.G. Gardiner wrote an extraordinarily shrewd and admiring assessment of Churchill, which concluded equivocally: ' "Keep your eye on Churchill" should be the watchword of these days. Remember, he is a soldier first, last and always. He will write his name big on our future. Let us take care he does not write it in blood.'

Now, amidst the crisis precipitated by Hitler's blitzkrieg, Churchill's contemporaries could not forget that he had been wrong about much even in the recent past, and even in the military sphere in which he professed expertise. During the approach to war, he described the presence of aircraft over the battlefield as a mere 'additional complication'. He claimed that modern anti-tank weapons neutered the powers of 'the poor tank', and that 'the submarine will be mastered . . . There will be losses, but nothing to affect the scale of events.' On Christmas Day 1939 he wrote to Sir Dudley Pound, the First Sea Lord: 'I feel we may compare the position now very favourably with that of 1914.' He had doubted that the Germans would invade Scandinavia. When they did so, Churchill told the Commons on 11 April: 'In my view, which is shared by my skilled advisers, Herr Hitler has committed a grave strategic error in spreading the war so far to the north . . . We shall take all we want of this Norwegian coast now, with an enormous increase in the facility and the efficiency of our blockade.' Even if some of Churchill's false prophecies and mistaken expressions of confidence were unknown to the public, they were common currency among ministers and commanders.

His claim upon his country's leadership rested not upon his contribution to the war since September 1939, which was equivocal,

but upon his personal character and his record as a foe of appeasement. He was a warrior to the roots of his soul, who found his being
upon battlefields. He was one of the few British prime ministers to
have killed men with his own hand – at Omdurman in 1898. Now
he wielded a sword symbolically, if no longer physically, amid a
British body politic dominated by men of paper, creatures of committees and conference rooms. 'It may well be,' he enthused six years
before the war, 'that the most glorious chapters of our history have
yet to be written. Indeed, the very problems and dangers that encompass us and our country ought to make English men and women of
this generation glad to be here at such a time. We ought to rejoice
at the responsibilities with which destiny has honoured us, and be
proud that we are guardians of our country in an age when her life
is at stake.' Leo Amery had written in March 1940: 'I am beginning
to come round to the idea that Winston with all his failings is the
one man with real war drive and love of battle.' So he was, of course.
But widespread fears persisted, that this erratic genius might lead
Britain in a rush towards military disaster.

Few of the ministers whom he invited to join his all-party coalition were equal to the magnitude of their tasks. If this is true of
all governments at all times, it was notably unfortunate now. Twenty-
one out of thirty-six senior office-holders were, like Halifax, David
Margesson, Kingsley Wood and Chamberlain himself, veterans of the
previous discredited administration. 'Winston has not been nearly
bold enough with his changes and is much too afraid of the
[Conservative] Party,' wrote Amery, who had led the Commons
charge against Chamberlain.

Of the Labour recruits – notably Clement Attlee, A.V. Alexander,
Hugh Dalton, Arthur Greenwood and Ernest Bevin – only Bevin was
a personality of the first rank, though Attlee as deputy prime minister
would provide a solid bulwark. Sir Archibald Sinclair, the Liberal
leader who had served as an officer under Churchill in France in
1916 and now became Secretary for Air, was described by those
contemptuous of his subservience to the new prime minister as 'head
of school's fag'. Churchill's personal supporters who received office

or promotion, led by Anthony Eden, Lord Beaverbrook, Brendan Bracken and Amery, were balefully regarded not only by Chamberlain loyalists, but also by many sensible and informed people who were willing to support the new prime minister, but remained sceptical of his associates.

Much of the political class thought Churchill's administration would be short-lived. 'So at last that man has gained his ambition,' an elderly Tory MP, Cuthbert Headlam, noted sourly. 'I never thought he would. Well – let us hope that he makes good. I have never believed in him. I only hope that my judgement . . . will be proved wrong.' The well-known military writer Captain Basil Liddell Hart wrote gloomily on 11 May: 'The new War Cabinet appears to be a group devoted to "victory" without regard to its practical possibility.' Lord Hankey, veteran Whitehall *éminence grise* and a member of the new government, thought it 'perfectly futile for war' and Churchill himself a 'rogue elephant'.

Even as Hitler's Panzer columns drove for Sedan and pushed onward through Holland and Belgium, Churchill was filling lesser government posts, interviewing new ministers, meeting officials. On the evening of 10 May Sir Edward Bridges, the shy, austere Cabinet Secretary, called at Admiralty House, where Churchill still occupied the desk from which he had presided as First Lord. Bridges decided that it would be unbecoming for an official who until that afternoon had been serving a deposed prime minister, too obsequiously to welcome the new one. He merely said cautiously: 'May I wish you every possible good fortune?' Churchill grunted, gazed intently at Bridges for a moment, then said: 'Hum. "Every good fortune!" I like that! These other people have all been congratulating me. Every good fortune!'

At Churchill's first meeting with the chiefs of staff as prime minister on 11 May, he made two interventions, both trifling: he asked whether the police should be armed when sent to arrest enemy aliens, and he pondered the likelihood of Sweden joining the war on the Allied side. Even this most bellicose of men did not immediately attempt to tinker with the movements of Britain's army on the Continent. When Eden, the new Secretary for War, called on the prime minister that day, he noted in his diary that Churchill 'seemed well satisfied with the way events were shaping'. If these words reflected a failure to perceive the prime minister's inner doubts, it is certainly true that he did not perceive the imminence of disaster.

Churchill cherished a faith in the greatness of France, the might of her armed forces, most touching in a statesman of a nation traditionally wary of its Gallic neighbour. 'In Winston's eyes,' wrote his doctor later, 'France is civilisation.' Even after witnessing the German conquest of Poland and Scandinavia, Churchill understood little about the disparity between the relative fighting powers of Hitler's Wehrmacht and Luftwaffe, and those of the French and British armies and air forces. He, like almost all his advisers, deemed it unthinkable that the Germans could achieve a breakthrough against France's Maginot Line and the combined mass of French, British, Dutch and Belgian forces.

In the days that followed his ascent to Downing Street on 10 May, Churchill set about galvanising the British machinery of war and government for a long haul. As war leader, he expected to preside over Britain's part in a massive and protracted clash on the Continent. His foremost hope was that this would entail no such slaughter as that which characterised the 1914–18 conflict. If he cherished no expectation of swift victory, he harboured no fear of decisive defeat. On 13 May, headlines in *The Times* asserted confidently: 'BRITISH FORCES MOVING ACROSS BELGIUM – SUCCESSFUL ENCOUNTERS WITH ENEMY – RAF STRIKES AGAIN'.

Addressing the Commons that day, the prime minister apologised for his brevity: 'I hope that . . . my friends . . . will make allowance, all allowance, for any lack of ceremony with which it has been necessary to act . . . We have before us an ordeal of the most grievous kind. We have before us many, many long months of struggle and of suffering . . . But I take up my task with buoyancy and hope. I feel sure that our cause will not be suffered to fail among men. At this time I feel entitled to claim the aid of all, and I say: "Come then, let us go forward together with our united strength."'

Churchill's war speeches are usually quoted in isolation. This obscures the bathos of remarks by backbench MPs which followed those of the prime minister. On 13 May, Major Sir Philip Colfox, West Dorset, said that although the country must now pursue national unity, he himself much regretted that Neville Chamberlain had been removed from the premiership. Sir Irving Albery, Gravesend, recalled the new prime minister's assertion: 'My policy is a policy of war.' Albery said he thought it right to praise his predecessor's commitment to the cause of peace. Colonel John Gretton, Burton, injected a rare note of realism by urging the House not to waste words, when 'the enemy is almost battering at our gates'. The bleakest indication of the Conservative Party's temper came from the fact that while Neville Chamberlain was cheered as he entered the chamber that day, Churchill's appearance was greeted with resentful Tory silence.

This, his first important statement, received more applause from abroad than it did from some MPs. The *Philadelphia Inquirer* editorialised: 'He proved in this one short speech that he was not afraid to face the truth and tell it. He proved himself an honest man as well as a man of action. Britain has reason to be enheartened by his brevity, his bluntness and his courage.' *Time* magazine wrote: 'That smart, tough, dumpy little man, Prime Minister Winston Churchill, knows how to face facts . . . Great Britain's tireless old firebrand has changed the character of Allied warmongering.'

That day, 13 May, the threat of German air attack on Britain caused Churchill to make his first significant military decision: he rejected a proposal for further fighter squadrons to be sent to France to reinforce the ten already committed. But while the news from the Continent was obviously bleak, he asserted that he was 'by no means sure that the great battle was developing'. He still cherished hopes of turning the tide in Norway, signalling to Admiral Lord Cork and Orrery on 14 May: 'I hope you will get Narvik cleaned up as soon as possible, and then work southward with increasing force.'

Yet the Germans were already bridging the Meuse at Sedan and Dinant, south of Brussels, for their armoured columns emerging from the Ardennes forests. A huge gap was opening between the

French Ninth Army, which was collapsing, and the Second on its left. Though the BEF in Belgium was still not seriously engaged, its C-in-C Lord Gort appealed for air reinforcements. Gort commanded limited confidence. Like all British generals, he lacked training and instincts for the handling of large forces. One of the army's cleverest staff officers, Colonel Ian Jacob of the war cabinet secretariat, wrote: 'We have for twenty years thought little about how to win big campaigns on land; we have been immersed in our day-to-day imperial police activities.'

This deficiency, of plausible 'big battlefield' commanders, would dog British arms throughout the war. Gort was a famously brave officer who had won a VC in World War I, and still carried himself with a boyish enthusiasm. Maj.Gen. John Kennedy, soon to become Director of Military Operations at the War Office, described the BEF's C-in-C as 'a fine fighting soldier' – a useful testimonial for a platoon commander. In blunter words, the general lacked brains, as do most men possessed of the suicidal courage necessary to win a Victoria Cross or Medal of Honor. A shrewd American categorised both Gort and the Chief of the Imperial General Staff, Sir Edmund Ironside, as 'purely physical soldiers who had no business in such high places'. Yet Sir Alan Brooke or Sir Bernard Montgomery would have been no more capable of averting disaster in 1940, with the small forces available to the BEF. Unlike most of Continental Europe, Britain had no peacetime conscription for military service until 1939, and thus no large potential reserves for mobilisation. The army Gort commanded was, in spirit, the imperial constabulary of inter-war years, starved of resources for a generation.

On 14 May, for the first time Churchill glimpsed the immensity of the Allies' peril. Paul Reynaud, France's prime minister, telephoned from Paris, reporting the German breakthrough and asking for the immediate dispatch of a further ten RAF fighter squadrons. The chiefs of staff committee and the war cabinet, which met successively at 6 and 7 o'clock, agreed that Britain's home defences should not be thus weakened. At seven next morning, the 15th, Reynaud telephoned personally to Churchill. The Frenchman spoke emotionally, asserting in English: 'The battle is lost.' Churchill urged him to steady himself, pointing out that only a small part of the French army was engaged, while the German spearheads were now far extended and thus should be vulnerable to flank attack.

When Churchill reported the conversation to his political and military chiefs, the question of further air support was raised once more. Churchill was briefly minded to accede to Reynaud's pleas. But Chamberlain sided with Air Chief Marshal Sir Hugh Dowding, C-in-C of Fighter Command, who passionately demurred. No further fighters were committed. That day Jock Colville, the prime minister's twenty-five-year-old junior private secretary and an aspiring Pepys, noted in his diary the understated concerns of Maj.Gen. Hastings 'Pug' Ismay, chief of staff to Churchill in his capacity as Minister of Defence. Ismay was 'not too happy about the military situation. He says the French are not fighting properly: they are, he points out, a volatile race and it may take them some time to get into a warlike mood.'

Sluggish perception lagged dreadful reality. Churchill cabled to US president Franklin Roosevelt: 'I think myself that the battle on land has only just begun, and I should like to see the masses engage. Up to the present, Hitler is working with specialized units in tanks and air.' He appealed for American aid, and for the first time begged the loan of fifty old destroyers. Washington had already vetoed a request that a British aircraft-carrier should dock at an American port to embark uncrated, battle-ready fighters. This would breach the US Neutrality Act, said the president. So too, he decided, would the dispatch of destroyers.

In France on the 15th, the RAF's inadequate Battle and Blenheim bombers suffered devastating losses attempting to break the Germans' Meuse pontoon bridges. A watching Panzer officer wrote: 'The summer landscape with the quietly flowing river, the light green of the meadows bordered by the darker summits of the more distant heights, spanned by a brilliantly blue sky, is filled with the racket of war . . . Again and again an enemy aircraft crashes out of the sky, dragging a long black plume of smoke behind it . . . Occasionally from the falling machines one or two white parachutes release themselves and float slowly to earth.' The RAF's sacrifice was anyway too late. Much of the German armour was already across the Meuse, and racing westward.

On the morning of the 16th it was learned in London that the Germans had breached the Maginot Line. The war cabinet agreed to deploy four further fighter squadrons to operate over the battle-field. At 3 o'clock that afternoon the prime minister flew to Paris, accompanied by Ismay and Gen. Sir John Dill, Ironside's Vice-CIGS. Landing at Le Bourget, for the first time they perceived the desper-ation of their ally. France's generals and politicians were waiting upon defeat. As the leaders of the two nations conferred at the Quai d'Orsay, officials burned files in the garden. When Churchill asked about French reserves for a counter-attack, he was told that these were already committed piecemeal. Reynaud's colleagues did not conceal their bitterness at Britain's refusal to dispatch further fighters. At every turn of the debate, French shoulders shrugged. From the British embassy that evening, Churchill cabled the war cabinet urging the dispatch of six more squadrons. 'I . . . emphasise the mortal gravity of the hour,' he wrote. The chief of air staff, Sir Cyril Newall, proposed a compromise: six further squadrons should operate over France from their British airfields. At 2 a.m., Churchill drove to Reynaud's flat to communicate the news. The prime minister thereafter returned to the embassy, slept soundly despite occasional distant gunfire, then flew home via Hendon, where he landed before 9 a.m. on the 17th.

He wore a mask of good cheer, but was no longer in doubt about the catastrophe threatening the Allies. He understood that it had become essential for the BEF to withdraw from its outflanked pos-itions in Belgium. Back in Downing Street, after reporting to the war cabinet he set about filling further minor posts in his government, telephoning briskly to prospective appointees, twelve that day in all. Harold Nicolson recorded a typical conversation:

'Harold, I think it would be wise if you joined the Government and helped Duff [Cooper] at the Ministry of Information.'

16

'There is nothing I should like better.'

'Well, fall in tomorrow. The list will be out tonight. That all right?'

'Very much all right.'

'OK.'

Sir Edward Bridges and other Whitehall officials were impressed by Churchill's 'superb confidence', the 'unhurried calm with which he set about forming his government'. At the outset, this reflected failure to perceive the immediacy of disaster. Within days, however, there was instead a majestic determination that his own conduct should be seen to match the magnitude of the challenge he and his nation faced. From the moment Churchill gained the premiership, he displayed a self-discipline which had been conspicuously absent from most of his career. In small things as in great, he won the hearts of those who became his intimates at Downing Street. 'What a beautiful handwriting,' he told Jock Colville when the private secretary showed him a dictated telegram. 'But, my dear boy, when I say stop you must write stop and not just put a blob.' Embracing his staff as an extension of his family, it never occurred to him to warn them against repeating his confidences. He took it for granted that they would not do so – and was rewarded accordingly.

Churchill lunched on 17 May at the Japanese embassy. Even in such circumstances, diplomatic imperatives pressed. Japan's expansionism was manifest. Everything possible must be done to promote its quiescence. That afternoon he dispatched into exile former Foreign Secretary Sir Samuel Hoare, most detested of the old appeasers, to become ambassador to Spain. He also established economic committees to address trade, food and transport. A series of telegrams arrived from France, reporting further German advances. Churchill asked Chamberlain, as Lord President, to assess the implications of the fall of Paris – and of the BEF's possible withdrawal from the Continent through the Channel ports. His day, which had begun in Paris, ended with dinner at Admiralty House in the company of Lord Beaverbrook and Brendan Bracken.

Posterity owes little to Churchill's wayward son Randolph, but a debt is due for his account of a visit to Admiralty House on the morning of 18 May:

> I went up to my father's bedroom. He was standing in front of his basin and shaving with his old-fashioned Valet razor . . .
>
> 'Sit down, dear boy, and read the papers while I finish shaving.' I did as told. After two or three minutes of hacking away, he half turned and said: 'I think I see my way through.' He resumed his shaving. I was astounded, and said: 'Do you mean that we can avoid defeat?' (which seemed credible) 'or beat the bastards?' (which seemed incredible).
>
> He flung his Valet razor into the basin, swung around and said: –
> 'Of course I mean we can beat them.'
>
> Me: 'Well, I'm all for it, but I don't see how you can do it.'
>
> By this time he had dried and sponged his face and turning round to me, said with great intensity: 'I shall drag the United States in.'

Here was a characteristic Churchillian flash of revelation. The prospect of American belligerence was remote. For years, Neville Chamberlain had repeatedly and indeed rudely cold-shouldered advances from Franklin Roosevelt. Yet already the new prime minister recognised that US aid alone might make Allied victory possible. Eden wrote that day: 'News no worse this morning, but seems to me too early to call it better. PM and CIGS gave, however, optimistic survey to Cabinet.' Whatever Churchill told his colleagues, he was now obliged to recognise the probability – though, unlike France's generals, he refused to bow to its inevitability – of German victory on the Continent. Reports from the battlefield grew steadily graver. Churchill urged the chiefs of staff to consider bringing large reinforcements from India and Palestine, and holding back some tank units then in transit from Britain to the BEF. The threat of a sudden German descent on England, spearheaded by paratroops, seized his imagination, unrealistic though it was.

A Home Intelligence report suggested to the government that national morale was badly shaken: 'It must be remembered that the defence of the Low Countries had been continually built up in the press . . . Not one person in a thousand could visualise the Germans breaking through into France . . . A relieved acceptance of Mr Churchill as prime minister allowed people to believe that a change of leadership would, in itself, solve the consequences of Mr Chamberlain. Reports sent in yesterday and this morning show that disquiet and personal fear have returned.'

That evening of 18 May, the war cabinet agreed that Churchill should broadcast to the nation, making plain the gravity of the emergency. Ministers were told that Mussolini had rejected Britain's proposal for an Italian declaration of neutrality. This prompted navy minister A.V. Alexander to urge the immediate occupation of Crete, as a base for operations against Italy in the Mediterranean. Churchill dismissed the idea out of hand, saying that Britain was much too committed elsewhere to embark upon gratuitous adventures.

On the morning of Sunday, 19 May, it was learned that the BEF had evacuated Arras, increasing the peril of its isolation from the main French forces. Emerging together from a meeting, Ironside said to Eden: 'This is the end of the British Empire.' The Secretary for War noted: 'Militarily, I did not see how he could be gainsaid.' Yet it was hard for colleagues to succumb to despair when their leader marvellously sustained his wit. That same bleak Sunday, the prime minister said to Eden: 'About time number 17 turned up, isn't it?' The two of them, at Cannes casino's roulette wheel in 1938, had backed the number and won twice.

At noon, Churchill was driven across Kent to Chartwell, his beloved old home, shuttered for the duration. He sought an interlude of tranquillity in which to prepare his broadcast to the nation. But he had been feeding his goldfish for only a few minutes when he was interrupted by a telephone call. Gort, in France, was seeking sanction to fall back on the sea at Dunkirk if his predicament worsened. The C-in-C was told instead to seek to re-establish contact with the French army on his right, with German spearheads in between. The French, in their turn, would be urged to counter-attack towards him. The Belgians were pleading for the BEF to hold a more northerly line beside their own troops. The war cabinet determined, however, that the vital priority was to re-establish a common front with the main French armies. The Belgians must be left to their fate, while British forces redeployed south-westwards towards Arras and Amiens.

Broadcasting to the British people that night, Churchill asserted a confidence which he did not feel, that the line in France would be stabilised, but also warned of the peril the nation faced. 'This is one of the most awe-striking periods in the long history of France and Britain. It is also beyond doubt the most sublime. Centuries ago words were written to be a call and a spur to the faithful servants of Truth and Justice: "Arm yourselves, and be ye men of valour . . . for it is better for us to perish in battle than to look upon the outrage of our nation and our altar. As the will of God is in Heaven, even so let it be."'

This was the first of his great clarion calls to the nation. It is impossible to overstate its impact upon the British people, and indeed upon the listening world. He asserted his resolve, and his listeners responded. That night he dispatched a minute to Ismay, reasserting his refusal to send further RAF squadrons to France. Every fighter would be needed 'if it becomes necessary to evacuate the BEF'. It was obvious that this decision would be received badly by the French, and not all his subordinates supported it. His personal scientific and economic adviser, Frederick Lindemann – 'the Prof' – penned a note of protest.

Britain's forces could exert only a marginal influence on the outcome of the battle for France. Even if every aircraft the RAF possessed had been dispatched to the Continent, such a commitment would not have averted Allied defeat. It would merely have sacrificed the squadrons that later won the Battle of Britain. In May 1940, however, such things were much less plain. As France tottered on the brink of collapse, with five million terrified fugitives clogging roads in a fevered exodus southwards, the bitterness of her politicians and generals mounted against an ally that matched extravagant rhetoric with refusal to provide the only important aid in its gift. France's leaders certainly responded feebly to Hitler's blitzkrieg. But their rancour towards Britain merits understanding. Churchill's perception of British self-interest has been vindicated by history, but scarcely deserved the gratitude of Frenchmen.

He sent an unashamedly desperate message to Roosevelt, regretting America's refusal to lend destroyers. More, he warned that while his own government would never surrender, a successor administration might parley with Germany, using the Royal Navy as its 'sole remaining bargaining counter . . . If this country was left by the United States to its fate, no one would have the right to blame those men responsible if they made the best terms they could for the surviving inhabitants. Excuse me, Mr President, putting this nightmare bluntly.' In Hitler's hands, Britain's fleet would pose a grave threat to the United States.

If this was a brutal prospect to lay before Roosevelt, it was by no means a bluff. At that moment Churchill could not know that Parliament and the British people would stick with him to the end. Chamberlain remained leader of the Conservative Party. Even before the crisis in France, a significant part of Britain's ruling class was susceptible to a compromise peace. Following military catastrophe, it was entirely plausible that Churchill's government would fall, just as Chamberlain's had done, to be replaced by an administration which sought terms from Hitler. Only in the months which followed would the world, and Churchill himself, gradually come to perceive that the people of Britain were willing to risk everything under his leadership.

On the 20th he told the chiefs of staff that the time had come to consider whether residual Norwegian operations around Narvik should be sustained, when troops and ships were urgently needed elsewhere. On the Continent, the Germans were driving south and west so fast that it seemed doubtful whether the BEF could regain touch with the main French armies. Gort was still striving to pull back forces from the Scheldt. That night, German units passed Amiens on the hot, dusty road to Abbeville, cutting off the BEF from its supply bases. Still Churchill declined to despair. He told the war cabinet late on the morning of the 21st that 'the situation was more favourable than certain of the more obvious symptoms would indicate'. In the north, the British still had local superiority of numbers. Fears focused on the perceived pusillanimity of the French, both politicians and soldiers. That day, a British armoured thrust south from Arras failed to break through. The BEF was isolated, along with elements of the French First Army. Calais and Boulogne remained in British hands, but inaccessible by land.

The House of Commons on 20 May, with the kind of inspired madness that contributed to the legend of 1940, debated a Colonial Welfare Bill. Many people in Britain lacked understanding of the full horror of the Allies' predicament. Newspaper readers continued to receive encouraging tidings. The *Evening News* headlined on 17 May: 'BRITISH TROOPS SUCCESS'. On the 19th, the *Sunday Dispatch* headline read 'ATTACKS LESS POWERFUL'. Even two days later, the *Evening News* front page proclaimed 'ENEMY ATTACKS BEATEN OFF'. An editorial in the *New Statesman* urged that 'the government should at once grapple with the minor, but important problem of Anglo–Mexican relations'.

Gort's chief of staff, Lt.Gen. Henry Pownall, complained bitterly on 20 May about the absence of clear instructions from London: 'Nobody minds going down fighting, but the long and many days of indigence and recently the entire lack of higher direction . . . have been terribly wearing on the nerves of all of us.' But when orders did come from the prime minister three days later – for a counterattack south-eastwards by the entire BEF – Pownall was even angrier: 'Can nobody prevent him trying to conduct operations himself as a super Commander-in-Chief? How does he think we are to collect eight divisions and attack as he suggests? Have we no front to hold? He can have no conception of our situation and condition . . . The man's mad.'

The German advance

Only the port of Dunkirk still offered an avenue of escape from the Continent, and escape now seemed the BEF's highest credible aspiration. On the 22nd and 23rd, the British awaited tidings of the promised French counter-offensive north-eastward, towards Gort. Gen. Maxime Weygand, who had supplanted the sacked Gamelin as Allied supreme commander, declared this to be in progress. In the absence of visible movement Churchill remained sceptical. If Weygand's thrust failed, evacuation would become the only British option. Churchill reported as much to the King on the night of 23 May, as Boulogne was evacuated. On the night of the 24th he fumed to Ismay about Gort's failure to launch a force towards Calais to link up with its garrison, and demanded how men and guns could be better used. He concluded, in the first overtly bitter and histrionic words which he had deployed against Britain's soldiers since the campaign began: 'Of course, if one side fights and the other does not, the war is apt to become somewhat unequal.' Ironside, the CIGS, told the Defence Committee that evening that if the BEF was indeed evacuated by sea from France, a large proportion of its men might be lost.

Churchill was now preoccupied with three issues: rescue of Gort's men from Dunkirk; deployment of further units of the British Army to renew the battle in France following the BEF's withdrawal; and defence of the home island against invasion. Reynaud dispatched a bitter message to London on the 24th, denouncing the British retreat to the sea and blaming this for the failure of Weygand's counter-offensive – which in truth had never taken place. 'Everything is complete confusion,' Sir Alexander Cadogan, Permanent Under-Secretary at the Foreign Office, noted in his diary on the 25th, 'no communications and no one knows what's going on, except that everything's black as black.'

Churchill cabled to the Dominion prime ministers, warning that an invasion of Britain might be imminent. He rejoiced that reinforcements from the Empire were on their way, and asserted his confidence that the Royal Navy and RAF should be able to frustrate an assault, following which 'our land defence will deal with any sea-borne survivors after some rough work'. He rejected the notion of a public appeal to the United States. He feared, surely correctly, that such a message would have scant appeal to a nation already disposed to dismiss aid to Britain as wasted motion. In this, as in his judgement of shifting American moods through the months that followed, he displayed much wisdom. A Gallup poll showed Americans still over-whelmingly opposed, by thirteen to one, to participation in the European conflict.

On 25 May, Churchill dispatched a personal message to Brigadier Claude Nicholson, commanding the British force in Calais, ordering that his men must fight to the end. The Belgians were collapsing. Gort cancelled his last planned counter-attack southward, instead sending north the two divisions earmarked for it, to plug the gap between British and Belgian forces. That evening, at a meeting of the Defence Committee, Churchill accepted the conclusion which Gort, now out of contact with London, had already reached and begun to act upon. The BEF must withdraw to the coast for evacu-ation. The commander-in-chief's order, issued in advance of consent from Britain, represented his most notable contribution to the campaign, and by no means a negligible one. The prime minister ordered that six skeleton divisions in Britain should be urgently prepared for active service, though scant means existed to accom-plish this. Artillery, anti-tank weapons, transport, even small arms were lacking. He acknowledged that France's leaders, resigned to defeat, would probably depose Reynaud and make terms with Hitler. Henceforward, the future of the French fleet was much in his mind. In German hands, these warships might drastically improve the odds favouring a successful invasion of Britain. That night, Ironside resigned as CIGS, to become commander-in-chief home forces. The general had never commanded Churchill's confidence, while Sir John Dill, Ironside's vice-chief, did. Next day Dill, fifty-nine years old, clever and sensitive though seldom in good health, became head of the British Army.

At 9 o'clock on the morning of the 26th, Churchill told the war cabinet there was a good chance of 'getting off a considerable proportion of the British Expeditionary Force'. Paul Reynaud arrived in London. He warned the prime minister over lunch that if Germany occupied a large part of France, the nation's old hero Marshal Philippe Pétain would probably call for an armistice. Reynaud dismissed British fears that the Germans were bent on an immediate invasion of their island. Hitler would strike for Paris, he said, and of course he was right. Churchill told Reynaud that Britain would fight on, whatever transpired. Following a break while he met the war cabinet, the two leaders resumed their talks. Churchill pressed for Weygand to issue an order for the BEF to fall back on the coast. This was designed to frustrate charges of British betrayal. Reynaud duly requested such a message, to endorse the reality of what was already taking place.

At a four-hour war cabinet meeting that afternoon, following Reynaud's departure, the merits of seeking a settlement with Hitler were discussed. Churchill hoped that France might receive terms that precluded her occupation by the Germans. Halifax, the Foreign Secretary, expressed his desire to seek Italian mediation with Hitler, to secure terms for Britain. He had held preliminary talks with Mussolini's ambassador in London about such a course. Churchill was sceptical, saying this presupposed that a deal might be made merely by returning Germany's old colonies, and making concessions in the Mediterranean. 'No such option was open to us,' said the prime minister.

Six Alexander Cadogan, who joined the meeting after half an hour, found Churchill 'too rambling and romantic and sentimental and temperamental'. This was harsh. The prime minister bore vast burdens. It behoved him to be circumspect in all dealings with the old appeasers among his colleagues. There were those in Whitehall who, rather than being stirred by Churchill's appeals to recognise a great historic moment, curled their lips. Chamberlain's private secretary, Arthur Rucker, responded contemptuously to the ringing phrases in one of the prime minister's missives: 'He is still thinking of his books.' Eric Seal, the only one of Churchill's private secretaries who established no close rapport with him,* muttered about 'blasted rhetoric'.

---

* Seal departed from Downing Street in 1941.

A substantial part of the British ruling class, MPs and peers alike, had since September 1939 lacked faith in the possibility of military victory. Although Churchill was himself an aristocrat, he was widely mistrusted by his own kind. Since the 1917 Russian Revolution, many British grandees, including such dukes as Westminster, Wellington and Buccleuch, and such lesser peers as Lord Phillimore, had shown themselves much more hostile to Soviet communism than to European fascism. Their patriotism was never in doubt. However, their enthusiasm for a fight to the finish with Hitler, which they feared would end in rubble and ruin, was less assured. Lord Hankey observed acidly before making a speech to the House of Lords early in May that he 'would be addressing most of the members of the Fifth Column'.

Lord Tavistock, soon to become Duke of Bedford, a pacifist and plausible quisling, wrote to former prime minister David Lloyd George that Hitler's strength was 'so great . . . it is madness to suppose we can beat him by war on the continent'. On 15 May, Tavistock urged Lloyd George that peace should be made 'now rather than later . . . If the Germans received fair peace terms a dozen Hitlers could never start another war on an inadequate . . . pretext.' Likewise, some financial magnates in the City of London were sceptical of any possibility of British victory, and thus of Churchill. Harold Nicolson wrote: 'It is not the descendants of the old governing classes who display the greatest enthusiasm for their leader . . . Mr Chamberlain is the idol of the business men . . . They do not have the same personal feelings for Mr Churchill . . . There are awful moments when they feel that Mr Churchill does not find them interesting.'

There were also defeatists lower down the social scale. Muriel Green, who worked at her family's garage in Norfolk, recorded a conversation at a local tennis match with a grocer's roundsman and a schoolmaster on 23 May. 'I think they're going to beat us, don't you?' said the roundsman. 'Yes,' said the schoolmaster. He added that as the Nazis were very keen on sport, he expected 'we'd still be able to play tennis if they did win'. Muriel Green wrote: 'J said Mr M. was saying we should paint a swastika under the door knocker ready. We all agreed we shouldn't know what to do if they invade.

After that we played tennis, very hard exciting play for 2 hrs, and forgot all about the war.'

In those last days of May, the prime minister must have perceived a real possibility, even a likelihood, that if he himself appeared irrationally intransigent, the old Conservative grandees would reassert themselves. Amid the collapse of all the hopes on which Britain's military struggle against Hitler were founded, it was not fanciful to suppose that a peace party might gain control in Britain. Some historians have made much of the fact that at this war cabinet meeting Churchill failed to dismiss out of hand an approach to Mussolini. He did not flatly contradict Halifax when the Foreign Secretary said that if the Duce offered terms for a general settlement 'which did not postulate the destruction of our independence . . . we should be foolish if we did not accept them'. Churchill conceded that 'if we could get out of this jam by giving up Malta and Gibraltar and some African colonies, he would jump at it'. At the following day's war cabinet he indicated that if Hitler was prepared to offer peace in exchange for the restoration of his old colonies and the overlordship of central Europe, a negotiation could be possible.

It seems essential to consider Churchill's words in context. First, they were made in the midst of long, weary discussions, during which he was taking elaborate pains to appear reasonable. Halifax spoke with the voice of logic. Amid shattering military defeat, even Churchill dared not offer his colleagues a vision of British victory. In those Dunkirk days, the Director of Military Intelligence told a BBC correspondent: 'We're finished. We've lost the army and we shall never have the strength to build another.' Churchil did not challenge the view of those who assumed that the war would end, sooner or later, with a negotiated settlement rather than with a British army marching into Berlin. He pitched his case low because there was no alternative. A display of exaggerated confidence would have invited ridicule. He relied solely upon the argument that there was no more to lose by fighting on, than by throwing in the hand.

How would his colleagues, or even posterity, have assessed his judgement had he sought at those meetings to offer the prospect of

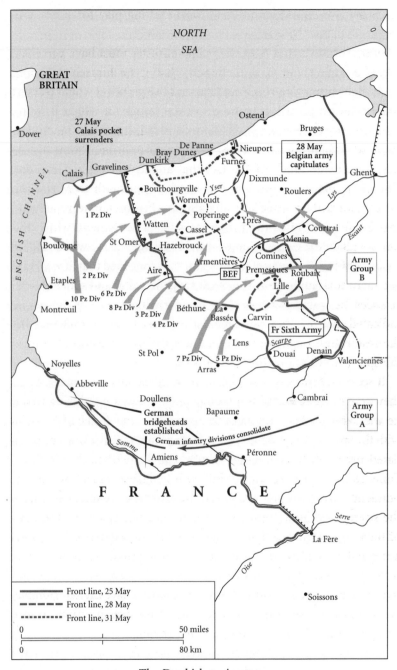

The Dunkirk perimeter

military triumph? To understand what happened in Britain in the summer of 1940, it is essential to acknowledge the logic of impending defeat. This was what created tensions between the hearts and minds even of staunch and patriotic British people. The best aspiration they, and their prime minister, could entertain was a manly determination to survive today, and to pray for a better tomorrow. The war cabinet discussions between 26 and 28 May took place while it was still doubtful that any significant portion of the BEF could be saved from France.

At the meeting of 26 May, with the support of Attlee, Greenwood and eventually Chamberlain, Churchill summed up for the view that there was nothing to be lost by fighting on, because no terms which Hitler might offer in the future were likely to be worse than those now available. Having discussed the case for a parley, he dismissed it, even if Halifax refused to do so. At 7 o'clock that evening, an hour after the war cabinet meeting ended, the Admiralty signalled the Flag Officer Dover, Vice-Admiral Bertram Ramsay: 'Operation *Dynamo* is to commence.' The destroyers of the Royal Navy, aided by a fleet of small craft, began to evacuate the BEF from Dunkirk.

That night yet another painful order was forced upon Churchill. The small British force at Calais, drawn from the Rifle Brigade, had only nuisance value. But everything possible must be done to distract German forces from the Dunkirk perimeter. The Rifles had to resist to the last. Ismay wrote: 'The decision affected us all very deeply, especially perhaps Churchill. He was unusually silent during dinner that evening, and ate and drank with evident distaste.' He asked a private secretary, John Martin, to find for him a passage in George Borrow's 1843 prayer for England. Martin identified the lines next day: 'Fear not the result, for either thy end be a majestic and an enviable one, or God shall perpetuate thy reign upon the waters.'

On the morning of the 27th, even as British troops were beginning to embark at Dunkirk, Churchill asked the leaders of the armed forces to prepare a memorandum setting out the nation's prospects of resisting invasion if France fell. Within a couple of hours the chiefs of staff submitted an eleven-paragraph response that identified the key issues with notable insight. As long as the RAF was 'in being', they wrote, its aircraft together with the warships of the Royal Navy should be able to prevent an invasion. If air superiority was lost, however, the navy could not indefinitely hold the Channel. Should the Germans secure a beachhead in south-east England, British home forces would be incapable of evicting them. The chiefs pinpointed the air battle, Britain's ability to defend its key installations, and especially aircraft factories, as the decisive factors in determining the future course of the war. They concluded with heartening words: 'The real test is whether the morale of our fighting personnel and civil population will counter-balance the numerical and material advantages which Germany enjoys. We believe it will.'

The war cabinet debated at length, and finally accepted, the chiefs' report. It was agreed that further efforts should be made to induce the Americans to provide substantial aid. An important message arrived from Lord Lothian, British ambassador in Washington, suggesting that Britain should invite the US to lease basing facilities in Trinidad, Newfoundland and Bermuda. Churchill opposed any such unilateral offer. America had 'given us practically no help in the war', he said. 'Now that they saw how great was the danger, their attitude was that they wanted to keep everything that would help us for their own defence.' This would remain the case until the end of the battle for France. There was no doubt of Roosevelt's desire to help, but he was constrained by the terms of the Neutrality Act imposed by Congress. On 17 May Gen. George Marshall, chief of the army, expounded to US Treasury Secretary Henry Morgenthau his objections to shipping American arms to the Allies: 'It is a drop in the bucket on the other side and it is a very vital necessity on this side and that is that. Tragic as it is, that is it.' Between 23 May and 3 June US Secretary of War Harry Woodring, an ardent isolationist, deliberately delayed shipment to Britain of war material condemned as surplus. He insisted that there must be prior public advertisement before such equipment was sold to the Allies. On 5 June, the Senate foreign relations committee rejected an administration proposal to sell ships and planes to Britain. The US War Department declined to supply bombs to fit dive-bombers which the French had already bought and paid for.

In the last days of May, a deal for Britain to purchase twenty US patrol torpedo boats was scuttled when news of it leaked to isolationist Senator David Walsh of Massachusetts. As chairman of the Senate's Navy Affairs Committee, Walsh referred the plan to the attorney-general – who declared it illegal. In mid-June, the US chiefs of staff recommended that no further war material should be sent to Britain, and that no private contractor should be allowed to accept an order which might compromise the needs of the US armed forces. None of this directly influenced the campaign in France. But it spoke volumes, all unwelcome in London and Paris, about the prevailing American mood towards Europe's war.

It was a small consolation that other powerful voices across the Atlantic were urging Britain's cause. The *New York Times* attacked Colonel Charles Lindbergh, America's arch-isolationist flying hero, and asserted the mutuality of Anglo-American interests. Lindbergh, said the *Times*, was 'an ignorant young man if he trusts his own premise that it makes no difference to us whether we are deprived of the historic defense of British sea power in the Atlantic Ocean'. The Republican *New York Herald Tribune* astonished many Americans by declaring boldly: 'The least costly solution in both life and welfare would be to declare war on Germany at once.' Yet even if President Roosevelt had wished to heed the urgings of such interventionists and offer assistance to the Allies, he had before him the example of Woodrow Wilson, in whose administration he served. Wilson was renounced by his own legislature in 1919 for making commitments abroad – in the Versailles Treaty – which outreached the will of the American people. Roosevelt had no intention of emulating him.

Chamberlain reported on 27 May that he had spoken the previous evening to Stanley Bruce, Australian high commissioner in London, who argued that Britain's position would be bleak if France surrendered. Bruce, a shrewd and respected spokesman for his dominion, urged seeking American or Italian mediation with Hitler. Australia's prime minister, Robert Menzies, was fortunately made of sterner stuff. From Canberra, Menzies merely enquired what assistance his country's troops could provide. By autumn, three Australian divisions were deployed in the Middle East. Churchill told Chamberlain to make plain to Bruce that France's surrender would not influence Britain's determination to fight on. He urged ministers – and emphasised the message in writing a few days later – to present bold faces to the world. Likewise, a little later he instructed Britain's missions abroad to entertain lavishly, prompting embassy parties in Madrid and Berne. In Churchill's house, even amid disaster there was no place for glum countenances.

At a further war cabinet that afternoon, Halifax found himself unsupported when he returned to his theme of the previous day, seeking agreement that Britain should solicit Mussolini's help in exploring terms from Hitler. Churchill said that at that moment, British prestige in Europe was very low. It could be revived only by defiance. 'If, after two or three months, we could show that we were still unbeaten, we should be no worse off than we should be if we were now to abandon the struggle. Let us therefore avoid being dragged down the slippery slope with France.' If terms were offered, he would be prepared to consider them. But if the British were invited to send a delegate to Paris to join with the French in suing for peace with Germany, the answer must be 'no'. The war cabinet agreed.

Halifax wrote in his diary: 'I thought Winston talked the most frightful rot. I said exactly what I thought of [the Foreign Secretary's opponents in the war cabinet], adding that if that was really their view, our ways must part.' In the garden afterwards, when he repeated his threat of resignation, Churchill soothed him with soft words. Halifax concluded in his diary record: 'It does drive one to despair when he works himself up into a passion of emotion when he ought to make his brain think and reason.' He and Chamberlain recoiled from Churchill's 'theatricality', as Cadogan described it. Cold men both, they failed to perceive in such circumstances the necessity for at least a semblance of boldness. But Chamberlain's eventual support for Churchill's stance was critically important in deflecting the Foreign Secretary's proposals.

Whichever narratives of these exchanges are consulted, the facts seem plain. Halifax believed that Britain should explore terms. Churchill must have been deeply alarmed by the prospect of the Foreign Secretary, the man whom only three weeks earlier most of the Conservative Party wanted as prime minister, quitting his government. It was vital, at this moment of supreme crisis, that Britain should present a united face to the world. Churchill could never thereafter have had private confidence in Halifax. He continued to endure him as a colleague, however, because he needed to sustain the support of the Tories. It was a measure of Churchill's apprehension about the resolve of Britain's ruling class that it would be another seven months before he felt strong enough to consign 'the Holy Fox' to exile.

The legend of Britain in the summer of 1940 as a nation united in defiance of Hitler is rooted in reality. It is not diminished by asserting that if another man had been prime minister, the political faction resigned to seeking a negotiated peace would probably have prevailed. What Churchill grasped, and Halifax and others did not, was that the mere gesture of exploring peace terms must impact disastrously upon Britain's position. Even if Hitler's response proved unacceptable to a British government, the clear, simple Churchillian posture, of rejecting any parley with the forces of evil, would be irretrievably compromised.

It is impossible to declare with confidence at what moment during the summer of 1940 Churchill's grip upon power, as well as his hold upon the loyalties of the British people, became secure. What is plain is that in the last days of May he did not perceive himself proof against domestic foes. He survived in office not because he overcame the private doubts of ministerial and military sceptics, which he did not, but by the face of courage and defiance that he presented to the nation. He appealed over the heads of those who knew too much, to those who were willing to sustain a visceral stubbornness. 'His world is built upon the primacy of public over private relationships,' wrote the philosopher Isaiah Berlin in a fine essay on Churchill, 'upon the supreme value of action, of the battle between simple good and simple evil, between life and death; but above all battle. He has always fought.' The simplicity of Churchill's commitment, matched by the grandeur of the language in which he expressed this, seized popular imagination. In the press, in the pubs and everywhere that Churchill himself appeared on his travels across the country, the British people passionately applauded his defiance. Conservative seekers after truce were left beached and isolated; sullenly resentful, but impotent.

Evelyn Waugh's fictional Halberdier officer, the fastidious Guy Crouchback, was among many members of the British upper classes who were slow to abandon their disdain for the prime minister, displaying an attitude common among real-life counterparts such as Waugh himself:

> Some of Mr Churchill's broadcasts had been played on the mess wireless-set. Guy had found them painfully boastful and they had, most of them, been immediately followed by the news of some disaster ... Guy knew of Mr Churchill only as a professional politician, a master of sham-Augustan prose, an advocate of the Popular Front in Europe, an associate of the press-lords and Lloyd George. He was asked: 'Uncle, what sort of fellow is this Winston Churchill?' 'Like Hore-Belisha [sacked Secretary for War, widely considered a char-latan], except that for some reason his hats are thought to be funny' ... Here Major Erskine leant across the table. 'Churchill is about the only man who may save us from losing this war,' he said. It was the first time that Guy had heard a Halberdier suggest that any result, other than complete victory, was possible.

Some years before the war, the diplomat Lord D'Abernon observed with patrician complacency that 'An Englishman's mind works best when it is almost too late.' In May 1940, he might have perceived Churchill as an exemplar of his words.

TWO

The Two Dunkirks

On 28 May, Churchill learned that the Belgians had surrendered at dawn. He repressed until much later his private bitterness, unjustified though this was when Belgium had no rational prospect of sustaining the fight. He merely observed that it was not for him to pass judgement upon King Leopold's decision. Overnight a few thousand British troops had been retrieved from Dunkirk, but Gort was pessimistic about the fate of more than 200,000 who remained, in the face of overwhelming German air power. 'And so here we are back on the shores of France on which we landed with such high hearts over eight months ago,' Pownall, Gort's chief of staff, wrote that day. 'I think we were a gallant band who little deserve this ignominious end to our efforts . . . If our skill be not so great, our courage and endurance are certainly greater than that of the Germans.' The stab of self-knowledge reflected in Pownall's phrase about the inferior professionalism of the British Army lingered in the hearts of its intelligent soldiers until 1945.

That afternoon at a war cabinet meeting in Churchill's room at the Commons, the prime minister again – and for the last time – rejected Halifax's urgings that the government could obtain better peace terms before France surrendered and British aircraft factories were destroyed. Chamberlain, as ever a waverer, now supported the Foreign Secretary in urging that Britain should consider 'decent terms if such were offered to us'. Churchill said that the odds were a thousand to one against any such Hitlerian generosity, and warned that 'nations which went down fighting rose again, but those which surrendered tamely were finished'. Attlee and Greenwood, the Labour members, endorsed Churchill's view. This was the last stand of the old appeasers. Privately, they adhered to the view, shared by former prime minister Lloyd George, that sooner or later negotiation with Germany would be essential. As late as 17 June, the Swedish ambassador reported Halifax and his junior minister R.A. Butler declaring that no 'diehards' would be allowed to stand in the way of peace 'on reasonable conditions'. Andrew Roberts has convincingly argued that Halifax was not directly complicit in remarks made during a chance conversation between Butler and the envoy. But it remains extraordinary that some historians have sought to qualify verdicts on the Foreign Secretary's behaviour through the summer of 1940. It was not dishonourable – the lofty eminence could never have been that. But it was craven.

Immediately following the 28 May meeting, some twenty-five other ministers – all those who were not members of the war cabinet – filed into the room to be briefed by the prime minister. He described the situation at Dunkirk, anticipated the French collapse, and expressed his conviction that Britain must fight on. 'He was quite magnificent,' wrote Hugh Dalton, Minister of Economic Warfare, 'the man, and the only man we have, for this hour . . . He was determined to prepare public opinion for bad tidings . . . Attempts to invade us would no doubt be made.' Churchill told ministers that he had considered the case for negotiating with 'that man' – and rejected it. Britain's position, with its fleet and air force, remained strong. He concluded with a magnificent peroration: 'I am convinced that every man of you would rise up and tear me down from my place if I were for one moment to contemplate parley or surrender. If this long island story of ours is to end at last, let it end only when each one of us lies choking in his own blood upon the ground.'

He was greeted with acclamation extraordinary at any assembly of ministers. No word of dissent was uttered. The meeting represented an absolute personal triumph. He reported its outcome to the war cabinet. That night, the British government informed Reynaud in Paris of its refusal of Italian mediation for peace terms.

A further suggestion by Halifax of a direct call upon the United States was dismissed. A bold stand against Germany, Churchill reiterated, would carry vastly more weight than 'a grovelling appeal' at such a moment. At the following day's war cabinet, new instructions to Gort were discussed. Halifax favoured giving the C-in-C discretion to capitulate. Churchill would hear of no such thing. Gort was told to fight on at least until further evacuation from Dunkirk became impossible. Mindful of Allied reproaches, he told the War Office that French troops in the perimeter must be allowed access to British ships. He informed Reynaud of his determination to create a new British Expeditionary Force, based on the Atlantic port of Saint-Nazaire, to fight alongside the French army in the west.

All through those days, the evacuation from the port and beaches continued, much hampered by lack of small craft to ferry troops out to the larger ships, a deficiency which the Admiralty strove to make good by a public appeal for suitable vessels. History has invested the saga of Dunkirk with a dignity less conspicuous to those present. John Horsfall, a company commander of the Royal Irish Fusiliers, told a young fellow officer: 'I hope you realise your distinction. You are now taking part in the greatest military shambles ever achieved by the British Army.' Many rank-and-file soldiers returned from France nursing a lasting resentment towards the military hierarchy that had exposed them to such a predicament. Horsfall noticed that in the last phase of the march to the beaches, his men fell unnaturally silent: 'There was a limit to what any of us could absorb, with those red fireballs flaming skywards every few minutes, and I suppose we just reached the point where there was little left to say.' They were joined by a horse artillery major, superb in Savile Row riding breeches and scarlet and gold forage cap, who said: 'I'm a double blue at this, old boy – I was at Mons [in 1914].' A young Grenadier Guards officer, Edward Ford, passed the long hours of waiting for a ship reading a copy of Chapman's Homer which he found in the sands. For the rest of his days, Ford was nagged by unsatisfied curiosity about who had abandoned his Chapman amid the detritus of the beaches.

Though the Royal Navy's achievement at Dunkirk embraced its

highest traditions, many men noted only the chaos. 'It does seem to me incredible that the organisation of the beach work should have been so bad,' wrote Lt. Robert Hichens of the minesweeper *Niger*, though he admired the absence of panic among embarking soldiers.

We were told that there would be lots of boats and that the embarkation of the troops would all be organised . . . That was what all the little shore boats were being brought over from England for . . . One can only come to the conclusion that the civilians and small boats packed up and went home with a few chaps instead of staying there to ferry to the big ships which was their proper job. As for the shore organisation, it simply did not exist . . . It makes one a bit sick when one hears the organisers of the beach show being cracked up to the skies on the wireless and having DSOs showered upon them, because a more disgraceful muddle and lack of organisation I have never seen . . . If a few officers had been put ashore with a couple of hundred sailors . . . the beach evacuation would have been a different thing . . . When the boats were finally hoisted I found that I was very tired and very hoarse as well as soaking wet. So I had a drink and then changed. I had an artillery officer in my cabin who was very interesting. They all seem to have been very impressed by the dive bombers and the vast number of them, and by the general efficiency of the German forces. The soldiers are not very encouraging, but they were very tired which always makes one pessimistic, and they had been out of touch for a long time. This officer did not even know that Churchill had replaced Chamberlain as Premier.

Pownall arrived in London from France to describe to the defence committee on 30 May Gort's plans for holding the Dunkirk perimeter. 'No one in the room,' wrote Ian Jacob of the war cabinet secretariat, 'imagined that they could be successful if the German armoured divisions supported by the Luftwaffe pressed their attack.' It was, of course, a decisive mercy that no such attack was 'pressed'. In the course of the Second World War, victorious German armies displayed a far more consistent commitment to completing the destruction of

their enemies when opportunity offered than did the Allies in similarly advantageous circumstances. Dunkirk was an exception. Most
of the BEF escaped not as a consequence of Hitler's forbearance, but
through a miscellany of fortuities and misjudgements. Success beyond
German imagination created huge problems of its own. Commanders'
attention was fixed upon completing the defeat of Weygand's forces,
of which large elements remained intact. The broken country around
Dunkirk was well suited to defence. The French First Army, south
of the port, engaged important German forces through the critical
period for the BEF's escape, a stand which received less credit from
the British than it deserved.

On 24 May von Rundstedt, commanding Army Group A, ordered
his Panzers, badly in need of a logistical pause, not to cross the Aa
canal and entangle themselves with British 'remnants', as Gort's
army was now perceived. Hitler supported his decision. He was
amenable to Goering's eagerness to show that his aircraft could
complete the destruction of the BEF. Yet, in the words of the most
authoritative German history, 'The Luftwaffe, badly weakened by
earlier operations, was unable to meet the demands made on it.'
In the course of May, Goering's force lost 1,044 aircraft, a quarter
of them fighters. Thanks to the efforts of the RAF's Fighter
Command over Dunkirk, the German Fourth Army's war diary
recorded on the 25th: 'The enemy has had air superiority. This is
something new for us in this campaign.' On 3 June the German air
effort was diverted from Dunkirk, to increase pressure on the French
by bombing targets around Paris.

Almost the entire RAF Air Striking Force was reduced to charred
wreckage, strewn the length of northern France. It scarcely seemed
to the Germans to matter if a few thousand British troops escaped
in salt-stained battledress, when they left behind every tool of a
modern army – tanks, guns, trucks, machine-guns and equipment.
Hitler's failure to complete the demolition of the BEF represented a
historic blunder, but an unsurprising one amid the magnitude of
German triumphs and dilemmas in the last days of May 1940. The
Allies, with much greater superiority, indulged far more culpable

strategic omissions when they returned to the Continent for the campaigns of 1943–45.

Ian Jacob was among those impressed by the calm with which Churchill received Pownall's Dunkirk situation report of 30 May. Thereafter, the war cabinet addressed another budget of French requests: for troops to support them on the Somme front; more aircraft; concessions to Italy; a joint appeal to Washington. Churchill interpreted these demands as establishing a context for French surrender, once Britain had refused them. The decision was taken to withdraw residual British forces from north Norway. The prime minister determined to fly again to Paris to press France to stay in the war, and to make plain that Britain would dissociate itself from any parley with Germany mediated by the Italians. Next morning, as Churchill's Flamingo took off from Northolt, he knew that 133,878 British and 11,666 Allied troops had been evacuated from Dunkirk.

The prime minister's old friend Sir Edward Spears, viewed by his fellow generals as a mountebank, was once more serving as a British liaison officer with the French, a role he had filled in World War I. Spears, waiting at Villacoublay airfield to meet the party, was impressed by the prime minister's imposture of gaiety. Churchill poked the British officer playfully in the stomach with his stick, and as ever appeared stimulated by finding himself upon the scene of great events. He beamed upon the pilots of the escorting Hurricanes which had landed behind him, was driven into Paris for lunch at the British embassy, then went to see Reynaud at the Ministry of War.

Amid the gloom that beset all France's leaders, gathered with her prime minister, Pétain and Admiral Jean François Darlan showed themselves foremost in despair. As Ismay described it: 'A dejected-looking old man in plain clothes shuffled towards me, stretched out his hand and said: "Pétain." It was hard to believe that this was the great Marshal of France.' The rationalists, as they saw themselves, listened unmoved to Churchill's outpouring of rhetoric. He spoke of the two British divisions already in north-western France, which he hoped could be further reinforced to assist in the defence of Paris.

He described in dramatic terms the events at Dunkirk. He declared in his extraordinary franglais, reinforced by gestures, that French and British soldiers would leave arm in arm – '*partage – bras dessus, bras dessous*'. On cabinet orders, Gort was to quit Dunkirk that night. If, as expected, Italy entered the war, British bomber squadrons would at once strike at her industries. Churchill beamed once more. If only France could hold out through the summer, he said, all manner of possibilities would open. In a final surge of emotion, he declared his conviction that American help would come. Thus this thirteenth meeting of the Allied Supreme War Council concluded its agenda.

Reynaud and two other ministers were guests for dinner that night at the palatial British embassy in the rue Saint-Honoré. Churchill waxed lyrical about the possibility of launching striking forces against German tank columns. He left Paris next morning knowing he had done all that force of personality could achieve to breathe inspiration into the hearts of the men charged with saving France. Yet few believed a word of it. The Allies' military predicament was irretrievably dire. It was impossible to conceive any plausible scenario in which Hitler's armies might be thrown back, given the collapse of French national will.

Paul Reynaud was among a handful of Frenchmen who, momentarily at least, remained susceptible to Churchill's verbiage. To logical minds, there was an absurdity about almost everything the Englishman said to ministers and commanders in Paris. Britain's prime minister paraded before his ally his own extravagant sense of honour. He promised military gestures which might further weaken his own country, but could not conceivably save France. He made wildly fanciful pledges of further military aid, though its impact must be insignificant. Britain's two divisions in the north-west were irrelevant to the outcome of the battle, and were desperately needed to defend the home island. But Churchill told the war cabinet in London on 1 June that more troops must be dispatched across the Channel, with a suitable air component. Even as the miracle of Dunkirk unfolded, he continued to waver about dispatching further fighters to the Continent. He trumpeted the success of the RAF in preventing the Luftwaffe from frustrating the evacuation, which he declared a splendid omen for the future.

Chamberlain and Halifax urged against sending more men to France, but Churchill dissented. He felt obliged to respond to fresh appeals from Reynaud. He envisaged a British enclave in Brittany, a base from which the French might be inspired and supported to maintain 'a gigantic guerrilla . . . The B.E.F. in France must immediately be reconstituted, otherwise the French will not continue in the war.' Amid the dire shortage of troops, he committed to France 1st Canadian Division, which had arrived in Britain virtually untrained and unequipped. The prime minister told one of the British generals who would be responsible for sustaining the defence of north-west France that 'he could count on no artillery'. An impromptu new 'division' was created around Rouen from lines of communications personnel equipped with a few Bren and anti-tank guns which they had never fired, and a single battery of field artillery that lacked dial sights for its guns. Until Lt.Gen. Alan Brooke, recently landed from Dunkirk, returned to France on 12 June, British forces there remained under French command, with no national C-in-C on the spot.

By insisting upon resumption of an utterly doomed campaign, Churchill made his worst mistake of 1940. It is unsurprising that his critics in the inner circle of power were dismayed. The strength of Churchill's emotions was wonderful to behold. But when sentiment drove him to make deployments with no possibility of success, he appalled his generals, as well as the old Chamberlainite umbrella-men. Almost every senior civilian and uniformed figure in Whitehall recognised that the Battle of France was lost. Further British commitments threatened to negate the extraordinary deliverance of Dunkirk. The Air Staff closed ranks with Halifax, Chamberlain and others to resist Churchill's demands that more fighters should be sent to France, in addition to the three British squadrons still operating there. On the air issue, Churchill himself havered, then reluctantly gave way. This was the first of many occasions on which he mercifully subordinated his instincts to the advice of service chiefs and colleagues. Chamberlain and Halifax were not wrong about everything. The moral grandeur in Churchill's gestures towards his ally in the first days of June was entirely subsumed by the magnitude of France's tragedy and Britain's peril.

The Dunkirk evacuation approached a conclusion on 4 June, by which time 224,328 British troops had been evacuated, along with 111,172 Allied troops, most of whom subsequently elected to be repatriated to France rather than fight on as exiles. For thirty-five minutes that afternoon, Churchill described the operation to the Commons, concluding with some of his greatest phrases: 'We shall fight on the beaches, we shall fight on the landing grounds, we shall fight in the fields and in the streets, we shall fight in the hills, we shall never surrender.'

That evening he found time to dispatch brief notes, thanking the King for withdrawing his objections to Brendan Bracken's membership of the Privy Council on the grounds of character; and to former prime minister Stanley Baldwin, expressing appreciation for a letter offering good wishes. Churchill apologised for having taken a fortnight to respond. 'We are going through v[er]y hard times & I expect worse to come,' he wrote; 'but I feel quite sure better days will come; though whether we shall live to see them is more doubtful. I do not feel the burden weigh too heavily, but I cannot say that I have enjoyed being Prime Minister v[er]y much so far.'

The German drive on Paris began on 5 June. Anglo–French exchanges in the days that followed were dominated by increasingly passionate appeals from Reynaud for fighters. Five RAF squadrons were still based in France, while four more were operating from British bases. The war cabinet and chiefs of staff were united in their determination to weaken Britain's home defence no further. On 9 June, Churchill cabled to South African premier Jan Smuts, who had urged the dispatch of more aircraft, saying: 'I see only one sure way through now, to wit, that Hitler should attack this country, and in so doing break his air weapon. If this happens he will be left to face the winter with Europe writhing under his heel, and probably with the United States against him after the Presidential election is over.' The Royal Navy was preoccupied with fears about the future of the French fleet. Admiral Sir Dudley Pound, the First Sea Lord, declared that only its sinking could ensure that it would not be used by the Germans.

Yet perversely, and indeed indefensibly, Churchill continued to dispatch troops to France. The draft operation order for 1st Canadian Division, drawn up as it embarked on 11 June, said: 'The political object of the re-constituted BEF is to give moral support to the French Government by showing the determination of the British Empire to assist her ally with all available forces . . . It is the intention . . . to concentrate . . . in the area North and South of Rennes . . . A division may have to hold 50 miles of front.' At a meeting of ministers in London that day, Dill was informed that a study was being undertaken for the maintenance of a bridgehead in Brittany, 'the Breton redoubt'. As late as 13 June, Royal Engineers were preparing reception points and transit camps on the Brittany coast, to receive further reinforcements from Britain.

Churchill recognised the overwhelming likelihood of French surrender, yet still cherished hopes of maintaining a foothold across the Channel. It seemed to him preferable to face the difficulties of clinging on in France, rather than those of mounting from Britain a return to a German-defended coast. He sought to sustain French faith in the alliance by the deployment of a mere three British divisions. He seemed unmoved by Mussolini's long-expected declaration of war on 10 June, merely remarking to Jock Colville: 'People who go to Italy to look at ruins won't have to go as far as Naples and Pompeii again.' The private secretary noted his master's bitter mood that day. On the afternoon of 11 June, Churchill flew with Eden, Dill, Ismay and Spears to the new French army headquarters at Briare on the Loire, seventy miles from Paris, to meet the French government once again. The colonel who met their plane, wrote Spears, might have been greeting poor relations at a funeral. At their destination, the Château du Muguet, there was no sense of welcome. At that evening's meeting of the Supreme War Council, after the

French had unfolded a chronicle of doom, Churchill summoned all his powers. He spoke with passion and eloquence about the forces which Britain could deploy in France in 1941 – twenty, even twenty-five divisions. Weygand said dismissively that the outcome of the war would be determined in hours, not days or weeks. Dill, pathetically, invited the supreme commander to use the makeshift British forces now in France wherever and however he saw fit.

The French, with the Germans at the gates of Paris, could scarcely be blamed for thinking themselves mocked. Eden wrote: 'Reynaud was inscrutable and Weygand polite, concealing with difficulty his scepticism. Marshal Pétain was overtly incredulous. Though he said nothing, his attitude was obviously "*C'est de la blague*" – "It's a joke."' The harshest confrontation came when Weygand asserted that the decisive point had been reached, that the British should commit every fighter they had to the battle. Churchill replied: 'This is not the decisive point. This is not the decisive moment. The decisive moment will come when Hitler hurls his Luftwaffe against Britain. If we can keep command of the air over our own island – that is all I ask – we will win it all back for you.' Britain would fight on 'for ever and ever and ever'.

Reynaud seemed moved. The newly appointed army minister, Brigadier-General Charles de Gaulle, was much more impressed by the prime minister's representation of himself as an Englishman than as an ally: 'Mr Churchill appeared imperturbable, full of buoyancy. Yet he seemed to be confining himself to a cordial reserve towards the French at bay, being already seized – not, perhaps, without an obscure satisfaction – with the terrible and magnificent prospect of an England left alone in her island, with himself to lead her struggle towards salvation.' The other Frenchmen present made nothing of the prime minister's words. Though courtesies were sustained through a difficult dinner that night, Reynaud told Britain's leader over brandy that Pétain considered it essential to seek an armistice.

To his staff, Churchill fumed at the influence upon Reynaud of his mistress, the comtesse de Portes, an impassioned advocate of surrender: 'That woman . . . will undo everything during the night that I do during the day. But of course she can furnish him with facilities that I cannot afford him. I can reason with him, but I cannot sleep with him.' For all the hopes which Churchill reposed in Reynaud, even at his best the French prime minister never shared the Englishman's zest for war *à l'outrance*. The American Under-Secretary of State, Sumner Welles, reported a conversation with France's leader earlier that summer: 'M. Reynaud felt that while Mr C[hurchill] was a brilliant and most entertaining man with a great capacity for organization, his kind has lost elasticity. He felt that Mr C could conceive of no possibility other than war to the finish – whether that resulted in utter chaos and destruction or not. That, he felt sure, was not true statesmanship.' This seems a convincing representation of Reynaud's view in June 1940. Like a significant number of British politicians in respect of their own society, the French prime minister perceived, as Churchill did not, a limit to the injury acceptable to the fabric and people of France in the cause of sustaining the struggle against Nazism.

Next morning, 12 June, Churchill told Spears to stay with the French, and to do everything possible to sustain them: 'We will carry those who will let themselves be carried.' Yet Britain had no power to 'carry' France. Pétain absented himself from the ensuing meeting of the Supreme War Council. His own decision was reached. Churchill raged at news that a planned RAF bombing mission to Italy the previous night had been frustrated by farm carts pushed across the runway by French airmen. Reynaud said that any further such missions must be launched from England. At Briare airfield, Ismay observed encouragingly that with no more allies to worry about, 'We'll win the Battle of Britain.' Churchill stared hard at him and said: 'You and I will be dead in three months' time.' There is no reason to doubt this exchange. Churchill claimed later that he had always believed Britain would come through. He certainly had a mystical faith in destiny, however vague his attachment to a deity. But it is plain that in the summer of 1940 he suffered cruel moments of rationality, when defeat seemed far more plausible than victory, when the huge effort of will necessary to sustain the fight was almost too much for him.

Six months later, Eden confessed to the prime minister that during the summer he and Pound, the First Sea Lord, had privately acknowledged despair to each other. Churchill said: 'Normally I wake up buoyant to face the new day. Then, I awoke with dread in my heart.' In the fevered atmosphere of the time, some MPs panicked. Harold Macmillan was among the prime movers in the so-called 'undersecretaries' revolt' by Tories demanding that the old 'men of Munich' should be summarily expelled from the government. 'All this,' in Leo Amery's words, 'on the assumption that France is going out altogether and that we shall be defeated.' The young turks were squashed.

When so many others were dying, Churchill could scarcely take for granted his own survival. A German bomb, a paratroop landing in Whitehall, an accident by land, sea or air such as befell many other prominent wartime figures, could extinguish him at any time. His courage, and that of those who followed and served him, lay in defying probability, sweeping aside all thought of the most plausible outcome of the struggle, and addressing each day's battles with a spirit undaunted by the misfortunes of the last. That Wednesday morning of 12 June, his Flamingo hedgehopped home over the lovely countryside of Brittany. Near the smoking docks of Le Havre, the pilot dived suddenly to avoid the attentions of two German planes which were strafing fishing boats. The Flamingo escaped unseen, landing safely at Hendon, but this was one of Churchill's closest calls. Later in the afternoon he told the war cabinet that it was obvious French resistance was approaching an end. He spoke admiringly of De Gaulle, whose resolution had made a strong impression on him.

Churchill had been back in London less than thirty-six hours when Reynaud telephoned, soon after midnight, demanding a new and urgent meeting at Tours, to which he had now retreated. The prime minister left next morning, accompanied by Halifax and Beaverbrook, driving through the incongruous London summer shopping crowds. He was greeted at Hendon with news that bad weather required a take-off postponement. 'To hell with that,' he growled. 'I'm going, whatever happens. This is too serious a situation to bother about the weather!' They landed at Tours amid a thunderstorm, on an airfield which had been heavily bombed the previous night, and solicited transport from a jaded rabble of French airmen. Churchill, Beaverbrook and Halifax crowded with difficulty into a small car which took them to the local prefecture, where they wandered unrecognised through the corridors. At last a staff officer escorted them to a nearby restaurant for cold chicken and cheese. This was black comedy. It is not difficult to imagine Halifax's disdain for the ordeal to which Churchill had exposed him.

Back at the prefecture, the British waited impatiently for Reynaud. It was essential that they take off again in daylight, because the bomb-cratered and unlit runway was unfit for night operations. At last the French prime minister arrived, with Spears. He told the English party that while Weygand was ready to surrender, it was still possible that he could persuade his colleagues to fight on – if he received a firm assurance that the Americans would fight. Otherwise, would Britain concede that it was now impossible for France to continue the war? Churchill responded with expressions of sympathy for France's agony. He concluded simply, however, that Britain would sustain its resistance: no terms, no surrender. Reynaud said that the prime minister had not answered his question. Churchill said he could not accede to a French capitulation. He urged that Reynaud's government should make a direct appeal to President Roosevelt before taking any other action. Some of the British party were dismayed that nothing was said about continuing the fight from France's North African empire. They were fearful that Reynaud's nation would not only cease to be their ally, but might join Germany as their foe. They were acutely aware that, even though the French leader still had some heart, his generals, excepting only De Gaulle, had none.

In the courtyard below, a throng of French politicians and officials, emotional and despairing, milled around Churchill as he left. Hands were wrung, tears shed. The prime minister murmured to De Gaulle: '*L'homme du destin.*' He ignored an impassioned intervention by the comtesse de Portes, who pushed forward crying out that her country was bleeding to death, and that she must be heard. French officials told the assembled politicians that Churchill at this last meeting of the Supreme War Council had shown full understanding of France's position, and was resigned to her capitulation. Reynaud did not invite Churchill to meet his ministers, as they themselves wished. They felt snubbed in consequence, though the omission changed nothing.

Churchill landed back at Hendon after a two-and-a-half-hour flight. At Downing Street he learned that President Roosevelt had responded to an earlier French appeal with private promises of more material aid, and declared himself impressed that Reynaud was committed to fight on. Churchill told the war cabinet that such a message came as close to an American declaration of war as was possible without Congress. This was, of course, wildly wishful thinking. Roosevelt, on Secretary of State Cordell Hull's advice, rejected Churchill's plea that he should allow his cable to be published.

On 12 June, the 51st Highland Division at Saint-Valery was forced to join a local capitulation by troops of the French Tenth Army, to which the British formation was attached. Had an order been given a few days earlier, it is plausible that the troops could have been evacuated to Britain through Le Havre. Instead, they became a sacrifice to Churchill's commitment to be seen to sustain the campaign. That same day, Gen. Sir Alan Brooke arrived with orders to lead British forces to the aid of the French. Reinforcements were still landing at the Brittany ports on the 13th.

When Ismay suggested that British units moving to France should hasten slowly, Churchill said: 'Certainly not. It would look very bad in history if we were to do any such thing.' This was of a piece with his response to chancellor Kingsley Wood's suggestion a few weeks later, that since Britain was financially supporting the Dutch administration in exile, in return the government should demand an increased stake in the Royal Dutch Shell oil company. 'Churchill, who objected to taking advantage of another country's misfortunes, said that he never again wished to hear such a suggestion.' At every turn, he perceived his own words and actions through the prism of posterity. He was determined that historians should say: 'He nothing common did or mean upon that memorable scene.' Indeed, in those days Marvell's lines on King Charles I's execution were much in his mind. He recited them repeatedly to his staff, and then to the House of Commons. Seldom has a great actor on the stage of human affairs been so mindful of the verdict of future ages, even as he played out his own part and delivered his lines.

On 14 June, the Germans entered Paris unopposed. Yet illusions persisted in London that a British foothold on the Continent might even now be maintained. Jock Colville wrote from Downing Street that day: 'If the French will go on fighting, we must now fall back on the Atlantic, creating new lines of Torres Vedras behind which British divisions and American supplies can be concentrated. Paris is not France, and . . . there is no reason to suppose the Germans will be able to subdue the whole country.' Colville himself was a very junior civil servant, but his fantasies were fed by more important people. That evening, Churchill spoke by telephone to Brooke in France. The prime minister deplored the fact that the remaining British formations were in retreat. He wanted to make the French feel that they were being supported. Brooke, with an Ulster bluntness of which Churchill would gain much more experience in the course of the war, retorted that 'it was impossible to make a corpse feel'. After what seemed to the soldier an interminable and absurd wrangle, Churchill said: 'All right, I agree with you.'

In that conversation, Brooke saved almost 200,000 men from death or captivity. By sheer force of personality, not much in evidence among British generals, he persuaded Churchill to allow his forces to be removed from French command and evacuated. On the 15th, orders were rushed to Canadians en route by rail from the Normandy coast to what passed for the battlefront. Locomotives were shunted from the front to the rear of their trains, which then set off once more for the ports. At Brest, embarking troops were ordered to destroy all vehicles and equipment. However, some determined and imaginative officers laboured defiantly and successfully to evacuate precious artillery. For the French, Weygand was further embittered by tidings of another British withdrawal. It seems astonishing that his compatriots did nothing to impede the operation, and even something to assist it.

Much has been written about Churchill's prudence in declining to reinforce defeat by dispatching further fighter squadrons to France in 1940. The contrary misjudgement is often passed over. Alan Brooke understood the prime minister's motive – to demonstrate to the French that the British Army was still committed to the fight. But he rightly deplored its futility. If Dunkirk represented a miracle, it was scarcely a lesser one that two weeks later it proved possible to evacuate almost all of Brooke's force to Britain through the north-western French ports. There were, in effect, two Dunkirks, though the latter is much less noticed by history. Churchill was able to escape the potentially brutal consequences of his last rash gesture to Reynaud, because of Brooke's resolution and the Germans' preoccupation with completing the destruction of the French army. Had not providence been merciful, all Brooke's men might have been lost, a shattering blow to the British Army's prospects of reconstitution.

On 15 June, at Churchill's behest Dill telephoned Brooke on a weak, crackling line, and told him to delay evacuation of 52nd Division from Cherbourg. In London there were renewed hopes of clinging to a foothold in France, though these had no visible foundation in reality. The French anyway discounted all such British aspirations. Brooke was exasperated. He told the CIGS: 'It is a desperate job being faced with over 150,000 men and a mass of material, ammunition, petrol, supplies etc, to try to evacuate or dispose of, and nothing to cover this operation except the crumbling French army . . . We are wasting shipping and precious hours.' Next day, London grudgingly agreed that the 52nd Division could continue returning to Britain. Yet administrative confusion persisted. Some troops were embarked at Le Havre for Portsmouth, only to be offloaded at Cherbourg and entrained for Rennes. A ship arrived at Brest on the morning of the 18th, bearing artillery and ammunition from England. At a dozen north-west French ports, tens of thousands of British troops milled in chaos, many of them lacking orders and officers.

German preoccupation with the French army alone made it possible to get the men and a few heavy weapons away, amid chaos and mismanagement. There were skirmishes between British and enemy forces, but no fatal clash. Between 14 and 25 June, from Brest and Saint-Nazaire, Cherbourg and lesser western French ports, 144,171 British troops were successfully rescued and brought home, along with 24,352 Poles and 42,000 other Allied soldiers. There were losses, notably the sinking of the liner *Lancastria* at a cost of at least 3,000 lives;* but these were negligible in proportion to the forces at risk – two-thirds of the numbers brought back from Dunkirk.

It is hard to overstate the chaos of British command arrangements in France during the last three weeks of the campaign, even in areas where formations were not much threatened by the Germans. Two trainloads of invaluable and undamaged British tanks were gratuitously abandoned in Normandy. 'Much equipment had been unnecessarily destroyed,' in the angry words of Maj.Gen. Andrew McNaughton, commanding 1st Canadian Division. Though the war had been in progress for almost nine months, Lt.Gen. Sir Henry Karslake, commanding at Le Mans until Brooke's arrival, wrote in a report: 'The lack of previous training for our formations showed itself in many ways.' Men of the 52nd Division arrived in France in June with equipment issued two days earlier, never having fired their anti-tank guns or indeed seen a tank. Karslake was appalled by the perceived indiscipline of some regular units, even before they were engaged: 'Their behaviour was terrible!' Far more vehicles, stores and equipment could have been evacuated, but for administrative disorder prevailing at the ports, where some ships from England were still being unloaded while, at nearby quays, units embarked for home. The commitment to north-west France represented a serious

---

* Estimates that as many as 8,000 people perished on the *Lancastria* are rendered implausible by the overall casualty figures for the campaign in France, which show a total British loss of life of only 11,000.

misjudgement by Churchill, which won no gratitude from the French, and could have cost the Allies as many soldiers as the later disasters in Greece, Crete, Singapore and Tobruk put together.

While the horror of Britain's predicament was now apparent to all those in high places and to many in low, Churchill was visibly exalted by it. At Chequers on the warm summer night of 15 June, Jock Colville described how tidings of gloom were constantly telephoned through, while sentries with steel helmets and fixed bayonets encircled the house. The prime minister, however, displayed the highest spirits, 'repeating poetry, dilating on the drama of the present situation . . . offering everybody cigars, and spasmodically murmuring: "Bang, bang, bang, goes the farmer's gun, run rabbit, run rabbit, run, run, run."' In the early hours of morning, when US ambassador Joseph Kennedy telephoned, the prime minister unleashed upon him a torrent of rhetoric about America's opportunity to save civilisation. Then he held forth to his staff about Britain's growing fighter strength, 'told one or two dirty stories', and departed for bed at 1.30, saying, 'Goodnight, my children.' At least some part of this must have been masquerade. But it was a masquerade of awesome nobility. Churchill's private secretary Eric Seal thought him much changed since 10 May, more sober, 'less violent, less wild, less impetuous'. If this was overstated, there had certainly been an extraordinary accession of self-control.

On 16 June the war cabinet dispatched a message to Reynaud, now in Bordeaux, offering to release France from its obligation as an ally to forswear negotiations with Germany, on the sole condition that the French fleet should be sailed to British harbours. De Gaulle, arriving in London, was invited to lunch with Churchill and Eden at the Carlton Club. He told the prime minister that only the most dramatic British initiative might stave off French surrender. He urged formalising a proposal for political union between France and Britain over which the cabinet had been dallying for days. Amid crisis, these desperate men briefly embraced this fanciful idea. An appropriate message, setting forth the offer in momentous terms, was dispatched to Reynaud. Churchill prepared to set forth once more for France, this time by sea, to discuss a draft 'Proclamation of Union'. He was already aboard a train at Waterloo with Clement Attlee, Archibald Sinclair and the chiefs of staff, bound for embarkation on a destroyer, when word was brought that Reynaud could not receive them. With a heavy heart, the prime minister returned to Downing Street. It was for the best. The proposal for union was wholly unrealistic, and could have changed nothing. France's battle was over. Reynaud's government performed one last service to its ally: that day in Washington, all the French nation's American arms contracts were formally transferred to Britain.

During the night, it was learned at Downing Street that Reynaud had resigned as prime minister and been replaced by Marshal Pétain, who was seeking an armistice. Pétain's prestige among the French people rested first upon his defence of Verdun in 1916, and second upon an ill-founded belief that he possessed a humanity unique among generals, manifested in his merciful handling of the French army during its 1917 mutinies. In June 1940 there is little doubt that Pétain's commitment to peace at any price reflected the wishes of most French people. Reynaud, however, probably committed a historic blunder by agreeing to forsake his office. Had he and his ministerial colleagues chosen instead to accept exile, as did the Norwegian, Belgian and Dutch governments, he could have prevented his nation's surrender of democratic legitimacy, and established French resistance to tyranny on strong foundations in London. As it was, he allowed himself to be overborne by the military defeatists, led by Pétain and Weygand, and denied himself a famous political martyrdom.

A British sergeant named George Starr, who escaped from the Continent through Dunkirk, belatedly reached home in Yorkshire on 18 June. He found his father listening to the radio announcement of France's surrender. The Starr family had for many years run a travelling circus on the Continent. George's father switched off the set, shook his head and said: 'The French will never forgive us for this.' His son could not understand what he meant. Later in the war, however, George Starr spent three years as a British agent with the French Resistance. He enjoyed ample opportunity to explore the sense of betrayal harboured by many French people towards Britain, which never entirely faded.

De Gaulle, Reynaud's army minister, almost alone among prominent Frenchmen chose to pitch camp in London, and secured the evacuation of his wife. The war cabinet opposed his request that he should be permitted to broadcast to his people on the BBC. Churchill however, urged on by Spears, insisted that the renegade – for so De Gaulle was perceived by many of his own people – should be given access to a microphone. The general's legal adviser, Professor Cassin, enquired of his new chief what was the status of his embryo movement in Britain. De Gaulle answered magnificently: 'We are France! . . . The defeated are those who accept defeat.' The general had an answer, too, to the problem of establishing his own stature: 'Churchill will launch me like a new brand of soap.' The British government indeed hired an advertising agency, Richmond Temple, to promote Free France. De Gaulle would need all the help he could get. Few Frenchmen, even those evacuated to Britain from the battle-field, were willing to fight on if their government quit. De Gaulle asked the captain of the French destroyer *Milan*, which carried him across the Channel, if he would serve under British colours. The naval officer answered that he would not. Most of his compatriots proved like-minded. 'Mr Churchill finds that there are not enough French and German bodies to satisfy him,' declared a sulphurous front-page editorial in the Paris paper *Le Matin*, in one of its first issues after the surrender. 'We ask if the British prime minister has lost his head. If so, what a pity that our ministers did not perceive it sooner.' The paper went on to denounce De Gaulle, and to accuse the British of fomenting revolt in France's overseas empire.

In 1941 and 1942, the prime minister would be obliged to preside over many British defeats, and indeed humiliations. Yet no trauma was as profound, no shock as far-reaching, as that which befell him in his first weeks of office, when the German army destroyed France as a military power, and swept the British from the Continent. Henceforward, the character of the war thus became fundamentally different from that of 1914–18. All assumptions were set at naught upon which Allied war policy, and Churchill's personal defiance of Hitler, had been founded. Whatever Britain's continuing capabilities at sea and in the air, since September 1939 it had been taken for granted that the British Army would confront the Nazi legions along-side the French, in the frankly subordinate role demanded by its inferiority of numbers – just ten divisions to ninety-four French on the western front. The British Army could never alone aspire to dispute a battlefield with the Wehrmacht, and this knowledge dominated British strategy.

It was hard for many people, even the highest in the land, to absorb the scale of the disaster which had befallen Allied arms, and which now threatened to overwhelm Britain. Alan Brooke was struck by a Churchillian observation about human nature. The prime minister said that the receptive capacity of a man's mind was like a three-inch pipe running under a culvert. 'When a flood comes the water flows over the culvert whilst the pipe goes on handling its 3 inches. Similarly the human brain will register emotions up to its "3 inch limit" and subsequent additional emotions flow past un-registered.' So it now seemed to Brooke himself, and to a host of others. They perceived that a catastrophe was unfolding, but their hearts could not keep pace with the signals from their brains about its significance. Harold Nicolson wrote in his diary on 15 June: 'My reason tells me that it will now be almost impossible to beat the Germans, and that the probability is that France will surrender and that we shall be bombed and invaded . . . Yet these probabilities do not fill me with despair. I seem to be impervious both to pleasure and pain. For the moment we are all anaesthetised.'

Another eye-witness, writer Peter Fleming, then serving as an army staff officer, identified the same emotional confusion: 'This period was one of carefree improvisation as far as most civilians were concerned. It was as though the whole country had been invited to a fancy-dress ball and everybody was asking everybody else "What are you going as?" A latent incredulity, and the fact that almost everybody had more than enough to do already, combined to give problems connected with invasion the status of engrossing digressions from the main business of life . . . The British, when their ally was pole-axed on their doorstep, became both gayer and more serene than they had been at any time since the overture to Munich struck up in 1937.'

British casualties in France were large in relation to the size of the BEF, but trifling by comparison with those of the French, and with the infinitely more intense struggles that would take place later in the war. The army lost just 11,000 killed and missing, against at least 50,000 French military dead. In addition, 14,070 British wounded were evacuated, and 41,030 BEF prisoners fell into German hands. The loss of tanks, artillery and weapons of all kinds was, of course, calamitous. It is a familiar and ill-founded cliché that the 1940 British Expeditionary Force was ill-equipped. In reality it was much better supplied with vehicles than the Germans, and had good tanks if these had been imaginatively employed. When Hitler's Field Marshal Fedor von Bock saw the wreckage at Dunkirk, he wrote in astonishment: 'Here lies the material of a whole army, so incredibly well-equipped that we poor devils can only look on with envy and amazement.' The BEF was driven from Dunkirk after relatively light fighting and very heavy retreating, because it lacked mass to change the outcome of the campaign once the French front was broken, and was outfought by German formations with better leadership, motivation and air support. The British Army was now, for all practical purposes, disarmed. Almost a thousand RAF aircraft were gone, half of these fighters.

But Britain had human material to forge a new army – though not one that alone could ever be large enough to face the Germans in a Continental war – if only time was granted before it must fight again. An American correspondent reported home that Londoners received news of the French surrender in grim silence rather than with jokes or protestations of defiance. The Battle of France was over, Churchill told the British people on the following night. The Battle of Britain was about to begin. The position of Churchill's nation on 17 June was scarcely enviable. But it was vastly better than had seemed possible a month earlier, when the BEF faced annihilation.

THREE

Invasion Fever

In the months after September 1939, Britain found itself in the bleak – indeed, in some eyes absurd – position of having declared war on Germany, while lacking means to undertake any substantial military initiative, least of all to save Poland. The passivity of the 'Phoney War' ate deeply into the morale of the British people. By contrast, the events of May and June 1940 at least had the merit, brilliantly exploited by Churchill, that they thrust before the nation a clear and readily comprehended purpose: to defend itself against assault by an overwhelmingly powerful foe. The Royal Irish Fusiliers, back from Dunkirk, staged a mess party to celebrate news that the French had surrendered. 'Thank heavens they have,' said an officer gaily. 'Now at last we can get on with the war.' A middle-aged court shorthand writer named George King, living in Surrey, wrote in a diary letter intended for his gunner son, left behind in France and on his way to captivity in Germany: 'Winston Churchill has told us just exactly where we stand. We are on our own, and have got to see this thing through; and we can do it, properly led. Goodness knows what the swines will try, but somehow we've got to stick it.'

Naval officer Robert Hichens wrote on 17 June: 'Now we know that we have got to look to ourselves only, I have an idea that England will respond wonderfully to this setback. She is always greatest in taking reverses.' After Churchill addressed the Commons on the 18th, a Labour backbencher, Dr Hastings Lees-Smith of Keighley, stood up: 'My hon. friends on these benches have asked me on their behalf to say one or two sentences. They wish to say to the PM that in their experience among the broad masses of the people of this country never in their lives has the country been more united than it is today in its support of the PM's assertion that we shall carry on right to the end. One sentence can summarise what we feel. Whatever the country is asked for in the months and, if necessary, in the years to come, the PM may be confident that the people will rise to their responsibilities.'

Yet, if the grit displayed by King, Hichens and Lees-Smith was real enough, it would be mistaken to suppose that it was universal. Not all sceptics about Britain's chances of survival were elderly politicians or businessmen. An RAF Hurricane pilot, Paul Mayhew, wrote in a family newsletter: 'Now I suppose it's our turn and though my morale is now pretty good . . . I can't believe that there's much hope for us, at any rate in Europe. Against a ferocious and relentless attack, the Channel's not much of an obstacle and with the army presumably un-equipped, I don't give much for our chances. Personally I have only two hopes; first that Churchill is more reliable than Reynaud and that we will go on fighting if England is conquered, and secondly that Russia, in spite of our blunders, will now be sufficiently scared to stage a distraction in the East. In America I have little faith; I suppose in God's own time God's own country will fight. But at present their army is smaller than the Swiss, their Air Force is puny and rather "playboy", and I doubt whether we need their Navy.' A week later, Mayhew apologised to his family for being 'ludicrously defeatist'. But here was a young airman voicing fears widely shared among his elders.

The summer and autumn of 1940 were poor seasons for truth-telling in Britain. That is to say, it was hard for even good, brave and honourable men to know whether they better served their country by voicing their private thoughts, allowing their brains to function, or by keeping silent. Logic decreed that Britain had not the smallest chance of winning the war in the absence of American participation, which remained implausible. Churchill knew this as well as anyone. Yet he and his supporters believed that the cause of freedom, the defiance of tyranny, made it essential that the British people should fight on regardless, sweeping aside all calculations of relative strengths and strategic disabilities. Posterity has heaped admiration upon the grandeur of this commitment. Yet at the time it demanded from intelligent men and women a suspension of reason which some rejected. For instance, Captain Ralph Edwards, Director of Naval Operations at the Admiralty, was an almost unwavering sceptic. On 17 June he noted in his diary: '[Captain] Bill Tennant came in to say that he'd told Sir Walter Monckton of all our misgivings about the higher direction of the war.' And again on the 23rd: 'Our cabinet with that idiot Winston in charge changes its mind every 24 hours ... I'm rapidly coming to the conclusion that we're so inept we don't deserve to win & indeed are almost certain to be defeated. We never do anything right.' Through the lonely eighteen months ahead, Churchill was galled that such scourges as Aneurin Bevan MP taxed him in the Commons with unwelcome facts of which he was thoroughly aware, painful realities such as he confronted every hour. From the outset, while he always insisted that victory would come, his personal prestige rested upon the honesty with which he acknowledged to the British people the gravity of the ordeal they faced.

Churchill told MPs on 4 June: 'Our thankfulness at the escape of our Army and so many men, whose loved ones have passed through an agonising week, must not blind us to the fact that what has happened in France and Belgium is a colossal military disaster. I have myself full confidence that if all do their duty, if nothing is neglected, and if the best arrangements are made, as they are being made, we shall prove ourselves once again able to defend our island home, to ride out the storm of war, and to outlive the menace of tyranny, if necessary for years, if necessary alone. That is the resolve of His Majesty's Government.' After the prime minister sat down, as always exchanges between MPs degenerated into commonplaces. Dr Lees-Smith delivered words of appreciation. Glaswegian maverick Jimmy Maxton, an Independent Labour MP, raised a point of order, which led to cross words and pettiness. Captain Bellenger of Bassetlaw rebuked Mr Thorne of Plaistow, whom Bellenger believed had impugned his courage: 'You have no right to make remarks of that kind.'

Clausewitz wrote in 1811: 'A government must never assume that its country's fate, its whole existence, hangs on the outcome of a single battle, no matter how decisive.' Churchill's conduct after the fall of France exasperated some sceptics who perceived themselves as clear thinkers, but conformed perfectly to the Prussian's dictum. His supreme achievement in 1940 was to mobilise Britain's warriors, to shame into silence its doubters, to stir the passions of the nation, so that for a season the British people faced the world united and exalted. The 'Dunkirk spirit' was not spontaneous. It was created by the rhetoric and bearing of one man, displaying powers that will define political leadership for the rest of time. Under a different prime minister, the British people in their shock and bewilderment could as readily have been led in another direction. Nor was the mood long-lived. It persisted only until winter, when it was replaced by a more dogged, doubtful and less exuberant national spirit. But that first period was decisive: 'If we can get through the next three months, we can get through the next three years,' Churchill told the Commons on 20 June.

Kingsley Martin argued in that week's *New Statesman* that Churchill's 18 June 'finest hour' broadcast to the nation was too simplistic: 'He misunderstood [the British people's] feelings when he talked of this as the finest moment of their history. Our feelings are more complex than that. To talk to common people in or out of uniform is to discover that determination to defend this island is coupled with a deep and almost universal bitterness that we have been reduced to such a pass.' Yet the prime minister judged the predominant mood much more shrewdly than the veteran socialist. In 1938 the British had not been what Churchill wanted them to be. In 1941 and thereafter they would often disappoint his hopes. But in 1940, to an extraordinary degree he was able to shape and elevate the nation to fulfil his aspirations.

Mollie Panter-Downes wrote in the *New Yorker* of 29 June:

It would be difficult for an impartial observer to decide today whether the British are the bravest or merely the most stupid people in the

63

world. The way they are acting in the present situation could be used to support either claim. The individual Englishman seems to be singularly unimpressed by the fact that there is now nothing between him and the undivided attention of a war machine such as the world has never seen before. Possibly it's lack of imagination; possibly again it's the same species of dogged resolution which occasionally produces an epic like Dunkirk. Millions of British families, sitting at their well-stocked breakfast tables eating excellent British eggs and bacon, can still talk calmly of the horrors across the Channel, perhaps without fully comprehending even now that anything like that could ever happen in England's green and pleasant land.

Many Americans, by contrast, thought it unlikely that Britain would survive. In New York, 'one thing that strikes me is the amount of defeatist talk', wrote US General Raymond Lee, 'the almost pathological assumption that it is all over bar the shouting . . . that it is too late for the United States to do anything'. Key Pittman, chairman of the Senate Foreign Relations Committee, called on Churchill to send the British fleet to the New World: 'It is no secret that Great Britain is totally unprepared for defense and that nothing the US has to give can do more than delay the result . . . It is to be hoped that this plan will not to be too delayed by futile encouragement to fight on. It is conclusively evident that Congress will not authorize intervention in the European war.' *Time* magazine reported on 1 July: 'So scared was many a US citizen last week that he wanted to shut off aid to Britain for fear that the US would weaken its own defenses, wanted to have the US wash its hands of help for Britain, for fear of getting involved on the losing side.'

A *Fortune* opinion survey showed that even before France collapsed, most Americans believed that Germany would win the war. Only 30.3 per cent saw any hope for the Allies. A correspondent named Herbert Jones wrote a letter to the *Philadelphia Inquirer* which reflected widespread sentiment: 'The great majority of Americans are not pacifists or isolationists, but, after the experience of the last war and Versailles, have no desire to pull Britain's chestnuts out of the fire for her, under the slogan of "Save the World for Democracy". They rightly feel that that little is to be gained by pouring out our money and the lives of our young men for the cause of either the oppressor of the Jews and Czechs or the oppressor of the Irish and of India . . .' Richard E. Taylor of Apponaugh, Rhode Island, wrote to a friend in England urging him to draw the attention of the authorities to the danger that the Germans might tunnel under the Channel.

Yet some Americans did not despair. An 'aid to Britain' committee gathered three million signatures on petitions to the White House. The organisation spawned a Historians' Committee under Charles Seymour of Yale; a Scientists' Committee under Nobel Prize-winner Harold Urey; a Theatre Committee under playwright and Roosevelt speechwriter Robert Sherwood. Americans were invited to set aside their caricature view of Britain as a nation of stuffed-shirt sleepy-heads, and to perceive instead battling champions of freedom. Novelist Somerset Maugham, arriving in New York, predicted a vastly different post-war Britain, and hinted at the beginnings of one more sympathetic to an American social vision: 'I have a feeling . . . that in the England of the future evening dress will be less important than it has been in the past.' America was still far, far from belliger-ence, but forces favouring intervention were stirring.

In 1941 Churchill devoted immense energy to wooing the US. But in 1940, once his June appeals to Roosevelt had failed, for several weeks he did not write to the president at all, and dismissed sugges-tions for a British propaganda offensive. 'Propaganda is all very well,' he said, 'but it is events that make the world. If we smash the Huns here, we shall need no propaganda in the United States . . . Now we must live. Next year we shall be winning. The year after that we shall triumph. But if we can hold the Germans in this coming month of July . . . our position will be quite different from today.'

But how to 'hold them'? the anglophile General Raymond Lee, military attaché at the London embassy, wrote: 'One queer thing about the present situation is that it is one which has never been studied at the Staff College. For years [British officers] had studied our [American Civil War] Valley campaign, operations in India,

Afghanistan, Egypt and Europe, had done landings on a hostile shore, but it had never occurred to them that some day they might have to defend the non-combatants of a country at war.' An MP recounted Churchill saying at this time: 'I don't know what we'll fight them with – we shall have to slosh them on the head with bottles – empty ones, of course.' This joke was almost certainly apocryphal, but as the prime minister himself observed of the manner in which spurious Churchilliana accrued, he became 'a magnet for iron filings'.

On 8 June, Britain's Home Forces boasted an inventory of just fifty-four two-pounder anti-tank guns, 420 field guns with 200 rounds of ammunition apiece, 613 medium and heavy guns with 150 rounds for each; 105 medium and heavy tanks and 395 light tanks. There were only 2,300 Bren light machine-guns and 70,000 rifles. Visiting beach defences at St Margaret's Bay in Kent on 26 June, Churchill was told by the local brigadier that he had three anti-tank guns, with six rounds of ammunition apiece. Not one shot must be wasted on practice, said the prime minister. He dismissed a suggestion that London might, like Paris, be declared an open city. The British capital's dense streets, he said, offered peerless opportunities for local defence. So dire was the shortage of small arms that when a consignment of World War I-vintage rifles arrived from the US on 10 July, Churchill decreed that they must be distributed within forty-eight hours. He rejected a proposal that Britain should try to deter Spain from entering the war by promising talks about the disputed sovereignty of Gibraltar as soon as peace returned. The Spanish, he said, would know full well that if Britain won, there would be no deal.

His wit never faltered. When he heard that six people had suffered heart failure following an air-raid warning, he observed that he himself was more likely to die of overeating. Yet he did not want to perish quite yet, 'when so many interesting things were happening'. Told that the Luftwaffe had bombed ironworks owned by the family of Stanley Baldwin, arch-appeasing thirties prime minister, he muttered, 'Very ungrateful of them.' When his wife Clementine described how she had marched disgusted out of a service at St Martin-in-the-Fields after hearing its preacher deliver a pacifist sermon, Churchill said: 'You ought to have cried "Shame," desecrating the House of God with lies.' He then turned to Jock Colville: 'Tell the Minister of Information with a view to having the man pilloried.' General Sir Bernard Paget exclaimed to Colville: 'What a wonderful tonic he is!'

Between June and September 1940, and to a lessening degree for eighteen months thereafter, the minds of the British government and people were fixed upon the threat that Hitler would dispatch an army to invade their island. It is a perennially fascinating question, how far such a peril was ever realistic – or was perceived as such by Winston Churchill. The collapse of France and expulsion of the British Army from the Continent represented the destruction of the strategic foundations upon which British policy was founded. Yet if the German victory in France had been less swift, if the Allies had become engaged in more protracted fighting, the cost in British and French blood would have been vastly greater, while it is hard to imagine any different outcome. John Kennedy was among senior British soldiers who perceived this: 'We should have had an enormous army in France if we had been allowed to go on long enough, and it would have lost its equip[men]t all the same.' Sir Hugh Dowding, C-in-C of Fighter Command, claimed that on news of the French surrender 'I went on my knees and thanked God,' because no further British fighters need be vainly destroyed on the Continent. Only German perceptions of the BEF's marginal role permitted so many of Britain's soldiers to escape from the battlefield by sea not once, but twice, in June 1940. No staff college war game would have allowed so indulgent an outcome. Though it was hard to see matters in such terms at the time, if French defeat had been inevitable, Britain escaped from its consequences astonishingly lightly.

The British in June 1940 believed that they were threatened by imminent invasion followed by likely annihilation. Unsurprisingly, they thought themselves the focus of Hitler's ambitions. Few comprehended his obsession with the East. They could not know that Germany was neither militarily prepared nor psychologically committed to launch a massive amphibious operation across the Channel. The Wehrmacht needed months to digest the conquest of France and the Low Countries. The Nazis' perception of Britain and its ruling class was distorted by pre-war acquaintance with so many aristocratic appeasers. Now, they confidently awaited the displacement of Churchill's government by one which acknowledged realities. 'Are the English giving in? No sure signs visible yet,' Goebbels wrote in his diary on 26 June. 'Churchill still talks big. But then he is not England.' Some historians have expressed surprise that Hitler prevaricated about invasion. Yet his equivocation was matched by the Allies later in the war. For all the aggressive rhetoric of Churchill and Roosevelt, the British for years nursed hopes that Germany would collapse without an Allied landing in France. The Americans were much relieved that Japan surrendered without being invaded. No belligerent nation risks a massive amphibious operation on a hostile shore until other options have been exhausted. Germany in 1940 proved no exception.

Churchill's people might have slept a little easier through that summer had they perceived that they were more happily placed to withstand the siege and bombardment of their island than any other conceivable strategic scenario. Their army had been delivered from the need to face the Wehrmacht on the battlefield, and indeed would not conduct major operations on the Continent for more than three years. The Royal Navy, despite its Norwegian and Dunkirk losses, remained an immensely powerful force. A German fleet of towed barges moving across the Channel at a speed of only three or four knots must remain within range of warship guns for many hours. On 1 July, the German navy possessed only one heavy and two light cruisers, together with four destroyers and some E-boats, available for duty as escorts. The Royal Air Force was better organised and equipped to defend Britain against bomber attack than for any other operation of war. If a German army secured a beachhead, Churchill's land forces were unfit to expel it. But in the summer of 1940 England's moat, those twenty-one miles of choppy sea between rival chalk cliffs, represented a formidable, probably decisive obstacle to Hitler's landlubbing army.

Among the government's first concerns was that of ensuring that the Vichy French fleet did not become available to Hitler. During days of cabinet argument on this issue, Churchill at one moment raised the possibility that the Americans might be persuaded to purchase the warships. In the event, however, a more direct and brutal option was adopted. Horace Walpole wrote two centuries earlier: 'No great country was ever saved by good men, because good men will not go to the lengths that may be necessary.' At Mers-el-Kebir, Oran, on 3 July, French commanders rejected an ultimatum from Admiral Sir James Somerville, commanding the Royal Navy's Force H offshore, either to scuttle their fleet or sail to join the British. The subsequent bombardment of France's warships was one of the most ruthless acts by a democracy in the annals of war. It resulted from a decision such as only Churchill would plausibly have taken. Yet it commands the respect of posterity, as it did of Franklin Roosevelt, as an earnest of Britain's iron determination to sustain the struggle. Churchill told the House of Commons next day: 'We had hoped until the afternoon that our terms would be accepted without bloodshed.' As to passing judgement on the action, he left this 'with confidence to Parliament. I leave it also to the nation, and I leave it to the United States. I leave it to the world and to history.'

As MPs cheered and waved their order papers in a curiously taste-less display of enthusiasm for an action which, however necessary, had cost 1,250 French lives, Churchill resumed his seat with tears pouring down his face. He, the francophile, perceived the bitter fruits that had been plucked at Oran. He confided later: 'It was a terrible decision, like taking the life of one's own child to save the State.' He feared that the immediate consequence would be to drive Vichy to join Germany in arms against Britain. But, at a moment when the Joint Intelligence Committee was warning that invasion seemed imminent, he absolutely declined to acquiesce in the risk that French capital ships might screen a German armada.

Pétain's regime did not declare war, though French bitterness about Oran persisted for years to come. The bombardment was less decisive in its strategic achievement than Churchill claimed, because one French battle-cruiser escaped, and a powerful fleet still lay at Toulon under Vichy orders. But actions sometimes have consequences which remain unperceived for long afterwards. This was the case with the attack on Mers-el-Kebir, followed by the failure two months later of a Free French attempt to take over Dakar, the capital of France's African colony Senegal. When General Francisco Franco, Spain's dictator, submitted to Hitler his shopping list for joining the Axis, it was headed by a demand that Hitler should transfer to Spain French colonies in Africa. Yet Vichy France's rejection of both British diplomatic advances and military threats, together with the refusal of most of France's African colonies to 'rally' to De Gaulle, persuaded Hitler to hope that Pétain's nation would soon become his fighting ally. He therefore refused to satisfy Franco at French expense. The attack on Oran, a painful necessity, and Dakar, an apparent fiasco, contributed significantly to keeping Spain out of the war.

One part of the British Commonwealth offered no succour to the 'mother country': the Irish Free State, bitterly hostile to Britain since it gained independence in 1922, sustained nominal allegiance by a constitutional quirk under the terms of the island's partition treaty. Churchill had heaped scorn upon Neville Chamberlain's 1938 surrender of Britain's Irish 'Treaty Ports' to the Dublin government. As First Lord of the Admiralty in 1939 he contemplated military action against Eire, as the southern Irish dominion was known. Amid the desperate circumstances of June 1940, however, he responded cautiously to a suggestion by Chamberlain – of all people – that Ireland should be obliged by force to yield up its harbours, which might play a critical role in keeping open Britain's Atlantic lifeline. Churchill was moved to oppose this by fear of a hostile reaction in the United States. Instead, the British government urged Lord Craigavon, prime minister of the Protestant north, which remained part of the United Kingdom, to seek a meeting with Irish prime minister Éamon de Valera to discuss the defence of their common island. Craigavon, like most of his fellow Ulstermen, loathed the Catholic southerners. He dismissed this notion out of hand.

Yet in late June, London presented a remarkable and radical secret proposal to Dublin: Britain would make a principled commitment to a post-war united Ireland in return for immediate access to Irish ports and bases. Britain's ambassador in Dublin reported De Valera's stony response. The *Taoiseach* would commit himself only to the neutrality of a united Ireland though he said unconvincingly that he 'might' enter the war after the British government made a public declaration of commitment to union.

The British government nonetheless urged Dublin to conduct talks with the Belfast regime about a prospective union endorsed by Britain, in return for Eire's belligerence. Chamberlain told the cabinet: 'I do not believe that the Ulster government would refuse to play their part to bring about so favourable a development.' De Valera again declined to accept deferred payment. MacDonald cabled London, urging Churchill to offer personal assurances. The prime minister wrote in the margin of this message: 'But all contingent upon Ulster agreeing & S. Ireland coming into the war.'

On 26 June Chamberlain belatedly reported these exchanges to Craigavon, saying: 'You will observe that the document takes the form of an enquiry only, because we have not felt it right to approach you officially with a request for your assent unless we had first a binding assurance from Eire that they would, if the assent were given, come into the war . . . If therefore they refuse the plan you are in no way committed, and if they accept you are still free to make your own comments or objections as may think fit.' The Ulsterman cabled back: 'Am profoundly shocked and disgusted by your letter making suggestions so far-reaching behind my back and without any pre-consultation with me. To such treachery to loyal Ulster I will never be a party.' Chamberlain, in turn, responded equally angrily to what he perceived as Craigavon's insufferable parochialism. He concluded: 'Please remember the serious nature of the situation which requires that every effort be made to meet it.'

The war cabinet, evidently unimpressed by Craigavon's anger, now strengthened its proposal to Dublin: 'This declaration would take the form of a solemn undertaking that the Union is to become at an early date an accomplished fact from which there shall be no turning back.' When Craigavon was informed, he responded: 'Your telegram only confirms my confidential information and conviction De Valera is under German dictation and far past reasoning with. He may purposely protract negotiations till enemy has landed. Strongly advocate immediate naval occupation of harbours and military advance south.'

Craigavon asserted in a personal letter to Churchill that Ulster would only participate in an All-Ireland Defence Force 'if British martial law is imposed throughout the island'. The two men met in London on 7 July. There is no record of their conversation. It is reasonable to assume that it was frosty, but by then Churchill could assuage the Ulsterman's fears. Two days earlier, De Valera had finally rejected the British plan. He, like many Irishmen, was convinced that Britain was doomed to lose the war. He doubted Churchill's real willingness to coerce Craigavon. If he ever seriously contemplated accepting London's terms, he also probably feared that once committed to belligerence, Ireland would become a British puppet.

Churchill makes no mention of the Irish negotiation in his war memoirs. Since the British offer to Dublin was sensational, this suggests that recollection of it brought no pleasure to the prime minister. Given De Valera's implacable hostility, the Irish snub was inevitable. But it represented a massive miscalculation by the Irish leader. Ernest Bevin wrote in confidence to an academic friend who was urging a deal on a united Ireland: 'There are difficulties which appear at the moment almost insurmountable. You see, De Valera's policy is, even if we get a united Ireland, he would still remain neutral. On that, he is immovable. Were it not for this attitude, I believe a solution would be easy . . . You may rest assured that we are watching every possible chance.' If Ireland had entered the war on the Allied side at any time, even after the US became a belligerent in December 1941 and Allied victory was assured, American cash would have flooded into the country, perhaps advancing Ireland's economic take-off by two generations.

The exchanges of July were not quite the end of the story. In December 1940, Churchill suggested in a letter to President Roosevelt that 'If the Government of Eire would show its solidarity with the democracies of the English-speaking world . . . a Council Of Defence of all Ireland could be set up out of which the unity of the island would probably in some form or other emerge after the war.' Here was a suggestion much less explicit than that of the summer, obviously modified by the diminution of British peril. It is impossible to know whether, if De Valera had acceded to the British proposal of June 1940, Churchill would indeed have obliged the recalcitrant Ulster Protestants to accept union with the south. Given his high-handed treatment of other dominions and colonies in the course of the war – not least the surrender of British overseas bases to the United States – it seems by no means impossible. So dire was Britain's predicament, of such vital significance in the U-boat war were Irish ports and airfields, that it seemed worth almost any price to secure them.

Churchill threw himself into the struggle to prepare his island to resist invasion. He decreed that if the Germans landed, all measures including poison gas were to be employed against them. On 6 July he inspected an exercise in Kent. 'Winston was in great form,' Ironside wrote in his diary, 'and gave us lunch at Chartwell in his cottage. Very wet but nobody minded at all.' A consignment of 250,000 rifles and 300 old 75mm field guns arrived from America – poor weapons, but desperately welcome. Ironside expected the German invasion on 9 July, and was surprised when it did not come. On 10 July, instead, the Luftwaffe launched its first big raid on Britain, by seventy aircraft against south Wales dockyards. Churchill knew this was the foretaste of a heavy and protracted air assault. Two days later he visited RAF Hurricane squadrons at Kenley, to the south of London. Straining to harness every aid to public morale, he demanded that military bands should play in the streets. He urged attention to gas masks, because he feared that Hitler would unleash chemical weapons. He resisted the evacuation of children from cities, and deplored the shipment of the offspring of the rich to sanctuary in the US. He argued vigorously against over-stringent rationing, and deplored pessimism wherever it was encountered. Dill, less than two months head of the army, was already provoking his mistrust: the CIGS 'strikes me as tired, disheartened and over-impressed with the might of Germany', wrote the prime minister to Eden. In Churchill's eyes, all through the long months which followed, defeatism was the only crime beyond forgiveness.

On 19 July, Ironside was dismissed as C-in-C Home Forces, and replaced by Sir Alan Brooke. Ironside wanted to meet an invasion with a thin crust of coastal defences, and to rely chiefly upon creating strong lines inland. Brooke, by contrast, proposed swift counter-attacks with mobile forces. Brooke and Churchill were surely correct in perceiving that if the Germans secured a lodgement and airfields in south-east England, the battle for Britain would be irretrievably lost. Inland defences were worthless, save for sustaining a sense of purpose among those responsible for building them.

Peter Fleming argued in his later history of the period that although the British went through the motions of anticipating invasion, they did not in their hearts believe in such an eventuality, because they had no historical experience of it: 'They paid lip-service to reality. They took the precautions which the Government advised, made the sacri-fices which it required of them and worked like men possessed . . . But . . . they found it impossible, however steadfastly they gazed into the future, to fix in a satisfactory focus the terrible contingencies which invasion was expected to bring forth.' Fleming added a percep-tive observation: 'The menace of invasion was at once a tonic and a drug . . . The extreme and disheartening bleakness of their long-term prospects was obscured by the melodramatic nature of the predica-ment in which . . . the fortunes of war had placed them.'

Churchill understood the need to mobilise the British people to action for its own sake, rather than allowing them time to brood, to contemplate dark realities. He himself thought furiously about the middle distance. 'When I look around to see how we can win the war,' he wrote to Beaverbrook on 10 July, 'I see only one sure path. We have no continental army which can defeat the German military power. The blockade is broken and Hitler has Asia and probably

Africa to draw upon. Should he be repulsed here or not try invasion, he will recoil eastward and we have nothing to stop him. But there is one thing that will bring him back and bring him down, and that is an absolutely devastating, exterminating attack by very heavy bombers from this country upon the Nazi homeland.' Likewise at Chequers on 14 July: 'Hitler must invade or fail. If he fails he is bound to go east, and fail he will.' Churchill had no evidential basis in intelligence for his assertion that the Germans might lunge towards Russia. At this time only a remarkable instinct guided him, shared by few others save Britain's notoriously erratic ambassador in Moscow, the Independent Labour MP Sir Stafford Cripps. Not until March 1941, three months before the event, did British intelligence decide that a German invasion of the Soviet Union was likely.

As for aircraft production, while fighters were the immediate need, the prime minister urged the creation of the largest possible bomber force. This, a desperate policy born out of desperate circumstances, absolute lack of any plausible alternative, would achieve destructive maturity only years later, when victory was assured by other means. Churchill appointed Admiral Sir Roger Keyes, the brainless old hero of the 1918 Zeebrugge raid, to become Director of Combined Operations, with a brief to prepare to launch raids on the Continent of Europe. He wanted no pinprick fiascos, he said, but instead attacks by five to ten thousand men. He ordered the establishment of Special Operations Executive, SOE, under the direction of Hugh Dalton as Minister of Economic Warfare, with a mandate to 'Set Europe ablaze.' He endorsed De Gaulle as the voice and leader of Free France. Brooke, at Gosport with Churchill on 17 July, found him 'in wonderful spirits and full of offensive plans for next summer'. Most of the commitments made in those days remained ineffectually implemented for years to come. Yet they represented earnests for the future that inspired Churchill's colleagues; which was, of course, exactly as he intended.

And above all in those days, there were his words. 'Faith is given to us to help and comfort us when we stand in awe before the unfurling scroll of human destiny,' he told the British people in a broadcast on

14 July, Bastille Day, in which he recalled attending a magnificent military parade in Paris just a year before. 'And I proclaim my faith that some of us will live to see a Fourteenth of July when a liberated France will once again rejoice in her greatness and her glory.' He continued:

> Here in this strong City of Refuge which enshrines the title-deeds of human progress and is of deep consequence to Christian civilization; here, girt about by the seas and oceans where the Navy reigns; shielded from above by the prowess and devotion of our airmen – we await undismayed the impending assault. Perhaps it will come tonight. Perhaps it will come next week. Perhaps it will never come. We must show ourselves equally capable of meeting a sudden violent shock or – what is perhaps a harder test – a prolonged vigil. But be the ordeal sharp or long, or both, we shall seek no terms, we shall tolerate no parley; we may show mercy – we shall ask for none.

One of the prime minister's listeners wrote: 'Radio sets were not then very powerful, and there was always static. Families had to sit near the set, with someone always fiddling with the knobs. It was like sitting round a hearth, with someone poking the fire; and to that hearth came the crackling voice of Winston Churchill.' Vere Hodgson, a thirty-nine-year-old London woman, wrote: 'Gradually we came under the spell of that wonderful voice and inspiration. His stature grew larger and larger, until it filled our sky.' Vita Sackville-West wrote to her husband Harold Nicolson, saying that one of Churchill's speeches 'sent shivers (not of fear) down my spine. I think that one of the reasons why one is stirred by his Elizabethan phrases is that one feels the whole massive backing of power and resolve behind them, like a great fortress: they are never words for words' sake.' Mollie Panter-Downes told readers of the *New Yorker*: 'Mr Churchill is the only man in England today who consistently interprets the quiet but completely resolute national mood.'

Isaiah Berlin wrote: 'Like a great actor – perhaps the last of his kind – upon the stage of history, he speaks his memorable lines with a large, unhurried, and stately utterance in a blaze of light, as is appropriate to a man who knows that his work and his person will remain the objects of scrutiny and judgement to many generations.' Tory MP Cuthbert Headlam wrote on 16 July: 'It is certainly his hour – and the confidence in him is growing on all sides.' Churchill's sublime achievement was to rouse the most ordinary people to extraordinary perceptions of their own destiny. Eleanor Silsby, an elderly psychology lecturer living in south London, wrote to a friend in America on 23 July 1940: 'I won't go on about the war. But I just want to say that we are proud to have the honour of fighting alone for the things that matter much more than life and death. It makes me hold my chin high to think, not just of being English, but of having been chosen to come at this hour for this express purpose of saving the world . . . I should never have thought that I could approve of war . . . There is surprisingly little anger or hate in this business – it is just a job that has to be done . . . This is Armageddon.' Churchill was much moved by receiving through the post a box of cigars from a working girl who said that she had saved her wages to buy them for him. One morning at Downing Street, John Martin found himself greeting a woman who had called to offer a £60,000 pearl necklace to the service of the state. Told of this, Churchill quoted Macaulay:

> Romans in Rome's quarrel,
> Spared neither land nor gold

Much of the German press editorialised about Churchill's 14 July speech, describing him as 'Supreme Warlord of the Plutocracy'. The *Deutsche Allgemeine Zeitung* was among the titles which suggested that his foolish determination to fight to the last would bring down upon London the same fate as had befallen other conquered cities: 'The unscrupulous rulers of Warsaw did not perceive the consequences of obstinacy until their capital lay in ruins and ashes. Likewise, Rotterdam paid the price for its failure to reach a rational

decision, such as saved other Dutch cities and – at the eleventh hour
– Paris.' German forces, Hitler's people were told, felt well rested after
the French campaign, and now stood poised to launch an assault on
Britain whenever the Führer gave the order. Meanwhile, the
Luftwaffe's air attacks on Churchill's country, which had hitherto
been on a small scale, would escalate dramatically. A quick victory
over Britain was to be confidently anticipated. German radio's
English-language propaganda broadcasts conveyed the same message,
of imminent doom.

On 19 July Hitler addressed the Reichstag and the world, publicly
offering Britain a choice between peace and 'unending suffering and
misery'. Churchill responded: 'I don't propose to say anything in
reply to Herr Hitler's speech, not being on speaking terms with him.'
He urged Lord Lothian, Britain's ambassador in Washington, to press
the Americans to fulfil Britain's earlier request for the 'loan' of old
destroyers. On 1 August he delivered a magisterial rebuke to the
Foreign Office for the elaborate phrasing of its proposed response
to a message from the King of Sweden, who was offering to mediate
between Britain and Germany. 'The draft errs,' he wrote, 'in trying
to be too clever, and to enter into refinements of policy unsuited to
the tragic simplicity and grandeur of the times and the issues at
stake.' That day, Hitler issued his Directive No. 17, unleashing the
Luftwaffe's massive air campaign against Britain.

FOUR

The Battle of Britain

Thus began the events that will define for eternity the image of Britain in the summer of 1940. Massed formations of German bombers with their accompanying fighter escorts droned across blue skies towards Kent and Sussex, to be met by intercepting Hurricanes and Spitfires, tracing white condensation trails through the thin air. The most aesthetically beautiful aircraft the world has ever seen, their grace enhanced in the eyes of posterity by their role as the saviours of freedom, pierced the bomber formations, diving, twisting, banking, hammering fire. Onlookers craned their heads upwards, mesmerised by the spectacle. Shop-workers and housewives, bank clerks and schoolchildren, heard the clatter of machine-guns; found aircraft fragments and empty cartridge cases tinkling onto their streets and littering suburban gardens; sometimes even met fallen aircrew of both sides, stumbling to their front doors.

Stricken planes spewing smoke plunged to the ground in cascades of churned-up earth if their occupants were fortunate enough to crash-land, or exploded into fiery fragments. This was a contest like no other in human experience, witnessed by millions of people continuing humdrum daily lives, bemused by the fact that kettles boiled in kitchens, flowers bloomed in garden borders, newspapers were delivered and honey was served for tea a few thousand feet beneath one of the decisive battlefields of history. Pilots who faced oblivion all day sang in their 'locals' that night, if they lived. Their schoolboy slang – 'wizard prang' and 'gone for a Burton' – passed into the language, fulfilling the observation of a French writer quoted by Dr Johnson: '*Il y a beaucoup de pueril-ities dans la guerre.*'

Once bombs began to fall on Britain's cities in August, blast caused a layer of dust to settle upon every surface, casting over the urban fabric of the country a drab greyness which persisted throughout the blitz. Yet islands of seasonal beauty survived. John Colville was struck by the tortoiseshell butterflies fluttering gaily over the lawn behind Downing Street: 'I shall always associate that garden in summer, the corner of the Treasury outlined against a china-blue sky, with 1940.' Churchill, intensely vulnerable to sentiment, witnessed many scenes which caused him to succumb. While driving to Chequers one day, he glimpsed a line of people. Motioning the driver to stop, he asked his detective to enquire what they were queuing for. Told that they hoped to buy birdseed, Churchill's private secretary John Martin noted: 'Winston wept.'

10 July was later officially designated as the first day of the Battle of Britain, though to the aircrew of both sides it seemed little different from those which preceded and followed it. The next month was characterised by skirmishes over the Channel and south coast, in which the Luftwaffe never lost more than sixteen aircraft in a day's combat – on 25 July – and Fighter Command no more than fifteen. Churchill insisted that coastal convoys should continue to sail the Narrows, partly to assert British rights of navigation, partly to provoke the Luftwaffe into action on what were deemed favourable terms for the RAF. On 11 August, attrition sharply increased: thirty British aircraft were shot down for thirty-five German. In the month thereafter, Goering launched his major assault on Fighter Command, its airfields, control centres and radar stations. Between 12 and 23 August, the RAF lost 133 fighters in action, a further forty-four to mishaps, while the Luftwaffe lost 299 aircraft to all causes.

By early autumn, British casualties and damage to installations had reached critical proportions. Among Dowding's squadron commanders, eleven out of forty-six were killed or wounded in July and August, along with thirty-nine of ninety-seven flight commanders. One Fighter Command pilot, twenty-one-year-old George Barclay of 249 squadron, a Norfolk parson's son, wrote after the bitter battles of 7 September: 'The odds today have been unbelievable (and we are all really very shaken!) . . . There are bombs and things falling around tonight and a terrific gun barrage. Has a blitz begun? The wing-commander's coolness is amazing and he does a lot to keep up our morale – very necessary tonight.' As in every battle, not all participants showed the stuff of heroes. After repeated German bombings of the RAF's forward airfield at Manston, ground crews huddled in its air-raid shelters and rejected pleas to emerge and service Hurricanes. The work was done by off-duty Blenheim night-fighter crews.

The prime minister intently followed the progress of each day's clashes. The Secret Intelligence Service warned that a German landing in Britain was imminent. Yet it was not easy to maintain the British people at the highest pitch of expectancy. On 3 August, Churchill felt obliged to issue a statement: 'The Prime Minister wishes it to be known that the possibility of German attempts at invasion has by no means passed away.' He carried this spirit into his own household. Downing Street and the underground Cabinet War Rooms were protected by Royal Marine pensioners, Chequers by a Guards company. The prime minister took personal charge of several practice alerts against the possibility of German paratroop landings in St James's Park. 'This sounds very peculiar today, but was taken quite seriously by us all in the summer of 1940,' a war cabinet secretariat officer recalled.

Churchill practised with a revolver and with his own Mannlicher rifle on a range at Chequers, entirely in earnest and not without pleasurable anticipation. It was odd that the Germans, having used special forces effectively in the May blitzkrieg on the Continent, never thereafter showed much interest in their possibilities. A direct assault on Churchill in 1940, most plausibly by a paratroop landing at Chequers, could have paid handsome dividends. Britain was fortunate that such piratical ventures loomed far less prominently in Hitler's mind, and in Wehrmacht doctrine, than in Churchill's imagination. In the summer of 1940 the Germans had yet to understand how pivotal to Britain's war effort was the person of the prime minister.

The supply of aircraft to Fighter Command was a critical factor.

While propaganda lauded the achievements of the Ministry of Aircraft Production, in Whitehall its conduct by Lord Beaverbrook provoked bitter criticism. For some weeks he ran the department from his private residence, Stornoway House in Cleveland Row, behind the Ritz Hotel. It is easy to perceive why many people, Clementine Churchill prominent among them, deplored the press baron, then sixty-one. He was a former appeaser, who had secretly subsidised the pre-war political career of Sir Samuel Hoare, most egregious of Chamberlain's ministers. In January 1940 Beaverbrook addressed the Duke of Windsor, the former King Edward VIII, about a possible peace offer to Germany. On 6 May he asserted in his own *Daily Express* that London would not be bombed, and that the Germans would not attack the Maginot Line. Deputy Führer Rudolf Hess later told Beaverbrook: 'Hitler likes you very much.' The historian G.M. Young suggested that Beaverbrook looked like a doctor struck off for performing an illegal operation. It was once said of his newspapers that they never espoused a cause which was both honourable and successful. The King opposed his inclusion in the cabinet, but among all men Churchill chose this old colleague from the 1917–18 Lloyd George government as his luncheon companion on 10 May 1940.

Beaverbrook cast a spell over Churchill which remained unbroken by his old friend's petulance, disloyalty and outrageous mischief-making. The Canadian-born magnate's command of wealth, such as the prime minister had always craved, impressed him. Churchill recognised in 'dear Max' a fellow original, full of impish fun, which was scantily available in Downing Street that summer. It is often remarked that Churchill had acolytes, but few intimates. More than any other person save his wife, Beaverbrook eased the loneliness of the prime minister's predicament and responsibilities. Churchill's belief in his old comrade's fitness for government was excessive. But who among Beaverbrook's cabinet colleagues was more blessed with dynamism and decision, such as seemed vital to meet the challenges of 1940?

As a minister, Beaverbrook trampled on air marshals, browbeat industrial chiefs, spurned consultation and cast aside procedure in pursuit of the simple objective of boosting fighter output. He ruled by row. Jock Colville once suggested that Beaverbrook took up more of Churchill's time than Hitler. The prime minister himself remarked a resemblance between Beaverbrook and the film star Edward G. Robinson, most notable for his portrayals of gangsters. It is hard to dispute that Beaverbrook was a monster. The Royal Air Force detested him. Much of his success in increasing aircraft output was achieved in consequence of decisions and commitments made before he took office. Yet for a brief season he deserved gratitude for injecting into the key element of British weapons production an urgency which matched the needs of the hour. He was supported by three great civil servants – Eaton Griffiths, Edmund Compton and Archibald Rowlands – together with Sir Charles Craven, former managing director of Vickers Armstrong, and Patrick Hennessy, forty-one-year-old boss of Ford at Dagenham. His other key prop, and sometimes adversary, was Air Marshal Sir Wilfred Freeman, who loathed Beaverbrook as a man, but grudgingly conceded his usefulness that summer.

Daily pressures upon the prime minister were unrelenting. The war cabinet met 108 times in the ninety-two days between 10 May and 31 July. His black dispatch box contained a pile of papers which seemed never to diminish, 'a farrago of operational, civil, political and scientific matters'. Overriding War Office objections, he promoted Maj. Millis Jefferis, a clever soldier engaged in weapons experimental work, and ordered that he should report directly to Lindemann at the Cabinet Office. He insisted that the maverick armoured enthusiast Maj.Gen. Percy Hobart should be given suitable employment, over-ruling Dill's objections with the assertion that he should remember that not only good boys help to win wars: 'It is the sneaks and stinkers as well.' He harassed the service chiefs in support of one of 'the Prof's' most foolish personal initiatives, aerial rocket deployments against enemy aircraft. Sir Hugh Dowding of Fighter Command wanted his pilots to kill German aircrew who took to their parachutes. Churchill, recoiling from what he perceived as dishonourable conduct, would have none of this. Travelling with Roger Keyes at the end of July, he told the admiral that he had 'many detractors' as chief of combined operations. Keyes responded tartly: 'So had you, but you are now there in spite of it.' Churchill said: 'There are no competitors for my job now – I didn't get it until they had got into a mess.'

Beyond pressing the urgency of fighter production, Churchill made few tactical interventions in the Battle of Britain, but one of the most justly celebrated took place in the Downing Street cabinet room on 21 June. There was fierce controversy between Lindemann and Sir Henry Tizard, chairman of the Aeronautical Research Committee, about a suggestion from air intelligence that the Luftwaffe intended to use electronic beams to guide its night raiders to British targets. Tizard dismissed the feasibility of such a technique. Churchill summoned him, together with Lindemann and senior airmen, to a meeting attended by twenty-eight-year-old scientific intelligence officer R.V. Jones. It soon became obvious that Jones alone understood the issue. Though awed by finding himself in such company, he said to the prime minister: 'Would it help, sir, if I told you the story right from the start?' Churchill was initially taken aback, then said: 'Well, yes, it would!' Jones spent twenty minutes explaining how his own researches, aided by 'Ultra' German signals decrypted by the codebreakers at Bletchley Park – still fragmentary at this stage of the war – had led him to an understanding of the Luftwaffe's navigational aids. Churchill, characteristically, found himself paraphrasing in his mind lines from the parodic nineteenth-century folklore collection *The Ingoldsby Legends*: 'But now one Mr Jones/Comes forth and depones/That fifteen years since, he had heard certain groans.'

When Jones finished, Tizard expressed renewed scepticism. Churchill overruled him, and ordered that the young scientist should be given facilities to explore the German beams. Initially much dismayed by Jones's revelations, he thrilled when the young 'boffin' told him that, once wavelengths were identified, the transmissions could be jammed. Jones himself, of course, was enchanted by the prime minister's receptiveness: 'Here was strength, resolution, humour, readiness to listen, to ask the searching question and, when convinced, to act.' The beams were indeed jammed. Jones became one of the outstanding British intelligence officers of the war. Tizard's career was, alas, virtually destroyed by his misjudgement. He was an old enemy of Lindemann, who now possessed ammunition with which to discredit him. Though a man of exceptional ability who had made a critical contribution to the creation of Britain's radar defences, never again did Tizard wield important influence. But the 'beams' episode showed Churchill at his best: accessible, imaginative, penetrating, decisive, and always suggestible about technological innovation.

From the summer of 1940 onwards, decrypts of German signals assumed a steadily rising importance to the British war effort. Selected samples codenamed *Boniface* were delivered to Churchill daily, in a special box to which even the private secretaries were denied a key. The chiefs of staff deplored his direct access to Ultra, arguing that he often derived false impressions from raw intelligence, and misjudged the significance of enemy exchanges. Yet Ultra armed the prime minister for the direction of the war in a fashion unknown to any other national leader in history. It played a critical role in guiding Churchill's own perceptions of strategy, both for good and ill, and fortified his confidence in overruling commanders.

The Bletchley Park codebreaking operation, still in its infancy in 1940, was the greatest British achievement of the war, and from 1941 became the cornerstone of its intelligence operations. The Secret Intelligence Service was directed by Brigadier Sir Stewart Menzies, 'C', a quintessential officer and gentleman, former president of 'Pop' and captain of the cricket XI at Eton, Life Guardsman and member of White's club. Menzies owed his appointment to Halifax. His record was more impressive as a Whitehall intriguer than as a spymaster. SIS never gained significant 'humint' – agent intelligence – about the Axis high command. Before Ultra got into its stride, most of Menzies's assessments of – for instance – German intentions in 1940–41 were wildly mistaken. He had little to do with the pre-war development of Bletchley Park, but by a skilful coup gained administrative control of its operations. He made it his business to deliver personally to the prime minister the most delectable codebreakers' delicacies, and in consequence was always a welcome visitor at Downing Street. All national leaders gain a frisson of excitement from access to secret intelligence. This was especially and understandably so of Churchill. Menzies, purveyor of Bletchley's golden eggs, gained exaggerated credit as owner of the goose.

Amid the great issues of national defence there were constitutional responsibilities, including regular meetings with the monarch. The King and Queen were 'a little ruffled', Jock Colville learned, 'by the offhand way he treated them – says he will come at six, puts it off until 6.30 by telephone, then comes at seven'. Only a king would dare to resent his prime minister's tardiness when Churchill had to supervise the creation of the Takoradi aircraft ferry route across Africa to Egypt, visit blitzed airfields, bully the Treasury into paying compensation for private homes destroyed by bombs, and write at length in his own hand to Neville Chamberlain, now stricken with the cancer that would kill him within three months. There were certainly difficulties, the prime minister acknowledged to his predecessor in a letter of 31 August: 'however when all is said and done I must say I feel pretty good about this war'. But Churchill was exasperated on 10 August when Sir Stafford Cripps, the Moscow ambassador, submitted to him a paper detailing proposals on post-war reconstruction. There would come a time for such things, but it was not the summer of 1940. Only a fool could have thought otherwise.

Meanwhile, Britain was running out of money. The war was costing £55 million a week, and Washington was implacable in its demands for immediate cash payment for every ton of weapons and supplies shipped across the Atlantic. Kingsley Wood, the chancellor, suggested melting down the nation's gold wedding rings, which would raise £20 million. The prime minister said that the Treasury should hold back from such a drastic measure, unless it became necessary to make a parade of it to shame the United States. On 16 August he visited Fighter Command's 11 Group Operations Room, and intently watched progress of the day's fighting on the huge plotting board. On the way back to Chequers in his car, 'Pug' Ismay, his chief of staff, made some remark. Churchill said: 'Don't speak to me. I have never been so moved.' After a few minutes' silence he leaned forward and said, 'Never in the field of human conflict has so much been owed by so many to so few.' Ismay wrote: 'The words burned into my brain.' That day, the Combined Intelligence Centre reported its belief that Hitler would make no decision about invasion until the outcome of the air battle became clear. On 24 August the first German bombs fell on outer London, and Fighter Command's airfields were again badly hit.

Sunday, 1 September, yet another day when intelligence suggested that invasion might come, passed without incident. On the 3rd, for the second time the war cabinet met in the new underground Central War Room. Churchill declared it to be 'lamentable' that only 500,000 rifles were scheduled to be produced by British manufacturers before the end of 1941. On 5 September he used the same adjective to deplore the 'passivity' to which the Royal Navy seemed reduced when it declined to bombard new German batteries at Cap Gris Nez, only twenty miles from the English south coast. He told Cunningham, Mediterranean C-in-C, that the supposed vulnerability of his fleet to Italian aircraft was 'exaggerated'. He urged the swift construction of landing craft to facilitate the raids on enemy shores he was so impatient to launch.

A wag in the War Office discovered in the Book of Job a description of a warhorse which the generals thought entirely fitting to their political master: 'He paweth in the valley, and rejoiceth in his strength; he goeth on to meet the armed men. He mocketh at fear, and is not affrighted; neither turneth he back from the sword. The quiver rattleth against him, the glittering spear and the shield. He swalloweth the ground with fierceness and rage . . . He saith among the trumpets, Ha, ha; and he smelleth the battle afar off, the thunder of the captains, and the shouting.' Yet while Churchill never disdained the gestures and symbols of warriorhood, he strove also for substance. Each night, he told Colville, 'I try myself by court martial to see if I have done anything effective during the day. I don't mean just pawing the ground – anyone can go through the motions – but something really effective.'

It is hard for a historian, as it was for Churchill's contemporaries, to conceive what it was like for a man to bear sole responsibility for preserving European civilisation. Harold Nicolson wrote of the prime minister's remoteness from ordinary mortals. His eyes were 'glaucous, vigilant, angry, combative, visionary and tragic . . . the eyes of a man who is much preoccupied and is unable to rivet his attention on minor things . . . But in another sense they are the eyes of a man faced by an ordeal or tragedy, and combining vision, truculence, resolution and great unhappiness.' Throughout the war there were moments when Churchill was oppressed by loneliness, which only Beaverbrook's company seemed able to assuage. It was by his personal choice, indeed unflagging insistence, that he delegated to others few of the responsibilities of supreme command. But the thrill and exaltation of playing out his role gave way, at times, to a despondency which required all his powers to overcome. In 1940 he sustained his spirit wonderfully well, but in the later war years he became prone to outbursts of self-pity, often accompanied by tears.

His personal staff's awareness of the prime minister's burden caused them to forgive his outbursts of discourtesy and intemperance. Ministers and commanders were less sympathetic. Their criticisms of Churchill's behaviour were human enough, and objectively just. But they reflected lapses of imagination. Few men in human history had borne such a load, which was ever at the forefront of his consciousness, and even subconsciousness. Dreams drifted through his sleep, though he seldom revealed their nature to others. What is astonishing is that in his waking hours he preserved such gaiety. Although an intensely serious man, he displayed a capacity for fun as remarkable as his powers of concentration and memory, his unremitting commitment to hard labour. Seldom, if ever, has a great national leader displayed such power to entertain his people, stirring them to laughter even amid the tears of war.

Churchill never doubted his own genius – subordinates often wished that he would. But there were many moments when his confidence in a happy outcome faltered amid bad tidings from the battlefield. He believed that destiny had marked him to enter history as the saviour of Western civilisation, and this conviction coloured his smallest words and deeds. When a Dover workman said to his mate as Churchill passed, 'There goes the bloody British Empire,' the prime minister was enchanted. '*Very* nice,' he lisped to Jock Colville, his face wreathed in smiles. But, in profound contrast to Hitler and Mussolini, he preserved a humanity, an awareness of himself as mortal clay, which seldom lost its power to touch the hearts of those who served him, just as the brilliance of his conversation won their veneration.

He was fearless about everything save the possibility of defeat. Hurrying from Downing Street to the Annexe with Colville one day, in his customary uniform of short black coat, striped trousers and white-spotted blue bow tie, they heard the whistle of descending bombs. The young official took cover as two explosions resounded nearby. He rose to observe the prime minister still striding up King Charles Street, gold-headed walking stick in hand.

Disraeli said: 'Men should always be difficult. I can't bear men who come and dine with you when you want them.' Churchill, with his tempestuous moods and unsocial hours, certainly fulfilled this requirement. The prime minister's typists were expected instantly to comprehend the meaning of some mumbled injunction such as 'Gimme "Pug"!' When taking dictation, they were required to respect every nuance of his precision of language. Alan Brooke was once outraged when Churchill shouted down the telephone to him: 'Get off, you fool!' It required intercession by the staff to soothe the general's ruffled feathers with the explanation that the prime minister, who was in bed when he called Brooke, had been telling Smokey the black cat to stop biting his toes. Jock Colville and the King's assistant private secretary Tommy Lascelles, lunching together one day, debated 'whether very great men usually had a touch of charlatanism in them', and of course they were thinking of the prime minister. Some fastidious souls recoiled from Churchill's perceived ruthlessness, though US military attaché Raymond Lee applauded him as 'an unscrupulously rough-and-tumble fighter . . . perfectly at home in his dealings with Hitler and Mussolini'.

Churchill was self-obsessed, yet displayed spasms of concern for his intimates just often enough to prevent them from becoming disgusted by his selfishness. After one outburst, he suddenly put his hand on private secretary John Martin's shoulder and said, 'You know, I may seem to be very fierce, but I am fierce only with one man – Hitler.' He expressed regret that he had lacked leisure to get to know Martin at the start of their relationship, back in May.

He was always happy to reminisce about himself, but had no small talk, in the sense of being willing to display a polite interest in the affairs of others, save those important to the state. He was reluctant even to pretend to pay attention to people who failed to capture his interest. Leo Amery contrasted him with Britain's First World War leader: 'Ll[oyd] G[eorge] was purely external and receptive, the result of intercourse with his fellow men, and non-existent in their absence, while Winston is literary and expressive of himself with hardly any contact with other minds.' 'Pug' Ismay shook his head in dismay when the prime minister once wantonly kept an entire ship's crew waiting half an hour to be addressed by him: 'It's very naughty of the PM. It's this unbridled power.'

Churchill's doctor Sir Charles Wilson wrote of 'the formidable ramparts of indifference which he presents to women', and which only his wife Clementine and their daughters were sometimes capable of scaling. Clementine – highly strung, intensely moral, sensitive to vulgarity – was often ignored, mauled, taken for granted. Yet beyond her fierce loyalty to her husband she marvellously sustained her commitment to rebuke his excesses, to repair the fractured china of his relationships. On 27 June she wrote a letter which has become justly famous:

Darling Winston, One of the men in your entourage (a devoted friend) has been to me & told me that there is a danger of your being generally disliked by your colleagues and subordinates because of your rough sarcastic & overbearing manner . . . My darling Winston – I must confess that I have noticed a deterioration in your manner; & you are not so kind as you used to be. It is for you to give the Orders & if they are bungled – except for the King, the Archbishop of

90

Canterbury & the Speaker you can sack anyone & everyone. Therefore with this terrific power you must combine urbanity, kindness & if possible Olympic [sic] calm . . . I cannot bear that those who serve the country & your self should not love you as well as admire and respect you. Besides you won't get the best results by irascibility & rudeness. They will breed either dislike or a slave mentality – 'Rebellion in War Time being out of the question!' Please forgive your loving devoted & watchful

    Clemmie

This note, of which the signature was decorated with a cat drawing, she tore up. But four days later she pieced it together and gave it to her husband – the only letter she is known to have written to him in 1940. The country, as much as he, owed a debt to such a wife. More than any other human being, Clementine preserved Churchill from succumbing to the corruption of wielding almost absolute authority over his nation.

Churchill seldom found a moment to read a book in 1940, but he addressed with close attention each day's newspapers, windows upon the minds of the British people. His hunger for information was insatiable. Not infrequently he telephoned personally to the *Daily Telegraph* or *Daily Express* at midnight to enquire what was their front-page 'splash' for next day. One night at Chequers he caused Colville to ring the Admiralty three times in quest of news. On the third occasion, the exasperated duty captain at the other end gave way to invective. The prime minister, overhearing the babble of speech from the other end, assumed that at least a cruiser must have been sunk. He seized the receiver from Colville's hand, 'to find himself subjected to a flow of uncomplimentary expletives which clearly fascinated him. After listening for a minute or two he explained with great humility that he was only the Prime Minister and that he had been wondering whether there was any naval news.'

He detested wanton as distinct from purposeful physical activity, and enjoyed relaxing with bezique or backgammon, which could be indulged without abandoning conversation. His companions remarked his lack of manual dexterity, evident when his pudgy fingers shuffled a pack of cards. 'He has more wit than humour,' suggested Charles Wilson. Colville noticed that while Churchill often smiled and chuckled, he never laughed outright, perhaps perceiving this as a vulgarity. The devotion he inspired in most of those who served him derived from a deportment which was at once magnificent and devoid of pomposity. In the early hours of a Sunday morning in his bedroom at Chequers, Colville recorded that Churchill 'collapsed between the chair and the stool, ending in a most absurd position on the floor with his feet in the air. Having no false dignity, he treated it as a complete joke and repeated several times, "a real Charlie Chaplin!"' He displayed a lack of embarrassment about his own nakedness characteristic of English public schoolboys, soldiers, and patricians accustomed to regard servants as mere extensions of the furniture.

He inspired more equivocal sentiments in his ministers and service chiefs. They were obliged to endure his monologues, and sometimes rambling reminiscences, when it would have been more useful for him to heed their reports and – so they thought – their opinions. 'Winston feasts on the sound of his adjectives,' wrote Charles Wilson, 'he likes to use four or five words all with the same meaning as an old man shows you his orchids; not to show them off, but just because he loves them. The people in his stories do not come to life; they are interred in a great sepulchre of words . . . So it happens that his audience, tired by the long day, only wait for the chance to slip off to bed, leaving Winston still talking to those who have hesitated to get up and go.'

His changeability, sometimes on matters of the utmost gravity, exasperated those who themselves bore large responsibilities. Ian Jacob observed: 'No one could predict what his mind would be on any problem.' It was galling for an exhausted general or administrator, denied the prime minister's powers of choosing his hours, to hear that Churchill could not discuss vital matters in the afternoon, because a note bearing the sacrosanct word 'Resting' was pinned to his bedroom door. Then the hapless officer or minister found himself summoned to do business at midnight or later.

The most damaging criticism of Churchill made by important people was that he was intolerant of evidence unless it conformed to his own instinct, and was sometimes wilfully irrational. Displays of supreme wisdom were interspersed with outbursts of childish petulance. Yet when the arguments were over, the shouting done, on important matters he usually deferred to reason. In much the same way, subordinates exasperated by his excesses in 'normal' times – insofar as war admitted any – marvelled at the manner in which the prime minister rose to crisis. Bad news brought out the best in him. Disasters inspired responses which compelled recognition of his greatness. Few colleagues doubted his genius, and all admired his unswerving commitment to waging war. John Martin wrote of 'the ferment of ideas, the persistence in flogging proposals, the goading of commanders to attack – these were all expressions of that blazing, explosive energy without which the vast machine, civilian as well as military, could not have been moved forward so steadily or steered through so many setbacks and difficulties'. Churchill conducted the affairs of his nation with a self-belief which was sometimes misplaced, but which offered an elixir of hope to those chronically troubled by rational fears. Amid Britain's sea of troubles, he represented a beacon of warmth and humanity, as well as of will and supreme courage, for which most of even the most exalted and sceptical of his fellow countrymen acknowledged gratitude.

A widespread illusion persists that in 1940 Churchill broadcast constantly to the British people. In reality he delivered only seven speeches through the BBC between May and December, roughly one a month. But the impact of these was enormous upon a nation which in those days clung to its radio receivers as storm-bound sailors once lashed themselves to the masts of their ships. There were no advancing British armies to follow on the map, no fleets reporting victories. Instead the prime minister's rolling periods, his invincible certainties in a world of raving tyrants, anchored his people and their island.

Few interventions of his own that summer were more significant than that which he made on 23 August, at the height of the perceived peril of German invasion. Britain's threadbare defences were further denuded by the dispatch to Gen. Sir Archibald Wavell's Middle East Command of 154 priceless tanks, to resist the anticipated Italian assault on Egypt. Besides the armour, forty-eight twenty-five-pounder guns, twenty Bofors, 500 Brens and 250 anti-tank rifles were sent. This was one of Churchill's most difficult decisions of the war. Eden and Dill deserve credit for urging it, at first in the face of the prime minister's doubts. It is impossible that they could have made such a commitment without a profound, almost perverse, belief that Hitler would not risk invasion – and perhaps also a recognition that Britain's defence rested overwhelmingly on the Royal Navy and RAF rather than the army.

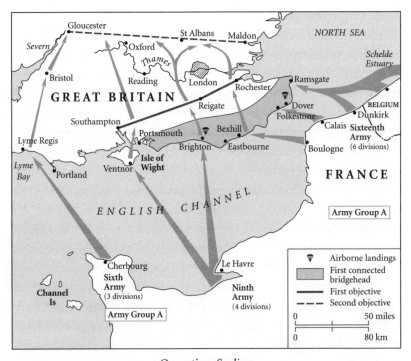

Operation *Sealion*

It is not surprising that an ignorant civilian such as 'Chips' Channon should have written on 16 September of expecting 'almost certain invasion'. It is more remarkable that Britain's military commanders and intelligence chiefs shared this fear, supposing that a massive German descent might take place without warning. Amphibious operations, opposed landings where port facilities are unavailable, do not require mere mechanical transfers of troops from sea to shore. They rank among the most difficult and complex of all operations of war. Two years of planning and preparation were needed in advance of the return to France of Allied armies in June 1944. It is true that in the summer of 1940 Britain lay almost naked, while four years later Hitler's Atlantic Wall was formidably fortified and garrisoned. In 1940 Britain lacked the deep penetration of German wireless traffic which was attained later in the war, so that the chiefs of staff had only the patchiest picture of the Wehrmacht's movements on the Continent.

Nonetheless it remains extraordinary that, at every suitable tide until late autumn, Britain's commanders feared that a German army might arrive on the southern or eastern coast. The navy warned – though the prime minister disbelieved them – that the Germans might achieve a surprise landing of 100,000 men. The most significant enemy preparation for invasion was the assembly of 1,918 barges on the Dutch coast. Hitler's military planners envisaged putting ashore a first wave of three airborne regiments, nine divisions – and 125,000 horses – between Ramsgate and Lyme Bay, a commitment for which available shipping was wholly inadequate. Another serious problem, never resolved, was that the Wehrmacht's desired initial dawn landing required an overnight Channel passage. It would be almost impossible to embark troops and concentrate barges without attracting British notice. The German fleet, never strong, had been gravely weakened by its losses in the Norwegian campaign. The defenders would be granted at least six hours of darkness in which to engage German invasion convoys, free from Luftwaffe intervention. The Royal Navy deployed around twenty destroyers at Harwich, and a similar force at Portsmouth, together with powerful cruiser elements. Channel invasion convoys would have suffered shocking, probably fatal losses. Once daylight came, German pilots had shown themselves much more skilful than those of the RAF and Fleet Air Arm in delivering attacks on shipping. The defending warships would have been badly battered. But for a German amphibious armada, the risk of destruction was enormous. The Royal Navy, outnumbering the German fleet ten to one, provided that decisive deterrent to *Sealion*.

The British, however, with the almost sole exception of the prime minister, perceived all the perils on their own side. Dill, the CIGS, seemed 'like all the other soldiers . . . very worried and anxious about the invasion, feeling that the troops are not trained and may not be steady'. Brooke, as C-in-C Home Forces, wrote on 2 July of 'the nakedness of our defences'. The Royal Navy was apprehensive that if German landings began, it might not receive adequate support from the RAF. Admiral Sir Ernle Drax, C-in-C Nore, expressed himself 'not satisfied that . . . the co-operation of our fighters was assured'.

The service chiefs were justified in fearing the outcome if German forces secured a beachhead. Alan Brooke believed, probably rightly, that if invaders got ashore, Churchill would seek to take personal command of the ground battle – with disastrous consequences. In the absence of a landing, of course, the prime minister was able to perform his extraordinary moral function. The British generals' fears of an unheralded assault reflected the trauma which defeat in France had inflicted upon them. It distorted their judgement about the limits of the possible, even for Hitler's Wehrmacht. Churchill, by contrast, was always doubtful about whether the enemy would come. He grasped the key issue: that invasion would represent a far greater gamble than Germany's 10 May attack in the West. Operation *Sealion* could not partially succeed. It must achieve fulfilment, or fail absolutely. Given Hitler's mastery of the Continent, and the impotence of the British Army, he had no need to stake everything upon such a throw.

But the prime minister was committed body and soul to prosecution of the war. In the summer and autumn of 1940, preparing a defence against invasion was not merely essential, it represented almost the only military activity of which Britain was capable. It was vital to incite the British people. If they were allowed to lapse into passivity, staring fearfully at the array of German might, all-conquering beyond the Channel, who could say whether their will for defiance would persist? One of Churchill's great achievements in those months was to convince every man and woman in the country that they had roles to play in the greatest drama in their history, even if the practical utility of their actions and preparations was often pathetically small. Young Lt. Robert Hichens of the Royal Navy wrote: 'I feel an immense joy at being British, the only people who have stood up to the air war blackmail.'

Between 24 August and 6 September the Luftwaffe launched 600 sorties a day. British civilians were now dying in hundreds. Devastation mounted remorselessly. Yet 7 September marked the turning point of the Battle of Britain. Goering switched his attacks from the RAF's airfields to the city of London. A sterile debate persists about whether Britain or Germany first provoked attacks on each other's cities. On 25 August, following civilian casualties caused by Luftwaffe bombs falling on Croydon, Churchill personally ordered that the RAF's Bomber Command should retaliate against Berlin. Some senior RAF officers resisted, on the grounds that such an attack, by the forces available, could make little impact and would probably incite the Germans to much more damaging action against British urban areas. Churchill overruled them, saying: 'They had bombed London, whether on purpose or not, and the British people and London especially should know that we could hit back. It would be good for the morale of us all.' Some fifty British aircraft were dispatched to Berlin, and a few bombs fell on the city. Though the material damage was negligible, the Nazi leadership was indeed moved to urge a devastating response against London, though this would assuredly have come anyway.

On the night of 7 September, 200 Luftwaffe aircraft raided the capital. Air Vice-Marshal Keith Park, commanding 11 Group, wrote on 8 September: 'It was burning all down the river. It was a horrid sight. But I looked down and said: "Thank God for that."' Next day, Churchill visited the capital's stricken East End. He saw misery and destruction, but knew how vastly these were to be preferred in Bethnal Green and Hackney than at Biggin Hill airfield or the south coast radar sites. The Germans had made a decisive strategic error. Thereafter, urban centres of Britain paid a heavy price for the Luftwaffe's raids, first by day and then by night. Daylight fighting continued over southern England until the end of October. But never again was Fighter Command's survival in doubt. In a broadcast on 11 September, Churchill told the British people that the German air force had 'failed conspicuously' to gain air mastery over southern England. As for invasion, 'We cannot be sure that they will try at all.' But the danger persisted, and every precaution must be taken.

On 12 September, when the prime minister visited Dungeness and North Foreland on the Kent coast with the C-in-C Home Forces, Alan Brooke wrote: 'His popularity is astounding, everywhere crowds rush up and cheer him wildly.' US general Raymond Lee perceived an improvement of temper even among the governing class, formerly so sceptical of Britain's prospects. He wrote in his diary on 15 September: 'Thank God ... the defeatist opinions expressed after Dunkirk are now no longer prevalent.' On 17 September, Churchill told the Commons that in future its sessions should not be advertised beforehand: 'We ought not to flatter ourselves by imagining that we are irreplaceable,' he said, addressing his fellow MPs in masterly language which suggested that he was confiding in a band of brothers, 'but at the same time it cannot be denied that two or three hundred by-elections would be a quite needless complication of our affairs at this particular juncture.'

Once more, he asserted serene confidence: 'I feel as sure as the sun will rise tomorrow that we shall be victorious.' He harangued Dalton, Minister of Economic Warfare, with what that assiduous diarist described as his 'usual vigorous rhetorical good sense', pacing up and down his room the while: 'This is a workman's war ... The public will stand everything except optimism ... The nation is finding the war not so unpleasant as it expected ... The air attacks are doing much less damage than was expected before the war began ... Don't be like the knight in the story who was so slow in buckling on his armour that the tourney was over before he rode into the ring.'

The bombs that were now falling upon city streets, as well as upon aircraft factories and dockyards, at first caused some government alarm. Cheering cockneys cried, 'Stick it, Winnie!' and 'We can take it!' as the prime minister toured blitz-stricken areas. But was this true? Tens of thousands of fugitives from cities became 'trekkers', plodding out into the countryside at dusk to escape the night raiders. There was evidence of near social breakdown in some bombed areas. Fighter Command, with its primitive air interception radar, had no effective counter to Luftwaffe assaults in darkness. Industrial production suffered severely. The destruction of homes and property, the incessant fear of bombardment, ate deep into many people's spirits.

Yet as the blitz continued, the nation learned to live and work with its terrors and inconveniences. Ministers' fears about morale subsided. Churchill rang Fighter Command one September night to complain irritably to its duty officer: 'I am on top of the Cabinet Office in Whitehall and can neither see nor hear a raider. Why don't you clear London of the Red warning? We have all been down too long.' The RAF's daily reports of losses inflicted on the enemy cheered Churchill and his people, but were heavily exaggerated. On 12 August, for instance, Churchill was told that sixty-two German aircraft had been shot down for twenty-five British. In reality, the Luftwaffe had lost only twenty-seven planes. Likewise two days later, Fighter Command claimed seventy-eight for three British losses, whereas Goering had lost thirty-four for thirteen RAF fighters shot down. The Duxford Wing once alleged that it had destroyed fifty-seven Luftwaffe aircraft. The real figure proved to be eight.

This chasm between claims and actuality persisted through the battle, and indeed the war. It attained a climax after the clashes of 11 September, when the RAF suggested that eighty-nine enemy aircraft had been lost for twenty-eight of its own. In fact, twenty-two German planes had been shot down for thirty-one British. Yet the inflated figures were very serviceable to British spirits, and a towering reality persisted: Goering's air groups were suffering unsustainable losses, two-to-one against those of Dowding's squadrons. This was partly because almost all shot-down German aircrew became prisoners, while parachuting RAF pilots could fight again. More important still, British aircraft factories were out-producing those of Germany. In 1940, the Luftwaffe received a total of 3,382 new single- and twin-engined aircraft, while 4,283 single-engined machines were delivered to the RAF. The wartime direction of British industry was flawed by many misjudgements and failures. Here, however, was a brilliant and decisive achievement.

Air Chief Marshal Sir Hugh Dowding, C-in-C of Fighter Command, was a difficult man, not for nothing nicknamed 'Stuffy'. He made his share of mistakes in the Battle of Britain, for instance in being slow to reinforce 11 Group when it became plain that the German effort was overwhelmingly directed against south-east England. Most of Fighter Command's initial tactical doctrine proved mistaken. But Dowding was more far-sighted than the Air Ministry, for instance early in the war urging the need for radar-equipped night fighters and long-range escorts. He displayed notable tenacity of purpose and made fewer blunders than the other side, which is how all battles are won.

His most significant contribution derived from understanding that his purpose must be to sustain Fighter Command in being, rather than to hazard everything upon the destruction of enemy aircraft. Each day, he husbanded reserves for the next. Churchill never acknowledged this refinement. Dowding's policy offended the prime minister's instinct to hurl every weapon against the foe. The airman, an austere spiritualist, could not offer Churchill congenial comradeship. Dowding's remoteness rendered him unpopular with some of his officers. It was probably right to enforce his scheduled but delayed retirement when the battle was won. Nonetheless, the brutally abrupt manner in which this was done was a disgrace to the leaders of the RAF. Dowding's cautious management of his squadrons contributed importantly to British victory.

Some historians today assert that Hitler was never serious about invading Britain. This view seems quite mistaken. It is true that the

German armed forces' preparations were unconvincing. British fears of imminent assault were unfounded, and reflected poorly upon the country's intelligence and defence chiefs. But Hitler the opportunist would assuredly have launched an armada if the Luftwaffe had gained control of the air space over the Channel and southern England. Mediterranean experience soon showed that in a hostile air environment, the Royal Navy would have found itself in deep trouble.

The Luftwaffe failed, first, because Fighter Command and its associated control facilities and radar stations were superbly organised. Second, the RAF had barely sufficient Hurricanes and Spitfires, and just enough skilled pilots, to engage superior numbers of enemy aircraft – though not as much superior as contemporary legend suggested. The Luftwaffe started its campaign with 760 serviceable Messerschmitt Bf109 fighters, its most important aircraft, against some 700 RAF Hurricanes and Spitfires. Almost as important, the Bf 109 carried only sufficient fuel to overfly Britain for a maximum of thirty minutes. The Luftwaffe had the technology to fit its planes with disposable fuel tanks, but did not use it. If the Bf109s had indeed possessed greater endurance, Fighter Command's predicament would have been much worse. As it was, the Germans could not sustain decisively superior forces over the battlefield, and were handicapped by failures of strategy and intelligence. In the early stages of the battle, Luftwaffe fighter tactics were markedly superior to those mandated by Fighter Command. But Dowding's pilots learned fast, and by September matched the skills of their opponents.

The Royal Air Force, youngest and brashest of the three services, was the only one which thoroughly recognised the value of publicity, and exploited it with notable success. The Battle of Britain caused the prestige of the nation's airmen to ascend to heights where it remained through the ensuing five years of the war. The RAF gained a glamour and public esteem which never faded. Senior military and naval commanders, by contrast, disdained the press. 'Publicity is anathema to most naval officers,' Admiral Sir Andrew Cunningham, C-in-C Mediterranean, wrote grumpily, 'and I was no exception.

I could not see how it would help us to win the war.' Despite frequent nagging from the prime minister, the navy and army exposed themselves only sulkily to media attention.

Cunningham's lofty attitude, commonplace in his service, was mistaken. As Churchill always recognised, modern war is waged partly on battlefields, and partly also on air waves, front pages, and in the hearts of men and women. When Britain's powers were so small, it was vital to create an inspiriting legend for the nation, and for the world. To this in 1940 the RAF contributed mightily, both through its deeds and the recording of them. The RAF was a supremely twentieth-century creation, which gained Churchill's admiration but incomplete understanding. He displayed an enduring emotionalism about the courage and sacrifices of aircrew. The men of Bomber as well as Fighter Command were never subjected to the accusations of pusillanimity which the prime minister regularly hurled at Britain's soldiers, and also sometimes sailors. Like the British people, he never forgot that, until November 1942, the RAF remained responsible for their country's only visible battlefield victory, against the Luftwaffe in 1940.

On the night of 2 October, Churchill passed some cold, wet, unrewarding hours visiting anti-aircraft positions in Surrey amid the stygian gloom of the blackout. In the car returning to Downing Street with General Sir Frederick Pile, who commanded the AA defences, he suddenly said: 'Do you like Bovril?' pronouncing the first syllable long, as in Hove. It was 4.30 a.m. Pile responded that he did. The prime minister lapsed into silence for a few moments, then said, 'Bovril and sardines are very good together . . . We will see what the commissariat can do for us as soon as we get back to No. 10.' Pile wrote: 'Very shortly afterwards we drew up in front of the door. The Prime Minister had a walking stick with him with which he rapped the door sharply: When the butler opened it the Prime Minister said: "Goering and Goebbels coming to report," and added: "I am *not* Goebbels."'

On 11 October at Chequers, Churchill said: 'That man's effort is flagging.' Goering's Luftwaffe was by no means a spent force.

The months of night blitz that lay ahead inflicted much pain and destruction, which Fighter Command lacked adequate technology to frustrate. When John Martin telephoned the Reform Club from Downing Street one night to enquire how it had been affected by a nearby blast, the porter responded serenely: 'The club is burning, sir.' But the RAF had denied the Germans daylight control of Britain's air space, and inflicted an unsustainable rate of loss. The Luftwaffe lacked sufficient mass to inflict decisive damage upon Britain. Hitler, denied the chance of a cheap victory, saw no need to take further risks by continuing the all-out air battle. Churchill's nation and army remained incapable of frustrating his purposes on the Continent, or challenging his dominion over its peoples. German attention, as Churchill suspected, was now shifting eastwards, in anticipation of an assault upon Russia.

The Luftwaffe continued its night blitz on Britain for months into 1941, maintaining pressure upon the obstinate island at minimal cost in aircraft losses. It was long indeed before the British themselves felt secure from invasion. Home defence continued to preoccupy Churchill and his commanders. He suffered spasms of renewed concern, which caused him to telephone the Admiralty and enquire about Channel conditions on nights thought propitious for a German assault. But the coming of autumn weather, and the Luftwaffe's abandonment of daylight attacks, rendered Britain almost certain of safety until spring. Churchill had led his nation through a season which he rightly deemed critical for its survival.

Across the Atlantic, a host of Americans were dazzled by his achievement. Nazi propagandists sought to exploit a famous photo of Churchill wielding a tommy-gun to suggest an image of Britain's prime minister as a gangster. But instead the picture projected an entirely positive image to Roosevelt's nation. Over there, what counted was the fact that the weapon was US-made. Americans were shown the leader of Britain putting to personal use a gun shipped from their country, and they loved it. By 30 September, a Gallup survey showed that 52 per cent of Americans favoured giving assistance to Churchill's people, even at risk of war. *Time*'s cover story, 'The Battle of Britain', declared that 'Winston Churchill so aptly and lovingly symbolizes Great Britain's unwillingness to give up when apparently cornered . . . There is an extraordinary fact about English democracy – namely, that at almost any given time some English leader turns out to be a perfect symbol of his people. At the time of Edward VIII's abdication, Stanley Baldwin was the typical Englishman. At the time of the Munich crisis, Neville Chamberlain was pathetically typical. But as of the fourth week of September 1940, Winston Churchill was the essence of his land. The three men are as dissimilar as fog, rain and hail, which are all water. But the country they ruled has changed. This England is different . . . [Churchill] is a Tory, an imperialist, and has been a strike-breaker and Red-baiter; and yet, when he tours the slums of London, old women say: "God bless you, Winnie."' A few weeks later, by American readers' acclamation Churchill became *Time*'s Man of the Year.

One evening at Chequers, in an irresistibly homely metaphor, he compared himself to 'a farmer driving pigs along a road, who always had to be prodding them on and preventing them from straying'. He professed that he 'could not quite see why he was so popular'. For all his undoubted vanity, almost everything that he had to tell the British people was bleak. His public confidence masked private uncertainty which goes far to explain his caution about government appointments and dismissals in 1940. For more than a decade he had been an outcast, clinging precariously to a handhold on the parapet of power. Though from May 1940 he acted the part of prime minister with supreme outward conviction, it was many months before he became assured of his own authority. 'For something like a year after he took office, Winston had no idea of his political strength among the voters, which is a mercy,' observed his aide Major Desmond Morton.

Ivan Maisky, the Soviet ambassador in London, displayed in his reports home an increasing enthusiasm for Churchill: 'One can now say confidently,' he told Moscow at the end of June, 'that the government's decision to continue the war has gained overwhelming popular support, especially among the working class. The confusion and despondency which I reported in the first days of the war are gone. Churchill's speeches have played a great part in this . . . Although Churchill thus far commands the support of the working class, the ruling classes are clearly split . . . [The faction] headed by Chamberlain is terribly fearful and willing to make peace with Germany on any acceptable terms . . . these elements are the real "Fifth Column" in England . . . The problem is that, for all Churchill's determination to continue the war, he is afraid to split the Conservative Party and rely upon a workers' coalition.'

Maisky's view of political divisions in Britain was not entirely fanciful. He was wrong to ascribe leadership of a peace party to Chamberlain, but correct in asserting that some old Chamberlain supporters, as well as a few Labour MPs, remained eager to parley with the Axis. In late June, Labour MP Richard Stokes was among a faction which wanted a negotiated settlement. In a letter to Lloyd George, Stokes claimed to speak for an all-party group of thirty MPs and ten peers. On 28 July, 'Chips' Channon MP wrote deploring the news that Chamberlain was stricken with cancer: 'Thus fades the last hope of peace.' Lord Lothian, Britain's ambassador in Washington, telephoned Halifax at about the same time, begging him to say nothing publicly that would close the door to possible negotiated terms. Harold Nicolson expressed relief that Halifax appeared unmoved by Lothian's 'wild' appeal. Raymond Lee wrote after a conversation with a businessman: '[He] was very interesting about the City . . . he . . . confirmed my belief that the City is ready for appeasement at any time and is a little bit irritated because it has no hold at all on Churchill.' David Kynaston, distinguished historian of the City of London, notes that Lee gave no evidence for this asser- tion. But Montagu Norman, governor of the Bank of England, as late as autumn 1940 clung to hopes that Neville Chamberlain would 'come back into his own'. City grandee Sir Hugo Cunliffe-Owen expressed a desire that Churchill might be supplanted by Labour's A.V. Alexander.

Privately, the prime minister expressed concerns about the staunchness of the upper classes. Among some of Britain's ruling caste, admiration for his dazzling oratory did not confirm his fitness for the premiership. At dinner tables in some great houses, traditional arbiters of power muttered into their soup about the perceived vulgarities, follies and egomania of the chubby cuckoo whom fate had so rashly planted in Downing Street and entrusted with Britain's destinies. Some people in high places – senior officers as well as politicians – resented his popularity with the public. They failed to perceive how desperately the nation needed to suppose itself led by a superman. How else might its survival be secured?

The House of Commons, through the summer, was swept along by the national mood and Churchill's stunning speeches. George Lambert, a Liberal MP since 1891, told the House at a secret session on 30 July that he had not heard such oratory since Gladstone. But old Chamberlainites continued to sulk, withholding trust as well as warmth from the prime minister. More than a few Tories still expected his administration to be short-lived, and hankered to identify a credible replacement. 'Feeling in the Carlton Club is running high against him,' wrote 'Chips' Channon on 26 September. When Chamberlain died in November, it was deemed unavoidable but regrettable that Churchill should be elected in his place as Tory leader. Not until much later in the war did Conservative MPs display towards the prime minister anything of the affection they had conferred upon his predecessor.

Clementine strongly advised him against embracing the inescapably partisan role of Tory leader. He would have enhanced his stature as national warlord by declining. But acceptance fulfilled a lifelong ambition. More important, he knew how fickle was the support of public and Parliament. He was determined to indulge no possible alternative focus of influence, far less power, such as the election of another man as Tory leader – most plausibly Anthony Eden – might create. There remained a small risk, and an intolerable one, that if Churchill refused, the Tories' choice might fall upon Halifax. It seemed to the prime minister essential to ensure control of the largest voting bloc in the Commons. Subsequent experience suggested that he was probably right. Had he placed himself beyond party, in the dog days of 1942 he might have become dangerously vulnerable to a party revolt.

As autumn turned to winter, the toll of destruction imposed by the Luftwaffe mounted. But so too did government confidence in the spirit of the nation. Some British people seemed to derive an almost masochistic relish from their predicament. London housewife Yolande Green wrote to her mother: 'I think it's a good thing that we've suffered all the reverses we have this last year for it has shaken us all out of our smug complacency better than any pep talk by our politicians . . . last weekend we had a nice quiet time in spite of six [air raid] alarms – one gets so used to them they hardly disturb one nowadays.' By October Churchill, drawing on a great cigar as he sat at the Chequers dining table in his siren suit, was able to observe with equanimity that he thought 'this was the sort of war which would suit the English people once they got used to it. They would prefer all to be in the front line taking part in the battle of London than to look on hopelessly at mass slaughters like Passchendaele.'

Bombing created mountains of rubble, obliterated historic buildings, killed thousands of people, damaged factories and slowed production. But it became progressively apparent to Churchill and his colleagues that the industrial fabric of Britain stretched too wide to be vulnerable to destruction from the air. The blitz never came close to threatening Britain's ability to continue the war. The aerial bombardment of cities, which a few years earlier had been perceived by many strategists as a potential war-winning weapon, now proved to have been much exaggerated in its effects, unless conducted with a weight of bombs undeliverable by the Luftwaffe – or, for years to come, by the Royal Air Force.

Millions of British people maintained existences compounded in equal parts of normality inside their own homes, and perils that might at any moment destroy everything around them which they held dear. Almost eighty years earlier, the novelist Anthony Trollope visited the United States during its Civil War. He noted the banalities of domestic life amid the struggle, and suggested with droll prescience: 'We . . . soon adapt ourselves to the circumstances around us. Though three parts of London were in flames, I should no doubt expect to have my dinner served to me, if I lived in the quarter which was free from fire.' In 1940 Lady Cynthia Colville echoed Trollope, observing at breakfast one morning that 'If one looked on all this as ordinary civilian life it was indeed hellish, but if one thought of it as a siege then it was certainly one of the most comfortable in history.'

Churchill himself was sometimes very weary, especially after striving to arbitrate on a dozen intractable strategic issues, and enduring perceived petulance from MPs in the Commons. 'Malaya, the Australian government's intransigence and "nagging" in the House was more than any man could be expected to endure,' he grumbled crossly one night to Eden. Yet his generosity of spirit seldom weakened, even towards the enemy. For all his frequent jibes at 'the horrible Huns', and at a moment when Britain's very existence was threatened, he displayed no vindictiveness when discussing a post-war vision. 'We [have] got to admit that Germany should remain in the European family,' he observed. 'Germany existed before the Gestapo.'

His energy seemed inexhaustible. That same evening at Chequers on which he likened himself to a swineherd, he conferred with two generals about Home Guard tasks in the event of invasion. He then studied aircraft production charts, which prompted him to marvel aloud that Beaverbrook had genius, 'and also brutal ruthlessness'. He led his guests for a moonlit walk in the garden, then settled down to quiz an officer newly returned from Egypt about tactics in the Western Desert. In both London and Buckinghamshire he received an endless stream of visitors. The exiled Polish prime minister, General Wladyslaw Sikorski, came to request some foreign exchange, and provoked a memorable Churchillian sortie into franglais: '*Mon général, devant la vieille dame de Threadneedle Street je suis impotent.*' There was always time for Americans. Whitelaw Reid, twenty-eight-year-old London correspondent of the *New York Herald Tribune*, was awed to find himself invited to lunch with the prime minister at Downing Street. Rear-Admiral Robert Ghormley of the

US Navy, on a mission to London, was presented with inscribed copies of the four volumes of Churchill's *Life of Marlborough*.

The death of Neville Chamberlain on 9 November roused Churchill to one of his most notable displays of magnanimity. His private view of the former prime minister was contemptuous: 'the narrowest, most ignorant, most ungenerous of men'. He felt gratitude for Chamberlain's loyal service as his subordinate since 10 May, and admiration for the courage with which he faced his mortal illness, but none for his record as prime minister. Now, however, he summoned his utmost powers of statesmanship to draft a tribute. He called his private secretary Eric Seal from bed to read it: 'Fetch the seal from his ice floe.' Next day, he delivered to the House of Commons a eulogy which forfeited nothing of its power and dignity by the fact that it memorialised a man so uncongenial to him:

In paying a tribute of respect and regard to an eminent man who has been taken from us, no one is obliged to alter the opinions which he has formed or expressed upon issues which have become a part of history; but at the Lychgate we may all pass our own conduct and our own judgements under a searching review. It is not given to human beings – happily for them, for otherwise life would be intolerable – to foresee or to predict to any large extent the unfolding course of events. In one phase men seem to have been right, in another they seem to have been wrong . . . History with its flickering lamp stumbles along the trail of the past, trying to reconstruct its scenes, to revive its echoes, and kindle with pale gleams the passion of former days. What is the worth of all this? The only guide to a man is his conscience; the only shield to his memory is the rectitude and sincerity of his actions. It is very imprudent to walk through life without this shield, because we are so often mocked by the failure of our hopes and the upsetting of our calculations; but with this shield, however the fates may play, we march always in the ranks of honour.

It fell to Neville Chamberlain in one of the supreme crises of the world to be contradicted by events, to be disappointed in his hopes, and to be deceived and cheated by a wicked man. But what were these high hopes in which he was disappointed? What were these wishes in which he was frustrated? What was that faith that was abused? They were surely among the most noble and benevolent instincts of the human heart – the love of peace, the toil for peace, the strife for peace, the pursuit of peace, even at great peril, and certainly to the utter disdain of popularity or clamour.

It was a supreme political act, to exhibit such grace towards the memory of a man who had failed the British people, and whom Churchill himself justly despised. Yet by November 1940 he could afford to display generosity. His mastery of the nation was secure. His successful defiance of Hitler commanded the admiration of much of the world. He had displayed gifts of self-discipline and political management such as had hitherto been absent from his career. His speeches were recognised as among the greatest ever delivered by a statesman, in war or peace. All that now remained was to devise some means of waging war against an enemy whose control of the Continent was unchallengeable, and whose superiority over Britain remained overwhelming. For Winston Churchill, the hardest part began when the achievement of 'the Few' was already the stuff of legend.

FIVE

Greek Fire

1 Seeking Action

In the autumn of 1940, even Churchill's foes at Westminster and in Whitehall conceded that since taking office he had revealed a remarkable accession of wisdom. He had not become a different person from his old self, but shed the maverick's mantle. He looked and sounded a king, 'Ay, every inch a king,' albeit one movingly conscious that he was the servant of a democracy. In a few months he had achieved a personal dominance of the country which rendered his colleagues acolytes, almost invisible in the shadow of his pedestal. Only Eden and Bevin made much impact on the popular imagination.

Among politicians and service chiefs, however, widespread uncertainty persisted, even if it was discreetly expressed. Though the Germans had not invaded Britain, what happened next? What chance of victory did Britain have? The well-known military writer Captain Basil Liddell Hart saw no prospect beyond stalemate, and thus urged a negotiated peace. In September Dalton reported Beaverbrook as 'very defeatist', believing that Britain should merely 'sit tight and defend ourselves until the USA comes into the war'. But would this ever happen? Raymond Lee, US military attaché in London, was among many Americans bemused about what President Roosevelt meant when he promised that their country would aid the British 'by all means short of war'. Lee sought an answer from senior diplomats at his own embassy: 'They say no one knows, that it depends on what R thinks from one day to another. I wonder if it ever occurs to the people in Washington that they have no God-given right to declare war. They may wake up one day to find that war has suddenly been declared upon the United States. That is the way Germany and Japan do business. Or, can it be that this is what Roosevelt is man-oeuvring for?'

Once the Battle of Britain was won, the foremost challenge facing Churchill was to find another field upon which to fight. In July 1940, Lee was filled with admiration for Britain's staunchness amid the invasion threat. But he suggested sardonically that if Hitler instead launched his armies eastward, 'in a month's time England would go off sound asleep again'. Likewise MP Harold Nicolson: 'If Hitler were to postpone invasion and fiddle about in Africa and the Mediterranean, our morale might weaken.' As long as Britain appeared to face imminent catastrophe, its people displayed notable fortitude. Yet it was a striking feature of British wartime behaviour that the moment peril fractionally receded, many ordinary people allowed themselves to nurse fantasies that their ordeal might soon be over, the spectre of war somehow banished. Soldier Edward Stebbing wrote on 14 November: 'I have heard a good many members of this unit say that they wished the war would end whether we win or lose . . . almost every day I hear some variations of the same idea, the common reason being that most of us are fed up with the whole business . . . The government is criticised for its lack of aggressiveness.'

A trades union correspondent wrote to Ernest Bevin from Portsmouth: 'At our weekly meeting last night of delegates representing thousands of workers . . . the members were very disappointed at your not telling the public that the government intended to prosecute the war more vigorously, and take the offensive, instead of always being on the defensive . . . We have retired service officers who tell us that we have no leaders. We have not won a battle since the war started and it is for that reason no country will join us, knowing full well that Germany will attack and swallow them, whilst our own government are debating the issue . . . Our workers' clubs contain Unionists, Liberals and Labour, all united to push the present government out of office at the first chance, and if something don't happen soon, the leaders will not be able to hold the workers.'

Yet how could Britain display aggressiveness, a capability to do more than merely withstand Axis onslaughts by bombers and U-boats? Clementine Churchill enquired at lunch one day: 'Winston, why don't we land a million men on the continent of Europe? I'm sure the French would rise up and help us.' The prime minister answered with unaccustomed forbearance that it would be impossible to land a million men at once, and that the vanguards would be shot to pieces. Back in 1915, as Lt.Col. Winston Churchill prepared to lead a battalion of the Royal Scots Fusiliers into the trenches, he told his officers: 'We will go easy at first: a little digging and feeling our way, and then perhaps later on we may *attempt a deed*.' This latter proposition commanded little enthusiasm among his comrades at the time, and even less among his generals a generation later. But by the winter of 1940 Churchill knew that a 'deed' must be attempted, to sustain an appearance of momentum in Britain's war effort.

At home, there could be no German invasion before spring. The nation's city-dwellers must bear the blitz, while the Royal Navy sustained the Atlantic lifeline against U-boats and surface commerce raiders. The navy had already suffered heavily, losing since 1939 one battleship, two aircraft-carriers, two cruisers, twenty-two submarines and thirty-seven destroyers. More ships were building, but 1941 losses would be worse. Churchill pinned great hopes on the RAF's offensive against Germany, but as he himself observed on 1 November 1940, 'the discharge of bombs is pitifully small'. It would remain so for a long time to come. CIGS Sir John Dill instructed his director of military operations, Maj.Gen. John Kennedy, to draft a strategy paper on how the war might be won. Kennedy said the best that he could offer was a plan for averting defeat. To make victory possible, American belligerence was indispensable.

Lt.Gen. Henry Pownall attended an army conference addressed by the prime minister in November 1940, and was impressed by his robust good sense: 'No more than anyone else did he see clearly how the war was going to be won, and he reminded us that for four years in 1914–18 nobody could foretell the final collapse of Germany, which came so unexpectedly . . . All we could do for the present, as during the Great War, was to get on with it and see what happened . . . He talked as well as ever, and I was much impressed by the very broad and patient view that he took of the war as a whole.' Churchill expressed the same sentiments to senior RAF officers conferring at Downing Street: 'As the PM said goodnight to the Air Marshals, he told them he was sure we were going to win the war, but confessed he did not see clearly how it was to be achieved.'

A chiefs of staff paper on Future Strategy, dated 4 September 1940, suggested that Britain should aim 'to pass to the general offensive in all spheres and in all theatres with the utmost possible strength in the Spring of 1942'. If even this remote prospect was fanciful, what meanwhile was the army to do? Churchill, with his brilliant intuitive understanding of the British people, recognised the importance of military theatre, as his service chiefs often did not. The soldiers' caution might be prudent, but much of the public, like unheroic Edward Stebbing and his comrades, craved action, an outcome, some prospect beyond victimhood. There was a rueful War Office joke at this time, prompted by the blitz, that Britain's soldiers were being put to work knitting socks for the civilians in the trenches.

Here was one of the foremost principles of wartime leadership which Churchill got profoundly right, though he often erred in implementation. He perceived that there must be action, even if not always useful; there must be successes, even if overstated or even imagined; there must be glory, even if undeserved. Attlee said later, very shrewdly: 'He was always, in effect, asking himself . . . "What must Britain do now so that the verdict of history will be favourable?" . . . He was always looking around for "finest hours", and if one was not immediately available, his impulse was to manufacture one.'

Churchill addressed the conduct of strategy with a confidence that dismayed many of his commanders, but which had evolved over a lifetime. As early as 1909, he wrote to Clementine about Britain's generals: 'These military men v[er]y often fail altogether to see the simple truths underlying the relationship of all armed forces . . . Do you know I would greatly like to have some practice in the handling of large forces. I have much confidence in my judgement on things, when I see clearly, but on nothing do I seem to feel the truth more than in tactical combinations.' While he was travelling to America in 1932, Clementine read G.F.R. Henderson's celebrated biography of Stonewall Jackson. She wrote to her husband: 'The book is full of abuse of politicians who try to interfere with Generals in the field – (Ahem!).' Her exclamation was prompted, of course, by memories of his battles with service chiefs during the First World War.

Churchill believed himself exceptionally fitted for the direction of armies, navies and air forces. He perceived no barrier to such a role in the fact that he possessed neither military staff training nor experience of higher field command. He wrote in his own history of the First World War:

> A series of absurd conventions became established, perhaps inevitably, in the public mind. The first and most monstrous of these was that the Generals and Admirals were more competent to deal with the broad issues of the war than abler men in other spheres of life. The general no doubt was an expert on how to move his troops, and the admiral upon how to fight his ships . . . But outside this technical aspect they were helpless and misleading arbiters in problems in whose solution the aid of the statesman, the financier, the manufacturer, the inventor, the psychologist, was equally required . . . Clear leadership, violent action, rigid decision one way or the other, form the only path not only of victory, but of safety and even of mercy. The State cannot afford division or hesitation at the executive centre.

Tensions between his instincts and the judgements of Britain's professional commanders would characterise Churchill's leadership. A Polish officer, attending a lecture at the British staff college on principles of war, rose at its conclusion to suggest that the speaker had omitted the most important: 'Be stronger.' Yet where might Britain achieve this? As Minister of Defence, Churchill issued an important directive. Limitations of numbers, he said, 'make it impossible for the

Army, except in resisting invasion, to play a primary role in the defeat of the enemy. That task can only be done by the staying power of the Navy and above all by the effect of Air predominance. Very valuable and important services may be rendered Overseas by the Army in operations of a secondary order, and it is for these special operations that its organization and character should be adapted.' After a British commando raid on the Lofoten Islands, Churchill wrote to the C-in-C Home Fleet: 'I am so glad you were able to find the means of executing "*Claymore*". This admirable raid has done serious injury to the enemy and has given an immense amount of innocent pleasure at home.' The latter proposition was more plausible than the former.

Churchill and his military chiefs renounced any prospect of engaging Hitler's main army. They committed themselves to a strategy based on minor operations which persisted, in substantial measure, until 1944. Pantellaria, the tiny Italian island between Tunis and Sicily, exercised a baleful fascination upon the war cabinet. After a dinner at Chequers in November 1940, Churchill fantasised about an assault 'by 300 determined men, with blackened faces, knives between their teeth and revolvers under their tails'. Eden in 1940–41 cherished absurd notions of seizing Sicily: 'The Sicilians have always been anti-fascist,' he enthused. A War Office plan dated 28 December called for a descent on the island by two infantry brigades. There was talk of Sardinia, and of the Italian-held Dodecanese islands. The chiefs of staff learned to dread mention of north Norway in the prime minister's flights of fancy.

None of these schemes was executed, save a brief and embarrassingly unsuccessful foray into the Dodecanese, because the practical objections were overwhelming. Even the most modest raid required scarce shipping, which could not sensibly be hazarded within range of the Luftwaffe unless air cover was available, as it usually was not. It was hard to identify credible objectives for 'butcher and bolt' forays, and to gather sufficient intelligence to give them a reasonable chance of success. However strongly the prime minister pressed for British forces to display initiative and aggression, the chiefs of staff resolutely opposed operations which risked substantial losses in exchange for mere passing propaganda headlines.

In the autumn of 1940, Africa offered the only realistic opportunities for British land engagement. Libya had been an Italian colony since 1911, Abyssinia since 1936. Churchill owed a perverse debt of gratitude to Mussolini. If Italy had remained neutral, if her dictator had not chosen to seek battle, how else might the British Army have occupied itself after its expulsion from France? As it was, Britain was able to launch spectacular African campaigns against one of the few major armies in the world which it was capable of defeating. Not all Italian generals were incompetents, not all Italian formations fought feebly. But never for a moment were Mussolini's warriors in the same class as those of Hitler. North Africa, and the *Duce*'s pigeon-chested posturing as an Axis warlord, offered Britain's soldiers an opportunity to show their mettle. If the British Army was incapable of playing in a great stadium against top-class opposition, it could nonetheless hearten the nation and impress the world by a demonstration in a lesser league.

Britain's chiefs of staff, however, remained sceptical about the strategic value of any big commitment in the Middle East, win or lose. The Suez Canal route to the East was anyway unusable, because the Mediterranean was too perilous for merchant shipping, and remained so until 1943. The Persian oilfields fuelled British military operations in Middle East C-in-C Sir Archibald Wavell's theatre, but lay too far from home by the Cape route to provide petrol for Britain, which instead relied upon American supplies. It is often forgotten that in those days the US was overwhelmingly the greatest oil producer in the world. Dill advocated reinforcing the Far East against likely Japanese aggression, and remained in his heart an opponent of the Middle East commitment throughout his tenure as head of the army. The CIGS understood the political imperatives facing Churchill, but foremost in his mind was a fear that acceptance of unnecessary new risk might precipitate further gratuitous disaster. The prime minister overruled him. He believed that the embarrassment of inertia in the

Middle East much outweighed the perils of seizing the initiative. In the midst of a war, what would the world say about a nation that dispatched large forces to garrison its possessions on the far side of the world against a possible future enemy, rather than engage an actual one much nearer to hand?

In September 1940 an Italian army led by Marshal Graziani, 200,000 strong and thus outnumbering local British forces by four to one, crossed the east Libyan frontier and drove fifty miles eastward into Egypt before being checked. Meanwhile in East Africa, Mussolini's troops seized the little colony of British Somaliland and advanced into Kenya and Sudan from their bases in Abyssinia. Wavell ordered Somaliland evacuated after only brief resistance. He remained impenitent in the face of Churchill's anger about another retreat.

This first of Britain's 'desert generals' was much beloved in the army. In World War I, Wavell won an MC and lost an eye at Ypres, then spent 1917–18 as a staff officer in Palestine under Allenby, whose biography he later wrote. A reader of poetry, and prone to introspection, among soldiers Wavell passed as an intellectual. His most conspicuous limitation was taciturnity, which crippled his relationship with Churchill. Many who met him, perhaps over-impressed by his enigmatic persona, perceived themselves in the presence of greatness. But uncertainty persisted about whether this extended to mastery of battlefields, where a commander's strength of will is of greater importance than his cultural accomplishments.

On 28 October 1940, the Italians invaded north-west Greece. Contrary to expectations, after fierce fighting they were evicted by the Greek army and thrown back into Albania, where the rival forces languished in considerable discomfort through five months that followed. British strategy during this period became dominated by Mediterranean dilemmas, among which aid to Greece and offensive action in Libya stood foremost. Churchill constantly incited his C-in-C to take the offensive against the Italians in the Western Desert, using the tanks shipped to him at such hazard during the summer. Wavell insisted that he needed more time. Now, however, overlaid upon this issue was that of Greece, about which Churchill repeatedly changed his mind. On 27 October, the day before Italy invaded, he dealt brusquely with a proposal from Leo Amery and Lord Lloyd, respectively India and colonial secretaries, that more aid should be dispatched: 'I do not agree with your suggestions that at the present time we should make any further promises to Greece and Turkey. It is very easy to write in a sweeping manner when one does not have to take account of resources, transport, time and distance.'

Yet as soon as Italy attacked Greece, the prime minister told Dill that 'maximum possible' aid must be sent. Neville Chamberlain in March 1939 had assured the Greeks of British support against aggression. Now, Churchill perceived that failure to act must make the worst possible impression upon the United States, where many people doubted Britain's ability to wage war effectively. At the outset he proposed sending planes and weapons to Greece, rather than British troops. Dill, Wavell and Eden – then visiting Cairo – questioned even this. Churchill sent Eden a sharp signal urging boldness, dictated to his typist under the eye of Jock Colville.

He lay there in his four-post bed with its flowery chintz hangings, his bed-table by his side. Mrs Hill [his secretary] sat patiently opposite while he chewed his cigar, drank frequent sips of iced soda-water, fidgeted his toes beneath the bedclothes and muttered stertorously under his breath what he contemplated saying. To watch him compose some telegram or minute for dictation is to make one feel that one is present at the birth of a child, so tense is his expression, so restless his turnings from side to side, so curious the noises he emits under his breath. Then out comes some masterly sentence and finally with a 'Gimme' he takes the sheet of typewritten paper and initials it, or alters it with his fountain-pen, which he holds most awkwardly half way up the holder.

On 5 November Churchill addressed MPs, reporting grave shipping losses in the Atlantic and describing a conversation he had held on his way into the Commons with the armed and helmeted guards at its doors. One soldier offered a timeless British cliché to the prime minister: 'It's a great life if you don't weaken.' This, Churchill told MPs, was Britain's watchword for the winter of 1940: 'We will think of something better by the winter of 1941.' Then he adjourned to the smoking room, where he devoted himself to an intent study of the *Evening News*, 'as if it were the only source of information available to him'. Forget for a moment the art of his performance in the chamber. What more brilliant stagecraft could the leader of a democracy display than to read a newspaper in the common room of MPs of all parties, in the midst of a war and a blitz? ' "How are you?" he calls gaily to the most obscure Member . . . His very presence gives us all gaiety and courage,' wrote an MP. 'People gather round his table completely unawed.'

Despite Wavell's protests, Churchill insisted upon sending a British force to replace Greek troops garrisoning the island of Crete, who could thus be freed to fight on the mainland. The first consignment of material dispatched to Greece consisted of eight anti-tank guns, twelve Bofors, and 20,000 American rifles. To these were added, following renewed prime ministerial urgings, twenty-four field guns, twenty anti-tank rifles and ten light tanks. This poor stuff reflected the desperate shortage of arms for Britain's soldiers, never mind those of other nations. Some Gladiator fighters, capable of taking on the Italian air force but emphatically not the Luftwaffe, were also committed. Churchill was enraged by a cable from Sir Miles Lampson, British ambassador in Egypt, dismissing aid to Greece as 'completely crazy'. The prime minister told the Foreign Office: 'I expect to be protected from this kind of insolence.' He dispatched a stinging rebuke to Lampson: 'You should not telegraph at Government expense such an expression as "completely crazy" when applied by you to grave decisions of policy taken by the Defence Committee and the War Cabinet after considering an altogether wider range of requirements and assets than you can possibly be aware of.'

On the evening of 8 November, however, the prospect changed again. Eden returned from Cairo to confide to the prime minister first tidings of an offensive Wavell proposed to launch in the Western Desert the following month. This was news Churchill craved: 'I purred like six cats.' Ismay found him 'rapturously happy'. The prime minister exulted: 'At long last we are going to throw off the intolerable shackles of the defensive. Wars are won by superior will-power. Now we will wrest the initiative from the enemy and impose our will on him.' Three days later, he cabled Wavell: 'You may . . . be assured that you will have my full support at all times in any offensive action you may be able to take against the enemy.' That same night of 11 November, twenty-one Swordfish biplane torpedo bombers, launched from the carrier *Illustrious*, delivered a brilliant attack on the Italian fleet at Taranto which sank or crippled three battleships. Britain was striking out.

Churchill accepted that the North African offensive must now assume priority over all else, that no troops could be spared for Greece. A victory in the desert might persuade Turkey to come into the war. His foremost concern was that Wavell, whose terse words and understated delivery failed to generate prime ministerial confidence, should go for broke. Dismayed to hear that Operation *Compass* was planned as a limited 'raid', Churchill wrote to Dill on 7 December: 'If, with the situation as it is, General Wavell is only playing small, and is not hurling in his whole available forces with furious energy, he will have failed to rise to the height of circumstances . . . I never "worry" about action, but only about inaction.' He advanced a mad notion, that Eden should supplant Wavell as Middle East C-in-C, citing the precedent of Lord Wellesley in India during the Napoleonic wars. Eden absolutely refused to consider himself for such an appointment.

On 9 December, at last came the moment for the 'Army of the Nile', as Churchill had christened it, to launch its assault. Wavell's 4th Indian and 7th Armoured Divisions, led by Lt.Gen. Sir Richard O'Connor, attacked the Italians in the Western Desert. Operation *Compass* achieved brilliant success. Mussolini's generals showed themselves epic bunglers. Some 38,000 prisoners were taken in the first three days, at a cost of just 624 Indian and British casualties. 'It all seems too good to be true,' wrote Eden on 11 December. Wavell decided to exploit this success, and gave O'Connor his head. The little

British army, by now reinforced by 6th Australian Division, stormed along the coast into Libya, taking Bardia on 5 January. At 0540 on 21 January 1941, red Verey lights arched into the sky to signal the start of O'Connor's attack on the port of Tobruk. Bangalore torpedoes blew gaps in the Italian wire. An Australian voice shouted: 'Go on, you bastards!'

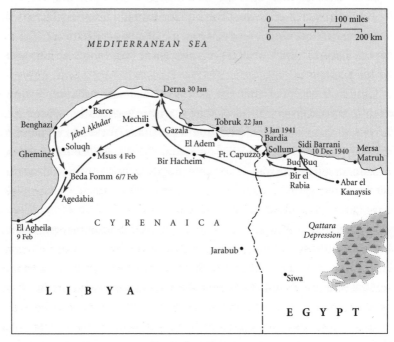

Operation *Compass*

At 0645, British tanks lumbered forward. The Italians resisted fiercely, but by dawn next day the sky was lit by the flames of their blazing supply dumps, prisoners in thousands were streaming into British cages, and the defenders were ready to surrender. O'Connor dispatched his tanks on a dash across the desert to cut off the retreating Italians. The desert army was in a mood of wild excitement. 'Off we went across the unknown country in full cry,' wrote Michael Creagh, one of O'Connor's division commanders. In a rare exhibition of emotion, O'Connor asked his chief of staff: 'My God, do you think it's going to be all right?' It was indeed 'all right'. The British reached Beda Fomm ahead of the Italians, who surrendered. In two months, the desert army had advanced 400 miles and taken 130,000 prisoners. On 11 February another of Wavell's contingents advanced from Kenya into Abyssinia and Somaliland. After hard fighting – much tougher than in Libya – here too the Italians were driven inexorably towards eventual surrender.

For a brief season, Wavell became a national hero. For the British people in the late winter and early spring of 1940–41, battered nightly by the Luftwaffe's bombardment, still fearful of invasion, conscious of the frailty of the Atlantic lifeline, success in Africa was precious. It was Churchill's delicate task to balance exultation about a victory with caution about future prospects. Again and again in his broadcasts and speeches he emphasised the long duration of the ordeal that must lie ahead, the need for unremitting exertion. To this purpose he continued to stress the danger of a German landing in Britain: in February 1941 he demanded a new evacuation of civilian residents from coastal areas in the danger zone.

Churchill knew how readily the nation could lapse into inertia. The army's home forces devoted much energy to anti-invasion exercises, such as *Victor* in March 1941. *Victor* assumed that five German divisions, two armoured and one motorised, had landed on the coast of East Anglia. On 30 March, presented with a report on the exercise, Churchill minuted mischievously, but with serious intent: 'All this data would be most valuable for our future offensive operations. I should be very glad if the same officers would work out a scheme for our landing an exactly similar force on the French coast.' Even if no descent on France was remotely practicable, Churchill was at his best in pressing Britain's generals again and again to forswear a fortress mentality.

But public fear and impatience remained constants. 'For the first time the possibility that we may be defeated has come to many people – me among them,' wrote Oliver Harvey, Eden's private secretary, on 22 February 1941. 'Mr Churchill's speech has rather sobered me,' wrote London charity worker Vere Hodgson after a prime ministerial broadcast that month. 'I was beginning to be a little optimistic. I even began to think there might be no Invasion . . . but he thinks there will, it seems. Also I had a feeling the end might soon be in sight; he seems to be looking a few years ahead! So I don't know what is going to happen to us. We seem to be waiting – waiting, for we know not what.'

Churchill had answers to Miss Hodgson's question. 'Here is the hand that is going to win the war,' he told guests at Chequers, who included Duff Cooper and General Sikorski, one evening in February. He extended his fingers as if displaying a poker hand: 'A Royal Flush – Great Britain, the Sea, the Air, the Middle East, American aid.' Yet this was flummery. British successes in Africa promoted illusions that were swiftly shattered. Italian weakness and incompetence, rather than British strength and genius, had borne O'Connor's little force to Tobruk and beyond. Thereafter, Wavell's forces found themselves once more confronted with their own limitations, in the face of energetic German intervention.

In the autumn of 1940 Hitler had declared that 'not one man and not one pfennig' would he expend in Africa. His strategic attention was focused upon the East. Mussolini, with his ambition to make the Mediterranean 'an Italian lake', was anyway eager to achieve his own conquests without German aid. But when the Italians suffered humiliation, Hitler was unwilling to see his ally defeated, and to risk losing Axis control of the Balkans. In April he launched the Wehrmacht into Yugoslavia and Greece. An Afrika Korps of two divisions under Erwin Rommel was dispatched to Libya. A new chapter of British misfortunes opened.

Churchill's decision to dispatch a British army to Greece in the spring of 1941 remains one of the most controversial of his wartime premiership. When the commitment was first mooted back in October, almost all the soldiers opposed it. On 1 November Eden, the Secretary for War, cabled from Cairo: 'We cannot, from Middle East resources, send sufficient air or land reinforcements to have any decisive influence upon course of fighting . . . To send such forces there . . . would imperil our whole position in the Middle East and jeopardize plans for offensive operations.' These remarks prompted a tirade from the prime minister, and caused Eden to write in his diary two days later: 'The weakness of our policy is that we never adhere to the plans we make.'

It seemed extraordinarily unlikely that a mere four divisions – all that could be spared from Wavell's resources – would make the difference between Greek victory and defeat. Aircraft were lacking. With German intervention looming in North Africa, such a diversion of forces threatened Britain's desert campaign. Kennedy told Dill on 26 January that he would have liked to see the chiefs of staff adopt much firmer resistance to the Greek proposal – 'We were near the edge of the precipice . . . CIGS said to me that he did not dissent, and considered the limitation placed upon the first reinforcements to be offered to the Greeks to be a sufficient safeguard. This seemed to me to be frightfully dangerous . . . If the Germans come down to Salonika the whole thing is bound to collapse, and nothing short of 20 divisions and a big air force, maintained by shipping we cannot afford, would be of any use . . . What we should do is keep the water in front of us. Anything we send to Greece will be lost if the Germans come down.' As so often with the counsels of Churchill's generals, this view represented prudence. Yet what would the British people say, never mind Goebbels, if the British lion skulked timorous beside the Nile?

Churchill changed his mind several times about Greece. Probably the most significant indication of his innermost belief derives from remarks to Roosevelt's envoy Harry Hopkins early in January. Hopkins reported to Washington on the 10th: 'He thinks Greece is lost – although he is now reinforcing the Greeks and weakening his African army.' Just as the prime minister's heart had moved him to dispatch more troops to France in June 1940 against military logic, so now it inspired him to believe that the Greeks could not be abandoned to their fate. An overriding moral imperative, his familiar determination to do nothing common or mean, drove the British debate in the early months of 1941. He nursed a thin hope that, following the success of *Compass*, Turkey might join the Allies if Britain displayed staunchness in the Balkans.

It is likely that Churchill would have followed his instinct to be seen to aid Greece even if Wavell in the Middle East had sustained opposition. As it was, however, the C-in-C provoked amazement among senior soldiers by changing his mind. When Dill and Eden arrived in Cairo in mid-February on a second visit, they found Wavell ready to support a Greek commitment. On the 19th, the general said: 'We have a difficult choice, but I think we are more likely to be playing the enemy's game by remaining inactive than by taking action in the Balkans.' Now it was Churchill's turn to wobble. 'Do not consider yourself obligated to a Greek enterprise if in your hearts you feel it will only be another Norwegian fiasco,' he signalled Eden on 20 February. Dill, however, said that they believed there was 'a reasonable chance of resisting a German advance'. Eden said to Wavell: 'It is a soldier's business. It is for you to say.' Wavell responded: 'War is an option of difficulties. We go.' On the 24th, Churchill told his men in Cairo: 'While being under no illusions, we all send you the order "Full Steam Ahead".'

The Greek commitment represented one of Anthony Eden's first tests as Foreign Secretary, the role to which he had been translated in December, on the departure of Lord Halifax to become British ambassador in Washington. In the eyes of many of his contemporaries, Eden displayed a highly-strung temperament, petulance and lack of steel which inspired scant confidence. An infantry officer in the First World War, endowed with famous charm and physical glamour, he established his credentials as an anti-appeaser by resigning from Chamberlain's government in 1938. Throughout the war, as afterwards, he cherished a passionate ambition to succeed Churchill in office, which the prime minister himself encouraged. Churchill valued Eden's intelligence and loyalty, but the soldiers thought him incorrigibly 'wet', with affectations of manner which they identified with those of homosexuals. Sir James Grigg, Permanent Under-Secretary at the War Office, and later Secretary for War, dismissed Eden as 'a poor feeble little pansy', though it should be noted that Grigg seldom thought well of anyone. In a world in which talent is rarely, if ever, sufficient to meet the challenges of government, it remains hard to identify a better candidate for the wartime foreign secretaryship. Eden often stood up to Churchill in a fashion which deserves respect. But his reports to Downing Street from the Mediterranean in 1940–41 reflected erratic judgement and a tendency towards vacillation.

Dill, head of the army, remained deeply unhappy about sending troops to Greece. But in the Middle East theatre, Wavell's was the decisive voice. Many historians have expressed bewilderment that this intelligent soldier should have committed himself to a policy which promised disaster. Yet it does not seem hard to explain Wavell's behaviour. For months the Middle East C-in-C had been harassed and pricked by the prime minister, who deplored his alleged pusillanimity. As early as August 1940, when Wavell visited London, Eden described the general's dismay at Churchill's impatience with him: 'Found Wavell waiting for me at 9am. He was clearly upset at last night's proceedings and said he thought he should have made it plain that if the Prime Minister could not approve his dispositions and had not confidence in him he should appoint someone else.' Though this early spat was patched up, the two men never established a rapport. Churchill wrote down Wavell as 'a good average colonel . . . [who] would make a good chairman of a Tory association'. The general displayed remarkable social gaucheness, for instance pitching his camp during visits to London later in the war at the home of 'Chips' Channon, one of the most foolish, if richest, men in Parliament. All through the autumn of 1940, bad-tempered signals flew to and fro between Downing Street and Cairo, provoked by the prime minister's impatience with Wavell's caution, and his C-in-C's exasperation with Churchill's indifference to military realities as he himself perceived them.

Again and again Churchill pressed Wavell, and indeed all his generals, to overcome their fears of the enemy, to display the fighting spirit which he prized above all things, and which alone, he believed, would enable Britain to survive. It seems necessary to recognise the loneliness of wartime commanders, thrust onto centre stage in a blaze of floodlights. Unlike ministers, most of whom had for years been famous men in the cockpit of affairs, even the highest-ranking of Britain's soldiers, sailors and airmen had passed their careers in obscurity, unknown beyond the ranks of their own services. Now, suddenly, such a man as Wavell found himself the focus of his nation's hopes. Even after the Libyan battlefield successes of recent months, the C-in-C in Cairo would have been less than human had he not been galled by Churchill's goading. In 1939 Poland had been left to face defeat alone, for it lay beyond the reach of a British or French army. In 1940 many Frenchmen and Belgians believed themselves betrayed by their Anglo-Saxon ally. In 1941 Britain's prime minister almost daily urged the peoples of the free world to join hands to contest mastery with the Nazis. Was a British army now to stand ingloriously idle, and watch Greece succumb?

In early March, Eden and Dill flew to meet the Athens government. Their brief from the prime minister was to expedite aid to Greece, where British troops began to land on the 4th, and to incite the Turks to belligerence. Churchill was under few delusions about the risks: 'We have taken a grave and hazardous decision to sustain the Greeks and to try and make a Balkan front,' he wrote to Smuts on 28 February. Bulgaria joined the Axis on 1 March. Yugoslavia was threatened. The Turks remained resolutely neutral, and the chiefs of staff anyway feared that Turkey as an ally would prove a liability. Yet now that the British were committed, and amid acute political and diplomatic difficulties, Eden and Dill laboured to give effect to earlier declarations of goodwill. Their reports to London remained unfailingly gloomy. Air Marshal Sir Arthur Tedder, commanding the Desert Air Force, was scornful about the haverings of almost all the politicians and senior officers making decisions in the Middle East. 'Wavell, I think, is a fine man,' he wrote, 'but the rest?!!! They swing daily from easy optimism to desperate defeatism and vice versa.'

At a war cabinet meeting in London on 7 March, attended by Australian prime minister Robert Menzies, Churchill's enthusiasm for the Greek commitment caused him, as so often, to talk roughshod over inconvenient material realities. He asserted, for instance: 'We should soon have strong air forces in Greece.' On the contrary, the RAF's feeble contingent – barely a hundred aircraft strong – was drastically outnumbered by the 1,350 planes of the Axis. Tokenism dominated the subsequent campaign. The British bombed Sofia's railyards in an attempt to hamper German supply movements to Yugoslavia. Yet this night attack was carried out by just six Wellingtons, a force insufficient convincingly to disrupt an exercise on Aldershot ranges. The nine squadrons committed by the RAF chiefly comprised obsolete and discredited aircraft, Gladiator biplane fighters and Blenheim light bombers. After achieving some early successes against the Italians, faced with modern German fighters such types could contribute nothing. Their destruction also entailed the loss of precious pilots. From January onwards, as the Luftwaffe ranged increasingly assertively over the Mediterranean, the Royal Navy was obliged to operate almost without air cover – and paid the price. By 14 April, the RAF in Greece had just forty-six serviceable planes.

There is no objective test by which the moral benefits of attempting to aid Greece can be measured against the cost of subjecting yet another British army to defeat. The official historians of wartime intelligence have highlighted one misjudgement in the spring of 1941: Churchill and his generals failed to perceive, because Ultra signal intercepts did not tell them, that Hitler's fundamental purpose in the Balkans was not offensive, but defensive. He sought to protect the Romanian oilfields and secure his southern flank before attacking Russia. It is unlikely, however, that even had this been recognised in London, it would have caused Churchill to opt for inaction. Throughout its history, Britain has repeatedly sought to ignore the importance of mass on the battlefield, dispatching inadequate forces to assert moral or strategic principles. This was the course Churchill adopted in March 1941. It has been suggested that Wavell should have resigned, rather than send troops to Greece. But field commanders have no business to make such gestures. Wavell did his utmost to support his nation's purposes, though he knew that, as commander-in-chief, he would bear responsibility for what must follow. On

7 April, when he bade farewell to Dill as the CIGS left Cairo for London with Eden, he said, 'I hope, Jack, you will preside at my court martial.'

The outcome was as swift as it was inevitable. The Germans crushed Yugoslav resistance during two days' fighting in Macedonia on 6–7 April, then embarked upon a series of dramatic outflanking operations against the Greeks. The Greek army was exhausted and demoralised following its winter campaign against the Italians. Its initial achievement in pushing forward into Albania, which had so impressed the British, represented the only effort of which it was capable. Within days, 62,000 British, Australian and New Zealand troops in Greece found themselves retreating southwards in disarray, harried at every turn by the Luftwaffe. A 6 April air raid on Piraeus blew up a British ammunition ship, wrecking the port. The RAF's little fighter force was ruthlessly destroyed.

Worse, even before the Germans occupied Greece, the Afrika Korps attacked in Libya. On 3 April the British evacuated Benghazi, then found themselves retreating pell-mell back down the coast road eastwards along which they had advanced in triumph two months earlier. By 11 April, when Rommel reached the limit of his supply chain, he had driven the British back almost to the start-line of their *Compass* offensive. It was fortunate that Hitler had dispatched to Libya too small a force and inadequate logistical support to convert British withdrawal into outright disaster. So much was wrong with the leadership, training, weapons and tactics of Wavell's desert army that it is questionable whether it could have repulsed the Afrika Korps even in the absence of the Greek diversion. Inevitably, however, Greece was deemed responsible for defeat in Libya.

The desert fiasco brought out both the worst and best in Churchill. He offered absurd tactical suggestions. He chafed at the navy's failure to bombard Tripoli, Rommel's supply base – an intolerable risk beneath the German air threat. On land, he urged foolishly: 'General Wavell should regain unit ascendancy over the enemy and destroy his small raiding parties, instead of our own being harassed and hunted by them. Enemy patrols must be attacked on every occasion, and our own patrols should be used with audacity. Small British parties in armoured cars, or mounted on motor-cycles, or, if occasion offers, infantry, should not hesitate to attack individual tanks with bombs and bombards, as is planned for the defence of Britain.' By contrast, the prime minister was at his best in overruling objections from the chiefs of staff and accepting the huge risk of dispatching a convoy, codenamed *Tiger*, direct through the Mediterranean to Egypt, instead of by the much safer but longer Cape route, with reinforcements of tanks.

Dill returned from Cairo steeped in gloom. John Kennedy, the DMO, sought to revive his spirits, but the CIGS dismissed reassuring words about the outlook. 'I think it is desperate. I am terribly tired.' Next day Kennedy noted: 'CIGS is miserable & feels he has wrecked the Empire.' That evening Kennedy, at dinner with a friend, discussed possible evacuation of the entire Middle East. 'On balance it was doubtful if we gained more than we lost by staying there. Prestige and effect on Americans perhaps the biggest arguments for staying.' Like most senior soldiers, Kennedy was appalled by events in Greece, and by Britain's role in the débâcle: 'Chiefs of staff overawed & influenced enormously by Winston's overpowering personality . . . I hate my title now, for I suppose outsiders think I really "direct" oper[atio]ns & am partly responsible for the foolish & disastrous strategy which our armies are following.' The self-confidence of Britain's senior soldiers was drained by successive battlefield defeats. They felt themselves incapable of opposing Churchill, but likewise unable to support many of his decisions with conviction. They saw themselves bearing responsibility for losing the war, while offering no alternative proposals for winning it. Left to their own devices, the generals would have accepted battle only on the most favourable terms. Churchill, however, believed that operational passivity must spell doom for his hopes both of preventing the British people from succumbing to inertia and persuading the Americans to belligerence.

Following the suicide of the Greek prime minister, Alexander Koryzis, on 18 April, the will of his nation's leadership collapsed. In London, Robert Menzies wrote after a war cabinet on 24 April 1941:

'I am afraid of a disaster, and understand less than ever why Dill and Wavell advised that the Greek adventure had military merits. Of the moral merits I have no doubt. Better Dunkirk than Poland or Czechoslovakia.' Menzies added two days later: 'War cabinet. Winston says "We will lose only 5000 men in Greece." We will in fact lose at least 15000. W is a great man, but he is more addicted to wishful thinking every day.'

Towards the end of April, a young soldier on leave in Lancashire who was visiting housewife Nella Last got up and left the living room as the family tuned to a broadcast by the prime minister. Mrs Last said: 'Aren't you going to listen to Winston Churchill?' Her guest demurred, as she recorded in her diary: 'An ugly twist came to his mouth and he said "No, I'll leave that for all those who like dope." I said, "Jack, you're liverish, pull yourself together. We believe in Churchill – one must believe in someone." He said darkly, "well, everyone is not so struck."' Mrs Last, like the overwhelming majority of British people, yearned to sustain her faith in the prime minister. Yet it seemed hard to do so on such an evening as this: 'Did I sense a weariness and . . . foggy bewilderment as to the future in Winston's speech – or was it all in my tired head, I wonder? Anyway, I got no inspiration – no little banner to carry. Instead I felt I got a glimpse of a horror and carnage that we have not yet thought of . . . More and more do I think it is the "end of the world" – of the old world, anyway.' The poor woman acknowledged that she was unhappy and frightened. 'Its funny how sick one can get, and not able to eat – just through . . . fear.' Harold Nicolson, Parliamentary Under-Secretary at the Ministry of Information, wrote: 'All that the country really wants is some assurance of how victory is to be achieved. They are bored by talks about the righteousness of our cause and our eventual triumph. What they want are facts indicating how we are to beat the Germans. I have no idea at all how we are to give them those facts.'

In Greece, the retreating army was much moved by the manner of its parting from the stricken people: 'We were nearly the last British troops they would see and the Germans might be at our heels,' wrote Lt.Col. R.P. Waller of his artillery unit's withdrawal through Athens, 'yet cheering, clapping crowds lined the streets and pressed about our cars . . . Girls and men leapt on the running boards to kiss or shake hands with the grimy, weary gunners. They threw flowers to us and ran beside us crying "Come back – You must come back again – Goodbye – Good luck."' The Germans took the Greek capital on 27 April. They had secured the country with a mere 5,000 casualties. The British lost 12,000 men, 9,000 of these becoming prisoners. The rest of Wavell's expeditionary force was fortunate to escape to Crete from the ports of the Peloponnese.

Dill broadcast his gloom beyond the War Office. 'He himself took a depressed view of our prospect in Libya, Syria and even Irak,' Lord Hankey recorded after a conversation with the CIGS, 'and said that the German armoured forces are superior to ours both in numbers and efficiency – even in the actual Tanks. He was evidently very anxious about invasion, and seemed to fear that Winston would insist on denuding this country of essential defensive forces. He asked what a CIGS could do if he thought the PM was endangering the safety of the country.' In such a case he should resign, said Hankey, an increasingly malevolent critic of the prime minister. Dill mused aloud: 'But can one resign in war?' It is extraordinary that the head of Britain's army allowed himself to voice such defeatist sentiments at such a moment in the nation's fortunes, even to a member of the government such as Hankey was. Yet it would be another six months before Churchill ventured to sack Dill. The general's limitations reflected a chronic shortage of plausible warrior chieftains at the summit of Britain's armed forces. It was not that Dill was a stupid man – far from it. Rather, he displayed an excess of rationality, allied to an absence of fire, which deeply irked the prime minister.

On 20 May, three weeks after Greece was occupied, General Kurt Student's Luftwaffe paratroops began landing on Crete – to face slaughter at the hands of 40,000 British defenders commanded by Major-General Bernard Freyberg. Thanks to Ultra, the entire German plan, and even its timings, were known to the British. On the first day, the battle appeared a disaster for the Germans. The British 14th Brigade defeated them at Heraklion, and the Australians were likewise victorious at Rethymnon. New Zealand infantrymen, perhaps the finest Allied fighting soldiers of the Second World War, held Maleme airfield. But that evening the New Zealanders' commanders made a fatal mistake, withdrawing from Maleme to reorganise for a counter-attack next day. On the afternoon of 21 May, a fresh battalion of German mountain troops crash-landed there in Junkers transports. Having secured the airfield, reinforcements poured in. Freyberg's force began to withdraw eastwards. The Royal Navy inflicted heavy losses on the German seaborne reinforcement convoy, but itself suffered gravely. 'We hold our breath over Crete,' wrote Vere Hodgson on 25 May. '. . . I feel Churchill is doing the same. He did not seem to mind evacuation of Greece, but he will take the loss of Crete very hard.'

As the Germans strengthened their grip on the island and Freyberg received Wavell's consent to evacuate, the Luftwaffe pounded the British fleet. Two battleships, an aircraft-carrier and many lesser vessels were damaged, four cruisers and six destroyers sunk. Crete became the costliest single British naval campaign of the Second World War. On shore, the defenders lost 2,000 men killed and 12,000 taken prisoner. Eighteen thousand were rescued and carried to Egypt by the navy. Freyberg persuaded Churchill to assert in his post-war memoirs that the campaign had cost the Germans 15,000 casualties. The true figure, well-known by that time, was 6,000, including 2,000 dead. Some 17,500 German invaders had defeated a British and Commonwealth force more than twice as numerous. By 1 June, it was all over.

Strategically, the fall of Crete was a much less serious matter for the British than would have been the loss of Malta. Admiral Cunningham believed that if the island had been held the British would have paid a heavy price for continuing to supply it, in the face of overwhelming German air superiority. It was Hitler's mistake to allow Student to deploy his parachute division against Freyberg's garrison, rather than commit the *Fallschirmjäger* against Malta, Britain's key Mediterranean island, which the Germans could probably have taken. But Churchill had promised the British people, and the world, that Crete would be staunchly defended. Its loss was a heavy blow to his authority, and even more so to his faith in the fighting power of the British Army. Thoughtful civilians, too, perceived the limitations of their own forces. 'The difference between the capability of the B[ritish] Army when dealing with the Italians and with the Germans is surely too plain to be missed,' Elizabeth Belsey, a communist living in Huntingdon who was deeply cynical about her nation's rulers, wrote to her soldier husband. 'One can detect here and there, especially in Churchill's speeches, hints that Britain realises the stickiness of her position.'

The prime minister was driven to offer threadbare explanations for the Mediterranean disaster, telling the House of Commons on 10 June: 'A very great number of the guns which might have usefully been employed in Crete have been, and are being, mounted in merchant vessels to beat off the attacks of the Focke Wulf and Heinkel aircraft, whose depredations have been notably lessened thereby.' But then he tired of his own evasions, saying: 'Defeat is bitter. There is no use in trying to explain defeat. People do not like defeat, and they do not like the explanations, however elaborate or plausible, which are given to them. For defeat there is only one answer. The only answer to defeat is victory. If a government in time of war gives the impression that it cannot in the long run procure victory, who cares for explanations ? It ought to go.'

Churchill believed, surely rightly, that Crete could have been held. Yet Freyberg had been his personal choice to lead its defence. The New Zealander, like Gort a World War I VC, was the sort of hero whom he loved. Freyberg was a fine and brave man, but on Crete he showed himself unfit for command responsibility. Many of his troops were fugitives from Greece. The British Army never had the skill which the Germans later displayed for welding 'odds and sods' into effective impromptu battle groups. A shortage of wireless sets crippled British communications, and Freyberg's understanding of the battle. There was little transport to move troops, and the Luftwaffe wrought havoc on such roads as existed. It was possible to argue that the British, Australian and New Zealand combat units on Crete – as distinct from the great 'tail', which degenerated into a rabble during the evacuation – fought well. They were baffled and angry when, after savaging Student's paratroopers, they found themselves ordered to withdraw. Failure on Crete was the responsibility of British – and New Zealand – higher commanders. But the ultimate verdict remained inescapable: once again, an imperial army had been beaten, in a battle conducted on terms which should have favoured the defenders.

Churchill a few months later claimed to regret the Greek commitment, which he described to Colville as the only error of judgement his government had made. Wavell should have garrisoned Crete, he said, and advised the Athens government to make the best terms with Germany that it could. But this was a view expressed while Britain was still struggling for survival. In the longer run of history, the nobility of his purpose in Greece commands respect. As Robert Menzies and others perceived, British passivity in the face of the destruction of Greek freedom would have created a sorry impression upon the world, and especially the United States. Nonetheless, events in the Mediterranean dismayed every enemy of Nazism. A Bucharest Jew, Mikhail Sebastian, wrote: 'Once more Germany gives the impression of an invincible, demonic, overwhelming force. The general feeling is one of bewilderment and impotence.' A German war correspondent, Kurt Pauli, approached some British prisoners near Corinth and struck a posture of chivalrous condescension. 'You've lost the game,' he said. Not so, the PoWs replied defiantly: 'We've still got Winston Churchill.'

Was this enough, however? Alan Brooke wrote later of 'the utter darkness of those early days of calamities when no single ray of hope could pierce the depth of gloom'. It was astonishing that the prime minister maintained his exuberance. Robert Menzies wrote: 'The PM in conversation will steep himself (and you) in gloom on some grim aspect of the war . . . only to proceed to fight his way out while he is pacing the floor with the light of battle in his eyes. In every conversation he inevitably reaches a point where he positively enjoys the war: "Bliss in that age was it to be alive." (He says) "Why do people regard a period like this as years lost out of our lives

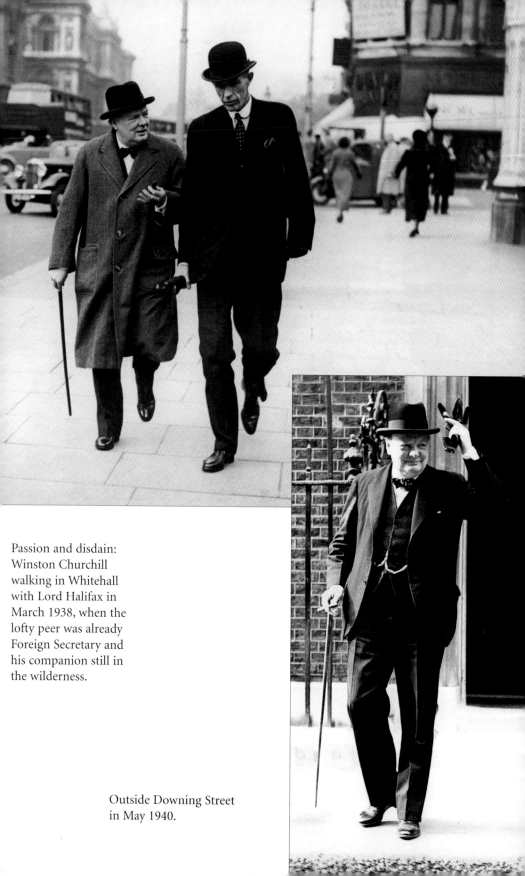

Passion and disdain:
Winston Churchill
walking in Whitehall
with Lord Halifax in
March 1938, when the
lofty peer was already
Foreign Secretary and
his companion still in
the wilderness.

Outside Downing Street
in May 1940.

Blitzkrieg: German columns advancing through France in May 1940.

In Paris on 31 May 1940 with Dill, Attlee and Reynaud.

Disaster and deliverance: Dunkirk.

Invasion fever: (*left*) Inspecting an unconvincing roadblock, and (*below*) the Mid-Devon Hunt combine business with pleasure by patrolling Dartmoor.

French warships blaze at Mers-el-Kebir under British bombardment, 3 July 1940.

The Battle of Britain: Hurricane pilots scramble.

The cockpit of war in 1940: the filter room at RAF Fighter Command, Bentley Priory.

A classic image, sometimes branded as faked for the benefit of German propaganda, but nonetheless symbolic: a Luftwaffe Heinkel over the London docks in September 1940.

The blitz: a street scene repeated a thousand times across the cities of Britain.

A study in defiance: Churchill portrayed by Cecil Beaton in the Cabinet Room at 10 Downing Street on 20 November 1940.

when beyond question it is the most interesting period of them? Why do we regard history as of the past and forget we are making it?"'

The near Middle East was only one among many theatres from which bad tidings crowded in upon Britain's prime minister. On 30 April, Iraqi troops attacked the RAF's Habbaniya air base outside Baghdad, prompting Churchill and Eden to conclude that they must seize Iraq to pre-empt a German takeover. The Luftwaffe's blitz on Britain continued relentlessly, and had by now killed more than 30,000 civilians. On 10 May, the demented deputy führer Rudolf Hess parachuted into Scotland on a personal peace mission which perversely served Nazi propaganda interests better than British. Bewildered people, especially in Moscow and Washington, supposed that some parley between Britain and Germany must indeed be imminent. Fears persisted that Spain would join the Axis. Although foreign exchange was desperately short, the government somehow found the huge sum of $10 million to bribe Spanish generals to keep their country out of the war. The payments, arranged through Franco's banker Juan March, were made into Swiss accounts. There is no evidence that this largesse influenced Spanish policy, but it represented an earnest of British anxiety about Franco's neutrality.

On 20 May, Germans began to appear in Vichy French Syria, causing Churchill to decree, once more against Wavell's opposition: 'We must go in.' British, Australian and Free French troops were soon fighting a bitter little campaign against the Vichyites, who resisted. Churchill observed crossly that it was a pity they had not displayed the same determination against the Germans in 1940. Pétain's troops were finally overcome. Britain's seizure of Iraq and Syria attracted little popular enthusiasm at the time, and has not attracted much interest or applause from historians since. Yet these two initiatives reflected Churchill's boldness at its best. British actions removed dangerous instability on Wavell's eastern flank. The diversion of troops caused much hand-wringing in Cairo, but represented strategic wisdom. If the Germans had been successful in their tentative efforts to rouse the Arab world against Britain, its predicament in the Middle East would have worsened dramatically. The most authoritative modern German historians of the war, the authors of the monumental Potsdam Institute series, consider British successes in Syria, Iraq and Abyssinia more important to the 1941 strategic pattern than defeat on Crete. Churchill, they say, 'was right when he asserted that on the whole, the situation in the Mediterranean and the Middle East was far more favourable to Britain than it had been a year earlier'. Yet it did not seem so at the time to the sorely tried British people.

On 23 May, a Friday, the battlecruiser *Hood* blew up during a brief engagement with the *Bismarck*. The days that followed, with the German battleship loose in the North Atlantic, were terrible ones for the prime minister. His despondency lifted only on the 27th, when as he addressed the House of Commons he received news that the *Bismarck* was sunk. Atlantic convoy losses remained appalling. American assistance fell far short of British hopes, and Churchill not infrequently vented his bitterness at the ruthlessness of the financial terms extracted by Washington. 'As far as I can make out,' he wrote to chancellor Kingsley Wood, 'we are not only to be skinned, but flayed to the bone.'

The Middle East remained Britain's chief battleground. Despite success in securing the eastern flank in Syria and seizing control of Iraq, Churchill's confidence in his C-in-C, never high, was ebbing fast. 'He said some very harsh things about Wavell, whose excessive caution and inclination to pessimism he finds very antipathetic.' For a few weeks, confidence flickered about a fresh offensive, *Battleaxe*. Admiral Cunningham was told that if this succeeded, and Wavell's forces reached Tripoli, the next step would be a landing in Sicily. Such fantasies were swiftly crushed. On 17 June it was learned in London that *Battleaxe* had failed, with the loss of a hundred priceless tanks. Churchill was exasperated to hear that Wavell wanted to evacuate Tobruk. This was militarily rational, for the port's logistic value was small, yet seemed politically intolerable. In April Churchill had described Wavell in a broadcast as 'that fine commander whom we cheered in good days and will back through bad'. Now, on 20

June, he sacked the Middle East C-in-C, exchanging him with Sir Claude Auchinleck, C-in-C India, whose seizure of Iraq had been executed with impressive efficiency. Wavell was given the Delhi command only because Churchill feared that to consign him to oblivion would play poorly with the public, to whom the general had been represented as a hero.

Clementine Churchill once wrote contemptuously to her husband about the deposed Middle East C-in-C: 'I understand he has a great deal of personal charm. This is pleasant in civilized times but not much use in total War.' Too many of the British Army's senior officers were agreeable men who lacked the killer instinct indispensable to victory. Wavell's best biographer, Ronald Lewin, has observed that he seemed destined for greatness in any field save that of high command in battle. It might more brutally be suggested that there was less to Wavell than his enigmatic persona led admirers to suppose. He once said to Pownall: 'My trouble is that I am not really interested in war.' This was a surprisingly common limitation among Britain's senior soldiers. It goes far to explain why Winston Churchill was much better suited to his own role than were some of his generals to theirs.

2 The War Machine

It is sometimes suggested that in the Second World War there was none of the mistrust, and indeed hostility, between generals and politicians, 'brass' and 'frocks', which characterised the British high command in the 1914–18 conflict. This is untrue. Ironside, when he was CIGS in 1939, remarked contemptuously to a staff officer as he set out for a war cabinet meeting: 'Now I'm going to waste a morning educating these old gentlemen on their job.' Though Churchill was not then prime minister, he was categorised among the despised 'old gentlemen'.

Lt.Gen. Henry Pownall wrote of Churchill's cabinet: 'They are a pretty fair lot of gangsters some of them – Bevin, Morrison and above all Beaverbrook who has got one of the nastiest faces I ever saw on any man.' John Kennedy wrote later in the war: 'It is a bad feature of the present situation, that there is such a rift between the politicians and the services. Winston certainly does not keep his team pulling happily in harness together. It is very wrong of him to keep abusing the services – the cry is taken up by other politicians & it is bad for the Service advisers to be made to feel ashamed of their uniforms.'

Yet the evidence of events suggests that the prime minister's criticisms of his soldiers were well merited. The shortcomings of the wartime British Army form the theme of a later chapter. By a notable irony, Churchill's machinery for directing the war effort was much more impressive than the means for implementing its decisions in the field. The war cabinet was Britain's principal policy-making body, regularly attended by the chiefs of staff as well as by its own eight members – in 1941 Churchill, Attlee, Eden, Bevin, Wood, Beaverbrook, Greenwood and Sir John Anderson. Some 400 committees and sub-committees, of varying membership and importance, devolved from it. Service business was addressed by the chiefs at their own gatherings, usually in Churchill's absence. Of 391 chiefs of staff meetings in 1941, Churchill presided at only twenty-three, whereas he chaired ninety-seven of 111 meetings of the war cabinet. He also conducted sixty out of sixty-nine meetings of its defence committee's operational group, and twelve out of thirteen meetings of its supply group.

Formalities were always maintained, with the prime minister addressing ministers and commanders by their titles rather than names. On Churchill's bad days, his subordinates were appalled by his intemperance and irrationality. But on his good ones – and what an astonishing number of these there were! – his deportment went far to render a war of national survival endurable for those conducting it. 'When he is in the right mood, no entertainment can surpass a meeting with him,' wrote a general. 'The other day he presided over a meeting on supply of equipment to allies and possible allies. He bustled in and said "well, I suppose it is the old story – too many little pigs and not enough teats on the old sow."'

The chiefs of staff met every day save Sunday at 10.30 a.m., in a room beneath the Home Office connected to the Cabinet War Rooms. Sessions customarily continued until 1 p.m. In the afternoons, chiefs worked in their own offices, to which they returned after dinner unless a further evening meeting had been summoned, as happened at moments of crisis, of which there were many. Every Monday evening the chiefs attended war cabinet. The 1914–18 conflict precipitated the beginnings of a historic shift in the balance of decision-making from commanders in the field towards the prime minister and his service chiefs in London. In the Second World War this became much more pronounced. Generals at the head of armies, admirals at sea, remained responsible for winning battles. But modern communications empowered those at the summit of national affairs to influence the conduct of operations in remote theatres, for good or ill, in a fashion impossible in earlier ages. Alan Brooke wrote later: 'It is a strange thing what a vast part the COS [committee] takes in the running of the war and how little it is known or its functions appreciated! The average man in the street has never heard of it.'

For any minister or service chief successfully to influence the prime minister, it was essential that he should be capable of sustaining himself in argument. Churchill considered that unless commanders had stomach to fight him, they were unlikely to fight the enemy. Few found it easy to do this. Admiral Sir Dudley Pound, the First Sea Lord, was one of many senior officers who cherished ambivalent attitudes towards Churchill: 'At times you could kiss his feet, at others you feel you could kill him.' Pound was a capable organiser whose tenure as chairman of the chiefs until March 1942 was crippled, first, by a reluctance to assert his own will against that of the prime minister, later by worsening health. Captain Stephen Roskill, official historian of the wartime Royal Navy, believed that Pound was never a big enough man for his role. The admiral had doubts about his own capacities, and once asked Cunningham whether he should resign his post. Churchill bears substantial blame for allowing Pound to keep his job when his failing body, as well as inadequate strength of character, had become plain. It was fortunate for the Royal Navy that the admiral had some able and energetic subordinates.

Admiral Sir Andrew Cunningham, the Mediterranean C-in-C who succeeded Pound when he became mortally stricken, was frustrated by his own inarticulacy: 'I . . . have to confess to an inherent difficulty in expressing myself in verbal discussion, which I have never got over except on certain occasions when I am really roused . . . I felt rather like a spider sitting in the middle of a web vibrating with activity.' Soon after Cunningham took up his post at the Admiralty, one Saturday afternoon the telephone rang at his Hampshire home. The prime minister wanted to talk on the scrambler. Cunningham explained that he possessed no scrambler. Churchill said impatiently that a device would be installed immediately. The admiral and his wife were kept awake until engineers finished their task at 1 a.m., when a call was duly put through to Downing Street. The prime minister was by then asleep. Cunningham, considerably cross, was told that the emergency had passed.

Air Chief Marshal Sir Charles Portal, who assumed direction of the RAF in October 1940, was widely considered the cleverest of the chiefs of staff. 'Peter' Portal displayed notable diplomatic gifts, especially later, in dealing with the Americans. Like many senior airmen, his principal preoccupation was with the interests of his own service, and above all its bomber offensive. His personality lacked the bright colours, his conduct the anecdotage, which enabled a man to shine at dinner tables or in the historiography of the war, but Ismay's key subordinate Brigadier Leslie Hollis paid tribute to Portal's incisive mind and infectious calm: 'I never saw him ruffled,' said Hollis, 'even under vicious and uninformed attacks on the Air Force. He would sit surveying the critic coldly from beneath his heavy-lidded eyes, never raising his voice or losing his temper, but replying to rhetoric with facts.' The army was envious of the skill with which Portal exercised his influence upon the prime minister, often more successfully than the CIGS. Gen. Sir John Dill was liked and respected by his colleagues, but by the summer of 1941 he was deeply scarred by the failures of his service; his fires were flickering, his self-confidence had ebbed. Chiefs of staffs' meetings throughout 1941–42 were pervaded by consciousness of the army's inability to deliver victories, and of the prime minister's consequent disaffection towards its leaders.

Major-General Hastings 'Pug' Ismay, throughout Churchill's premiership his chief of staff as Minister of Defence and personal representative on the chiefs of staff committee, was sometimes criticised as a courtier, too acquiescent to his master's whims. John Kennedy, for instance, disliked Ismay: 'I am thankful I have so little to do with him . . . Ismay is such a devotee of PM's that he is a danger. He said the other evening in the club "if the PM came in & said he'd like to wipe his boots on me, I'd lie down & let him do it. He is such a great man everything should be done for him." This is a dangerous attribute for a man who has such an influence on military advice.'

Yet this was a minority view. Most people – ministers, commanders and officials alike – respected Ismay's tact and discretion. He perceived his role as that of representing the prime minister's wishes to service chiefs, and vice versa, rather than himself acting as a prime mover. He never offered strategic advice because he believed, surely rightly, that this would usurp the chiefs' functions. He was a superb diplomat, who presided over a small staff of which the principal members were Hollis, who had served as a Royal Marine officer aboard a cruiser at the 1916 battle of Jutland, and the brilliant, austere, bespectacled Colonel Ian Jacob, a field marshal's son. Ismay himself was usually to be found in the prime minister's anteroom, while the secretariat was based in Richmond Terrace, around the corner from Downing Street. There, Jacob established the Defence Registry, which logged every incoming signal from commanders in the field, including those addressed to the chiefs of staff. Whatever mistakes were made by the British high command, however acute became personal tensions between the prime minister, his generals, admirals and air marshals, throughout Churchill's war premiership, the highest standards of coordination, staff discipline and exchange of information prevailed between Downing Street and the service ministries.

On the civil side, the prime minister was served by a remarkable group of officials. Cabinet Secretary Sir Edward Bridges preserved an enthusiasm for cerebral diversions, even amid the blitz. He presided over self-consciously intellectual debates in the Downing Street staff mess at supper, such as one in pursuance of the theme 'Is there any evil except in intent?' Bridges had the additional merit that he was as passionately committed as the prime minister to victory at any cost, and in June 1940 rejected out of hand proposals to establish skeleton Whitehall departments in Canada, against the eventuality of German occupation of Britain.

The Downing Street staff understood, as some outsiders did not, that while the prime minister's regime might be unusual, it was remarkably disciplined. Minutes were typed and circulated within an hour or two of meetings taking place, even after midnight. The private secretaries – for most of the war Leslie Rowan, John Martin, Tony Bevir and John Colville – worked in shifts through the day and much of the night. 'The chief difficulty is understanding what he says,' wrote Martin in the early days of his service, 'and great skill is required in interpreting inarticulate grunts or single words thrown out without explanation. I think he is consciously odd in these ways.' Colville, as a young patrician – he was the grandson of Lord Crewe – who had also attended Harrow, Churchill's old school, basked in paternalistic indulgence from his master. His social self-assurance, indeed conceit, enabled him to gossip among potentates at the prime minister's dinner table without awe, though his role was only that of a humble official. As a diarist Colville fulfilled a priceless historical function as chronicler of the prime minister's domestic routine.

Churchill's personal followers inspired mistrust outside the 'secret circle', and sometimes inside it also. There was frequent criticism of his willingness to indulge old friends and family connections in significant posts. Later in the war, his son-in-law Duncan Sandys made himself deeply unpopular as a junior army minister. Alan Brooke swore that he would resign if, as was rumoured likely though it never became a reality, Sandys was promoted to become Secretary for War. It was often asserted that Beaverbrook, Cherwell and Brendan Bracken were unsuitable intimates for the prime minister, just as important

Americans resented Harry Hopkins's relationship with Roosevelt. Yet in judging Churchill's chosen associates, the only relevant issue is whether acolytes – the so-called 'cronies' – improperly influenced his decisions.

Beaverbrook was the most wilful and intrusive. Whether in or out of office, he occupied an astonishing amount of the prime minister's time and attention. Churchill never appeared to notice Beaverbrook's physical cowardice, unusual in any member of his circle, and widely remarked by colleagues during the blitz, when as often as possible he retired to the country, and on the long wartime journeys abroad. The press baron exercised notable power as Minister of Aircraft Production in 1940, then as Minister of Supply in 1941. He remained thereafter one of the few civilians to whose views Churchill listened. Beaverbrook made much mischief about personalities. His contempt embraced the entire wartime Commons. 'In truth it is only a sham of a parliament,' he wrote to Hoare in Madrid in May 1941. 'The Front Bench is part of the sham. There Attlee and Greenwood, a sparrow and a jackdaw, are perched on either side of the glittering bird of paradise.' It is easy to identify issues on which Beaverbrook urged the prime minister to do the wrong thing, of which more will be said later. It is much harder to discover a case in which his imprecations were successful.

Brendan Bracken, Churchill's familiar for a decade before the war, enjoyed ready access, much resented by rivals. But his influence was deemed greater than it was, because the garrulous Bracken boasted so much about it. Fellow ministers and officials were sometimes shocked by the familiarity with which he addressed the prime minister as 'Winston'. He and Beaverbrook were dubbed the 'knights of the bath' in recognition of the implausible rendezvous they sometimes shared with Churchill. Nonetheless, this clever, elusive Irishman, his bespectacled features surmounted by what looked like a wig of red steel wool, provided Churchill with a useful source of intelligence and gossip about domestic affairs, and served as a successful Minister of Information from July 1941 to 1945. Forty in 1941, Bracken had high intelligence and a remarkable capacity for private kindness. As a pocket press baron himself, owner of the *Economist* and chairman of the *Financial News*, he thoroughly understood the demands of the media. He frequently intervened to improve journalists' access to the services, and to curb the prime minister's rage when newspapers were deemed to have exceeded the bounds of reasonable criticism. He exercised no influence on strategy, and was seldom present when it was discussed.

Professor Frederick Lindemann, the prime minister's personal scientific adviser who became Lord Cherwell in June 1941, was the most widely disliked of Churchill's intimates. His cleverness was not in doubt, but his intellectual arrogance and taste for vendettas bred many enemies. Fifty-five in 1941, Cherwell had inherited a fortune gained from waterworks in Germany. He enjoyed flaunting his wealth before less fortunate scientific colleagues, often arriving for Oxford meetings in a chauffeur-driven Rolls-Royce. His habit of crossing roads looking straight ahead, indifferent to oncoming traffic, reflected his approach to issues of state and war. A bachelor and a vegetarian, of strongly right-wing and indeed racist convictions, he was an unselfconscious eccentric. When three of his Cabinet Office staff insisted on being transferred to the Merchant Navy to play a more active part in the war, he was alarmed by the secrets they would take with them to sea. He told them: 'If you see that you are about to be captured, you must kill yourselves immediately!'

When the scientist's judgement was mistaken, his obstinacy did considerable harm. He campaigned obsessively for aerial mines as a defence against air attack, wasting significant design and production effort. His advocacy of 'area bombing' was founded on a misreading of data, and caused him to injure the Royal Navy's cause in the Battle of the Atlantic. Because Churchill trusted Cherwell, 'the Prof's' errors were disproportionately damaging. The prime minister sometimes abused Cherwell's statistics to advance rash theses of his own. Ian Jacob described him as a 'licensed gadfly'. On balance, however, Cherwell's contribution to Churchill's governance was positive. It enabled him to support with evidence argument on a vast range of issues.

Among lesser figures, the booming Major Desmond Morton was

an able intelligence officer who provided important information to Churchill in his pre-war wilderness years, and exercised considerable influence at Downing Street in 1940. Thereafter, however, Morton became marginalised, with a significant voice only on French matters. Charles Wilson, the prime minister's physician, who became Lord Moran in 1943, inspired the post-war anger of Churchill's staff by publishing intimate diaries of his experiences. Jock Colville wrote contemptuously of the self-regarding doctor: 'Moran was seldom, if ever, present when history was made; but he was quite often invited to dinner afterwards.' This was to address a gerbil with an elephant gun. Moran was never a policy-maker, nor even wielded influence. It seems enough that he served Churchill well in his medical capacity, and proved an acceptable companion on the prime minister's historic journeys.

The 'cronies' were viewed by Churchill's critics as charlatans. Yet each had real merits, above all brains. There were no fools in the prime minister's entourage, though steadiness of judgement was less assured. None of his chosen associates was a conformist. All were loners who walked by themselves, however readily they embraced social intercourse as a tool of influence. In Whitehall and at Westminster, less gifted men, both in and out of uniform, denounced the false prophets who supposedly led the prime minister astray. Yet most of Churchill's wilder schemes derived from his own supremely fertile imagination, not from mischief-makers in his inner circle. 'He always retained unswerving independence of thought,' wrote Jock Colville. 'He approached a problem as he himself saw it and of all the men I have ever known he was the least liable to be swayed by the views of even his most intimate counsellors.' In the same fashion, Churchill formed his own judgements of men, favourable or otherwise, and was deeply resistant to the influence of others in adjusting them.

Many misunderstandings of Churchill's conduct of governance by his contemporaries, including some close to the seat of power, derived from the promiscuity of his conversation. Every day, whether in the company of generals, ministers, visitors or personal staff, he gave vent to impulsive and intemperate judgements on people and plans. These sometimes amused, often alarmed and appalled, even those with long experience of him. Yet his intimates, above all the officers of the war cabinet secretariat, knew that nothing Churchill said was intended as a basis for action, unless subsequently confirmed in writing. They knew that he often spoke merely as a means of helping himself to formulate ideas. It has been remarked that he had an undisciplined mind, the source of a cornucopia of ideas, some brilliant, others absurd. Ismay called him 'a child of nature'. Yet the most notable aspect of the machine for the direction of Britain's war was that it was better ordered than that of any other belligerent, notably including those of Germany and later the US. A cynic might suggest that Churchill created a system to protect himself from his own excesses. In remarkable degree, this was successful.

The late spring of 1941 found the British no nearer than they had been six months earlier to perceiving a path to victory. When General Raymond Lee returned to London after a trip to Washington in April, he wrote: 'The people strike me . . . as being much more solemn than they were in January.' Churchill's enthusiasm for special forces and raiding operations derived from his awareness of the need to strive constantly to sustain a semblance of momentum. A story was told to a general by his brother, which achieved wide circulation in the War Office. As a boy, the narrator had been a guest at a game shoot at Blenheim Palace, where Churchill attempted an absurdly long shot at a hare. The boy asked him why he had wasted a cartridge. 'Young man,' replied Churchill blithely, 'I wished that hare to understand it was taking part in these proceedings.' The same spirit, addressed to matters of vastly greater import, impelled Churchill in the spring and summer of 1941. The War Office deemed it futile to hold Tobruk after Rommel had bypassed it in April. Only Churchill's insistence prompted deployment there of an Australian garrison which was soon more numerous than the German force encircling it. But in that season of defeats, the saga of Australia's infantrymen – the 'diggers' – withstanding the 'siege of Tobruk' was elevated by British propaganda into a serviceable legend.

Military theatre had its limitations, however. Churchill had a grossly exaggerated belief in the power of boldness alone to overcome material and numerical deficiencies. 'War,' he wrote, 'consists of fighting, gnawing and tearing, and . . . the weaker or more frail gets life clawed out of him by this method. Manoeuvre is a mere embellishment, very agreeable when it comes off . . . Fighting is the key to victory.' Yet the events of 1940–41 showed, and subsequent experience confirmed, that British forces could defeat those of the Wehrmacht only when they were substantially stronger. If Hitler had dispatched to North Africa even a further two or three divisions from his vast order of battle, it is likely that Britain would have been driven from Egypt in 1941. Many senior soldiers thought this outcome likely, though they underrated Rommel's logistics problems. 'I suppose you realise that we shall lose the Middle East,' Dill said to Kennedy on 21 June, a remark which emphasised his unfitness for the post he occupied. Kennedy, in his turn, incurred Churchill's ire merely by mentioning that contingency in his presence. The British were spared from disaster in the Mediterranean in 1941 because Hitler's strategic priorities lay elsewhere. On 22 June, Germany invaded Russia.

SIX

Comrades

The German invasion of Russia on 22 June 1941 transformed the Second World War. The British, through Ultra intercepts, had long been aware of Hitler's impending onslaught. They persuaded themselves that their intervention in Greece had imposed a delay upon Operation *Barbarossa*. In reality, a late thaw and German equipment shortages were the decisive factors in causing the assault to take place later than Hitler had wished. The British and American peoples to this day perceive their contribution to the eastern war in terms of convoys heroically fought across the Arctic to Murmansk, bearing massive Western aid. Reality was less simple. In 1941–42, both Britain and the US were desperately short of war material for their own armed forces, and had little to spare for Stalin's people. For eighteen months after Russia was invaded, the period during which its survival hung in the balance, Western aid was much more marginal than the rhetoric of Winston Churchill and Franklin Roosevelt suggested, and ordinary citizens in the West were encouraged to suppose.

In June 1941, the immediate impact of *Barbarossa* in Britain was surprisingly muted. The shocks of the previous year had imposed an anaesthetising effect. In people's gratitude at finding themselves still unscathed at their breakfast tables each morning, their island spared from Nazi pillage, many received tidings of this epochal event with surprising insouciance. Edward Stebbing, a twenty-one-year-old soldier whose impatience with the struggle was cited earlier, felt bewildered: 'There is nothing straightforward about this war. In the maze of lies and treachery it is almost impossible to find the truth.'

The *Financial Times* columnist Lex wrote on 23 June: 'Markets spent the morning trying to make up their minds whether the German aggression against Russia was a bull or a bear . . . The majority concluded that whatever happened we could hardly be worse off as a result of Hitler's latest somersault.' Here was another manifestation of Churchill's 'three-inch pipe' theory about human emotions. Amid a surfeit of drama and peril, many people took refuge in the sufficient cares of their own daily lives, and allowed a torrent of world news, good and ill, to flow past them to the sea.

Most of Britain's ruling class, from the prime minister downwards, regarded the Soviet Union with abhorrence. The Russians had rebuffed all British diplomatic advances since the outbreak of war, and likewise London's warnings of Nazi intentions. Until the day of the German assault, under the terms of the 1939 Nazi–Soviet pact Stalin provided Hitler with huge material assistance. Only a few months earlier Vyacheslav Molotov, Stalin's foreign minister, was bargaining with the Nazis, albeit unsuccessfully, for a share of the spoils of British defeat. The extravagance of Soviet demands provided Hitler with a final pretext for launching *Barbarossa*.

In addressing the history of the Second World War it is necessary to recognise the huge moral compromises forced upon the nations fighting under the banner of democracy and freedom. Britain, and subsequently America, strove for the triumph of these admirable principles wherever they could be secured – with the sometimes embarrassing exceptions of the European overseas empires. But again and again, hard things had to be done which breached faith with any definition of absolute good. If this is true of politics at all times, it was especially so between 1939 and 1945. Whether in dealing with France, Greece, Iraq, Persia, Yugoslavia or other nations, attitudes were struck and courses adopted by the Allies which no moral philosopher could think impeccable. British wartime treatment of its colonies, of Egypt and above all India, was unenlightened. But if Churchill's fundamental nobility of purpose is acknowledged, most of his decisions deserve sympathy.

He governed on the basis that all other interests and considerations must be subordinated to the overarching objective of defeating the Axis. Those who, to this day, argue that Churchill 'might have saved the British Empire' by making a bargain with Hitler, leaving Russia and Germany to destroy each other, ignore the practical difficulty of making a sustainable deal with the Nazi regime, and also adopt a supremely cynical insouciance towards its turpitude. The moral and material price of destroying Hitler was high, but most of mankind has since acknowledged that it had to be paid. In the course of the war the prime minister was repeatedly called upon to decide not which party, nation or policy represented virtue, but which must be tolerated or supported as the least base available. This imperative was never more conspicuous than in Britain's dealings with the Soviet Union.

Between 1917 and 1938, Churchill sustained a reputation as an implacable foe of Bolshevism. Yet in the last years before attaining the premiership he changed key, displaying a surprising willingness to reach out to the Russians. In October 1938, against Chamberlain's strong views he urged an alliance with Moscow, and counselled the Poles to seek an accommodation with Stalin. This line did as much to raise his standing with British Labour MPs as to lower it among Tories. In September 1939 he urged Chamberlain to perceive the Soviet advance into Poland as a favourable development: 'None of this conflicts with our main interest, which is to arrest the German movement towards the East and South-East of Europe.' In a broadcast a fortnight later, he said: 'That the Russian armies should stand on this line [in Poland] was clearly necessary for the safety of Russia against the Nazi menace.' In January 1940, it is true, he became an enthusiastic supporter of Finland, then beset by the Russians. He once enquired about the possibility of bombing Russian oilfields at Baku in the Caucasus, to stem fuel deliveries to Germany. Excepting this interruption, however, Churchill showed himself willing to make common cause with the Russians if they would share the burden of defeating Hitler. This was probably because he could not see how else this was to be accomplished.

The prime minister was at Chequers on that June Sunday morning when news came of *Barbarossa*. He immediately told Eden, a house guest, of his determination to welcome the Soviet Union as a partner in the struggle, then spent the rest of the day roaming restlessly under hot sunshine, refining themes and phrases for a broadcast. He communed with Beaverbrook and Sir Stafford Cripps, the Moscow ambassador who chanced to be in Britain, but did not trouble to summon the cabinet. When at last he sat before the BBC microphone that evening, he began by acknowledging his own past hostility towards the Soviets: 'The Nazi regime is indistinguishable from the worst features of Communism. It is devoid of all theme and principle except appetite and racial domination. No one has been a more consistent opponent of Communism than I have for the last twenty-five years. I will unsay no word that I have spoken about it.' But then he asserted, in bold and brilliant terms, Britain's commitment to fight alongside Stalin's Russia:

> The past, with its crimes, its follies, and its tragedies flashes away. I see the Russian soldiers standing on the threshold of their native land, guarding the fields which their fathers tilled from time immemorial. I see them guarding their homes where mothers and wives pray – ah, yes, for there are times when all pray – for the safety of their loved ones, the return of the bread-winner, of their champion, of their protector. I see the ten thousand villages of Russia where the means of existence is wrung so hardly from the soil, but where there are still primordial human joys, where maidens laugh and children play.
>
> I see advancing upon all this in hideous onslaught the Nazi war machine, with its clanking, heel-clicking Prussian officers, its crafty expert agents from the cowing and tying down of a dozen countries. I see also the dull, drilled, docile, brutish masses of the Hun soldiery plodding on like a swarm of crawling locusts. I see the German bombers and fighters in the sky, still smarting from many a British whipping, delighted to find what they believe is an easier and a safer prey.
>
> I have to declare the decision of His Majesty's Government ... Any man or state who fights on against Nazi-dom will have our aid ... We shall give whatever aid we can to Russia and the Russian people

... The Russian danger is therefore our danger, and the danger of the
United States, just as the cause of any Russian fighting for his hearth
and home is the cause of free men and free people in every quarter
of the globe.

Not for the first time in the war, Churchill's words received the
acclaim of most British people, while inspiring doubts among some
Tory MPs and senior officers. Repugnance towards the bloodstained
Soviets ran deep through the upper echelons of British society. Leo
Amery, the India Secretary, recoiled from making common cause
with communists. Col. John Moore-Brabazon, Minister of Aircraft
Production, was rash enough publicly to assert a desire to see the
Germans and Russians exterminate each other. Jock Colville described
this as 'a sentiment widely felt'. Lt.Gen. Pownall complained about
the limp-wristed attitude he perceived in approaches towards the
Russians by Foreign Secretary Anthony Eden and the diplomats of
his department. 'They think they are dealing with normal people.
They are not. Russians are orientals and need treating quite differently and far more roughly. They are not Old Etonians.' Tory MP
Cuthbert Headlam observed with curious detachment: 'I don't
suppose that the "conquest" of Russia will take very long. And what
then – presumably either Hitler will make some kind of peace offer
based upon our acceptance of the "New Order", or he will try his
hand at an invasion here or push on in the [Middle] Eastern theatre.'
Headlam thought Churchill's posture tactically sensible, but like
many other people found himself unable to anticipate a happy ending
without the Americans. He fell back upon hopes of loftier assistance:
'One feels that God is on our side – that's the great thing.'

Among the British left, however, and the public at large,
enthusiasm for Churchill's declaration of support for Russia was
overwhelming. Independent Labour MP Aneurin Bevan, an almost
unflagging critic of Churchill's leadership, nonetheless congratulated
him on his welcome to the Russians as comrades-in-arms: 'It was an
exceedingly clever statement, a very difficult one to make, but made
with great wisdom and strength.' Surrey court shorthand-writer

George King wrote: 'I glory in all this. I have always had a soft spot for the Russians, and never blamed them for their dislike of us. We gave them good cause in the years after the last war . . . Thank God for Russia. They have saved us from invasion this year.' Londoner Vere Hodgson wrote on 22 June: 'The Russians have not been too nice to us in the past, but now we have to be friends and help one another . . . So we have got one fighting ally left in Europe. I felt my morale rising.' She added in the following month, with notable sagacity: 'Somehow I think Stalin is more a match for Hitler than any of us . . . he looks such an unpleasant kind of individual.' In this she was entirely right. It was never plausible that, in order to defeat Hitler, British people would have been willing to eat each other. But Russians did so during the siege of Leningrad. Indeed, they endured many worse things between 1941 and 1945, which spared the Western Allies choices such as the British prime minister never flinched from, but his people did.

British communists, many of whom had hitherto been indifferent to the war, now changed tune dramatically. Some, like Mrs Elizabeth Belsey, henceforward matched impassioned admiration for Mother Russia's struggle with unremitting scorn for Britain's leaders. She wrote to her soldier husband:

I was agreeably surprised . . . that Churchill received Russia so promptly into the circle of our gallant allies. I had thought he might either continue his own war, ignoring Russia's, or clear out & let Russia hold the baby. On mature reflection, I realise that the course he took was for him the only realistic one. His speech disgusted me . . . The damnably sloppy picture he drew of the Russians 'defending their soil', and the even-atheists-pray-sometimes attitude towards Soviet women! And the way in which every single speaker on the subject makes it quite frankly clear that whereas we supported Greece for the Greeks, Norway for the Norwegians, Abyssinia for the Abyssinians and so on, we are now supporting Russia solely for ourselves . . . And as for Churchill's personal record! Who's going to remind him of his statement that if he had to choose between communism & fascism he wasn't sure he'd choose communism?

Churchill derived Micawberish satisfaction from the fact that Hitler's lunge eastward signified that 'something had turned up'. But he shared with his generals a deep scepticism about Russia's ability to withstand the Wehrmacht. A year earlier, tiny Finland had humiliated the Red Army. British national pride argued that it was wildly implausible for Russia to repulse Hitler's legions, where the combined might of the French and British armies had failed to do so in 1940. Pownall wrote on 29 June: 'It's impossible to say how long Russian resistance will last – three weeks or three months?' The best that Britain's service chiefs sought from the new eastern front, following the launching of *Barbarossa*, was that the Russians might hold out until winter. British troops continued making preparations against a German descent on the home shore, partly because there was no other credible occupation for them. Pownall expressed scepticism: 'I don't believe Winston is at heart a believer in invasion of this country. Of course he can't say that, because everyone would then immediately slacken off.'

Much of the British Army – a substantially larger part than that deployed in the Middle East – stayed in Britain, where it would remain for three more years, to the chagrin of the Russians and later also of the Americans. Of some twenty-five infantry and four armoured divisions at home, only perhaps ten were battleworthy. There was no purpose in shipping formations to the Middle East, or for that matter to Britain's Eastern Empire, any faster than they could be equipped with tanks, anti-tank guns, automatic weapons and artillery. All these things remained in short supply. It was considered necessary to sustain production of weapons and aircraft known to be obsolete, because introduction of new designs imposed delays that seemed unacceptable. A host of ill-equipped, half-trained, profoundly bored British soldiers lingered in their own country month after month, and eventually year after year, while much smaller numbers of their comrades fought abroad. Alan Brooke, C-in-C Home

Forces, complained how difficult it was to hone units to fighting pitch when they lacked the stimulus of action.

Moreover, the overwhelming bulk of the RAF's fighter strength continued to be deployed in southern England, conducting 'sweeps' over northern France which were deemed morally important, but cost the RAF greater losses than the Luftwaffe – 411 pilots between June and September, for 103 Luftwaffe aircraft shot down (though the RAF claimed 731). Generals and admirals chafed at this use of air resources. Fighters were of priceless value in the Middle East and over the Mediterranean. When Admiral Cunningham was told that he was to become a Knight Grand Cross of the Bath, he responded tartly that he would rather be given three squadrons of Hurricanes. 'Why the authorities at home apparently could not see the danger of our situation in the Mediterranean without adequate air support passed my comprehension,' he wrote. There was a further difficulty, which would handicap the RAF for the rest of the war: the Spitfire and Hurricane were superb interceptors, ideal for home defence, but had very limited fuel endurance. The further afield the war extended, the more severely Britain suffered from the absence of long-range fighters. The Royal Navy lacked good carrier aircraft until American types became available in 1944–45. The large home deployment of fighters was justified by the chiefs of staff on the grounds that if Hitler launched an invasion, the RAF would play the critical role in national defence. It nonetheless seems an important strategic mistake that throughout 1941–42 Britain retained extravagantly large air forces on domestic airfields – seventy-five squadrons of day fighters against thirty-four in the whole of the Middle East in late 1941 – even after most of the Luftwaffe had departed for the eastern front. Britain remained heavily over-insured against invasion well into 1942, at important cost to its overseas battlefield forces.

If Hitler, rather than turn east, had instead chosen to increase pressure on Britain in 1941, and even if he still flinched from invasion, he might have intensified the night blitz, seized Gibraltar and Malta, reinforced Rommel, and expelled the Royal Navy from the Mediterranean. Had these things come to pass, it is by no means assured that Churchill could have retained the premiership. As it was, providence lifted the spectre of immediate catastrophe in the west – if only the Atlantic convoy routes could be kept open. Here, in mid-1941, Ultra's role became critical. More and more German naval signals, above all orders to U-boats at sea, were being broken at Bletchley Park in 'real time'. From July, some convoys were successfully diverted away from known submarine concentrations, substantially reducing losses.

The critical choice for Britain, after 22 June 1941, was how far to deplete its own inadequate armoury to aid the Russians. The Cretan experience intensified British paranoia about paratroops. It was feared that German night airborne landings in southern England might negate all calculations about the Royal Navy's and RAF's ability to frustrate an amphibious armada. On 29 June Churchill offered the War Office one of his more fanciful projections: 'We have to contemplate the descent from the air of perhaps a quarter of a million parachutists, glider-borne or crash-landed aeroplane troops. Everyone in uniform, and anyone else who likes, must fall upon these wherever they find them and attack them with the utmost alacrity – "Let every one/Kill a Hun".'

Against this background, the service ministers and chiefs of staff strongly opposed sending planes and tanks to Russia. Here was a mirror image of the debate in Washington about Britain. Churchill's soldiers, sailors and airmen displayed as much reluctance as their American brethren had done a year earlier to dispatch precious weapons to a nation that might be defeated before they could be put to use.

The Russians scarcely assisted their own cause. On the one hand, they made fantastic demands upon Churchill's government: for twenty-five British divisions to be shipped to Russia; for an army to stage an immediate landing on the Continent, to force the Germans to fight on a 'second front' – a phrase of which much more would be heard. On the other hand, they confronted British diplomats and soldiers in Russia with a wall of silence about their own struggle. An American guest at a London lunch party dominated by political grandees wrote afterwards: 'It was quite evident that all of the Britishers were deeply distrustful of the Russians. Nobody really knew much about what was happening.'

Until the end of the war, the British learned more about the eastern front from Ultra intercepts of enemy signals than from their supposed allies in Moscow. Many German operational reports were swiftly available in London. Rigorous security sought to conceal from the enemy the fact that Bletchley Park was breaking their codes. Churchill was much alarmed by a report which appeared in the *Daily Mirror* headed 'Spies trap Nazi code'. The story began: 'Britain's radio spies are at work every night ... taking down the Morse code messages which fill the air ... In the hands of experts they might produce a message of vital importance to our Intelligence Service.' The *Mirror* piece was published in absolute ignorance of Ultra, and merely described the activities of British amateur radio 'hams'. But Churchill wrote to Duff Cooper, then still Information Minister, deploring such reporting. He was morbidly sensitive to the peril of drawing the slightest German attention to their radio security.

Yet there were dangerous indiscretions, including one by the prime minister himself in a BBC broadcast on 24 August, in which he drew upon Ultra intercepts to highlight the numbers of civilians being murdered by the SS in Russia. The Germans noticed. Hitler's top police general, SS Oberstgruppenführer Kurt Daluege, signalled all his units on 13 September: 'The danger of enemy decryption of wireless messages is great. For this reason only non-sensitive information should be transmitted.' It was fortunate that the German high command failed to draw more far-reaching conclusions from Churchill's words.

In the first weeks after the Panzers swept across the Soviet frontier, intelligence revealed that the Russians were suffering colossal losses of men, tanks, planes, territory. Everything the War Office could learn confirmed the generals' predisposition to assume that Stalin would be beaten. Only two important powers in Britain pressed the case for aid to Russia. The first was public opinion. Beyond the orbit of senior officers, aristocrats and businessmen who disliked the Soviets, *Barbarossa* unleashed a surge of British sentiment, indeed sentimentality, in favour of the Russian people, which persisted until 1945. Factories and shipyards, where communist trades unionists had hitherto shown lukewarm support for a 'bosses' war', were suddenly swept by enthusiasm for Russia. Communist Party membership in Britain rose – not least because frank discussion of the Soviet regime's barbarity was suspended for the duration. The British people nursed a shame about their own defeats, a guilt that their nation was accomplishing so little towards the defeat of Hitler, which would be ever more stridently articulated in the years ahead.

Then there was the prime minister. In the matter of Russia, as in his defiance of Hitler a year earlier, he embraced a policy which entirely accorded with the public mood: all aid to Britain's new comrades-in-arms. American military attaché Raymond Lee found it droll to see the Soviet ambassador, Ivan Maisky, 'almost a pariah in London for so many years', now communing constantly with Churchill, Eden and US ambassador 'Gil' Winant. Churchill's bigness on this issue emphasised the smallness of most of his colleagues. He perceived that whatever the difficulties, however slight the prospect of success, it must not be said that Russia suffered defeat because Britain failed to do what it could to assist her. At first, following *Barbarossa*, he pressed the chiefs of staff for a landing in north Norway, to open a direct link to the Red Army. When this notion was quashed, chiefly because Norway lay beyond range of land-based air cover, he ordered that every possible tank and aircraft, including some bought by Britain from the Americans, should be shipped to Stalin. There persisted, however, a very long day's march – much longer than most historians have allowed – between intent and effective implementation. Through the summer of 1941, while Russia's survival hung in the balance, pitifully little war material was dispatched.

As for the United States, the country was at first uncertain what to make of the new situation. Roosevelt sounded insouciant, almost flippant, in a letter to US ambassador Admiral William Leahy in Vichy on 26 June: 'Now comes this Russian diversion. If it is more than just that it will mean the liberation of Europe from Nazi domination – and at the same time I do not think we need worry about any possibility of Russian domination.' But the isolationist *Chicago Tribune* asked why the US should ally itself with 'an Asiatic butcher and his godless crew'. The *New York Times* remained hesitant even in August: 'Stalin is on our side today. Where will he be tomorrow?' Senator Bennett Champ Clark of Missouri shrugged: 'It's a case of dog eat dog.' Arch-isolationist Senator Burton K. Wheeler declared his matching contempt for Stalin, Churchill and Roosevelt.

The US chiefs of staff were even more reluctant to see weapons shipped to Russia than to Britain. Though the president forcefully expressed his determination to aid Stalin's people, months elapsed before substantial US material moved. At the beginning of August, Roosevelt fiercely abused the State and War Departments for their failure to implement his wishes on aid: 'The Russians feel that they have been given the run-around in the United States.' By the end of September, only $29 million-worth of supplies had been dispatched. There was a sharp contrast between US financial treatment of Britain and Russia. Where Britain in 1940–41 was obliged to sell its entire negotiable assets to pay American bills before receiving Lend-Lease aid, when Washington put a similar proposal to Moscow, it was angrily rejected. The Russians refused to part with their gold. Roosevelt acquiesced with a docility the British would have welcomed for themselves. US supplies to Russia were provided gratis, under Lend-Lease. But progress towards implementation remained slow. As in Britain, there was a lack of will as well as of immediate means.

The absence of Western aid made it all the more urgent that Britain should be seen to fight in the west, that the desert army should once more take the offensive. Auchinleck, 'an obstinate, high-minded man', as Churchill described him in an unpublished draft of his war memoirs, insisted that he could not attack before autumn. Operation *Crusader*, as the new desert push was codenamed, was repeatedly postponed. Churchill chafed and fulminated, even muttering implausibly about replacing Auchinleck with Lord Gort. But he continued to receive the same message from Cairo. The only bright spot in

North Africa was the continuing defence of Tobruk by 7th Australian Division. Churchill was exasperated beyond measure later in the year when the Australian government in Canberra, by then led by Labor's John Curtin after Robert Menzies' eviction from power, insisted that this formation should be evacuated from the beleaguered port, to be replaced by British troops. On 25 August, British forces entered Persia after the pro-Nazi Shah's rejection of an ultimatum from London demanding the expulsion of several hundred Germans from the country. Churchill and Eden shared an embarrassment about the Persian incursion, intensified when Russian forces moved into the north of the country. Persia became an important supply route for aid to Stalin, but the British were conscious that their seizure of power there echoed Hitler's method of doing business.

At home, Churchill urged the RAF's Bomber Command to intensify its night attacks on German industry. Yet these were not merely ineffectual, they were also shockingly costly. Between 1 and 18 August alone, 107 British bombers were lost over Germany and France. The night blitz on Britain had incurred Luftwaffe losses of less than 1 per cent for each raid, a substantial proportion of these to accidents. Yet the RAF's wartime bomber losses averaged 4 per cent. This was a sobering statistic for young aircrew obliged to carry out thirty sorties to complete a tour of operations. Meanwhile, the Royal Navy's heroic and bloody Mediterranean convoy battles to sustain the defence of Malta commanded much media attention, but did nothing to divert German attention from the east.

As the Russians fell back, whole armies disintegrating before the Nazi juggernaut, Stalin was infuriated when Eden and Lord Moyne, government leader in the House of Lords, made speeches ruling out any prospect of an early Second Front. The ministers' intention was, of course, to quash speculation at home, but in Moscow their remarks were perceived as crass. They obliged Hitler by explicitly forswearing any threat to his rear. Stalin cabled Maisky at the end of August: 'The British government, by its passive, waiting policy, is helping the Nazis. The Nazis want to knock off their enemies one at a time – today the Russians, tomorrow the British . . . Do the British understand this?

I think they do. What do they want out of this? They want us to be weakened. If this suspicion is correct, we must be very severe in our dealings with the British.'

British efforts to guard secrets from their new co-belligerent were fatally compromised by the plethora of communist sympathisers, headed by Donald Maclean and John Cairncross, who had access to privileged information. More British documents, cables, committee minutes and Ultra intercepts were passed to the Soviet Union than Russia's intelligence service had resources to translate. For instance Beria, Stalin's intelligence chief, reported to his leader on 28 August 1941: 'We would like to inform you on the contents of a telegram from the Ministry of Foreign Affairs of England dated 18 August this year addressed to the English ambassador to the USA. Contents of this telegram have been obtained by the Intelligence Department of NKVD of the USSR in London using our agents. "In response to Paragraph 3 of your telegram No.3708 of 8 August. Our attitude towards Russians will be determined entirely on the principle of reciprocity. We must make them open their military installations and other objects of interest to our people in Russia. So far we have shown Russians almost nothing. In the near future they will be shown factories producing standard weapons. They will not, however, be admitted to experimental plants. Chiefs of staff have established the general principle for all institutions, whereby Russians can only be given such information or reports as would be useless to the Germans even if they gained possession of them . . . We hope that American authorities will not exceed the limits to which we adhere."' Knowledge of British attitudes did nothing to persuade the Russians to lift the obsessive secrecy cloaking their own military and industrial activities.

For all Churchill's professions of enthusiasm about dispatching war material from Britain, precious little was happening. Within his own government, the policy commanded wholehearted support only from Eden and Beaverbrook. Lord Hankey was among those who openly opposed aiding Stalin, urging instead a higher priority for the Atlantic battle. Churchill declared in a BBC broadcast on 9 September that 'large supplies are on the way' to the Soviet Union. Three weeks later he told the House of Commons: 'In order to enable Russia to remain indefinitely in the field as a first-class war-making power, sacrifices of the most serious kind and the most extreme efforts will have to be made by the British people, and enormous new installations or conversions from existing plants will have to be set up in the United States, with all the labour, expense and disturbance of normal life which these entail.'

Yet the chiefs of staffs' objections delayed even a shipment of 200 US-built Tomahawk fighters and a matching number of Hurricanes promised to Stalin by the prime minister. These planes reached Russia at the end of August. Otherwise, Britain's main contribution by autumn was a consignment of rubber. Churchill's people were as bemused as Moscow was angered by Britain's failure to employ its own forces in some conspicuous emergency action to distract the Germans. Surrey shorthand-writer George King wrote on 16 September: 'Hitler is throwing all he has got into the Eastern battles. I think we all wish here we could strike him somewhere in the West, but I suppose we are not ready yet.' And again a few weeks later: 'The marvellous Russians are still holding the enemy.'

Late in September, the British government undertook an important initiative. Lord Beaverbrook, now Minister of Supply, sailed for Russia with a twenty-two-strong British delegation including Ismay, Churchill's chief of staff, and accompanied – remarkably, given that the US was still a non-belligerent – by eleven Americans led by Roosevelt's emissary Averell Harriman. 'Make sure we are not bled white,' Churchill told Beaverbrook at parting. But Beaverbrook was determined to stretch out a hand to Stalin, to demonstrate a goodwill and generosity beyond anything the British government and chiefs of staff had mandated. In three meetings with Stalin, at which the Russian leader displayed insatiable curiosity about Churchill, Beaverbrook deployed all his charm and enthusiasm. He swallowed Stalin's insults – 'What is the use of an army if it does not fight? . . . The paucity of your offers shows you want to see the Soviet Union defeated.' The press lord sought to amuse as well as encourage the warlord. A civil servant observed cynically that Beaverbrook and Stalin achieved a rapport because they were both racketeers. The British promised tanks, planes and equipment – explicitly 200 aircraft and 250 tanks a month – while Harriman, on behalf of the Americans, offered matching largesse. The British proposal represented between a quarter and a third of 1941–42 domestic production of fighters, and more than one-third of tank output. It was as much as any minister could have offered, but the Russians considered it nugatory in the context of the titanic struggle to which they were committed.

Beaverbrook returned to London on 10 October in messianic mood. In public, he praised to the skies Stalin and his nation. To the defence committee of the war cabinet he wrote: 'There is today only one military problem – how to help Russia. Yet on that issue the chiefs of staff content themselves with saying that nothing can be done.' So violently did he press the Russian case that Ian Jacob of the war cabinet secretariat became persuaded that he aspired to supplant Churchill as prime minister. Beaverbrook urged an immediate landing in Norway, while from Moscow Cripps cabled proposing that British troops should be sent to reinforce the Red Army. Thenceforward Beaverbrook became the foremost advocate of an early Second Front, exploiting his own newspapers to press the case. It is sometimes suggested that he made his only important contribution to Britain's war effort during the summer of 1940, as Minister of Aircraft Production. But his intervention in the autumn of 1941, to demand supplies for Russia, was of even greater significance. At a time when many others in London, commanders and ministers alike, were dragging their feet, the press baron's intemperate zeal made a difference to both public and political attitudes.

Beaverbrook's subsequent Second Front campaign, of which more will be said, was irresponsible and disloyal. He displayed naïveté or worse in his extravagant eulogies of the Soviet Union, ignoring and even denying the bloodstained nature of Stalin's tyranny in a fashion Churchill never stooped to. Alan Brooke was among those who harboured lasting bitterness about the commitments Beaverbrook made in Moscow, which he considered irresponsibly generous. Yet as

Minister of Supply, Beaverbrook grasped a fundamental point that more fastidious British politicians, generals and officials refused to acknowledge. Whatever the shortcomings of Russia as an ally, the outcome of the struggle in the east must be decisive in determining the fate of Britain. The North African campaign might loom large in British perceptions and propaganda, but was of negligible importance alongside Stalin's war. If Hitler overwhelmed Russia, he might become invincible in Europe even if America later entered the war.

Until March 1942, when the Germans awoke to the importance of interdicting Allied supplies and strongly reinforced their air and naval forces in north Norway, convoys to Russia were almost unmolested, and only two British ships were lost. Churchill appointed Beaverbrook chairman of a new Allied Supplies Executive, to plan and supervise deliveries. Yet even with his support, shipments remained modest. The British dispatched obsolescent and poorly crated Hurricane fighters, many of which arrived damaged; US-built Tomahawk fighters, which the Russians found unreliable, and for a time grounded; together with tanks and Boyes anti-tank rifles which the British Army recognised as inadequate. The second so-called 'PQ' convoy to Russia sailed only on 18 October 1941, the third on 9 November. In their desperation, the Russians came as near as ever in the war to displaying gratitude. A Soviet admiral said later: 'I can still remember with what close attention we followed the progress of the first convoys in the late autumn of 1941, with what speed and energy they were unloaded in Archangel and Murmansk.'

Lord Hankey, however, wrote with malicious satisfaction about the perceived hypocrisy of Beaverbrook's enthusiasm for arming Russia, when as Minister of Supply he was responsible for the shortcomings of British tank production: 'Now I have to bring to light the fact that he is building nothing but dud tanks when he is vociferously appealing to the workers to work all day and all night to produce for Russia innumerable Tanks – all dud Tanks.' The Russians valued the Valentine, which coped with the conditions of the eastern front much better than the Matilda, which was also shipped in quantity. But they quickly grasped that most of the weapons dispatched from Britain were those its own forces least wanted. They scarcely helped themselves by contemptuously dismissing British offers of technical instruction. The new users' unfamiliarity caused much equipment to be damaged or destroyed. Several Russian pilots killed themselves by attempting to take off without releasing their Tomahawks' brakes.

When large-scale American supplies began to reach Russia in 1943–44, these exercised a dramatic influence on the feeding and transport of the Red Army. The Russians soon lost interest in tanks and planes, which they preferred to build for themselves, seeking instead American trucks, boots, technical equipment, aluminium and canned meat. It is arguable that food deliveries narrowly averted starvation in Russia in the winter of 1942–43. US shipments eventually totalled £2.5 billion, against Britain's £45.6 million. Allied aid is thought to have contributed 10 per cent to the Soviet war effort in 1943–44 – but only 5 per cent in 1942, and a negligible proportion in 1941. Chris Bellamy, among the best-informed Western historians of the Soviet Union's war, suggests that while such a contribution seems marginal, when the Soviet Union hung close to defeat it may have been decisive.

In 1941–42 the British and Americans cannot realistically be blamed for dispatching so little to Russia, because both weapons production and shipping were inadequate to meet their own needs. The relevant point is merely that there was a chasm between Anglo-American rhetoric and the real Western contribution. In the first year after *Barbarossa* was launched, of 2,443 tanks promised by the Western powers only 1,442 arrived on time, together with 1,323 of 1,800 aircraft. During this period, the Russians were themselves producing 2,000 tanks a month – most of notably higher quality than those shipped to Murmansk and Archangel. The Red Army sometimes lost a thousand tanks a week on the battlefield.

By the autumn of 1941, the tension between popular enthusiasm in Britain for Stalin's people, and contempt for the Russians in some parts of the war machine, was imposing intense pressure on the prime minister. An *Observer* columnist suggested that Russia's entry into the war fed Britain's instinctive complacency: 'The effect upon us psychologically is unhealthy. We have found a short cut to victory . . . We settle back to read with satisfaction how our air offensive against Germany is helping our great Soviet ally. With Russia and U.S.A. on our side, now surely all will be well.' Edward Stebbing, discharged from the army and working as a laboratory technician, wrote in October: 'My main feeling is one of bitter, flaming anger at the inertia of our government . . . our help to Russia has been almost negligible.'

Even as Stebbing was penning his angry reflections, the prime minister warned Middle East command of 'the rising temper of the British people against what they consider our inactivity'. To his son Randolph in the Middle East on 31 October, he described the sniping of his critics in Parliament and Beaverbrook's frequent threats of resignation: 'Things are pretty hard here . . . The Communists are posing as the only patriots in the country. The Admirals, Generals and Air Marshals chant their stately hymn of "Safety First" . . . In the midst of this I have to restrain my natural pugnacity by sitting on my own head. How bloody!' Gen. John Kennedy wrote in his diary in September: 'The fundamental difficulty is that altho we want the Germans to be knocked out above all, most of us feel . . . that it would not be a bad thing if the Russians were to be finished as a military power too . . . The CIGS constantly expresses his dislike of the Russians . . . The Russians on their side doubtless feel the same about us.'

Pownall, Dill's vice-chief, wrote in October: 'Would that the two loathsome monsters, Germany and Russia, drown together in a death grip in the winter mud.' Oliver Harvey at the Foreign Office was astonished by the strength of ill-will towards Moscow within the government: 'The Labour ministers . . . are as prejudiced as the P.M. against the Soviets because of their hatred and fear of the Communists at home.' Churchill himself, according to the diplomat, was prone to spasms of doubt about how far aid to Russia was cost-effective: 'After his first enthusiasm, he is now getting bitter as the Russians become a liability and he says we cannot afford the luxury of helping them with men, only with material.'

Yet Churchill recognised how fortunate his nation had been, thus far to wage war at relatively small cost in lives compared to those lost by Poland and France, not to mention Russia. He marvelled: 'In two years struggle with the greatest military Power, armed with the most deadly weapons, barely 100,000 of our people have been killed, of which nearly half are civilians.' Such a cool assessment of what would, in other times, have been deemed a shocking 'butcher's bill' helps to explain his fitness for the nation's leadership. Robert Menzies, when still Australian prime minister, noted this: 'Winston's attitude to war is much more realistic than mine. I constantly find myself looking at "minor losses" and saying "there are some darkened homes." But he is wise. War is terrible and it cannot be won except by lost lives. That being so, don't think of them.'

Churchill, once more desperate for military theatre, urged the War Office to accelerate plans for raids on the Continent. 'The Army must do something – the people want it,' he told John Kennedy and the Director of Military Intelligence during a lunch at Downing Street. 'Surely this [is] within our powers – The effects might be enormous – The Germans engaged in Russia – now [is] the time.' Kennedy wrote: 'Winston is in a difficult position. He is hard pressed politically to take action while Russia is struggling so desperately. He keeps saying "I cannot hold the position." The difficulty is that with a disaster the position may be harder to hold.' News from the eastern front was unremittingly grim. The Red Army's losses were appalling. A great swathe of Stalin's empire had already fallen to Hitler. Churchill, after a meeting with his generals on 11 October, bade them farewell with a mournful headshake: 'Yes, I am afraid Moscow is a gone coon,' he said, padding off along the Downing Street passage towards his afternoon nap.

The Soviet Union had not the smallest moral claim upon Britain. Even if Churchill had stripped his own nation's armed forces and dispatched heavier shipments to Murmansk after *Barbarossa* was launched, the impact on the early eastern front campaigns would have been small. As it was, the chiefs of staff were dismayed by the impact of aid to Russia upon British tank and aircraft strengths in the Middle and Far East, which were anyway grievously inadequate. Worse, American deliveries to Britain were significantly cut so that Roosevelt could meet his own commitments to Stalin. Given the weakness of British arms in 1941, it was unrealistic to suppose that Churchill could have done much more to aid the Russians. In 1942, however, a yawning gap opened between British and American undertakings, and quantities of material delivered. It was ironic, of course, that the boundlessly duplicitous Soviets should thereupon have proclaimed, and even sincerely harboured, moral indignation towards Britain and the United States. But the principal reality of subsequent military operations would be that Russians did most of the dying necessary to undo Nazism, while the Western powers advanced at their own measured pace towards a long-delayed confrontation with the Wehrmacht.

For many years after 1945, the democracies found it gratifying to perceive the Second World War in Europe as a struggle for survival between themselves and Nazi tyranny. Yet the military outcome of the contest was overwhelmingly decided by the forces of Soviet tyranny, rather than by Anglo-American armies. Perversely, this reality was better understood by many contemporary British people than it has been by their descendants.

SEVEN

The Battle of America

1 Strictly Cash

Throughout 1941, even after torrents of blood began to flow across the plains of Russia, Churchill's foremost priority remained the enlistment of the US as a fighting ally. As he followed the fortunes of Britain's desert battles, the pursuit of the *Bismarck*, Atlantic convoy struggle, campaign in Greece and faltering bomber offensive, his American vision dominated the far horizon. Unless or until the US joined the war, Britain might avert defeat, but could not aspire to victory. Among Churchill's priceless contributions to Britain's salvation was his wooing of the USA, when many of his compatriots were rash enough to indulge rancour towards what they perceived as the fat, complacent nation across the Atlantic. 'I wonder if the Americans realise how late they are leaving their intervention,' wrote John Kennedy in May 1941, 'that if they wait much longer we may be at the last gasp.' In a notable slip of the tongue, a BBC announcer once referred to the threat of 'American' rather than 'enemy' parachutists descending on Britain.

It would be hard to overstate the bitterness among many British people, high and low, about the United States's abstention from the struggle. The rhetoric of Roosevelt and Churchill created an enduring myth of American generosity in 1940–41. Cordell Hull, the Secretary of State, wrote of 'rushing vast quantities of weapons to Britain in the summer of 1940'. In truth, however great the symbolic importance of early US consignments, their practical value was small.

American-supplied artillery and small arms were obsolete, and made a negligible contribution to Britain's fighting power. Aircraft deliveries in 1941 were moderate both in quantity and quality. The fifty old destroyers loaned by the US in exchange for British colonial basing rights were scarcely seaworthy: just nine were operational at the end of 1940, and the rest required long refits. Only from 1942 onwards, when Britain received Grant and Sherman tanks, 105mm self-propelled guns, Liberator bombers and much else, did US war material dramatically enhance the capabilities of Churchill's forces.

Moreover, far from guns, tanks and planes shipped across the Atlantic representing American largesse, until the end of 1941 these were cash purchases. Under the terms of the Neutrality Act imposed by Congress, no belligerent could be granted credit. For the first two years of the war the US reaped huge profits from arms sales. 'The United States Administration is pursuing an almost entirely American policy, rather than one of all possible aid to Britain,' Eden wrote to Churchill on 30 November 1940. Roosevelt anticipated British bankruptcy, and adopted the notion of 'loaning' supplies, an idea which originated with New York's Century Association, before Churchill asked him to do so. But the president was furious when Lord Lothian, in October 1940 still British ambassador in Washington, told American journalists: 'Well boys, Britain's broke. It's your money we want.' There is doubt whether the ambassador used these exact words, but the thrust of his remarks was undisputed.

Roosevelt told Lothian there could be no suggestion of American subsidy until Britain had exhausted her ability to pay cash, for Congress would never hear of it. There was a widespread American belief in British opulence, quite at odds with reality. Amid the Battle of Britain, the US administration questioned whether Churchill's government had honestly revealed its remaining assets. Washington insisted upon an audited account, a demand British ministers found humiliating. Churchill wrote to Roosevelt on 7 December 1940, saying that if Britain's cash drain to the US continued, the nation would find itself in a position in which 'after the victory was won with our blood and sweat, and civilization saved and the time gained for the United States to be fully armed against all eventualities, we should stand stripped to the bone. Such a course would not be in the moral or economic interests of either of our countries.'

In responding to Churchill, Roosevelt never addressed this point, and his evasion was significant. He acknowledged a strong US national interest in Britain's continued resistance – displaying extraordinary energy and imagination in moving public and congressional opinion – but not in its post-war solvency. American policy throughout the war emphasised the importance of strengthening its competitive trading position *vis-à-vis* Britain by ending 'imperial preference'. The embattled British began to receive direct aid, through Lend-Lease, only when the last of their gold and foreign assets had been surrendered. Many British businesses in America were sold at fire-sale prices. The Viscose rayon-manufacturing company, jewel in the overseas crown of Courtaulds and possessing assets worth $120 million, was knocked down for a mere $54 million, because Treasury Secretary Henry Morgenthau insisted that the cash should be realised at a week's notice. New York bankers pocketed $4 million of this sum in commission on a riskless transaction. Shell, Lever Bros, Dunlop Tyre and British insurance interests were alike compelled to sell up their US holdings for whatever American rivals chose to pay. The governor of the Bank of England, Montagu Norman, wrote in March 1941: 'I have never realised so strongly as now how entirely we are in the hands of American "friends" over direct investments, and how much it looks as if, with kind words and feelings, they were going to extract these one after another.'

The British government exhausted every expedient to meet US invoices. The Belgian government-in-exile lent £60 million-worth of gold which had been brought out of Brussels, although their Dutch and Norwegian counterparts refused to sell gold for sterling. An American cruiser collected from Cape Town Britain's last £50 million in bullion. Lend-Lease came with ruthless conditions constraining British overseas trade, so stringent that London had to plead with Washington for minimal concessions enabling them to pay for Argentine meat, vital to feeding Britain's people. Post-war British commercial aviation was hamstrung by the Lend-Lease terms. If Roosevelt's behaviour was founded upon a pragmatic assessment of political realities and protection of US national interests, only the imperatives of the moment could have obliged Churchill to assert its 'unselfishness'. Whatever US policy towards Britain represented between 1939 and 1945, it was never that. 'Our desperate straits alone could justify its terms,' wrote Eden about the first round of Lend-Lease.

Most of the British did not anyway care for their transatlantic cousins. Anti-Americanism was pronounced among the aristocracy. Halifax, whom Churchill dispatched to Britain's Washington embassy in December 1940, told Stanley Baldwin: 'I have never liked Americans, except odd ones. In the mass I have always found them dreadful.' Lord Linlithgow, a fellow grandee who was viceroy of India, wrote to commiserate with Halifax on his posting: 'the heavy labour of toadying to your pack of pole-squatting parvenus! What a country, and what savages those who inhabit it!' Halifax told Eden that he had proposed him as an alternative candidate for the ambassadorship: 'I only said that I thought you might hate it a little less than myself!'

Installed at the embassy, the former Foreign Secretary endured much suffering in the service of Britain, not least during a visit to a Chicago White Sox baseball game in May 1941, at which he found himself invited to eat a hot dog. This was too much for the fastidious ambassador, who declined. During a trip to Detroit he was pelted with eggs and tomatoes by a group calling itself 'The Mothers of America'. Oliver Harvey, Eden's private secretary, described the aloof Halifax's performance in his role as 'pretty hopeless – the old trouble of being unable to make real personal contacts . . . All business in the U.S.A. is now transacted by telephoning and "popping-in", both of which H can't abide. He only goes to see the President on business – and naturally usually to ask for things – he has never got on to a more intimate chat basis with him.' Dalton related a mischievous story that Halifax broke down and wept soon after his arrival in Washington, 'because he couldn't get on with these Americans'.

Many Tory MPs shared the grandees' distaste for the US. Cuthbert Headlam, admittedly something of an old woman, wrote of Americans with condescension: 'They really are a strange and unpleasing people: it is a nuisance that we are so dependent on them.' A Home Intelligence Report found 'no great enthusiasm for the US or for US institutions among any class of the British people . . . There was an underlying irritation largely due to American "apathy".' Fantastically, some British officers questioned whether it would be in Britain's interests for America to become a belligerent. Air Marshal Sir John Slessor, with the British Mission in Washington in April 1941, noted that some of his colleagues believed 'it wouldn't really pay us for the US to be actively engaged in the war'. Air Marshal Sir Arthur Harris, later C-in-C of Bomber Command, wrote with characteristic intemperance about the difficulties of representing the RAF in Washington in 1941. It was hard to make progress, he said bitterly,

> when one is dealing with a people so arrogant as to their own ability and infallibility as to be comparable only to the Jews and the Roman Catholics in their unshakeable conviction that they alone possess truth. As to production generally out here. This country is now at a crossroads. Up to date they have had a damn fine war. On British dollars. Every last one of them. The result has been a magnificent boom after long years of black depression and despair . . . They lose no opportunity of impressing upon us individually how magnificently they are fighting (sic) and how inept, inefficient and idiotic and cowardly is our conduct of those few miserable efforts we ourselves are making in battle and in industry . . . Such production of war materials as has been achieved up to date has therefore been all to their profit and in no way to their inconvenience . . . They will come in when they think that we have won it. Not before. Just like they did last time. They will then tell the world how they did it. Just like they did last time.

If Harris's tone was absurdly splenetic, it was a matter of fact that Britain and France provided the surge of investment that launched America's wartime boom. In 1939, US gross national output was still

below its 1929 level. Anglo-French weapons orders and cash thereafter galvanised US industry, even before Roosevelt's huge domestic
arms programme took effect. Between 1938 and the end of 1942
average income per family in Boston rose from $2,418 to $3,618, in
Los Angeles from $2,031 to $3,469, admittedly boosted by inflation
and longer working hours. It could be argued – indeed was, by the
likes of Harris – that Britain exhausted its gold and foreign currency
reserves, and sold out its investments, to fund America's resurrection from the Depression.

In London, ministers and generals found it irksome to be required
to lavish extravagant courtesies upon American visitors. Hugh Dalton
grumbled about attending a party given at the Savoy by the *Sunday
Express* for American broadcaster Raymond Gram Swing: 'It is just
a little humiliating, though we shall soon get more and more used
to this sort of thing, that the majority of the Ministers of the Crown
plus foreign diplomats, British generals and every kind of notability
in the press world have to be collected to help to boost this, I am
sure, quite admirable and well-disposed American broadcaster.'
Dalton was disgusted when the guest of honour asked him blithely
whether there were factions in Britain willing to make peace with
Germany. Nor was such impatience confined to ministers. Kenneth
Clark of the Ministry of Information suggested the need for a
campaign against 'the average man's . . . unfavourable view of the
United States as being a country of luxury, lawlessness, unbridled
capitalism, strikes and delays'.

The British were exasperated by American visitors who told them
how to run their war, while themselves remaining unwilling to fight.
A British officer wrote of Roosevelt's friend, the flamboyant Col.
William 'Wild Bill' Donovan: 'Donovan . . . is extremely friendly to
us & a shrewd and pleasant fellow and good talker. But I could not
but feel that this fat & prosperous lawyer, a citizen of a country not in
the war, & which has failed to come up to scratch even in its accepted
programme of assistance, possessed very great assurance to be able
to lay down the law so glibly about what we and other threatened
nations should & sh[ou]ld not do.'

It is against this background of British resentment and even hostility towards the US that Churchill's courtship of Roosevelt must be perceived. The challenge he faced was to identify what D.C. Watt has called 'a possible America', able and willing to deliver. This could only be sought through the good offices of its president. Churchill, least patient of men, displayed almost unfailing public forbearance towards the USA, flattering its president and people, addressing with supreme skill both American principles and self-interest. He was much more understanding than most of his countrymen of American Utopianism. On the way to Chequers one Friday night late in 1940, he told Colville 'he quite understood the exasperation which so many English people feel with the American attitude of criticism combined with ineffective assistance; but we must be patient and we must conceal our irritation. (All this was punctuated with bursts of "Under the spreading Chestnut Tree".)'

Churchill himself knew the United States much better than most of his compatriots, having spent a total of five months there on visits in 1895, 1900, 1929 and 1931. 'This is a very great country, my dear Jack,' he wrote enthusiastically to his brother back in 1895, when he stopped by en route to the Spanish war in Cuba. 'What an extraordinary people the Americans are!' He was shocked by the spartan environment of West Point Military Academy, but much flattered by his own reception there: 'I was . . . only a Second Lieutenant, but I was . . . treated as if I had been a General.' During his December 1900 lecture tour he was introduced in New York by Mark Twain, and told an audience in Boston: 'There is no one in this room who has a greater respect for that flag than the humble individual to whom you, of the city which gave birth to the idea of a "tea party", have so kindly listened. I am proud that I am the natural product of an Anglo-American alliance; not political, but stronger and more sacred, an alliance of heart to heart.'

He had met presidents Theodore Roosevelt, Woodrow Wilson and Herbert Hoover, along with Vanderbilts and Rockefellers, Hollywood stars, Henry Morgenthau, William Randolph Hearst and Bernard Baruch. He had lectured to American audiences in 1931–32 about the perceived shared destiny of the English-speaking peoples. Many of his British contemporaries saw in Churchill American behavioural traits, above all a taste for showmanship, that his own class disliked, but which were now of incomparable value. Humble London spinster Vere Hodgson perceived this, writing in her diary: 'Had he been pure English aristocracy he would not have been able to lead in the way he has. The American side gives him a superiority complex – in a way that Lord Halifax would not think in good taste – but we need more than good taste to save Britain at this particular moment.'

In 1940–41, Churchill sometimes displayed private impatience towards perceived American pusillanimity. 'Here's a telegram for those bloody Yankees,' he said to Jock Colville as he handed the private secretary a cable in the desperate days of May 1940. In dispatches to Washington, the malignant US ambassador Joseph Kennedy made the worst of every such remark which he intercepted. He translated Churchill's well-merited dislike of himself into allegations that the prime minister was anti-American. Kennedy's dispatches inflicted some injury on Britain's cause in Washington, cauterised only when Roosevelt changed ambassadors in 1941, replacing Kennedy with John 'Gil' Winant, and Churchill embarked upon personal relationships with the president, Harry Hopkins and Averell Harriman. Churchill's broadcasts, however, already commanded large American audiences, and imposed his personality upon Roosevelt's nation in 1940–41 almost as effectively as upon his own people. By late 1941, Churchill ran second only to the president in a national poll of US radio shows' 'favourite personality'. 'Did you hear Mr Churchill Sunday?' Roscoe Conkling Simmons asked his readers in the *Chicago Defender* on 3 May 1941. 'You may be against England, but hardly against England as Mr Churchill paints her . . . Did you note how he laid on the friendship of Uncle Sam?' Churchill's great phrases were repeated again and again in the American press, 'blood, toil, tears and sweat' notable among them.

If Churchill had not occupied Britain's premiership, who among his peers could have courted the US with a hundredth part of his

warmth and conviction? There was little deference in his make-up
– none, indeed, towards any of his own fellow countrymen save the
King and the head of his own family, the Duke of Marlborough. Yet
in 1940–41 he displayed this quality in all his dealings with Americans,
and above all their president. When the stakes were so high he was
without self-consciousness, far less embarrassment. To a degree that
few of his fellow countrymen proved able to match between 1939
and 1945 he subordinated pride to need, endured slights without
visible resentment, and greeted every American visitor as if his
presence did Britain honour.

By far the most important of these was, of course, Harry Hopkins,
who arrived on 8 January 1941 as the president's personal emissary,
bearing a letter to King George VI from his fellow head of state,
saying that 'Mr Hopkins is a very good friend of mine, in whom I
repose the utmost confidence.' Hopkins was a fifty-year-old Iowan,
a harness-maker's son who had been a lifelong crusader for social
reform. He met Roosevelt in 1928, and the two men formed an intimacy. Hopkins, the archetypal New Dealer, in 1932 became federal
relief administrator, and one of the strongest influences on the
administration. Roosevelt liked him in part because he never asked
for anything. It was the heady scent of power that Hopkins savoured,
not position or wealth, though he had a gauche enthusiasm for night-
clubs and racetracks, and was oddly flattered by press denunciations
of himself as a playboy. He cherished contrasting passions for fungi
and the poetry of Keats. The high spot of his only pre-war visit to
London, in 1927, was a glimpse of Keats's house. A lonely figure after
the death of his second wife from cancer in 1937, he was invited by
FDR to live at the White House. Hopkins had pitched camp there
ever since, with the title of Secretary of Commerce and undeclared
role of chief of staff to the president, until he was given responsibility
for making Lend-Lease work.

Hopkins's influence with the president was resented by many
Americans, not all of them Republicans. He was widely unpopular,
being described by critics as 'FDR's Rasputin', an 'extreme New Dealer'.

At the outset of World War II he had been an instinctive isolationist, writing to his brother: 'I believe that we really can keep out of it. Fortunately there is no great sentiment in this country for getting into it, although I think almost everyone wants to see England and France win.' Physically, he cut an unimpressively dishevelled figure, his long neck and gaunt features ravaged by the stomach cancer that had almost killed him. Many people who met Hopkins perceived, through the haze from the cigarettes he chain-smoked, 'a walking corpse'. A *Time* photograph of him carried the caption: 'He can work only seven hours a day.' Brendan Bracken, sent to greet Hopkins off the flying-boat that brought him to Poole harbour, was appalled to find this vital visitor slumped apparently moribund in his seat, unable even to unfasten his seatbelt. The relationship with the British upon which the envoy now embarked became the last important mission of his life.

On 10 January 1941 Churchill welcomed Hopkins for the first time in the little basement dining room of Downing Street – the house was somewhat battered by bomb blast – for a *tête-à-tête* lunch that lasted three hours. The guest opened their conversation with the forthrightness that characterised Hopkins's behaviour: 'I told him there was a feeling in some quarters that he, Churchill, did not like America, Americans or Roosevelt.' This was Joseph Kennedy's doing, expostulated the prime minister, and a travesty. He promised absolute frankness. He said that he hoped Hopkins would not go home until he was satisfied 'of the exact state of England's need and the urgent necessity of the exact material assistance Britain requires to win the war'. He then deployed all his powers to charm his guest, with unqualified success.

Hopkins's intelligence and warmth immediately endeared him to Churchill. Throughout his political life the president's man had decided upon courses of action, then pursued them with unstinting energy. If he arrived in Britain with a relatively open mind, within days he embraced the nation, its leader and cause with a conviction that persisted for many months, and did incalculable service. That first Friday evening, the American drove to join the prime minister and his entourage at Ditchley in Oxfordshire, Churchill's weekend residence on moonlit nights during the blitz, when Chequers was perceived to be vulnerable to the Luftwaffe. The text of the Lend-Lease Bill, now beginning its hazardous passage through Congress, had just been published. Britain's dependence on the outcome was absolute. However, Churchill warned the chancellor, Kingsley Wood, that he himself would say nothing to Washington about looming British defaults on payments for arms, should Lend-Lease fail to pass the US legislature: 'We must trust ourselves to [the president].'

Hopkins was extraordinarily forthcoming to his hosts, who welcomed his enthusiasm after the cold scepticism of Joseph Kennedy. That first weekend, on the way to see Churchill's birthplace at Blenheim Palace, the envoy told Brendan Bracken that Roosevelt was 'resolved that we should have the means of survival and of victory'. Hopkins mused to the great CBS broadcast correspondent Ed Murrow, then reporting from London: 'I suppose you could say – but not out loud – that I've come to try to find a way to be a catalytic agent between two prima donnas.' Churchill, for his part, diverted his guest during the month of his visit with a succession of mono-logues, strewing phrases like rose petals in the path of this most important and receptive of visitors. At dinner at Ditchley, the prime minister declared:

We seek no treasure, we seek no territorial gain, we seek only the right of man to be free; we seek his rights to worship his God, to lead his life in his own way, secure from persecution. As the humble labourer returns from his work when the day is done, and sees the smoke curling upwards from his cottage home in the serene evening sky, we wish him to know that no rat-a-tat-tat – [here he rapped on the table] of the secret police upon his door will disturb his leisure or interrupt his rest. We seek government with the consent of the people, man's freedom to say what he will, and when he thinks himself injured, to find himself equal in the eyes of the law. But war aims other than these we have none.

Churchill's old colleagues – the likes of Balfour, Lloyd George, Chamberlain, Baldwin, Halifax – had for years rolled their eyes impatiently in the face of such outpourings. Familiarity with Winston's extravagant rhetoric rendered them readily bored by it, especially when it had been deployed in support of so many unworthy and unsuccessful causes in the past. Yet now, at last, Churchill's words and the mood of the times seemed perfectly conjoined. His sonorous style had an exceptional appeal for Americans. Hopkins had never before witnessed such effortless, magnificent dinner-table statesmanship. He was entranced by his host: 'Jesus Christ! What a man!' He was impressed by the calm with which the prime minister received news, often bad. One night during the usual evening film at Ditchley, word came that the cruiser *Southampton* had been sunk in the Mediterranean. The show went on.

During the weeks that followed, Hopkins spent twelve evenings with Churchill, travelled with him to visit naval bases in Scotland and blitzed south coast towns. He marvelled at his host's popularity and absolute mastery of Britain's governance, though he was less impressed by the calibre of Churchill's subordinates: 'Some of the ministers and underlings are a bit trying,' he told Roosevelt. Eden, for instance, he thought talked too much. Hopkins attained a quick, shrewd grasp of the private distaste towards the prime minister that persisted among Britain's ruling caste: 'The politicians and upper crust pretend to like him.' He was in no doubt, however, about the fortitude of the British people. 'Hopkins was, I think, very impressed by the cheerfulness and optimism he found everywhere,' wrote Churchill's private secretary Eric Seal. 'I must confess that I am surprised at it myself . . . PM . . . gets on like a house afire with Hopkins, who is a dear, & is universally liked.' Roosevelt's envoy told Raymond Lee: 'I have never had such an enjoyable time as I had with Mr Churchill.'

Back in Washington, the president was much tickled by reports of Hopkins's popularity in Britain, as the Interior Secretary Harold Ickes noted: 'Apparently the first thing that Churchill asks for when he gets awake in the morning is Harry Hopkins, and Harry is the last one he sees at night.' Maybe so, growled the cynical Ickes, but even if the president had sent a bubonic plague-carrier, Britain's prime minister would have found it expedient to see plenty of him. Among the envoy's most important functions was to brief Churchill about how best to address the American people and assist Roosevelt's efforts to assist Britain. Above all, the prime minister was told, he should not suggest that any commitment of US ground troops was either desirable or likely. Hopkins concluded his report to the president: 'People here are amazing from Churchill down,' he wrote, 'and if courage alone can win – the result will be inevitable. But they need our help desperately.'

When the envoy landed back at New York's LaGuardia airport in February 1941, the new ambassador-designate to Britain, 'Gil' Winant, called out to him as he descended from his plane: 'Are they going to hold out?' Hopkins shouted back 'Of course they are.' This was a self-consciously theatrical exchange for the benefit of the assembled throng of reporters, but nonetheless sincere. Thereafter, Hopkins's considerable influence upon the president was exercised towards gaining maximum American support for Britain. Londoner Vere Hodgson was among those who thrilled to a BBC broadcast by Roosevelt's envoy: 'He finished with really glorious words of comfort: "People of Britain, people of the British Commonwealth of Nations, you are not fighting alone." I felt after this the War was won.'

Yet, however successful was the Hopkins visit from a British perspective, it did not alter fundamentals. 'Winston is completely certain of America's full help,' the Australian prime minister, Robert Menzies, wrote doubtingly during a visit to Chequers at the end of February 1941. 'Is he right? I cannot say.' Franklin Roosevelt was conducting his nation's policy in accordance with a belief that he could not move faster than public opinion would allow. Such opinion was moving Britain's way. To the boundless relief of the prime minister, on 8 February the Lend-Lease Bill passed the House by 260 votes to 165, and on 8 March was endorsed by the Senate, sixty votes to thirteen. For months thereafter, the last of Britain's foreign exchange continued to be drained to pay for supplies – only 1 per cent of war material used by Britain in 1941 represented fruits of Lend-Lease. But the new measure ensured that even when Britain's cash was exhausted, shipments kept coming. Importantly, 1940 Republican presidential candidate Wendell Willkie supported it – and Britain.

The president extracted for the British through Lend-Lease the most generous terms a US legislature would swallow, much preferable to the straight loans of World War I, which Britain alienated US opinion by failing to repay. A substantial minority of Americans, including many at the summits of industry and commerce, not merely opposed Roosevelt's policies, but hated the man. He perceived his own power as circumscribed, in a fashion which the prime minister underestimated. Unlike Churchill, Roosevelt never led a coalition government, though he included some prominent Republicans such as Henry Stimson in his cabinet. He always faced substantial opposition in Congress – sometimes only on lesser matters, but sometimes also on great ones. There was no doubt of his sincerity in desiring British victory. Having overcome his initial uncertainties about Churchill, partly thanks to Hopkins, by March 1941 he could declare to the American people: 'In this historic crisis, Britain is blessed with a brilliant and great leader.' But Roosevelt considered himself lacking any mandate to dispatch American soldiers to fight in Europe. Until December 1941, while he provided increasing aid to Britain – 'We must become the great arsenal of democracy,' a phrase borrowed from the French economist Jean Monnet by way of the American judge Felix Frankfurter – he remained unwilling to lead a charge towards war. In this he was assuredly wise. If the United States had plunged into belligerence with Germany before Pearl Harbor, and even in the unlikely event that Roosevelt could have pushed a declaration of war through Congress, he would thereafter have led a divided country.

The British historian Michael Howard, in 1941 a student at Oxford awaiting a summons to the army, has written: 'It is never very easy for the British to understand that a very large number of Americans, if they think about us at all, do so with various degrees of dislike and contempt . . . In the 1940s the Americans had some reason to regard the British as a lot of toffee-nosed bastards who oppressed half the world and had a sinister talent for getting other people to do their fighting for them.' Melville Troy was an American cigar importer living in London. Though he admired the fortitude of the British amid the blitz, he was deeply anxious to see his own country spared from its horrors: 'Personally I am very sorry to see America turning her pruning hooks and ploughshares into implements of war, and wish we had a Woodrow Wilson to keep us out of it.' Many of Troy's fellow countrymen thought likewise.

There was much, much more British wooing to be done. The extravagant courtesies shown by the government to Harry Hopkins were outdone when Winant arrived as ambassador. He was met at Bristol by Brendan Bracken and the Duke of Kent. A special train took him to Windsor, where King George VI was waiting at the station. The monarch then drove Winant in his own car to the Castle. Never in history had a foreign envoy been received with such ceremony. Meanwhile, implementation of the Lend-Lease programme enlisted another key American player in Britain's cause. Averell Harriman, fifty-year-old son of a railroad millionaire, was a supremely gilded product of Groton and Yale, a polo player and skier, international banker and collector of Impressionist paintings, a cosmopolitan of considerable gifts. Roosevelt explained Harriman's new mission to reporters at the White House: 'As soon as the Lend-Spend, Lend-Lease – whatever you call it – bill is perfected, more or less, he will go over and – Oh, I suppose you will ask all about his title, so I thought I would invent one . . . we decided it was a pretty good idea to call him an "Expediter". That's a new one for you. I believe it is not in the diplomatic list or any other list. So he will go over as "Defense Expediter".'

In the spring of 1941 Harriman became an important American advocate of aid to Britain. Nonetheless, in Washington Hopkins and Henry Stimson, the Secretary for War, remained the only prominent members of the administration wholeheartedly committed to such a policy. Other leading Americans remained sceptical. In the War

Department, US generals cloaked dogged resistance to shipping abroad arms that were needed at home in a mantle of complaints about allegedly amateurish British purchasing policy. One officer, contemptuous of the informality of the Hopkins mission, told Harriman: 'We can't take seriously requests that come late in the evening over a bottle of port.'

Among chief of the army Gen. George Marshall's key subordinates there were deep divisions about the merits of participation in the war, and of the British as prospective allies. Some senior officers unashamedly reserved their admiration for the Germans. Maj.Gen. Stanley Embick was a former chief of the War Plans Division who had become sceptical about Churchill and his people during service in France in World War I. Now he believed that Britain's war effort would fare better if the country changed prime minister. He thought that US aid should stop far short of belligerency. Like his son-in-law, Major Albert Wedemeyer of the War Plans Division, Embick addressed every Anglo-American issue with a determination that his country should not be duped into pulling British chestnuts out of the fire. Maj.Gen. Charles 'Bull' Wesson hated the British, because he had once been dispatched from Washington to London with a message for the chiefs of staff, and was kept waiting to deliver it. Raymond Lee wrote: 'He resented this so much that it led to a wrangle and almost hatred on his part for the British, which he exploits at every opportunity. So small an act of discourtesy, either real or imagined, which took place many years ago, is having ill effects in the relations between the two countries today.'

By contrast Colonel – soon to be lieutenant-general and a key figure in Marshall's team – Joseph McNarney, who had visited Britain, believed it was vital to American national security that Churchill's island should not fall. Marshall himself was less implacably hostile to the British than Embick, but in the summer of 1941, in the words of his biographer, 'If rather than when continued to dominate his thinking about American involvement.' Nor was such caution confined to senior officers. *Time* and *Life* magazines interviewed US Army draftees, and reported their morale to be low. At a camp movie night in Mississippi, men booed when FDR and Marshall appeared on a newsreel.

Averell Harriman was in no doubt that America should fight. But he departed for London on 15 March 1941 fearful that Roosevelt was still unwilling to lead the US anywhere near as far or fast as was necessary to avert a Nazi triumph: 'I was deeply worried the president did not have a policy and had not decided how far he could go . . . The President obviously hoped that he would not have to face an unpleasant decision. He seemed unwilling to lead public opinion or to force the issue but [he] hoped . . . that our material aid would let the British do the job.' Few doubted that Roosevelt already stood among America's greatest presidents. But he was often also a notably cautious one.

Harriman noted in a memorandum of 11 March: 'I must attempt to convince the Prime Minister that I, or someone, must convey to our people his war strategy or else he cannot expect to get maximum aid.' Like Hopkins, he was received in Britain on the reddest of carpets. He was met at Bristol by Commander 'Tommy' Thompson, Churchill's administrative aide, who led him aboard a plane which took them straight to Chequers. Harriman's guest gift to Clementine Churchill was a box of tangerines, which she received with unfeigned gratitude. The envoy was enfolded in a warm prime ministerial embrace. Kathleen Harriman, who accompanied her father's mission, wrote to her sister: 'The PM is much smaller than I expected and a lot less fat . . . and looks rather like a kindly teddy bear . . . I'd expected an overpowering, rather terrifying man. He's quite the opposite: very gracious, has a wonderful smile and isn't at all hard to talk to. He's got the kind of eyes that look right through you. Mother [Clementine] is a very sweet lady. She's given up her whole life to her husband and takes a back seat graciously. Everyone in the family looks upon him as God and she's rather left out.'

In London, Harriman established himself on the second floor of a Grosvenor Square building adjoining the US embassy, and was also given his own office at the Admiralty. Churchill invited him to attend the weekly meetings of the cabinet's Atlantic Committee.

Of Harriman's first eight weekends in Britain, he spent seven at Chequers, though like most American guests he found his sense of privilege tempered by dismay at the coldness of the house. Churchill convoyed him, like Hopkins, as a prize exhibit on his own travels around the country. Here, he told the British people, was a living earnest of America's commitment – the president's personal representative.

In private to Harriman, 'the PM bluntly stated that he could see no prospect of victory until the United States came into the war'. If Japan attacked, said Churchill, the British naval base of Singapore would be at risk. At every turn the prime minister sought to balance his desire to convince Roosevelt that Britain was a prospective winner against the need to exert pressure by emphasising the threat of disaster if America held back. Harriman urged Churchill to bolster Britain's case by publishing details of its appalling shipping losses. Between February and April 1941, 142 ships totalling 818,000 tons had gone to the bottom, more than double the rate of sinkings in the early months of the war. At a Defence Committee meeting in May, Eden and Beaverbrook suggested that at least meat ship losses might be disclosed, to emphasise the gravity of the food situation. Churchill, with the support of several other ministers, opposed this, 'believing that we shall get the Americans in by showing courage and boldness and prospects of success and not by running ourselves down'. Moreover, figures which privately frightened the British government would deal a shocking blow to domestic morale if they were revealed, and must provide a propaganda gift to Hitler.

Some Americans displayed a condescension which irked the recipients of their aid. Kathleen Harriman described British reluctance to enthuse about American Spam and cheese: 'The great difficulty is re-educating the people,' she wrote to her sister. 'They prefer to go hungry rather than change their feeding habits.' A Tory MP wrote: 'The idea of being our armoury and supply furnishers seems to appeal to the Yanks as their share in the war for democracy . . . They are a quaint lot – they are told that if we lose the war they will be next on Hitler's list . . . and yet they seem quite content to leave the actual fighting to us; they will do anything except fight.' Duff Cooper, as Minister of Information, told newspaper editors on 21 March 1941: 'The great thing is not to antagonise the United States ... When we offered the bases against the [fifty loaned] destroyers we imagined, in Winston's words, that we were exchanging "a bunch of flowers for a sugar cake". But not at all. The Americans have done a hard business deal.' After Lend-Lease became operational Franks, British driver to US military attaché Raymond Lee, told his master that he noticed more goodwill towards Americans. 'Well, yes,' agreed Lee sardonically. 'Perhaps you might describe it that way, but it is only natural, don't you think, that for seven thousand million dollars – that's nearly a billion pounds – we ought to be entitled to a little bonhomie!' 'Oh yes, sir, yes, sir, quite. That's just what I mean, sir. I should say there is quite a bit more bonhomie in the air, sir.' This was only half-true. Most British people considered that the US was providing them with minimal means to do dirty work that Americans ought properly to be sharing themselves.

The threat of Japanese aggression against the British Empire in the Far East dogged Churchill that summer of 1941. Germany was fully committed in Russia. Britain's land forces in North Africa seemed to have a real prospect of victory against the Italians and such German troops as Hitler could spare from the eastern front. But if Japan attacked, the strategic balance would once more be overturned. Cadogan, at the Foreign Office, wrote in July that Churchill was 'frightened of nothing but Japan'. The prime minister expressed confidence that if Tokyo moved against the British Empire, the Americans would intervene. His ministers, generals and officials were much less convinced. It was a nightmare prospect, that Britain might find itself at war in the East while America remained neutral. Some thought it likely that Japan would join Germany's attack on Russia, rather than strike at Malaya. Eden asked Churchill what he would do in such an eventuality. The prime minister replied firmly that Britain would never herself initiate hostilities with Japan, unless the United States did so. Month after month of 1941, he sought to promote the illusion that Britain's war effort was viable and purposeful. In private, however, he recognised its ultimate futility unless Roosevelt's nation came in with both feet.

2 Walking Out

That summer, countless hours were expended by British diplomats, staff officers and the prime minister himself, weighing and debating every subtlety of US behaviour and opinion. Few lovers expended as much ink and thought upon wartime correspondence as did the prime minister on his long letters to Roosevelt, sometimes dispatched twice or thrice weekly, in which he described the progress of Britain's war. He adopted a confiding tone, taking it for granted that the president shared his own, and his country's, purposes. He extended his courtship to the president's people. On 16 June, the award *in absentia* of an honorary doctorate from Rochester University, New York, inspired one of his finest radio broadcasts to Americans:

A wonderful story is unfolding before our eyes. How it will end we are not allowed to know. But on both sides of the Atlantic we all feel – I repeat, all – that we are a part of it, that our future and that of many generations is at stake. We are sure that the character of human society will be shaped by the resolves we take and the deeds we do. We need not bewail the fact that we have been called upon to face such solemn responsibilities. We may be proud, and even rejoice amid our tribulations, that we have been born at this cardinal time for so great an age and so splendid an opportunity of service here below. Wickedness – enormous, panoplied, embattled, seemingly triumphant – casts its shadow over Europe and Asia. Laws, customs, and traditions are broken up. Justice is cast from her seat. The rights of the weak are trampled down. The grand freedoms of which the President of the United States has spoken so movingly are spurned and chained. The whole stature of man, his genius, his initiative, and his nobility, is ground down under systems of mechanical barbarism and of organized and scheduled terror.

Churchill's words moved many people in his audience. Yet in Washington, Halifax observed wearily that trying to pin down the Americans was like 'a disorderly day's rabbit-shooting'. Roosevelt offered much to Britain – aircrew training, warship repair facilities, the loan of transports, an American garrison to replace British troops in Iceland, secret military staff talks throughout February and March, growing assistance to Atlantic convoy escorts. But still the US stood well short of belligerence. In July, Roosevelt's Draft Renewal Bill passed the House of Representatives by only one vote. Churchill hankered desperately for a meeting with the president. More than that, he persuaded himself that if such an encounter took place, it would presage a decisive change in the Anglo–American relationship.

When, at last, Roosevelt fixed an August rendezvous at Placentia Bay, off Newfoundland, the prime minister's hopes were unbounded. He wrote to the Queen before his departure on the 4th: 'I must say I do not think our friend would have asked me to go so far for what must be a meeting of world-wide notice, unless he had in mind some further forward step.' He was in tearing spirits on the rail journey north, as was his entourage on discovering the lavish scale of catering provided. From Scapa Flow he cabled the president, using language that assumed a community of purpose far closer than that which Roosevelt acknowledged: 'We are just off. It is 27 years ago to-day that Huns began their last war. We must make a good job of it this time. Twice ought to be enough.' Then, in Colville's words, 'with a retinue which Cardinal Wolsey might have envied', Churchill set sail aboard the great battleship *Prince of Wales* for Newfoundland. Harry Hopkins, newly returned from Moscow and once more in a state of collapse, joined them for the passage. That marvellously brave man had travelled most of the way from Russia in the gun blister of a Catalina flying boat.

One of the few useful purposes fulfilled by British battleships in the Second World War was to convey Churchill on his wartime journeys in a style befitting the arbiter of an embattled empire. There was an irony about his presence aboard *Prince of Wales*. Only a few weeks earlier, he had demanded courts martial of officers deemed to have lacked resolution in the navy's contest with the *Bismarck*. He was furious that *Prince of Wales* had broken off action after *Hood*'s sinking, even though the British battleship was severely damaged. The court martial proposal was dropped only when Sir John Tovey, C-in-C Home Fleet, said that if any such retribution was attempted, he himself would resign his post and serve as 'prisoner's friend'.

En route to the Atlantic rendezvous, much less work was done than became usual on later voyages. There was no agenda to prepare, because the British delegation had no notion how the meeting might evolve. They seized the opportunity for rest. Churchill read with relish three of C.S. Forester's *Hornblower* novels, tales of derring-do about the Royal Navy in the Napoleonic wars. He fantasised enthusiastically about a possible sortie from north Norway by the *Tirpitz*, which might enable him to participate in a great naval engagement. Mothersill pills were much in demand as specifics against seasickness.

Humble members of the British delegation, such as a cluster of clerks, were amazed by manifestations of the prime minister's informality. 'Working in H[arry] H[opkins]'s cabin this morning,' Corporal Geoffrey Green wrote in his diary, '& WSC came in wearing only pyjama coat & cigar – no pants – grinned at us and said "good morning" – too amazed to reply properly!' The ship's storerooms were packed with delicacies from Fortnum & Mason, together with ninety grouse, killed ahead of the usual shooting season to provide a treat for the prime minister's exalted guests. On the American side, Hopkins cabled Washington suggesting that hams, wine and fruit, especially lemons, would be acceptable to the British party.

Placentia Bay is a rocky inlet on the south coast of Newfoundland, where some five hundred inhabitants occupied a fishing settlement ashore. The British discerned a resemblance to a Hebridean sea loch. Early on the morning of 9 August, *Prince of Wales* began to stand in. Then her officers realised that the ship's clocks were set ahead of North American time. The ship turned and ploughed a lazy course offshore for ninety minutes, before once more heading into the anchorage. At 9 a.m. her anchors rattled down a few hundred yards from the US cruiser *Augusta*, which bore the president. The British remarked the contrast between the zig-zag camouflage of their own vessel, dressed for battle, and the pale peacetime shading of the American warship's paintwork.

No one knows exactly what was said at the encounters aboard *Augusta* between Churchill and Roosevelt. But Hopkins, who was present, described the mood. The president adopted his almost unfailing geniality, matched by the opacity which characterised his conversation on every issue of delicacy. As for his companion, no intending suitor for marriage could have matched the charm and enthusiasm with which the prime minister of Great Britain addressed the president of the United States. Churchill and Roosevelt were the most fluent conversationalists of their age. Even when substance was lacking in their exchanges, there was no danger of silences. They had in common social background, intense literacy, love of all things naval, addiction to power, and supreme gifts as communicators. Both were stars on the world stage. In the twenty-first century, when physical fitness is a preoccupation of many national leaders, it may also be remarked that neither of the two greatest statesmen on earth seemed much reduced by the fact that one was a fifty-nine-year-old cripple, the other a man of sixty-six famous for his over-indulgence in alcohol and cigars.

One of Roosevelt's intimates, Marguerite 'Missy' LeHand, declared him 'really incapable of a personal friendship with anyone'. Yet for all his essential solitariness, the president had a gift for treating every new acquaintance as if the two had known each other all their lives, a capacity for forging a semblance of intimacy which he exploited ruthlessly. Churchill, by contrast, had scant social interest in others. After the untimely death of his close friend F.E. Smith, Lord Birkenhead, in 1930, he was unwilling to interest himself in any other human being, save possibly Beaverbrook and Jan Smuts, for long enough to establish a social, as distinct from political, communion. Indeed, at Placentia he pricked the president's vanity by forgetting that the two had met earlier – in London in 1918.

Churchill loved only himself and Clementine, while to Roosevelt's mistresses it was rumoured – though probably mistakenly – that he had recently added the exiled Crown Princess Marthe of Norway. While Roosevelt sometimes uttered great truths, he was a natural dissembler. Henry Morgenthau claimed to be baffled by the president's contradictions: 'weary as well as buoyant, frivolous as well as grave, evasive as well as frank . . . a man of bewildering complexity of moods and motives'. Roosevelt was much more politically imaginative than Churchill. He told Wendell Willkie in the spring of 1941 that he thought Britain would experience a social revolution when the war was over, and he was right. Churchill, meanwhile, gave scarcely a moment's thought to anything that might follow Britain's desperate struggle for survival against the Axis, and was implacably hostile to socialism. Roosevelt, like his people, regarded the future without fear. Optimism lay at the heart of his genius as US national leader through the Depression. Churchill, by contrast, was full of apprehension about the threats a new world posed to Britain's greatness.

At Placentia Bay the prime minister strove to please the president, and Roosevelt, fascinated by the prime minister's personality, was perfectly willing to be pleased. However, the shipboard meetings between British and American service chiefs were tense and stilted. Generals George Marshall and Henry 'Hap' Arnold, and Admirals Harold Stark and Ernest King, were wary. On security grounds, Roosevelt had given them no warning of the intended meeting until they boarded *Augusta*. They had thus prepared nothing, and were determined to say nothing, which committed their nation an inch further than existing policy avowed. The British – CIGS Sir John Dill, First Sea Lord Sir Dudley Pound and Vice-Chief of Air Staff Sir Wilfred Freeman – were bemused by the fact that the US Army and Navy preferred to conduct briefings separately, and outlined entirely different strategic viewpoints.

When Marshall spoke of creating a US Army of four million men, the British expressed amazement. There seemed no prospect, they said, that land fighting would take place in the continental United States. Shipping did not exist to transport and supply a large army overseas. What need could there be for such a mobilisation? Churchill himself was at pains to assure the mothers of America that even if their nation entered the war, their sons would not be required to shed blood on the battlefields of Europe. A month before Placentia, he rebuked Auchinleck for telling journalists that US troops were needed. Such remarks, said the prime minister, strengthened the hand of American isolationists, and ran 'contrary to what I have said about our not needing the American Army this year, or next year, or any year that I could foresee'. British strategic calculations denied a requirement for British or US land forces capable of engaging the Wehrmacht on the Continent, because Dill and his colleagues did not perceive this as a viable objective.

At Placentia, Arnold said little on behalf of the US Air Force, while Marshall talked more about equipment than strategy. The Americans said they found it hard to satisfy British demands for weapons. They claimed that requests were submitted in muddled profusion, through a variety of channels. The British felt a chasm between their own mindset, formed and roughened by the experience of war, and that of their American counterparts, still imbued with the inhibitions of peace. It was not easy for men with lesser gifts of statesmanship than the prime minister to subdue their consciousness that the leaders of America's armed forces resented shipping to Britain arms which they wanted for themselves. It was hard for Dill and his colleagues not to be irked by the caution of these rich, safe Americans, when they themselves were battered by the responsibility of conducting Western civilisation's struggle for survival. The Royal Navy's officers noted the lack of curiosity displayed by the Americans, notably Admiral King, about their experiences of battle, for instance against the *Bismarck*. Privately, US sailors mocked Dudley Pound, 'the old whale' as British soldiers called him. Dill got on well with Marshall, but Ian Jacob wrote bleakly in his diary: 'Not a single American officer has shown the slightest keenness to be in the war on our side. They are a charming lot of individuals, but they appear to be living in a different world from ourselves.'

Roosevelt was irritated to learn that the prime minister had brought with him two well-known journalists, H.V. Morton and Howard Fast. Though they were barred from filing dispatches until back on British soil, this was a reminder that Churchill sought to extract from the meeting every ounce of propaganda capital. Roosevelt, meanwhile, was determined to keep open every option, to proceed with utmost caution. The reporters were denied access to US ships.

It is important to recognise that both the British and the Americans still expected Russia to suffer defeat, leaving Britain alone once more to face the Nazi empire – and soon also, perhaps, the Japanese. Churchill urged Roosevelt to offer the strongest possible warnings to Tokyo against further aggression. It has been suggested that he went further, pleading for pre-emptive US military action in the Far East, but this seems implausible. Several times during the conference, Churchill asked Averell Harriman if the president liked him. Here was an admission of the prime minister's vast anxiety, and vulnerability.

'It would be an exaggeration to say that Roosevelt and Churchill became chums at this conference, or at any subsequent time,' wrote Robert Sherwood, White House familiar and later biographer of Harry Hopkins. 'They established an easy intimacy, a joking informality and a moratorium on pomposity and cant – and also a degree of frankness in intercourse which, if not quite complete, was remarkably close to it. But neither of them ever forgot for one instant what he was and represented or what the other was and represented . . . They were two men in the same line of business – politico-military leadership on a global scale . . . They appraised each other through the practised eyes of professionals, and from this appraisal resulted a degree of admiration and sympathetic understanding of each other's professional problems that lesser craftsmen could not have achieved.' While the prime minister eagerly succumbed to sentiment in forming a view of his fellow potentate, the president did not reciprocate. Churchill and Roosevelt achieved a friendship of state. The American and British peoples felt that they understood their respective leaders, but the British had better reason to make the claim. Churchill was what he seemed. Roosevelt was not.

The prime minister brilliantly stage-managed his part of the Placentia meeting, himself choosing hymns for the Sunday church service beneath the huge guns of *Prince of Wales*, before a pulpit draped with the flags of the two nations – 'Onward Christian Soldiers', 'O God Our Help in Ages Past' and 'Eternal Father Strong to Save'. Scarcely a man present went unmoved. 'My God, this is history!' muttered a fellow clerk 'in a hushed, awed voice' to Corporal Geoffrey Green. As excited photographers clicked shutters from vantage points on the turrets and upperworks, a colleague said to Ian Jacob that the occasion must fulfil the fantasies of a pressman high on hashish.

That afternoon Churchill took a launch on a brief visit to the shore, wandering a while with Cadogan, the Prof and his secretaries, and somewhat unexpectedly picking wildflowers. Senior officers of the two nations continued to shuttle to and fro between their ships, each arrival and departure being greeted with full ceremonial by bands and honour guards, which ensured that the anchorage was never tranquil. Next day there were further talks, desultory as before, between the service chiefs. Roosevelt marginally raised the stakes in the Atlantic war by agreeing that US warships should escort convoys as far east as Iceland. He justified this measure back in Washington by asserting that there was little purpose in providing American supplies to Britain without seeking to ensure that they reached their destination.

The most substantial outcome of the president and prime minister's encounter was the Atlantic Charter, a strange document. It had its origin in a suggestion by Roosevelt that the two leaders should issue a statement of common principles. As published, it represented a characteristically American expression of lofty intentions. Yet it was drafted by Sir Alexander Cadogan, the attendant Foreign Office mandarin. The Charter was signalled to London for approval by the war cabinet, whose members were dragged out of bed for the purpose. In the small hours of the next morning – another drizzly affair, like most in Newfoundland – an officer reported to Churchill just as he was going to bed that London's reply had arrived. 'Am I going to like it?' the prime minister demanded – in Jacob's words 'like a small boy about to take medicine'. Yes, he was told, all was well. His ministers had endorsed the Anglo–American statement. When published, its noble phrases in support of a common commitment to freedom rang around the world, and gave hope to colonial subjects in a fashion that Churchill certainly did not intend. Back in the USA, however, the Charter roused little popular enthusiasm. It was never signed, because this would have made it necessary to present the document to the Senate for ratification as a treaty.

Before they parted, the president offered the prime minister warm words of goodwill and a further 150,000 old rifles. But there was nothing that promised America's early belligerence. This was what Churchill had come for, and he did not get it. By 2.50 p.m. on 12 August it was all over. Low cloud cut off the ships' view of the shore. *Augusta* slid away into a fog as sailors lined the side of *Prince of Wales* to salute the departing president. Then the British set their own course for home. 'It was hard to tell whether Churchill returned from Newfoundland entirely satisfied with his conference with Roosevelt,' wrote Ian Jacob. The prime minister told his son Randolph that he had enjoyed 'a very interesting and by no means unfruitful meeting with the president . . . and in the three days when we were continually together, I feel we made a deep and intimate contact of friendship. At the same time one is deeply perplexed to know how the deadlock is to be broken and the United States brought boldly and honourably into the war.'

Churchill revealed nothing of his private disappointment in the exuberant rhetoric with which he addressed his colleagues and the nation on returning to Britain. He felt obliged to satisfy their craving for good news, and told the war cabinet that American naval commanders were bursting with impatience to join the struggle, though others at Placentia detected nothing of the kind. His report of Roosevelt's private remarks appears wilfully to have exaggerated the president's carefully equivocal expressions of support. Pownall, now Dill's vice-CIGS, wrote in his diary: 'Roosevelt is all for coming into the war, and as soon as possible . . . But he said that he would never declare war, he wishes to provoke it.' Uncertainty persists about whether the president really used these words, or whether Churchill put them into his mouth on returning to London. Even such sentiments fell short of British hopes. For all the president's social warmth, he never indulged romantic lunges of the kind to which Churchill was prone. If not quite an anglophobe, Roosevelt never revealed much private warmth towards Britain. He left Placentia with the same mindset he had taken there. He was bent upon assisting the British by all possible means to avert defeat. But he had no intention of outpacing congressional and popular sentiment by leading a dash towards US belligerence. American public opinion was vastly more supportive of its government's oil embargo against Japan, in response to Tokyo's descent on Indochina, than it was of Roosevelt's increasing naval support for Britain in the Battle of the Atlantic; this, ironically, though the embargo provoked the Japanese to bomb America into the war.

Churchill, at an off-the-record British newspaper editors' briefing on 22 August, predicted that Japan would not attack in the East, and observed that the Battle of the Atlantic was going better. Suggesting that German U-boats would be reluctant to risk tangling with American warships, which were now operating actively in the western Atlantic, he said: 'I assume that Hitler does not want to risk a clash with Roosevelt until the Russians are out of the way.' The flush of British excitement faded. The prime minister's lofty rhetoric could not overcome a sense of anti-climax, which extended across the nation. A War Office clerk seemed to a British general to judge Placentia rightly when he dismissed Churchill's broadcast describing the meeting as 'nothing dressed up very nicely'.

Vere Hodgson, the Notting Hill charity worker, heard the BBC promise 'an important government announcement' on the afternoon of 14 August, and expected a declaration of Anglo–American union. When, instead, radio listeners heard the words of the Atlantic Charter, she wrote in disappointment: 'There was a statement of War Aims. All very laudable in themselves – the only difficulty will be in carrying them out.' Churchill cabled Hopkins, revealing unusually explicit impatience: 'I ought to tell you that there has been a wave of depression through cabinet and other informed circles here about

President's many assurances about no commitments and no closer to war, etc . . . If 1942 opens with Russia knocked out and Britain left again alone, all kinds of dangers may arise. I do not think Hitler will help in any way . . . You know best whether anything more can be done . . . Should be grateful if you could give me any sort of hope.'

At Downing Street, Churchill observed irritably that Americans had committed themselves to suffer all the inconveniences of war, 'without its commanding stimuli'. Over dinner with Winant, the US ambassador, on 29 August, he again appealed explicitly for American belligerence. Colville recorded: 'The PM said that after the joint declaration [the Atlantic Charter], America could not honourably stay out . . . If R declared war now . . . they might see victory as early as 1943; but if she did not, the war might drag on for years, leaving Britain undefeated but civilization in ruins.' Influential American visitors continued to be courted with unflagging zeal. The journalist John Gunther was entertained at Chequers. A tedious Pennsylvania Democrat, Congressman J. Buell Snyder, chairman of the House Military Sub-Committee on Appropriations, was warmly received at Downing Street. Yet at the end of August Charles Peake, minister at Britain's Washington embassy, expressed profound gloom about the prospect of the United States entering the war soon, perhaps at all. He even questioned – as did some members of the US administration – whether Roosevelt desired such an outcome. Although America could no longer be deemed neutral, it seemed plausible that it might cling indefinitely to its non-belligerent status. There was, and remains, no evidence that Roosevelt was willing to risk a potentially disastrous clash with Congress. Unless America became a fighting ally, Lend-Lease would merely suffice to stave off British defeat.

The autumn of 1941 was one of many wartime seasons which must be viewed without hindsight about what followed. British prospects everywhere seemed bleak. An American diplomat who spent ten days in Scotland returned to report to his embassy: 'The attitude of the people he had been with, most of them big industrialists and realists in their points of view, is that the British are now losing the war, and that it is ridiculous to talk about subduing the German Army by bombing cities inside Germany . . . The German Army . . . must be beaten somehow or other on the ground, or the war is lost.' Churchill agreed. 'It will not be possible for the whole British Army (other than those in the Middle East) to remain indefinitely inert and passive as a garrison of this island against invasion,' Churchill wrote to Ismay on 12 September. 'Such a course, apart altogether from military considerations, would bring the Army into disrepute. I do not need to elaborate this.'

Moscow regarded the meeting of Churchill and Roosevelt with its accustomed paranoia. A Soviet biographer of Churchill, writing more than thirty years later, asserted that at Placentia Bay, 'plans were worked out to establish Anglo–American domination of the post-war world. The leaders of Britain and the USA were drawing up these plans while the USSR was bearing the brunt of the war and America had not yet entered it.' Stalin, in desperate straits, wanted 30,000 tons of aluminium, together with 400 planes and 500 tanks a month from Britain. Churchill told Ambassador Maisky that Moscow would have to be content with half these quantities, and look to the Americans for the rest. On 15 September, Stalin demanded that twenty-five British divisions should be sent to the Russian front via Iran or Archangel. He had already asked Harry Hopkins to solicit Roosevelt to dispatch an American army to Russia. Hopkins, suitably amazed, said that even if the US entered the war, it was unlikely that she would dispatch soldiers to fight in the Caucasus.

It was a measure of Churchill's anxiety to appease Moscow that he agreed in principle to send British troops to Russia. He speculated wildly that Wavell, a Russian-speaker, might command such a force. To try to assist the Russians and fail, he declared, was better than to make no attempt. He was flailing. On 23 October, the notion was formally abandoned. Stalin complained that badly crated British aircraft were arriving 'broken' at Archangel. The British hoped against hope that dire Russian threats to seek a separate peace were as much bluff as their own mutterings about launching a Second Front.

*   *   *

As Britain's merchant fleet suffered relentless attrition in the Atlantic, food minister Lord Woolton briefed the cabinet on the necessity to ration canned goods. Churchill murmured in sorrowful jest: 'I shall never see another sardine!' In reality, of course, he suffered less than any other British citizen from the exigencies of war, and occasionally professed embarrassment that he had never lived so luxuriously in his life. If his energy was somewhat diminished by age, he had less need than ever before to trouble himself about personal wants, which were met by his large staff of domestics and officials. No ministerial colleague enjoyed his privileges in matters of diet, comfort, domestic and travel arrangements. Eden, as Foreign Secretary, waxed lyrical about being offered a slice of cold ham at a Buckingham Palace luncheon, and oranges at the Brazilian embassy. Every wartime British government diarist fortunate enough to travel, including the most exalted ministers and generals, devoted much space to applauding the food they enjoyed abroad, because the fare at home was so dismal.

The prime minister seldom ate in other people's houses, but enjoyed an occasional meal at Buck's club. He sometimes attended gatherings at the Savoy of the Other Club, the dining group he and F.E. Smith had founded in 1910. There, more often than not, he sat beside Lord Camrose, proprietor of the *Daily Telegraph*, a friend who vainly coveted a government job. One night in the autumn of 1941 he slipped out of Downing Street with Eden and Beaverbrook to dine at the Ritz. Reminiscing, he said he would like to have his old First War colleagues Balfour and Smith with him now. Beaverbrook suggested that if Churchill had played his cards better, he might have become prime minister in 1916. Churchill said that the worst moment of his life came when Lloyd George said there was no place for him in the new cabinet.

The housekeepers at both Downing Street and Chequers were issued with unlimited supplies of diplomatic food coupons for official entertaining. These enabled Churchill and his guests to indulge a style unknown to ordinary citizens. The costs of Chequers rose dramatically in the Churchill years from those of Neville Chamberlain, matching the expansiveness of the hospitality. The Chequers Trust's solicitor agreed with Kathleen Hill, Churchill's secretary, in January 1942 that 'the Food Account was very high'. The family made a modest regular cash contribution to compensate the trustees for the Churchills' private share of the house's costs, including paying a quarter of the bill for a little Ford car used by Clementine.

Privileged though the family's domestic circumstances might be, the prime minister's wife often found it no easier than her compatriots to purchase acceptable food. This caused dismay to insensitive visitors. Once in the following year, when Eleanor Roosevelt and other Washingtonians were guests in the No.10 Annexe, Mrs Churchill apologised for the fare: 'I'm sorry dear, I could not buy any fish. You will have to eat macaroni.' Henry Morgenthau noted without enthusiasm: 'Then they gave us little left-over bits made into meat loaf.' By contrast, some of Churchill's guests recoiled from his self-indulgence at a time when the rest of the country was enduring whale steaks. One night when Churchill took a party to the Savoy, the Canadian prime minister Mackenzie King was disgusted that his host insisted on ordering both fish and meat, in defiance of rationing regulations. The ascetic King found it 'disgraceful that Winston should behave like this'.

Churchill's wit served better than his hospitality or the war news to sustain the spirit of his colleagues. At a vexed Defence Committee meeting to discuss supplies for Russia, he issued Cuban cigars, recently arrived as a gift from Havana. 'It may well be that these each contain some deadly poison,' he observed complacently as those so inclined struck matches. 'It may well be that within days I shall follow sadly the long line of your coffins up the aisle of Westminster Abbey – reviled by the populace as the man who has out-borgiaed Borgia!' Eden, arriving for a Chequers weekend, was shown upstairs by Churchill, who himself lit his guest's bedroom fire. The Foreign Secretary wrote a trifle cattily: 'I know no-one with such perfect manners as a host – especially when he feels like it.'

While great men discussed affairs of state at Downing Street or Chequers, below stairs the staff gossiped about The Master in the fashion of every patrician household. 'Oh, Miss, you'll never guess what he did next,' Nellie the Downing Street parlourmaid would say to Elizabeth Layton, one of the prime minister's three typists. Mrs Landemore the cook was a fount of tittle-tattle about the British aristocracy, while Sawyers the prime minister's valet dispensed glasses of wine diverted from the dining room among the staff. Every Friday afternoon, or sometimes Saturday morning, a column of three big black cars stood waiting by the garden gate of Downing Street to waft the prime minister to Chequers at breakneck speed, his journey hastened by police outriders and sirens. Unless he took with him in the car some visitor with whom he wished to converse, he customarily dictated to a typist all the way. Arrived at his destination one day, he said to Elizabeth Layton: 'Now run inside and type like HELL.' The staff late shift were seldom released to their beds before 3 a.m.

Churchill was exultant when, on 8 September, Roosevelt issued a 'shoot first' order to US warships in the Atlantic, dramatically raising his nation's stakes against Germany's U-boats. But two weeks later, when Eden dined with the Churchills and Oliver Lyttelton, the Middle East Minister of State, who was just back from Cairo, 'Winston was depressed at outset, said he felt that we had harsh times ahead.' The prime minister knew from intercepted Japanese diplomatic traffic that Tokyo was winding down its foreign missions and evacuating nationals from British territory. Sir Stewart Menzies, 'C', showed him a cable from Berlin to Tokyo in which Hitler's staff assured the Japanese that 'in the event of a collision between Japan and the United States, Germany would at once open hostilities with America'. After Churchill was glimpsed by Bletchley codebreakers one Saturday, visiting their dank hutted encampment, four of its most senior staff wrote to him personally, appealing for more resources. This prompted an 'Action This Day' note to 'C': 'Make sure they have all they want on extreme priority.'

On 20 October Churchill told the Defence Committee he 'did not believe that the Japanese would go to war with the United States and ourselves'. After many months in which he had wilfully exaggerated the prospect of America entering the war, the chances of such a development were now greater than he avowed. It may be that, following so many disappointments, he did not dare to hope too much. The terrible, nagging fear persisted that Tokyo might launch a strike only against British possessions, without provoking the US to fight. The views of the British and American governments were distorted by logic. Both now possessed strong intelligence evidence of an impending Japanese assault. Yet it remained hard to believe that the Tokyo regime would start a war with the United States that it could not rationally hope to win.

The dispatch of a naval battle squadron to the Far East, supposedly to deter Japanese aggression, was the prime minister's personal decision, and reflected his anachronistic faith in capital ships. Likewise, the squadron's commander, Admiral Tom Phillips – ironically one of Churchill's severest critics in the Admiralty – was his own choice, and a poor one, because Phillips's entire war experience had been spent in shore-based staff appointments. Churchill likened the prospective impact of British battleships in the Far East to that achieved by the presence of Hitler's *Tirpitz* in Arctic waters, 'a threat in being'. Just as the Americans absurdly overrated the deterrent power of deploying a mere thirty-six USAAF B-17 bombers in the Philippines, so the prime minister failed to grasp the fact that, with or without Admiral Phillips's squadron, British forces in the Far East were woefully deficient in strength and leadership.

The Director of Naval Operations, Captain Ralph Edwards, wrote in his diary when the battleship commitment was made: 'Another Prayer from the prime minister, who wishes us to form a squadron of "fast, powerful modern ships – only the best to be used" in the Indian Ocean. This, he avers, will have a paralysing effect on the Japanese – why it should, the Lord alone knows . . . This, mind you, at the same time as he wishes to form a force at Malta, reinforce the Mediterranean, help Russia and be ready to meet a break-out by the *Tirpitz*. The amount of unnecessary work which that man throws on the Naval Staff would, if removed, get us all a month's leave . . . If only the honourable gentleman were to confine himself to statesmanship and politics and leave naval strategy to those properly concerned, the chances of winning the war would be greatly enhanced. He is without doubt one of history's worst strategists.' Churchill wrote to Roosevelt, reporting the dispatch of *Prince of Wales*, *Repulse* and the carrier *Indomitable*: 'There is nothing like having something that can catch and kill anything.' This was a bizarre assertion, after two years of war had demonstrated both the vulnerability of capital ships and the shortcomings of the Fleet Air Arm.

In almost all respects, during the Second World War the Royal Navy showed itself the finest of Britain's three fighting services, just as the US Navy was the best of America's. Axis submarines and air attack inflicted heavy losses, but British seamen displayed consistent high courage and professionalism. The navy's institutional culture proved more impressive than that of the army, perhaps also of the RAF. The Battle of the Atlantic was less dramatic and glamorous than the Battle of Britain, but preservation of the convoy routes was an equally decisive achievement. The sea service's chronic weaknesses, however, were air support and anti-aircraft defence. From beginning to end of the war, the Fleet Air Arm's performance lagged far behind that of the US Navy's air squadrons, partly because of inadequate aircraft, partly because the British did not handle them so well, and partly because there were never enough carriers. Churchill served the navy's interests poorly by failing to insist that the RAF divert more long-range aircraft to maritime support operations, and especially to the Atlantic convoys.

As autumn turned to winter there seemed little cause for optimism at sea, in the air or on land. Wise old Field-Marshal Smuts cabled Churchill from South Africa in considerable dismay on 4 November: 'I am struck by the growth of the impression here and elsewhere that the war is going to end in stalemate and thus fatally for us.' Many Americans perceived the British sitting idle behind their Channel moat, waiting for the United States to ride to their rescue. Averell Harriman wrote a personal letter to Churchill from Washington: 'People are wondering why you don't do something offensively. In my opinion it is important that more should be said about what you are doing.' The diplomat urged energetic media promotion of the RAF's bomber offensive, and of the Royal Navy's convoys to Russia.

Smuts, meanwhile, believed that Russia was being beaten, and that the US was still determined to avoid belligerence. This view was widely shared in London. Britain's army vice-chief of staff remained fearful of a German invasion of Britain, and baffled about how his own side might win the war: 'Whatever may happen on the Russian front, it is only by successful invasion of these islands that Hitler can definitely win the war . . . I wish we had so clear an idea of how we could win. At present we cling rather vaguely to a combination of dissatisfied populations, lowering of morale amongst Germans and German troops, blockade and somewhat inaccurate bombing at night . . . America . . . seems further removed now from coming into the war than she was last April.'

Yet there is evidence that Churchill's personal view was shifting towards an expectation of US belligerence. He asserted to Lord Camrose at the Other Club on 14 November that he was confident the Americans would soon be in the war. Camrose was sufficiently impressed to write to his son, repeating the prime minister's words. On the 19th, Churchill told guests during a lunch at Downing Street that he expected to land the second of four possible 'prizes'. The first would be US entry into the war without involving Japan; the second would be America's accession as an ally, matched by that of Japan as an enemy; the third would be that neither country entered the war; the fourth, that Japan became an enemy, while the United States remained neutral. Yet to others privy to secret intelligence of Japanese motions, the prime minister's hopes seemed ill-founded.

Churchill strove to provide cause for Americans to modify their impression of British passivity. Briefing Commodore Lord Louis Mountbatten on his new role as 'chief adviser' to Combined Operations, soon translated into overall command, the prime minister said: 'Your whole attention is to be concentrated on the offensive.' This was another of the periods when he enthused about a possible descent on Norway, heedless of the intractable reality that its coastline was beyond British fighter range. Eden expressed dismay about this plan to his private secretary: 'A.E. is much perplexed – he feels as I do so many of W.'s gorgeous schemes have ended in failure . . . a false step – a faulty short-cut – would set us back years.'

In Churchill's fevered search for aggressive commanders he cast a jaundiced eye upon many incumbents. He harboured a persistent animus towards General Sir Ronald Adam, Adjutant-General and one of the army's ablest staff officers, partly because Adam created the Army Bureau of Current Affairs, a perceived socialist propaganda instrument. Churchill talked of sacking Tedder, commander of the Desert Air Force, soon to be recognised as one of the outstanding airmen of the war. Sir Wilfred Freeman, vice-chief of air staff, called on the chronically disaffected Hankey to ask what Portal, his boss, should do if Churchill insisted on Tedder's removal. Hankey offered his usual answer: resign. Freeman asserted that in such an event he himself would quit also: 'He said he had no use for Churchill at all.'

The prime minister often felt oppressed by the perceived pettiness and petulance of Parliament. In the House on 11 November 1941 he faced a barrage of questions and supplementaries: first about alleged Italian atrocities in Montenegro, then about the government's apparent unwillingness to allow the RAF to bomb Rome. When he answered evasively, Sir Thomas Moore, Member for Ayr, demanded: 'Does my right hon. friend really think it wise to provide a hide-out for this rat Mussolini?' Churchill responded: 'I think it would be as well to have confidence in the decisions of the Government, whose sole desire is to inflict the maximum of injury upon the enemy.' Another MP drew attention to shortages of equipment, described in Lord Gort's recently published dispatch on the 1940 campaign in France. Churchill brusquely rejected calls for an inquiry. He might have suggested that such matters came under the heading of archaeology, rather than conduct of the war.

Another Member demanded information about the precise composition of the prime minister's party at the Placentia Bay meeting, and asked 'whether in view of the fact that we are fighting for our existence, he will consider removing from Government service all persons of German education and of German origin'. Churchill invited the questioner to be explicit. This the MP declined to do, but the House readily comprehended the enquiry as an attack upon Lord Cherwell. Other MPs then raised questions in which Cherwell was named. 'The Prof' was widely perceived as a pernicious influence upon the prime minister. MPs who did not dare to attack Churchill himself instead vented their frustrations upon his associates. The prime minister defended Cherwell. But he bitterly resented being obliged to do so.

At the same question time, an MP urged that greyhound racing should be banned on working days, to deter absenteeism from factories and pits. Others called for a review and modification of Regulation 18B, under which aliens were detained without trial. These exchanges occupied twelve columns of Hansard, and caused Churchill to return to Downing Street in dudgeon. Who could blame him? How pettifogging seemed the issues raised by MPs, how small-minded the pinpricks of their criticisms, alongside the great issues with which he wrestled daily. If self-pity about the intrusions of democracy is in some measure common to all prime ministers in war or peace, such carping became infinitely irksome to the leader of a nation struggling for survival against overwhelming odds.

The best news in November was of Auchinleck's long-delayed offensive in the desert, Operation *Crusader*, which began on 18 November. Churchill trumpeted its progress: 'For the first time, the Germans are getting a taste of their own bitter medicine.' On the 20th, before the House of Commons, he described the North African assault in the most dramatic terms: 'One thing is certain – that all ranks of the British Empire troops involved are animated by a long-pent-up and ardent desire to engage the enemy . . . This is the first time that we have met the Germans at least equally well-armed and equipped.' The prime minister knew from Ultra that Auchinleck had launched 658 tanks against Rommel's 168, that the RAF deployed 660 aircraft against 642 of the Luftwaffe's. Yet, in *Crusader*'s first days, the British suffered much heavier losses than the Germans. Churchill continued to cherish hopes of the tangled, messy desert fighting, but there was no sign of a breakthrough. On 23 November Auchinleck sacked Alan Cunningham, commander of the newly christened Eighth Army, and replaced him with his own chief of staff, Neil Ritchie. Rommel had destroyed the career of yet another British general. The Germans were once again fighting harder, faster and more effectively than the British.

It was at this time that Churchill's patience with his senior soldier, Sir John Dill, chief of the Imperial General Staff since May 1940, at last expired. Dill's difficulty was that, like his predecessor 'Tiny' Ironside, he suffered from a surfeit of realism. This inspired in both men successively a gloom about their own nation's prospects which grated intolerably upon the prime minister. Dill was exhausted by Churchill's insistence on deciding every issue of strategy through trial by combat, testing arguments to destruction at interminable Downing Street meetings. 'Winston's methods were frequently repulsive to him,' wrote Alan Brooke. Dill recoiled from the need to work with the Russians, whom he abhorred, believed that whenever Hitler chose to reinforce Rommel, the Middle East would be lost, and feared that neglect of Britain's Far East defences would precipitate disaster if the Japanese attacked. Dill never doubted Churchill's greatness as national leader, but he considered him wholly unfit to direct strategy.

Churchill, in his turn, had told John Kennedy many months earlier that he found Dill 'too much impressed by the enemy's will'. The CIGS was an intelligent man, possessed of famous charm. But, like many other British officers, he lacked steel to bear the highest responsibilities in a war of national survival. On 16 November 1941 Churchill told Dill he must go, designating as his replacement Sir Alan Brooke, C-in-C Home Forces. The change provoked dismay in high places. This was partly because, as a man, Dill was widely liked. Colleagues and friends indulged that fatal British sympathy for agreeable gentlemen, however inadequate to their appointed tasks. Dill was perceived as a victim of Churchill's determination to bar dissent from his own conduct of the war. There is no doubt, however, that his removal was right. Never a driving force, he was now a spent one.

His successor proved the outstanding British command appointment of the Second World War. Brooke – like Dill, Montgomery and Alexander – was a Northern Irishman. He was fifty-eight years old. He had characteristics often identified with Protestant Ulster: toughness, diligence, intolerance, Christian commitment, and a brusqueness that sometimes tipped over into ill-temper. His sharp brain was matched by extraordinary strength of purpose. A passionate bird-watcher, Brooke saved his softer side for his feathered friends, his adored second wife Benita and their two young children. He had a low opinion of his fellow men, fellow soldiers and allies, expressed in his wartime diaries with a heavy dressing of exclamation marks. His booming voice and thick-rimmed spectacles intimidated strangers. Intensely active and indeed restless, Brooke was so little seen in the War Office that it was said of him that he knew his way to only two rooms there – his own and the lavatory.

Though the new CIGS was often charmed by the prime minister's puckish wit, and did not doubt his greatness, he and Churchill never achieved full mutual understanding. Brooke was disgusted by the selfishness of Churchill's working habits, late hours and strategic flights of fancy. Like Dill and Wavell, he loathed war as much as the prime minister relished it. But he displayed a tenacity and resolve in the face of difficulties and Churchillian follies which Dill lacked. David Margesson, the Secretary for War, said that Brooke was sustained by 'his ability to shake himself like a dog coming out of water after unpleasant interviews with Winston, and . . . his power of debate (& his rasping voice)'. The new CIGS was a harsh and ruthless man. These qualities equipped him to fulfil his role far more effectively than the mild-mannered Dill.

Brooke proved a superb planner and organiser. He gained nothing like the public celebrity of Montgomery and Alexander. The CIGS and the prime minister could not be described as brothers in arms. But they forged a partnership in the direction of British strategy which, however stormy, served their nation wonderfully well. Churchill, so often accused of surrounding himself with acolytes and 'yes' men, deserves the utmost credit for appointing and retaining as CIGS an officer who, when their views differed, fought him to the last gasp. The ascent of Brooke, on the eve of another critical turning point in the war, was a great day for British arms.

In the first days of December a flood of intelligence revealed Japanese forces redeploying in South-East Asia. The suspense was very great as the British waited for Tokyo to reveal its objectives. To the end, there was apprehension that a Nipponese whirlwind might bypass the USA and its possessions. On Sunday, 7 December, Churchill learned that Roosevelt proposed to announce in three days' time that he would regard an attack on British or Dutch possessions in the Far East as an attack on America. That day at lunch, US ambassador 'Gil' Winant was among the guests at Chequers. Churchill asserted vigorously that if the Japanese attacked the United States, Britain would declare war on Japan. Winant said he understood that, for the prime minister had declared it publicly. Then Churchill demanded: 'If they declare war on us, will you declare war on them?' Winant replied: 'I can't answer that, Prime Minister. Only the Congress has the right to declare war under the United States constitution.' Churchill lapsed into silence. That terrible apprehension persisted, of facing the Japanese alone. Then he said, with his utmost charm: 'We're late, you know. You get washed and we will go in to lunch together.'

Harriman, a fellow guest at dinner that night, found Churchill 'tired and depressed. He didn't have much to say throughout dinner and was immersed in his thoughts, with his head in his hands part of the time.' Then they heard the radio news of Japan's attack on Pearl Harbor, and looked incredulously at each other. Churchill jumped up and started for the door, saying, 'We shall declare war on Japan.' Within a few minutes he and Winant were speaking by phone to Roosevelt. Soon afterwards the Admiralty called, reporting Japanese attacks on Malaya.

Churchill could not claim that his long campaign of seduction was responsible for US entry into the war. This had followed only upon Japanese aggression. America's policy of deterrence in the East, fortified by sanctions, had instead provoked Tokyo to fight. Though the 'day of infamy' resolved many dilemmas and uncertainties, it is unlikely that Roosevelt viewed Pearl Harbor with the same enthusiasm as the prime minister. Events had produced an outcome which the president, left to himself, might not have willed or accomplished for many months, if ever. What is certain is that Churchill had sown seeds of a fertility such as only he could have nurtured, for a harvest which he now gathered. He possessed a stature, and commanded an affection among the American people, incomparably greater than anything won by the faltering performance of Britain's war machine. In the years ahead, his personality would enable him to exercise an influence upon American policies which, for all its limitations, no other British leader could have aspired to.

When Britain's Tokyo ambassador Sir Robert Craigie later submitted a valedictory dispatch, he was sharply censured by the prime minister for describing Japan's assault in the East as 'a disaster for Britain'. On the contrary, said Churchill, it was 'a blessing . . . Greater good fortune has never happened to the British Empire.' That night of 7 December 1941, Churchill wrote in a draft of his memoirs: 'saturated and satiated with emotion and sensation, I went to bed and slept the sleep of the saved and thankful. One hopes that eternal sleep will be like that.'

EIGHT

A Glimpse of Arcadia

De Gaulle said after Pearl Harbor: 'Well then, this war is over. Of course, there are more operations, battles and struggles ahead; but . . . the outcome is no longer in doubt. In this industrial war, nothing can resist the power of American industry. From now on, the British will do nothing without Roosevelt's agreement.' The US president told Churchill: 'Today all of us are in the same boat with you and the people of the Empire, and it is a ship which will not and cannot be sunk.' Unlike Churchillian assertions earlier in the war, born of blind faith, Roosevelt's words were rooted in realities of power.

Harold Nicolson wrote on 11 December: 'We simply can't be beaten with America in. But how strange it is that this great event should be recorded and welcomed here without any jubilation. We should have gone mad with joy if it had happened a year ago . . . Not an American flag flying in the whole of London. How odd we are!' Part of the explanation was given by London charity worker Vere Hodgson. Like many of her compatriots, she felt that Pearl Harbor served the Americans right: 'Though I do not wish anyone to be bombed, a little wholesome shaking-up is good for people who contemplate the sufferings of others with equanimity . . . Poor dear people in those islands of bliss, sunshine and fruit drinks. They must have had an unpleasant Sunday afternoon . . . I should think Colonel Lindbergh has retired to a room with dark blinds – not to be heard of for many a long day.'

A Home Intelligence report said: 'While the public are prepared to make any sacrifices necessary to help Russia . . . they have no such disposition towards America . . . America is "too damned wealthy" . . . Americans are too mercenary-minded, and . . . the hardship and suffering of war "will do them a lot of good".' Few British people felt minded to thank the Americans for belatedly entering the war not from choice or principle, but because they were obliged to. Some were fearful that US belligerence would check the flow of supplies to Britain and Russia. It was left to the prime minister to open his arms to a transatlantic embrace which many of his compatriots were foolish enough to grudge.

In the days following Pearl Harbor, from everywhere save Malaya the war news reaching Churchill briefly brightened. The Royal Navy was faring better in its struggle with Hitler's U-boats. Auchinleck continued to signal optimistically about the progress of *Crusader* in the desert. 'Consider tide turned,' he reported from Cairo on 9 December, and two days later: 'We are pressing pursuit vigorously.' The Russians were still holding Moscow, Leningrad and the Baku oilfields. Churchill told the House of Commons on 8 December: 'We have at least four-fifths of the population of the globe upon our side. We are responsible for their safety and for their future. In the past we have had a light which flickered, in the present we have a light which flames, and in the future there will be a light which shines over all the land and sea.'

On 10 December came ghastly tidings, of the destruction of *Prince of Wales* and *Repulse* by Japanese air attack off Malaya. Churchill was stunned. Their deployment reflected his personal decision, their loss an indictment of his misplaced faith in 'castles of steel' amid oceans now dominated by air and submarine power. It is often claimed that the fate of the two capital ships was sealed by the absence of the carrier *Indomitable*, prevented by accidental damage from joining the battle squadron. Given the shortcomings of the Fleet Air Arm and its fighters, it seems more plausible that if *Indomitable* had been at sea off Malaya, as intended by Churchill and the Admiralty, it would have been lost with *Prince of Wales* and *Repulse*.

Yet even this blow was endurable in the context of American belligerency. On 11 December Germany and Italy removed a vital lingering doubt by declaring war on the USA. Next day Churchill cabled to Eden, who was en route to Moscow: 'The accession of the United States makes amends for all, and with time and patience will give certain victory.' There were short-term hazards. Washington would cut overseas weapons shipments to meet the needs of its own armed forces. Ten RAF squadrons en route to Persia to support Stalin's southern front must be diverted to the Far East. But these were mere inconveniences alongside the glittering prospect opened by American might.

The prime minister's first priority was to meet Roosevelt and his military chiefs face to face, to cement the alliance created by events, though never ratified by formal treaty. Henceforward, Anglo–American dealings would be influenced by formal agreements on material issues, above all Lend-Lease, but governed chiefly by personal understandings, or lack of them, between the leaders of the two nations and their chiefs of staff. When Churchill proposed an immediate descent on Washington, the president demurred. On security grounds he suggested a rendezvous in Bermuda, which he said that he could not himself attend before 7 January 1942. In reality, Roosevelt was hesitant about making space at the White House for the overpowering personality of Britain's prime minister and the torrent of rhetoric with which he would assuredly favour the American people. Nonetheless, in the face of Churchill's chafing, the president agreed that he should come to Washington before Christmas.

As the prime minister prepared to sail, there was a flurry of last-minute business. He cabled Eden that while it might be desirable for Russia to declare war on Japan, Stalin should not be pressed too hard on this issue, 'considering how little we have been able to contribute' to the Soviet war effort. The Foreign Secretary was told, however, that on no account should he appear willing to satisfy Moscow's demands for recognition of the frontiers which the Russians had established for themselves by agreement with Hitler, absorbing eastern Poland and the Baltic states. Not only would such action be unprincipled, it would discomfit the Americans, who were at that time even more hostile than the British to Stalin's territorial ambitions.

Meanwhile, Attlee was urged not to implement a threatened cut in the British people's rations: 'We are all in it together and [the Americans] are eating better meals than we are.' Reducing supplies would savour of panic, said the prime minister. From Gourock on the Clyde on the morning of 13 December he telephoned Ismay to urge that 'everything that was fit for battle' should be dispatched to the Far East. Then, with his eighty-strong party which included Beaverbrook and the chiefs of staff – Dill still representing the army while Brooke took over at the War Office – he boarded the great battleship *Duke of York*, sister of the lost *Prince of Wales*.

The passage was awful. Day after day, *Duke of York* ploughed through mountainous seas which caused her to pitch and roll. Max Beaverbrook, who had been invited partly to provide companionship for 'the old man' and partly because he was alleged to be popular with Americans, wheezed that he was being borne across the Atlantic in 'a submarine masquerading as a battleship'. Churchill, almost alone among the passengers, was untroubled by seasickness. Patrick Kinna, his shorthand-taker, found his own misery worsened by the cigar smoke that choked the prime minister's cabin high in the superstructure. A stream of bad news reached the party at sea: the Japanese landed in north Borneo on 17 December, on Hong Kong island next day. Churchill minuted the chiefs of staff on the 15th, urging the vital importance of ensuring that Singapore was held: 'Nothing compares in importance with the fortress.' Heedless of the pitching of the storm-tossed warship, he dictated a succession of long memoranda, setting out his views on the way ahead.

Supplies for Russia from both Britain and the US must be sustained, he said, for only thus 'shall we hold our influence over Stalin and be able to weave the mighty Russian effort into the general texture of the war'. He proposed that American troops should be sent to Northern Ireland, to provide an additional deterrent against German landings. By 1943, he said, Britain would be 'more strongly prepared against invasion than ever before'. The possibility of a German descent on Britain continued to feature in his calculations. If Russia was knocked out, as still seemed likely, the Nazis could again turn west.

Hitler must recognise the urgency of completing the conquest of Europe before America became fully mobilised. Churchill suggested that US bombers should deploy in Britain to join the growing air offensive against Germany. He expected Singapore to be defended for at least six months.

He interrupted his dictation to tell Kinna to make some sailors stop whistling outside his cabin. This was a distraction and a vulgarity which he could not abide – he once said that an aversion to whistling was the only trait he shared with Hitler. Kinna duly retired, but was too nervous of his likely reception to address the offending seamen, who lapsed into silence spontaneously. Oblivious of the towering seas outside, the pitching of the huge ship, Churchill resumed composition of his *tour d'horizon*. He wanted the Americans to land in French North Africa in 1942. The following year, he anticipated launching attacks against some permutation of Sicily, Italy, Norway, Denmark, Holland, Belgium, the French Channel or Atlantic coasts, possibly the Balkans. In his memoranda he made some wild assertions, for instance anticipating that when the time came to invade the Continent 'the uprising of the local populations for whom weapons must be brought will supply the corpus of the liberating offensive'. But he also looked with imaginative foresight to the creation of improvised aircraft-carriers, which would indeed play a key role later in the war, and urged a carrier-borne air assault on Japan.

On 21 December he wrote a long letter to Clementine: 'I do not know when or how I shall come back. I shall certainly stay long enough to do all that has to be done, having come all this way at so much trouble and expense.' He told her he had no patience with those who denounced Britain's unreadiness in the Far East: 'It is no good critics saying "Why were we not prepared?" when everything we had was already fully engaged.' In this he was surely justified. Those, like Dill, who had favoured reinforcing Malaya at the expense of the Middle East, were mistaken. It would have been absurd to dispatch desperately needed aircraft, tanks and troops to meet a putative threat in the Far East, at the likely cost of losing Egypt to an enemy already at its gates. It is hard to imagine any redeployment of available British resources in the autumn of 1941 which would have prevented disaster. So far-reaching were British weaknesses of leadership, training, tactics, air support and will in Malaya and Burma that the Japanese were all but certain to prevail.

The heavy seas imposed delays which caused *Duke of York*'s passage to seem to its passengers interminable. Churchill fulminated at the waste of time, but was obliged to concede that he could not subdue the elements. A five-day crossing stretched to nine, then ten. The chiefs of staff delivered their comments upon Churchill's long strategic memoranda, which were discussed at a series of meetings under his chairmanship. They opposed a firm commitment to opening the major 'Second Front' in Europe in 1943. Germany, they said, must first be weakened by intensified and protracted bombing. They urged acknowledgement of the fact that 'the Japanese will be able to run wild in the Western Pacific' until Germany and Italy were disposed of. Churchill, who was undergoing one of his periodic bouts of scepticism about bombing, resisted any declaration of excessive faith in its potential. He warned against expecting the Americans to take as insouciant a view of Japanese Pacific advances as the chiefs proposed. He said it was essential to promote an offensive vision, rather than merely to advocate counter-measures against Axis thrusts. All this was very wise.

On 22 December *Duke of York* at last stood into Hampton Roads. The British party landed, and Churchill and his immediate staff boarded a plane for the short flight to Washington. Through its windows they peered down through gathering darkness, fascinated by the bright lights of the American capital after the gloom of blacked-out London. There to meet the prime minister at the airport was Franklin Roosevelt, whose guest he became for the next three weeks. If this was a tense time for the British delegation, it was also an intensely happy one for Churchill. Who could deny his deserving of it, after all he had endured during the previous eighteen months? That first Anglo–American summit was codenamed *Arcadia*, paradise of ancient Greek shepherds. To the prime minister Washington indeed seemed paradisiacal. Installed in the White House, he enthused to Clementine: 'All is very good indeed; and my plans go through. The Americans are magnificent in their breadth of view.'

From his first meeting with Roosevelt he emphasised the danger that Hitler might seize Morocco, and thus the urgent need that Allied forces should pre-empt him. Less convincingly, he cited the French battleships *Jean-Bart* and *Richelieu*, sheltering in North Africa, as 'a real prize'. He was galled when Dill suggested that shipping short-ages might make it impossible to convey an American army across the Atlantic in 1942, and swept this argument aside. The two national leaders and their chiefs of staff discussed, then dismissed, arguments for creating a war council on which all the Allies and British domin-ions would be represented. It was agreed that while the dominions should be consulted, policy must be made between the Big Three. This latter outcome was inevitable, but sowed the seeds of future unhappiness around the Empire, and especially in Australia.

While in Washington, Churchill learned of the crippling of the battleships *Valiant* and *Queen Elizabeth* by Italian human torpedoes in Alexandria harbour, together with the loss of two cruisers at sea. He was furious to hear that his deputy prime minister had informed the Australians and Canadians of the drastic weakening of the Mediterranean fleet. 'I greatly regret that this vital secret should be spread about the world in this fashion,' he cabled Attlee. 'We do not give our most secret information to the Dominions.'

The British and American chiefs of staff held twelve joint meetings. To the relief of Churchill and his delegation, the US leadership imme-diately confirmed the conclusion of earlier 'ABC' Anglo–American staff talks that the Allies should pursue the policy of 'Germany First'. It is sometimes insufficiently recognised how far Allied decisions for 1942 were influenced by shipping imperatives. The British were shocked, in the first weeks after Pearl Harbor, to discover how few bottoms would be available in the year ahead, before the huge US 'liberty ship' building programme achieved maturity. Britain required thirty million tons of imports a year to sustain itself, which must be borne across the Atlantic by merchant fleets much diminished by sinkings.

With the limited capacity available, there was much more scope for American action against the Germans, by supplying Russia and deploying US troops in the west, than against the Japanese in the Pacific. The Asian war required three or four times the freighting effort of the European one, because of the distances involved. A merchant ship could make only three round trips a year to the Pacific theatre. The 'Germany first' strategy thus represented not only strategic sense, but also logistic necessity. Yet, given the much greater popular animosity towards Japan in the US, it should never be taken for granted. Harold Macmillan observed later of the prime minister: 'No one but he (and that only with extraordinary patience and skill) could have enticed the Americans into the European war at all.' This overstated the case. But the US commitment to the western conflict indisputably represented a diplomatic triumph for Britain.

When Roosevelt introduced the prime minister to a throng of American pressmen, Churchill roused cheers and applause by climbing onto a chair so they could see him better. Asked whether it was true that Singapore was the key to the Far East war, he parried skilfully: 'The key to the whole situation is the resolute manner in which the British and American democracies are going to throw themselves into the conflict.' How long would it last? 'If we manage it well, it will only take half as long as if we manage it badly.' His exuberance was increased by further optimistic signals from Auchinleck in North Africa about the progress of *Crusader*.

On Christmas Eve, standing beside Roosevelt on the balcony as the White House tree lights were illuminated before a huge crowd, he said: 'I cannot feel myself a stranger here in the centre and at the summit of the United States. I feel a sense of unity and fraternal association which, added to the kindliness of your welcome, convinces me that I have a right to share your Christmas joys . . . Let the children have their night of fun and laughter. Let the gifts of Father Christmas delight their play. Let us grown-ups share to the full in their unstinted pleasures before we turn again to the stern task and the formidable years that lie before us, resolved that, by our sacrifice and daring, these same children shall not be robbed of their inheritance or denied their right to live in a free and decent world.'

He found his pulse racing after the balcony appearance, from which his words were broadcast: 'It has all been very moving.' That evening it was also a struggle to overcome private dismay: he learned of the fall of Hong Kong.

Roosevelt, matching the prime minister courtesy for courtesy and jest for jest, taunted him at dinner about having fought on the wrong side in the Boer War. When Churchill was asked about the quality of US food supplies to Britain, he complained: 'Too many powdered eggs.' He cabled Auchinleck, urging that now the desert campaign seemed to be progressing so well he should release an armoured brigade and four RAF squadrons for the Far East. On Christmas evening he left the rest of the presidential party watching a movie, and stumped off upstairs murmuring about 'homework'. He was writing next day's speech to the US Congress.

Washington Post reporter Hope Ridings Miller wrote: 'Senators' . . . office telephones carried call after call from friends – wondering if there was some way, somehow, something could be done to obtain tickets for the biggest show on the season's calendar.' It was late in the morning when Churchill, wearing a blue polka-dot bow tie, clambered to his feet in the chamber on Capitol Hill. He grinned, donned spectacles, blinked back the tears that so often filled his eyes at dramatic moments. Congressman Frank McNaughton saw 'a stubby, granite little man . . . dumpy, heavy-shouldered, massive-jawed, with a solid bald crown flecked with straggles of grey hair'. Hands on hips, Churchill began to address the audience beyond the dense bank of microphones. 'Smiling, bowing, and looking very much at home,' wrote Miller, 'the Prime Minister flushed slightly as the ovation ushering him in increased in volume and burst into an ear-splitting crescendo. Compared with that demonstration, the tone in which he began his speech was so low those of us in the press gallery had a difficult time catching all his opening lines . . . A consummate actor, who carefully times his speech so that each word and each syllable is given the exact emphasis it should have, Mr Churchill also pauses at the proper time for applause . . .'

In the knowledge that Americans, and especially their legislators, were deeply wary of Britain as a suppliant, he said nothing of dependency, real though this was. Instead he talked of partnership, shared burdens. He flourished his own American parentage: 'I shall always remember how each Fourth of July my mother would wave an American flag before my eyes.' He reached his peroration: 'Lastly, if you will forgive me for saying it, to me the best tidings of all is that the United States, united as never before, has drawn the sword for freedom, and cast aside the scabbard.' He unsheathed an imaginary blade, and brandished it aloft. Then he sat down, sweating freely.

As one man, the chamber rose. The applause echoed on and on, until at last with a little wave Churchill left the rostrum. Hope Ridings Miller reported: 'I never saw Congress in a more enthusiastic mood, and some diplomats, who habitually sit on their hands at a joint Congressional meeting, lest one gesture of applause might be diplomatically misinterpreted, clapped louder and longer than anybody.' Interior Secretary Harold Ickes called him 'the greatest orator in the world . . . I doubt if any other Britisher could have stood in that spot and made the profound impression that Churchill made.' It was just after 1 o'clock. The prime minister, pouring himself a whisky in the Senate Secretary's office, said to Charles Wilson, his doctor: 'It is a great weight off my chest.' At an informal lunch after his speech, he told congressmen: 'The American people will never know how grateful we are for the million rifles sent us after Dunkirk. It meant our life and our salvation.' If this was a flourish of flattery, it promoted a legend that Americans cherished. That night Wilson was alarmed to discover that Churchill had suffered an attack of angina pectoris. But there was nothing to be done, no change in the schedule to be considered. It would have been a political catastrophe if the world saw Britain's elderly war leader flag.

Churchill used Roosevelt's personal train to travel to Ottawa to address the Canadian Parliament, where he achieved another wonderful success. Back at the White House, he wrote happily to Attlee: 'We live here a big family, in the greatest intimacy and informality.' Peerless phrases slipped from his lips in even the most banal circumstances. At the White House lunch on New Year's Day, as he transferred hash and poached egg to his plate, the egg slipped off. The prime minister restored it to the hash, with a glance at his hostess, 'to put it on its throne'. It was fortunate that conversation sparkled, for the food at the Roosevelt White House was notoriously awful. After the meal, in her sitting room Eleanor Roosevelt and her secretary Malvina Thompson compared notes on the two leaders with another guest, the first lady's friend and confidant Joseph Lash. Lash said the prime minister had the richer temperament, but the president was a more dependable, steadier man in a crisis. '"Tommy" clapped her hands and said she and Mrs Roosevelt felt the same. The president was more hardheaded, they felt. He was less brilliant, but more likely to do the right thing. The president also gave the impression of being more under control, of never letting himself go.'

It is striking how many of those who worked with Roosevelt deferred to his greatness, but disliked his personality. Diplomat Charles Bohlen, for instance, observed that despite the president's pose of informality, 'the aura of the office was always around him'. If Churchill's outbursts of ill-temper sometimes irked colleagues, Roosevelt's associates were made uneasy by his bland geniality, his reluctance to display anger, or indeed to reveal any frank sentiment at all. Where Churchill sought clarity of decision by working on paper, Roosevelt preferred to do business verbally. No minutes were taken of his cabinet meetings. This approach led to many confusions, on issues of war and domestic policy alike. The president prided himself on his powers of persuasion, and had raised to an art form the ability to send every visitor out of his presence confident that he had got what he wanted. Both Churchill and Roosevelt were often accused of betraying their own social class, but the president was a much more skilled politician. De Gaulle described him as 'a patrician democrat whose every simple gesture is carefully studied'.

Halifax wrote with condescension but some justice about Churchill's late-night sessions with the chiefs of staff at the White House: 'Winston's methods, as I have long known, are exhausting for anybody who doesn't happen to work that way; discursive discussions, jumping like a water bird from stone to stone where the current takes you. I am sure the faults that people find with him arise entirely from overwhelming self-centredness, which with all his gifts of imagination make him quite impervious to other people's feelings.' Some of Roosevelt's intimates were struck by Churchill's single-minded obsession with the war. The occupant of the White House, by contrast, was obliged to devote far more of his energies to domestic matters, and to managing Congress. 'The difference between the President and the prime minister,' wrote his secretary William Hassett, 'is the prime minister has nothing on his mind but the war: the President must also control the government of the United States.'

Churchill felt able to take more for granted with his own nation's legislature than did Roosevelt with his. Yet while the Americans perceived Britain's government as entirely dominated by Churchill, the British took a legitimate pride in the effectiveness of their bureaucratic machine. Churchill's team were bemused by the whimsical fashion in which the US government seemed to be conducted. Ian Jacob thought the Oval Office 'one of the most untidy rooms I have ever seen. It is full of junk. Half-opened parcels, souvenirs, books, papers, knick-knacks and all kinds of miscellaneous articles lie about everywhere, on tables, on chairs, and on the floor. His desk is piled with papers; and alongside his chair he has a sort of bookcase also filled with books, papers, and junk of all sorts piled just anyhow. It would drive an orderly-minded man, or woman, mad.' FDR's famous dog, Fala, had to be evicted from a meeting in the cabinet room for barking furiously during a Churchillian harangue.

Cadogan asked Halifax with mandarin disdain: 'How *do* these people carry on?' They were unimpressed by Roosevelt as a warlord. Jacob wrote: 'By the side of the Prime Minister he is a child in military affairs, and evidently has little realisation of what can and what cannot be done . . . To our eyes the American machine of Government seems hopelessly disorganised . . . They will have first to close the gap between their Army and Navy before they can work as a real team with us.' Had any American senior officer read these words, he would have answered that it was pretty rich for a British soldier thus to patronise the USA and its armed forces, when Britain's record since 1939 was of almost unbroken battlefield failure, while her economic survival rested upon American largesse. Criticisms of Roosevelt's working methods had substance, but ignored America's untold wealth and achievements.

The British, in the years ahead, would persistently underestimate US capabilities, and feed American resentment by revealing their sentiments. They failed, for instance, to recognise the potency of Roosevelt's personal commitment to supplying Russia. Just as Churchill and Beaverbrook faced opposition on this issue in Britain, so the president was obliged to overcome critics at the top of the armed forces, in Congress and the media, who were fiercely reluctant to offer Stalin open cheques on the US Treasury. Roosevelt, like Churchill, stood head and shoulders above his military advisers in his determination to support Russia's war. If American deliveries, like those of Britain, lagged far behind promises, without the exercise of the president's formidable personal authority the Soviet Union would have been denied food, commodities, vehicles and equipment that became vital to its war effort.

In Washington, the Allies agreed a vast increase in US weapons production – Beaverbrook made a useful contribution by urging the feasibility of this on Roosevelt. It would be more than two years before the full effects became apparent on the battlefield. The Americans, including George Marshall, were slow to grasp the length of the inevitable delay between decisions to arm and achievement of capability to unleash upon the enemy the vast war machine they planned to create. But a powerful beginning was made at *Arcadia*. On 5 January 1942 Churchill flew to Florida for five days' warmth, rest and work. He revised the strategy papers he had composed on the voyage from Britain. Amid the obvious determination of the US chiefs of staff to grapple the German army, he committed himself to 'large offensive operations' in Europe in 1943. This even though news from the battlefronts was turning sour again. Rommel had been able to extricate seven German and Italian divisions from the desert battle, and was regrouping in Tripolitania. The Japanese were storming down the Malay peninsula, prompting the first stab of apprehension about Singapore. Large reinforcements were being rushed to 'the fortress', as Churchill so mistakenly called the island.

Then there were a few more days with Roosevelt. 'They tell me I have done a good job here,' Churchill said to Bernard Baruch. The financier replied: 'You have done a one hundred per cent job. But now you ought to get the hell out of here.' The visitor was in danger of outstaying his welcome. The president had grown bored with the relentless, self-indulgent sparring between the prime minister and Beaverbrook. While never lacking confidence in the superior might of the nation which he himself led, Roosevelt found that it became tiring to live alongside the Englishman's bombastic presence. He was glad to see his guests go. Churchill wrote in his memoirs: 'The time had now come when I must leave the hospitable and exhilarating atmosphere of the White House and of the American nation, erect and infuriate against tyrants and aggressors. It was to no sunlit prospect that I must return.' He knew with what dismay the British nation must greet the torrent of ill-tidings from the Far East, which had yet to reach a flood.

The president said to the prime minister at their parting: 'Trust me to the bitter end.' Then Churchill took off in a Boeing Clipper flying-boat, one of three such aircraft purchased from the Americans the previous year. The Clipper flew low and slow, but offered its passengers a magnificent standard of comfort and cuisine. Dinner, served between Bermuda and Plymouth, consisted of consommé, shrimp cocktail, filet mignon with fresh vegetables, pudding, dessert, coffee, champagne and liqueurs. Then the passengers were able to retire to bunks, though Churchill wandered restlessly during the night. They landed in Britain on the morning of 17 January, after an eighteen-hour flight. That evening the prime minister briefed the war cabinet. 'An Olympian calm' prevailed at the White House, he said. 'It was perhaps rather isolated. The president had no adequate link between his will and executive action.' The British found the State Department 'jumpy'. Secretary of State Cordell Hull had been enraged by the unheralded Free French seizure of the tiny

Vichy-held islands of Saint-Pierre and Miquelon off Newfoundland, a development which wasted precious Anglo–American time and goodwill to resolve. Amery noted wryly that in Churchill's report to the cabinet he did not trouble to mention his visit to Canada.

But the prime minister's mood was exultant, as well it might be. He had achieved a personal triumph in the United States, such as no other Englishman could have matched. He told the King that after many months of walking out, Britain and America were at last married. If there was no doubt that henceforward Britain would be junior partner in the Atlantic alliance, Churchill had imposed his greatness on the American people, in a fashion that would do much service to his country in the years ahead.

There were important nuances about this first visit, however. First, at a time when most of the decision-makers of both Britain and the US still thought it likely that Russia would be defeated, they failed to perceive the extent to which the war against Hitler would be dominated by the struggle in the East. At the turn of 1941–42, Roosevelt and Churchill in Washington supposed that they were shaping strategy for the destruction of Nazism. They had no inkling of the degree to which Stalin's nation would prove the most potent element in achieving this. Though the USA was by far the strongest global force in the Grand Alliance, Russia mobilised raw military power more effectively than either Western partner would prove able to do.

As for Anglo–American relations, Charles Wilson wrote of Churchill: 'He wanted to show the President how to run the war, and it has not quite worked out like that.' Eden told the cabinet: 'There is bound to be difficulty in practice in harmonizing day-to-day Anglo–Russian co-operation with Anglo–American co-operation. Soviet policy is amoral: United States policy is exaggeratedly moral, at least where non-American interests are concerned.' Despite the success of Churchill's Washington visit, it would be mistaken to suppose that all Americans succumbed to the magic of his personality. His great line to Congress, 'What kind of people do they think we are?', prompted widespread editorialising. But in the weeks that followed by no means all of this was favourable to Britain. The *Denver*

Post said sourly: 'There is one lesson the United States should learn from England. That is to put our own interests ahead of those of everybody else.' The *Chicago Tribune*'s attitude was predictably rancid: 'It is unfortunate that Mr Roosevelt has had the example of Mr Churchill constantly before him as a guide. Mr Churchill is a man of very great capacity in many directions, but as a military strategist he has an almost unbroken record of disappointments and failures.'

Some of the foremost personalities at *Arcadia* found each other unsympathetic. Henry Morgenthau, the Treasury Secretary, thought Max Beaverbrook cocky to the point of impertinence. In the absence of the newly appointed Alan Brooke, the British chiefs of staff made a weak team. The Americans liked Charles Portal, but the airman rarely imposed himself. Admiral Dudley Pound seemed a cipher, whose fading health disqualified him from meaningful participation. The Americans were too polite to allude in the visitors' presence to Britain's resounding military failures, but these were never far from their minds when they discerned extravagant assertiveness in Churchill or his companions. They had respect for the Royal Navy and RAF, but scarcely any for the British Army. Scepticism about British military competence would persist throughout the war in the upper reaches of the US Army, colouring its chiefs' attitudes in every strategic debate.

As for the president and the prime minister, Hopkins said: 'There was no question but that [Roosevelt] grew genuinely to like Churchill.' This seems at best half-true. Their political convictions were far, far apart. For all Franklin Roosevelt's irrepressible bonhomie, excessive doses of Churchill palled on him. A joke did the rounds in Washington, and indeed featured in *Time* magazine, that the first question the president asked Harry Hopkins on his return from Britain in February 1941 was: 'Who writes Churchill's speeches for him?' The prime minister sought to display courtesy by pushing the president's wheelchair each evening from the drawing room to the lift. Yet it seems plausible that this gesture was misjudged, that it merely emphasised the contrast between the host's enforced immobility and the guest's exuberant energy. British witnesses at the White

House observed Churchill striving to overcome his own irrepressible instinct to talk, and instead to listen to the president. It is hard to believe that Roosevelt's profound vanity was much massaged by Churchill's presence in his home.

The president's respect for the British prime minister's abilities was not in doubt, any more than was his commitment to the alliance to defeat Germany and Japan. But he was a much cooler man than Churchill. 'Even those closest to Roosevelt,' wrote Joseph Lash, who knew him well, 'were always asking, "What does he really think? What does he really feel?"' At no time did Roosevelt perceive himself engaged with the prime minister in a matched partnership. He was no mere leader of a government, but a head of state, who wrote to monarchs as equals. Churchill felt no deep sense of obligation to America for its provision of supplies. In his eyes, Britain for more than two years had played the nobler part, pouring forth blood and enduring bombardment in a lone struggle for freedom. Roosevelt had scant patience with such pretensions. He paid only lip service to Britain's claims on the collective gratitude of the democracies. Churchill's nation was now mortgaged to the hilt to the US. Sooner or later, the president had every intention of exercising his power as holder of his ally's title deeds.

Roosevelt had visited Britain several times as a young man, but never revealed much liking for the country. As president he repeatedly rejected invitations to go there. He perceived hypocrisy in its pretensions as a bastion of democracy and freedom while it sustained a huge empire of subject peoples denied democratic representation. Cooperation with Churchill's nation was essential to the defeat of Hitler. Thereafter, in the words of Michael Howard, Roosevelt 'proposed to reshape the world in accordance with American concepts of morality, not British concepts of realpolitik'. Roosevelt's acquaintance with foreign parts had been confined to gilded European holidays with his millionaire father, and a 1918 battlefield tour. He nonetheless had a boundless appetite to alter the world. Eden was appalled when he later heard the president expound a vision of Europe's future: 'The academic yet sweeping opinions which he built . . . were alarming in their cheerful fecklessness. He seemed to see himself disposing of the fate of many lands, allied no less than enemy.' The president mentioned, *inter alia*, a liking for the notion that the French colonial port of Dakar should become a US naval base. His hubris shocked not only the British, but also such wise Americans as Harriman.

Eden claimed that Churchill regarded Roosevelt with almost religious awe. Yet the Foreign Secretary almost certainly misread as credulity Churchill's supremely prudent recognition of necessity. In no aspect of his war leadership did the prime minister exercise a more steely self-discipline than in this relationship. 'My whole system is founded on friendship with Roosevelt,' he told Eden later. He knew that without the president's goodwill, Britain was almost impotent. He could not afford not to revere, love and cherish the president of the United States, living embodiment of American might. He dismissed doubts and reservations to the farthest recesses of his mind. For the rest of the war he sought to bind himself to Roosevelt in an intimacy from which the president often flinched. Churchill was determined upon marriage; Roosevelt acknowledged the necessity for a ring, but was determined to maintain separate beds, friends and bank accounts. The prospect of ultimate divorce, once the war was won, held no terrors for him.

The second strand in that first alliance conference was the attitude of the US chiefs of staff. They were appalled by the spectacle of Britain's prime minister establishing himself for weeks on end at the White House, engaged in strategic discussions with the president from which they were often absent. Marshall, an intensely moral man, deplored casual intermingling of professional and social intercourse – so much so that he always refused invitations to stay at Hyde Park, the Roosevelt estate on the Hudson River in upstate New York. So strict was his personal austerity that when he added a chicken run to his quarters at Fort Myer, he insisted upon paying personally for the materials used in its construction. Unfamiliar with the promiscuity of Churchill's conversation, he resented every moment of the visitor's intimacies with Roosevelt. 'The British,' wrote

Henry Stimson, 'are evidently taking advantage of the president's well-known shortcomings in ordinary administrative methods.' Hopkins cautioned Roosevelt against agreeing military decisions in the absence of Marshall. Yet, to the chief of the army's fury, Roosevelt accepted Churchill's proposal that if the Philippines fell, residual American forces should be redeployed to Singapore.

Marshall was even more hostile than Roosevelt to British imperial pretensions. And while from the outset the president's imagination was seized by the notion of a North African landing, Marshall's was not. He and his colleagues were irked by a perceived British assumption that they could now draw on US manpower and weapons 'as if these had been swept into a common pool for campaigns tailored to suit the interests and convenience of Great Britain', in the words of Marshall's biographer. 'From the British standpoint it was easy to conclude that a course of action favorable to their national interest was simply good strategic sense and that failure of the Americans to agree showed inexperience, immaturity and bad manners.' From the first day of the war, Marshall was bent upon engaging the Germans in north-west Europe at the earliest possible date, and avoiding entanglement in British 'sideshows'.

The only British officer with whom the chief of the army forged a close relationship was Dill. Ironically, the discarded CIGS now became a significant figure in the Anglo–American partnership. By an inspired stroke, when Churchill went home he left behind in Washington a somewhat reluctant Dill, who was shortly afterwards appointed chief of the British military mission. Between the embassy and the mission – housed in the US Public Health Building on Constitution Avenue – there were soon nine thousand British uniformed and civilian personnel in Washington. Dill also became British representative on the newly created Combined Chiefs of Staff Committee when it met in Washington in the absence of Pound, Brooke and Portal. Halifax, as ambassador, achieved no intimacy with the Americans, and it was never plausible that he should do so. Dill was understandably bemused by his new appointment: 'It is odd that Winston should want me to represent him here when he clearly was glad of an excuse to get me out of the CIGS job.' But he became Marshall's confidant, a sensitive interpreter of the two nations' military aspirations. In the years that followed Dill made a notable contribution to the Grand Alliance, calming transatlantic storms and explaining rival viewpoints. He prospered as a diplomat where he had failed as a director of strategy.

Churchill's first visit to Washington was thus a public triumph, a less assured private one. But he was wise to bask while he could in the sunshine of the new American relationship. Back at home, many troubles awaited him. History perceives 1940, when Britain stood alone, as the pivotal year for the nation's survival. Yet 1942 would prove the most torrid phase of Churchill's war premiership. The British people, so staunch amid the threat of invasion, two years later showed themselves weary and fractious. Amid the reality of crushing defeats, they tired of promises of prospective victories. In peace or war, the patience of democracies is seldom great. That of Britain had been progressively eroded by bombardment, privation and battle-field humiliation. In the press, the Commons and on the streets of Britain, Churchill now faced criticism more bitter and sustained than he had known since assuming office.

NINE

'The Valley of Humiliation'

Throughout history, societies have enthused about victorious over-seas conflicts, and recoiled from unsuccessful ones. The US declarations of war represented the fulfilment of all Churchill's hopes since May 1940. Yet 1942 proved, until its last weeks, the most unhappy year of his premiership. It was not only that Britain suffered a further succession of defeats. It was that public confidence in the prime minister's leadership waned in a fashion unthinkable during the Battle of Britain. Even if it remained improbable that he would be driven from office, he was beset by critics who questioned his judgement and sought to constrain his powers. Between his return from the United States in late January and the battle of Alamein in November, there were no moments of glory, and almost unremitting bad news. The British Empire suffered the heaviest blows in its history, which only the American alliance rendered endurable.

On the train back to London after his flying-boat landed from Washington, Churchill indulged a last flicker of complacency. He told his doctor: 'I have done a good job of work with the President . . . I am sure, Charles, the House will be pleased with what I have to tell them.' A glance at the day's newspapers disabused him. He laid down the *Manchester Guardian* without enthusiasm. 'There seems to be plenty of snarling,' he said. In the days that followed, ill tidings crowded forward. Naval losses in the Mediterranean meant that in the forthcoming months Britain could deploy no battle fleet from Alexandria. Amid reports from Malaya that the British Army was falling back routed upon Singapore, Churchill enquired whether there was a case for writing off 'the fortress', diverting reinforcements and aircraft elsewhere. His message was passed in error to the Australian representative to the war cabinet, Sir Earle Page – a man 'with the mentality of a greengrocer', in Brooke's scornful phrase – who in turn forwarded it to Canberra. Prime minister John Curtin responded with an indignant cable to Churchill, asserting that to abandon Singapore would be 'an inexcusable betrayal'.

Relations between the Australian government and London, never cordial, entered a new phase of acrimony. Churchill valued Australia's fighting men, but was contemptuous of its weak Labor government. He contrasted Australian pusillanimity – what would now be called 'whingeing' – unfavourably with the staunchness of New Zealand. Throughout the war he treated all the self-governing dominions as subject colonies, mere sources of manpower. Dominion politicians visiting London were accorded public courtesy, private indifference. Robert Menzies, the former Australian prime minister who was now opposition leader, commanded respect, but even Menzies had been moved to protest back in 1940, when his government heard of the Dakar operation only on reading about it in the press. The sole imperial figure to enjoy Churchill's confidence was Field Marshal Jan Smuts, South Africa's prime minister, a friend since the end of the Boer War. It was Smuts who said: 'We should thank God for Hitler. He has brought us back to a realization of brute facts . . . He has, in fact, taken the lid off Hell, and we have all looked into it.'

Churchill's impatience with the dominions was understandable. Their governments – with the notable exception of New Zealand – often displayed a parochialism irksome to a British prime minister directing a global struggle for survival. Neither Canada nor Australia, for instance, introduced universal conscription for overseas service until the last stages of the conflict. But Churchill's condescension towards Canberra and Ottawa was no more likely to please sensitive colonial governments than his absolute dismissal of Indian opinion won friends in the subcontinent. 'The PM is not really interested in Mackenzie King,' wrote Charles Wilson about Canada's prime minister. 'He takes him for granted.'

The *New Statesman* complained: 'Mr Churchill has been unwilling to give so much as a gracious word to win the support of India and Burma.' The prime minister's later reluctance to release scarce shipping to relieve the Bengal famine, which killed some three million people, appalled both the viceroy and Amery, Secretary of State for India. When Amery wished to make a broadcast to explain British policy, the prime minister vetoed it, saying that such action 'is making too much of the famine and sounding apologetic'. More than any other aspect of his wartime behaviour, such high-handedness reflected the nineteenth-century imperial vision of Churchill's youth. As the Far East situation deteriorated, for four months there seemed a real possibility that Australia would be invaded. The Canberra government turned openly to the US for protection, in default of reassurance backed by reinforcements which the threadbare 'mother country' could not provide.

On 27 January, amid increasing parliamentary criticism, Churchill faced the Commons. 'It is because things have gone badly, and worse is to come, that I demand a Vote of Confidence,' he said. This was a deliberate device, to force his critics to show their hands, or flinch. Having won the subsequent division by a majority of 464 to one, he walked beaming through the throng in the central lobby on the arm of Clementine, who had come to lend support. But he knew that this outcome represented no ending of his troubles. He was unwell, nagged by a cold he could not shake off. On 9 February Eden's private secretary Oliver Harvey told his chief that he should be prepared to take over the premiership, and noted in his diary: 'I think he is.' Beyond the risks inherent in Churchill's wartime travels, the health of a man of sixty-seven, labouring under huge strains, might collapse at any time. Such a contingency was never far from his colleagues' consciousness.

Churchill signalled Wavell, newly appointed as Anglo-American supreme commander in the Far East, urging that when the Russians on the eastern front and Americans on Luzon in the Philippines were fighting so staunchly, it was essential that the army in Malaya should be seen to give of its best: 'The whole reputation of our country and our race is involved.' Two days later, on 11 February, in response to continuing domestic criticism of his government and Beaverbrook's desire to resign, he offered Stafford Cripps, whom he despised but who had a large popular following, the ministry of supply. Churchill grumbled about Cripps's demand to sit in the war cabinet: 'Lots of people want to. You could fill the Albert Hall with people who want to be in the War Cabinet.' Denied a seat, Cripps declined office. The prime minister fumed amid his frustrations. Brooke, less than two months in his job as CIGS, told Dalton at dinner on 10 February: 'Sometimes . . . the PM is just like a child who has lost his temper. It is very painful and no progress can be made with the business.'

There was a new shock on 12 February. The German battlecruisers *Scharnhorst* and *Gneisenau* left Brest and steamed at full speed up the English Channel, assisted by fog. Churchill's secretary Elizabeth Layton entered the cabinet room at 3 p.m. to take dictation, where she found the prime minister 'striding up and down, all on edge. He dictated four telegrams like a whirlwind, and then phoned this and phoned that. I wondered if I should go, and once did slip out, but was recalled. Did another telegram, he marched up and down, talking to himself, a mass of compressed energy. Presently he sat down and said, "There's a bloody great battle going on out there." I said, "Do you think we might get them?" He said, "Don't know. We winged 'em, but they aren't dead yet."' The navy did not 'get them'. The German squadron reached Wilhelmshaven. Ultra informed Churchill that the ships had been severely damaged by mines on the last stage of their passage, but this was small comfort, and could not be revealed because of its source. The British people saw only that the Royal Navy and RAF were unable to stop Hitler's capital ships passing with impunity through British home waters.

Headlines screamed, the public was affronted. The *Daily Mirror* asked on 14 February: 'Is it any longer true that we trust the Prime Minister, but do not trust his Government?' The *News Chronicle* likewise: 'Have we not been hypnotised by Mr Churchill's personality . . . into acquiescence in an inefficient war direction?' The *Daily Mail* wrote that there were two Churchills: '1. The Inspirer of the Nation. 2. The Controller of the War.' The British people were perplexed by the second Churchill, who claimed 'that it was the duty of Parliament and Press to maintain the Government with the implication that any weakening of his own position would be a weakening of its cause'. The *Mail* rejected this view: 'No man is indispensable.' Sir William Beveridge wrote a major article for *The Times*, urging the creation of a 'proper' war cabinet of ministers without portfolios. A Glasgow secretary, Pam Ashford, wrote on 5 March: 'Defeatism is in the air, and . . . I feel it too.' When the opinion-monitoring group Mass-Observation quizzed its observers about the prime minister, they were startled by the vehemence of criticism of his conduct as warlord. A London clerk said: 'I think it is time he went. After all, the only connection in which one thinks of Churchill now is with regard to high strategy, whatever that may be. High strategy stinks to high heaven . . . This view I have confirmed with quite a few people. His speeches are no longer listened to.'

If this attitude was untypically strident, there was a yearning at every level of British society for a defence supremo who could deliver battlefield success, as the prime minister seemed unable to do. Many people sought a new deliverer, an aspiration no less strongly felt because it was unrealistic, and unsupported by identification of an appropriate candidate. There was no appetite to change national leaders, but much enthusiasm for delegating Churchill's military powers. The prime minister said to his old friend Violet Bonham Carter: 'I'm fed up . . . I feel very biteful and spiteful when people attack me.' He was constantly urged to add talent to his cabinet, 'But where is the galaxy? I can't get the victories. It's the victories that are so hard to get.' In a fit of pique about press savaging of the government, information minister Brendan Bracken told parliamentary lobby correspondents that it would be their fault if Britain lost the war.

On 15 February, Singapore surrendered. This time there was no Dunkirk, no miraculous escape for the garrison. Almost twice as many imperial troops fell into captivity as in France in 1940. Jock Colville, temporarily removed from Downing Street to train in South Africa as a fighter pilot, heard Churchill's broadcast addressing the disaster. He was deeply moved: 'The nature of his words and the unaccustomed speed and emotion with which he spoke convinced me that he was sorely pressed by critics and opponents at home. All the majesty of his oratory was there, but also a new note of appeal, lacking the usual confidence of support ... There was something about his voice and delivery which made me shiver.' The broadcast was much less well received than most of Churchill's performances. In private, the prime minister was angry and depressed. 'We have so many men in Singapore, so many men,' he lamented. 'They should have done better.' At a Pacific War Council meeting he said of the Japanese: 'They moved quicker and ate less than our men.'

He suggested to his naval aide, Captain Richard Pim, that this might be the moment for him to surrender the premiership. Pim said: 'But my God, sir, you cannot do that.' It is unlikely that Churchill seriously considered resignation, but his despair was real enough. What use was it, that he himself displayed a warrior's spirit before the world, if those who fought in Britain's name showed themselves incapable of matching his rhetoric? In Norway, France, Greece, Crete, Libya and now Malaya, the British had been beaten again and again. Alan Brooke wrote in his diary: 'If the army cannot fight better than it is doing at the present, we shall deserve to lose our Empire.'

Some blame attached to Wavell, not for failing to achieve victory, but for declining to avow the inevitability of Singapore's fall, and to make an uncompromising recommendation to halt reinforcements and evacuate every possible man. Brooke had done exactly this in France in June 1940. The British 18th Division landed at Singapore on 29 January 1942, by which date there was no prospect of saving the campaign. Almost the entire army fell into captivity a fortnight later. It remains hard to understand why Churchill deluded himself that Singapore could be held. Every soldier knew that its fate must be decided in southern Malaya, that the island in isolation was indefensible, and the chiefs of staff made this plain to the prime minister on 21 January. It was regrettable that commanders on the spot did not adopt a more trenchant tone. While Wavell's signals about Malaya were unfailingly pessimistic, they did not explicitly acknowledge that Singapore's demise was inevitable until it was too late to save any portion of its garrison. It was true that he exercised his short-lived command amid draconian signals from Churchill, demanding a last-man, last-round defence. But whereas it should have been possible to hold Crete, Singapore was doomed.

British and imperial forces in Malaya were ill-trained, ill-equipped, and poorly led at every level. They faced an enemy who commanded the air, but two years later German and Japanese soldiers displayed extraordinary resilience in the face of vastly stronger air forces than the Luftwaffe deployed in Greece, the Japanese in Malaya. It was the absence of any scintilla of heroic endeavour, any evidence of last-ditch sacrifice of the kind with which British armies through the centuries had so often redeemed the pain of defeats, that shocked Churchill. In Malaya there was no legend to match that of Sir John Moore's retreat to Corunna in the Napoleonic wars, of Rorke's Drift in Zululand, of the defence of Mafeking and Ladysmith in the Boer War. The Americans forged a propaganda epic, however spurious, out of their defence of the Bataan peninsula between December 1941 and April 1942. The British salvaged nothing comparable from South-East Asia. Their soldiers gave up pitifully easily. *The Times* of 16 February offered its readers crumbs of comfort for Singapore: 'The sacrifice and the suffering and the incomparable gallantry of the defence were not wholly in vain.' This was nonsense. There was only abject defeat, surrender to numerically inferior enemies who had proved themselves better and braver soldiers. It is brutal, but seems valid, to suggest that Malaya might have been defended with greater determination had British, Indian and Australian soldiers known the fate that awaited them in Japanese captivity.

Who could wonder that Churchill should be plunged into despair? 'At the back of his mind and unconsciously, I believe,' wrote Oliver Harvey shrewdly, 'the PM is jealous of Stalin and the successes of his armies.' Even if American aid enabled Britain to survive the war, how could the nation hold up its head in the world, be seen to have made a worthy contribution to victory, if the British Army covered itself with shame whenever exposed to a battlefield? Lack of shipping remained a massive constraint on deployments. John Kennedy wrote: 'We have masses of reinforcements we cannot move.' At any one moment of 1942, 2,000 British and American merchantmen were afloat on the Atlantic shuttle, three or four hundred of them vulnerable to U-boat attack. In peacetime, a cargo ship took an average thirty-nine days to complete a round trip between Europe and North America. Now, the same rotation took eighty-six days, with forty-three spent in port instead of a peacetime fourteen, mostly waiting for convoys. Dill cabled the chiefs of staff from Washington, saying that this seemed a time for the Allies to focus on essentials: security of the British Isles and United States, and preventing a junction of German and Japanese forces on the Indian Ocean: 'These simple rules might help us to stick to things that matter in these difficult days.' Yet, as so often with British generals' strategic visions, this one was entirely negative.

Churchill told the Commons on 24 February: 'The House must face the blunt and brutal fact that if, having entered a war yourself unprepared, you are struggling for life with two well-armed countries, one of them possessing the most powerful military machine in the world, and then, at the moment when you are in full grapple, a third major antagonist with far larger military forces than you possess suddenly springs upon your comparatively undefended back, obviously your task is heavy and your immediate experiences will be disagreeable.' Many MPs nonetheless voiced discontent. James Griffiths, Labour Member for the Welsh mining constituency of Llanelli, said that at the time of Dunkirk people had responded to the call. By contrast, 'We believe that now there is a feeling of disquiet in the nation. We ought not to resent it.' Commander Sir Archibald Southby, Epsom, spoke of the German 'Channel dash' and the fall of Singapore as two events which 'shook not only the Government but the British Empire to its foundations. Nay, it would be fair to say that they influenced opinion throughout the world. They produced the most unfortunate reverberations in the United States of America just at a time when harmony and understanding between the two nations was of paramount importance.'

Sir George Schuster, Walsall, said he thought the public wanted to feel that it was being told the truth, and was beginning to doubt this. People had been assured that in Libya the British Army was now meeting the enemy on equal terms. Then, after Rommel's dramatic comeback, they heard that the Germans had a better anti-tank gun, that our guns were inadequate to pierce enemy armour. 'That was a shock to public opinion. They felt they had been misled.' He also suggested that the public wanted to see fewer civilians 'getting away with it' – escaping their share of sacrifice to the war effort – and more discipline in factories.

During lunch at Buckingham Palace that day, Churchill told the King that Burma, Ceylon, Calcutta, Madras and parts of Australia might well be lost. The defence of Burma had already begun badly. Brooke noted with his customary spleen that some politicians allowed the bad news to show. 'This process does not make Cabinet Ministers any more attractive,' he wrote to a friend. 'But Winston is a marvel. I cannot imagine how he sticks it.' Clementine Churchill wrote to Harry Hopkins: 'We are indeed walking through the Valley of Humiliation.'

In consequence of the disasters on the battlefield, Churchill was obliged to make changes in his government, more painful and embarrassing than some historians have acknowledged. The only agreeable aspect of the reshuffle was the sacking of Lord Hankey, whose rancour had become intolerable. Hankey thereafter became prominent among Churchill's critics, a would-be conspirator against his continuance in office. Beaverbrook finally resigned. Stafford Cripps was given his seat in the war cabinet, as Lord Privy Seal and Leader of the Commons. For the prime minister this was a bitter pill. It was a measure of the weakness of his position that he accepted Cripps. The two men, wrote Eden wonderingly, had 'always been as distant as a lion and an okapi'. Churchill is alleged to have said of Libya: 'There are miles and miles of nothing but arid austerity. How Cripps would like it!'

Cripps was fifty-two, a product of Winchester and New College Oxford, and nephew of the socialist intellectual Beatrice Webb. He became first a research chemist, then a successful commercial barrister. A pacifist in World War I, he was elected as a Labour MP in 1931 and served briefly in Ramsay MacDonald's government before refusing to join his coalition. A vegetarian and teetotaller, in the 1930s he became converted to Marxism, an uncritical enthusiast for the Soviet Union whose name was often coupled with that of Aneurin Bevan. In 1939 he was expelled from the parliamentary Labour Party after differences with Attlee. When he was in Moscow between 1940 and 1942, Churchill was not displeased to note that Stalin showed much less enthusiasm for the ambassador, and for his company, than his British admirer displayed for the Soviet leader.

In many respects a foolish man, Cripps nonetheless became temporarily an important one in 1942. A fine broadcaster, his commitment both to the Soviet Union and to a socialist post-war Britain won him a large popular following. He spoke passionately, and without irony, of Russian workers 'fighting to keep their country free', and of the alliance between 'the free workers of England, America and Russia'. Amid the mood of the times such sentiments struck a powerful chord, contrasting with the stubborn conservatism of many other MPs – and of the prime minister. In a poll that invited voters to express a preference as prime minister if some misfortune befell Churchill, 37 per cent of respondents named Eden, but 36 per cent opted for Cripps.

Churchill was well aware that his new minister aspired to the premiership. For most of 1942 he felt obliged to treat Cripps as a potential threat to his authority. Amid so many misfortunes, some surprising people supported the Lord Privy Seal's ambitions. Private conclaves of MPs, editors, generals and admirals discussed Churchill and his government in the most brutal terms. John Kennedy dined at Claridge's on 5 March 1942 with Sir Archie Rowlands of the ministry of aircraft production and John Skelton, news editor of the *Daily Telegraph*: 'The talk was very much about Winston and very critical. It was felt that Winston was finished, that he had played his last card in reforming the government. S[kelton] is very hostile to Winston and thinks Cripps should be put in his place. He feels that we shall lose the whole Empire soon and be driven back on G.B. It is easy to make a case for this.' Averell Harriman wrote to Roosevelt on 6 March:

Although the British are keeping a stiff upper lip, the surrender of their troops at Singapore has shattered confidence to the core – even in themselves but, more particularly, in their leaders. They don't intend to take it lying down and I am satisfied we will see the rebirth of greater determination. At the moment, however, they can't see the end to defeats. Unfortunately Singapore shook the Prime Minister himself to such an extent that he has not been able to stand up to this adversity with his old vigor. A number of astute people, both friends and opponents, feel it is only a question of a few months before his Government falls. I cannot accept this view. He has been very tired but is better in the last day or two. I believe he will come back with renewed strength, particularly when the tone of the war improves.

The Battle of the Atlantic had taken a serious turn for the worse. In January the German navy introduced a fourth rotor into its Enigma ciphering machines. This refinement defied British codebreakers through the bloody year of convoying that followed. Charles Wilson, Churchill's doctor, noticed that the prime minister carried in his head every statistical detail of Atlantic sinkings. Nonetheless, Wilson wrote, 'he is always careful to consume his own smoke; nothing he says could discourage anyone . . . I wish to God I could put out the fires that seem to be consuming him.' Mary Churchill noted in her diary that her father was 'saddened – appalled by events . . . . He is desperately taxed.' Cadogan wrote likewise: 'Poor old P.M. in a sour mood and a bad way.'

On 6 March, Rangoon was abandoned. Next day, Churchill wrote to Roosevelt urging that the Western Allies should concede Russian demands for recognition of their 1941 frontiers – which Britain had staunchly opposed the previous year. The Americans demurred, but the prime minister's change of attitude reflected intensified awareness of the Allies' vulnerability. He was now willing to adopt the most unwelcome expedients if these might marginally strengthen Russia's resolve. Amid alarm that Stalin might be driven to parley with Hitler, eastern Poland became expendable. In the same spirit,

Churchill cabled Moscow promising that if the Germans employed poison gas on the eastern front, as some feared was imminent, the British would retaliate as if such a weapon had been used against themselves. Stalin promptly asked for technical information about both British chemical weapons and counter-measures against them. There is no evidence that the former was forthcoming, but the British strove by every means to convince the Russians of their commitment as allies. Western fears that Stalin might seek a separate peace persisted for many months.

Beyond the great issues on Churchill's desk, he was obliged to address myriad lesser ones. He warned about the risk of a possible German commando raid, launched from a U-boat, to kidnap the Duke of Windsor, now serving as governor-general of the Bahamas. The Nazis, said the prime minister, might be able to exploit the former king to their advantage. Having inspired the creation of the Parachute Regiment, which carried out its first successful operation against a German radar station at Bruneval on France's northern coast on 28 February, Churchill pressed for the expansion of airborne forces on the largest possible scale. Four Victoria Crosses were awarded for the Royal Navy's 28 March attack on the floating dock at Saint-Nazaire. This generous issue of decorations was designed to make the survivors feel better about losses – 500 men killed, wounded or captured. Propaganda made much of Saint-Nazaire. The public was assured that the Germans had suffered heavily, though in reality their casualties were many fewer than those of the raiders. Meanwhile, ministers solicited Churchill about appointments, honours, administrative issues. Such nugatory matters were hard to address when the Empire was crumbling.

Churchill's obsession with capital ships persisted even in the third year of the war. He asserted that the destruction of the 42,000-ton *Tirpitz*, sister ship of the *Bismarck*, anchored in a Norwegian fjord where it posed a permanent threat to Arctic convoys, would be worth the loss of a hundred aircraft and 500 men. On 9 March, twelve Fairey Albacores of the Fleet Air Arm attacked the German behemoth, without success. Churchill asked the First Sea Lord 'how it was that 12 of our machines managed to get no hits as compared with the extraordinary efficiency of the Japanese attack on *Prince of Wales* and *Repulse*?' How not, indeed? Though the RAF made an important contribution to interdicting Rommel's Mediterranean supply line in 1942, the RAF and Fleet Air Arm's record of achievement in attacks upon enemy surface ships remained relatively poor until the last months of the war. Churchill thought so, minuting Pound in the following year that it seemed 'a pregnant fact' that the Fleet Air Arm had suffered only thirty fatalities out of a strength of 45,000 men in the three months to the end of April. The 1940 attack on Taranto and the 1941 crippling of the *Bismarck* were the only really impressive British naval air operations of the war.

During the winter of 1941–42, Churchill had become unhappily conscious of the failure of British 'precision bombing' of Germany. He was party to the critical change of policy which took place in consequence, largely inspired by his scientific adviser. Lord Cherwell's intervention about bombing was his most influential of the war. It was a member of his Cabinet Statistical Office staff, an official named David Butt, who produced a devastating report based on a study of British bombers' aiming-point photographs. This showed that only a small proportion of aircraft were achieving hits within miles, rather than yards, of their targets. Cherwell convinced the prime minister, who was shocked by Butt's report, that there must be a complete change of tactics. Since, under average weather conditions, RAF night raiders were incapable of dropping an acceptable proportion of bombs on designated industrial objectives, British aircraft must henceforward instead address the smallest aiming points they were capable of identifying: cities. They might thus fulfil the twin objectives of destroying plant and 'dehousing' workers, to use Cherwell's ingenuous phrase. No one in Whitehall explicitly acknowledged that the RAF was thus to undertake the wholesale killing of civilians. But nor did they doubt that this would be the consequence, though British propaganda for the rest of the war shrouded such ugly reality in obfuscation, not least from the aircrew conducting bomber operations at such hazard to themselves.

Churchill always considered himself a realist about the horrors and imperatives of war. Yet as recently as 1937 he had proclaimed his opposition to air attacks upon non-combatants, during a Commons debate on air-raid precautions: 'I believe,' he said, 'that if one side in an equal war endeavours to cow and kill the civil population, and the other attacks steadily the military objectives . . . victory will come to the side . . . which avoids the horror of making war on the helpless and weak.' Now, however, after thirty months of engagement with an enemy who was prospering mightily by waging war without scruple, Churchill accepted a different view. Bomber Command had failed as a rapier. Instead, it must become a blunt instrument. Operational necessity was deemed to make it essential to set aside moral inhibitions. For many months, indeed years, ahead, bombing represented the only means of carrying Britain's war to Germany. The prime minister approved Cherwell's new policy.

On 22 February 1942, Air Chief Marshal Sir Arthur Harris became C-in-C of Bomber Command. Contrary to popular myth, Harris was not the originator of 'area bombing'. But he set about implementing the concept with a single-minded fervour which has caused his name to be inextricably linked with it ever since. The first significant event of Harris's tenure of command was a raid on the Renault truck plant in the Paris suburb of Billancourt. The war cabinet hoped that this would boost French morale, which seemed unlikely when it emerged that more than 400 civilians had been killed. On 28 March, 134 aircraft carried out a major attack upon the old German Hanse town of Lübeck. The coastal target was chosen chiefly because it was easy for crews to find. The closely packed medieval centre was, in Harris's contemptuous words, 'built more like a fire-lighter than a human habitation'. The raid left much of Lübeck in flames, and was judged an overwhelming success. Four successive attacks on the port of Rostock in late April achieved similar dramatic results, causing Goebbels to write hysterically in his diary: 'Community life in Rostock is almost at an end.' On 30 May, Harris staged an extraordinary *coup de théâtre*. Enlisting the aid of training and Coastal Command aircraft

247

he dispatched 1,046 bombers against the great city of Cologne, inflicting massive damage.

The chief merit of the 'Thousand Raid', together with others that followed against Essen and Bremen, lay less in the injury they inflicted upon the Third Reich – a small fraction of that achieved in 1944–45 – than in the public impression of Britain striking back, albeit in a fashion which rendered the squeamish uncomfortable. Some 474 Germans died in the 'Thousand Raid' on Cologne, but on 2 June the *New York Times* claimed that the death toll was 20,000. Churchill cabled Roosevelt: 'I hope you were impressed with our mass air attack on Cologne. There is plenty more to come.'

Throughout 1942 and 1943, British propaganda waxed lyrical about the achievements of the bomber offensive. Churchill dispatched a stream of messages to Stalin, emphasising the devastation achieved by the RAF. The British people were not, on the whole, strident in yearning for revenge upon Germany's civilian population. But many sometimes succumbed to the sensations of Londoner Vere Hodgson, who wrote: 'As I lay in bed the other night I heard the deep purr of our bombers winging their way to Hamburg . . . This is a comfortable feeling. I turned lazily in bed and glowed at the thought, going back in my mind to those awful months when to hear noise overhead was to know that the Germans were going to pour death and destruction on us . . . One cannot help feeling that it is good for the Germans to know what it feels like. Perhaps they won't put the machine in motion again so light-heartedly.'

Later in the war, when great Allied armies took the field, Churchill's enthusiasm for bombing ebbed. But in 1942 he enthused about the strategic offensive because he had nothing else. Again contrary to popular delusion, he never found Sir Arthur Harris a soulmate. The airman sometimes dined at Chequers, because his headquarters at High Wycombe was conveniently close. But Desmond Morton was among those who believed that the prime minister thought Harris an impressive leader of air forces, but an unsympathetic personality. Churchill said of Bomber Command's C-in-C after the war: 'a considerable commander – but there was a certain coarseness about him'. In the bad times, however – and 1942 was a very bad time – he recognised Harris as a man of steel, at a time when many other commanders bent and snapped under the responsibilities with which he entrusted them.

From the outset, area bombing incurred criticism on both strategic and moral grounds, both inside and outside Parliament. Clement Attlee, leader of the Labour Party and deputy prime minister, was a persistent private critic, on both moral and pragmatic grounds. He stressed the value of bombers in support of ground and naval operations. In the public domain, the *New Statesman* argued that it was perverse to heap praise on the fortitude of the civilian population of Malta in enduring Axis air attack, without perceiving the lesson for Britain's own forces attacking Germany. 'The disaster of this policy is not only that it is futile,' the distinguished scientist Professor A.V. Hill, MP for Cambridge University, told the House of Commons, 'but that it is extremely wasteful, and will become increasingly wasteful as time goes on.' But Hill's words reflected only a modest minority opinion.

There was a powerful case for accepting the necessity for area bombing. A major British industrial commitment was made to creating a massive force of heavy aircraft. This attained fulfilment only in the very different strategic circumstances of 1944–45. The most pertinent criticism of 1942–43 bombing policy was that the airmen's fervour to demonstrate that their service could make a decisive independent impact on the war caused them to resist, to the point of obsession, calls for diversions of heavy aircraft to other purposes, above all the Battle of the Atlantic. John Kennedy wrote in May 1942 that the bomber offensive 'can be implemented only at severe cost to our command of the sea and our military operations on land. I have just been looking at an old paper of [Winston's], written in Sept.1940, which begins "the Navy can lose us the war, but only the Air Force can win it . . . " I am convinced that events will prove this to have been a profound delusion.'

Cherwell supported Harris in resisting calls for the reinforcement of Coastal Command, but they were both surely wrong. Evidence is strong that even a few extra squadrons could have achieved more in fighting the U-boats, a deadly menace well into 1943, than they did over Germany in the same period. But the navy made its case without much skill or subtlety. Admiral Sir John Tovey, C-in-C Home Fleet, denounced the bomber offensive as 'a luxury, not necessity'. His words infuriated the prime minister, who was also irked by Tovey's reluctance to hazard his ships within reach of Norwegian-based German air power. He described Tovey as 'a stubborn and obstinate man', and was delighted when in May 1943 he was replaced by the supposedly more aggressive Sir Bruce Fraser. The admirals' difficulty was that while their service's function of holding open the sea routes to the US, Russia, Malta, Egypt and India was indispensable, it was also defensive. As Churchill said, the fleet was responsible for saving Britain from losing the war, but its ships could not win it. The Admiralty damaged its own case by insisting that the RAF lavish immense effort, and accept heavy casualties, bombing the impregnable U-boat pens of north-west France, and patrolling the Bay of Biscay. The sailors would have done better to emphasise the issue of direct air cover for the Atlantic convoy routes, which drastically impeded the operations of German submarines.

Churchill thought better of the Royal Navy as a fighting service than he did of most of its commanders. They seemed relentlessly negative towards his most cherished projects. He was justifiably angry that, despite repeated encouragement, the navy had failed to master techniques for refuelling warships at sea, thus severely restricting the endurance of capital ships. But, even after the loss of *Prince of Wales* and *Repulse*, he remained cavalier about their vulnerability to air attack. Most of his naval commanders were fine professional seamen, whom Britain was fortunate to have. It was galling for them to have their courage implicitly and even explicitly impugned, when they were justly anxious to avoid gratuitous losses of big ships which would take years to replace. Nonetheless, like the generals, the admirals might have shown more understanding of the prime minister's fundamental purpose: to demonstrate that Britain was willing and able to carry the fight to the enemy; to do more than merely survive blockade and air bombardment.

Herein lay the case for the bomber offensive. Churchill seems right to have endorsed this, when Britain's armed forces were accomplishing so little elsewhere, but mistaken to have allowed it to achieve absolute priority in the RAF's worldwide commitments. Concentration of force is important, but so too is a prudent division of resources between critical fronts, of which the Atlantic campaign was assuredly one. By a characteristic irony of war, Churchill enthused most about bombing Germany during 1941–42, when it achieved least. Thereafter, he lost interest. In 1943, Bomber Command began to make a real impact on Ruhr industries, and might have achieved important results if the economic direction of Harris's operations had been more imaginative. In 1944–45, its impact on Germany's cities became devastating, but American targeting policies enabled the USAAF to achieve the critical victories of the air war, against the Luftwaffe and German synthetic oil plants. The last volume of Churchill's war memoirs mentions Bomber Command only once, in passing and critically.

On 1 April 1942, Churchill wrote to Roosevelt: 'I find it very difficult to get over Singapore, but I hope we shall redeem it ere long.' Instead, however, bad news kept coming. On the 4th a Japanese battle fleet, ranging the Indian Ocean, launched planes to bomb Ceylon. In the days that followed, enemy aircraft sank two Royal Navy cruisers and the carrier *Hermes*. Mandalay fell, and it was plain that the British must withdraw across the Chindwin river out of Burma, into north-east India. Malta was in desperate straits, under relentless Axis air attack. Convoys to Russia were suffering shocking losses from German air and U-boat attack: PQ13 in April lost five ships of nine. Only eight ships of twenty-three dispatched in the next convoy reached their destination, fourteen having been turned back by pack ice. Churchill urged Stalin to provide more air and sea cover for the Royal Navy in the later stages of the Arctic passage, but the Russians lacked both means and competence. There was also little goodwill. British sailors and airmen venturing ashore at Murmansk and Archangel were disgusted by the frigidity of their reception. Nowhere, it seemed, did the sun shine upon British endeavours. That spring, Alan Brooke found the prime minister very difficult: 'CIGS says WSC is often in a very nasty mood these days,' noted John Kennedy on 7 April.

Even at this dire period of the war, it was remarkable how many newspaper column inches were devoted to the needs and prospects of post-war reconstruction. This galled the prime minister. He expressed exasperation at having to bother with what he called 'hypo-thetical post-war problems in the middle of a struggle when the same amount of thought concentrated on the question of types of aeroplane might have produced much more result'. Yet many ordin-ary citizens found the war a less rewarding, more dispiriting experience than did Winston Churchill. The present seemed endurable only by looking beyond it to a better future.

Articles and correspondence constantly appeared in print, addressing one aspect or another of a world without war. As early as 4 September 1940, a letter-writer to *The Times* named P.C. Loftus urged that 'this nation not be found unprepared for peace as we were found unprepared for war'. A correspondent signing himself 'Sailor' wrote to the *New Statesman* on 21 February 1942: 'Men wonder what they are fighting for. The old empty jingoisms about "Freedom" and "Homeland" no longer satisfy. There is a suspicion that all will not be well after the peace – that, after all, we are fighting for property and private interests.' The prominent socialist intellectual Harold Laski complained of Churchill's refusal to declare a commitment to social change: 'He does not seem to see that the steps we take now necessarily determine the shape of the society we shall enter when the war is over.' A *Statesman* editorial said: 'It is difficult to find any alert & active member of the Labour Party who does not believe that the end of the war will find the forces of privilege more strongly entrenched in power than they were at the beginning.'

Such sentiments, a gnawing dissatisfaction with British society, extended well beyond the confines of the political left. 'This nation has become very soft,' John Kennedy wrote sadly in his diary on 23 February 1942. 'The people do not want to fight for the Empire.

Mostly, I suppose, they do not care whether they have an empire or not so long as they have an easy and quiet life. They do not realise that German domination will be very unpleasant . . . I think something more is wanted on the political side. There is a great lack of any sense of urgency everywhere. We do not know what we are fighting for. The Atlantic Charter is not good enough an ideal up against the fanaticism of the Germans and the Japs.' Officers commanding two army primary training centres told a morale investigator that the great majority of their recruits 'lack enthusiasm and interest in the war and betray ignorance of the issues involved in it'.

On 6 March 1942, an editorial in the *Spectator* declared: 'The national fibre is today unmistakably different from what it was in those days of 1940 which the Prime Minister could speak of, in accents which carried universal conviction, as our finest hour. No one can pretend that we are living through our finest hour today.' The writer, like his counterpart on the *New Statesman*, felt that the British people lacked a core of belief to move them, as the Russian people were moved: 'Why do men and women in Britain today wait for inspiration from outside? Why are they listening for a voice? Have we no voice within us? Are we ignorant of what is needed?'

In May 1942, America's *Fortune* magazine published an entire issue about the post-war world. Henry Luce, proprietor of *Fortune*, invited Britain's Foreign Secretary to contribute an article about his own country's vision. Eden declined, prompting an official in the American department of the Foreign Office, one C.R. King, to express dismay. It seemed to him a serious mistake to snub Luce. Yet he recognised the problem. Eden had no idea what to say: 'I do not know that HMG have formulated (much less announced) any ideas on these problems beyond those that find expression in the Atlantic Charter.' King added that there was wide agreement in the United States 'that America will emerge, after total victory, militarily and economically supreme'. The *Economist* challenged Churchill in an editorial: 'When has the Prime Minister made one of his great and compelling speeches on the theme, not of world strategy, but of the hopes and fears of the British people? So long as he is silent,

Conservatism, the dominant political attitude in Britain, is silent, and Americans inevitably believe that maybe the Conservatives are out to do nothing but conserve.'

Few intellectuals liked Churchill, and he repaid their distaste. He harboured a special animus against the left-wing journalist Michael Foot, one of the authors of *Guilty Men*, the famous 1940 indictment of the pre-war appeasers. Churchill considered it rank hypocrisy, as indeed it was, that the authors should have attacked the 'men of Munich', when Foot's own Labour Party opposed pre-war rearmament. The intellectuals' preoccupation with post-war Britain exasperated the prime minister, when he was struggling to find means to avert the destruction of European freedom. But in this matter, his instincts were ill-attuned to those of the public. When *Picture Post* devoted an entire issue to 'the Britain we hope to build when the war is over', the magazine received 2,000 letters from readers. Churchill's indifference to the Beveridge Report, which laid the foundations of the Welfare State, on its publication in December 1942 was wholly at odds with the popular enthusiasm that greeted it. Sir William Beveridge himself frequently criticised Britain's wartime governance in print. Before his report was even written, one day when the cabinet was debating the 'unsatisfactory attitude of the workers generally . . . Archie Sinclair suggested that what we really needed to reassure the public was a victory. Winston summed up by saying that clearly what we wanted is a victory over Beveridge.'

Early in April, Churchill's honeymoon with Roosevelt was rudely interrupted. The prime minister had planned himself to go to India, to address its defence and constitutional future, but crises elsewhere made it seem inappropriate for him to leave London and travel so far. Stafford Cripps was dispatched in his stead, with a mandate to discuss with India's nationalist leaders prospective post-war self-government. Talks quickly collapsed. The Hindu-majority Indian National Congress rejected delay, and insisted upon immediate admission to political power. Cripps reported accordingly to London, and was told to come home. Churchill had expected, and indeed wished, no other outcome. He was content that the gesture had been made, and that it was Cripps who bore the odium of failure.

On 11 April, however, Roosevelt cabled Churchill urging that Cripps should remain in India and preside over the creation of a nationalist government. The president asserted that American opinion was overwhelmingly hostile to Britain on this issue: 'The feeling is almost universally held that the deadlock has been caused by the unwillingness of the British Government to concede to the Indians the right of self-government . . . [if] minor concessions would be made by both sides, it seems to me that an agreement might yet be found.' Many Americans explicitly identified India's contemporary predicament with that of their own country before the Revolution of 1776. 'You're the top/You're Mahatma Gandhi!' wrote Cole Porter euphorically, reflecting the huge enthusiasm of his countrymen for the guru of the Indian independence movement. Such sentiment was wormwood to Churchill. At the best of times he had little patience with the Indian people. His view was unchanged since he served among them as a cavalry subaltern in the 1890s. Leo Amery, the India Secretary, found Churchill 'a strange combination of great and small qualities . . . He is really not quite normal on the subject of India.' The prime minister opposed, for instance, granting Indian commissioned officers disciplinary powers over British other ranks. He expostulated against 'the humiliation of being ordered about by a brown man'.

Churchill was ruthlessly dismissive of Indian political aspirations, when the Japanese army was at the gates. He could scarcely be expected to forget that the Mahatma had offered to mediate Britain's surrender to Hitler, whom the standard-bearer of non-violence and Indian freedom described as 'not a bad man'. Gandhi in 1940 wrote an open letter to the British people, urging them to 'lay down arms and accept whatever fate Hitler decided. You will invite Herr Hitler and Signor Mussolini to take what they want of the countries you call your possessions. Let them take possession of your beautiful island with your many beautiful buildings. You will give all these, but neither your souls nor your minds.'

Much worse, however, was the US president's attempt to meddle with what the prime minister perceived as an exclusively British issue. It would never have occurred to Churchill to offer advice to Roosevelt about the future governance of America's Philippines dependency. He deemed it rank cant for a nation which had itself colonised a continent, dispossessing and largely exterminating its indigenous population, and which still practised racial segregation, to harangue others about the treatment of native peoples.

Here was an early, wholly unwelcome foretaste of the future. The USA, principal partner and paymaster of the alliance to defeat fascism, was bent upon exercising decisive influence on the post-war global settlement. Churchill, who thought of nothing save victory, and knew how remote this was in April 1942, found Roosevelt's heavy-handedness irksome. He lost no time in flagging both his determination to stand fast against the Indian National Congress's demands, and his sensitivity about American meddling. 'Anything like a serious difference between you and me would break my heart,' he wrote to the president on the 12th, 'and would surely deeply injure both our countries at the height of this terrible struggle.' Roosevelt's belief that the day of empires was done would achieve post-war vindication with a speed even he might have found surprising. Britain's exercise of power over the Indian people between 1939 and 1945 was clumsy and ugly, and Churchill must bear some of the blame. But the prime minister was surely right that to transfer power in the midst of a world war was unthinkable, especially when the Indian Congress's attitude to the Allied cause was equivocal.

The spring of 1942 brought some lifting of Allied spirits, especially after the US Navy inflicted heavy damage on the Japanese in the 4 May Battle of the Coral Sea. Churchill changed his mind yet again about acceding to Russian demands for recognition of their territorial claims on Poland and the Baltic states. 'We must remember that this is a bad thing,' he told the cabinet. 'We oughtn't to do it, and I shan't be sorry if we don't.' On 5 May, British forces landed in Madagascar, seeking to pre-empt a possible Japanese coup. Churchill wrote to his son Randolph: 'The depression following Singapore has been replaced by an undue optimism, which I am of course keeping in proper bounds.' He was much wounded by the criticisms that had fallen upon him since January. Before he made a national broadcast on 10 May, he drafted a passage which he subsequently – and surely wisely – omitted to deliver, but which reflected the pain he had suffered in recent months:

> Everyone feels safer now, and in consequence the weaker brethren become more vocal. Our critics are not slow to dwell upon the misfortunes and reverses which we have sustained, and I am certainly not going to pretend that there have not been many mistakes and shortcomings. In particular, I am much blamed by a group of ex-ministers for my general conduct of the war. They would very much like to reduce my power of direction and initiative.
>
> Though I have to strive with dictators, I am not, I am glad to say, a dictator myself. I am only your servant. I have tried to be your faithful servant but at any moment, acting through the House of Commons, you can dismiss me to private life. There is one thing, however, which I hope you will not do; I hope you will never ask me or any successor you may choose to bear the burden of responsibility in times like these without reasonable authority and the means of taking decisions.

Hugh Dalton wrote on 12 May 1942: 'Dinner with [Tory MP] Victor Cazalet, who thinks we cannot possibly win the war with the present PM. He has, however, no good alternative.' King George VI, of all people, suggested to his prime minister at luncheon one day that the burden of also serving as defence minister was too much for him, and enquired gauchely what other aspect of public affairs he was interested in. Yet Churchill's difficulty henceforward was that the most formidable challenge to his authority came not from his British critics, but from the nation's overwhelmingly more powerful partner, the US. When Harry Hopkins addressed MPs at the House of Commons on 15 April, he sought to bolster Churchill's standing by asserting that he was 'the only man who really understands Roosevelt'. But the American also declared bluntly, as Harold Nicolson reported, that 'there are many people in the USA who say that we are yellow and can't fight'.

Dill mused in a letter to Wavell from Washington, 'One trouble is that we want everything from them from ships to razor blades and have nothing but services to give in return – and many of the services are past services.' A shrewd British official, Arthur Salter, wrote early in 1942: 'It must be accepted that policy will increasingly be decided in Washington. To proceed as if it can be made in London and "put over" in Washington, or as if British policy can in the main develop independently and be only "co-ordinated" with America, is merely to kick against the pricks.' The prime minister led a nation whose role in the war seemed in those days confined to victimhood, not only at the hands of the enemy, but also at those of its mighty new ally. He yearned inexpressibly to recover the initiative on some battlefield. His generals, however, offered no prospect of offensive action before autumn. Amid the deep public disaffection of spring and summer, this seemed to Churchill an eternity away.

TEN

Soldiers, Bosses and 'Slackers'

1 An Army at Bay

Churchill was reconciled to the fact that Britain's defeats by Japan were irreversible until the tide of the war turned. Henceforward, recognising American dominance of Far East strategy, he devoted much less attention to the Japanese struggle than to the war against Germany. He remained bitterly dismayed, however, by the failures of Auchinleck's forces in the Western Desert, where paper comparison of strengths, showing significant British superiority, suggested that victory should be attainable. At a meeting with his military chiefs he asserted repeatedly: 'I don't know what we can do for that Army – all our efforts to help them seem to be in vain.' Back in 1941, Cadogan at the Foreign Office wrote: 'Our soldiers are the most pathetic amateurs, pitted against professionals . . . The Germans are magnificent fighters and their Staff are veritable Masters of Warfare. Wavell and suchlike are no good against them. It's like putting me up to play Bobby Jones over 36 holes. We shall learn, but it will be a long and bloody business.' Yet a year later, there seemed no evidence that the British Army and its commanders had yet 'learned'. Cadogan wrote after the Far East disasters: 'What will happen if the Germans get a footing here? Our army is the mockery of the world!'

Britain's generals were conscious of their service's low standing, but deemed it unjust that their own prime minister should sustain a barrage of harassment, criticism and even scorn against it. Especially between 1940 and 1942, they perceived themselves obliged to conduct campaigns with inadequate resources, in consequence of inter-war defence policies imposed by the very Conservative Party which still dominated the government – though not, of course, by Churchill himself. Generals often found themselves licking wounds inflicted by the prime minister at the United Services club in Pall Mall, and more junior ranks at its near neighbour the Army & Navy club – the 'Rag' – which played an important social role. These were not mere corn exchanges for service gossip, but rendezvous for earnest conclaves. Amid the daily dining-room parade of red-tabbed officers in gleaming Sam Brownes there was a less privileged audience of retired warriors, prone to eavesdrop and solicit employment. These eventually caused 'Pug' Ismay to decamp to White's club in St James's Street. Its membership was socially grand but strategically insensitive, which enabled him to eat lunches in peace. His table companions 'had no bright ideas for winning the war, and were careful not to embarrass me by asking questions which it would have been difficult to answer'.

Until 1943, and in lesser degree thereafter, the prestige of Britain's soldiers lagged far behind that of its sailors and airmen. Churchill's intemperate goading caused much anger and distress to naval officers. He often threatened to sack dissenting or allegedly insufficiently aggressive admirals, including Sir Andrew Cunningham, Sir James Somerville of Force 'H' and the Home Fleet's Sir John Tovey. But even when the navy suffered severe setbacks and losses, its collective honour and reputation remained unchallenged. This was not so of the army. It enjoyed a more secure social place in British national life than did its US counterpart, and attracted into its smart regiments successive generations of aristocratic younger sons. It was much less effective, however, as a military institution. For every clever officer such as Brooke, Ismay or Jacob, there were a hundred others lacking skill, energy and imagination, who nonetheless performed their duties in a cloud of cultural complacency. Their courage was seldom in doubt, but much else was.

Churchill spent much of the first half of the war searching in mounting desperation for commanders capable of winning victories on land. Throughout his own long experience of war, he had been impressed by many heroes, but few British generals. In his 1932 work *Great Contemporaries*, he painted an unsympathetic portrait of Field Marshal Sir Douglas Haig, principal conductor of the nation's armies through the World War I bloodbath in France and Flanders:

> He presents to me in those red years the same mental picture as a great surgeon before the days of anaesthetics, versed in every detail of such science as was known to him: sure of himself, steady of poise, knife in hand, intent upon the operation: entirely removed in his professional capacity from the agony of the patient, the anguish of relations, or the doctrines of rival schools, the devices of quacks, or the first-fruits of new learning. He would operate without excitement, or he would depart without being affronted; and if the patient died, he would not reproach himself.

Churchill was determined that no British army in 'his' war would be commanded by another such officer. Every general between 1939 and 1945 carried into battle an acute awareness of the animosity of the British people, and of their prime minister, towards the alleged 'butchers' of 1914–18. In this baggage, indeed, may be found a source of the caution characteristic of their campaigns. Yet Britain's military limitations went much deeper than mere generalship. It might have been profitable for Churchill to divert some of the hours he devoted to scanning the countenances and records of commanders, instead to addressing the institutional culture of the British Army. John Kennedy expressed the War Office's bafflement: 'We manage by terrific efforts to pile up resources at the necessary places and then the business seems to go wrong, for lack of generalship and junior leadership and bad tactics and lack of concentration of force at decisive points.'

Clausewitz laid down principles, rooted in his experience of the Napoleonic wars, when he perceived all European armies as possessing approximately the same quality of weapons, training and potential. Thus, the Prussian believed that outcomes were determined by relative mass, and by the respective skills of rival commanders. If this was true in the early nineteenth century, it certainly was not in the Second World War, when Allied and Axis armies displayed widely differing levels of ability and commitment. Superior weapons systems deployed by one side or the other sometimes produced decisive effects. Clausewitz distinguished three elements of war – policy, strategy and tactics. Churchill addressed himself with the keenest attention to the first two, but neglected the third, or rather allowed his commanders to do so.

Britain could take pride in its distaste for militarism. But its inability to deploy effective armies until a late stage of the Second World War was a grievous handicap. Even competent British officers found it hard to extract from their forces performances good enough to beat the Germans or Japanese, who seemed to the prime minister to try much harder. Conversely, Axis troops sometimes achieved more, especially in defence, than indifferent generalship by local commanders entitled Hitler or Hirohito to expect. Rommel, who in 1941–42 became a British obsession, was a fine leader and tactician, but his neglect of logistics contributed much to his own difficulties in North Africa. His triumphs over the British reflected the institutional superiority of his little German force as much as his own inspired opportunism. The Australian war correspondent Alan Moorehead, an exceptionally perceptive eye-witness, wrote from the desert in August 1942, in an assessment laid before British readers while the war was still being fought: 'Rommel was an abler general than any on the British side, and for this one reason – because the German army was an abler army than the British army. Rommel was merely the expression of that abler German army.'

This seems to identify a fundamental Allied difficulty. Eighth Army's defeats in North Africa in 1941–42, almost invariably by German troops inferior in numbers and armoured strength, certainly reflected inadequate generalship. But they were also the consequence of shortcomings of method and determination. The British public was increasingly conscious of these. Glasgow secretary Pam Ashford wrote on 24 June 1942: 'There is a general feeling that there is something wrong with our Forces . . . Mrs Muir thought it was our generals who were not equal to the German generals, they get out-manoeuvred every time.' Young laboratory technician and former soldier Edward Stebbing wrote: 'The feeling is growing that we are having our present reverses in Libya and the Far East not merely because of inferiority in numbers and equipment, but also because the enemy are really too clever for us, or rather that we are too stupid for the enemy.'

Ivan Maisky, the Russian ambassador in London, once observed to Hugh Dalton that he found British soldiers unfailingly stiff and formal, unlike their counterparts of the other services. The army, he suggested, lacked the Royal Navy's and RAF's collective self-confidence. This was so. Gen. Pownall wrote after the Far East disasters:

> Our [career officers] regard [war] as an upsetting, rather exhausting and distinctly dangerous interlude in the happier, more comfortable and more desirable days of peace-soldiering . . . We need . . . a tougher Army, based on a tougher nation, an Army which is regarded by the people as an honourable profession to which only the best can gain admittance; one which is prepared and proud to live hard, not soft, in peace. One whose traditions are not based on purely regimental history but on the history of the whole British Army; where the competition is in efficiency, not in games or pipe-blowing and band concerts . . . Training must be harder, exercises must not be timed to suit meal-times. Infantry shouldn't be allowed to say that they are tired . . . We must cultivate mobility of mind as well as of body, i.e. imagination; and cut out the great hampering 'tail' which holds back rather than aids the 'teeth'.

The regimental system was sometimes an inspirational force, but often also, as was implied by Pownall's remarks, a source of parochialism, an impediment to the cohesion of larger formations. German, American and Russian professional soldiers thought in divisions; the British always of the regiment, the cherished 'military family'. Until the end of the war, the dead hand of centralised, top-down command methods, together with lack of a fighting doctrine common to the entire army, hampered operations in the field. Eighth Army's techniques for the recovery of disabled vehicles from the battlefield – a vital skill in maximising combat power – lagged badly behind those of the Afrika Korps. British armoured units, imbued with a cavalry ethos, remained childishly wedded to independent action. In the desert, as in the Crimea a century earlier, British cavalry charged – and were destroyed. This, when since 1940 the Germans had almost daily demonstrated the importance of coordinating tanks, anti-tank guns and infantry in close mutual support.

British unit as well as army leadership left much to be desired. On the battlefield, local elements seldom displayed initiative, especially if outflanked. Troops engaged in heavy fighting sometimes displayed resolution, but sometimes also collapsed, withdrew or surrendered more readily than their commanders thought acceptable. The sybaritic lifestyle of the vast rear headquarters nexus around Cairo shocked many visitors, especially Americans but also including British ministers Oliver Lyttelton and Harold Macmillan. Here, indeed, was a new manifestation of the 'château generalship' condemned by critics of the British Army in the First World War, and this time focused upon Shepheard's hotel and the Gezireh club.

Sloth and corruption flourished in the workshops and bases of the rear areas, where tens of thousands of British soldiers indifferent to the progress of the war were allowed to pursue their own lazy routines, selling stores, fuel and even trucks for private profit. 'Petrol, food, NAAFI supplies, vehicle engines, tools, tyres, clothing – all rich booty – were pouring into Egypt, free for all who dared,' wrote a disgusted colonel responsible for a network of ordnance depots, who was as unimpressed by the lack of 'grip' in high places as by the systemic laziness and corruption he perceived throughout the rear areas of Middle East Command. It was a serious indictment of the army that such practices were never checked. Even at the end of 1943, Harold Macmillan complained of the then Middle East C-in-C, Sir Henry 'Jumbo' Maitland-Wilson, that 'The Augean stables are still uncleaned.' Since shipping shortages constrained all Allied

Germany triumphs in both west and east. (*Above*) Blazing shore facilities on Crete in May 1941, and (*right*) one of some three million Russian soldiers who surrendered to the Wehrmacht during the first year of Operation *Barbarossa*.

Friendship of state. (*Above*) Harry Hopkins and his host pose outside Downing Street on 10 January 1941, with Brendan Bracken behind; (*left*) FDR and Churchill at Placentia Bay on 10 August, the president leaning on the arm of his unlovable son Elliot.

War in the desert. (*Right*) British troops advance through a minefield. (*Below*) Some of the tens of thousands of Italian prisoners who fell into British hands during Wavell's Operation *Compass*.

Civilian chroniclers of the
wartime experience: Vere
Hodgson and George
King in Home Guard
battle dress.

Whitehall diarists: Sir
John Kennedy; Sir
Alexander Cadogan;
Harold Nicolson.

Clockwise from top left: Charles Wilson, Lord Moran; Hugh Dalton; Leo Amery; Cuthbert Headlam; Oliver Harvey; Lt. Gen Henry Pownall.

Working on his train, with a secretary's 'silent' typewriter at hand to take dictation.

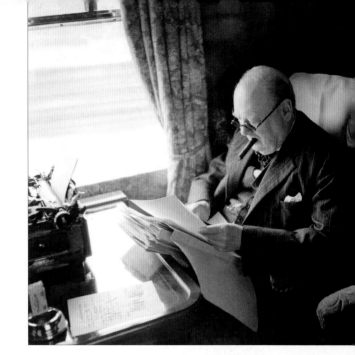

Viewing new aircraft with (*left to right*) Lindemann, Portal and Pound.

Jock Colville's September 1941 farewell to Downing Street gathering, on the steps to the garden. *Left to right*: Colville, Leslie Rowan, 'Master', John Peck, John Martin, Miss Watson, Commander 'Tommy' Thompson, Tony Bevir, Charles Barker.

Return from Arcadia: Churchill briefly at the controls of the British plane which brought him home from Washington in January 1942.

One of the many impassioned Second Front rallies held in Britain's cities in 1942–43.

operations, waste of material and supplies transported at such cost to theatres of war was a self-inflicted handicap. The Allies provided their soldiers with amenities and comforts quite unknown to their enemies. These became an acceptable burden in the years of victory, but bore hardly upon the war effort in those of defeat.

Throughout the conflict, in Britain's media there was debate about the army's equipment deficiencies, tactics and commanders. The government vacillated about how far to allow criticism to go. In December 1941, Tom Wintringham wrote an article for *Picture Post* entitled 'What has Happened in Libya?' He attacked the army's leadership, tanks and guns. As a result, *Picture Post* was briefly banned both from distribution in the Middle East and from British Council offices worldwide. Few people doubted that what Wintringham said was true. The difficulty was to reconcile expression of realities with the need to sustain the morale of men risking their lives on the battlefield equipped with these same inadequate weapons, and sometimes led by indifferent officers.

In March 1942 the popular columnist John Gordon delivered a withering blast against Britain's service chiefs in Beaverbrook's *Sunday Express*. They were, he said, men who had achieved high rank merely by staying on in uniform in pursuit of 'cushy billets' after the last war ended in 1918, while their betters earned civilian livings. 'All this,' noted a general who read Gordon's rant, 'has a devastating effect on army morale. When soldiers are in a tight corner, how can they be expected to fight if they have been led to believe that their leaders are men of straw?'

Brooke, Alexander and others believed that some of the army's difficulties derived from the fact that its best potential leaders, who should have been the generals of World War II, had been killed in the earlier Kaiser's war. It may be of marginal significance that the German army husbanded the lives of promising junior officers with more care than did the British, at least until the 1918 campaigns, but it seems mistaken to make too much of this. The core issue was that Germany's military culture was more impressive. That of the pre-war British Army militated against recruitment and promotion of clever, imaginative, ruthless commanders, capable of handling large forces – or even of ensuring that they were equipped with weapons to match those of the enemy. All too many senior officers were indeed men who had chosen military careers because they lacked sufficient talent and energy to succeed in civilian life. Brooke privately agreed with much of what John Gordon wrote. His own fits of melancholy were often prompted by reflections on the unfitness of the British Army to engage the Wehrmacht: 'We are going to lose this war unless we control it very differently and fight it with more determination . . . It is all desperately depressing . . . Half our Corps and Divisional Commanders are totally unfit for their appointments, and yet if I were to sack them I could find no better! They lack character, imagination, drive and powers of leadership.'

When some 1,600 army officers of various ranks in Home Forces were relieved in 1942, in an attempt to introduce new blood, cynics observed that their replacements seemed socially and professionally indistinguishable from those they supplanted. Churchill attempted one lunge towards altering the social ethos at the top of the army: when he made up his mind to sack Dill as CIGS, he dallied with appointing as his successor Gen. Sir Archibald Nye. Nye's virtue – in the eyes of politicians, anyway – was that as the son of a sergeant-major he could not be denounced as a 'toff'. Eventually, however, Churchill allowed himself to be persuaded that Nye lacked the experience and gifts to be given the top job, and merely promoted him to become Brooke's deputy.

Harold Macmillan saw the wartime army at close quarters, and thought little of most of its senior officers. He accused both the British and US chiefs of staff of surrounding themselves with a host of acolytes 'too stupid to be employed in any operational capacity'. Observing that one British commander was 'a bit wooden', Macmillan continued:

These British administrative generals, whose only experience of the world is a military mess at Aldershot or Poona, are a curiously narrow-minded lot. They seem to go all over the world without observing anything in it – except their fellow-officers and their wives . . . and the various Services clubs in London, Cairo, Bombay, etc., but they are honourable, hard-working, sober, clean about the house and so on. At the end of their careers, they are just fit to be secretaries of golf clubs. War, of course, is their great moment. In their hearts (if they were honest with themselves) they must pray for its prolongation.

This was harsh, but not unjust. Churchill was imbued with a belief that the execution of Admiral Sir John Byng in 1757, for failing to relieve Minorca, had a salutary effect on the subsequent performance of the Royal Navy. He was right. Following Byng's shooting, from the Napoleonic wars through the twentieth century, the conduct of British naval officers in the face of the enemy almost invariably reflected an understanding that while they might be forgiven for losing a battle, they would receive no mercy if they flinched from fighting one. After the sacking of General Sir Alan Cunningham in Libya, Churchill muttered to Dill about the virtues of the Byng precedent. The then CIGS answered sharply that such a view was anachronistic.

Dill could justly argue that displays of tigerish zeal such as the prime minister wanted were inappropriate to a modern battlefield, and frequently precipitated disasters. Neither Marlborough nor Wellington won his battles by heroic posturing. But the prime minister was surely correct to believe that generals should fear disgrace if they failed. The British Army's instinctive social sympathy for its losers was inappropriate to a struggle of national survival. Even the ruthless Brooke anguished over the dismissal of Ritchie, a conspicuous failure as Eighth Army commander in Libya: 'I am devoted to Neil and hate to think of the disappointment this will mean to him.' Some middle-ranking officers who proved notoriously unsuccessful in battle continued to be found employment: Ritchie was later allowed to command a corps in north-west Europe – without distinction. It would have been more appropriate to consign proven losers to professional oblivion, as the Americans often did. But this was not the British way, nor even Brooke's.

Fundamental to many defeats in the desert was an exaggerated confidence in manoeuvre, an inadequate focus on firepower. Until 1944, successive models of tank and anti-tank guns lacked penetrative capacity. It was extraordinary that, even after several years' experience of modern armoured warfare, British- and American-made fighting vehicles continued to be inferior to those of the Germans. Back in 1917, in the first flush of his own enthusiasm for tanks, Churchill had written to his former battalion second-in-command Archie Sinclair, urging him to forsake any thought of a life with the cavalry, and to become instead an armoured officer: 'Arm yourself therefore my dear with the panoply of modern science of war . . . Embark in the chariots of war and slay the malignants with the arms of precision.' Yet a world war later, Churchill was unsuccessful in ensuring that the British Army deployed armour capable of matching that of its principal enemy. From 1941 onwards the British usually deployed more tanks than the Germans in the desert, sometimes dramatically more. Yet the Afrika Korps inflicted devastating attrition, by exploiting its superior weapons and tactics.

Again and again MPs raised this issue in the Commons, yet it proved beyond military ingenuity or industrial skill to remedy. American tanks were notably better than British, but they too were outmatched by those of the Germans. Until almost the end of the war, both nations adopted a deliberate policy of compensating by tank quantity for well-recognised deficiencies of quality. It is impossible to overstate the significance of this failure in explaining defeats.

Nor was the problem of inadequate weapons restricted to tanks. In 1941, when the War Office was offered a choice of either 100 six-pounder anti-tank guns or six times that number of two-pounders, it opted for the latter. By that winter Moscow was telling London not to bother sending any further two-pounders to Russia, because the Red Army found them useless – as did Auchinleck's units in the desert. Only late in 1942 did six-pounders become available in substantial numbers. The War Office struggled in vain to match the superb German 88mm dual-purpose anti-aircraft and anti-tank gun, which accounted for 40 per cent of British tanks destroyed in North Africa, against 38 per cent which fell to Rommel's panzers.

British tank and military-vehicle design and production were non-standardised and dispersed among a ragbag of manufacturers. Given that the RAF and the Royal Navy exploited technical innovations with striking success, the failure of Britain's ground forces to do so, certainly until 1944, must be blamed on the army's own procurement chiefs. It was always short of four-wheel-drive trucks. Mechanical serviceability rates were low. Pre-war procurement officers, influenced by the experience of colonial war, had a visceral dislike for platoon automatic weapons, which they considered wasteful of ammunition. The War Office of the 1920s dismissed Thompson sub-machine guns as 'gangster weapons', but in 1940 found itself hastening to import as many as it could buy from the Americans. Only in 1943–44 did British Stens become widely available. Infantry tactics were unimaginative, especially in attack. British artillery, always superb, was the only real success story.

Until late in 1942, Eighth Army in North Africa was poorly supported by the RAF. Air force leadership was institutionally hostile to providing 'flying artillery' for soldiers, and only sluggishly evolved liaison techniques such as the Luftwaffe had practised since 1939. Churchill strongly defended the RAF's right to an independent strategic function, asserting that it would be disastrous to turn the air force into 'a mere handmaid of the Army'. But it proved mistaken to permit the airmen such generous latitude in determining their own priorities. Close air support for ground forces was slow to mature.

One of the most damaging errors of aircraft production policy was 'the tendency to bridge over waiting periods for new types delayed in development by means of "stop-gap" orders for older types', in the words of an official historian. 'Three aircraft especially, the Battle, the Blenheim and Whitley, were repeatedly ordered long after the replacement date originally set for them had arrived.' There was a mistaken belief that it must be better to provide the RAF with any aircraft than none. Yet Battles and Blenheims, especially, added nothing to British combat power, and merely provided coffins for the unfortunate aircrew obliged to fly them in 1940–41. Whitley bombers remained in production until mid-1943, even though the

RAF latterly ceased to sacrifice them over Germany. Better planes were coming. Aircraft design proved one of Britain's real successes in the second half of the war. But in 1942 there were still pathetically few of the new Mosquito and Lancaster bombers, or of upgraded models of the Spitfire and Hurricane. Almost all the latest types were deployed at British airfields, rather than in support of the army's battles in the Middle and Far East.

'In all its branches, the German war machine appeared to have a better and tighter control than our army,' wrote Alan Moorehead. 'One of the senior British generals said to the war correspondents . . . "We are still amateurs. The Germans are professionals."' This was an extraordinary admission in mid-1942. The army's performance improved during the latter part of that year. But, to prevail over the Germans, British – and American – forces continued to require a handsome superiority of men, tanks and air support.

There remained one great unmentionable, even in those newspapers most critical of Britain's military performance: the notion that, man for man, the British soldier might be a less determined fighter than his German adversary. The 'tommy' was perceived – sometimes rightly – as the victim of his superiors' incompetence, rather than as the bearer of any personal responsibility for failures of British arms. In private, however, and among ministers and senior officers, this issue was frequently discussed. George Marshall deplored the manner in which Churchill spoke of the army's Other Ranks as 'the dull mass', a phrase which reflected the prime minister's limited comprehension of them. There was an embarrassing moment at Downing Street when following a cabinet meeting Randolph Churchill joined a discussion about the army, and shouted: 'Father, the trouble is your soldiers won't fight.' Churchill once observed of his son: 'I love Randolph, but I don't like him.' It was astonishing that, in the midst of debates about great matters, he indulged his son's presence, and expected others to do so. On this occasion, however, Randolph's intervention might have been hyperbolic, but was to the point. Many British officers perceived their citizen soldiers as lacking the will and commitment routinely displayed by the

Germans and Japanese. Underlying the conduct of Churchill's wartime commanders was a fundamental nervousness about what their men would, or would not, do on the battlefield.

Churchill understood that if British troops were to overcome Germans, they must become significantly nastier. This represented a change of view. In 1940 he favoured civility towards the enemy, reproaching Duff Cooper as Minister of Information for mocking the Italians: 'It is a well-known rule of war policy to praise the courage of your opponent, which enhances your own victory when gained.' Likewise in January 1942 he declared his admiration for Rommel on the floor of the House of Commons: 'a very daring and skilful opponent . . . and, may I say across the havoc of war, a great general'. Progressively, however, the prime minister came to think it mistaken to suggest that Axis soldiers were honourable foes. Such courtesies encouraged British troops to surrender too readily. As the war matured, Churchill deplored newspaper reports of chivalrous German behaviour: 'These beastly Huns are murdering people wholesale in Europe and have committed the most frightful atrocities in Russia, and it would be entirely in accordance with their technique to win a reputation for treating British and American soldiers with humanity on exceptional and well-advertised occasions.'

In the spring and summer of 1942, Churchill was right to believe that the British Army's performance in North Africa was inadequate. Many of his outbursts about the soldiers' failures, which so distressed Brooke and his colleagues, were justified. It remains debatable whether remedies were available, when positions of military responsibility must perforce be filled from the existing pool of regular officers. Most were captives of the culture to which they had been bred. Its fundamental flaw was that it required only moderate effort, sacrifice and achievement, and produced only a small number of leaders and units capable of matching the skill and determination of their enemies. The army's institutional weakness would be overcome only when vastly superior Allied resources became available on the battlefield.

2 Home Front

The secretary of the Tory backbench 1922 Committee one day took Leo Amery aside in the Commons smoking room. He told the India Secretary there was deep restlessness among MPs, 'because they did not feel that there was anyone inside the Cabinet who stood for the Conservative point of view at all'. This was largely true. Almost everything about Britain's wartime domestic policies seemed socialistic. Centralisation, planning, rationing and regulation were fundamental to mobilisation of the nation's resources, to fair distribution of food, fuel, clothing. Every British citizen cursed wartime bureaucracy, transport shortages, queues, the relentlessly dispiriting influence of the blackout, the food and privileges still available to those with money to pay for them. But the country was, for the most part, notably well administered. For this the prime minister deserved full credit, for putting the right men in charge.

Clement Attlee, leader of the Labour Party and deputy prime minister, wielded no authority over the military machine, but exercised wide influence on domestic policy. A mild-mannered man whom some made the mistake of underrating, Attlee conducted himself with unfailing dignity, discretion and good sense. There were many moments when he would have been justified in losing his temper with Churchill, but he remained unruffled. The prime minister was seldom less than courteous to Labour members of his government, but they were rarely invited to join his table or to weekend at Chequers. To share private moments, he almost invariably chose Conservative ministers. Even in a coalition administration, this was probably inevitable, and Attlee displayed no sign of resentment, or indeed of any wish to join Churchill's circle.

During the prime minister's increasingly frequent absences abroad his deputy presided over the cabinet and war cabinet, taking the decisions that had to be made, but never overreaching his authority. There were often complaints by critics that the cabinet allowed itself to be a mere rubber-stamp, that Attlee and his colleagues failed to restrain Churchill's excesses. But it is only necessary to consider the damage that would have been done had the Labour leader used his position to lead an opposition to the prime minister and fracture the government's unity, to applaud his statesmanship. He believed that Churchill, for all his imperfections, was the only possible man to lead Britain through the war. He served the prime minister loyally, and chaired a host of important committees.

Ernest Bevin towered over his socialist colleagues in the esteem not only of the public, but of Churchill. Hugh Dalton, a renegade Etonian socialist, called the Minister of Labour 'by far the best of all my colleagues, in spite of his mountainous defects of egoism, garrulity and peasant-minded suspicion'. Bevin, sixty-two, the son of a Somerset farm labourer, left school at eleven. Though almost uneducated, he displayed the highest intelligence and force of personality. Until co-opted into government in 1940 he had been secretary of Britain's largest union, the Transport & General Workers. He disliked communists as much as the prime minister, and wielded his immense popular authority to curb trade union excesses as much as any man could. He deserves much of the credit for the fact that Britain mobilised its population, and especially its women, more effectively than any other belligerent nation, save possibly Russia. He was never less than blunt: Churchill was probably undismayed when Bevin once told Stafford Cripps in cabinet that 'he didn't know why he didn't mind his own bloody business'.

Sir John Anderson, as Lord President of the Council, presided over a domestic counterpart of the war cabinet. A ponderous, humourless former civil servant who had served as governor of Bengal, Anderson commanded little affection but much respect. His memory, and grasp of facts and figures, were so prodigious that a colleague once enquired whether he boasted an elephant on his coat of arms. Though he sat in the Commons as MP for the Scottish Universities, his biographer observed: 'He never really understood the House. He naturally regarded all men, and, in particular, men in public positions ... as being rational in their words and actions ... When this did not seem to him to be so, it distressed him and even offended his sense of propriety. "I am shocked at their irresponsibility," he once remarked of MPs.'

Churchill never warmed to Anderson – no one could – but he valued his abilities: 'There is no better warhorse in the government,' he said. Anderson acted as economic coordinator, with responsibility for wages and manpower, then became in1943 – less successfully – chancellor of the Exchequer. In his invariable wing collar and formal Whitehall attire, he was nicknamed 'Jehovah', which caused Attlee to open a committee meeting one morning with the jocular greeting: 'Here we all are, Jehovah's witnesses.' Churchill nominated Anderson as successor to the premiership in the event that both he and Eden were killed on one of their wartime journeys.

Anderson undertook only one uncharacteristic action in his life. As a lonely widower of fifty-nine, he married a raffish young widow, Ava Wigram, whose late husband Ralph had passed secret intelligence to Churchill in the 1930s. The Andersons bought a millhouse together in Sussex, where one day he fell off a small bridge into the river. The Lord President swam round in circles in his pork pie hat, which reduced Ava to hysterical laughter. Anderson demanded angrily: 'Would you have your husband drown?' She was eventually persuaded to assist him. In the country, he was once observed churning butter with one hand, while doing his ministerial boxes with the other. This austere, unimaginative man, who bore responsibility with the ease of long experience, managed a host of matters that were vital, but which bored the prime minister.

Anderson's most notable colleague was the food minister, Lord Woolton, another outstanding figure of Britain's war. Woolton – Frederick Marquis before his elevation – was a former boss of the department store chain John Lewis. He was not only an inspired administrator, directing the operations of 40,000 people handling the national rationing and distribution system, but also a natural communicator. Save for the prime minister, no member of the government proved more accomplished in explaining himself to the nation through the BBC's microphones. 'Woolton pie', made with cheap, nutritious and – above all – available ingredients, became a lasting memory of the war for millions of people. Woolton once displayed dismay at criticism in the Lords of a 'government in slumberland'. Hugh Dalton observed patronisingly, from the view-point of a career politician: 'He has had no political training to harden his skin and his sensibilities.'

Dalton himself, a socialist intellectual but a considerable social climber who loved to lunch with such hostesses as Lady Colefax, was moved from the Ministry of Economic Warfare to the Board of Trade in the February 1942 reshuffle, having allegedly fumbled the manage-ment of Special Operations Executive, SOE. Dalton was grieved to lose control of the sabotage organisation, which excited him, but thereafter did useful work grappling with the intractable coal industry. He was one of the best Whitehall diarists of the war, an ardent intriguer, bitchy and self-obsessed. After one of his own platform performances, he wrote: 'I am in exceptionally good form and make a very good speech, full of impromptu jokes.' His admiration for Churchill was not reciprocated. He was never on the guest list for Chequers, and like most of his colleagues seldom saw the prime minister privately.

Herbert Morrison was a controversial Home Secretary, not much esteemed by his colleagues, least of all Bevin, with whom he feuded. Morrison, a World War I conscientious objector, had made his repu-tation in London local government. In Whitehall, his conceit was deemed to exceed his abilities. Lord Leathers as Minister of War Transport, by contrast, a peacetime shipping magnate, was highly regarded by almost everyone except Alan Brooke. A group of notably talented civil servants and academics supported the cabinet team, the economist Maynard Keynes prominent among them. Beaverbrook complained that the government was run by 'the three profs – Cherwell, Keynes and [the economist Lionel] Robbins'.

Churchill was often criticised for taking insufficient interest in domestic affairs. Yet he seems to deserve full credit for ensuring that those to whom he entrusted them were, almost without exception, men of notable ability. The British people were exasperated by petty restriction. Some factories suffered from poor management, outdated production methods, lack of quality control and a recalcitrant work-force – shortcomings which had hampered the nation's economic progress through the previous half-century. But many industries achieved remarkable results, and reaped the harvest of Britain's astonishing wartime record of scientific innovation. The overall achievement was impressive.

Wartime unity was a considerable reality. The majority of the British people remained staunch. Yet class tensions ran deep. Significant groups, above all shop-floor workers, displayed disaffection. Sections of Britain's industrial workforce perceived no contradiction between supporting Churchill and the crusade against Nazism, while sustaining the class struggle which had raged since the beginning of the century. Strikes were officially outlawed for the duration by the government's March 1941 Essential Work Order, but legislation failed to prevent wildcat stoppages, above all in coal pits, shipyards and aircraft plants, often in support of absurd or avaricious demands. At the depth of the Depression, in 1932, just 48,000 working days were lost to strikes in the metal, engineering and shipbuilding industries. In 1939, by contrast, 332,000 days were lost; in 1940, 163,000; 1941, 556,000; 1942, 526,000; 1943, 635,000; 1944, 1,048,000; 1945, 528,000. This was a better record than that achieved in 1917, when stoppages in the same industries cost three million days of production. Nonetheless, it suggests a less than wholehearted commitment to the war effort in some factories, also manifested by dockyard workers who, to the disgust of ships' crews, were guilty of systematic pilferage, including on occasion lifeboat rations.

Few workers broke ranks during the Dunkirk period, but as the war news improved they perceived less urgency about the struggle for national survival. 'I gather that production is not nearly good enough,' wrote Tory MP Cuthbert Headlam in December 1940, 'that the work people in airplane and other gov[ernment] factories are beginning to go ca'canny; that the dockers at the ports are giving trouble . . . communists active – I only hope that much of this gossip is exaggerated, but it is alarming nonetheless.' In September 1941, when Churchill visited the Armstrong-Siddeley factory at Coventry, where Whitley bombers were being manufactured, he was warned that the plant was 'a hotbed of communism'. Jock Colville wrote:

'I was disgusted to hear that their production tempo had not really grown until Russia came into the war.' Nine thousand men at Vickers-Armstrong in Barrow went on unofficial strike in a dispute over piecework rates. When a tribunal found against them, the strike committee held a mass meeting at a local football ground, and put forward a motion suggesting that the men should resume work 'under protest'. This was overwhelmingly defeated, and the dispute dragged on for weeks.

Of eight serious strikes in the aircraft industry between February and May 1943, six concerned pay, one was sparked by objections to an efficiency check on machine use, and one by refusal to allow two fitters to be transferred to different sections of the same shop. There were twenty-eight lesser stoppages prompted by disputes about canteen facilities, alleged victimisation of a shop steward, the use of women riveters, and refusal by management to allow collections for the Red Army during working hours. A report on De Havillands at Castle Bromwich noted 'a marked absence of discipline . . . slackness . . . difficulty in controlling shop stewards'. Ernest Bevin reported that the aircraft industry 'had failed to improve its productivity in proportion to the amount of labour supplies'. A total of 1.8 million working days were lost during 1,785 disputes in 1943, a figure which rose to 3.7 million in 2,194 disputes in 1944.

'Strikes continue to cause much discussion,' declared a 1943 Home Intelligence report. 'The majority feeling is that strike action in wartime is unjustified . . . Fatigue and war-weariness, combined with the belief that we are "out of the wood" and victory now certain, are thought by many to account for the situation.' American seamen arriving in Britain were shocked by the attitudes they encountered among dockers. Walter Byrd, chief officer of the US merchantman SS *J. Marshall*, 'made very strong criticism of the attitude of stevedores and other dockworkers in the port of Glasgow. He accused them of complete indifference to the exigencies of any situation, however urgent.' Byrd complained to harbour security officers that many trucks and tanks were being damaged by reckless handling during offloading. It was decided to dispatch some shipworkers to work in US yards on British vessels. At a time when passenger space was at a premium, service chiefs were enraged when these men refused to sail without their wives – and their demand was met: 'I do not see why the country sh[oul]d not be mobilised and equality of sacrifice demanded,' a senior army officer commented indignantly.

Of all wartime industrial disputes, 60 per cent concerned wages, 19 per cent demarcation, 11.2 per cent working arrangements. A strong communist element on Clydeside was held responsible by managements for many local difficulties. Some trades unionists adopted a shameless view that there was no better time to secure higher pay than during a national emergency, when the need for continuous production was so compelling. Those who served Britain in uniform were poorly rewarded – the average private soldier received less than a pound a week – but industrial workers did well out of the war. The Cost of Living Index rose from eighty-eight in 1939 to 112.5 in 1945, while average wages rose from 106 to 164. The highest-paid men, handling sheet metal on fuselage assembly in aircraft factories, received £20–£25 a week, though £12 was nearer the average for a sixty-hour week. Average civilian weekly earnings in July 1944 were just over £6.

In the coal industry, wage increases were much steeper, from an indexed 109 to 222. But these did nothing to stem a relentless decline in production – by 12 per cent between 1938 and 1944 – which alarmed the government and bewildered the public. The mines employed 766,000 workers in 1939, 709,000 in 1945. Loss of skilled labour from the pits to the services provided an inadequate explanation for the fall in per capita output, since the German coal industry achieved dramatic increases under the same handicap.

Absenteeism was rife among the British mine workforce, rising from 6.4 per cent in 1938 to 8.3 per cent in 1940; 12.1 per cent in 1943; 16.3 per cent in 1945. Almost half of those missing were reckoned to have downed tools by choice. In addition, miners' strikes accounted for half of all working days lost to industrial disputes in 1943, two-thirds in 1944. Almost everything was wrong with the coal industry: poor management, a high accident and disease rate, rail transport problems and stubborn miners' resistance to mechanisation. Early in 1941, according to the official wartime history of British coal, 'it became necessary to bring home to the industry the urgency of production'. The Essential Work (Coalmining) Order was introduced, providing a guaranteed wage, but banning absenteeism. In July 1942 a despairing government took operational control of the industry. Yet still production languished, and stoppages persisted.

A report by the Ministry of Fuel and Power said in 1942: 'The mining community, more than all other industrial groups . . . tends to see present events in the light of the history of their own community and their own experience . . . Underlying the feeling against the owners and suspicion of the miners' leaders is a more general attitude of disbelief in the statements of those in authority.' Here was the core of the problem: alienation of miners, especially in south Wales, from the purposes of government, and even from Britain's war. The official historians wrote later: 'One can hardly overstress the effect of the Depression years upon the morale of the mining community . . . many miners . . . felt a sardonic satisfaction in finding themselves for once able to call the tune. Their attitude was not antisocial. It was only un-social . . . We have to consider how far these narrowed and embittered men could be expected to respond to inducements wrung from the authorities by the urgency of war.'

In 1944, three million tons of coal production were lost by strikes. A team of American technical experts who studied Britain's mining industry reported to the government: 'The center of the problem . . . is the bad feeling and antagonism which pervade the industry and which manifests itself in low morale, non-cooperation and indifference. In almost every district we visited, miners' leaders and mine owners complained of men leaving the mines early, failure to clear the faces and voluntary absenteeism.' The cabinet decided against publishing this report.

Class divisions sustained notable variations in communities' health. The south-east had prospered economically in the last years before war came, but other regions remained blighted by the Depression. In 1942, while four babies of every thousand born in south-east England died, seven perished in south Wales, the north-west and the north-east. Measles produced four times as many fatalities among children in the latter areas as in the former, and tuberculosis rates were much higher. A 1943 Ministry of Health study found that 10 per cent of a sample of 600 children were ill-nourished: 'many of the people had lived for years past in poverty and unemployment, and had given up the struggle to maintain a decent standard of housekeeping and cooking'. The condition of many children evacuated from blitzed cities shocked those who received them. Of 31,000 registered in Newcastle, for instance, 4,000 were deficient in footwear, 6,500 in clothing. Authorities in Wales reported that among evacuees from Liverpool there were 'children in rags', in a personal condition that 'baffles description'. Many of the families from which such offspring came perceived the war in less than idealistic terms.

At the opposite end of the social spectrum a Conservative MP, Thomas Dugdale, noted that many of his colleagues, conscious of the punitive taxes which the propertied classes were now paying and the shrunken wealth of their own kind, were disgusted by 'the exceedingly high wages being paid to war workers . . . the many reports of slackness, absenteeism etc in the factories'. Cuthbert Headlam asserted bitterly that the left was fomenting class war: 'From the way men like J.B. Priestley speak, one might imagine that nothing was being done for the great mass of the population and this country was preserved solely for an idle crowd of parasites who never lifted a finger for the public good.' On 24 February 1942, Lt.Col. Rayner, Tory MP for Totnes, complained in the Commons that the response of the British people to two fanatical enemies was inadequate: 'We are not showing ruthless purpose today. Hundreds of thousands of people are not pulling their weight. Slackness is widespread, sacrifice in many directions is most remarkable by its absence, and vested interests of one sort and another are still acting as a brake on our war activities.' Labour MPs, in turn, resented such slights on workers, and believed that employers and managers were largely to blame. Aneurin Bevan and fifteen other MPs voted against Regulation 1AA, introduced by Ernest Bevin, the labour minister, which imposed penalties upon those instigating unofficial strikes.

Churchill himself was always reluctant to join attacks on the industrial workforce. 'We are told how badly labour is behaving,' he said in a debate on war production on 29 July 1941,

> and then a lot of people who never did a day's hard work in their lives are out after them . . . People speak of workmen getting £6, £7, or £8 a week and not giving a fair return to the State . . . I come to the remark of my hon. Friend the Member for Kidderminster [Sir John Wardlaw-Milne], who said that 'our people are only working up to 75 per cent of their possible efficiency.' 75 per cent of what? . . . I take as the datum line the three months after Dunkirk. Then, it will be admitted, our people worked to the utmost limit of their moral, mental and physical strength. Men fell exhausted at their lathes, and workmen and working women did not take their clothes off for a week at a time. Meals, rest and relaxation all faded from their minds . . . There are certainly . . . reasons why we cannot wholly recapture and maintain indefinitely the intense personal efforts of a year ago . . . If we are to win this war . . . it will be largely by staying power. For that purpose you must have reasonable minimum holidays for the masses of workers.

Churchill suggested that the conditions of manual workers had worsened in consequence of their wartime diet: 'Except for our Fighting Services, we have been driven back to a large extent from the carnivore to the herbivore. That may be quite satisfactory to the dietetic scientists who would like to make us all live on nuts, but undoubtedly it has produced, and is producing, a very definite effect upon the energetic output of the heavy worker. We want more meat in the mines and the foundries, and we want more cheese.' He noted left-wing attacks on Ernest Bevin, Minister for Labour: 'He makes mistakes, as I do, though not so many or so serious – he has not the same opportunities . . . And if you tell me that the results he produces do not compare with those of totalitarian systems of government and society, I reply by saying "We shall see about that when we get to the end of the story."'

Churchill had much greater faith in the British people than did his ministers, which helps to explain his bitterness when they expelled him from office in 1945. Most Conservative politicians were fearful of the working class, conscious of deep popular discontent with the old order. Many voters would never forget the perceived betrayals of the Depression and the pre-war foreign policy which had permitted the ascent of Hitler. Thoughtful Tories knew this. Halifax once wrote to Duff Cooper: 'We [Chamberlain's ministers in early 1940] were all conscious of the contrast between the readiness of the Nation . . . to spend £9 million a day in war to protect a certain way of life, and the unwillingness of the administrative authorities in peace to put up, shall we say, £10 million to assist in the reconditioning of Durham unless they could see the project earning a reasonable percentage.'

Many of Britain's 'haves' were acutely nervous of its 'have-nots', especially when popular enthusiasm for Russia was running high. Fear of 'the reds', and of malign consequences from the boost the war provided to their prestige, was a pervasive theme among Britain's political class. Those with a taste for blunt speaking asserted that Russian communists seemed to be conducting their war effort more impressively than British capitalists. Self-consciousness about this state of affairs was never far from the minds of either Churchill or his people in 1942–43. A deep, persistent discontent about perceived Western Allied inertia, contrasted with Soviet achievement, prevailed in many of the humblest homes in Britain.

ELEVEN

'Second Front Now!'

On 3 April 1942, Roosevelt dispatched to London Harry Hopkins and the chief of the army, bearing a personal letter from himself to the prime minister. 'Dear Winston,' this began, 'What Harry and Geo Marshall will tell you all about has my heart and mind in it. Your people & mine demand the establishment of a front to draw off pressure on the Russians, & these peoples are wise enough to see that the Russians are to-day killing more Germans & destroying more equipment than you & I put together. Even if full success is not attained, the big objective will be. Go to it!'

The mission of Hopkins and Marshall was to persuade the British to undertake an early landing in France. This was the US chief of the army's first encounter with Alan Brooke, and each man was wary of the other. They were a match in stubbornness, but little else. The Ulsterman was bemused when Marshall told him that he sometimes did not see Roosevelt for six weeks: 'I was fortunate if I did not see Winston for 6 hours.' The British were offered two alternative US plans. The first called for a 1943 invasion by thirty US and eighteen British divisions, with the strategic objective of securing Antwerp. Marshall, acutely mindful of the urgency of the Russians' plight, favoured the second and less ambitious option: an operation to be launched in September 1942 by mainly British forces, supported by 2½ US divisions – 'no very great contribution', as Brooke observed acidly. The American general acknowledged that it might be impossible indefinitely to hold a beachhead on the Continent in the face of a rapid German build-up. He nonetheless considered that the benefits of drawing enemy forces from the eastern front at such a critical moment made even a short-lived incursion into France worthwhile.

It was almost intolerably galling for the British that after suffering German bombardment and siege through thirty-one months, for twenty-seven of which the Americans had sat comfortably in the dress circle, they should now be urged to sacrifice another army in compliance with bustling US impatience for action. Brooke wrote of Marshall: 'In many respects he is a very dangerous man while being a very charming one!' The CIGS told his staff that the highest aspiration of any credible Anglo–American operation in France in 1942 would be to seize and hold the Cherbourg peninsula across the twenty-mile width of its neck. Measured against the war in the east, said Brooke, where the Russians were fighting across a thousand-mile front, so feeble an initiative would make the Western Allies the laughing stock of the world. John Kennedy commented on Soviet demands for a French invasion: 'The extraordinary thing is that the Russians seem to have no idea of our real strength. Or if they do, they are so obsessed with their own point of view that they do not care what happens to us.' It was odd that a British general should expect anything else from Moscow. It was much more dismaying, however, to find the Americans prey to the same strategic fantasy, arguing the case for a sacrificial, even suicidal sortie into France, of a kind Japanese samurai might have applauded.

Churchill nonetheless responded enthusiastically to the president's letter, 'your masterly document', as he called it. 'I am in entire agreement in principle with all you propose, and so are the chiefs of staff. If, as our experts believe, one can carry this whole plan through successfully, it will be one of the grand events in all the history of war.' Here the prime minister set the tone for all British dealings with the Americans about the Second Front, as the invasion concept was popularly known – the 'First Front' was, of course, in Russia. Though Churchill had not the slightest intention of leading an early charge back into Europe, he enthused to his visitors about the prospect. He accepted the need for Allied land forces to engage the enemy on the Continent, for he knew how dear was this objective to American hearts, and especially that of George Marshall. Attlee and Eden joined the prime minister in declaring how warmly they welcomed Washington's plan. Churchill and his commanders then set about ensuring that nothing should be done to implement it.

They relied upon the difficulties to make the case for themselves. In a series of meetings that began at Chequers, Marshall made his pitch. On 14 April he told Churchill and the British chiefs that 'within the next three or four months, we were very likely to find ourselves in the position when we were forced to take action on the continent'. Mountbatten, now a member of the chiefs' committee as head of combined operations, emphasised the dire shortage of landing craft. The prime minister cautioned that it was scarcely feasible to break off operations in all the other theatres in which Allied troops were engaged. Marshall, unimpressed by Britain's extravagant commitments, as he perceived them, in the Middle East, observed that 'great firmness' would be needed to avoid 'further dispersions'.

The American visitors were generously plied with courtesies. They returned to Washington aware that Churchill and his commanders had doubts about a 1942 landing, but wrongly supposing that they were persuadable. Only slowly did Marshall and his colleagues grow to understand that British professions of principled enthusiasm were unmatched by any intention of early commitment. The US chief of the army was too big a man to succumb to anglophobia, as did some of his colleagues. But henceforward this stiff, humourless officer, who concealed considerable passion beneath his cool exterior, had a mistrust of British evasions, verbal and strategic, which persisted for the rest of the war. Churchill's nation, he considered, was traumatised by its defeats, morbidly conscious of its poverty and obsessed with fear of heavy casualties. The British refused to accept what seemed to the Americans a fundamental reality: that it was worth paying any price to keep Russia fighting.

Throughout the war, the military leaders of the United States displayed a strategic confidence much greater than that of their British counterparts. The fact that Americans were never obliged to face the prospect of invasion of their homeland, still less the reality of bombardment of their cities, removed a significant part of the tension and apprehension which suffused British decision-making. American forces endured setbacks abroad, but never the storm of shell at home and abject defeats abroad which characterised British experience for three years. On the issue of the Second Front, Marshall's judgement was almost certainly gravely mistaken. The 1942 strategic view adopted by Churchill and Brooke was right. But the British damaged their relationship with the chief of the army and his colleagues by persistent dissimulation. There was Churchill's cable to Roosevelt of 17 April, acknowledging American enthusiasm for an early landing in France, and asserting that 'we are proceeding with plans and preparations on that basis'. As late as 20 June he was writing, albeit amid a thick hedge of qualifications: 'Arrangements are being made for a landing of six or eight Divisions on the coast of Northern France early in September.' The British prevaricated because they feared that frankness would provoke the Americans to shift the axis of their national effort westward, towards the Pacific. Indeed, Marshall once threatened to do this.

The debate was further complicated by the fact that Marshall's view accorded with that of the British and American publics. A host of ordinary people responded to the Russians' plight with a warmth and sympathy absent from the attitudes of British ministers and service chiefs. The *New Statesman* of 14 February 1942 quoted an officer who had been a pre-war Labour parliamentary candidate: 'Everywhere there is a feeling that some groups of people – perhaps Big Business, perhaps the politicians – are thwarting our natural development. A few more Russian victories and Far East defeats may force Westminster to understand that the most deep-seated feeling in England today is one of envy – envy of the Russians, who are being allowed to fight all out.' Envy was surely the wrong word to ascribe to public sentiment, but guilt there was in plenty, among British people who felt that their own country was doing embarrassingly little to promote the defeat of the Axis.

On Sunday, 29 March, 40,000 people massed in Trafalgar Square for a demonstration in support of a Second Front. Among other speakers, *Sunday Express* columnist John Gordon addressed the theme 'Strike in Europe now!' In April the government lost two parliamentary by-elections, one in Rugby to an independent candidate standing on a 'Second Front Now' ticket. On 1 May the left-wing weekly *Tribune* carried an unsigned article by Frank Owen, then undergoing armoured training as a soldier, headlined: 'Why Churchill?' Its author posed the question: 'Have we time to afford Churchill's strategy?' – meaning the delay to a Second Front. Brooke wrote in his diary, voicing sentiments which would persist through the next two years: 'This universal cry to start a second front is going to be hard to compete with, and yet what can we do with some 10 divisions against the German masses? Unfortunately the country fails to realize the situation we are in.' The Germans, operating with good land communications and a strong air force, could crush a miniature invasion without significantly depleting the vast Axis army, over 200 divisions, engaged on the eastern front.

If Churchill must expect to endure the slings and arrows of critics ignorant of British military weakness, it was harsh that he also faced a barrage from one man who should have known better. Beaverbrook had resigned from the government allegedly on grounds of exhaustion. The shrewd civil servant Archie Rowlands believed, however, that the press lord perceived Churchill's administration failing, and wished to distance himself from its fate. Since Beaverbrook's visit to Moscow, this arch-capitalist had become obsessively committed to Stalin's cause, and to British aid for Russia. His newspapers campaigned stridently for the Second Front, intensifying the pressure on Churchill.

Visiting New York as a semi-official emissary of the British government, Beaverbrook addressed an audience of American newspaper and magazine publishers on 23 April. He told them: 'Communism under Stalin has won the applause and admiration of all the western nations.' He asserted that there was no persecution of religion in the USSR, and that 'the church doors are open'. He urged: 'Strike out to help Russia! Strike out violently! Strike even recklessly!' Here was rhetoric that went far beyond the courtesies necessary to placate Stalin and encourage his people, and that flaunted Beaverbrook's irresponsibility. Yet when Churchill telephoned next day from London, instead of delivering the stinging rebuke which was merited, he sought to appease the erratic press baron by offering him stewardship of all Britain's missions in Washington. Happily this proposal was rejected, but it reflected Churchill's perception of his own political beleaguerment.

Beaverbrook preened himself before Halifax about the huge fan mail he claimed to be receiving. His egomania fed extravagant ambition. The ambassador recorded in his diary that Beaverbrook told him: 'I might be the best man to run the war. It wants a ruthless, unscrupulous, harsh man, and I believe I could do it.' It is possible that, at a time when there was widespread clamour for the ministry of defence to be divorced from the premiership, Beaverbrook saw himself in the former role. Yet he demonstrated notable naïveté about strategic realities, given that he was privy to so much secret information about British weakness. When challenged about the difficulties of providing air cover for an early landing in France, Beaverbrook asserted that this could be provided by Beaufighters. Any man who supposed that twin-engined aircraft could contest air superiority with German Bf109s showed himself unfit to participate in strategic decision-making. Monstrously, Beaverbrook threatened that his newspapers would campaign for recognition of Stalin's claims in Eastern Europe and the Baltic states. Yet Churchill never lost faith in his friend, nor expelled him from his circle, as Clementine so often urged him to do. The prime minister's loyalty to 'the Beaver' was as ill-deserved as it proved unrewarding.

Molotov, Stalin's foreign minister, arrived in Britain for talks on 21 May 1942. Following his first encounter with the prime minister he reported to Moscow: 'Concerning the second front, Churchill made a brief statement during the morning session, stating that the British and American governments are in principle committed to mounting such an operation in Europe, with maximum available resources, at the earliest possible date, and are making energetic preparations for this.' After subsequent meetings, however, at which the British made much of the practical difficulties of staging an invasion of the Continent, he told Moscow that it would be rash to expect early action. Molotov was a grey bureaucrat so slavishly loyal to Stalin that during the thirties purges he signed an arrest order for his own wife. By such means he, almost alone among prominent old Bolsheviks, had escaped the executioners and clung to office. It must have strained to the limits Churchill's obedience to political imperatives to entertain such a man at Downing Street and Chequers, which the Russian remembered chiefly, and contemptuously, for its lack of showers.

If further evidence was needed of Beaverbrook's mischief-making, Molotov reported on 27 May, following two encounters with the press lord: 'He advised me to push the British government [for an invasion], and assured me that Roosevelt is a proponent of the second front.' Beyond Russian secretiveness, Churchill was also obliged to contend with Moscow's susceptibility to fantasies. Stalin appeared sincerely to believe that Japanese aircraft were being flown by German pilots, and that the British had for some unfathomable reason provided Japan with 1,500 combat aircraft.

Molotov's main business in London was to negotiate a treaty of alliance. He was dismayed by British refusal to meet the demands which Russia had been making ever since entering the war, for recognition of its hegemony not only over the Baltic states, but also over eastern Poland. Stalin, however, was less concerned. He cabled Molotov on the 24th, telling him to accept the vaguely worded draft about post-war security offered by Eden: 'We do not consider this a meaningless statement, we regard it as an important document. It does not contain that paragraph [proposed in a Russian draft] on border security, but probably this is not so bad as it leaves our hands free. We will resolve the issue of frontiers, or rather, of security guarantees for our frontiers . . . by force.' Much more serious, in Russian eyes, was the perceived inadequacy of British arms shipments. Stalin emphasised the need for fighters and tanks, especially Valentines, which had proved best suited, or least unsuited, to Russian conditions. The British, however, remained evasive about further reinforcement of their convoys to Archangel. Joan Beaumont, one of the most convincing chroniclers of wartime Western aid to Russia, has written: 'It is the irony of the commitment to the Soviet Union that while . . . consensus on its necessity grew in the first half of 1942, so also did the obstacles in the way of putting this into effect.'

Grandiose American promises of aid – initially eight million tons for 1942–43, half of this food – foundered on the Allies' inability to ship anything like such quantities. By the end of June 1943 less than three million tons had been delivered of a pledged 4.4 million. Joan Beaumont again: 'Considerable though these achievements and sacrifices were, they seemed poor in contrast to the promises which had been made . . . At the time when the Russian need was greatest, the assistance from the West . . . was at its most uncertain.' There was special Soviet bitterness about British refusal of repeated requests for Spitfires. The most strident of Russia's propagandists, Ilya Ehrenburg, denounced to his millions of Soviet readers the fact that the Allies were 'sending very few aircraft, and not the best they have either'. The Russians claimed to be insulted on discovering that some Hurricanes they received were reconditioned rather than new. Given the poor quality of planes and tanks provided, Moscow began to focus its demands upon trucks and food.

Molotov flew on from London to Washington, where the White House butler reported to Roosevelt that Russia's foreign minister had arrived with a pistol in his suitcase. The president observed that they must simply hope it was not intended for use on him. Following a meeting at the White House on 30 May, Molotov displayed in his report to Moscow a frustration at Roosevelt's evasive bonhomie that would have struck a chord with the British. Dinner, the Russian complained, 'was followed by a lengthy but meaningless conversation . . . I said that it would be desirable to engage at least 40 German divisions at the Western front in the summer and autumn of this year. Roosevelt and Marshall responded that they very much wanted to achieve this, but faced immediate shipping difficulties in moving forces to France.' The Russian pleaded that if there was no Second

Front in 1942, Germany would be much stronger in 1943. 'They offered no definite information.' However, the president said that 'preparations for the second front are under way . . . he, Roosevelt is trying to persuade the American generals to take the risk and land 6 to 10 divisions in France. It is possible that it will mean another Dunkirk and the loss of 100,000–120,000 men, but the sacrifices have to be made to provide help in 1942 and shatter German morale.'

Stalin cabled again on 3 June, first rebuking Molotov for the brevity of his reports. The Soviet leader said that he did not want to be told mere essentials. He needed trivial details as well, to provide a sense of mood. 'Finally, we think it absolutely necessary that both [British and American] communiqués contain paragraphs about establishing the second front in Europe, and state that full agreement had been reached on this issue. We also think it necessary that both communiqués should include specifics on deliveries of material from Britain and the USA to the Soviet Union.'

Here were the same imperatives pressing Stalin as had weighed upon Churchill in 1940–41. First, and as the Russian leader acknowledged in his cables to Molotov, it was vital to persuade Hitler that there was a real threat of an Allied invasion of France, to deter him from transferring further divisions to the eastern front. Second, morale was as important to the peoples of the Soviet Union as to those of the democracies. Every gleam of hope was precious. Stalin nursed no real expectation that Anglo-American armies would land on the Continent in 1942. But, just as Churchill in 1941 promoted in Britain much more ambitious expectations of American belligerence than the facts merited, so Stalin wished to trumpet to the Russian people Roosevelt's and Churchill's assurances that a Second Front was coming, even though he himself did not believe them. If the British and Americans later breached such assurances, this would provide useful evidence of capitalist perfidy. For embattled Russia in the summer of 1942, 'later' seemed scarcely to matter.

Back in London on 9 June, Molotov met Churchill once more, before the signing of a treaty of alliance. If the Russian's purpose was to promote discord between London and Washington, he was by no means unsuccessful. The prime minister was much disturbed when Molotov told him of Roosevelt's aspirations for the post-war world, including international trusteeship for the Dutch and French empires in Asia, and enforced disarmament of all save the Great Powers. Then the foreign minister outlined his exchanges at the White House about the Second Front:

> I mentioned among other things that Roosevelt agreed with the point of view that I had set forth, i.e., that it could prove harder to establish a second front in 1943 than in 1942 due to possible grave problems on our front. Finally, I mentioned that the president attached such great importance to the creation of a second front in 1942 that he was prepared to gamble, to endure another Dunkirk and lose 100,000 or 120,000 men ... I stressed however that I thought the number of divisions which Roosevelt proposed to commit insufficient, i.e., six to ten.
>
> Here Churchill interrupted me in great agitation, declaring that he would never agree to another Dunkirk and a fruitless sacrifice of 100,000 men, no matter who recommended such a notion. When I replied that I was only conveying Roosevelt's view, Churchill responded: 'I shall tell him my view on this issue myself.'

Oliver Harvey recorded the same conversation: 'Roosevelt had calmly told Molotov he would be prepared to contemplate a sacrifice of 120,000 men if necessary – our men. PM said he would not hear of it.'

Molotov said years later: 'We had to squeeze everything we could get out of [the Allies]. I have no doubt that Stalin did not believe [that a Second Front would happen]. But one had to demand it! One had to demand it for the sake of our own people. Because people were waiting, weren't they, to see whether help [from the Allies] would come. That sheet of paper [the Anglo–Soviet agreement] was of great political significance to us. It cheered people up, and that meant a lot then.'

The Anglo–Soviet Treaty signed on 26 May merely committed 'the

High Contracting Parties . . . to afford one another military and other assistance and support of all kinds'. But in Moscow after Molotov's return from London, *Pravda* reported: 'The Day is at hand when the Second Front will open.' On 19 June the newspaper described a meeting of the Supreme Soviet, whose members were told that the accords reached between the Soviet Union, Britain and the US reflected the fact 'that complete agreement had been achieved about the urgency of opening of the second front in Europe in 1942'. This announcement, said the paper, was received with protracted applause, as was a subsequent statement that 'these agreements are of the highest importance for the nations of the Soviet Union, since the opening of the second front in Europe will create insurmountable difficulties for Hitler's armies on our front'. All this was untrue, and well understood to be so by Stalin and Molotov. But among so many other deceits, what was one more, deemed so necessary to the spirit of the Russian people? And in this case the Russians were entirely entitled to declare that the Americans, and in lesser degree the British, were making promises in bad faith.

Molotov, in old age, asserted that he found Churchill 'smarter' than Roosevelt: 'I knew them all, these capitalists, but Churchill was the strongest and cleverest . . . As for Roosevelt, he believed in dollars. Not that he believed in nothing else, but he thought that they were so rich and we so poor, and that we would become so weakened that we would come to the Americans and beg. This was their mistake . . . They woke up when they'd lost half of Europe. And here of course Churchill found himself in a very foolish predicament. In my opinion, Churchill was the most intelligent of them, as an imperialist. He knew that if we, the Russians, defeated Germany, then England would start losing its feathers. He realised this. As for Roosevelt, he thought: [Russia] is a poor country with no industry, no grain, they are going to come and beg. There is no other way out for them. And we saw all this completely differently. The entire nation had been prepared for the sacrifices, for struggle.' This was, of course, a characteristic Soviet post-facto exposition of what took place in 1942–43. But Molotov seems right to have perceived in the Americans' behaviour a fundamental condescension, of the same kind that underlay their attitude towards Britain. It was rooted in a belief that when the conflict ended, US power would be unchallengeable by either ally.

Gen. Dwight Eisenhower wrote to his old friend George Patton on 20 July 1942: 'This war is still young.' For Americans, this was true. But the British, after almost three years of privation, defeat, intermittent bombardment and enforced inaction, saw matters very differently. Washington was seeking to browbeat Churchill into sacrificing a British army, with token American participation, as a gesture of support for the Soviet Union. Marshall's cardinal mistake was failure to perceive that the scale of a battle in France was beyond the power of the Allies to determine. The Allies might seek to conduct a minor operation, but the Germans could mass forces to convert this into a major disaster.

There was never the smallest possibility that the prime minister and his generals would accede to the US proposal. 'I do not think there is much doing on the French coast this year,' the prime minister minuted the chiefs of staff on 1 June. Britain in mid-1942 had fifteen divisions in the Middle East, ten in India and thirty at home, few of the latter ready for war. None of the fifteen first-line infantry divisions in Home Forces was fully equipped, while nine 'lower establishment' divisions were in worse case. Two-thirds of weapons and equipment emerging from factories were being shipped directly overseas, where they were needed 'at the sharp end', while Home Forces continued to queue for resources.

That spring Churchill pressed two proposals upon his chiefs of staff against their wishes. He prevailed on one, though not the other. He overruled Brooke's judgement that the seizure of Vichy-held Madagascar was unnecessary. Troops landed on the island in May, quickly capturing the main port, then fighting a six-month campaign against dogged Vichy resistance before the entire island was subdued in November. This was a wise precautionary move. If the Japanese, at the floodtide of their conquests, had fulfilled their ambitions to take Madagascar, British communications with India and the Middle East would have been critically threatened. The other Churchillian proposal, however, for a landing in north Norway, was defeated by all-service objections. It should have been within the powers of the British Army in 1942 to seize and hold a Norwegian perimeter, thus frustrating further attacks on convoys to Russia by the Luftwaffe and German navy. But given the proven shortcomings of the army and Fleet Air Arm, Brooke was probably right to quash the plan. Such an operation would have fatally compromised Churchill's North African ambitions, which promised larger gains for lesser hazards.

The British and American publics were, however, ignorant of the weakness of the Western Allies' armed forces in comparison to those of their enemies. For most of 1942 they debated the Second Front with a fervour that exasperated the prime minister and his commanders. Churchill was disgusted by a *Time* magazine article which described Britain as 'oft-burned, defensive-minded', and wrote to Brendan Bracken: 'This vicious rag should have no special facilities here.' The British embassy in Washington reported to London: 'Advocacy of a second front has increased largely as a result of the Russian reverses. An influential section of editorial opinion . . . has been insisting that the danger of such an operation now is more than outweighed by the greater danger likely to arise if it is delayed.' The British were constantly provoked by manifestations of American ignorance about operational difficulties. A US officer at dinner in London one night demanded of a British general why more fighters could not be flown to Malta, to protect Mediterranean convoys. The visitor was oblivious of the fact, irritably explained by his host, that Malta was far beyond the range of Spitfires or Hurricanes flying from Gibraltar.

The British were increasingly troubled by the difficulties of conveying their views to an American leadership of which both the political and military elements seemed resistant to its ally's opinions. A British official in Washington wrote to London in May 1942: 'No Englishman here has the close relationship with Hopkins and the President which are necessary. There is no one who can continually represent to the White House the Prime Minister's views on war direction. The Ambassador does not regard it within his sphere.

Dill dare not as he would ruin his relationship with the US chiefs of staff if he saw Hopkins too often.' Brigadier Vivian Dykes of the British Military Mission wrote: 'We simply hold no cards at all, yet London expects us to work miracles. It is a hard life.'

Churchill concluded that only another personal meeting with Roosevelt could resolve the Second Front issue, or more appropriately the alternative North African landing scheme – Operation *Torch* – in Britain's favour. He took off once more with Alan Brooke, in a Boeing flying-boat. By the afternoon of 19 June he was being driven around Roosevelt's Hyde Park estate, *tête-à-tête* with his host. Here was exactly the scenario which Churchill wanted, and which the US chiefs of staff deplored. Their commander-in-chief was talking alone with Britain's fiercely persuasive prime minister. Churchill wrote in his memoirs that the two men thus got more business done than at conferences. This was disingenuous. What he meant, of course, was that he was free from impassioned and hostile interventions by Marshall and his colleagues. At Hyde Park the prime minister was enchanted to be treated as 'family', though his staff sometimes overreached themselves in exploiting guest privileges. Private secretary John Martin was sternly rebuked by Roosevelt's telephonist, Louise Hachmeister, when she found him ensconced in her master's study, using the president's direct line to Washington.

On 20 June at Hyde Park, Churchill handed Roosevelt a masterly note on strategy. Arrangements for a landing in France in September were going forward, said the prime minister. However, the British continued to oppose such an operation unless there was a realistic prospect of being able to stay. 'No responsible British military authority has so far been able to make a plan for September 1942 which has any chance of success unless the Germans become utterly demoralised, of which there is no likelihood. Have the American staffs a plan? If so, what is it? If a plan can be found which offers a reasonable prospect of success His Majesty's Government will cordially welcome it and will share to the full with their American comrades the risks and sacrifices . . . But in case no plan can be made in which any responsible authority has good confidence . . . what else are we going to do? Can we afford to stand idle in the Atlantic theatre during the whole of 1942?' It was in this context, urged Churchill, that a North African landing should be studied.

That evening, president and prime minister flew to the capital. They were together at the White House when a pink message slip was brought to Roosevelt, who passed it wordlessly to Churchill. It read: 'Tobruk has surrendered, with 25,000 men taken prisoner.' Churchill was initially disbelieving. Before leaving Britain he had signalled to Auchinleck, stressing the importance of holding the port: 'Your decision to fight it out to the end most cordially endorsed. Retreat would be fatal. This is a business not only of armour but of will power. God bless you all.' Now the prime minister telephoned Ismay in London, who confirmed the loss of Tobruk, together with 33,000 men, 2,000 vehicles, 5,000 tons of supplies and 1,400 tons of fuel. A chaotic defence, left in the hands of a newly promoted and inexperienced South African major-general, had collapsed in the face of an unexpected German thrust from the south-east. The débâcle was characterised by command incompetence, a pitiful indolence and lack of initiative among many units. Maj.Gen. Klopper's last signal from Tobruk was an enigmatic study in despair: 'Situation shambles . . . Am doing the worst. Petrol destroyed.'

The prime minister was stunned, humiliated. It seemed unbearable that such news should have come while he was a visitor, indeed a suppliant, in Washington. Roosevelt, perceiving his guest's despondency, responded with unprecedented spontaneity, generosity and warmth. 'What can we do to help?' he asked. After consultation with his chiefs of staff, the president briefly entertained a notion of dispatching a US armoured division to fight in Egypt. On reflection, it was agreed instead to send the formation's 300 Sherman tanks and 100 self-propelled guns, for British use. This reinforcement, of quality equipment, was critical to later British victory at Alamein. Roosevelt's gesture, which required the removal of new weapons from a US combat formation, prompted the deepest and best-merited British gratitude towards the president of the war.

The American historian Douglas Porch, one of the ablest

chroniclers of the Mediterranean campaigns, believes that Churchill fundamentally misjudged American attitudes towards Britain's war effort. The prime minister wanted a victory in the Middle East, to dispel US scepticism about British fighting capability. Porch argues, however: 'It was Britain's beleaguered helplessness that evoked most sympathy in Washington and helped to prepare the American people psychologically to intervene in the war.' It was certainly true that Americans pitied British material weakness. Yet an enduring source of US resentment, reflected in polls throughout much of the war, was a belief that the British were not merely ill-armed, but also did not try hard enough. It was one thing for the US to provide food and arms to a defiantly struggling democracy, it was quite another to see the British apparently content to sit tight in their island, and conduct lethargic minor operations in North Africa, while the Russians did the real business, and paid the horrific blood price, of destroying Hitler's armies.

It was remarkable how much the mood in Washington had shifted since January. This time, there was no adulation for Churchill the visitor. 'Anti-British feeling is still strong,' the British embassy reported to London, 'stronger than it was before Pearl Harbor . . . This state of affairs is partly due to the fact that whereas it was difficult to criticise Britain while the UK was being bombed, such criticism no longer carries the stigma of isolationist or pro-Nazi sympathies.' Senator Allen Ellender of Louisiana declared sourly that 'there was little point in supplying the British with war material since they invariably lost it all'. Roosevelt's secretary, William Hassett, wrote in his diary: 'These English are too aggressive except on the battlefront, as assertive as the Jews, always asking for a little more and then still more after that.' Hassett admitted that the president found Churchill 'a delightful companion', but added: 'With a softie for president, Winnie would put rollers under the Treasury and open Second, Third, or Fourth Fronts with our fighting men.'

As for the general public, an Ohioan wrote to the White House: 'Tell that Churchill to go home where he belongs . . . All he wants is our money.' An anonymous 'mother of three' sought to address

Britain's prime minister from California: 'Every time you appear on our shores, it means something very terrible for us. Why not stay at home and fight your own battles instead of always pulling us into them to save your rotten necks?' A New Yorker's letter to a friend in Somerset, intercepted by the censors, said: 'I knew when I saw your fat-headed PM was over here that there was another disaster in the offing.' Such views were untypical – most Americans retained warm respect for Churchill. But they reflected widespread scepticism about his nation's willingness to fight, and doubt whether the prime minister's wishes coincided with American national interest. 'All the old animosities against the British have been revived,' wrote an analyst for the Office of War Information. 'She didn't pay her war debts after the last war. She refuses to grant India the very freedom she claims to be fighting for. She is holding a vast army in England to protect the homeland while her outposts are lost to the enemy.'

A further report later in the summer detected a marginal improvement of sentiment, but found confidence in the British still much below that of the previous autumn. It noted: 'Phrases such as "the British always want someone to pull their chestnuts out of the fire" and "England will fight to the last Frenchman" have attained considerable currency.' The OWI's July survey invited Americans to say which nation they thought was trying hardest to win the war. A loyal 37 per cent answered the United States, 30 per cent named Russia, 14 per cent China, 13 per cent offered no opinion. Just 6 per cent identified the British as most convincing triers. A similar poll the following month asked which belligerent was perceived as having the best fighting spirit. Some 65 per cent said America, 6 per cent named Britain. The same survey highlighted Americans' stunning ignorance about the difficulties of mounting an invasion of Europe. A 57 per cent majority said they thought the Allies should launch a Second Front 'within two to three months'. A similar 53 per cent thought that such an operation would have a 'pretty good' chance of success, while 29 per cent reckoned the odds 50–50, and only 10 per cent feared that an invasion would fail. A remarkable 60 per cent of respondents thought not merely that an invasion of France should happen inside three months – they anticipated that it would.

US Supreme Court Justice Felix Frankfurter wrote on 9 July 1942 to Stafford Cripps, who had expressed concern about Anglo–American relations: 'The dominant underlying feeling is not bad . . . But there is a central difficulty. It is, as I see it, a lack of continuing conscious-ness of comradeship between the two peoples, not only in staving off an enemy that threatens everything we hold dear, but comrade-ship in achieving a common society having essentially the same gracious and civilized ends.' Columnist Walter Lippmann expressed similar views to Maynard Keynes. There was a need, suggested Lippmann, for a new political understanding between Britain and the US about the future of its empire: 'The Asiatic war has revived the profound anti-imperialism of the American tradition.'

The Foreign Office was dismayed by remarks made by the anglophile Wendell Willkie during a visit to Moscow. He told British ambassador Sir Archibald Clark Kerr that US public opinion towards Britain was shaping 'dangerously', and that he was 'scared' by it. Not one of the Americans he had met on his journey between Washington and Moscow, from truck drivers to ambassadors, had a good word for British behaviour abroad. He urged that the prime minister should make a speech on post-war policy showing that he realised that 'old-fashioned imperialism' was dead. Churchill, of course, had no intention of doing any such thing.

A 6 July report to the Foreign Office about the British embassy in Washington was almost flagellatory about the American view of Halifax's mission: 'The Embassy . . . has a quite fantastically low reputation. It is regarded as snobbish, arrogant, patronising, dim, asleep and a home of reactionary and generally disreputable ideas.' The report then listed popular American objections to Britain, headed by its class system, which was alienating workers – 'the British are going red'; imperialism; 'British bunglers in high places: over-cautious, contemptuous of all new ideas and defensively minded, tired old men bored with their own task . . . British sitting safely in own island with 3.5 million men under arms, Brits always being defeated ... Lend-Lease is stripping America to supply the British who have not even paid their [First] war debts ... Anti-British sentiment is a part of the central patriotic American tradition ... Anglophobia is a proof of vigorous Americanism, socially acceptable in a way anti-Catholicism and anti-semitism are not ... All the Roosevelt-haters hate the English because they are held to be popular with the President.'

British postal censorship reported to the Foreign Office on a cross-section of US opinion monitored in mail intercepts. From Newark, New Jersey, a man wrote to a friend in Britain: 'Believe me we here are disgusted reading of British retreats and nobody blames the Tommy. We blame the Brass Hats for their inefficiency and being outmanoeuvred by Jerry every time.' On 11 September, a New Yorker wrote in the same vein: 'There is no doubt that something is rotten about the British command everywhere ... It isn't always lack of material – it is more often blind stupidity.' Another New Yorker, posted to Australia, wrote to a British friend in Stoke-on-Trent: 'English imperialism is responsible for more of our griefs and wars than you can shake a stick at. Incidentally I'm surprised to find that a great many Aussies hate the set-up in England more than I do! You IMPOSSIBLE English!'

Eden's Minister of State Richard Law, son of former prime minister Bonar Law, dispatched an extraordinarily emotional report to the Foreign Office during a visit to America. He claimed that in US Army training camps 'anti-British feeling was beyond belief ... deliberately inculcated by certain higher officers, notably General [Brehon] Somervell, who mocked that Churchill lacked the "sustained excitement" to execute a cross-channel attack'. Throughout the higher command of the US Army, claimed Law, anti-British feeling was intense. There was violent jealousy of the prime minister, who was regarded as dominating and bamboozling the president. The American chiefs of staff 'were about as friendly to the British as they would be to the German general staff if they sat round a table with them'. This was an extravagant assessment of Anglo–American tensions. But it illustrates the scale of concern in British official circles in 1942, when the nation's military reputation was at its lowest ebb.

Churchill knew that his nation and his soldiers had to be seen to fight. If they could not engage in Europe, they must do so in the Middle East. The long periods of passivity which gripped Eighth Army in North Africa, however necessary logistically, inflicted immense harm upon both British self-esteem and the nation's image abroad. At a war cabinet meeting presided over by Attlee, Bevin declaimed theatrically: 'We must have a victory! What the British public wants is a victory!' When John Kennedy was summoned to Downing Street, the prime minister talked of current operations in North Africa, 'then added a dig at the British Army (which unfortunately he can never resist) saying, "if Rommel's army were all Germans, they would beat us."' Later, the DMO reported the conversation to Brooke: 'I told him what Winston had said about the Germans being better than our troops & he said he must speak to Winston about this. His constant attacks on the Army were doing harm – especially when they were made in the presence of other politicians, as they so often were.' Yet so ashamed was Kennedy, as a soldier, about the fall of Tobruk that for some time he avoided his beloved 'Rag' – the Army & Navy club – to escape unwelcome questions about the army's lamentable showing.

While Churchill was in Washington in June, some American newspapers suggested that his government would fall. He was sufficiently alarmed by what he read to telephone Eden from the White House for reassurance that there was no critical threat to his leadership. Nothing important had changed, he was told, but Tory MP Sir John Wardlaw-Milne had tabled a censure motion in the Commons. Public opinion was fragile. 'The people do not like him being away so much in such critical times,' wrote a naval officer. A Mass-Observation diarist, Rosemary Black, deplored Churchill's absence in America at a time when the British people were enduring so much bad news: 'I myself felt pretty disgusted with him when I saw a photograph of him enjoying himself at the White House again. If only he'd keep those great gross cigars out of his face once in a way.'

London voluntary worker Vere Hodgson, bewildered as the rest of the nation by the fall of Tobruk, wrote crossly in her diary: 'The enemy did not seem to understand what was expected of them, and failed to fall in with our plans. Grrr! As Miss Moyes says, it makes you see green, pink and heliotrope. I woke up in the middle of Sunday night, and thought of that convoy delivered with so much blood, sweat and losses to Tobruk on Saturday – to fall like ripe fruit into German mouths. I squirmed beneath the bedclothes and ground my teeth with rage.' She added after the prime minister broadcast two weeks later: 'Mr Churchill's speech did not contain much comfort. He dominated us as he always does, and we surrender to his over-powering personality – but he knows no more than any of us why Tobruk fell.'

George King wrote to his son from Sanderstead in Surrey: 'We heard yesterday that we have lost Tobruk; the same old story – rotten leadership. The Yanks will yet show us how to do the job. The "red tabs" form the only rotten part of the British Army!' Lancashire house-wife Nella Last, intensely loyal to Churchill, mused in bewilderment to her diary on 25 June 1942: 'Where can soldiers go where they have a reasonable chance? Tobruk has gone – what of Egypt, Suez and India? Nearly three years of war: WHY don't we get going – what stops us? Surely by now things should be organised better in some way. Why should our men be thrown against superior mechanical horrors, and our equipment not standardised for easier management and repair? There is no flux to bind us – nothing. It's terrifying. Not all this big talk of next year and the next will stop our lads dying uselessly. If only mothers could think that their poor sons had not died uselessly – with a purpose . . . It's shocking.'

A report of the Home Intelligence Division of the Ministry of Information declared: 'Russian successes continue to provide an antidote to bad news from other fronts . . . "Thank God for Russia" is a frequent expression of the very deep and fervent feeling for that country which permeates wide sections of the public.' Membership of Britain's Communist Party rose from 12,000 in June 1941 to 56,000 by the end of 1942. The British media provided no hint of the frightful cruelties through which Stalin sustained the Soviet Union's defence, nor of the blunders and failures which characterised its war effort in 1941–42.

In informed political and military circles there was no scintilla of the guilt about Soviet sacrifices that prevailed among the wider public. From Churchill downwards, there was an overwhelming and not unreasonable perception that whatever miseries and losses fell upon the Russian people, the policies of their own government – above all the 1939 Nazi–Soviet Pact – were chiefly responsible. Brooke wrote disgustedly about British aid to Russia: 'We received nothing in return except abuse for handling the convoys inefficiently.' John Kennedy expressed bewilderment about public attitudes: 'There is an extraordinary and misguided enthusiasm for the Russians. Stalin is more of a hero than the King or even Winston.' A naval officer, Commander Andrew Yates, wrote to a friend in America: 'Little as I formerly liked him, the man who killed a million Germans, Jo Stalin, becomes my friend for life.' A Ministry of Information official cautioned, however, against exaggerated fears that popular applause for Soviet military prowess equated with a mass conversion to communism, such as some Tory MPs perceived: 'That danger will never come through admiration of the achievements of another country, but only through dissatisfaction with our own – dissatisfaction savage enough to cherish a revolutionary programme.'

Nonetheless, perceptions of the Red Army as braver and more willing for sacrifice than their own soldiers were a source of anger and shame among Churchill's people, which persisted throughout the summer of 1942. The public could not be told that Stalin's armies achieved their remarkable feats under draconian compulsion; that if Russian soldiers sometimes displayed more fortitude than British or American ones, this was chiefly because if they flinched they faced execution by their own commanders, a sanction imposed upon hundreds of thousands of Stalin's men in the course of the war. Debate about British military inertia and failure continued to dominate the press. 'Reactionary attitudes are spreading,' complained communist Elizabeth Belsey. 'The *Spectator* this week sounds much opposed to the 2nd front. What do all these people suppose Russia is to do without the 2nd Front? Continue fighting with faith instead of oil?'

Maggie Joy Blunt, a journalist of left-wing sympathies, wrote on 7 August 1942: 'Why is not Mr Churchill, rather than his critics, standing on the plinth of the Nelson column shouting for a Second Front and demanding greater efforts from every man and woman in the country? The desire to make that effort is there. The people would respond instantly to the right word from Churchill. We have the feeling, strongly, that Powers That Be wish to see Russian might crippled before they will move a finger to help. They do not want Russia to have any say in the peace terms. Capitalist interests are still vastly strong, and the propertied bourgeois, although a minority, have still an enormous influence on the conduct of our affairs and are terrified of the idea of Socialism. Socialism is inevitable.' Londoner Ethel Mattison wrote to her sister in California on 1 August: 'When the Anglo–Soviet Alliance was signed, and . . . the Second Front was one of the main points . . . [It] rather tended to make people sit back and wait for it. However, the waiting has been so long and the Russians are suffering so terribly that it seems the idea must be pushed into realisation by the force of public opinion. Everywhere you go, in buses, trains and in lifts you hear fragments of conversation in connection with it.'

The Russian press, unsurprisingly, devoted much space to the Second Front lobby. *Pravda* carried a story reporting the mass rallies in Britain in support of early action under the headline 'English people are willing to help their Russian comrades'. It quoted Associated Press correspondent Drew Middleton declaring after a tour of Britain that there was overwhelming public support for an invasion, that shipping difficulties could be overcome, that bombing of Germany was recognised as an insufficient support to Russia. *Pravda* also described Second Front demonstrations in Canada. Through the months that followed there was much more Moscow press comment on the same theme. On 9 August *Pravda* headlined: 'No time to lose – British press on the Second Front'. On 15 August: 'Time has come to act, say American newspapers'. Next day, a report described a deputation representing 105,000 British workers from seventy-eight companies calling at Downing Street to present a Second Front petition to Churchill. On the 19th, *Pravda* headlined: 'English public organisations demand offensive against Germany', and on the 23rd: 'We have no right to wait – English trades unions demand opening Second Front'.

The narrative of the Second World War presented by most historians is distorted by the fact that it focuses upon what happened, rather than what did not. Until November 1942, weeks and sometimes months passed without much evidence of activity by British land forces. Between June 1941 and the end of the war, British newspapers and BBC broadcasts were often dominated by reports of the struggle on the eastern front, where action appeared continuous. Countless editorials paid tribute to the deeds of 'our gallant Russian allies'. This goes far to explain why Russia commanded such admiration in contemporary Britain. Accounts of the eastern fighting were vague and often wildly inaccurate, but they coalesced to create a valid impression of vigorous, hideously costly and increasingly successful action by the Red Army. The battle for Stalingrad, which now began to receive massive coverage, intensified public dismay about the contrast between British and Russian achievements. 'Every week of successful defence,' reported the Ministry of Information on 9 October 1942, 'confirms the popularity of the Russians and there is much uneasiness and unhappiness at the spectacle of our apparent inaction.'

Ismay said that he admired Churchill as much for the courage with which he resisted a premature Second Front as for the vigour with which he promoted other projects. He observed that a lesser man might have given in to the vociferous lobbyists. He deplored the public's inescapable ignorance of the fact that real partnership with the Russians was impossible, given their implacable secretiveness. To understand the British public temper in World War II, it is necessary to recognise how little people knew about anything beyond the visible movements of armies and the previous night's bomber raids on

Germany. Information which is commonplace in time of peace becomes the stuff of high secrecy in war: industrial production figures, weapons shortages, shipping movements and losses, details of aid to Russia or lack of it. Many reports in newspapers, especially those detailing Allied combat successes and enemy losses, were fanciful. The prime minister offered the nation only the vaguest and most general notion of its likely prospects. This was prudent, but obliged millions of people to exist for years in a miasma of uncertainty, which contributed decisively to the demoralisation of 1941–42.

A study of contemporary British newspapers surprises a modern reader, because in contrast to twenty-first-century practice, greater attention was paid to events than to personalities, even that of Churchill himself. He received much less coverage than does a modern prime minister, partly because little detail about his personal life was revealed outside his inner circle. For security reasons his travels were often unreported until he had left a given location. His speeches and public appearances were, of course, widely covered, but many days of the war passed without much press reference to the prime minister. While battlefield commanders such as Alexander and Montgomery became household names, other key figures remained almost unknown. Sir Alan Brooke, for instance, whose military role was second in importance only to that of Churchill, was scarcely mentioned in the wartime press. Above all, accurate prophecy was rendered impossible by the fact that the condition of the enemy, the situation 'on the other side of the hill', remained largely shrouded in mystery even to war leaders privy to Ultra secrets. Conditions in occupied Europe, as well as the state of Hitler's war machine, were imperfectly understood in London. It was widely reported that the Nazis were conducting appalling massacres, killing many Jews in death camps. But the concept of systematic genocide embracing millions of victims was beyond popular, and even prime minis-terial, imagination. Entire books have been written about Churchill and the Holocaust, yet the fundamentals may be expressed succinctly: the prime minister was aware from 1942 onwards that the Nazis were pursuing murderous policies towards the Jews. British Jewish leaders sought to urge upon him that their people were subject to unique and historically unprecedented horrors. He responded with words of deep sympathy, indeed passion, and once urged that the RAF should do whatever was possible to check the slaughter. But he did not himself pursue the issue when told of 'operational difficulties' – which meant that the airmen did not believe that attempts to destroy railway tracks in Eastern Europe were as useful to the war effort as continuing the assault on Germany's cities. Churchill perceived the killing of the Jews in the context of Hitler's wider policies of massacre, which embraced millions of Russians, Poles, Yugoslavs, Greeks and other races. He believed that the only way to address these horrors was by hastening the defeat of Germany and liberation of the occupied nations. This assumption also guided public sentiment.

Public ignorance fed endless speculation, embracing a range of possibilities from the war's ending within months to its indefinite continuation. When Harold Macmillan became British minister in the Mediterranean, he wrote: 'The trouble . . . is that no one really has any idea as to the future course of the war. One minute people rush to an extreme of pessimism – and think it will never end. The next they become so excited by a favourable battle that they regard it as more or less over. And the experts cannot give us any guidance. The better they are, the less willing I find them (I mean men like Cunningham, Tedder and Alexander) to express a view.' A contributor to *Punch* composed a poem about his own 'befuddlement amid one bright star of England'. This struck a chord with Alan Lascelles, assistant private secretary to King George VI, who wrote in his diary: 'I suppose that, with the exception of some thirty or forty High Esoterics – the War Cabinet and its immediate minions – I get as much illumination on the drear fog of war as anyone in this country. Yet I am befogged, all right.' For a humble citizen to keep going it was necessary to hope blindly, because evidence for informed optimism was lacking.

In the first two days of July, Churchill faced a debate on the censure motion tabled against him in the Commons. Sir John Wardlaw-Milne destroyed his own case in the first minutes of his speech by proposing that the Duke of Gloucester, the King's notoriously thick-headed brother, should become Britain's military supremo. The House burst into mocking laughter, and Churchill's face lit up. He knew, in that moment, that he could put his critics to flight. But he was nonetheless obliged to endure a barrage of criticism. Aneurin Bevan spoke with vicious wit: 'The prime minister wins debate after debate and loses battle after battle. The country is beginning to say that he fights debates like a war and the war like a debate.' Bevan also asserted that arms factories were producing the wrong weapons; that the army was 'riddled by class prejudice' and poorly commanded.

Then he delivered the sort of peroration which disgusted Churchill, but struck a powerful echo with the public: 'For heaven's sake do not let us make the mistake of betraying those lion-hearted Russians. Speeches have been made, the Russians believe them and have broken the champagne bottles on them. They believe this country will act this year on what they call the second front . . . they expect it and the British nation expects it. I say it is right, it is the correct thing to do . . . Do not in these high matters speak with a twisted tongue.' In the course of the Confidence debate, MPs voiced valid criticisms of the army's poor tanks and leadership. Much was said about the RAF's lack of dive-bombers, to which the British accorded exaggerated credit for German successes. Unsurprisingly, no one hinted that the British soldier was not the equal of his German counterpart, but there were fierce denunciations of the high command and class culture of the army, some of it from MPs less jaundiced than Bevan.

Americans were impressed that such strictures could be expressed. 'Polyzoides' wrote in the *Los Angeles Times*: 'The fact that, during one of the most critical periods in the history of the British Empire, there is still freedom of speech and criticism testifies to the greatness of the nation.' Such high-minded sentiments provided, however, small comfort to the prime minister. Leo Amery wrote: 'Winston is I think far too inclined to attribute to sheer personal malice the anxiety of various people to know what is really happening and makes no allowance either for the value in a democracy of telling our people the whole truth however unpalatable.' A housewife diarist, Mrs Clara Millburn, though a warm admirer of Churchill, was nonetheless impressed by the report of Wardlaw-Milne's performance in the Commons: 'His speech sounds very good to us at first hearing.' By contrast, she thought little of Oliver Lyttelton's opening speech for the government: 'Everyone seems to want C as PM, but they do not think he has chosen wisely for his Cabinet.' When the House divided, Churchill won by 475 votes to twenty-five. 'He is a giant among pygmies when it comes to a debate of this kind, and I think that everybody realizes it,' wrote Tory MP Cuthbert Headlam, often a sceptic. But he added that if the censure motion had been directed against the Ministry of Supply, he himself would not have voted against it. Next day, Mrs Millburn wrote: 'It is to be hoped that the PM takes some notice of the criticisms, for one feels some changes are necessary.'

Churchill's Commons success did nothing to stifle wide-ranging and bitter criticism of the government's conduct of the war. *The Times*, in an editorial on 10 July, though asserting that 'No responsible body of opinion dreams of changing the national leadership,' repeated its oft-made demand for a separation of the roles of prime minister and Minister of Defence. The paper returned to the charge on 20 July, observing: 'A British victory is urgently needed'; and again on the 22nd: 'All the evidence goes to show that the war machine is both cumbrous and unmethodical.' In *The Times*'s letters column, a correspondent named Clive Garcia, writing from the Army & Navy club, spoke of 'a vicious circle to which we have now grown accustomed: first, disaster; then a debate on the conduct of the war, voicing profound apprehension; then a vote of confidence in the Government . . . then a pause until the next disaster'. Meanwhile, asserted Garcia, 'defects in the war machine go uncorrected'.

Several other letter-writers addressed intelligently and pertinently the inadequacy of British tanks. *The Times* commented on their strictures: 'The simple question – though the answer may be complex – is how a great and inventive industrial country nearing the end of the third year of War has failed to supply its Army with weapons superior to those employed by the enemy, the nature of which was for the most part known?' An editorial in the *New Statesman* on 29 July asserted that the 'military situation of the [Allies] is graver than at any time since 1940'.

Within a few minutes of Churchill's return to Downing Street from the Commons on 2 July, Leo Amery arrived with his son Julian, an army officer just back from Egypt. To the fury of Alan Brooke, who was also present, young Amery – 'a most objectionable young pup', in the general's words – painted for the prime minister a picture of the desert army as demoralised, poorly equipped and bereft of confidence in its commanders. This confirmed Churchill's own views. In an unpublished draft of his war memoirs he characterised the 1942 desert defeats as 'discreditable' and 'deplorable'. In six months, Auchinleck's forces had been driven back 600 miles. Worst of all, Captain Amery played to the strongest instincts of the prime minister by urging that Churchill should go himself to the Middle East and resolve the situation. 'The cheek of the young brute was almost more than I could bear,' wrote Brooke. The CIGS had hoped to travel alone to Egypt to address the army's difficulties. Now, instead, the prime minister was determined to intervene personally, then fly on to Moscow to confront Stalin.

But first, there was another visit to London by Hopkins, Marshall and King. Before they arrived, former CIGS Sir John Dill wrote to Churchill from Washington: 'May I suggest with all respect that you must convince your visitors that you are determined to beat the Germans, that you will strike them on the continent of Europe at the earliest possible moment even on a limited scale, and that anything which detracts from this main effort will receive no support from you at all.' The general mused tendentiously about a possible landing in France: 'What does success mean? If invasion ultimately fails tactically but causes diversion from Russian front will it have succeeded?' Such maudlin reflections were unlikely to increase Churchill's confidence in Dill, who had gained some personal popularity in Washington because he was thought to favour an early

Second Front. 'Churchill, however, believes the other way,' wrote vice-president Henry Wallace. 'Apparently the ruling class in England is very anxious not to sacrifice too many British men. They lost so many in World War I that they feel they cannot afford to lose more in World War II. They want to wait until the American armies have been sufficiently trained so that losses will be at least fifty-fifty. Dill does not belong to this school of thought.' It was certainly true that some people in London believed the general had 'gone native' in Washington.

To the prime minister's annoyance, following Marshall, King and Hopkins's arrival in London on 19 July, they spent some hours communing with the newly appointed senior US officer in Europe, Gen. Dwight Eisenhower, before calling at Downing Street. When Anglo–American discussions began, the visitors repeated their familiar demand for a 1942 beachhead in France. They clung stubbornly to two propositions which the British deemed monstrous. First, they thought that a 'redoubt', such as Churchill had briefly favoured in June 1940, might be seized and held in northern France. Second, they considered that even if such an operation failed, the losses – destined to be overwhelmingly British – would be justified by the inconvenience imposed upon the Germans.

Brooke rehearsed familiar objections. The US chief of the army challenged him bluntly, demanding: 'Well, how are we going to win this war? You cannot win it by defensive action.' Churchill formally presented Marshall's proposal to the war cabinet, which unanimously rejected it. There was little more to be said. The Americans remained deeply unhappy, but knew that they could not impose a scheme dependent almost entirely upon the sacrifice of British lives. Marshall had come to London with a brief from Roosevelt to make this final attempt to reconcile the British to an invasion of France; then, if he failed, to accept the North African plan. On 22 July the president cabled acquiescence in British rejection of an early assault on the Continent. With utmost reluctance, Marshall committed himself to what became the *Torch* landings of November 1942.

Now the British were all smiles, and it was the Americans' turn to sulk. 'Gil' Winant, the ambassador, usually mild-mannered, expressed vehement objections to the North African plan. The American visitors spent a final weekend at Chequers, with the prime minister at his sunniest, then returned to Washington, nursing frustration.

For most of August, Marshall continued to agitate against *Torch*. From the moment Churchill first mooted the North African scheme back in December, the chief of the army had been willing to indulge it only if US troops could land unopposed, with Vichy French acquiescence. The Americans were fearful that if they were obliged to launch an amphibious assault, the Germans would swiftly reinforce North Africa through Franco's Spain, isolating any US forces deployed east of the Straits of Gibraltar. It is important to emphasise that in the late summer of 1942 the American chiefs believed that the British were doomed to lose Egypt. This would free Rommel's army to turn on a US invasion force. Marshall not only disliked committing American soldiers to the Mediterranean theatre: he feared that a campaign there could fail. A cynic such as Alan Brooke might have contrasted unfavourably the US chief of the army's insouciance about the perils of an abortive British descent on France with his sensitivity about the prospect of an unsuccessful American one on North Africa.

The *Torch* commitment represented one of Churchill's most important victories of the war. He had persuaded Roosevelt to impose a course of action on his chiefs of staff against their strongest wishes. As for the president, this was his most significant strategic intervention, one of the few occasions when he acted in earnest the part of commander-in-chief, instead of delegating his powers to his military advisers. The two national leaders displayed the highest wisdom. Roosevelt's decision was driven by the same political imperatives that Churchill recognised. Marshall later acknowledged this, saying of the US chiefs of staff: 'We failed to see that a leader in a democracy has to keep the people entertained. The people demand action.' Fulfilment of this requirement was matched by the president's acknowledgement that if the British did not choose to land in France in 1942, they could not be made to do so. At this stage also, Roosevelt was much more ready than in subsequent years to be influenced by Churchill's judgement. The US would land only an initial 70,000 men in North Africa, though thereafter these would be progressively reinforced. In 1942 a significant proportion of Marshall's available forces were committed to home defence of the United States, though it was hard to see who might mount an invasion.

The British sought to salve bruised US Army sensibilities by offering a strong endorsement of its ambitions for a landing in France in 1943. But Marshall knew that once American forces were fighting in the Mediterranean, it would be hard to get them out again in time for an invasion of France the following year. In the formal document decreeing the North African commitment, CCS94, the chiefs of staff acknowledged 'that it be understood that a commitment to [*Torch*] renders *Roundup* [an invasion of France] in all probability impracticable of successful operation in 1943'. Only much later did some prominent American soldiers grudgingly concede that Churchill might have been right; that his and Roosevelt's commitment to *Torch* saved the Allies from a colossal folly. And this was only when the US Army had experienced for itself the savage reality of fighting the Wehrmacht.

TWELVE

Camels and the Bear

Churchill travelled to the Middle East in austere and dangerous discomfort. 'What energy and gallantry of the old gentleman,' marvelled Oliver Harvey, 'setting off . . . across Africa in the heat of mid-summer.' This was true enough, but masked the reality that for the rest of the war Churchill was much happier in overseas theatres than amid the drabness of Britain, where he found scant romance, increasing pettiness and complaint. Though he cherished a vision of fortress Albion, its reality became increasingly uncongenial. Before his departure, the prime minister discussed with Eden whether another minister should join his party: 'He felt the need for company, especially in Moscow.' Here was a glimpse of Churchill's loneliness when he faced great challenges. He yearned for the comradeship of some peer figure such as Beaverbrook in whom he could confide, with whom he could exchange impressions and jokes. This time, however, it was decided that he should take in his entourage only civil servants and soldiers, Alan Brooke foremost among them. They would be joined for the Moscow leg by Averell Harriman, whose presence was designed to ensure Russian understanding that what the British asserted, the Americans endorsed, and by Sir Archibald Wavell, who had served in Russia in 1919 and spoke the language.

They travelled aboard a Liberator bomber which possessed desirable virtues of performance – range, speed and altitude – but none of the luxuries of the Boeing Clipper. Somewhat to the embarrassment of Britain's airmen, the safety of the prime minister was entrusted to a young Atlantic ferry pilot named Bill Vanderkloot, who hailed from Illinois. Vanderkloot was deemed to possess temperament, navigational skills and long-range experience which no available home-grown British pilot could match. The American admirably fulfilled expectations. His plane, however, was a cramped and unsuitable conveyance for an elderly man upon whose welfare, in considerable degree, the hopes of Western civilisation rested. It was so noisy that Churchill could communicate with his fellow passengers only by exchanging notes. The flight was long and cold. They made an African landfall over Spanish Morocco, then struck a course which took them well inland before turning east over the desert, flying high and using oxygen. In his mask, wrote one of the plane's crew, Churchill 'looked exactly as though he was in a Christmas party disguise'. He sat in the co-pilot's seat, reviving a host of youthful memories as they approached Cairo: 'Often had I seen the day break on the Nile.' Once on the ground, he began a long, painstaking grilling of soldiers and officials about the desert campaign, the army and its commanders.

All that he saw and heard confirmed his instincts back in London. Ever since 1939, visitors to Egypt had been dismayed by the lassitude pervading the nexus of headquarters, camps, villas, hotels and clubs that lay along the Nile. An air of self-indulgent imperialism, of a kind that confirmed the worst prejudices of Aneurin Bevan, persisted even in the midst of a war of national survival. 'Old Miles [Lampson, British ambassador to Egypt] leads a completely peacetime existence, a satrap,' wrote Oliver Harvey scornfully. 'He does no work at all.' The habits and complacency of peacetime also prevailed in many military messes. In 1941 Averell Harriman, no ascetic, was shocked by the indolence and luxury he saw around him on his first visit to Cairo. A year later, too many gentlemen still held sway over too few players. The former Republican presidential candidate Wendell Willkie, passing through Egypt, perceived a 'lackadaisical' attitude to the war which was 'painful'. Auchinleck had repeatedly disappointed Churchill's hopes. The good soldiers in the Middle East were tired. A staff officer wrote from Egypt in July 1942: 'There seem to me to be too many people at home who have had no war – through no fault of their own – and too many people out here who have had too much war.'

The desert army continued to suffer grave technical and tactical deficiencies. The cavalry ethos still dominated armoured operations, despite the frequent failures of British tanks' attempts to destroy German ones. 'The Auk's' formations seemed unable to master the Afrika Korps' art of using anti-tank guns to stop British armour before committing its own Panzers. The shoddiness of British industrial production was exposed when home-built tanks were offloaded in Egypt. Their bolts proved to have been only hand-tightened at the factories, and most had been inadequately packed and loaded for ocean passage. Weeks of labour were necessary in the workshops of the Nile Delta before armoured vehicles were fit for action. American Grant tanks, which now equipped some British armoured units, mounted a 75mm sponson gun capable of destroying German Panzers, but were otherwise outmatched by them. New Shermans were still in transit from the US.

Auchinleck's troops had been outfought again and again. British defeats in 1940–41 had been attributable to circumstances beyond commanders' control: pre-war neglect, lack of air support and German superiority. The failures of late 1941 and 1942, however, reflected culpable weaknesses. The two ablest airmen in Cairo, Arthur Tedder and 'Maori' Coningham, talked frankly to Churchill and Brooke about their perceptions of the army's shortcomings. Colonel Ian Jacob noted in his diary during the Cairo visit that there had been 'far too many cases of units surrendering in circumstances in which in the last war they would have fought it out . . . The discipline of the Army is no longer what it used to be . . . There is lacking in this war the strong incentive of a national cause. Nothing concentrate has replaced the old motto "For King and Country". The aims set before the people . . . are negative, and it still does not seem to have been brought home . . . that it is a war for their own existence.' War correspondent Alan Moorehead agreed: 'In the Middle East there was, in August, a general and growing feeling [among the troops] that something was being held back from them, that they were being asked to fight for a cause which the leaders did not find vital enough to state clearly. It's simply no good telling the average soldier that he is fighting for victory, for his country, for the sake of duty. He knows all that. And now he is asking, "For what sort of victory? For what sort of a post-war country? For my duty to what goal in life?"'

If this was indeed true – and Moorehead knew the desert army intimately – then the prime minister himself deserved some of the blame. It was he who, despite the urgings of ministers, refused to address himself to 'war aims', a post-war vision. Instead, he held out to British soldiers the promise of martial glory, writing to Clementine from Cairo: 'I intend to see every important unit in this army, both back and front, and make them feel the vast consequences which depend upon them and the superb honours which may be theirs.' In supposing such things to represent plausible or adequate incitements for citizen soldiers, Churchill was almost certainly mistaken. But it was not in his nature to understand that most men cared more about their prospects in a future beyond war than about ribbons and laurels to be acquired during the fighting of it.

In Churchill's eyes the first priority in Egypt was, as usual, to identify new commanders. By 6 August he had made up his mind to sack Auchinleck. The general received his dismissal ungraciously, and harboured bitterness for the rest of his life. Dill blamed Churchill for the Middle East C-in-C's failure, claiming that the prime minister 'had ruined Auchinleck . . . he had dwarfed him just as he dwarfs and reduces others around him'. This charge says more about Dill's limitations, as a shop steward for unsuccessful British generals, than about the prime minister's. Of course Churchill had harried Auchinleck. It has been suggested above that the general's failure in part reflected institutional weaknesses in the British Army. But 'the Auk' had been the man in charge through a succession of operations abysmally conducted by subordinates of his choice. British failure to defeat the Afrika Korps at Gazala in May–June 1942 reflected gross command incompetence. It was surely right to dismiss Auchinleck.

Churchill's first impulsive thought for his replacement was Alan Brooke. The CIGS was much moved by the proposal, but wisely and selflessly rejected it. He perceived himself as indispensable at the War Office – and he was right. The prime minister's next choice was Lt. Gen. William 'Strafer' Gott, who had gained a reputation for dashing leadership from the front, but in whom Brooke lacked confidence. Since 1939 the prime minister had been convinced that Britain's armed forces lacked leaders with fire in their bellies, and had sought to appoint to high command proven warriors, heroes. In this he was often mistaken. Steely professionalism was lacking rather than conspicuous personal bravery. There is something in the observation of the Russian writer who asserts that 'Courage often proves to be the best part of the man who possesses it.' Many of Churchill's favourite warriors lacked intellect. In 1940 he had elevated Admiral Sir Roger Keyes to become Director of Combined Operations. Keyes had conceit and a talent for bombast, but was quite unfit for his post, as Churchill was obliged to recognise the following year. Keyes's replacement, Mountbatten, caught Churchill's imagination by his exploits at sea. But the Royal Navy deemed 'Dickie' an indifferent destroyer flotilla leader, and admirals were disgusted that glamour, fluency and royal connections secured his meteoric promotion. Freyberg failed in Crete. Another Churchillian favourite, Maj. Gen. Sir Edward Spears, was responsible for many difficulties in relations with the Free French, especially in his role as senior British representative in Syria.

In 1942, Churchill chose Admiral Sir Henry Harwood to succeed Andrew Cunningham as naval C-in-C Mediterranean. Harwood had won the prime minister's approval by leading his cruiser squadron in the December 1939 Battle of the River Plate against the pocket battleship *Graf Spee*, but for all his undoubted courage he was a notoriously stupid officer whose removal soon became necessary. Yet Churchill's enthusiasm for naval heroes remained undiminished. When Dudley Pound died in September 1943, Churchill wanted Admiral Sir Bruce Fraser to replace him as First Sea Lord. Naval officers thought Fraser dim, but Churchill perceived him as a fighter. When the navy instead insisted on Cunningham, who had often locked horns with the prime minister, Churchill said petulantly: 'All right. You can have your Cunningham, but if the Admiralty don't do as they are told I will bring down the Board in ruins even if it means my coming down with it.'

Gott was yet another officer who commended himself to the prime minister because he had made a name as a thruster, yet it is most unlikely that he was competent to command Eighth Army. Fate intervened. En route to Cairo to receive his appointment, Gott's plane was shot down and he was killed. Instead Brooke's nominee, Sir Bernard Montgomery, was summoned from a corps command in England to head Eighth Army. Churchill had met Montgomery on visits to his units, and was impressed by his forceful personality, if not by his boorish conceit. But in accepting his appointment to the desert, the prime minister was overwhelmingly dependent on the CIGS's judgement. Gen. Sir Harold Alexander, a brave, charming but unassertive Guardsman who had recently presided over the British retreat from Burma, was appointed C-in-C Middle East. The prime minister, who found 'Alex' congenial and reassuring, expected him to play a far more important role in shaping future operations than Montgomery. Several senior subordinate officers were also earmarked for sacking and replacement.

Having set in motion wholesale change at the top, Churchill departed from Cairo on the most taxing stage of this epic excursion. He was to meet the Soviet Union's warlord, and deliver the unwelcome news that the Western Allies had determined against launching a Second Front in 1942. After a brief stopover in Tehran, on 12 August he made a 10½-hour flight to Moscow, accompanied by his personal staff and Averell Harriman. A few hours after landing, Churchill was summoned to the Kremlin. He asked Harriman to accompany him: 'I feel things would be easier if we all seemed to be together. I have a somewhat raw job.'

In truth, and as surprisingly few historians show recognition of, Stalin was already aware of all that Churchill feared to tell him. Whitehall and Washington were alike deeply penetrated by communist sympathisers. Among the most prominent, John Cairncross served as Lord Hankey's private secretary, with access to war cabinet papers until Hankey's sacking in 1942, when he was transferred to Bletchley Park. Anthony Blunt served in MI5, while Guy Burgess and Kim Philby worked for SIS. Donald Maclean had access to key Foreign Office material, especially concerning research on the atomic bomb. In the US government – which was anyway lax about securing its secrets from the Russians – Harry Dexter White worked for Henry Morgenthau, Nathan Silvermaster for the Board of Economic Warfare, Alger Hiss for the State Department. Harry Hopkins talked with surprising freedom, though surely not ill intent, to a key NKVD agent in the United States. Throughout the war, a mass of British and US government reports, minutes and decrypted Axis messages was passed to Moscow by such people, through their controllers in London and Washington. As a result, before every Allied summit the Russians were vastly better informed about Anglo-American military intentions, than vice versa. So much material reached Stalin from London that he rejected some of it as disinformation, plants by cunning agents of Churchill. When Kim Philby of SIS told his NKVD handler that Britain was conducting no secret intelligence operations in the Soviet Union, Stalin dismissed this assertion with the contempt he deemed it to deserve. Molotov and Lavrenti Beria, the Soviet intelligence and secret police chief, frequently concealed from their leader accurate intelligence which they believed would anger him.

Yet in August 1942 Stalin was thoroughly briefed about Western Allied strategy, thanks to highly placed Soviet agents. He had been told of the fierce Anglo-American arguments about the Second Front. On 4 August Beria reported:

Our NKVD resident in London sent the following information received from a source close to the English General Staff: A meeting about the second front took place on 21 July 1942. It was attended by Churchill, Lord Mountbatten, General Marshall and others. General Marshall sharply criticized the attitude of the English . . . He insisted that the second front should be opened in 1942 and warned that if the English failed to do this the USA would have to reconsider sending reinforcements to Great Britain and focus their attention on the Pacific. Churchill gave the following response to General Marshall: 'There is not a single top general who would recommend starting major operations on the continent.' A further meeting on the second front took place on 22 or 23 July 1942. This was attended on the English side by Churchill, Mountbatten and the chiefs of staff; on the American side by Marshall, Eisenhower and others. The participants discussed a plan for the invasion of the continent which has been developed by English and American military experts . . . English chiefs of staff unanimously voted against and were supported by Churchill who declared that he could not vote against his own chiefs of staff. NKVD resident in London also reported the following, based on information from agents which had been also confirmed earlier by a source close to American embassy: on 25 July the British war cabinet agreed that there should be no second front this year.

A further 12 August NKVD intelligence brief to Stalin included a note on the prime minister's political position: 'Churchill departed for the USSR in an atmosphere of growing domestic political crisis. The intensification of fighting on the Soviet–German front has had a marked effect on British public opinion . . . Source believes Churchill will offer a number of concessions to the Soviet Union BERIA.' Russian access to such insights should not be taken to mean that Stalin was always correctly informed. For instance, several times during the war NKVD agents reported to Moscow supposed parleys between the Western Allies and the Nazi leadership. On 12 May 1942 Beria passed to Stalin 'a report from the London resident on German attempts to start separate negotiations with the English': 'We know from a reliable source that an official from the German embassy in Sweden has flown to England from Stockholm on board a civilian aircraft.' Like other such claims, this one was fallacious, but it fuelled Soviet paranoia. NKVD information was entirely accurate, however, about Britain's position on the Second Front. Moscow was told that the prime minister's objections did not derive, as Stalin had supposed, from political hostility to the USSR, but instead from pragmatic military considerations.

Stalin had always displayed intense curiosity about Churchill, for a quarter of a century the arch-foe of Bolshevism. In June 1941 the Russian leader was surprised by the warmth with which Britain's prime minister embraced him as a co-belligerent. In the intervening fourteen months, however, little had happened to gain Stalin's confidence. Extravagant Western promises of aid had resulted in relatively meagre deliveries. *The Times* editorialist waxed lyrical on 6 January 1942 about the flow of British supplies to support the alliance with the Soviets: 'The first result of this collaboration has been the splendid performance of British and American tanks and aeroplanes on Russian battlefields.' This was a wild exaggeration of reality, based upon sunshine briefings of the media and Parliament by the British government. Not only were targets for shipments of aircraft and tanks to Russia unfulfilled, but much of the material dispatched was being sunk in transit.

Convoy PQ16 was the target of 145 Luftwaffe sorties, and lost eleven of its thirty-five ships. In July, when twenty-six out of thirty-seven ships carrying American and British supplies were lost with PQ17, 3,850 trucks, 430 tanks and 250 fighters vanished to the bottom. Following this disaster the Royal Navy insisted on cancelling all further convoys for the duration of the Arctic summer and its interminable daylight. Churchill, pressed by Roosevelt, reinstated the September convoys, and began moving supplies through Persia, where the British and Russians now shared military control. But the only important reality, in Moscow's eyes, was that aid consignments lagged far behind both Allied promises and Russian needs. Even more serious, the British had vetoed American plans for an early Second Front.

It was implausible that Stalin would display a sentimental enthusiasm for his British allies, any more than for any other human beings in his universe. He would never acknowledge that his nation's predicament was the consequence of his own awesomely cynical indulgence of Hitler back in 1939. But Russia's sense of outraged victimhood was none the less real for being spurious. The Soviets sought to bludgeon or shame the British and Americans into maintaining supply shipments, and landing an army in Europe at the earliest possible date. Russia was counting her dead in millions while the British cavorted in North Africa, paying a tiny fraction of the eastern blood sacrifice. In August 1942, Rostov-on-Don had fallen, Germany's armies were deep in the Caucasus and almost at the gates of Stalingrad. Posterity knows that Hitler had made a fatal mistake, splitting his principal summer thrusts in pursuit of the strategically meaningless capture of Stalin's name-city. The tide of the eastern war would turn decisively by the year's end. But Russians at the time could not see beyond cataclysm. They knew only that their predicament was desperate. They could no more regard Churchill's people as comrades-in-arms than might a man thrashing in a sea of sharks look in fellowship upon spectators cheering him on from a boat.

The prime minister wasted no time, at his first meeting with Stalin, before reporting the decision against a landing in Europe in 1942. He said that any such venture must be on a small scale, and thus assuredly doomed. It could do no service to Russia's cause. The British and American governments were, however, preparing 'a very great operation' in 1943. He told Stalin of *Torch*, the North African invasion plan, observing that he hoped the secret would not find its way into the British press – a jibe at ambassador Maisky's notorious indiscretions to journalists in London. He spoke much about the RAF's bombing of Germany, describing the beginnings of a long campaign systematically to destroy Hitler's cities with a ruthlessness he assumed the Soviet leader would applaud. 'We sought no mercy,' said the prime minister, 'and we would show no mercy.'

The substance of this first encounter, which lasted three hours and forty minutes, was made even less palatable by poor interpreting. All foreign visitors to the Kremlin were at first disconcerted that Stalin never looked into their eyes. Instead, this infinitely devious warlord, clad in a lilac tunic and cotton trousers tucked into long boots, gazed blankly at the wall or the floor as he listened and as he spoke. There were no immediate Soviet tantrums, though Stalin made plain his displeasure at the Second Front decision. 'A man who is not prepared to take risks,' he mocked, 'cannot win a war.' Given his prior knowledge of Churchill's 'revelation', at this meeting he was making sport of the prime minister. But he did so with his usual supreme diplomatic skill, maintaining his visitors' suspense about what their host really knew or thought. When they parted and Churchill returned to his villa, he signalled Attlee in London: 'He knows the worst, and we parted in an atmosphere of goodwill.' Harriman cabled Roosevelt: 'The prime minister was at his best and could not have handled the discussion with greater brilliance.' Next day, the 13th, Churchill conferred with Molotov about detailed aspects of Allied plans, and aid to Russia.

That afternoon Brooke, Wavell and Tedder arrived, in a Liberator delayed by technical trouble. They were in time to attend the prime minister's second meeting with Stalin, and were shocked by their glacial reception. The Soviet leader began by handing Churchill a formal protest about the delay to the Second Front: 'It is easy to understand that the refusal of the Government of Great Britain to create a second front in 1942 inflicts a mortal blow to the whole of Soviet public opinion . . . complicates the situation of the Red Army at the front and compromises the plans of the Soviet command.' What Churchill called 'a most unpleasant discussion' ensued. He was resolute in making plain that the Allied decision was irrevocable, and thus that 'reproaches were vain'. Stalin taunted him with the destruction of PQ17: 'This is the first time in history the British Navy has ever turned tail and fled from the battle. You British are afraid of fighting. You should not think the Germans are supermen. You will have to fight sooner or later. You cannot win a war without fighting.'

Harriman slipped a note to Churchill: 'Don't take this too seriously – this is the way he behaved last year.' The prime minister then addressed Stalin with unfeigned passion about Britain's past defiance and future resolution, his stream of rhetoric flowing far ahead of the interpreters. Stalin laughed: 'Your words are not important, what is vital is the spirit.' Churchill accused Stalin of displaying a lack of comradeship. Britain, he reminded the Georgian, had been obliged to fight alone for a year. In the early hours of 14 August the two delegations parted as frigidly as they had met. 'I am downhearted and dispirited,' Churchill told his British colleagues. 'I have come a long way and made a great effort. Stalin lay back puffing at his pipe, with his eyes half closed, emitting streams of insults. He said the Russians were losing 10,000 men a day. He said that if the British Army had been fighting the Germans as much as the Red Army had, it would not be so frightened of them.'

After a few hours' sleep, the British communed among themselves. Churchill was smarting from the drubbing he had received. All his latent animosity to the Soviets bubbled forth, revived by abuse from a leader who eighteen months earlier had been content to collude in Hitler's rape of Europe. He was also dismayed by an incoming signal from London, detailing heavy losses to the epic *Pedestal* convoy to Malta. Cabling Attlee to report the Russians' intransigence, he said that he made 'great allowances for the stresses through which they are passing'.

That night the British attended a banquet, accompanied by the usual orgy of toasts. Hosts and guests feasted in a fashion grotesque in a society on the brink of mass starvation. But what was one more grotesquerie, amid the perpetual black pageant of the Kremlin? Stalin shuffled among the tables, as was his habit, clinking glasses and making jokes, leaving Churchill often lonely and perforce silent in his own place. When the Soviet warlord sat down once more, the prime minister said: 'You know, I was not friendly to you after the last war. Have you forgiven me?' His host responded: 'All that is in the past. It is not for me to forgive. It is for God to forgive.' This literal translation obscures the proverbial meaning of the Russian phrase, probably missed by Churchill: 'I will never forgive.' The British delegation found it bizarre that Stalin, of all people, so often invoked the Deity, a habit he acquired as a young seminarian. He said of *Torch*: 'May God prosper this undertaking.' The most notable success of the evening was a speech by Wavell in Russian.

Even the Soviets were impressed by the quantities of alcohol consumed by both their own leader and Churchill. One guest, unfamiliar with the prime minister's usual diction, wrote afterwards: 'His speech was slurred as though his mouth was full of porridge.' The Russians decided that Churchill must be perpetrating some shocking indiscretion when they saw Brooke tugging insistently at his sleeve in a fashion no man would have dared do to Stalin. After the prime minister left the dining room, Stalin noticed that Alexander Golovanov, who commanded the Soviet air force's long-range bombers, was staring at him in some alarm. 'Don't be afraid,' said the Soviet leader, with unaccustomed docility. 'I am not going to drink Russia away.' He lapsed into silence for a few moments, then said: 'When great affairs of state are at stake, alcohol tastes like water and one's head is always clear.' Golovanov noted with respect that Stalin walked from the room steadily and unhurriedly.

Churchill left the banquet in sullen mood, deploring alike the food, his hosts' manners and the uncongenial setting. Next morning, a meeting between Brooke, Wavell and Stalin's senior officers proved abortive when the Russians flatly refused to disclose any details of their operations in the Caucasus, saying that they were authorised to discuss only the Second Front. The sole Soviet weapons system that inspired British enthusiasm was the Katyusha multiple rocket-launcher, of which the visitors requested technical details. These were never forthcoming.

On Saturday, Churchill and his colleagues entered the big Kremlin conference room overlooking the Moskva river with considerable apprehension. The prime minister told Stalin that he had considered it his duty to inform him personally of the Second Front decision. Exchanges between the two sides were more fluent, because Churchill had now enlisted the services of Major Birse, a bilingual member of Britain's Military Aid Mission. Stalin suddenly seemed more emollient. 'Obviously there are differences between us,' he said, 'but . . . the fact that the meeting has taken place, that personal contact has been established . . . is very valuable.' After more than an hour of talks, as they rose from the table Stalin suddenly, and apparently spontaneously, invited Churchill for drinks in his private apartment. There they adjourned for a further six hours of informal conversation, during which the prime minister believed that a better rapport was established. Stalin suggested a British landing in north Norway, a proposal which Churchill could endorse with unfeigned enthusiasm. The Russian said that it would be helpful for Britain to dispatch trucks rather than tanks to the Red Army, though this request reflected ignorance of British military-vehicle weaknesses. A sucking pig was brought in, which Stalin addressed avidly, and his guests sampled politely. A draft communiqué was agreed. At 2.30 a.m. Churchill parted from his host, with protestations of goodwill on both sides.

Back at his villa forty-five minutes later, the prime minister found that the Polish General Wladyslaw Anders had been awaiting him for many hours. 'Ah! My poor Anders,' said Churchill. 'I have been detained by M. Stalin and now I must fly off. But you come along to Cairo and we shall have a talk there.' Then he lay wearily down on a sofa, closed his eyes, and described to his party what had been said in Stalin's apartment. At 5.30 a.m. the British party took off for Cairo in four Liberators.

Churchill left Russia satisfied that his visit had achieved as much as was possible, in bleak circumstances. He had displayed the highest gifts of statesmanship, placing a brave face upon bad tidings, never flinching when his host flourished the knout. Ian Jacob wrote: 'No one but the Prime Minister could have got so far with Stalin, in the sense that we understand friendship. The thing that impressed me most about Stalin was his complete self-possession and detachment. He was absolutely master of the situation at all times . . . He had a gentle voice, which he never raised, and his eyes were shrewd and crafty.'

Harriman was full of admiration for Churchill's patience in the face of Russian insults, for his restraint in withholding the obvious rejoinder to Stalin's mockery – that the Soviet Union had forged a devil's bargain with Nazi Germany in 1939. Yet the prime minister had scarcely enjoyed the Moscow experience. Jacob wrote: 'Churchill was decidedly upset by the lack of comradeship that he had encountered. There was none of the normal human side to the visit – no informal lunches, no means of doing what he most liked, which was to survey at length the war situation in conversation, and to explore the mind of his interlocutor.' Churchill nonetheless deluded himself that he had established a personal connection with Russia's leader. No man could achieve that, least of all a British aristocrat famously hostile to all that the Soviet Union stood for. Brooke wrote: 'He appealed to sentiments in Stalin which I do not think exist there.'

Churchill's faith in the power of his personality to alter outcomes was occasionally justified in his dealings with Roosevelt, but never with Stalin. The Russians dispensed a modicum of amiability and fellowship in the last stage of the prime minister's Moscow visit, because unremitting hostility might threaten the Anglo–American supply line. In August 1942, as at every subsequent summit, Stalin had two notable advantages. First, the Western Allies would never press their own wishes beyond a certain point, because they feared that failure to indulge the Soviet warlord might provoke him to seek a separate peace with Hitler. If Stalin needed Anglo–American supplies, the Western Allies needed the Red Army more. Second, while visitors were obliged to improvise scripts as they went along, struggling to keep pace with apparent shifts of Soviet mood, Stalin's performance was precisely orchestrated from start to finish. He possessed almost complete knowledge of Allied military intentions, or lack of them, before Churchill landed in Moscow and delivered his budget of news at the Kremlin – and likewise at later 1943–45 meetings. Russia's leader was able to adjust every nicety of courtesy and insult accordingly. It is unlikely that Stalin made many, if any, genuinely spontaneous remarks or gestures while Churchill was in Moscow. He merely lifted or lowered British spirits as seemed expedient, with the assurance of an orchestral conductor.

The Russians missed no opportunity to work wedges between the British and Americans. One night when Churchill went to bed, Stalin urged Harriman to stay and talk. The diplomat pleaded exhaustion. When Harriman did find himself alone with the Russian leader, he was caressed with comparisons between US and British prowess: 'Stalin told me the British Navy had lost its initiative. There was no good reason to stop the convoys. The British armies didn't fight either – Singapore etc. The US Navy fought with more courage and so did the Army at Bataan. The British air force was good, he admitted. He showed little respect for the British military effort but much hope in that of the US.' Stalin's words were not wasted. When Harriman reported to Roosevelt back in Washington, he thought the president gratified by Churchill's discomfiture.

It is an outstanding curiosity of the Second World War that two such brilliant men as Winston Churchill and Franklin Roosevelt allowed themselves to suppose that the mere fact of discovering a common enemy in Hitler could suffice to make possible a real relationship, as distinct from an arrangement of convenience on specifics, between Britain, the United States and the Soviet Union. Stalin and his acolytes never for a moment forgot that their social and political objectives were inimical to those of their capitalist allies. British politicians, generals and diplomats were, however, foolish enough to hope that they might achieve some comradeship with the Soviets, without forswearing their visceral loathing for them. Few senior Americans were as hostile to the Russians as were the British, partly because they were so confident of US power, and correspondingly less fearful of Soviet ambitions. But the Americans too – with such notable exceptions as Harriman – harboured delusions about their ability to make friends with the Russians, or at least to exploit US might to bend the Soviet government to their will, which rational assessment of rival national purposes should have dispelled.

It is striking that Churchill's visit to Moscow failed to inspire any quickening of aid to Russia. Following the disaster to PQ17 in July, the British dispatched no further supplies to Archangel for two months, declining to risk another convoy in the relentless daylight of Arctic high summer. On and after 20 September, twenty-seven of PQ18's forty ships arrived safely. Thereafter, for four months the Royal Navy was too preoccupied with supporting the *Torch* landings to dispatch any Arctic convoys at all. At horrific risk, thirteen merchant ships sailed independently and unescorted to the Kola Inlet. Just five arrived. By January 1943 only two further convoys, thirty merchantmen in all, had reached Russia safely. Thereafter, as Allied resources grew and German strength in north Norway was weakened by diversions of Luftwaffe aircraft to other theatres, the picture changed dramatically. Massive consignments of vehicles, stores and equipment, most of American manufacture, were successfully shipped, half of them through Vladivostok. Such assistance made a critical contribution to the Red Army's advance to victory in 1944–45. But Stalin and his people were entitled to consider that they saved themselves until 1943 with only marginal foreign aid.

Soviet historians in comparatively modern times have continued to heap scorn upon the shortfalls of Western assistance. In 1978 Victor Trukhanovsky wrote: 'The deliveries were curtailed not so much by the difficulties of escorting convoys . . . as Churchill and British historians like to claim, as by the fact that in Britain there were influential circles which did not like the alliance with the USSR and hindered the normal development of relations between the two allies. Their influences affected the stance adopted by Churchill.' Although in reality shortages of weapons and shipping, together with Soviet intransigence, were the principal inhibiting factors, it was true that few senior figures in Britain wanted the Soviets to emerge strengthened from the war. Extravagant early assurances given to Moscow by both Washington and London were broken. Churchill's promise to dispatch twenty, even forty British air squadrons to support the Red Army went unfulfilled. There were readily identifiable reasons for this. But Stalin saw only one reality: that while his own nation was engulfed in blood and destruction, Britain remained relatively unscathed and America absolutely so.

Churchill was too wise to waste much consideration upon the moral superiority of Britain's position over that of the Soviet Union. All that now mattered to the British and Americans was that the three nations shared a common commitment to the defeat of Nazism. Nonetheless, it was hard to achieve even basic working relationships. Whatever courtesies Stalin accorded to such grandees as Churchill, Eden, Hopkins, Harriman and Beaverbrook, and whatever Soviet secrets he himself occasionally revealed to them, humbler Allied officers and diplomats were denied the most commonplace information. They were exposed to unremitting discourtesy on good days, to contemptuous abuse on bad ones. British and American sailors landing at Murmansk and Archangel suffered insults and humiliations. A later head of the British military mission to Moscow, Lt.Gen. Brocas

Burrows, had to be replaced at the Soviets' insistence after their hidden microphones caught him describing them as 'savages'.

The prime minister and his colleagues, like Roosevelt and Marshall, knew that Russia must be given assistance because, to put the matter bluntly, each Russian who died fighting the Germans was one less Englishman or American who must do so. But it would have been asking too much to expect the Westerners to like the Russians. Policy made it essential to pretend to do so, just as Stalin sometimes offered a charade of comradeship. But the Soviets behaved as brutes alike to their own people and to the Western Allies. Only the idealists of the left, of whom there were many in wartime Britain, though rather fewer in America, sustained romantic illusions about Mother Russia. They were fortunate enough never to glimpse its reality.

Back in Cairo on 17 August, Churchill briefly lapsed into exhaustion. After a rest, however, he quizzed Alexander about the prospective desert offensive, which there were hopes of launching in September. On the 19th, he drove 120 miles through sandy wastes landmarked with supply dumps and wired encampments to visit Montgomery at his headquarters and inspect troops. This was an outing which he thoroughly enjoyed. He claimed to detect a new mood among officers and men. His imagination surely ran ahead of reality, for the new regime had been in place only a week. But a perception of change buoyed his spirits. He slept in the plane back to Cairo, then attended a conference, dined, and sat chatting to Brooke in the warm night air on the embassy lawn until 2 a.m. He commissioned the ambassador's wife, Lady Lampson, to undertake a shopping expedition on behalf of Clementine, buying Worth scent, Innoxa and Chanel face cream, fifteen lipsticks – and silk to make the delicate underwear in which he loved to clothe himself.

A signal arrived from Mountbatten, describing the raid on Dieppe that had taken place that day. Of 6,000 men engaged, mostly Canadian, a thousand had been killed and 2,000 taken prisoner. More than a hundred aircraft had been lost in fierce air battles with the Luftwaffe. Yet the chief of combined operations reported, absurdly:

'Morale of returning troops reported to be excellent. All I have seen are in great form.' It was some time before Churchill fully grasped the disastrous character of the raid. Lessons were learned about the difficulties of attacking a hostile shore. Inflated RAF claims masked the reality that the Germans had that day shot down two British aircraft for every one which they themselves lost. Once more, a sense of institutional incompetence overlay the débâcle. The invaders bungled the amphibious assault in every possible way, while the Germans responded with their accustomed speed and efficiency. After almost three years of war, Britain was incapable of conducting a limited surprise attack against an objective and at a moment of its own choice. Mountbatten was successful in evading responsibility, much of which properly belonged to him – back in May, he had boasted to Molotov about 'his' impending operation. But leaders and planners had failed at every level. Incredibly, General Sir Archie Nye, acting CIGS in Brooke's absence, was unaware that the raid was taking place. It is scant wonder that Churchill lacked confidence in his commanders, and remained morbidly fearful that Britain's war-making instruments were doomed to break in his hand.

Only Beaverbrook, still banging a drum for the Second Front, seemed unchastened by the experience of Dieppe. His *Evening Standard* asserted that the shipping problems of an early invasion could be overcome if the chiefs of staff displayed more guts, declared the raid to have been a near-victory, and editorialised on 21 August 1942: 'The Germans cannot afford any more Dieppes either on land or in the air . . . Two or three simultaneous raids on a large scale would be too much for the three solitary Panzer divisions in France.' No general or minister doubted that such calls to arms were delivered at Beaverbrook's explicit behest. The pressures upon the prime minister not merely for action, but for success, were now greater than at any time since he assumed office.

THIRTEEN

The Turn of Fortune

Churchill's purge of desert generals was greeted in Britain with un-surprising caution. So many newly promoted officers had been welcomed as Wellingtons, only to be exposed as duffers. *The Times*'s military correspondent observed that commanders in the Middle East 'have changed so frequently that the subject can now be approached only with tempered enthusiasm'. Through the months that followed, the British media displayed a wariness close to cynicism about Eighth Army's prospects. A *Times* editorial on 26 August observed that neither the RAF's bomber offensive nor the raid on Dieppe had 'relieved the continuing sense of an inadequacy in the British mili-tary achievement at a time when our allies face a supreme crisis'. Journalist Maggie Joy Blunt wrote in her diary on 19 August, expressing dismay about Dieppe: 'While I grumble young Russia waits in agony for our Second Front. Here in England we are divided, despondent and without faith, ruled by old men, governed by money. The old fears, the old distrust are deeply rooted.' Such gloom was not confined to civilians. Brooke wrote later: 'When looking back at those days in the light of after events one may be apt to overlook those ghastly moments of doubt which at the time crowded in on me.'

Churchill, who read newspapers avidly, cannot have gained much pleasure from their cynicism about the command changes. However, he returned to London on 24 August still exhilarated by what he had seen in the desert and by the perceived success of his visit to Stalin. His boundless capacity for optimism was among his greatest virtues, at a time when those around him found it easier to succumb to gloom. On the night of 30 August, Rommel, desperately short of fuel, attacked at Alam Halfa. The British, forewarned by Ultra, inflicted a decisive repulse on the Afrika Korps. The prime minister now became passionately anxious that Montgomery's own offensive should be launched before the American North Africa landings, provisionally scheduled for October. There was fresh trouble with Washington, where Marshall was urging Roosevelt to limit the scale of *Torch*, and to omit Algiers from its objectives. Churchill feared that he would have to defy medical advice and fly once more to see the president. Only on 3 September did Roosevelt accede to Churchill's imprecations, which were supported by US generals Dwight Eisenhower and Mark Clark in London. *Torch* was to proceed on 8 November, with landings at Casablanca, Oran and Algiers.

But while Allied warlords nursed private excitement about the prospect of great happenings, the public and body politic perceived only continuing inactivity. Churchill indulged an outburst of self-pity on 24 September, telling Alan Brooke that he, the prime minister, 'was the only one trying to win the war, that he was the only one who produced any ideas, that he was quite alone in all his attempts, no one supported him ... Frequently in this oration he worked himself up into such a state from the woeful picture he had painted, that tears streamed down his face!'

It was inevitable that, having insisted upon assuming sole responsibility for direction of the war, Churchill should bear blame for the weaknesses which caused the armed forces so often to be seen to fail. Public dissatisfaction with Britain's wartime government attained its highest pitch during the last weeks before a dramatic change of fortune. Many ministers and generals, who readily accepted that only Churchill could be Britain's prime minister, were nonetheless convinced that he should divorce the premiership from the ministry of defence, delegating operational control of the war. But to whom? The mooted candidates were almost as unsuitable as had been the Duke of Gloucester. Leo Amery told Dill, home on leave, that he favoured appointing Wavell as 'super-chief of staff ... Dill agreed, but said nothing could get Winston to face up to it however bad the present arrangement may be.' This exchange says little for the judgement of either man, but much about the mood in Whitehall towards the prime minister. Even Eden, Churchill's most trusted colleague, was convinced that he should relinquish the ministry of defence.

Churchill later described September and October 1942 as his most anxious months of the war. Amery complained after a cabinet wrangle: 'It is an awful thing dealing with a man like Winston who is at the same moment dictatorial, eloquent and muddle-headed.' Beaverbrook, unswervingly mischievous and disloyal, told Eden on 8 October that the prime minister was 'a "bent" man, and couldn't be expected to last long . . . The future belonged to A.E.' Influential Canadian diplomat Humphrey Hume Wrong, in London on a fact-finding mission, wrote in his diary: 'The dominance of Churchill emerges from all these talks. Cripps on the shelf, Attlee a lackey, Bracken the Man Friday of Churchill. It isn't as bad as the political gossips make out, but it's bad enough.' On 17 October John Kennedy, who had been ill, attended a cabinet committee meeting with Churchill. 'He sat down and glowered all round, everybody waiting to see if he was in a good temper. He pressed the bell and told the sec[retar]y he had come without a handkerchief. His detective came in with one in an envelope. W. took it out & blew his nose & looked all round again. Then he got up & and spent a minute or two in adjusting the electric fire. Then sat down & glowered all round again. Then lit his cigar & took a sip from his tumbler of iced water . . . Then he saw me and with a twinkle in his eye . . . said "Glad to see you are better." Then to business.'

If Churchill's person was in Downing Street, his spirit was far away, in the drifting sands of Egypt. Montgomery was training troops, making plans, stockpiling ammunition, readying his new Sherman tanks. The foxy little general insisted upon launching Eighth Army's offensive according to his own timetable, heedless of the prime minister's impatience. A critical contribution to his campaign was already being made at sea. Guided by Ultra decrypts, the RAF and Royal Navy inflicted a series of devastating blows on the Italian tankers and supply ships fuelling and feeding the Afrika Korps. By late October, even before Eighth Army began its assault, the German logistical predicament in Egypt was desperate. The prime minister knew this from his *Boniface* decrypts, and dispatched a barrage of anxious, sometimes threatening, signals to Alexander. A British army strongly superior in men, tanks, guns and planes must surely be capable of defeating an enemy known to be almost immobilised for lack of fuel.

The operational value of Ultra material on the battlefield depended heavily on the receptiveness of individual commanders, and the quality of their intelligence chiefs. Some generals and admirals were astonishingly indifferent to the bounties they were offered. Montgomery was the first British desert commander to employ a top-class intelligence officer, in the person of Oxford academic Brigadier Bill Williams, and to heed his counsel. Ultra played a key role in enabling Montgomery to defeat Rommel's thrust at Alam Halfa. Admiral Sir Dudley Pound, First Sea Lord until 1943, often used intelligence poorly, most notoriously during the PQ17 Arctic convoy battle. By contrast, the Admiralty's submarine tracking room was brilliantly conducted, and played a decisive role in the Battle of the Atlantic. In 1942, however, Bletchley's inability to crack the U-boat cipher rendered Allied convoys appallingly vulnerable. November saw the worst losses of the war: some 721,700 tons of Allied shipping were sunk. Then, suddenly and dramatically, the code-breakers achieved another breakthrough, and once more provided the Royal Navy with means to track U-boat positions. From December onwards, convoys could again be routed away from the submarine wolfpacks. Thanks overwhelmingly to intelligence, the tide of the Atlantic battle, as well as of the Mediterranean campaign to inter-dict supplies to Rommel, turned decisively against Germany.

Montgomery launched his attack at Alamein on 23 October. Brendan Bracken said: 'If we are beaten in this battle, it's the end of Winston.' This was histrionic: within a fortnight the *Torch* landings far behind Rommel's front would have rendered the German position in Egypt untenable. That is why Correlli Barnett, Douglas Porch and others have described Alamein as 'the unnecessary battle'. But it was a desperately necessary one for the self-esteem of the British people. Bracken's words reflected the prevailing mood among even the prime minister's most loyal supporters. Churchill had presided over so many failures. There must be a success – a British success. Some post-war strategists have argued that if Montgomery had merely waited for *Torch*, he could then have fallen upon Rommel's retreating army in the open, and achieved a far more devastating and less costly victory. But this was never a credible political option for Eighth Army – nor for the prime minister.

On the night of 23 October, he attended a dinner for Eleanor Roosevelt at Buckingham Palace. A courtier wrote:

> Winston was like a cat on hot bricks, waiting for the news of the start of Alexander's offensive in Egypt. This . . . had begun at 8pm our time, and I had to go out in the middle to get the news by telephone from No. 10. After a brief interval, nothing would content Winston but to go to the telephone himself. His conversation evidently pleased him, for he walked back along the passage singing 'Roll Out The Barrel' with gusto, but with little evidence of musical talent. This astonished the posse of footmen through which he had to pass. I wondered what their Victorian predecessors would have thought had they heard Dizzy, or Mr G[ladstone], singing 'Knocked 'em in the Old Kent Road' in similar circumstances.

Back in June, Auchinleck had chosen to halt his retreat and defend a line at El Alamein. South of a narrow stretch of desert, there less than forty miles wide, hills rendered the position impervious to flank attack. In contrast to most North African battlefields, there was little room for manoeuvre: it was necessary for an attacker to batter a path by frontal assault through minefields, wire, deep defences. In August, when Rommel attacked, these circumstances profited the British. Seven weeks later they enabled 104,000 Germans and Italians to mount an unexpectedly staunch defence against 195,000 British troops and overwhelming firepower. Gen. Georg Stumme, acting as Axis commander during Rommel's absence on sick leave, was killed in the first days. Rommel returned. For almost a week, the British pounded and hammered at his positions. Churchill and the British people held their breath. The first news was good – but so it had often been before, to be followed by crushing disappointments. The British no longer dared to anticipate victory. One minister, Amery, wrote on 26 October: 'I am terribly anxious lest even with our superior weight of tanks and artillery and aircraft it might yet prove another Passchendaele, and we spend ourselves in not quite getting through.'

Churchill became seriously alarmed when, on the 28th, Montgomery paused and regrouped. He dispatched a threatening minute to Brooke: 'It is most necessary that the attack should be resumed before *Torch*. A standstill now will be proclaimed a defeat. We consider the matter most grave.' British armies had been here so often before. Auchinleck had achieved comparable successes, only to see them crumble to dust. Then, on 2 November, Montgomery launched his decisive blow, Operation *Supercharge*. 'How minute and fragile one felt, trapped in this maelstrom of explosive fury!' wrote a bewildered young British platoon commander. 'When we moved forward we scuttled like mice across the inhospitable sand . . . ready to sway and flatten ourselves to earth if a shell burst nearby . . . We were being fired upon. Though this was the very meaning of war, I felt a sense of outrage and betrayal. Someone had blundered. How could the chaos conceivably resolve itself into a successful attack? Yet all the major battles of history must have seemed like this, a hopeless shambles to the individual in front, with a coherence only discernible to those in the rear.'

Montgomery's men broke through. Ultra revealed to the British that Rommel considered himself beaten, and was in full retreat. Churchill rejoiced. At a Downing Street lunch he gleefully told guests, including MP Harold Nicolson: 'There is more jam to come. Much more jam. And in places where you least expect it.' After this coy hint at *Torch*, across the same lunch table he told Brendan Bracken to order the nation's church bells rung. When the proposal met doubts, he agreed to delay until 15 November, to ensure that no accident befell Allied arms. Thereafter, he was determined that the British people should recognise just cause for celebration.

Brooke wrote in his diary: 'If *Torch* succeeds we are beginning to stop losing this war.' Early on Sunday, 8 November, Allied forces

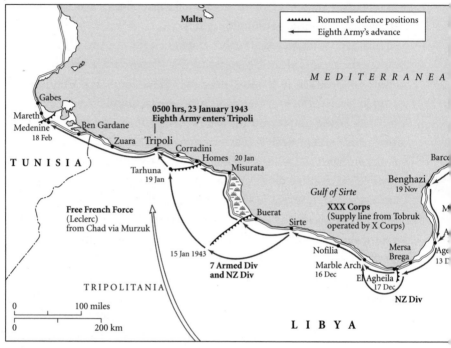

The North African campaign

landed in North Africa. Eisenhower's command was initially small, half the size of Montgomery's – 107,000 men, 35,000 of them British. But the symbolic significance of this first commitment of American ground troops against Hitler was immense. Though the invaders encountered some fierce resistance from Vichy forces, all the beachheads were swiftly secured. Churchill cabled congratulations to Marshall, adding wryly: 'We shall find the problems of success not less puzzling though more agreeable than those we have hitherto surmounted together.' *The Times* wrote of the prime minister's performance at the annual Mansion House dinner on 10 November: 'A sense of exaltation pervaded Mr Churchill's speech. It was the speaker's due. In the toil and sweat and tears to which

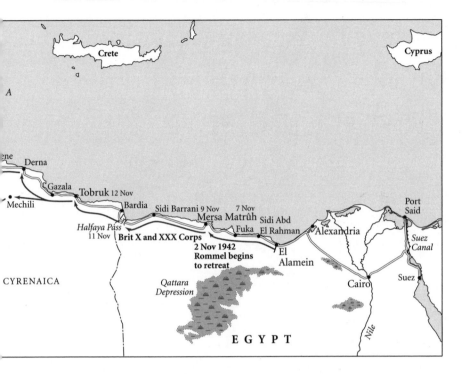

he summoned his country he has borne a leader's share.' Dalton
wrote on 12 November: 'The self-respect of the British Army is on
the way to being re-established. Last week . . . a British general was
seen to rush in front of a waiting queue at a bus stop and to leap
upon the moving vehicle. One onlooker said he would not have
dared to do this a week before.'

Alexander and Montgomery became Britain's military heroes of
the hour, and indeed of the rest of the war. The former was especially fortunate to find laurels conferred upon him, for his talents were
limited. Hereafter, Alexander basked in Churchill's favour. He
conformed to the prime minister's *beau idéal* of the gentleman
warrior. While forces under his command would endure many

341

Operation *Torch*

setbacks, they never suffered absolute defeat. Montgomery was a much more impressive personality, a superb manager and trainer of troops, the first important British commander to display the steel necessary to fight the Germans with success. Churchill famously observed of him: 'Pity our 1st victorious general should be a bounder of the 1st water.' Montgomery's conceit was notorious. In one of his proclamations in the wake of a victory, he asserted that it had been achieved 'with the help of God'. In the 'Rag', an officer observed sardonically that 'It was nice Monty had at last mentioned the Almighty in dispatches.' Yet Churchill and Brooke knew that diffidence and modesty are seldom found in successful commanders. Montgomery had few, if any, of the attributes of a gentleman. This was all to the good, even if it rendered him less socially congenial to the prime minister than Alexander. Gentlemen had presided over too many British disasters.

'Monty's' cold professionalism was allied to a shrewd understanding of what could, and could not, be demanded of a British citizen army in whose ranks there were many men willing to do their duty, but few who sought to become heroes. He does not deserve to rank among history's great captains, but he was a notable improvement upon the generals who had led Britain's forces in the first half of the Second World War. A carapace of vanity armoured him against prime ministerial harrowing of the kind that so wounded Wavell and Auchinleck. In the autumn and winter of 1942 it was the newcomers' good fortune to display adequacy at a time when the British achieved a formidable superiority of men, tanks, aircraft.

'We are winning victories!' exulted London charity worker Vere Hodgson on 29 November. 'It is difficult to get used to this state of things. Defeats we don't mind – we have all developed a stoical calm over such things in England. But actually to be advancing! To be taking places! One has an uneasy sense of enjoying a forbidden luxury.' Aneurin Bevan said nastily that the prime minister 'always refers to a defeat or a disaster as though it came from God, but to a victory as though it came from himself'. Throughout the war, Bevan upheld

Britain's democratic tradition by sustaining unflagging criticism of the government. To those resistant to Welsh oratory, however, his personality was curiously repellent. A dogged class warrior, he harried Churchill across the floor of the Commons as relentlessly when successes were being celebrated as when defeats were lamented. Bevan drew attention to the small size of the forces engaged at Alamein, and to the dominance of Commonwealth troops in Montgomery's army. His figures were accurate, but his scorn was at odds with the spirit of the moment – full of gratitude, as was the prime minister. At a cabinet meeting on 9 November, Churchill offered the government's congratulations to the CIGS and Secretary of State for the army's performance. This was, wrote Brooke sourly later, 'the only occasion on which he expressed publicly any appreciation or thanks for work I had done during the whole of the period I worked for him'.

For a generation after the Second World War, when British perceptions of the conflict were overwhelmingly nationalistic, Alamein was seen as the turning point. In truth, of course, Stalingrad – which reached its climax a few weeks later – was vastly more important. Montgomery took 30,000 German and Italian prisoners in his battle, the Russians 90,000 in theirs, which inflicted a quarter of a million losses on Hitler's Sixth Army. But Alamein was indeed decisive for Britain's prime minister. On 22 November he felt strong enough to allow Stafford Cripps to resign from the war cabinet, relegating him to the ministry of aircraft production. Churchill said of Cripps to Stalin: 'His chest is a cage, in which two squirrels are at war, his conscience and his career.' Cripps had pressed proposals for removing the direction of the war from the prime minister's hands. Now these could safely be dismissed, their author sidelined. His brief imposture as a rival national leader was over. In the ensuing thirty months of the German war, though the British people often grew jaded and impatient, never again was Churchill's mastery seriously questioned.

As Montgomery's forces continued to drive west across Libya, the prime minister looked ahead. Fortified by Ultra-based intelligence, he felt confident that the combination of Eighth Army's victory at

Alamein and the *Torch* landings ensured the Germans' expulsion from North Africa. No more than anyone else did he anticipate Hitler's sudden decision to reinforce failure, and the consequent prolongation of the campaign. In November 1942 it seemed plausible that the entire North African littoral would be cleared of the enemy by early new year. What, then, for 1943? The chiefs of staff suggested Sicily and Sardinia. This prompted a contemptuous sally from Downing Street: 'Is it really to be supposed that the Russians will be content with our lying down like this during the whole of 1943, while Hitler has a third crack at them?' Churchill talked instead of possible landings in Italy or southern France, perhaps even northwest Europe. Though he soon changed his mind, in November he still shared American hopes for *Roundup*, a major invasion of the Continent in 1943. He also remained mindful of his commitments to Stalin, and was acutely anxious not to be seen again to break faith. He told the War Office on 23 November: 'I never meant the Anglo-American Army to be stuck in North Africa. It is a springboard and not a sofa.'

The Americans were always unjust in supposing that Churchill shared the extreme caution of his generals. On the contrary, the prime minister was foremost among those urging commanders to act more boldly. As he told the House of Commons on 11 November, 'I am certainly not one of those who need to be prodded. In fact, if anything, I am a prod. My difficulties rather lie in finding the patience and self-restraint through many anxious weeks for the results to be achieved.' For most of the Second World War, Churchill was obliged to struggle against his military advisers' fear of battlefield failure, which in 1942 had become almost obsessive. Alan Brooke was a superbly gifted officer, who forged a remarkable partnership with Churchill. But if Allied operations had advanced at a pace dictated by the War Office, or indeed by Brooke himself, the conflict's ending would have come much later than it did. The British had grown so accustomed to poverty of resources, shortcomings of battlefield performance, that it had become second nature for them to fear the worst. Churchill himself, by contrast, shared with the Americans a desire to hasten forward Britain's creaky military machine. It was not that Britain's top soldiers were unwilling to fight – lack of courage was never the issue. It was that they deemed it prudent to fight slowly. Oliver Harvey noted on 14 November, with a cynicism that would have confirmed Stalin in all his convictions: 'The Russian army having played the allotted role of killing Germans, our Chiefs of Staff think by 1944 they could stage a general onslaught on the exhausted animal.'

This was an important and piercing insight upon British wartime strategy from 1942 onwards. There was a complacency, here explicitly avowed by Harvey, about the bloodbath on the eastern front. Neither Churchill nor Brooke ever openly endorsed the expressed desire of colleagues to see the Germans and Soviets destroy each other. But they certainly wanted the vast attritional struggle in the east to spare the Western Allies from anything similar. Most nations in most wars have no option save to engage an adversary confronting them in the field. The Anglo-Americans, by contrast, were quarantined from their enemies by eminently serviceable expanses of water, which conferred freedom of choice about where and when to join battle. This privilege was exercised wisely, from the viewpoint of the two nations. The lives of their young men were diligently husbanded. But such self-interested behaviour, almost as ruthless as Moscow's own, was bound to incur Russian anger.

The Allied invasion of French colonial Africa provoked a political crisis. By chance Admiral Jean Darlan, Vichy vice-president and foreign minister, was in Algiers when the Americans arrived. He assumed command of French forces which, to the surprise and dismay of US commanders, resisted their would-be liberators with considerable energy, inflicting some 1,400 casualties. There was then a negotiation, however, which caused Darlan to order his troops to lay down their arms, saving many more American lives. He was rewarded by Eisenhower, Allied supreme commander of *Torch*, with recognition as France's high commissioner, *de facto* ruler of North Africa. The British, unconsulted, were stunned. Darlan had collaborated enthusiastically with the Germans since 1940. It had seemed plausible that he might lead the French navy against Britain – De Gaulle thought

so. '*La France ne marchera pas*,' he told Churchill, '*mais la flotte –
peut-être*'; 'France will not march [on Britain]. But the fleet – perhaps.'
Now, Darlan's betrayal of Vichy demonstrated his moral bankruptcy.
In his new role he rejected requests for the liberation of Free French
prisoners in North African jails, and indeed treated such captives with
considerable brutality. Many exiled Frenchmen missed a great
opportunity in November 1942 to sink their differences and throw
themselves wholeheartedly into the struggle against the Axis. A British
senior officer wrote aggrievedly: 'Although the French hate the
Germans, they hate us more.' De Gaulle, Britain's anointed representative of 'Fighting France', was of course outraged by the Darlan
appointment, as was Eden. The Foreign Office had supported its lofty
French standard-bearer through many outbursts of Churchillian
exasperation, and in the face of implacable American hostility.

Throughout Churchill's life he displayed a fierce commitment to
France. He cherished a belief in its greatness which contrasted with
American contempt. Roosevelt perceived France as a decadent imperial power which had lacked British resolution in 1940. Entirely
mistakenly, given the stormy relationship between De Gaulle and
Churchill, the president thought the general a British puppet. He
was determined to frustrate any attempt to elevate De Gaulle to
power when the Allies liberated France. The Americans had none of
the visceral hatred for Vichy that prevailed in London. Since 1940
they had sustained diplomatic relations with Pétain's regime, which
in their eyes retained significant legitimacy. Here was a further manifestation of British sensitivities born of suffering and proximity, while
the US displayed a detachment rooted in comfortable inviolability.

In November 1942, British political and public opinion reacted
violently to Darlan's appointment. Just as the country was denied
knowledge of Stalin's excesses, so it had been told nothing of De
Gaulle's intransigence. British people knew only that the general
was a patriot who had chosen honourable exile in London, while
Darlan was a notorious anglophobe and lackey of the Nazis. When
Churchill addressed a secret session of the Commons about the
North African crisis on 10 December, the mood of MPs was angry

and uncomprehending. In private, since Darlan's appointment on 8 November Churchill had wavered. He disliked the admiral intensely. But he was also weary of De Gaulle's tantrums. He deemed the solidarity of the Anglo–American alliance to transcend all other considerations. He spoke to the House with remarkable frankness – such frankness, indeed, that after the war much of what he said was omitted from the published record of his speeches to the Commons' secret sessions.

'In war,' he said, 'it is not always possible to have everything go exactly as one likes. In working with allies it sometimes happens that they develop opinions of their own . . . I cannot feel that de Gaulle is France, still less that Darlan and Vichy are France. France is something greater, more complex, more formidable than any of the sectional manifestations . . . The House must not be left to believe that General de Gaulle is an unfaltering friend of Britain. On the contrary, I think he is one of those good Frenchmen who have a traditional antagonism ingrained in French hearts by centuries of war against the English . . . I could not recommend you to base all your hopes and confidence upon him.'

He went on to explain that General Henri Giraud, whom the Americans thought a more suitable national leader than De Gaulle, had been smuggled out of France by the Allies with the explicit intention that he should assume authority in North Africa. This purpose was confounded only when Giraud was rebuffed by senior French officers on the spot. Averell Harriman wrote: 'I have always deemed it tragic that the British picked De Gaulle and even more tragic that we picked Giraud.' On 10 December MPs, perhaps impressed by how fully Churchill confided in them, were placated by his arguments. In private, the British government redoubled its efforts to get Darlan removed from office. The Americans rejected London's proposal – an implausible one – that Harold Macmillan, British resident minister in the Mediterranean, should assume temporary authority in Algiers. Anglo–American relations were still steeped in acrimony on this issue when it was unexpectedly resolved. On 24 December a young French royalist burst into Darlan's office at the Summer Palace and shot him dead.

Responsibility for the assassination remains one of the last significant mysteries of the Second World War. The immediate perpetrator, one Fernand Bonnier de la Chapelle, was hurried before a firing squad two days later. Oliver Harvey, Eden's private secretary, expressed most undiplomatic dismay about the execution: 'It shows how wrong you get if once you compromise with evil. You find yourself shooting a good man for doing what you should have done yourself.' It was a relief to almost everyone else, however, that de la Chapelle was extinguished without revealing details of his plot. That a plot there was, is certain. A priest granted de la Chapelle absolution for his action before he walked into the Summer Palace, and modern conspiracy theorists have not failed to notice that Brigadier Menzies, chief of SIS, was in Algiers on Christmas Eve. The historian David Reynolds believes that the British were implicated. The most likely explanation, however, is that the killer was incited by a Free French group. Though there is no evidence of De Gaulle's personal complicity, the ruthless behaviour of his London organisation between 1940 and 1944 makes this credible.

If Darlan's murder was ugly, it lifted a heavy shadow from Anglo–American relations. General Giraud was installed in Darlan's place. After tortured negotiations between Churchill, Eden and De Gaulle in London, the two Frenchmen achieved a grudging and distant accommodation. Macmillan's attitude reflected that of many British politicians and diplomats: 'One comes away, as always after conversations with De Gaulle, wondering whether he is a demagogue or a madman, but convinced that he is a more powerful character than any other Frenchman with whom one has yet been in contact.' This widely shared view caused most British politicians and diplomats to conclude that De Gaulle must continue to be supported. Churchill kicked against such realism, demanding with extravagant verbosity that the general should be dumped. At the last, however, he sulkily acquiesced. De Gaulle remained recognised by London, though not by Washington, as principal representative of France in exile.

On 29 November 1942, Churchill minuted the chiefs of staff: 'I certainly think that we should make all plans to attack the French coast either in the Channel or in the Bay of Biscay, and that 12 July 1943 should be fixed as the target date.' Throughout this period he pressed Roosevelt repeatedly to expedite the US build-up in Europe so that the invasion of France could take place in 1943. Astonishingly, or even perversely, given his almost unflagging enthusiasm for attacking the supposed 'soft underbelly' of the Axis, on 1 December Churchill wrote to Brooke: 'It may be that we should close down the Mediterranean activities by the end of June with a view to *Round-Up* in August.' The US chiefs of staff were wholly justified in their belief that their British counterparts were unwilling to execute a 1943 cross-Channel attack. But they did an injustice to Churchill in supposing that he too had at this stage closed his mind. In the course of the next year, he vacillated repeatedly.

Marshall and his colleagues also underrated the professional skill and judgement of Brooke and his team. American practice was founded upon an expectation that means could always be found to fulfil chosen national objectives. Thus, Roosevelt's chiefs of staff decided upon a purpose, then addressed the practical problems of fulfilling it. The British chiefs, by contrast, forever struggling against straitened resources, declined to endorse any course of action unless they could see how it was to be executed. Such caution irked Churchill as much as the Americans: 'I do not want any of your own long-term projects,' he often expostulated to Brooke, shaking his fist in the CIGS's face. 'All they do is cripple initiative.'

In December 1942 it seemed to Britain's service chiefs that it would be impossible to mass sufficient landing craft to support a D-Day in 1943. Pressure on shipping was unrelenting in every theatre. There were never enough troops. British relations with the Australian government were further strained in December, by Canberra's insistence that 9th Australian Division should return home from North Africa, even though the threat of a Japanese invasion of Australia had been lifted. Churchill cabled Curtin, the Australian prime minister, that he did not consider this decision 'in accordance with the general strategic interests of the United

Nations', but Canberra remained implacable. Curtin's enthusiasm for leaving his men to fight at British discretion cannot have been enhanced by news that while only 6 per cent of the Allied troops at Alamein were Australian, they suffered 14 per cent of Montgomery's casualties in the battle.

And now the two North African campaigns faltered. The Allies were confounded by Hitler's decision to reinforce the theatre. If this was strategically foolish, it rendered much more difficult the immediate task of the British and US armies. American commanders and troops lacked experience. Though the Allies had numerical superiority in men, tanks and aircraft, the Germans fought with their usual skill and persistence. Alexander was famous for his courtesy and charm in addressing the Americans, but in private he railed at their military incompetence.

His reservations about Eisenhower's soldiers were just, but it ill became a British officer to express them. The British contingent in Ike's forces, designated as First Army, was led by Gen. Sir Kenneth Anderson. Anderson proved yet another in the long line of his nation's inadequate field commanders – 'not much good', in Brooke's succinct words of dismissal. Operations in Tunisia dispelled any notion that First Army's men were entitled to patronise their US counterparts. Eisenhower was more willing than most of his countrymen to hide frustrations about Allied shortcomings, but he wrote in his diary on 5 January 1943: 'Conversations with the British grow wearisome. They're difficult to talk to, apparently afraid that someone is trying to tell them what to do and how to do it. Their practice of war is dilatory.' A few days later, he added: 'British, as usual, are scared someone will take advantage of them even if we furnish everything.' In another entry he described the British as 'stiff-necked'. Richard Crossman of Britain's Political Warfare Executive thought that 'Getting on with Americans is frightfully easy, if only one will talk quite frankly and not give the appearance of being too clever, but v few English seem to have achieved it.' In North Africa, they were less than impressed by Eisenhower. Though Churchill's scepticism was later modified by necessity and experience, that winter he was sufficiently irritated by the

general's perceived blunders to evade fulfilment of Ike's request for a
signed photograph of himself.

At the beginning of December, the prime minister sketched a design
for 1943 based upon his expectation that Tunisia would be occupied
by the year's end, and North Africa cleared of Axis forces a month
later. By Christmas, this timetable was wrecked. Eighth Army's westward advance against Rommel progressed much more slowly than
Churchill had hoped in early November. The Russian convoy
programme was further dislocated by the need to keep large naval
forces in the Mediterranean. The British joint planners, unambitious
as ever, favoured making Sardinia the Allies' next objective. The prime
minister dismissed this notion, urging that Sicily was a much worthier
target. But he had begun to perceive that a 1943 D-Day in France
was implausible.

Churchill now wanted a conference of the 'Big Three', to settle
strategy. He loved summits, a coinage he invented, not least because
he believed that the force of his own personality could accomplish
ends more impressive than his nation's real strength could deliver,
in its fourth year of war. But Stalin declined a proposal to meet in
Khartoum, saying that he could not leave Moscow. Roosevelt was
often less enthusiastic than Churchill about personal encounters. Just
as the prime minister hoped for disproportionate results from these,
to the advantage of his own country, so the president knew that the
wealth and might of the United States spoke more decisively than
any words which he might utter at a faraway conference table. But
he liked the idea of visiting the theatre of war, and accepted Churchill's
proposal for a meeting to be held in liberated Casablanca, on the
Atlantic coast of North Africa.

The prime minister arrived in the Liberator *Commando* on 12
January 1943. His identification for security purposes as 'Air
Commodore Frankland' seemed absurd, from the moment he landed
at Casablanca to be greeted by a glittering array of brass. Ismay
muttered: 'Any fool can see that is an air commodore disguised as the
Prime Minister.' The 'air commodore' was then driven to his appointed

residence, the Villa Mirador, inside the closely guarded perimeter where the conference was to be held. He cabled Attlee: 'Conditions most agreeable. I wish I could say the same of the problems.'

The American service chiefs flew from Washington to Bathurst in West Africa, where the chief of the army was persuaded to disembark in a beekeeper's hood, to ward off mosquitoes. This was abandoned when Marshall found the welcoming party clad only in shorts. The Americans flew on to Casablanca with a lavish inventory of tents, cooking equipment and trinkets suitable for Arabs, lest they should be forced down in the desert, together with snowshoes and cold-weather clothing for a possible onward trip to Moscow. The British had their own embarrassments. They felt humiliated by their makeshift air transports, which obliged exalted passengers to disembark dirty and dishevelled from the bomb bays. Roosevelt reached Casablanca on the 14th, and was installed in a villa close to that of the prime minister. Churchill greeted him exuberantly. The two great men talked while their chiefs of staff embarked upon the bruising process of seeking an agreement which the president and prime minister could then be invited to endorse.

The Casablanca conference was the most important Anglo–American strategic meeting of the war, because it established the framework for most of the big things which were done thereafter. It represented the high point of British wartime influence, because it took place at a time when projected operations still depended on preponderantly British forces. Its deliberations were warmed by victories in Africa, and knowledge of looming Russian triumph at Stalingrad. At Alamein, in some degree the British Army had retrieved its fallen reputation. Churchill answered a question from correspondents about Eighth Army's pursuit of Rommel: 'I can give you this assurance – everywhere that Mary went the lamb is sure to go.' British staffwork for the conference was superb, aided by the presence offshore of a purpose-equipped command ship.

However powerful were the reservations of British service chiefs about their prime minister's strategic wisdom, an intimate working relationship ensured that they knew exactly what he wanted.

By contrast, even after thirteen months of war the US president was 'still something of an enigma to his American advisers', in the words of Marshall's biographer: 'Roosevelt imposed no unified plan.' His military chiefs 'still had twinges of doubt about Roosevelt's lack of administrative order, his failure to keep the Chiefs of Staff informed of private high-level discussions, and his tendency to ignore War Department advice in favour of suggestions from officials of other departments'. Marshall knew from the outset that he would lose his battle for a 1943 cross-Channel attack. In advance of the summit Roosevelt had displayed his customary opacity. However, he threw out enough hints to show that he, like the British, favoured the capture of Sicily. Admiral Ernest King, for the US Navy, was overwhelmingly preoccupied with the Pacific campaign. Quite uncharacteristically, the chief of the army was blustering in suggesting that an early invasion of France remained plausible.

In the combined chiefs' conference room at the Anfa Hotel, Alan Brooke echoed Churchill's recent protests to Roosevelt about the scale of the American Pacific build-up, which, said the British CIGS, threatened the agreed principle of 'Germany first'. The British thus wrongfooted Marshall by pressing him to justify the weight of resources committed to the Japanese war, to the detriment of Europe. This was a telling counter against American arguments that the British were prevaricating. Brooke then argued – implausibly in the eyes of history, and even in the context of January 1943 – that a massive combined bomber offensive against Germany, together with home-grown resistance among the peoples of occupied Europe, might relegate an invasion of France to a mere mopping-up operation. The Americans pressed the British for early offensive action in Burma, to assist the cause of China. This was perceived as a vital priority in Washington, a negligible one in London.

British politicians and generals had thus far found little to enjoy about the Second World War. But many of those at Casablanca – with the exception of Brooke, who seldom relished anything about the conflict – found the conference congenial. Harold Macmillan described 'a general atmosphere of extraordinary goodwill'. The weather was still cool, but flowers bloomed everywhere amid the palm trees and bougainvillea. Notice boards gave details of meeting venues and timings, then, 'when we got out of school at five o clock, you would see field marshals and admirals going down to the beach to play with the pebbles and make sand castles . . . The whole spirit of the camp was dominated by the knowledge that two men were there who rarely appeared in public, but whose presence behind the scenes was always felt . . . It was rather like a meeting of the later period of the Roman empire . . . There was a curious mixture of holiday and business in these extraordinarily oriental and fascinating surroundings . . . The whole affair was a mixture between a cruise, a summer school and a conference.'

Churchill, in the sunniest of moods in this sunny clime, wrote to Clementine on 15 January about the chiefs of staff's deliberations: 'At present they are working on what is called "off the record", and very rightly approaching the problems in an easy and non-committal fashion on both sides.' This reflected a wildly benign view. While courtesies were maintained, especially at social encounters, the first two days of conference sessions were tense and strained. Marshall asserted repeatedly that if the British were as serious as they professed about helping the Russians, they could only do this by executing *Roundup*, a landing in Europe in 1943. The British emphasised their support in principle for *Roundup*, but insisted that resources were lacking to undertake such a commitment.

There was a punishing schedule for *Symbol*, as the conference was codenamed. The combined chiefs of staff held thirty-one meetings in eleven days. Each involved gruelling exchanges between the principals, seeking to address a vast range of strategic and logistical issues. At later conferences in Quebec and elsewhere some closed sessions took place, without the usual congregation of staff officers in attendance, to allow a degree of frankness and indeed rudeness between the principals in breaking deadlocks. Ian Jacob was always conscious of American reservations about Brooke: 'I think CIGS's extremely definite views, ultra-swift speech and, at times, impatience, made them keep wondering whether he was not putting something over on them.'

Moran wrote of Brooke 'throwing down his facts in the path of understanding with a brusque gesture. In his opinion it was just common sense; he had thought it all out. Not for a moment did it occur to him that there might be another point of view.' At Casablanca Admiral King's temper, and passionate anglophobia, periodically broke out. During one meeting he asserted that American public opinion would never stand for certain courses. Brooke shrugged: 'Then you will have to educate them.' King, nettled, responded: 'I thank you [to remember that] the Americans are as well educated as the British.'

Churchill and Roosevelt attended only the conference plenary sessions, which took place in the evenings at the president's villa. Churchill wrote to Attlee about Roosevelt: 'He is in great form and we have never been so close.' Harold Macmillan observed that the prime minister handled the plenary meetings 'with consummate skill'. Away from the big table, 'his curious regime of spending the greater part of the day in bed and all the night up made it a little trying for his staff. I have never seen him in better form. He ate and drank enormously all the time, settled huge problems, played bagatelle and bezique by the hour, and generally enjoyed himself.' Churchill was dismayed that the British chiefs intended that a descent on Sicily should take place in September. This, he said, was much too late. If he did not accept the feasibility of a 1943 landing in France, he nonetheless wanted an alternative major Allied initiative by summer.

De Gaulle arrived, sulking, to meet Giraud. Churchill marvelled at his intransigence: 'The PM stood in the hall watching the Frenchman stalking down the garden path with his head in the air,' wrote his doctor, Charles Wilson. 'Winston turned to us with a whimsical smile: "His country has given up fighting, he himself is a refugee, and if we turn him down he's finished. Well, just look at him!" he repeated. "He might be Stalin, with 200 divisions behind his words. I was pretty rough with him. I made it quite plain that if he could not be more helpful we were done with it . . . He hardly seemed interested.

My advances and my threats met with no response."' Tears came to Churchill's eyes as he said: 'England's grievous offence in de Gaulle's eyes is that she has helped France. He cannot bear to think that she needed help. He will not relax his vigilance in guarding her honour for a single instant.'

If the British were enjoying themselves at Casablanca, most of the Americans were not. Ian Jacob wrote disdainfully: 'Being naturally extremely gullible, the Americans calmly repeat any hare-brained report they hear.' John Kennedy wrote of their senior officers: 'We feel that the Americans have great drive and bigger ideas than ours, but that they are weak in staff work and in some of their strategic conceptions. The Americans are extremely difficult to know. Under their hearty and friendly manner one feels there is suspicion and contempt in varying degrees according to personality.' This was so. A biographer of Eisenhower has written: 'Many American officers found their British opposite numbers to be insufferable not only in their arrogance but in their timidity about striking the enemy.' One of Ike's divisional commanders, Maj. Gen. Orlando Ward, wrote in disgust that Americans in North Africa found themselves reduced to the status of 'a pointer pup . . . If someone with a red mustache, a swagger stick and a British accent speaks to us, we lie down on the ground and wiggle.'

Harriman was dismayed by the eagerness of the US chiefs of staff, when in exclusively American company, to badmouth the British. In their hearts, he thought, Marshall and his colleagues recognised the intractability of mounting a cross-Channel attack in 1943 as surely as did the prime minister and Brooke. But, in Jacob's words, 'They viewed the Mediterranean as a kind of dark hole, which one entered into at one's peril. If large forces were committed . . . the door would suddenly and firmly be shut behind one.' They still seemed obsessed, in the eyes of the British chiefs, with fears that the Germans might intervene in North Africa through Spain. They deplored the sensation that the British, and explicitly Churchill, were exerting greater influence upon their president's decisions than themselves.

The strategic deadlock was broken, in the end, by a combination of harsh realities and skilful diplomacy, in which Dill played a key role. In January 1943, the Americans had 150,000 troops in the Mediterranean theatre. The British in the region fielded three times as many soldiers, four times as many warships and almost as many aircraft as the US. Once the North African campaign was wound up, the forces immediately available for follow-up operations would comprise four French divisions, nine American – and twenty-seven British. Churchill's own soldiers, sailors and airmen continued to predominate in the conflict with Germany, albeit employing an increasing proportion of US tanks and equipment. Until this balance of forces shifted dramatically in 1944, British wishes were almost bound to prevail. When Brooke grew close to despair at one point in discussions, on 18 January, during a lunchtime break Dill first told him that agreement was closer than he supposed. Then he warned that if this could not be achieved between the chiefs, Churchill and Roosevelt must be invited to arbitrate, which neither British nor American commanders wanted: 'You know what a mess they would make of it!'

That same afternoon, the major differences were resolved. The British formally endorsed American commitments for the Pacific, and promised to launch an offensive in Burma after the monsoon. The two nations committed themselves to a massive air programme against Germany, the Combined Bomber Offensive, to create conditions for a successful invasion of France in 1944. They agreed to invade Sicily in the summer of 1943, and left further follow-up operations against Italy to be decided in the course of events. A face-saving sop was agreed about a cross-Channel attack: if resources and landing craft proved available, there should be a major operation to seize a bridge-head in France in August 1943. It is unlikely that anyone present anticipated fulfilment of this condition, but lip-service continued to be paid to it for months ahead, not least in cables to Stalin. Churchill and Roosevelt added a few token points of their own for the combined chiefs' formal endorsement. They reasserted the importance of convoys to Russia and aid to China; the CCS were urged to try for a Sicilian landing as early as June; the need was emphasised to hasten concentration of forces in Britain for an invasion of France.

Roosevelt thanked Dill for his role in brokering an Anglo–American deal. The British officer responded: 'My object is to serve my country and to serve yours. I hope and I believe that our interests are identical and in every problem that arises I try to look at it not as a British or an American problem, but as an Anglo–American problem.' Yet Dill, customarily much more temperate than Brooke in his judgements on all things American, later wrote to the CIGS about the president: 'The better I get to know that man the more selfish and superficial I think him . . . of course, it is my job to make the most and the best of him.'

The Times adopted a complacent view of the status of Britain's leader at the Casablanca conference, news of which was given to the public only after the principals departed: 'Mr Churchill . . . takes his place at the President's side with equal and complementary authority. The light now beginning to break wherever allied forces are engaged shows his stature enhanced by the deep shadows through which his country has passed.' There was a deceitful assertion in the newspaper's report that De Gaulle and Giraud 'have come together in the utmost cordiality'.

Churchill perceived Casablanca as a great success. He was charmed by Roosevelt's geniality, though Harriman claimed that he was distressed by the president's announcement to the press at the close of the conference that the Allies would insist upon the unconditional surrender of the Axis powers: 'He was offended that Roosevelt should have made such a momentous announcement without prior consultation and I am sure he did not like the manner of it. I had seen him unhappy with Roosevelt more than once, but this time he was more deeply offended than before. I also had the impression that he feared it might make the Germans fight all the harder.' These remarks have bewildered historians. In reality, the president had discussed unconditional surrender with Churchill before his announcement. The prime minister, in his turn, signalled prior warning to the war cabinet in London.

If he was indeed irritated with Roosevelt, it was probably a matter of emphasis. There could be no possible negotiation with the Nazi regime, but Churchill might have liked to leave a margin of hope in the minds of prospective German anti-Nazis that their nation could expect some mercy if Hitler was deposed. Just before Pearl Harbor, in November 1941, Churchill reminded the cabinet that when Russia was invaded, 'we had made a public statement that we would not negotiate with Hitler or with the Nazi regime'. He added that he thought 'it would be going too far to say that we should not negotiate with a Germany controlled by the Army. It was impossible to forecast what form of Government there might be in Germany at a time when their resistance weakened and they wished to negotiate.' It is likely that in January 1943 his view had not changed much about the desirability of a constructive vagueness in the Allies' public position towards non-Nazi Germans, even following the vast accession of American strength, and the transformation of the war.

At Casablanca, Harriman told the president of Churchill's apparent distress about unconditional surrender. Roosevelt seemed unmoved. Likewise at dinner with the prime minister, he mused aloud about independence for Morocco, compulsory education, fighting disease and other social crusades. Churchill displayed impatience. Harriman believed that Roosevelt talked as he did for the fun of provoking the old British Tory. 'He always enjoyed other people's discomfort,' wrote the US diplomat. 'It never bothered him very much when other people were unhappy.' As at all their encounters, Churchill strove to create opportunities for *tête-à-tête* conversations with the president, but found it increasingly difficult to catch him alone. Roosevelt had grown wary of Churchill's special pleadings, impatient of his monologues, and was probably also mindful of Marshall's resentment about any strategic discussion from which the chief of the army was absent.

In the months that followed Casablanca, such disaffected figures as Albert Wedemeyer made no secret of their anger at the manner in which a strategy had been approved by their president against the wishes of US armed forces chiefs. They believed that British enthusiasm for Mediterranean operations was driven by imperialistic rather than military considerations. This remained their view through the ensuing two years. Such sentiments became known in Congress and the media, and were responsible for much future cross-Atlantic ill temper. But Marshall, with notable statesmanship, acknowledged the decisions graciously. He strove against the anti-British sentiment widespread among America's soldiers, writing to the army's public relations chief shortly after Casablanca, urging him to counter the 'insidious business of stirring up ill-feeling between the British and us'.

The conference broke up with fervent expressions of goodwill on all sides. Churchill gave his staff his usual instruction when it was time to pack, borrowed from memories of the back end of theatre programmes: 'Wigs by Clarkson.' The prime minister and president drove for four hours to Marrakesh, where they installed themselves at the Villa Taylor. That evening, as the sun was setting amid the snow-clad Atlas mountains, Churchill climbed to the roof to savour the scene, which had much moved him on a peacetime visit six years earlier. Now he insisted that the president must share the experience. Two servants locked hands to form a chair on which the president was carried up the winding stairs, 'his paralysed legs dangling like the limbs of a ventriloquist's dummy', as Charles Moran noted cruelly. The prime minister murmured: 'It's the most lovely spot in the whole world.'

It seems open to doubt whether Roosevelt gained equal pleasure from an experience which emphasised his own incapacity. Churchill could be notably insensitive to the vulnerabilities of others. Amid delight about winning his battle for the Italian commitment at Casablanca, he allowed himself to express an enthusiasm for Britain's ally which few of Roosevelt's conference team would have reciprocated: 'I love these Americans,' he told his doctor, 'they behave so generously.' Yet never again would his enthusiasm be so unqualified. If there had been a period of real intimacy between the US president and the British prime minister in 1941–42, when Roosevelt in some measure deferred to Churchill's experience of war, thereafter their relationship became steadily more distant. Mutual courtesies, affectionate rhetoric, were sustained. But perceptions of national interest diverged with increasing explicitness.

Before the two leaders parted, they dispatched a joint cable to

Moscow outlining the conference decisions. 'Whatever we decided to undertake in 1943 would have to be represented to Stalin as something very big,' wrote Ian Jacob. The Soviet warlord was now told that there would be a landing in Europe 'as soon as practicable'. Neither leader supposed, however, that their studied vagueness would fool Moscow. 'Nothing in the world will be accepted by Stalin as an alternative to our placing 50 or 60 divisions in France by the spring of this year,' observed Churchill. 'I think he will be disappointed and furious.' The prime minister was correct. To Marshal Georgy Zhukov, by now his most trusted commander, Stalin vented his anger about the inadequacy of Allied aid: 'Hundreds of thousands of Soviet people are giving their lives in the struggle against fascism, and Churchill is haggling with us about two dozen Hurricanes. And anyway those Hurricanes are crap – our pilots think nothing of them.'

There was one important aspect of the Casablanca conference, and indeed of Allied strategy-making for the rest of the war, which was never expressly articulated by Western leaders, and is still seldom directly acknowledged by historians. The Americans and British flattered themselves that they were shaping policies which would bring about the destruction of Nazism. Yet in truth, every option they considered and every operation they subsequently executed remained subordinate to the struggle on the eastern front. The Western Allies never became responsible for the defeat of Germany's main armies. They merely assisted the Russians to accomplish this. For all the enthusiasm of George Marshall and his colleagues to invade Europe, it remains impossible to believe that the US would have been any more willing than was Britain to accept millions of casualties to fulfil the attritional role of the Red Army at Stalingrad, Kursk, and in a hundred lesser bloodbaths between 1942 and 1945. Roosevelt and Churchill had the satisfaction of occupying higher moral ground than Stalin. But it is hard to dispute the Soviet warlord's superior claim to be called the architect of victory.

Roosevelt took off for home on 25 January. Churchill lingered, and in those surroundings which he loved created his only painting of the war, a view of the Atlas mountains. Then he embarked upon one of his most energetic rounds of wartime travelling, which pleased chiefly himself. Brooke was obliged to cancel a cherished scheme for two days' sightseeing and a Moroccan partridge shoot, to accompany his master to Turkey. The cabinet opposed this expedition, which ministers considered futile. Churchill overruled them, hankering to revive his grand design, which had foundered in 1941, to raise the Balkans against Hitler. He also rejoiced in the exhilaration of touring the Mediterranean as a victorious warlord, after the humiliations and frustrations of earlier years.

Arrived at the Cairo embassy early on 26 January, he recoiled from the ambassadress's offer of breakfast tea, demanding instead white wine. Brooke described the scene with fastidious amazement: 'A tumbler was brought which he drained in one go, and then licked his lips, turned to Jacqueline [Lampson] and said: "Ah! that is good, but you know, I have already had two whiskies and soda and 2 cigars this morning"!! It was then only shortly after 7.30am. We had travelled all night in poor comfort, covering some 2300 miles in a flight of over 11 hours, a proportion of which was at over 11,000 ft., and there he was, as fresh as paint, drinking wine on top of two previous whiskies and 2 cigars!!' In Cairo, Churchill held significant conversations with his former historical researcher, the Oxford don William Deakin, now an SOE officer handling Yugoslavia. Deakin described the modest help being dispatched to the royalist General Mihailovic and his Cetnik guerrillas. He briefed the prime minister for the first time about the significance of Josef Broz, 'Tito', who led a rapidly growing force of some 20,000 insurgents whom SOE believed to be less communist than they appeared. Deakin's views were supported by Ultra intercepts already known to Churchill, revealing German belief that the communists represented a much more substantial military threat than the Cetniks.

The prime minister endorsed approaches to Tito, and Deakin himself was soon parachuted to the Croat leader's headquarters. Unbeknown to the British, the partisan chief spent the spring of 1943 parleying with the Germans about a possible truce that would free his forces to destroy Mihailovic. Nazi intransigence, however, obliged the partisans to fight the Axis. The British, and especially officers of SOE, were guilty of persistent delusions about Tito's politics. But they were right about one big thing: Hitler's determination to defend Yugoslavia and its mineral resources caused him to deploy large forces in a country well-suited to guerrilla operations. There, as nowhere else in occupied Europe outside Russian territory, internal resistance achieved a significant strategic impact.

The military contingent in Churchill's party set off for neutral Turkey clad in borrowed and absurdly ill-fitting civilian clothes. Their visit to President Ismet Iononu on 30 January was no more successful than the cabinet had anticipated. The Turks were full of charm and protestations of goodwill. Always fearful of Stalin, they valued British good offices to deflect the Russians from aggression on their northern border. In the stuffy railway carriage in which the two sides met, the British were half-embarrassed, half-impressed by Churchill's insistence on addressing the Ankara delegation in his fluent but incomprehensible French. It would have made no difference had he spoken in Chinese. The Turks were uninterested in joining the war. Why should they have done so? It might be true that the Allies now looked like winners. But since the Anglo-Americans had no designs on Turkey, it was surely prudent for that impoverished nation to maintain its neutrality. Brooke fretted about the security risks to the prime minister, on an ill-guarded train in the middle of nowhere. Local rumour had broadcast news of the visit far and wide. The CIGS searched out Churchill's detective, whom he discovered eating a hearty supper in the dining car: 'I told him that the security arrangements were very poor and that he and his assistant must make a point of occasionally patrolling round Winston's sleeper through the night. He replied in an insolent manner: "Am I expected to work all night as well as all day?" I then told him that he had travelled in identical comfort with the rest of the party, and that I was certainly not aware that he had even started working that day.'

But the visit passed off safely until Churchill's Liberator, taxi-ing to take-off on his departure, bogged down on the runway at Adana. The prime minister made comic personal attempts to direct recovery operations, with much gesticulation to the Turks about the plane's sunken wheel, before having recourse to a spare aircraft. Back in Cairo on 1 February, he learned of the surrender of the German Sixth Army at Stalingrad. Cabling to congratulate Stalin, he enthused about 'a heavy operation across the Channel in August', involving seventeen to twenty British and US divisions. The Russians could scarcely be blamed for adopting a cynical view of their allies when the prime minister sought to sustain this charade within days of settling an entirely different agenda at Casablanca. He flew on to Montgomery's headquarters outside Tripoli. In a natural amphitheatre at Castel Benito, he addressed soldiers of Eighth Army. 'After the war,' he said, 'when a man is asked what he did it will be quite sufficient to say "I marched and fought in the Desert Army." And when history is written . . . your feats will gleam and glow and will be a source of song and story long after we who are gathered here have passed away.' With tears in his eyes, he took the salute as 51st Highland Division passed in review before him through the streets of Tripoli, led by its pipers. He visited the New Zealand Division and eulogised Freyberg, its commander.

In Algiers on 6 February, he told former Vichyite military leaders that 'if they marched with us, we would not concern ourselves with past differences'. At last the British were successful in achieving recognition for De Gaulle in North Africa. General Giraud was replaced as principal French authority by a national committee of uneasily mingled Gaullists and Giraudists. American distaste for De Gaulle persisted. But Washington grudgingly acknowledged that the Free French, whose soldiers had been fighting the Axis powers while Vichy's men collaborated with them, must be permitted some share in determining their nation's future.

At this, the end of Churchill's Mediterranean odyssey, he mused aloud about the possibility of his own death. Ian Jacob noted his remarks: 'It would be a pity to have to go out in the middle of such an interesting drama without seeing the end. But it wouldn't be a bad moment to leave – it is a straight run-in now, and even the cabinet could manage it.' His words were significant for two reasons.

First, he knew as well as any man how plausible it was that he should die on one of his wartime air journeys, as so many senior officers died. Two members of the Casablanca secretariat were killed when their plane was lost on the journey home, news which Brooke ordered to be temporarily withheld from Churchill when it came through on the eve of his own flight to Turkey. General Gott, the Polish General Sikorski, Air Marshal Sir Trafford Leigh-Mallory, Admiral Sir Bertram Ramsay, together with Arthur Purvis, the head of Britain's Washington purchasing mission, were only the most prominent figures killed on RAF wartime flights – interestingly, hardly any prominent USAAF passengers fell victim to similar misfortunes. Churchill observed, when a North African take-off was delayed by magneto failure, that it was nice of the magneto to fail on the ground. So indeed it was.

He was right also to perceive that the most critical period of his leadership was at an end. Many dramas still lay ahead, but Britain no longer faced any danger of falling victim to Nazi tyranny. The course was set towards Allied victory. Back in London on 11 February 1943, making a Commons statement about Casablanca, he observed that Great Britain and the US were formerly peaceful societies, ill-armed and unprepared. By contrast, 'they are now warrior nations, walking in the fear of the Lord, very heavily armed, and with an increasingly clear view of their own salvation'. Mindful of the resurgent U-boat threat in the Atlantic, he stressed the sea as the principal area of danger. In response to a foolish question about what plans existed for preventing Germany from starting another war, he replied that this would provide fit food for thought, 'which would acquire more precise importance when the present unpleasantness has been ended satisfactorily'.

It would be absurd to describe Churchill, in the early spring of 1943, as having become redundant. But after three years in which he had done many things which no other man could, he was no longer vital to Britain's salvation. If in 1940–41 he had been his nation's deliverer, in 1942–43 the Americans owed him a greater debt than they recognised, for persuading their president to the

Mediterranean strategy. His strategic judgement had been superior to that of America's chiefs of staff. Hereafter, however, his vision became increasingly clouded and the influence of his country waned. For the rest of the war Churchill would loom much larger in the Grand Alliance as a personality than as leader of its least powerful element. Henceforward, never far from the minds of both Roosevelt and Stalin was the brutal question which Napoleon asked about the Pope: 'How many divisions have the British?'

FOURTEEN

Out of the Desert

In 1943, to Winston Churchill and to many British, Russian and American people, it sometimes seemed that the Western Allies spent more time talking than fighting Hitler's armies. Granted, large forces of aircraft battered Germany in a bomber offensive of which much was made in newspapers and cables to Stalin. The Royal Navy, with growing strength, assurance and success, was still waging a vital defensive struggle to hold open the Atlantic convoy routes. US forces fought savage battles with the Japanese in the Pacific. But this was the last year of the war in which shortage of resources severely constrained Anglo-American ground action. In 1944 a vast array of ships, planes, weapons and equipment generated by US industrial mobilisation flooded forth onto the battlefields, arming Allied forces on land, at sea and in the air on a scale such as the world had never seen. Until then, however, Churchill's and Roosevelt's armies engaging the Axis remained pathetically small in comparison to those of the Soviets.

The British committed thirteen divisions to North Africa, the Americans six. Of these formations, eight would land in Sicily. Some eleven British divisions in varying states of manning and under-equipment remained at home, training for operations in France or wherever else the prime minister decided to commit them. Additionally, hundreds of thousands of British troops were scattered along the North African littoral, and throughout Egypt, Palestine, Syria, Iraq, Persia and India. These performed logistical and garrison functions of varying degrees of utility, but were not, as Churchill often reminded Alan Brooke, killing Italians, Germans or Japanese. The US Marine Corps was deployed in the Pacific, while General Douglas MacArthur directed a modest army contingent in Australia and New Guinea. In 1943 the latter campaign was dominated by three Australian divisions. A huge Indian Army in India, supplemented by British units, pursued desultory operations, but seldom that year proved able to deploy more than six divisions against the Japanese. At a time when Stalin and Hitler were pitting some 200 apiece against each other in the east, it is scarcely surprising that the Russians viewed their allies' Mediterranean activities with contempt.

Most Anglo-American historians agree that a D-Day in France in 1943 would have been a disaster. It is only necessary to consider the ferocity of the resistance the Germans mounted in Normandy between June and August 1944 to imagine how much more formidable could have been their response to an invasion a year earlier, when Hitler's power was much greater, that of the Allies much less. But it infuriated the Russians that the British and Americans exercised to the full their luxury of choice, such as Stalin lacked after June 1941, about when to engage a major German army. It is possible that the Allies might have got ashore in France in 1943, and stayed there. But the casualties of the campaign that followed would have been horrendous, dwarfing those of north-west Europe in 1944–45. While the Russians fought most of their war beneath the triple goads of patriotism, compulsion and indifference to human cost, the Anglo-Americans were able to husband lives until their industrial resources could be deployed to overwhelming advantage. They chose to deploy far smaller front-line ground combat forces in proportion to their national populations than either Russia or Germany. David French, author of an acute study of the British Army in World War II, observes: 'In absolute terms the British reduced their casualties simply by abstaining for long periods of the war from fighting the kind of intensive land battles in which they were bound to incur heavy losses.'

On 13 February 1943, when it was still hoped that the North African campaign could be wound up within a month, Churchill was exasperated to hear that the Sicilian landing could not take place before July. He cabled Hopkins in Washington: 'I think it is an awful thing that in April, May and June, not a single American or British soldier will be killing a single German or Italian soldier while the Russians are chasing 185 divisions around.' He, like the British people, was acutely conscious of the Russians' losses and – increasingly – of their victories in the Caucasus, at Kharkov and Stalingrad. He cabled Stalin constantly about the progress of the RAF's bomber offensive, and assured him mendaciously that the French invasion plan was being 'kept alive from week to week'. When the chiefs of staff asked him to press Moscow for information about Russian military plans, he demurred: 'I feel so conscious of the poor contribution the British and American armies are making . . . that I should not be prepared to court the certain rebuff which would attend a request for information.' In a flush of impatience, he asked his chiefs if the British could launch *Husky*, as the Sicily operation was now codenamed, on their own. No, was the firm reply. But in asking the question, Churchill discredited American suspicions that he was reluctant for his soldiers to fight.

February's defeat at the Kasserine pass in Tunisia, where a German thrust drove back in rout superior US forces, had no strategic significance. Within days Eisenhower's troops had regrouped and regained the lost ground. But it dealt a decisive blow to hopes of an early end of the campaign. On 27 February, Alexander reported on the state of US forces and the three French divisions, mostly colonial troops, now joining the campaign: 'Americans require experience and French require arms . . . Hate to disappoint you, but final victory in North Africa is not (repeat not) just around the corner.'

It was a perverse feature of the war, that while the British people sustained warm admiration for Russian achievements, they seldom displayed the same generosity towards Americans. The Grand Alliance spawned a host of Anglo–Soviet friendship groups in Britain, but few Anglo–American ones. A Home Intelligence report of 14 January 1943 declared: 'At the time of Pearl Harbor, public interest in the US received a momentary stimulus which soon declined and has (in marked contrast to the attitude to Russia and things Russian) remained low ever since.' When news of the Kasserine battle was released in Britain, Violet Bonham Carter recorded in her diary a friend's story of meeting a vegetable seller in Covent Garden who said: 'Good news today, sir!' 'Have the Russians done well?' 'No – the Americans have got the knock.' This, asserted Bonham Carter, represented 'the universal reaction' to news of the reverse that had befallen Eisenhower's armies. A best-selling novel of the time was *How Green was My Valley*; Attlee jested unkindly that Alexander in North Africa was now writing a sequel, *How Green is My Ally*. Churchill deleted from a draft of his memoirs a February letter to the King in which he wrote: 'The enemy make a great mistake if they think that all the troops we have there are in the same green state as are our United States friends.' Americans were irked to read the findings of a Gallup Poll that asked British people which ally was making the greatest contribution to winning the war. Some 50 per cent answered 'Russia', 43 per cent 'Britain', 5 per cent 'China', and just 3 per cent 'the United States'.

The British knew that the war was a long way from ending, and were resigned to that prospect. But after more than three years of bombardment, privation and defeats, weariness had set in. It is hard to overstate the impact of the blackout on domestic morale. Year after year, throughout the hours of darkness the gloom of Britain's cities was relieved by no visible chink of light. As the novelist Anthony Powell observed, few people's tempers were as sound in 1943 as they had been in 1939. The British were deeply sensitive to American triumphalism, of which echoes wafted across the Atlantic from these allies who still ate prodigiously and had never been bombed. Harold Macmillan wrote with lofty disdain about the Americans around him in the Mediterranean: 'They all look exactly alike to me – like Japanese or Chinese.'

Tory MP Cuthbert Headlam lamented news of a later US battlefield success: 'I am told that our efforts are scarcely noted in the American press. I fancy that the Americans after this war are likely to be more swollen-headed and tiresome than after the last; they may well be more troublesome to us than the Russians.' In their hearts, all these men knew that their country could accomplish nothing without the US, that only American resources made the defeat of Hitler possible. But it was sometimes hard to avoid indulging ungenerous sentiments, amid British consciousness that the struggle was reducing their own society to penury, while America grew relentlessly in wealth and might. If many upper-crust British people hoped that the Soviets and Nazis would destroy each other in the course of the war, most Americans seemed well pleased by the prospect of the British Empire becoming a casualty of victory.

The Russians expressed renewed impatience about lack of progress in the Mediterranean. Stalin cabled Churchill: 'The weight of the Anglo-American offensive in North Africa has not only not increased, but there has been no development of the offensive at all, and the time limit for the operations set by yourself was extended.' The Soviet leader said that thirty-six German divisions were being redeployed from the west to the eastern front, an unimpressive testimonial to Anglo-American efforts. Churchill persuaded himself that this show of anger reflected the influence of the Soviet hierarchy. He still cherished delusions that he possessed a personal understanding with Stalin, interrupted only when other members of the Moscow politburo demanded a harsher line with the imperialists. Anglo–Russian relations worsened again when the Admiralty insisted on cancellation of its March convoy to Archangel. German capital ships posed a continuing threat off north Norway, while British naval resources were strained to the limits by Mediterranean and Atlantic commitments. In early spring, for the last time in the war Allied decryption of U-boat signals was interrupted, with shocking consequences for several Atlantic convoys – forty-two merchant ships were lost in March, against twenty-six in February.

Churchill sought to placate Moscow by promising a dramatic increase in aircraft deliveries via Persia, and 240,000 tons of supplies in August. But once again, British assurances were unfulfilled because of shipping and convoying difficulties. Stalin cared nothing about these. Why should he have done? He saw only that his armies were being called upon to destroy those of Hitler, aided by more Western words than action. After the war, Brooke expressed surprise about his own diary: 'It is rather strange that I did not refer more frequently to the news from Russia.' Indeed it was. More than two million Russian soldiers – and millions more civilians – died in 1943, while British and American forces fighting the Germans lost around 70,000 killed, including bomber aircrew. In Moscow's eyes, it seemed characteristic that the Allies should again suspend supplies to Russia, where the real war was being fought, for the convenience of their own marginal operations in North Africa. Hugh Dalton asked Britain's Moscow ambassador, Sir Archibald Clark Kerr, if there was a danger of the Russians making a separate peace with Hitler: 'He says he would not rule this out, if we continue to seem to them to be doing nothing to help.'

Anglo–Soviet relations were further soured by the Germans' April announcement of the discovery of thousands of bodies of Polish officers killed by the Soviets in 1939 at Katyn, near Smolensk. On the 15th Churchill told General Sikorski, the Poles' leader in Britain: 'Alas, the German revelations are probably true. The Bolsheviks can be very cruel.' In the Commons smoking room, when Duff Cooper and Harold Nicolson mentioned Katyn to the prime minister, he answered tersely: 'The less said about that the better.' He urged Sikorski not to make much publicly of the story, to avoid provoking Moscow. Amid Polish rage, this warning went unheeded. The 'London Poles' publicly denounced the Russians, who promptly severed relations with them and announced the creation of their own Polish puppet regime. Churchill warned Stalin sharply that Britain, in its turn, would not recognise Moscow's Poles. Lines were now drawn. Moscow was bent upon a post-war settlement that brought Poland into a Soviet-dominated buffer zone. Churchill expended immense energy and political capital throughout the next two years in efforts to prevent such an outcome. Yet nothing could alter geography: Warsaw lay much closer to the armies of Stalin than to those of Churchill and Roosevelt.

It might be supposed that, in those days, Churchill's daily existence was eased by the facts that many of the big decisions were taken, his critics had been put to flight by battlefield success; Britain's survival was no longer in doubt. But there was no relaxation for a man who had chosen personally to direct the war effort, in the midst of a global struggle, and whose existence was entirely focused upon hastening Allied victory. Ian Jacob described him in bed of a morning: 'Sawyers brings the breakfast; then Kinna is sent for to take something down; meanwhile the bell is rung for the Private Secretary on duty who is asked for news, & told to summon someone, say CIGS or Pug. Then it is the candle for lighting cigars that is wanted. Then someone must get Hopkins on the phone. All this while the PM is half-sitting, half-lying in his bed, breathing rather stertorously, & surrounded by papers.'

Elizabeth Layton, one of Churchill's typists, remarked that he hated any of his staff to speak, unless they had something of substance to say. 'There is nothing in the world he hates more than to waste one minute of his time,' she wrote to her parents. 'He is so funny in the car; he may dictate, or he may just think for the whole hour, mumbling and grumbling away to himself; or he may be watching the various things we pass, suddenly making little ejaculations like "Oh – look at the lambs", or "What kind of aeroplane is that" – to which little reply is expected. I think he knows now that I have learned not to waste his time by making any fool observations, which one might have felt obliged to break the silence by doing.' That weekend, Churchill was at his most benign. 'We had good news about Tunisia,' Layton wrote to her parents, 'so the boss was in a good temper, and really I've seldom had such fun. He was very nice to us all and treated us like human beings for once! Poor man, don't think I ever blame him for not doing so – it is so understandable.'

The prime minister displayed no appetite for a respite from responsibility, and welcomed companionship only to provide himself with an audience. For all his sociability, paradoxically Churchill remained an intensely private person. Moran thought that he kept his own counsel, 'sharing his secret thoughts with no one . . . There is no one to whom he opens his heart. Brooke is too cold and critical; he always seems to be doubtful of the P.M.'s facts and often throws cold water on his pet projects.' Alexander, by contrast, was a notably skilled flat-terer. The accommodating Guardsman listened patiently to the prime minister's monologues. When he himself responded, 'He is always so reassuring,' in Moran's words, 'always so sure that the P.M.'s plans are right.' The companionship of courtiers and visitors sufficed to assuage Churchill's restlessness only for short periods. He was driven by a constant hunger for movement, action and the company of other great men, with whom he could advance great matters.

It had become plain that, even if other factors proved favourable, landing craft would be lacking for a French D-Day in 1943. Lack of shipping also made it necessary to abort a proposed amphibious landing in Burma. Churchill wanted to ensure that the Americans persevered with his Mediterranean strategy, and were neither deflected towards the Pacific nor persuaded to hold back their forces for a later descent on France. He was shocked and angry when he learned that Eisenhower had said that news of two German divisions deployed in Sicily might make it necessary to abort *Husky*. On 8 April he minuted the chiefs of staff that he was bewildered about how the American general could therefore have professed himself so eager for a 1943 invasion of France across the Channel, 'where he would have to meet a great deal more than two German divisions . . . I trust the chiefs of staff will not accept these pusillanimous and defeatist doctrines, from whomever they come.'

John Kennedy wrote, as he watched the prime minister compose one such missive: 'I had never seen him dictate before, and it was most interesting. He mouthed and whispered each phrase till he got it right, & then said it aloud to the typist.' Churchill suggested another meeting with Marshall and Hopkins in North Africa in April, but neither the war cabinet nor the Americans favoured such a rendezvous. Instead, he decided to go to Washington again. On 4 May he set off from London to Clydebank, and thence onward aboard the great liner *Queen Mary* to New York.

Throughout the first half of the war, Britain confronted predicaments rather than enjoying options. Henceforward, however, vastly improved circumstances conferred opportunities, promoted dilemmas. The North African campaign was at last approaching a close. On 8 May, British forces entered Tunis, and the Americans took Bizerta. Once more Britain's church bells rang for victory. At Casablanca the Americans had endorsed an overwhelmingly British vision for further Mediterranean operations. The two subsequent Anglo–American conferences of the year, codenamed *Trident* and *Quadrant*, were dominated by British efforts to sustain the US commitment made in January. Some of the contortions of Marshall and his colleagues reflected a desire to gain control of the Allied agenda, to resist British wishes simply because they were British. It seemed to the Americans intolerable that when their cash, supplies, aircraft, tanks and soon manpower would overwhelmingly dominate future Allied operations, Churchill and his colleagues should dictate the nature of these.

Each side also cherished its own unrealistic delusions. For instance, the Americans were uninterested in amphibious operations in South-East Asia, because these would contribute nothing towards fulfilling their principal strategic interest in the region, that of assisting Chiang Kai-shek's ramshackle war effort in China. On Churchill's part, he sailed to America in May determined to resist entanglement in the fever-ridden jungles of Burma, eager instead for 'an Asiatic *Torch*' – possible landings on Sumatra, Java or Malaya, all fanciful. Shrewd strategists, notably including the British General Bill Slim, understood that the American drive across the central Pacific would be the key element in Japan's defeat. British operations in Burma were chiefly designed to 'show willing' to the US, which goes far to explain the prime minister's cynicism about most things to do with the Asian war.

Churchill and his commanders were justified in their insistence that operations in Sicily, and thereafter some further exploitation in Italy, were indispensable. He told the chiefs of staff at a meeting aboard the *Queen Mary* on 10 May: 'The greatest step we could take in 1943 . . . would be the elimination of Italy.' But the British woefully underestimated the difficulties of conducting a campaign on the mainland, and the likely strength of German resistance. They were rash enough to urge upon the Americans a view, reflecting their

Cairo, August 1942. *Left to right*: Tedder, Smuts, Brooke, WSC, Harwood, Auchinleck, Richard Casey, Wavell.

Arrival in Moscow: the bespectacled Molotov stands beside Harriman and Churchill in front of their Liberator.

A British fiasco is matched by a Soviet triumph. (*Above*) A
scene on the beach at Dieppe after the disastrous August
1942 raid. (*Below*) Soviet troops advance towards their great
victory at Stalingrad at the turn of the year.

Out of the desert at last. (*Above*) The British advance at El Alamein in November 1942. (*Left*) American war leaders at Casablanca in January 1943: Marshall and King sit on either side of Roosevelt, while behind them stand Hopkins, Arnold, Somervell and Harriman.

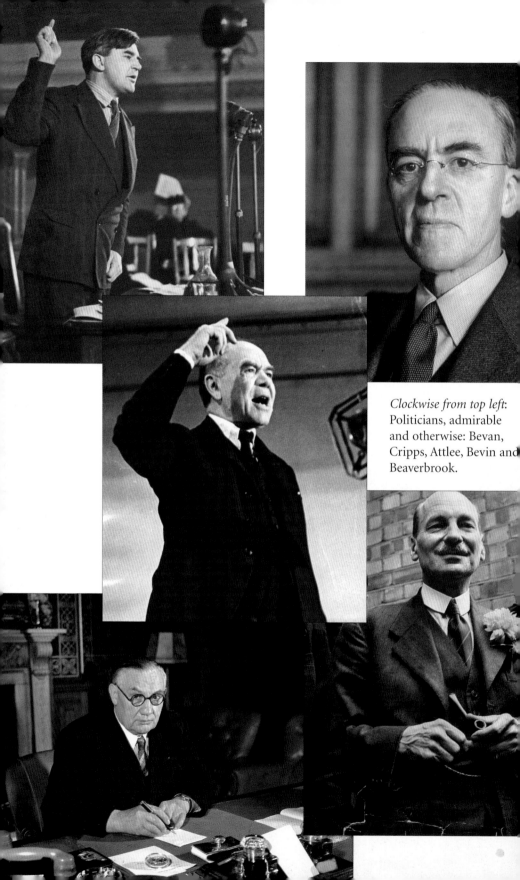

Clockwise from top left: Politicians, admirable and otherwise: Bevan, Cripps, Attlee, Bevin and Beaverbrook.

Churchill with General Anderson at the Roman amphitheatre at Carthage where he addressed men of Britain's desert army in May 1943.

The agony of Italy: US troops advance through characteristically intractable terrain.

Churchill's folly in the Dodecanese. (*Above*) Beaufighters attack German shipping off Kos on 3 October 1943. (*Below*) German troops land on the island, to achieve one of their last gratuitous military successes of the war.

At Algiers in June 1943 with (*left to right*) Eden, Brooke, Tedder, Cunningham, Alexander, Marshall, Eisenhower and Montgomery.

With Clementine in the saloon of his special train in Canada in August 1943.

The 'Big Three' at Tehran on 30 November 1943, Churchill's sixty-ninth birthday, with the US president visibly ailing.

Churchill's last major personal strategic initiative of the war, the Anzio landing of January 1944.

experience against Mussolini's troops in North Africa, that occupying most of Italy would be easy.

The Anglo-American armies needed to learn manifold lessons about command structures, air support and large-scale opposed amphibious landings. These the Mediterranean provided in 1943. But when the Russians were fighting huge and bloody battles in the east, it is unsurprising that American officers recoiled from the prospect that their own ambitions for the coming year should be so modest. Many senior figures in the US Army doubted that the British were sincere about supporting a French D-Day even in the spring of 1944. Marshall and his colleagues, and indeed Roosevelt, were apprehensive that once the Allies got themselves into Italy, they would not easily extricate the forces which it would be essential to shift to Britain before the end of the year.

During Churchill's first days in America he visited Roosevelt's retreat at Shangri-La in the Alleghenies, and delivered another magnificent oration to Congress on 19 May. When Halifax, at the Washington embassy, fussed that after the war the Americans might demand repayment of Britain's Lend-Lease debt, Churchill said truculently: 'Oh, I shall like that one. I shall say, yes by all means let us have an account . . . but I shall have my account to put in too, and my account is for holding the baby alone for eighteen months, and it was a very rough brutal baby . . . I don't quite know what I shall have to charge for it.' He was dismayed, however, by a perceived decline in Roosevelt's health. 'Have you noticed that the President is a tired man?' he demanded of Moran. 'His mind seems closed; he seems to have lost his wonderful elasticity.' If it was true that the president's health was declining, the real significance of his changed mood was that he was less amenable to Churchill's blandishments.

The prime minister would have been even more troubled had he known that at this very moment the president was secretly pursuing a bilateral meeting with Stalin, excluding Churchill, through the good offices of the pre-war US ambassador to Moscow, the egregious Joseph E. Davies. Davies, like Stafford Cripps, was a devoted admirer of the Soviet Union. During his time in Moscow he sought to persuade his wife that volleys she heard as NKVD firing squads executed victims of the purges were mere construction workers' jack-hammers. Davies formed a large art collection from works sold to him at knockdown prices by the Soviet authorities, looted from galleries or confiscated from murdered state enemies. His outrageous and adulatory memoir of his time in Russia was made into a 1943 Hollywood movie, *Mission to Moscow*, using a script authorised by himself. In May, Roosevelt provided a USAAF aircraft to fly Davies to Moscow carrying prints of the film for Stalin's edification. Though this deplorable figure failed to arrange the meeting Roosevelt sought, the president's willingness to employ him reflected shameless duplicity towards Churchill.

The combined chiefs of staff, meanwhile, were locked in close, tense, almost continuous sessions under Marshall's chairmanship. Brooke on 13 May made remarks which stunned and appalled the Americans. Dismissing prospects of an early invasion of France, he said that 'no major operations would be possible until 1945 or 1946, since it must be remembered that in previous wars there had always been some 80 French divisions available on our side . . . The British manpower position was weak.' Marshall responded icily: 'Did this mean that the British chiefs of staff regarded Mediterranean operations as the key to a successful termination of the European war?' Sir Charles Portal interjected, in a fashion surely designed to limit the damage done by Brooke's brutal assertion, that 'If Italy was knocked out this year, then in 1944 a successful re-entry into NW Europe might well be possible.' British scepticism, said Portal, focused on the notion that a force of twenty to twenty-five divisions could achieve important results across the Channel on the Continent of Europe 'unless almost the entire bulk of the German Army was in Russia or the Balkans'.

Brooke once again emphasised that the Red Army alone possessed sufficient mass to engage the full weight of the Wehrmacht: 'Russia was the only ally in possession of large ground forces and our strategy must aim to help her to the maximum possible effect.' He wrote in his diary that night: 'It was quite evident that Marshall was quite incapable of grasping the objects of our strategy nor the magnitude of operations connected with cross-Channel strategy.' The CIGS found the *Trident* conference one of the most gruelling and depressing experiences of his war. The exchanges that day illustrated his deep caution, indeed pessimism. Brooke's reputation as a strategist is significantly damaged by his remarks at the combined chiefs of staff meeting on 13 May. Though Marshall was often wrong in 1942–43, thereafter it was Brooke whose judgement was suspect. If the British view prevailed, it was hard to imagine that D-Day would take place in 1944. Never since December 1941 had the two allies' military leaderships seemed so far apart.

Yet as the Americans fought back, the British gave ground. At last, Brooke's team acknowledged a 'firm belief' that conditions for an invasion of France would exist in 1944. On the 19th the British accepted a target date of 1 May 1944 for a landing in northern France by twenty-nine divisions. Lt.Gen. Sir Frederick Morgan was appointed to lead the COSSAC* staff, to plan such an invasion. The outcome, Churchill cabled to Attlee on 21 May, was agreement that Britain should have 'a free hand' in the Mediterranean until November 1943. Success in Sicily would be exploited to advance the elimination of Italy from the Axis until concentration and redeployment of forces for the French landings began. Brooke wrote, after a meeting with Roosevelt and Churchill at the White House on 21 May: 'I do not think they realised how near we were to a failure to reach agreement!' He observed four days later that such conferences were

the most exhausting entertainments imaginable. I am convinced they do a lot of good in securing great understanding between us, and yet – they fall short insofar as our basic convictions remain unaltered. King still remains determined to press Pacific at the expense of all other fronts. Marshall wishes to ensure cross-Channel operation at expense of Mediterranean. [I still feel] that Mediterranean offers far more hope of adding to final success. Portal in his heart feels that if we left him a free hand bombing alone might well win the war. And dear old Dudley Pound when he wakes up wishes we would place submarine warfare above all other requirements . . . And Winston??

* Chief of Staff to the Supreme Allied Commander.

Thinks one thing at one moment and another at another moment. At times the war may be won by bombing . . . At others it becomes essential for us to bleed ourselves dry on the Continent because Russia is doing the same. At others our main effort must be in the Mediterranean . . . with sporadic desires to invade Norway and 'roll up the map in the opposite direction to Hitler'! But more often he wants us to carry out ALL operations simultaneously!

Churchill was at his most ebullient by the time he and Roosevelt parted. At a final press conference at the White House with Roosevelt on 26 May, he delighted the assembled correspondents by clambering onto a chair and giving his famous two-fingered V-sign. Then he boarded a Boeing Clipper for Algiers via Gibraltar, accompanied by George Marshall and Brooke. The three travelled together to brief Eisenhower about the conference decisions. En route, the aircraft was struck by lightning, awakening Churchill from a deep sleep. He wrote wryly: 'I had always wondered why aircraft did not mind being struck by lightning. To a groundsman it would seem quite a dangerous thing.' On the day of their later return from Gibraltar, on much the same course, a British plane whose passengers included the film star Leslie Howard was shot down by a German fighter, with the loss of all on board. If the hazards of many wartime flights were unavoidable, that of Churchill and his party to Algiers surely entailed extravagant risk. Had the US chief of the army perished with the prime minister and CIGS, the blow to the Grand Alliance would have been terrible indeed. The party arrived safely, however. As they neared the Rock, Brooke was curiously moved to see the prime minister, wearing what he described as a yachting cap, peering eagerly down through the clouds with a cigar clenched beneath his lips, looking out for the first sight of land. The soldier, so often exasperated by his master, perceived this as a glimpse of his 'very human & lovable side'.

Churchill spent eight happy days in Tunisia and Algeria, on one of them addressing a great throng of British troops in the ancient amphitheatre at Carthage. 'I was speaking,' he told guests at dinner that night, 'from where the cries of Christian virgins rent the air while roaring lions devoured them – and yet – I am no lion and certainly not a virgin.' Eisenhower and Montgomery expressed confidence about planning for the Sicilian landing. Marshall, however, made it plain that he was determined to reserve judgement about future Italian operations until the outcome of the Sicilian campaign became clear.

On 4 June, Churchill flew home to Britain by Liberator. Four days later he offered a survey of the war to the House of Commons which was justly confident, though Marshall and his colleagues might have disputed his sunny portrayal of Anglo–American relations: 'All sorts of divergences, all sorts of differences of outlook and all sorts of awkward little jars necessarily occur as we roll ponderously forward together along the rough and broken road of war. But none of these makes the slightest difference to our ever-growing concert and unity, there are none of them which cannot be settled face to face by heart-to-heart talks and patient argument. My own relations with the illustrious President of the United States have become in these years of war those of personal friendship and regard, and nothing will ever happen to separate us in comradeship and partnership of thought and action while we remain responsible for the conduct of affairs.' Here was, of course, an expression of fervent desire rather than of unfolding reality.

If Churchill expressed satisfaction about the progress of the war, Stalin did not. He cabled Roosevelt, copied to Churchill, to express dismay at Anglo-American postponements of D-Day, then wrote direct to the prime minister on 24 June: 'It goes without saying that the Soviet Government cannot put up with such disregard of the most vital Soviet interests in the war against the common enemy.' Two days later, Churchill responded by dispatching one of his toughest messages of the war to the Russian leader: 'Although until 22nd June 1941, we British were left alone to face the worst that Nazi Germany could do to us, I instantly began to aid Soviet Russia to the best of our limited means from the moment that she was herself attacked by Hitler. I am satisfied that I have done everything in human power to help you. Therefore the reproaches which you now cast upon your Western Allies leave me unmoved. Nor, apart from the damage to our military interests, should I have any difficulty in presenting my case to the British

Parliament and nation.' He was growing weary of the Russians, writing a fortnight later: 'Experience has taught me that it is not worthwhile arguing with Soviet people. One simply has to confront them with the new facts and await their reactions.'

Yet many British citizens sympathised with the Russian view. 'I am the last to plead Stalin's case,' Clark Kerr cabled from Moscow on 1 July, but it seemed to the British ambassador that the weakness in the British position lay 'not in our inability to open this second front but in our having led him to believe we were going to'. Beaverbrook, still chronically disloyal, wrote to Henry Luce, overlord of *Time* magazine, on 2 July: 'In my view there is an undercurrent of uncertainty [in Britain] whether an attack on Italy can, so far as Russia is concerned, attain the proportions of a real Second Front. The public are convinced that the chance has now come to take the fullest advantage of Russian successes. And no operation in the West which left unaffected the German dispositions in the East would for long meet with popular favour.' Surrey court shorthand-writer George King agreed with Beaverbrook: 'When Mr Churchill received the freedom of London last week,' he wrote on 7 July, 'he said it seemed clear that "before the leaves of autumn fall, real amphibious battles will be in progress." One hopes so, because much as all must dread the casualties, the Allies owe such an action to Russia and the slaves of Europe.' Oliver Harvey wrote from the Foreign Office: 'To some of the Government it is incredible, unforgivable, indeed inadmissible, that the Russian can be so successful. This is the attitude of the W[ar] O[ffice].'

On 10 July, Allied forces landed in Sicily under the command of Britain's Sir Harold Alexander. In Washington and London, ministers and generals knew that *Husky* was marred by all manner of blunders, great and small. The airborne assault was shambolic. Anglo–American command arrangements remained confused throughout the campaign. Italian troops showed no desire to fight seriously, but the two German divisions on the island displayed their usual high professionalism in resisting the attacks of Alexander's much superior forces. The British and American publics, however, knew little about the bungles. They perceived only the overriding realities that the landings were successful, and that within weeks Axis forces were driven from Sicily. Brooke, who had been profoundly worried about *Husky* because it reflected a British design, experienced a surge of relief. Churchill, rejoicing, urged the chiefs of staff on 13 July to plan ambitiously for follow-up operations in Italy: 'Why should we crawl up the leg like a harvest bug, from the ankle upwards? Let us rather strike at the knee.' He wanted early amphibious landings, even before Sicily was cleared, directed against Naples and Rome. On 16 July he told Smuts: 'I believe the President is with me: Eisenhower in his heart is naturally for it.'

Macmillan pitied Eisenhower, attempting to fulfil his role as Mediterranean supreme commander amidst a constant bombardment of cables marked 'private, personal and most immediate', and emanating variously from the combined chiefs of staff, Marshall, Roosevelt, Churchill direct, Churchill through the Foreign Office, or Eden through the Foreign Office. 'All these instructions,' observed Macmillan laconically, 'are naturally contradictory and conflicting.' He and Ike's chief of staff, Bedell Smith, endeavoured to sort and reconcile such communications and decide which should be acted upon.

Even as Churchill enthused about the prospects in the Mediterranean he began to waver again about *Overlord*, as D-Day in France would henceforward become known. On 19 July he told the chiefs of staff that he now had doubts whether the forces available in Britain by 1 May 1944 would suffice for a successful landing 'in view of the extra-ordinary fighting efficiency of the German Army, and the much larger forces they could so readily bring to bear against our troops even if the landings were successfully accomplished. It is right for many reasons to make every preparation with the utmost sincerity and vigour, but if later on it is realised by all concerned that the operation is beyond our strength in May and will have to be postponed till August 1944, then it is essential that we should have this other consideration up our sleeves.' He urged them to dust down *Jupiter*, his long-cherished scheme for a descent on north Norway.

The Italian campaign

Oliver Harvey wrote admiringly in his diary on 24 July about the firmness with which Churchill had dismissed a proposal from Henry Stimson, visiting London, to advance the 1 May D-Day date: 'On this, I'm thankful to say, the PM will refuse absolutely to budge. On military affairs he is instinctively right as he is wrong on foreign affairs. As a war minister he is superb, driving our own Chiefs of Staff, guiding them like a coach and four, applying whip or brake as necessary, with the confidence and touch of genius.' Even though Stimson's proposal was indeed misguided, Harvey's accolade was ill-timed. Churchill's renewed foot-dragging showed him at his worst. For eighteen months he had staved off Marshall's demands for early action in France. The British had the best of the arguments, at the cost of feeding American mistrust and resentment, which now ran deep. Back in May, Brooke had written, expressing exasperation with perceived American inconsistency of purpose: 'Agreement after agreement may be secured on paper, but if their hearts are not in it they soon drift away again.' Yet Marshall and his colleagues could have applied the same strictures to the British, with at least equal justice.

Lt.Gen. Sir Frederick Morgan, appointed by the chiefs of staff to plan *Overlord*, later became embittered when he perceived himself marginalised before D-Day eventually took place. Yet his post-war private observations cannot be wholly discounted. 'I firmly believe,' he told US historian Forrest Pogue in 1947, 'that [Churchill and his chiefs] returned from Casablanca fully determined to repudiate the agreement that they had been forced there to sign with the Americans [for an invasion of France] . . . Apart from a mere dislike of the project, the British authorities proceeded to make every possible step to impede progress in NW Europe by diverting their forces, as unobtrusively as possible, to other theatres of war.' He expressed his opinion that his own appointment was made in the expectation that he would eventually be sacrificed 'as a scapegoat when a suitable excuse should be found for withdrawing British support from the operation'. Morgan cited the scepticism about *Overlord* of Admiral Cunningham, whom he quoted as saying: 'I have already evacuated three British armies in the face of the enemy and I don't propose to evacuate a fourth.' Morgan thought far more highly of the US chiefs of staff and of Eisenhower than of the British leadership: 'On Br side . . . had suffered long series of disasters and had become casualty conscious to a very high degree. Br manpower sit. in a state of bankruptcy. Inconceivable that Br could play other than minor part in . . . reconquest of Europe from the Germans.'

The Americans did not, of course, read the prime minister's 19 July minute to his chiefs. But from the late summer of 1943 onwards they perceived continuing British wavering about D-Day which they were now implacably – and rightly – committed to override. Churchill's hesitation about an invasion in 1944 reflected an apprehension about the fighting power of an Anglo-American army against the Wehrmacht which was unworthy of the Grand Alliance now that its means were growing so great, its huge mobilisation at last approaching maturity.

Churchill's new strategic vision embraced some wild notions. On 25 July, Mussolini resigned and Italy's government fell into the hands of King Victor Emmanuel III and Marshal Pietro Badoglio. The Italian dictator's fall prompted Churchill to revive one of his favourite schemes, a descent on Italian-occupied Rhodes, designed to drag Turkey into the war. This ambition would precipitate a minor disaster later in the year, the Dodecanese campaign. Churchill's standing in American eyes would decline steadily between the summer of 1943 and the end of the war, and he himself bore a substantial share of responsibility for this. It is true that his wise warnings about the future threat posed by the Soviet Union were insufficiently heeded. But this was in significant part because the Americans lost faith in his strategic judgement.

He persuaded Washington that a new summit was now needed, to settle plans for Italy. This meeting, *Quadrant*, was to be held in Quebec. On 5 August 1943 he stood on the platform at Addison Road station in West Kensington, singing 'I go away/This very day/ To sail across the sea/Matilda.' Then his train slid from its platform northwards to Greenock, where his 200-strong delegation boarded the *Queen Mary*, bound for Canada. Churchill landed at Halifax on

9 August, and remained in North America until 14 September, by far his longest wartime sojourn there. Since it was plain that the big decisions on future strategy would be taken by Americans, as usual he sought to be on the spot, to deploy the weight of his own personality to influence them. While the combined chiefs of staff began their debates in Quebec, Churchill travelled by train with his wife and daughter Mary to stay with Roosevelt. At Niagara Falls he told reporters: 'I saw these before you were born. I was here first in 1900.' A correspondent asked fatuously: 'Do they look the same?' Churchill said: 'Well, the principle seems the same. The water still keeps flowing over.'

At Hyde Park it was stifling barbecue weather, with hamburgers and hot dogs. Churchill fumed about reports of Nazi mass killings in the Balkans. He sought to interest the president in the region, with little success. Then the two leaders travelled to join the discussions of their chiefs of staff. The venue had been chosen to suit common Anglo–American convenience, without much heed to the fact that it lay on Canadian soil. Moran wrote that Canada's premier, Mackenzie King, resembled a man who has lent his house for a party: 'The guests take hardly any notice of him, but just before leaving they remember he is their host and say pleasant things.' Secretary of State Cordell Hull was permitted by Roosevelt to make one of his rare summit appearances at *Quadrant*, not much to his own satisfaction. Unwilling to share Churchill's late hours, one midnight Hull announced grumpily that he was going to bed. The prime minister expressed astonishment: 'Why, man, we are at war!'

Many subsidiary matters reared their heads at the *Quadrant* conference. Churchill was still pressing to launch a British landing on Sumatra, evoking a rash historical precedent by asserting that 'in its promise of decisive consequences it invited comparison with the Dardanelles operation of 1915'. He introduced to the Americans two newly favoured heroes, Brigadier Orde Wingate, who had commanded a column of his Chindits behind the Japanese lines in Burma, and Wing-Commander Guy Gibson, who led the RAF's heroic May 1943 attack on the Ruhr dams. Wingate proved a short-lived protégé: closer acquaintance caused Churchill to realise that he was too mad for high command. Meanwhile the young airman's superiors, notably including Sir Arthur Harris, believed that the transatlantic trip 'spoiled young Gibson' by exposing him to a popular adulation in Canada and the US that went to his head. Stars of battle, like their artistic counterparts in peacetime, have seldom fitted comfortably into the entourages of prime ministers.

Meanwhile, Stalin was making threatening demands for a Russian voice in the governance of occupied territories. He cabled from Moscow demanding the creation of a joint military commission, which should hold its first meeting in Sicily. In Quebec, Churchill warned the Americans of 'bloody consequences in the future . . . Stalin is an unnatural man. There will be grave troubles.' He was correct, of course. Thereafter, the Russians perceived the legitimisation of their own conduct in Eastern Europe. Since the Western Allies decreed the governance of territories which they occupied, the Soviet Union considered itself entitled to do likewise in its own conquests.

But the central issue at stake at Quebec was that of *Overlord*. The Americans were implacably set upon its execution, while the British continued to duck and weave. Wedemeyer wrote before the meeting that it was necessary for the US chiefs to advance a formula which would 'stir the imagination and win the support of the Prime Minister, if not that of his recalcitrant planners and chiefs of staff'. Marshall's biographer, the magisterial American historian Forrest Pogue, remarks of Churchill in those days: 'As usual, he was full of guile.' This seems to misread the prime minister's behaviour. Opportunism and changeability, rather than studied cunning, guided most of his strategic impulses. Yet there is no period of the war at which American dismay about British behaviour seems better merited than autumn 1943, as Eden and others acknowledged. Churchill and his commanders had always professed themselves committed to launching an invasion of Europe in 1944. At the Casablanca and Washington conferences, the British had not argued against *Overlord* in principle, but merely fought for delay. Now, it seemed, they were altogether reneging.

Churchill opened his budget at Quebec by reasserting principled support for an invasion. But he pressed for an understanding that if, in the spring of 1944, the Germans deployed more than twelve mobile divisions in France, the operation should not take place. Lt. Gen. Sir Frederick Morgan, director of the Anglo–American COSSAC staff which had been planning the invasion, suggested that if the Germans appeared capable of deploying more than fifteen divisions against the beachhead in the two months following D-Day, a landing should not be launched. When the Germans flooded the river plains around Caen a few days before the conference began, COSSAC's operations division minuted: 'The full implications of this have not yet been assessed, but it is quite possible that it will finally "kill" *Overlord*.' Brooke made plain his continuing scepticism about the operation's feasibility.

The British case was that the immediate strategic priority was to seize the chances of the moment in the Mediterranean, rather than to stake everything upon a highly dangerous and speculative cross-Channel attack. In war, they argued, circumstances were always changing. They were more realistic than the Americans, in their understanding that a decision to enter Italy was irrevocable: 'If we once set foot on the Italian mainland,' wrote John Kennedy, 'we are in for a big commitment . . . The Americans I am sure do not realise that limited operations in Italy eg against Naples, are impossible. We must either stop at the Straits of Messina or go the whole hog.' On 17 August, Churchill received a characteristically triumphalist signal from Alexander: 'By 10am this morning, the last German soldier was flung out of Sicily.' The prime minister's enthusiasm for his favourite general seldom flagged, and he applauded the Sicilian operations as 'brilliantly executed'. Yet it had taken thirty-eight days for much superior Allied forces to expel less than three German divisions. Far from being 'flung out' of the island, inexcusably General Albert Kesselring's troops had been allowed to withdraw in good order across the Straits of Messina with most of their vehicles, guns and equipment.

At all the wartime conferences there was a stark contrast between the strains upon the principals, middle-aged and elderly men contesting great issues day and night, and the delights afforded to hundreds of attendant supporting staff who did not bear their responsibilities. The latter – staff officers, officials, clerks, ciphering personnel – worked hard at the summits, but also played hard. Duty officers were always in attendance upon the teletype machines which rattled forth signals and reports around the clock. Typists composed minutes of the day's meetings, and planners prepared drafts for the next. But it seemed to these young men and a few women miraculous to be delivered for a few weeks from rationed, battered, darkened England to bask in bright lights and prodigious quantities of food and drink, all of it free. Most danced and partied enthusiastically through the nights while their great men wrangled. The English visitors revelled in shopping opportunities unknown in Britain for four years.

Events did more than changes of heart to patch up Anglo–American differences at Quebec. The known readiness of the new Italian government to surrender made it plain to Marshall and his colleagues that Allied forces in Sicily must advance into Italy. It seemed unthinkable to leave a vacuum which the Germans could fill as they chose. The British, for their part, professed to endorse the *Overlord* plan presented by Morgan and the COSSAC team. There was much bickering about a cut-off date at which Allied divisions earmarked for France must be withdrawn from the Mediterranean, and thus about what objectives in Italy might feasibly be attained beforehand. Churchill, who dreamed of Allied armies driving towards Vienna, instead reluctantly endorsed a line from Livorno to Ancona by November, saying: 'If we can't have the best, these are very good second bests.' In the event, Livorno and Ancona would not be taken until late June 1944. But in the heady days of August the Allies still supposed that once the Italians surrendered, the Germans would not make much of a fight for Mussolini's country.

When the conference ended on 24 August, Ian Jacob wrote: 'There seems to be general satisfaction, though I can't see what has been decided which takes us much beyond *Trident*.' The 'general satisfaction' was merely a matter of public courtesy. Brooke wrote: 'The Quebec conference has left me absolutely cooked.' He subsequently acknowledged that at this time he was close to a nervous breakdown. The Americans were deeply unhappy about British conditionality towards *Overlord*. Churchill's team had not for a moment abandoned their determination to keep the Allies deeply engaged in Italy, even at risk to D-Day. After a brief break at a mountain camp for fly-fishing – not a pastime which Churchill indulged with much conviction – he travelled to Washington, where he spent the next five days urging the need to hasten operations in Italy. On 3 September, Italian representatives signed the surrender document at Cassibili in Sicily, while at dawn units of Eighth Army landed on the Italian mainland north of Reggio. Five days later, the British 1st Airborne Division seized the port of Taranto without opposition, which Churchill dubbed 'a masterstroke' in a laudatory signal to Alexander.

On 9 September, Mark Clark's Fifth Army staged an amphibious assault at Salerno, precipitating one of the bloodiest battles of the campaign, and a near-disaster. 'It was like fighting tanks bare-handed,' wrote an American infantry colonel facing a Panzer assault on the beachhead. 'I saw riflemen swarm over the top of moving German tanks trying to shoot through slits or throw grenades inside. Other tanks would machine-gun them off. They ran over wounded men . . . and spun their treads.' In the first hours, Clark was sufficiently panicked to order re-embarkation, until overruled by Alexander. At painful cost, a perimeter was established and held. That day, as German forces raced to occupy key strategic positions across southern Italy, the Italian fleet set off towards Malta to surrender. Its flagship, the battleship *Roma*, was sunk en route by German bombers, once again demonstrating the Luftwaffe's skills against maritime targets. A mad Allied plan for a parachute assault on Rome was mercifully cancelled at the last moment. Even the Anglo-Americans at their most optimistic were forced to acknowledge that, against the Germans, excessive boldness was invariably punished.

Churchill was mortified that, once again, he was in Roosevelt's company when bad news came. He had held out to the president a prospect of easy victory in Italy. Now, instead, they learned of savage German resistance at Salerno. The British were naïve in anticipating that a surrender by Italy's government must of itself deliver most of the country into Allied hands. Brooke had told the combined chiefs of staff on 13 May: 'He did not believe Germany would try to control an Italy which was not fighting.' He and Churchill were importantly deceived by Ultra decrypts which showed that the Germans intended to abandon most of Italy without a fight. In the event, however, and as so often, Hitler changed his mind. This was a direct consequence of the Allied armies' poor showing, in German eyes, on Sicily and at Salerno. Anglo-American commanders and men exposed their limitations. Montgomery's performance was no more impressive than that of Mark Clark. The Germans were astonished by the ease with which some British and American soldiers allowed themselves to be taken prisoner. Kesselring, the German commander on the spot, concluded that defending Italy against such an enemy might be less difficult than he had supposed. He reported accordingly to Hitler. The Führer responded by ordering a vigorous defence of the peninsula, a task which the field-marshal – who was appointed German supreme commander in Italy on 6 November – undertook with extraordinary energy and effectiveness. Allied fumbling of the first phase of operations in Italy thus had critical consequences for the rest of the campaign.

In those days in America, Churchill became excited by a possible landing on the Dalmatian coast, using 75,000 Polish troops and possibly the New Zealand Division. On 10 September Roosevelt departed for Hyde Park, leaving Britain's prime minister installed in America's capital: 'Winston, please treat the White House as your home,' said the president generously, urging him to invite whomever he liked. Churchill used this licence to the full, summoning Marshall to press upon him the case for hastening reinforcements to Italy. On 14 September, at last he returned to Halifax, to board the battle-cruiser *Renown* for home. His American hosts were glad to see him go. Their enthusiasm for his exhausting presence had worn as thin as their patience with his Mediterranean fantasies. Roosevelt's secretary

William Hassett wrote after their visitor's previous Washington departure in May: 'Must be a relief to the Boss for Churchill is a trying guest – drinks like a fish and smokes like a chimney, irregular routines, works nights, sleeps days, turns the clocks upside down . . . Churchill has brains, guts . . . and a determination to preserve the British Empire . . . He has everything except vision.' This was a view now almost universal within Roosevelt's administration. Harry Hopkins told Eden, when the Foreign Secretary visited Washington, that the president – and indeed Hopkins himself – 'loves W as a man for the war, but is horrified at his reactionary attitude for after the war'. Hopkins spoke of the prime minister's age, 'his unteachability'.

The leaders of the United States were justly convinced that the time for butterfly strategy-making was over. British evasions over a cross-Channel attack were no longer justifiable. If the Western Allies were to engage land forces on the Continent of Europe in time to affect outcomes before the Russians defeated Hitler on their own, *Overlord* must take place in 1944. Henceforth, commitments in Italy must be adjusted to fit the overriding priority of the invasion of north-west Europe, and not vice versa. Marshall and his colleagues could scarcely be blamed for their exasperation at the prime minister's renewed pleas for a descent on north Norway, and the fit of enthusiasm with which he was seized for operations in the eastern Mediterranean.

It was widely expected both in Washington and London that Marshall would command *Overlord*. Churchill had broken it to Brooke at Quebec that his earlier insouciant offer of this glittering appointment to the CIGS was no longer open. It was foolish of both the prime minister and the general to have supposed for a moment that a British officer might be acceptable for the role; and even more so of Brooke, by his own admission, to sulk for several months about his disappointment. He possessed a sublime, and exaggerated, conceit about his own strategic wisdom. He had grievously injured himself in American eyes by prevarications about *Overlord*, even more outspokenly expressed than those of the prime minister. It was absurd to suppose that Brooke might have claimed command of an operation which for months he had denounced as being launched prematurely.

Only an American could credibly lead this predominantly American crusade, but Roosevelt kept open until November his choice of appointee. Marshall wanted the job, sure enough. The chief of the army indulged a brief fantasy that Sir John Dill might be his deputy, or even – if the British persuaded the president that one of their own should command – that the former CIGS might be supreme commander. Stimson wanted Marshall, because he believed that the chief of the army alone had the authority and strength of character to overcome the 'mercurial inconstancy' of the prime minister.

There was always a paradox about Churchill as warlord. On the one hand, he had a wonderful instinct for the fray, more highly developed than that of any of his service advisers. Yet his genius for war was flawed by an enthusiasm for dashes, raids, skirmishes, diversions, sallies more appropriate – as officers who worked with him often remarked – to a Victorian cavalry subaltern than to the director of a vast industrial war effort. The doctrine of concentration of force, an obsession of the Americans and especially of Marshall, was foreign to his nature. Though Churchill addressed his duties with profound seriousness of purpose, he wanted war, like life, to be fun. This caused the American service chiefs, earnest men all, not infrequently to think him guilty of frivolity as well as of pursuing selfish nationalistic purposes. Brooke, meanwhile, was perhaps the greatest staff officer the British Army has ever known. But experience of fighting the Germans for four years on short commons had made him a cautious strategist, and by this stage of the war an unconvincing one. He shared the Americans' impatience, indeed exasperation, with Churchill's wilder schemes. But in the autumn of 1943, and indeed well into the winter, Brooke was joined to the prime minister in a common apprehension about *Overlord*. American resolution alone ensured that the operational timetable for D-Day was maintained. If Roosevelt and Marshall had been more malleable, the British would have chosen to keep larger forces in Italy, especially when Clark's and Montgomery's advances languished. D-Day would have been delayed until 1945.

The Allies were now committed to take the port of Naples, and exploit northwards to Rome. Thereafter, they had uneasily agreed that the future of the Italian campaign should be settled in the light of events. John Kennedy wrote on 3 September: 'It will be interesting to see whether the Americans have judged the Mediterranean war better than we have.' He himself bitterly regretted the scheduled diversion of forces from Italy to *Overlord*: 'But we cannot dictate and I doubt if we could have done more to persuade the Americans. They are convinced that the landing in France is the only way to win the war quickly, & will listen to no arguments as to the mechanical difficulties of the operation or the necessity of weakening & drawing off the Germans by means of operations in the Medn.' A month later, he was still writing about the arguments concerning 'the Mediterranean versus *Overlord* strategy', but the War Office seemed resigned to the likely triumph of the latter: 'In the end I suppose that we shall probably go into France with little opposition & the historians will say that we missed glorious opportunities a year earlier etc. etc.'

Beaverbrook had tabled a new motion in the House of Lords calling for a Second Front. Now he allowed himself to be wooed back into government as lord privy seal by Churchill's private assurance that the invasion was fixed for the following summer. Beaverbrook's recall exasperated many ministers. Churchill spoke passionately of his friend to W.P. Crozier of the *Manchester Guardian*: 'I need him, I need him. He is stimulating and, believe me, he is a big man.' Sir John Anderson felt it necessary to call the ministerial grumblers to order. 'He says we must not make things too hard for the PM 'who is conducting the war with great skill,' recorded Dalton. 'The PM was very unhappy during the period when Beaverbrook was not one of his colleagues. He is a sensitive artist, attaching great value to "presentation" and the quality of the spoken word. He likes to have around him certain people, whose responses will not be jarring or unwelcome. He has valued Beaverbrook for this for many years. We must not, therefore, be too particular, even if things are sometimes not done in quite the most regular or orderly way.'

Beaverbrook's irregularities included, at this time, assisting Randolph Churchill to pay his debts. Though such subsidy certainly did not influence the prime minister's conduct towards him, it reflected a fundamentally unhealthy relationship, such as Beaverbrook contrived with many of his acquaintance.

The Americans found much more substantial cause for complaint about the prime minister's behaviour. Transatlantic debate remained dominated by British attempts to regard the *Overlord* commitment as flexible, and by US insistence upon its inviolability. Given American primacy in the alliance, which was now increasingly explicit, Churchill and Brooke must have known in their hearts that D-Day was almost certain to happen the following summer. But their attempts to suggest otherwise ate deeply into the fretwork of Allied trust. The Americans were wrong in supposing that Churchill's policy was directed towards ensuring that *Overlord* never took place at all. The huge and costly infrastructure already being created in Britain to support an invasion of France – not least Churchill's cherished *Mulberry* artificial harbours – disproved that allegation. The prime minister's inconstancy related exclusively to timing, but was none the less injurious for that. As for the British public, Surrey shorthand-writer George King was unimpressed by Churchill's flowered phrases about the Italian campaign: 'He says a Second Front is in existence, but I can't see it myself.'

King's impatience with the progress of the war was widely shared. The left displayed astonishing venom towards the government. Communist Elizabeth Belsey, a highly educated woman of notable intellectual tastes, remarked in a letter to her husband that the sudden death of Sir Kingsley Wood, the chancellor, 'will save a piece of rope later on'. In September 1943 she wrote that she and friends 'amused ourselves making lists of the people who ought to be shot first when the time for shooting comes . . . [Walter] Citrine, [TUC General Secretary] Morrison, Halifax, [Lord] Londonderry, Lady Astor, [Sir James] Grigg and a heap more'. She was disgusted by the hostility towards Russia displayed by the Polish exile government in London, and exulted at the deaths in a Gibraltar plane crash of its leader,

General Sikorski, and the Tory MP Victor Cazalet: 'no loss . . . I never did like having that Sikorski person on our side, did you?'

The Russians, of course, welcomed every manifestation of public dissatisfaction with Allied operations. On 6 August, *Pravda* offered its readers one of its more temperate commentaries:

It would be wrong to belittle the importance of allied military operations – the bombing of Germany by British and American air forces, and the importance of supplies and military material being provided to us. Nonetheless, only four German divisions opposed our allies in Libya, a mere two German divisions and a few Italian ones in Sicily. These statistics suffice to show the true scale of their operations as compared to those on the Soviet–German front where Hitler had 180 German divisions and about 60 divisions of his 'allies' in the summer of 1942 . . . The armies of our British and American allies so far have had no serious encounters with the troops of Hitler's Germany. The Second Front so far does not exist.

What is the Second Front? There is no cause to heed the waffling of certain people who pretend that they don't know what we are talking about; who claim that there is already not only a second front, but also, a third, a fourth, and probably even a fifth and a sixth front (including the air and submarine campaigns, etc.). If we are to speak seriously about a second front in Europe, this would mean a campaign which, as comrade Stalin pointed out as early as the autumn of 1942, would divert, say, sixty German divisions and twenty of Germany's allies'.

We know all the excuses used to justify delays . . . for example, arguments about [Hitler's] mythological 'Atlantic Wall', and the allegedly insoluble shipping problem. The 'impregnable Atlantic Wall' exists only in the minds of those who want to believe in such lies . . . After the success of the big allied landing in North Africa last year, and that of the Allies' operation in Sicily, it seems ridiculous to cite 'shipping problems' where a landing in Western Europe is concerned.

Amid the torrent of Soviet propaganda, bombast and insults, it was hard for British and American ministers and diplomats to know what were Moscow's real views. Long after the war, Molotov conceded to a Russian interviewer that Stalin was much more realistic than he ever acknowledged to Churchill. The old Soviet foreign minister spoke gratefully of the Italian campaign:

> Even such help was serviceable to us. After all, we were not defending England, we were defending socialism, you see. And could we expect them to help the cause of defending socialism? Bolsheviks would have been idiots to expect this! We just needed to be able to press them, to say 'what villains you are!' . . . The [British] people of course realized that Russians were fighting while their own country wasn't. And not only did [the Anglo-Americans] hold back, they wrote and said one thing to us, but did something completely different. This made their own people see the truth and ask their own leaders: why are you playing tricks? This undermined faith in the imperialists. All this was very important to us.

At the end of June 1943, Stalin recalled Ivan Maisky to Moscow, and in August formally replaced him at the London embassy. Stalin told his appointed successor, a thirty-seven-year-old party apparatchik named Feodor Gusev, that Maisky 'had made himself much too busy trying to justify the English who are sabotaging the opening of the Second Front'. Churchill was dismayed by Maisky's recall, and unimpressed by Gusev, whose grasp of English was poor and social skills non-existent. At the prime minister's first meeting with the new envoy, he pushed into the Russian's unwilling hands a letter he had received from Stalin denouncing the tardy shipments of British supplies, and told him that he refused to accept such an insulting communication. Gusev wrote later: 'He literally shoved the envelope into my hand, turned away and walked back to his desk.' When he reported this exchange in some trepidation to Moscow, he was relieved to be told by Molotov: 'You behaved correctly about the envelope. We consider the return of the envelope simply as another of Churchill's hysterical gestures . . . From now on, you are to deliver letters from comrade Stalin and other documents only in Russian.

Remember that in Moscow the English only deliver documents to us in English, including letters to comrade Stalin.' It was six months before Churchill again agreed to receive Gusev.

In Britain in 1943 there were more miners' strikes than at any time since 1900. *The Times* editorialised on 3 September, amid another standstill in the pits: 'The disposition to strike . . . may have some common origin. There is a too prevalent view that the war is going so well that effort in industry can be relaxed.'

Trades unionist Jack Jones wrote to Brendan Bracken from Cardiff on 3 October 1943:

> I think I may claim to know the mind of our workers, who are quite as loyal as the men and women of the Forces. Yet they strike! And at a time when it is more important than ever that they shouldn't. There may be even more disastrous stoppages through the coming winter.
>
> Time itself induces war-weariness and frayed nerves, especially when what one is doing is unspectacular, out of the limelight and monotonous . . . A gnawing doubt is a sort of match ready to set aflame an undefined resentment against war conditions . . . What they want to steady them is a tonic. I remember during the last war the tonic effect on the South Wales miners of a visit and talk by L[loyd] G[eorge] . . . But this war dwarfs the last, and Mr Churchill has had much more on his plate than ever L.G. had . . . My faith in Mr Churchill's leadership is greater than ever. But I feel that now his capacity for inspiring others should, if it is humanly possible, be devoted to the steadying and inspiring of the splendid production line of our Home Front.

Churchill's failure to reach out explicitly to the industrial working class, beyond his national broadcasts and speeches, in part reflected disinclination. He preferred to address himself to the conduct of the war and foreign affairs; and in part also, there was the fact that he had little to say to the factory people which they would wish to hear. He left to Ernest Bevin, in particular, the task of rallying and rousing

Labour-voting miners and shop-floor workers. He himself could not offer such people the vision of post-war Britain, and especially of socialist change, on which their hearts and minds were set. Churchill's single-minded commitment to victory lay at the heart of his greatness as a war leader. But for a growing number of his people, in the autumn of 1943 this was not enough.

In that season, between the Italian and Normandy campaigns, he made one of his last attempts to implement an explicitly British strategic initiative, against American wishes. He believed that the eastern Mediterranean offered opportunities for exploitation which Washington was too blind to recognise. He therefore sought to address these with exclusively British forces. The consequence was a disaster, albeit minor in the scale of global war, which emphasised in the most painful fashion Germany's residual strength, together with the limitations of British power when the United States withheld its support.

FIFTEEN

Sunk in the Aegean

One of the most celebrated movie epics about the Second World War is Carl Foreman's *The Guns of Navarone*, based upon the 1957 thriller of that title written by Alastair Maclean. It depicts the landing of a British special forces team on a Greek island in the Aegean Sea. After stupendous feats of derring-do, they contrive the undoing of its German defenders, and safe passage for the Royal Navy's destroyers. Maclean's heroic fiction was rooted in an extraordinary series of episodes in the eastern Mediterranean in the autumn of 1943 which deserve to be better known to students of the war. This is not, however, because the saga ended in a British triumph, which it certainly did not, but because it provides a case study in folly which was overwhelmingly Winston Churchill's responsibility. The story merits rehearsal and analysis, as an example of the consequences of the prime minister's capacity for rash boldness. If the scale of the campaign was mercifully small, the blunders were many and large. They help to explain why strategists who worked most closely with Churchill sometimes despaired of his obsessions.

Rhodes and the much smaller islands of the Dodecanese to the north lie a few miles off the coast of Turkey, and are inhabited by Greeks. Italy had seized them in 1912. Three years later, France and Britain endorsed this shameless imperialist venture as part of the price for Italian accession to the Allied cause in World War I. The islands, which possessed few merits save their barren beauty and strategic location, had been garrisoned by Italian forces ever since. They first attracted Churchill's attention in 1940. He believed, surely wrongly, that if the Allies could dispossess the Italians, such a visible shift of power in the eastern Mediterranean would induce Turkey to enter the war. At his behest, British commandos staged an abortive raid in February 1941. During the ensuing two years the islands were recognised as beyond Allied reach. But as the Mediterranean skies brightened, Churchill's Aegean enthusiasm revived. At Casablanca he urged upon the Americans the importance of seizing Rhodes and the Dodecanese, and tasked his own chiefs of staff to prepare a plan. In addition to troops, landing craft would be necessary, together with American fighters. Twin-engined Lightnings and British Beaufighters were the only planes with range to provide air support over the Aegean from North African bases. The utmost 'ingenuity and resource', urged Churchill, should be deployed to secure the Dodecanese.

Plans were made for two alternative scenarios: the first was a 'walk in' to Rhodes with Italian acquiescence; the second was for Operation *Accolade*, an opposed invasion against German opposition. The priority of Sicily, however, meant that by late summer nothing had been done. John Kennedy wrote on 13 August: 'We shall have to shut down in the Aegean.' The War Office assumed that the invasion of Italy, together with the commitment to *Overlord*, rendered operations there implausible. Instead, however, impending Italian surrender imbued the prime minister's Aegean ambitions with a new urgency. He remained convinced that an Allied coup there would precipitate Turkish belligerence.

The Americans were uninterested alike in the operation and in the Turks as allies. They believed that British aspirations in the eastern Mediterranean were rooted in old-fashioned imperialism rather than contemporary strategy, and were resolutely opposed to any diversion of resources from Italy, never mind from *Overlord*. At the *Quadrant* conference in Quebec in August, they paid polite lip-service to British enthusiasm for an Aegean initiative, but made it plain that whatever Churchill chose to do about Rhodes and the Dodecanese must be accomplished exclusively with the resources available to General Sir Henry 'Jumbo' Maitland-Wilson, now Middle East

C-in-C in Cairo – 'his jumbonic majesty', as Macmillan referred to this large and unimaginative dignitary. In other words, the British were on their own. There would be no USAAF Lightning fighters and precious few landing craft. At a time when concentration of force upon the Allies' central purposes seemed more important than ever before, US leaders recoiled from an entirely gratuitous dispersal.

The prime minister was undeterred. He pressed Maitland-Wilson to land on Rhodes anyway. The general, not one of his country's great military thinkers but compliant to Churchill's wishes, earmarked 4th Indian Division to execute *Accolade*. Then, however, it was decided that the Indians were needed in Italy. Maitland-Wilson's cupboard was left almost bare of fighting units. He cabled Eisenhower on 31 August: 'Any enterprise against Rhodes or Crete except an un-opposed walk-in is now impossible.' The prime minister disagreed. The Germans were everywhere in retreat. On the eastern front they had just suffered devastating defeat at Kursk. They had been expelled from Sicily. Italy was about to quit the war. On every front, Ultra signal decrypts revealed German commanders bewailing their flagging strength in the face of Allied dominance. Surely, in such circum-stances, even small forces boldly handled could crush the residual German presence in the Aegean. If operations in the eastern Mediterranean were to be conducted on a modest scale, they held special lustre in the prime minister's eyes, because speed, dash and a touch of piracy might yield an exclusively British triumph.

Urged on by London, Maitland-Wilson resurrected *Accolade*, with such rag-bag forces as he could scrape together. On 9 September the prime minister greeted news of the blossoming of his cherished project with a notation: 'Good. This is a time to play high. Improvise and dare.' Four days later, he cabled Maitland-Wilson: 'The capture of Rhodes by you at this time with Italian aid would be a fine contribution to the general war. Can you improvise the necessary garrison? . . . What is your total ration strength? This is the time to think of Clive and Peterborough, and of Rooke's men taking Gibraltar . . .' The prime minister's reference to 'ration strength' was, of course, a goad designed to remind the C-in-C of the vast number of men under his command, scattered across hundreds of thousands of square miles, and mostly employed on logistical or garrison tasks. Churchill's stirring appeal to the memory of historic imperial triumphs ignored the fact that now Maitland-Wilson's troops would face the German army.

A fundamental doctrinal divide persisted throughout the war: the British liked minor operations, while the Americans, with the marginal exception of MacArthur, did not. US strategic thinking, like that of the Germans, was dominated by a belief in concentration of force. The US Army undertook very few raids such as the British, and Churchill in particular, loved – Vaasgo, Bruneval, Saint-Nazaire, Bardia, Dieppe and many more. Special forces absorbed a dismayingly high proportion of Britain's most ardent warriors, volunteers attracted by the prospect of early independent action, rather than deferred encounters within the straitjacket of a military hierarchy. Brooke deplored the proliferation of army and Marine commando units. He believed, probably rightly, that their functions could have been as well performed by regular units specially trained for specific tasks. The mushroom growth of British special forces reflected the prime minister's conviction that war should, as far as possible, entertain its participants and showcase feats of daring to inspire the populace. In this, elite 'private armies' fulfilled their purpose. But they ill served the wider interests of the British Army, chronically short of good infantrymen for the big battlefields. Too many of Britain's bravest soldiers spent the war conducting irregular and self-indulgent activities of questionable strategic value.

Operations in the Mediterranean since 1940 had inspired the creation of a range of exotic units which basked in the prime minister's support and were led by social grandees or inspired eccentrics, often both. The Special Air Service, Special Boat Squadron, Long Range Desert Group, Popski's Private Army, Special Interrogation Group and their kin provided much pleasure to the adventurous spirits who filled their ranks, and inflicted varying degrees of inconvenience upon the enemy. In the absence of more substantial forces, when Italy suddenly announced its accession to the Allied cause, Maitland-Wilson turned to one of the 'private armies', the Special Boat Squadron, to make the first moves in the Aegean. While its raiders began landing piecemeal on every island they could reach, the Middle East C-in-C dispatched its commander as an emissary to the Italians, to urge that they should turn on their local Germans without delay, and without waiting for British troops.

Major Earl Jellicoe, son of the World War I admiral, led the SBS with notable courage and exuberance. On the night of 9 September Jellicoe, abruptly plucked from the fleshpots of Beirut, was parachuted onto Rhodes with a wireless operator and an Italian-speaking Polish officer who served under the *nom de guerre* of 'Major Dolbey' and had never jumped before. Dolbey broke his leg on landing. Jellicoe, finding himself under fire as soon as he hit the ground, felt obliged to swallow the letter which he carried from General Maitland-Wilson to the Italian governor, Admiral Inigo Campioni. When the shooting stopped, however, Italian soldiers transported the British party to Campioni's quarters. There, with Dolbey interpreting amid acute pain from his shattered leg, Jellicoe set about persuading the governor to throw in his lot with the Allies.

At first, Campioni seemed enthusiastic. But when he learned that the British could hope to land only a few hundred men on Rhodes, while strong German forces were on the spot, his zeal ebbed. He was still prevaricating about active, as distinct from token, belligerence when 6,000 men of the German assault division on Rhodes staged their own coup, overran the whole island and made prisoner its 35,000-strong Italian garrison. Jellicoe and Dolbey were fortunate that Campioni allowed them to sail away and avoid capture. General Maitland-Wilson wrote later that the admiral's spirit 'was clearly affected by the delay and by the fact that the Germans were there while we were not'. The unfortunate Italian had the worst of all worlds. Having disappointed the British, he was later shot by the Germans.

Possession of Rhodes and its excellent airfields enabled Hitler's forces to dominate the Aegean. The only prudent course for the British was now to recognise that their gambit had failed, and to forsake their ambitions. Far from doing this, however, they set about reinforcing failure. If they could seize other nearby islands, they reasoned, these might provide stepping stones for an October landing on Rhodes, to reverse the verdict of 11 September. This was a reckless decision, for which immediate blame lay with Maitland-Wilson, but ultimate responsibility with Churchill, who dispatched a stream of signals urging him on. Not only did the British lack strong forces to fight in the Dodecanese, but an opposed assault on Rhodes would have required a bloodbath, in pursuit of the most marginal strategic objective. *The Times* of 18 September reported the launching of operations in the Dodecanese, and commented: 'Presumably the Germans will try to oust the Allies by landing parachutists, but it is hoped . . . that the Allied forces will be sufficient to thwart the German efforts. Thus the situation in the Aegean becomes pregnant with possibilities.'

These were not, however, to the advantage of the British. What followed in September and October 1943 was a débâcle, punctuated by piratical exploits and dramas, each one of which was worthy to become a movie epic. Patrols of the Long Range Desert Group, deprived of sands on which to fight since the North African campaign ended, began descending on the Dodecanese by landing craft, plane, naval launch, caïque, canoe and boats of the superbly named Raiding Forces' Levant Schooner Flotilla. A company of the Parachute Regiment was flown into Kos by Dakota. Men of Jellicoe's SBS reached Kastellorizo in two launches, and thereafter deployed to other islands. Companies of 234 Brigade, the only available British infantry force, were transported piecemeal to Kos and Leros as fast as shipping could be found to get them there.

A squadron of South African-manned Spitfires was deployed on Kos, which alone had an airfield. A British officer set up his headquarters there alongside that of the Italian garrison, conspicuously hesitant new allies. An officer of SOE landed on Samos, followed by several hundred troops. A general serving as military attaché in Ankara crossed from the Turkish coast. There were soon 5,000 British personnel scattered through the archipelago. Command arrangements were chaotic, with almost absolute lack of coordination between army, navy and air force. But in those naïve early days, many of the newcomers relished the sensation of adventuring upon azure seas and islands steeped in classical legend. Amid barren hills, olive groves and little white-painted village houses, British buccaneers draped in sub-machine guns and grenades mingled with the local Greeks, breathed deep the Byronic air, pitched camp and waited to discover how the Germans would respond.

The Dodecanese

They were not long left in doubt. Hitler had no intention of relinquishing control of the Aegean. The Germans began to meet tentative British incursions by sea and air with their usual energy and effectiveness. Almost daily skirmishes developed, with RAF Beaufighters strafing German shipping, Luftwaffe planes attacking Kos, LRDG patrols and elements of the SBS fighting detachments of Germans wherever they met them. An officer of yet another British intelligence group, MI9, found himself suddenly hijacked – and shot in the thigh – by pro-fascist sailors on an Italian launch ferrying him between local ports. These men changed sides when they heard on the radio of Mussolini's rescue from mountain captivity by Otto Skorzeny's Nazi commandos. On several islands Germans, Italians and British roamed in confusion, ignorant of each other's locations or loyalties. Two British officers being held prisoner found their Austrian guard offering to let them escape if he might come too. Captors and captives often exchanged roles as the tides of the little campaign ebbed and flowed.

The prevailing theme was soon plain, however. The Germans were winning. In Greece and the Aegean they deployed 362 operational aircraft, many of which were available to operate in the Dodecanese. The South African Spitfire squadron on Kos was hacked to pieces in the air and on the ground by Bf109s. RAF Beaufighters lost heavily in anti-shipping strikes which inflicted little damage upon the enemy. German bombing demoralised the British – and still more, their new Italian allies – as well as destroying Dakotas shuttling to Kos. The Royal Navy was dismayed by the difficulties of sustaining supply runs to tenuously held islands under German air attack. British troops in the area were a hotchpotch of special forces, intelligence personnel, gunners, infantry and 'odds and sods', lacking mass, coherence and conviction. The main force, 234 Brigade, had spent the previous three years garrisoning Malta, where its soldiers gained much experience of bombing, hunger and boredom, and none of battle. In the fifth year of the war, when in almost every other theatre the Allies were winning, in the eastern Mediterranean Churchill contrived a predicament in which they were locally vulnerable on land, at sea and in the air.

On the morning of 3 October, the 680 soldiers, 500 RAF air and ground crew and 3,500 Italians on Kos awoke to discover that German ships offshore were unloading a brigade-strong invasion force whose arrival had been unheralded, and whose activities were unimpeded. It was a tribute to German improvisation that such an operation could be staged with little of the training or specialist paraphernalia which the Allies deemed essential for amphibious landings. The Germans mounted the Kos invasion with a scratch force, supplemented by a paratroop landing, against which the RAF launched ineffectual air strikes. The British defenders lacked both mobility and will to leave their positions and mount swift counter-attacks.

The island was twenty-eight miles long by six wide, with a local population of 20,000. Its rugged hills, impervious to entrenchment, rose to a height of 2,800 feet. In two days' fighting, 2,000 Germans supported by plentiful Stuka dive-bombers secured Kos for a loss of just fifteen killed and seventy wounded. Some 3,145 Italians and 1,388 British prisoners fell into their hands, along with a mass of weapons, stores and equipment. Neither the Italians nor RAF personnel on the island showed much appetite for participation in the ground battle. It was a foolish delusion in London to have supposed that Italian troops, who for three years had shown themselves reluctant to fight the Allies, could any more readily be motivated to take on the Germans. The men of the Durham Light Infantry were outnumbered, inexperienced, and never perceived much prospect of success. Churchill described the defence of Kos as 'an unsatisfactory resistance'. While this was true enough, responsibility rested overwhelmingly with those who placed the garrison there. The worst victims were the Italians, who paid heavily for their brief change of allegiance. On Kefallonia, in the Ionian islands, the Germans had already conducted a wholesale massacre of 4,000 'treacherous' Italian troops who surrendered to them. On Kos, the victors confined themselves to executing eighty-nine Italian officers. A few dozen determined British fugitives escaped by landing craft and small boat.

In the days and weeks following the loss of Kos, Churchill in vain pressed Eisenhower to divert resources from Italy to recapture it. A game of hide-and-seek persisted on other islands, between Hitler's units and British special forces. The Germans staged a further airborne landing on Astipalaea. Luftwaffe aircrew, accustomed to the depressed spirits of many of their countrymen who knew that the war was being lost, were amazed to find exuberant paratroopers in Junkers transports en route to a drop zone singing, '*Kameraden*, today there is no going back.' At this late stage of the war, the obliging British had provided the *Fallschirmjäger* with a field on which there were still victories to be won.

The Long Range Desert Group, whose men were not organised, trained or equipped to fight as infantry, suffered heavily in desultory battles. The main British force left in the Dodecanese was now based on Leros, an island much smaller than Kos and twenty miles further north. When the British commander there heard that German prisoners on nearby Levitha had overpowered their captors and seized control, he packed fifty LRDG men onto two naval motor launches, and dispatched them to retake it. Once ashore, the LRDG fought a series of little actions with the Germans in which four raiders were killed and almost all the others captured. Just seven escaped at nightfall, by courtesy of the Royal Navy. Levitha remained firmly in German hands.

Churchill was dismayed by the unfolding misfortunes in the Aegean, as well he might be. Brooke wrote on 6 October: 'It is pretty clear in my mind that with the commitments we have in Italy we should not undertake serious operations in the Aegean . . . [but] PM by now determined to go for Rhodes without looking at the effects on Italy.' Churchill chafed to travel personally to North Africa to incite the Americans to address themselves to Aegean operations. Cadogan wrote: 'He is excited about Kos and wants to lead an expedition to Rhodes.' The prime minister tried in vain to persuade Washington that Marshall should fly to meet him in Tunisia, there to be persuaded of the virtues of the Aegean commitment. On 7 October he wrote personally to Roosevelt: 'I have never wished to send an army into the Balkans, but only by agents and commandos to stimulate the intense guerrilla activity there. This may yield results measureless in their consequence at very small cost to main operations. What I ask for is the capture of Rhodes and the other islands of the Dodecanese . . . Leros, which at the moment we hold so precariously, is an important naval fortress, and once we are ensconced in this area air and light naval forces would have a fruitful part to play . . . I beg you to consider this.' He argued that operations in the eastern Mediterranean were 'worth at least up to a first-class division'. The Americans disagreed. They transferred some Lightning squadrons to Libya, to operate in support of the Royal Navy in the Aegean. But, as other priorities pressed, after only four days these aircraft were withdrawn. Since the Germans were operating much superior Bf109 single-engined fighters, it is anyway unlikely that the twin-engined Lightnings could have altered the local balance of air power any more than did the RAF's Beaufighters. But the British were bitter that they were left to fight alone.

In London on 8 October, *The Times* said of the fall of Kos: 'It cannot be expected that every allied venture will be successful: but there is no denying that the state of affairs in the Dodecanese is causing disquietude.' The paper asked pertinent questions about why stronger Allied forces had not been committed. That day, Brooke wrote in his diary: 'I am slowly becoming convinced that in his old age Winston is becoming less and less well balanced! I cannot control him any more. He has worked himself into a frenzy of excitement about the Rhodes attack, has magnified its importance so that he can no longer see anything else and has set his heart on capturing this one island even at the expense of endangering his relations with the President and with the Americans, and also the whole future of the Italian campaign. He refuses to listen to any arguments or to see any dangers! . . . The whole thing is sheer madness, and he is placing himself quite unnecessarily in a very false position! The Americans are already desperately suspicious of him, and this will make matters far worse.'

All Brooke said was true. That same day, 8 October, Churchill wrote again to the Americans, addressing himself to both Eisenhower and the president: 'I propose . . . to tell Gen. Wilson that he is free if he judges the position hopeless to order the garrison [of Leros] to evacuate . . . I will not waste words in explaining how painful this decision is to me.' But Leros was not evacuated, as it should have been. Churchill cabled Maitland-Wilson on 10 October: 'Cling on if you possibly can . . . If after everything has been done you are forced to quit I will support you, but victory is the prize.'

On 13 October, John Kennedy wrote in his diary: 'It does seem amazing that the PM should spend practically a whole week on forcing forward his ideas about taking an island in the face of all military advice . . . Jumbo [Maitland-Wilson] chanced his arm in occupying Kos and the other Aegean islands.' Churchill cabled Maitland-Wilson on 14 October: 'I am very pleased with the way you used such poor bits and pieces as were left to you. *Nil desperandum.*' And again to Maitland-Wilson, copied to Eden: 'Keep Leros safely.' Churchill referred to Leros, absurdly, as a 'fortress', even less meaningful in this case than when he had used the same word of Singapore and Tobruk. The C-in-C, desperate not to disappoint the prime minister, persevered. Given the scepticism of Brooke, why did not the CIGS assert himself, and insist upon withdrawal from the Aegean? The most plausible answer is that, when he was fighting Churchill almost daily about much bigger issues, notably including the prime minister's enthusiasm for an invasion of Sumatra, Leros seemed insufficiently important to merit yet another showdown. Win or lose, the campaign represented only a marginal drain on resources. Brooke could not hope to overcome the prime minister's passions on every issue. Instead he stood back, and watched the subsequent fiasco unfold.

For five further bloody weeks, the British struggled on in the Aegean. The battles which took place in that period at sea, in the air and on land more closely resembled those of 1941 than most Allied encounters with the Germans in 1943. The Royal Navy's cruisers, destroyers, submarines and small craft sought to sink German shipping, and to bombard ports and shore positions, while subjected to constant air attacks by the Luftwaffe's Ju88s. With the loss of the field on Kos, the RAF's nearest base was now 300 miles away. Even old Stuka dive-bombers, powerless in the face of fighter opposition, became potent weapons when they could fly unchallenged.

There were many savage little naval actions in the narrow waters between the islands. On 7 October, for instance, the submarine *Unruly* conducted an unsuccessful torpedo attack on a German troop convoy, then in frustration surfaced and engaged the enemy with its four-inch deck gun until driven to submerge by the appearance of the Luftwaffe. *Unruly* later torpedoed a minelayer carrying 285 German troops. The cruisers *Sirius* and *Penelope* were caught by German bombers while attacking shipping, and *Penelope* was damaged. The destroyer *Panther* was sunk on 8 October, and the cruiser *Carlisle* so badly damaged by bombers that after limping back to port she never put to sea again. The Luftwaffe sustained constant attacks on Leros's port facilities, so that British warships had to dash in, dump supplies and sail again inside half an hour. The RAF's anti-shipping skills were still inferior to those of the Germans, and Beaufighter strikes cost the British attackers more heavily than their enemies. Even when raids were successful, such as one by Wellington bombers on the night of 18 October, the results were equivocal: the Wellingtons dispatched to the bottom ships carrying 204 Germans, but also 2,389 Italian and seventy-one Greek prisoners. By 22 October a total of 6,000 Italian prisoners had drowned when their transports succumbed to British air strikes, while 29,454 Italian and British PoWs had been successfully removed to the Greek mainland, and thence to Germany.

The cruisers *Sirius* and *Aurora* were badly damaged by Ju88s, while German mines accounted for several British warships including the submarine *Trooper*, which disappeared east of Leros. Almost every ship of the Royal Navy which ran the gauntlet to the Dodecanese, including launches, torpedo-boats and caïques, had to face bombs, heavy seas in the worsening autumn weather, and natural hazards inshore. The destroyer *Eclipse* was sunk on 23 October, while carrying 200 troops and ten tons of stores. The navy reluctantly decided that it could no longer sail destroyers in the Aegean during daylight, in the face of complete German air dominance. The RAF continued to suffer heavily – in a single day's operations on 5 November, six Beaufighters were destroyed, four crews lost.

On 31 October, the senior British airman in the Mediterranean, Air Chief Marshal Sir Arthur Tedder, wrote: 'We are being pressed to throw good money after bad. The situation is fundamentally unsound.' John Kennedy urged Alan Brooke on 28 October that 'the price we were paying [for Leros was] too great and the return too small to justify retention'. Brooke professed to agree, but told Kennedy that at that day's chiefs of staff meeting the decision had been made to hang on. It had now become too difficult to withdraw the garrison in the face of German air superiority. In his own diary, Brooke called Leros 'a very nasty problem, Middle East [Command] have not been either wise or cunning and have now got themselves into the difficult situation that they can neither hold nor evacuate Leros. Our only hope would be assistance from Turkey, the provision of airfields from which the required air cover could be provided.' Such aid was not forthcoming.

The final act of the Aegean drama began on 12 November, when the Germans attacked Leros. The British garrison there, some 3,000 strong together with 5,500 Italians, had had several weeks to prepare for the inevitable. Nonetheless, when the moment came, everything that could go amiss did so. Before the landing 234 Brigade was commanded by a short, red-faced and heavily moustached officer named Ben Brittorous, who embodied almost every deficiency of the wartime British Army. Brittorous was obsessed with military etiquette, and harassed officers and men alike about the importance of saluting him. In his weeks on Leros he made himself loathed by his troops, and made few effective preparations to meet a German landing. When the Luftwaffe started bombing in earnest, he retired to his tunnel headquarters, and stayed there until relieved of his command a week before the German descent, to be replaced by a gunner officer, Brigadier Robert Tilney. Tilney, newly promoted to lead in battle men whom he knew only slightly, was less disliked than Brittorous, but also seemed to lack conviction. He immediately redeployed his three infantry battalions around the island, with the intention of repelling a German landing on the beaches. Not only did this plan spread the defenders thin, but the brigade was very short of radios and telephones. Communication between Tilney and his units was tenuous even before the Germans intervened.

On 11 November, Ultra informed the British that a landing on Leros, Operation *Typhoon*, would be launched on the following day. Some 2,730 German troops were committed, a force inferior in size to that of the defenders. Yet the RAF and Royal Navy found themselves unable to do anything effective to interfere with enemy arrangements. Bad weather frustrated planned British bombing attacks on the Luftwaffe's Greek airfields. The commander of a Royal Navy destroyer flotilla in the area declined to brave a suspected minefield to attack the invasion convoy. The British official historian, Captain Stephen Roskill, wrote later: 'The enemy had boldly discounted any effective threat to the convoy by day, and by night he had concealed his vessels very skilfully; yet it seems undeniable that it should not have reached its destination virtually unscathed.'

While the German main body landed from the sea, *Fallschirmjäger* staged another superbly brave and determined air assault. RAF strikes against the landing ships were notably less effective than the Luftwaffe's close support of the invaders. A fourth British battalion, landed to reinforce 234 Brigade during the battle, failed to affect its outcome. Some of the island's defenders fought well, but others did not. The limited scale of British casualties indicates that this was no sacrificial stand. On Leros, from battalions of 500 men apiece the Royal West Kents lost eighteen killed in action, the Royal Irish Fusiliers twenty-two, the King's Own forty-five, the Buffs forty-two.

When the German parachutists landed, the defenders – in much superior numbers – should have launched an immediate counter-attack on the landing zone before the invaders could reorganise. Instead, British infantry simply sat tight and fired from their positions. As the Germans advanced across the island, one British officer was dismayed to see men of the King's Own fleeing for their lives in the face of mortar fire. At 1800 on the first day, call sign *Stupendous* of the Long Range Desert Group signalled bitterly from Leros: 'Lack of RAF support absolutely pitiful: ships sat around here all day, and Stukas just laughed at us.' The defence lacked mobility and, more important, motivation and competence to match that of the Germans. Jeffrey Holland, who served as an infantry sergeant on Leros, wrote later: 'As the battle progressed, it was evident that the enemy had deployed . . . first-class combat troops, who demonstrated consummate skill, courage and self-reliance.' An SBS man wrote of one scene he observed: 'We were amazed to see groups of British soldiers in open route order proceeding away from the battle area . . . The colonel stopped and interrogated them, and they said they had orders to retire to the south. Many were without arms, very dejected and exceedingly tired.'

Brigadier Tilney lost control of most of his force at an early stage, and was enraged to find units retiring without orders. He threatened two battalion commanders with court martial for refusing to order their units into attack. Jeffrey Holland wrote: 'The Germans moved quickly from one position to another, but never retreated; they seemed willing to accept a high rate of casualties. Their officers and NCOs exposed themselves to fire when directing an attack or defence. They seemed indifferent to the British fire which they sensed was tentative; neither well coordinated nor directed.'

Some courageous British counter-attacks were launched, in which a battalion CO and several company commanders were killed. At midnight on 14 November, Bletchley Park decrypted a German signal warning that the position of the invasion force on Leros was 'critical', and that it was essential to get heavy weapons ashore immediately to swing the battle. The Germans on Leros experienced nothing like the walkover they had enjoyed on Kos. But the defenders, having failed to take the initiative at the outset, never regained it. The terrain made it almost impossible for men to dig in, to protect themselves from bombing. Too often in World War II, British troops perceived enemy air superiority as a sufficient excuse to reconcile themselves to defeat.

Maitland-Wilson kept alive Churchill's hopes of salvaging the battle, signalling on 14 November that British troops on Leros, though 'somewhat tired', were 'full of fight and well fed'. To the end, the prime minister pressed for more energetic measures to support them. On the evening of the 16th, as he approached Malta en route to the Tehran conference, he signalled Air Chief Marshal Tedder: 'I much regret not to see you tonight, as I should have pressed upon you the vital need of sustaining Leros by every possible means. This is much the most important thing that is happening in the Mediterranean in the next few days . . . I do not see how you can disinterest your-self in the fate of Leros.' Tedder wrote scathingly afterwards: 'One would have thought that some of the bitter lessons of Crete would have been sufficiently fresh in mind to have prevented a repetition . . . It seems incredible now, as it did then, that after four years' expe-rience of modern war, people forgot that air-power relies on secure bases, weather, and effective radius of action.'

At 1600 hours on 17 November, the fifth day after the landing on Leros, Tilney surrendered. Some 3,000 British and 5,500 Italian soldiers became prisoners. Almost a hundred wounded men had been evacuated earlier. Several score bold spirits, including the inevitable and invincible Lord Jellicoe, escaped in small boats and eventually made their way to Turkey or small islands from which the navy rescued them. More than 3,000 British, Greek and Italian personnel were successfully evacuated from the nearby island of Samos before the Germans occupied this also. Including aircrew, the British lost around 1,500 killed in Aegean operations between September and November 1943 – 745 Royal Navy, 422 soldiers and 333 RAF. The Long Range Desert Group sacrificed more men in the Dodecanese than in three years of North African fighting. Five British infantry battalions were written off.

Hitler sent a congratulatory message to his Aegean commanders which was, for once, entirely merited: 'The capture of Leros, under-taken with limited means but with great courage, carried through tenaciously in spite of various setbacks and bravely brought to a victorious conclusion, is a military accomplishment which will find an honourable place in the history of war.' The British on Leros had advantages – notably that of holding the ground – which should have been decisive, even in the face of enemy air superiority. It was shameful that the German paratroopers were so easily able to over-come larger numbers of defenders who knew that they were coming.

Admiral Sir Andrew Cunningham, now First Sea Lord, castigated the army: 'I am still strongly of the opinion that Leros might have been held,' he wrote later. Brigadier Tilney, a German PoW until 1945, became principal scapegoat for the island's fall. Blame, however, properly ran all the way up through the chain of command to Downing Street. It was no more possible in 1943 than in 1941 for warships to operate successfully in the face of enemy air superiority. German aircrew were more proficient at attacking shipping than their British counterparts. British troops on Leros, as so often earlier in the war, showed themselves less effective warriors than their opponents. Far from being an elite, 234 Brigade was a second-rate unit which conducted itself as well as might have been expected in the circumstances. The best apology that can be made for its performance is that it would have served little purpose for men to display suicidal courage, or to accept sacrificial losses, in a campaign which was anyway almost certainly doomed, and at a time when overall Allied victory was not in doubt.

If the defenders of Leros had repulsed the German assault in mid-November, British prestige might have profited, but the balance of power in the Aegean would have remained unchanged, and the agony would have been protracted. The Royal Navy would still have been left with an open-ended commitment to supply Leros under German air attack. As long as Rhodes remained in enemy hands, the British presence in the Dodecanese was strategically meaningless. Far from Leros offering a launching pad for a prospective assault on Rhodes, as Churchill insisted, it was merely a beleaguered liability. The Royal Navy suffered much more pain than it inflicted in the Aegean campaign, and achieved as much as could have been expected. In all, four cruisers, five destroyers, five minesweepers, two submarines and assorted coastal craft were sunk or badly damaged. The RAF could not be blamed for the difficulties of conducting operations beyond the range of effective air cover, but its performance in the anti-shipping role was unimpressive. Some 113 aircraft were lost – the Beaufighter squadrons suffered especially heavily, losing 50 per cent of their strength. Once the airfields on Kos were gone, and with them any hope of operating single-engined fighters, the British should have cut their losses and quit.

In London, the news from the Aegean caused dismay and bewilderment in what was otherwise a season of Mediterranean victories.

Cadogan at the Foreign Office wrote on 16 November: 'Bad news of Leros. Talk of, and plans for, evacuation brings back the bad days of '40 and '41. But it's on a smaller scale of course.' A *Times* editorial on 18 November commented justly: 'The fall of Leros should be a reminder that well-established principles of strategy cannot be neglected with impunity.' A week later, the newspaper said that 'this lamentable episode' raised issues about 'the broad strategy of our whole Mediterranean campaign . . . on which British public opinion will require reassurance'.

Britain's Aegean commitment was trifling in the grand scheme of the war, but represented a blow to national pride and prestige, precipitated by the personal decisions of the prime minister. Once more, he was obliged to confront the limitations of his own soldiers against the Germans – and the vulnerability of British forces without the Americans. John Kennedy described the operation as 'a justifiable risk. [Maitland-Wilson] could not know how strongly the Boche would resist.' But four years' experience of making war against Hitler should have inoculated the prime minister and his generals against recklessness. Ultra intercepts warned London that the Luftwaffe was reinforcing the eastern Mediterranean before British troops were committed. Churchill repeatedly deluded himself that boldness would of itself suffice to gain rewards. This might be so against an incompetent or feeble enemy, but was entirely mistaken against a supremely professional foe who always punished mistakes. The daring of the prime minister's commitment was unmatched by the battlefield showing of those responsible for carrying it out. In the Aegean, as so often elsewhere, the speed of German responses to changing circumstances stood in stark contrast to faltering Allied initiatives.

Kennedy wrote that 'the PM on paper has full professional backing for all that has been done'. He meant that the chiefs of staff and Maitland-Wilson formally endorsed the prime minister's commitments to the Aegean. In truth, however, almost all the higher commanders had allowed his wishes to prevail over their own better judgement. Brooke, unreasonably, joined the prime minister in blaming the Americans for failing to provide support: 'CIGS feels that the war may have been lengthened by as much as six months by the American failure to realise the value of exploiting the whole Mediterranean situation and of supporting Turkey strongly enough to bring her into the war.' Yet why should the Americans have sought to save the British from the shipwreck of an adventure which they had always made it plain they did not believe in? There is, moreover, no reason to suppose that additional US air support would have altered outcomes. Likewise, the British official historian seems mistaken in lamenting the diversion from the Aegean in the first days of the campaign of six Royal Navy fleet destroyers, to escort battleships home to Britain. If the destroyers had remained, they would merely have provided the Luftwaffe with additional targets. Even had the British successfully seized Rhodes, it remains unlikely that Turkey would have entered the war, and debatable whether Turkish military assistance was worth much to the Allies.

Some of the same objections could be made to Churchill's 1943 commitment to the Aegean as to his early Balkan foray in 1915. The Dardanelles campaign, on which he impaled his First World War reputation, was designed to open the Black Sea route to arm Russia. Yet even had the passage been secured, the World War I Allies were chronically short of weapons for their own armies, and had next to none to spare for shipment to the Russians. Likewise in 1943, even if Turkey had joined the conflict its army would have been entirely dependent on Anglo-American weapons and equipment. It was proving difficult to supply the needs of Russian, US, British and French forces. As the Americans anticipated, Turkey would more likely have become a hungry mouth for the Allies to feed than a threat to German purposes in the Balkans.

Churchill bitterly described the Aegean campaign as the Germans' first success since Alamein. On 21 November he told his wife Clementine in a cable from North Africa: 'Am still grieving over Leros etc. It is terrible fighting with both hands tied behind one's back.' He was, of course, venting frustration that he had been unable to persuade the US to support his aspirations. In his war memoirs he described this as 'the most acute difference I ever had with General

Eisenhower'. He cabled Eden from Cairo, also on 21 November, to suggest that if questions were asked in Parliament about the Aegean, the Foreign Secretary should tell the House defiantly that the hazards of the operation were foreseen from the outset, 'and if they were disregarded it was because other reasons and other hopes were held to predominate over them. If we are never going to proceed on anything but certainties we must certainly face the prospect of a prolonged war.' This was lame stuff, to justify the unjustifiable.

Amazingly, at the meeting of the combined chiefs of staff in Cairo on 24 November, the prime minister renewed his pleas for an invasion of Rhodes. Marshall recalled: 'All the British were against me. It got hotter and hotter. Finally Churchill grabbed his lapels . . . and said: "His Majesty's Government can't have its troops standing idle. Muskets must flame."' Marshall responded in similarly histrionic terms: 'Not one American soldier is going to die on [that] goddam beach.' The US chiefs remained unwavering, even when Maitland-Wilson joined the meeting to press the Rhodes case. The British, having lost to the Germans, now lost to the Americans as well. In a letter to Clementine on 26 November, Churchill once more lamented the fall of Leros: 'I cannot pretend to have an adequate defence of what occurred.' Indeed, he did not. The Aegean campaign represented a triumph of impulse over reason that should never have taken place. It inflicted further damage upon American trust in the prime minister's judgement and commitment to the vital objectives of the Grand Alliance. It was fortunate for British prestige and for Churchill's reputation that it unfolded at a time when successes elsewhere eclipsed public consciousness of a gratuitous humiliation.

SIXTEEN

Tehran

In the eyes of the world, in the autumn of 1943 Churchill's prestige was impregnable. He stood beside Roosevelt and Stalin, the 'Big Three', plainly destined to become victors of the greatest conflict in the history of mankind. 'Croakers' at home had been put to flight by the battle-field successes denied to Britain between 1939 and 1942. Yet those who worked most closely with the prime minister, functionaries and service chiefs alike, were troubled by manifestations of weariness and erratic judgement. His government never lacked domestic critics. His refusal seriously to address issues of post-war reconstruction caused widespread dismay. 'His ear is so sensitively tuned to the bugle note of history,' wrote Aneurin Bevan – for once justly – 'that he is often deaf to the more raucous clamour of contemporary life.' Eden agreed: 'Mr Churchill did not like to give his time to anything not exclusively concerned with the conduct of the war. This seemed to be a deep instinct in him and, even though it was part of his strength as a war leader, it could also be an embarrassment.'

It was irksome for ministers responsible for addressing vital issues concerned with Britain's future to find their leader unwilling to discuss them, or to make necessary decisions. There would be growing difficulties in reconciling the views of the government's Labour and Tory members on post-war policy. Leo Amery wrote of a later meeting: 'Winston handled the debate [on the Town and Country Planning Bill] with considerable skill and impartiality, but the nearer we get to reconstruction the more difficult it will be to keep the team together.' On 29 November 1943, Bevin gained admission to the prime minister's bedroom, where so many remarkable scenes were played out in a setting sketched by Brooke: 'The red and gold dressing gown in itself was worth going miles to see, and only Winston could have thought of wearing it! He looked rather like some Chinese mandarin! The few hairs were usually ruffled on his bald head. A large cigar stuck sideways out of his face. The bed was littered with papers and despatches. Sometimes the tray with his finished breakfast was still on the bed table. The bell was continually being rung for secretaries, typists, stenographer, or his faithful valet Sawyers.'

On this occasion Bevin raised the issue of Lord Woolton's future role in post-war planning. Churchill said crossly that he was just leaving to see Stalin, was preoccupied with other things, 'and that it was really too much to go into detailed questions at the moment'. Bevin was as angry as the prime minister. There was never a right time to catch Churchill, to discuss matters which did not command his interest. Yet he was so often criticised for declining seriously to address post-war issues that it is salutary to compare his attitude with that of Hitler. The Nazis inflicted crippling economic, social and military damage upon their own empire by setting about forging a new 'Greater Germany' while the war's outcome was still unresolved. Churchill's single-minded preoccupation with achieving victory may have dismayed his colleagues, but it seems a fault on the right side.

The British people acknowledged him as the personification of their war effort. As the dominance of the US and Soviet Union grew, his rhetoric and statesmanship were the most formidable weapons his flagging nation could wield to sustain its place at the summit of the Grand Alliance. But in the last eighteen months of the war, while he received his share of the applause for Allied victories, he also suffered increasing frustrations and disappointments. At every turn, cherished projects were stillborn, favoured policies atrophied, because they could not be executed without American resources or goodwill, which were unforthcoming. This was by no means always to Britain's disadvantage. Some schemes, such as the Aegean campaign, were ill-conceived and unlikely to prosper. But no man less liked to be thwarted than Churchill. Much happened, or did not happen, in the years of American ascendancy which caused the prime minister to fume at his own impotence.

His words remained as magnificent in the years of victories as they had been in those of defeats. He enjoyed moments of exhilaration, because he had a large capacity for joy. But the sorrows were frequent and various. He refused to abandon his obsession with getting the Turks into the war, cabling Eden, en route back from Moscow, that it was necessary to 'remind the Turkey that Christmas was coming'. He dismissed proposals summarily to depose the king of Italy, saying, 'Why break off the handle of the jug before we get to Rome and have a chance of securing a new handle for it!' He told the cabinet one day, amid a discussion about Soviet perfidy in publishing claims in *Pravda* that Britain had opened unilateral peace negotiations with the Nazis: 'Trying to maintain good relations with a communist is like wooing a crocodile, you do not know whether to tickle it under the chin or beat it on the head. When it opens its mouth you cannot tell whether it is trying to smile, or preparing to eat you up.'

In those months Churchill's mind was overwhelmingly fixed upon the Mediterranean campaign. But it would have well served the interests of the British war effort had he also addressed another important issue which he neglected. Air Chief Marshal Sir Arthur Harris, C-in-C of Bomber Command, chose this moment to divert the bulk of his increasingly formidable force away from the Ruhr, where Lancasters and Halifaxes had been pounding factories for years, to attack Germany's capital. This was one of the major strategic errors of the RAF's war. The Berlin region was certainly industrially important, but it was far from Britain, heavily defended, and often shrouded in winter overcast. This assault continued until April 1944, at a cost in RAF losses that became prohibitive, without dealing the decisive blow Harris sought – and which he had promised the prime minister. Bomber Command lost the 'Battle of Berlin'.

Much more significant, however, was the respite granted to the Ruhr. Adam Tooze's important recent research on the Nazi economy has shown that in the autumn of 1943 the Ruhr's industries lay on the brink of collapse. If Bomber Command had continued its assault, instead of switching targets eastwards, the consequences for Hitler's war machine might have been dramatic. Allied intelligence about German production was poor. One of Harris's major mistakes as director of the bomber offensive was failure to grasp the importance of repeating blows against damaged targets. He allowed himself to be misled about his force's achievements by air photographs of devastated cities.

So, too, did the prime minister. To explain why he left the RAF to its own devices for much of the war, it is necessary to acknowledge how little reliable information was available about what bombing was, or was not, doing to Germany. The progress of Britain's armies was readily measured by following their advances or retreats on the map; that of the Royal Navy by examining statistics of sinkings. But once the Battle of Britain was won, the RAF's performance was chiefly judged by assessments, often spurious, produced by its own staff officers. Nobody, including Portal, Harris and Churchill, really knew what bombing was achieving, though soldiers and sailors believed it was much less than airmen claimed. The prime minister had a strong vested interest in thinking the best of British bombing. He trumpeted its achievements to the Americans, and even more to Stalin, to mollify their frustration about the shortcomings of Western ground operations. It would have been a major political embarrassment had evidence emerged that the strategic offensive was doing less than Harris claimed.

Thus, between 1942 and the 1944 controversy about bombing the French rail network ahead of *Overlord*, Churchill never sought an independent assessment of what Bomber Command was contributing, though it consumed around one-third of Britain's entire war effort. Harris persuaded the prime minister that his aircraft wreaked havoc, as they did. But dramatic images of flame and destruction in the Reich were unaccompanied by rigorous analysis of German industry, about which intelligence was anyway sketchy and most of the RAF's data plain wrong. Harris, like his American counterparts, was left free to fight his battle as he himself saw fit, to pursue an obsessive attempt to prove that bombing could win the war without much input of accurate evidence or imagination. This was a serious omission on the part of the prime minister, and a missed opportunity for the Royal Air Force.

In this later period of the war, the fatigue of Churchill's people grew alongside American and Russian might. The Aegean campaign represented a minor demonstration of British vulnerability, but larger ones lay ahead. In the late autumn of 1943, four issues dominated Britain's military agenda: the campaign in Italy; the commitment to *Overlord*; residual possibilities of ambitious adventures in the Balkans; and Operation *Buccaneer*, a putative amphibious landing in Burma. On 6 November, Sir Archibald Clark Kerr warned from Moscow of Russian fears that the British were still hostile to *Overlord*. Churchill responded: 'I will do everything in human power to animate the forward movement on which my heart is set at this moment.' But the words 'forward movement' embraced a range of possible operations, some in the Mediterranean, of which *Overlord* was only one. Dalton wrote after a cabinet meeting: 'In an expansive moment Winston told us his apprehensions about the "*Over-lord*" policy which the Americans have forced upon us, involving a dangerous and time-wasting straddle of our transport and landing craft between two objectives when we might have gone on more effectively in Italy and the Balkans.'

For some weeks Churchill had been pressing for a meeting with Roosevelt and Stalin, which he would dearly have liked to hold in London. It was unsurprising that the Russian leader rejected this notion out of hand, but the British felt snubbed when they learned that the US president was also unwilling to visit their country. Such a rendezvous would play badly with the American electorate in the forthcoming election year, claimed Roosevelt. After some dalliance, Tehran was found a mutually acceptable venue. Churchill sought an advance bilateral summit in Cairo, to which the Americans agreed. He sailed for the Mediterranean on the battlecruiser *Renown*, accompanied by his usual entourage and service chiefs, daughter Sarah and son Randolph. Harold Macmillan boarded the great warship at Gibraltar: 'We were greeted by her owner – or so he seemed – who was finding this an agreeable method of cruising.' But Churchill was in poor health. Disembarking at Malta, he spent two days in bed at the residence of Lord Gort, the governor.

Gort was no slave to creature comforts. When Ismay visited the ailing prime minister he was greeted by pathetic solicitations for enhanced rations and a bath: 'Do you think you could bring me a little bit of butter from that nice ship? . . . I only want a cupful of hot water, but I can't get it.' Churchill's bedroom overlooked a thorough-fare crowded with chattering Maltese. Moran recorded a touching moment: 'From the street below came a great hubbub of voices. His brow darkened. He threw his legs out of bed, and striding across the room thrust his head through the open window, bawling: "Go away, will you? Please go away and do not make so much noise."'

The chiefs of staff held an unsatisfactory meeting, crowded into the prime minister's bedroom. A few days earlier, John Kennedy expounded in his diary British policy for the encounter with the Americans: 'We have now crystallised our ideas as to the strategy to be advocated.' The Italian campaign should be continued, renewed efforts made to bring Turkey into the war through Allied activism in the Balkans, and the US urged 'to accept a postponement of *Overlord*'. The adjutant-general Sir Ronald Adam told a fellow officer: 'The PM's stock is not high with the President at the moment, and the latter is being dragged rather unwillingly to Cairo . . . The PM has now gone very Mediterranean-minded, and the future of *Overlord* is again in the melting-pot.'

Churchill chafed constantly about the slow progress of Allied operations in Italy. Winter weather had reduced campaigning to a crawl, and the Germans were resisting with their usual determination. 'The pattern of battle seldom varied,' wrote one veteran of the campaign, Fred Majdalany. 'The Germans would hold a position for a time until it was seriously contested: then pull back a mile or two to the next defendable place, leaving behind a trail of blown bridges, minefields and road demolitions . . . The Allied armies would begin with a night attack – ford a stream or river after dark, storm the heights on the far side, dig themselves in by dawn, and hope that by that time the Sappers, following on their heels, would have sufficiently repaired the demolitions and removed the obstacles to permit tanks to follow up . . . The Germans, watching these proceedings, would attempt to frustrate them by raining down artillery and mortar fire.'

The prime minister was infuriated that two British divisions had already been withdrawn from the line in advance of their return home to prepare for D-Day. In a minute to the chiefs on 20 November, he complained of Italian operations being compromised by 'the shadow of *Overlord*'. He said that Yugoslavia's partisans, whom he was eager to support more vigorously, were containing more Axis divisions than the British and American armies. He deplored American insistence on 1 May as the date for D-Day, 'with inflexible rigidity and without regard to the loss and injury to the Allied cause created thereby'. The consequence of this 'fixed target date', he said, was that 'our affairs will deteriorate in the Balkans and that the Aegean will remain firmly in German hands . . . for the sake of an operation fixed for May upon hypotheses that in all probability will not be realized by that date'. Churchill wanted all available resources directed first towards capturing Rome by January 1944, and second upon taking Rhodes later that month. None of this was likely to find favour with the Americans, nor deserved to.

The British delegation sailed on from Malta to Alexandria, and thence flew to Cairo, arriving on 21 November. Macmillan, seeing Churchill for the first time for some months, perceived his powers diminished, yet still remarkable: 'Winston is getting more and more dogmatic (at least outwardly) and rather repetitive. One forgets, of course, that he is really an old man – but a wonderful old man he is too . . . It is amusing to watch how he will take a point and reproduce it as his own a day or two later. He misses very little, although he does not always appear to listen.'

The first meeting of the *Sextant* conference took place on 23 November, and addressed the Far East. The US contingent was in irritable mood, because prior word of the gathering had leaked to correspondents, increasing the security risk. The British were galled by the attendance of Chiang Kai-shek and his wife, at American insistence. Much attention was given to Chinese issues. The British shared US faith neither in China's value as an ally nor in the massive commitment to provide aid 'over the Hump' of the Himalayas. They had not forgotten that a few months earlier Roosevelt had urged them to cede possession of Hong Kong to Chiang Kai-shek as a 'gesture of goodwill'. This caused Eden to observe to Harry Hopkins that he had not heard the president suggest any similar act of largesse at American expense. Smuts said emolliently: 'We are inclined to forget the President's difficulties. There is a very strong undercurrent against him. The things the Americans do are based partly on ignorance, partly on their determination to get power. We have learned hard lessons in the four years of the war. They have had no hard lessons. Yet we do not want to wait another four years while they learn them.'

The British were right about the intractability of China, but their dismissive attitude increased Anglo–American tensions. Churchill made much of plans to launch Orde Wingate and his Chindits on ambitious deep penetrations in north Burma. The Americans, however, regarded these as reflecting the characteristic British enthusiasm for sideshows at the expense of major operations. They favoured *Buccaneer*, a big coastal landing in Burma. The British, however, now argued that Mediterranean action, not to mention *Overlord*, would be fatally compromised by diverting landing craft to the Bay of Bengal.

At the second plenary session on the 24th, Churchill complained vigorously about the loss of Kos and Leros. He also said it was untrue that he favoured unlimited operations in Italy: he was committed to *Overlord* 'up to the hilt'. But he sought agreement that Allied armies should aim to reach a line between Pisa and Rimini. Eisenhower addressed the conference on the 26th. He was still only Mediterranean supreme commander, unaware that *Overlord* would soon become his personal responsibility. He said that he supported British aspirations both in the valley of the Po and the Aegean. 'He stressed the vital importance of continuing the maximum possible operations in an established theatre since much time was invariably lost when the scene of action was changed.' This was welcome to Churchill, if not to Marshall.

The conference's British administrators were at pains to offer hospitality matching that which the Americans had provided at Casablanca in January. But given Britain's impoverished state, they were embarrassed by their guests' locust-like response. The assembled throng of officials and service officers accounted for 20,000 cigarettes and seventy-five cigars. Each day, 500 beers, eighty bottles of whisky, twelve of brandy, and thirty-four of gin were consumed. It was decided that at future summits, out of respect for the rationed people of Britain, those attending should at least be asked to pay for their own drinks.

Between sessions, Churchill took Roosevelt to see the Pyramids, and talked enthusiastically to his staff about the warmth of their relationship. Yet Eden described the Cairo conference as 'among the most difficult I ever attended'. British fortunes in the Far East were at their lowest ebb. Imperial forces were apparently incapable of breaking through into Burma in the face of a numerically inferior Japanese army. Given Roosevelt's rambling approach to business, 'W. had to play the role of courtier and seize opportunities as and when they arose. I am amazed at the patience with which he does this . . . Though the role of attendant listener was uncongenial to him, the Prime Minister played it faultlessly all these days, so that we came through without the loss of any feathers, if not with our tails up.' But presidential needling of the prime minister was more pronounced than usual. Roosevelt reproached Churchill for allowing Eden to tell the king of Greece not to attempt to return home once his country was liberated until it was plain that his subjects wanted him. This was an odd intervention, given the Americans' subsequent hostility to the monarch. The British were furious with the president for encouraging Greek intractability.

Churchill lamented to the British delegation Roosevelt's casual approach to business, observing that while he was 'a charming country gentleman', his dilatory habits wasted time. The prime minister and his colleagues were surprised and irked by the Americans' failure to hold bilateral discussions with them before meeting Stalin. 'PM and President *ought* to have got together, with their staffs, before meeting the Russians but that through a series of mischances has not happened,' mused Cadogan. The British were slow to perceive that such evasion reflected policy rather than 'mischances'. This would be the president's first meeting with Stalin. Earlier in the year Roosevelt had sought a meeting with the Soviet leader without Churchill present. When his initiative came to nothing he coolly lied to the prime minister, asserting that the proposal had originated with Moscow, not himself. Roosevelt believed that he could forge a working relationship with Moscow, which must not be compromised by any appearance of excessive Anglo–American amity or collusion. It did not trouble him that to such an end Churchill must be discomfited.

Hopkins bemoaned the prime minister's 'bloody Italian war', and warned Moran: 'We are preparing for a battle at Tehran. You will find us lining up with the Russians.' The doctor wrote wonderingly of the American attitude to Churchill: 'They are far more sceptical of him than they are of Stalin.' Hopkins's enthusiasm for the prime minister had diminished, and so too had his influence in his own country. Roosevelt's secretary wrote pityingly: 'Poor Harry, the public is done with him. He is a heavy liability to the President.' The US delegation in Cairo leaked freely to correspondents. The *Washington Post* was among many newspapers which afterwards disclosed to the American public 'the reported recalcitrance of Churchill' towards US strategic wishes. No military agreements between the British and Americans had been reached by 27 November, when *Sextant* adjourned for the principals to fly on to Tehran.

Churchill seldom showed much concern for his own security, but raised an eyebrow when his car was almost engulfed by crowds as the convoy approached the British Legation in the Persian capital. Roosevelt had accepted lodgings in the Russian compound next door, and chose to meet Stalin for the first time alone. The opening session of the summit took place on the afternoon of 28 November, in the Soviet embassy under Roosevelt's chairmanship. It bears emphasis that, for every participant with a scintilla of imagination, these gatherings were awesome occasions. Even Brooke, tired and cynical, found it 'quite enthralling' to behold the 'Big Three' for the first time assembled together around a table. Those present knew that they were sharing in the making of history. Most strove to speak and act in a fashion worthy of the moment.

Churchill began by asserting his firm commitment to an advance to the Pisa–Rimini line in Italy; to a landing in southern France; and to *Overlord*, provided his preconditions about maximum German strength in the invasion area were met. 'It will be our stern duty,' he said, in a trumpet blast notably discordant with his haverings about the operation, 'to hurl across the Channel against the Germans every sinew of our strength.' Stalin enquired smoothly: 'Who will command *Overlord*?' This was a brilliant shaft. He said that he could not regard any operation entirely seriously until a leader had been named to direct it. Though Eden found Stalin's personality 'creepy' and chilling, like all the Western delegates the Foreign Secretary recognised a master of diplomacy: 'Of course the man was ruthless and of course knew his purpose. He never wasted a word. He never stormed, he was seldom even irritated. Hooded, calm, never raising his voice, he avoided the repeated negatives of Molotov which were so exasperating to listen to. By more subtle methods he got what he wanted without having seemed so obdurate.'

Roosevelt assured the Russian leader that a commander for *Overlord* would be appointed within days. Stalin – 'Ursus Major', as Churchill christened 'the Great Bear' – was satisfied. He even professed enthusiasm for the Italian campaign, despite his dismay that German divisions were still being transferred from the west to fight in Russia. Churchill praised the efforts of Tito's communist partisans in Yugoslavia, which he assumed would please Stalin, and declared his eagerness to provide them with greater assistance. The Russian leader said that the Soviet Union would enter the war against Japan as soon as Germany was defeated, which gratified the Americans.

Early each morning of the summit, NKVD officers – who included Beria's son Sergo – presented Stalin with transcripts of conversations intercepted by microphones planted in the American residence.

The Soviet leader expressed amazement at the freedom with which the Westerners talked among themselves, when they must realise that they were being overheard. Latterly, indeed, he began to wonder whether they were really so naïve that they did not guess: 'Do you think they know that we are listening?' He was gratified to find Roosevelt speaking well of him. Once, noting the president's assertion that there was 'no way to fool Uncle Joe', he grinned into his moustache and muttered: 'The old rascal is lying.' He was less amused by transcribed exchanges in which Churchill repeated to the president his reservations about *Overlord*. Young Beria was rewarded with a Swiss watch for the efficiency of his eavesdropping.

The most notorious episode at the conference arose from Stalin's brutal jest about shooting 50,000 German officers once the war was won, followed by Roosevelt's rejoinder that 49,000 would suffice. Elliott Roosevelt, the president's son, rose to say that he cordially agreed with Stalin's proposal, and was sure that the US would endorse it likewise. This caused Churchill to storm from the room in disgust. The Russians soothed the prime minister, but it was a grisly moment. When Stalin made his sally, Churchill knew him to be responsible for the cold-blooded massacre of at least 10,000 Polish officers – the true figure was almost 30,000 – as well as countless of his own people. Moreover, the US president's willingness to join in the joke suggested a heartlessness which was real enough, and which shocked the British leader. Finally, Elliott Roosevelt's intervention was intolerable. It was a curiosity of the war that great men saw fit to take their children on missions of state. Randolph Churchill's presence in North Africa, and everywhere else, was an embarrassment. Jan Smuts and Harry Hopkins both brought their sons to Cairo for *Sextant*. But none matched the crassness of the president's offspring. Churchill knew that, to sustain the Anglo–American relationship, he must endure almost anything which Roosevelt chose to say or do. But that moment in Tehran was hard for him. Marshall said of Stalin at the conference: 'He was turning his hose on Churchill all the time, and Mr Roosevelt, in a sense, was helping him. He [FDR] used to take a little delight in embarrassing Churchill.'

Cadogan recorded the distress of the British delegation that Roosevelt seemed willing to endorse almost everything Stalin proposed. When the future boundaries of Poland were discussed, Averell Harriman was dismayed by his president's visible indifference. Roosevelt wanted only enough to satisfy Polish-American voters, which was not much. Soviet eavesdroppers reported to Stalin Churchill's private warnings to Roosevelt about Moscow's preparations to install a communist government in Poland. According to Sergo Beria, Roosevelt replied that since Churchill was attempting to do the same thing by installing an anti-communist regime, he had no cause for complaint.

The American leader was much more interested in promoting Soviet support for the future United Nations organisation, an easy ball for the Russians to play. They indulged Roosevelt by ready acquiescence, though even Stalin expressed scepticism about the president's vision of China joining Russia, Britain and the US to police the post-war world. Harriman perceived the danger of flaunting before the Russians Roosevelt's carelessness about East European borders. The relentless advance of Stalin's armies would have rendered it difficult for the West to stem Soviet imperialism. Churchill was by now reconciled to shifting Poland's frontiers westwards, compensating the Poles with German territory for their eastern lands to be ceded to Russia. That proposal represented ruthlessness enough. But the US president's behaviour went further, making plain that Stalin could expect little opposition to his designs in Poland or elsewhere.

Roosevelt, bent upon creating a future in which the Great Powers acted in concert, seemed heedless of reality: that Stalin cared nothing for consensus, and was interested only in licence for pursuing his own unilateral purposes. Among the American team, Charles Bohlen and George Kennan of the State Department shared Harriman's misgivings about Roosevelt's belief that he shared a world vision with Stalin. The prime minister's fears for the future began to coalesce. 'That the President should deal with Churchill and Stalin as if they were people of equal standing in American eyes shocked Churchill profoundly,' wrote Ian Jacob.

Yet most of Roosevelt's delegation left the summit basking in a glow of satisfaction created by the formal commitment to *Overlord*, so long desired by both the US and Soviet Union. The persistent evasiveness of the British on this issue irked even the most anglophile Americans. The Tehran experience afterwards yielded one of Churchill's great sallies. The meeting, he said, caused him to realise how small Britain was: 'There I sat with the great Russian bear on one side of me, with paws outstretched, and on the other side the great American buffalo, and between the two sat the poor little English donkey who was the only one . . . who knew the right way home.'

Stalin was highly satisfied with the Tehran talks, at which he perceived himself as getting all that he wanted. He thought the US president a truth-teller, as Churchill was not, and told the Stavka on his return to Moscow: 'Roosevelt has given a firm commitment to launch large-scale operations in France in 1944. I think he will keep his word. But if he does not, we shall be strong enough to finish off Hitler's Germany on our own.'

Eden thought the 1943 meetings with the Russians the most satisfactory, or least unsatisfactory, of the war, before the steep deterioration of relations during 1944, when Soviet expansionism became explicit. But the British delegation at Tehran deplored the manner in which the Big Three's discussions roamed erratically across a wilderness of issues, bringing none to a decisive conclusion save that even Churchill would thereafter have found it difficult to escape the *Overlord* commitment. Cunningham and Portal declared the conference a waste of time. The British were especially dismayed that no attempt was made to oblige the Russians to recognise the legitimacy of the Polish exile government in London, in return for Anglo-American acceptance of Poland's altered borders.

After Tehran, Churchill cannot have failed to understand, in his own heart at least, how little Roosevelt cared for Britain, its interests or stature. Not for a moment did the prime minister relax his efforts to woo and cajole the president. But it became progressively harder for him to address the United States than Russia. With Stalin, Churchill continued to seek bargains, but his expectations were pitched low. The American relationship, however, was fundamental to every operation of war, to feeding the British people, to all prospect of sustaining the Empire in the post-war world. It seems extraordinary that some historians have characterised the relationship between Roosevelt and Churchill as a friendship. To be sure, the prime minister embraced the president in speech and correspondence as 'my friend'. In no aspect of his life and conduct as Britain's leader did he display more iron self-control than in his wartime dealings with the Americans. 'Every morning when I wake,' he once said, 'my first thought is how I can please President Roosevelt.' But much of what FDR served up to Churchill between 1943 and 1945 was gall and wormwood.

From Tehran, while Roosevelt went home to Washington, Churchill flew to Cairo. He was tired and indeed ill, yet meetings and dinners crowded in upon each other. He rebuked Mountbatten by signal for demanding the services of 33,700 fighting soldiers to address 5,000 Japanese in the Arakan – 'The Americans have been taking their islands on the basis of two-and-a-half to one. That your Generals should ask for six-and-a-half to one has produced a very bad impression.' He dined at the embassy on 10 December with a party which included Smuts, Eden, Cadogan and Randolph Churchill, then took off at 1 a.m. for Tunisia. His York landed at the wrong airfield, where Brooke saw him 'sitting on his suitcase in a very cold morning wind, looking like nothing on earth. We were there about an hour before we moved on and he was chilled through by then.'

After another brief flight they landed again, this time in the right place, and he was driven to Maison Blanche, Eisenhower's villa near Carthage. On 11 December he slept all day, then dined with Ike, Brooke, Tedder and others. He went to bed in pain from his throat. At 4 a.m. Brooke was awakened by a plaintive voice crying out, 'Hulloo, Hulloo, Hulloo.' The CIGS switched on a torch and demanded crossly: 'Who the hell is that?' His beam fell upon the prime minister in his dragon dressing gown, a brown bandage around his head, complaining of a headache and searching for his doctor.

Next day Churchill had a temperature, and Moran telegraphed for nurses and a pathologist. He was diagnosed with pneumonia.

Over the following days, though he continued to see visitors and dispatch a stream of signals, he lay in bed, knowing that he was very ill. 'If I die,' he told his daughter Sarah, 'don't worry – the war is won.' On 15 December he suffered a heart attack. Sarah read *Pride and Prejudice* aloud to him. News of Churchill's illness unleashed a surge of sentiment and sympathy among his people. A British soldier in North Africa wrote in his diary: 'We all hope and pray that he will recover. It would be a great thing if Mr Churchill will live to see the victorious end to his great fight against the Nazis.' On the afternoon of the 17th, Clementine Churchill arrived, escorted by Jock Colville, who had been recalled from the RAF to the Downing Street secretariat. The new M & B antibiotics were doing their work. While the prime minister remained weak, and suffered a further slight heart attack, he no longer seemed in peril of death. On the 19th Clementine wrote to her daughter Mary: 'Papa much better today. Has consented not to smoke and to drink only weak whisky and soda.'

He was now fuming about the 'scandalous . . . stagnation' of the Italian campaign, and especially about the failure to use available landing craft to launch an amphibious assault behind the German front. He urged Roosevelt to give swift consideration to British proposals for new command arrangements in the Mediterranean, now that Dwight Eisenhower had been named to direct *Overlord*. Roosevelt would almost certainly have given this role to Marshall, had the British been willing to agree that the chief of the army should become super-commander-in-chief of all operations against the Germans, in the Mediterranean as well as in north-west Europe. But Churchill and Brooke were determined to preserve at least one key C-in-C's appointment for a British officer. The president was unwilling to spare Marshall from Washington merely to command *Overlord*. On those terms he preferred to keep the chief of the army at home, as overall director of the US war effort.

The British chiefs of staff wanted Maitland-Wilson to succeed Eisenhower as Mediterranean supremo, and Air Chief Marshal Sir

Arthur Tedder to become Ike's deputy for *Overlord*. Churchill favoured Alexander for British commander on D-Day – as also did Eisenhower. The war cabinet demurred, urging Montgomery in deference to public opinion as well as military desirability. Surprisingly, Churchill acceded to their view. This was certainly the right appointment, for Montgomery was a much superior general. But it was unusual for Churchill to allow himself to be balked by ministers on a matter of such importance. Most likely, willingness to allow Alexander to remain in Italy reflected the importance he attached to operations there. He believed, mistakenly, that 'Alex' could provide the impetus which he perceived as lacking. Macmillan strongly urged Alexander's appointment, noting that Maitland-Wilson had been Middle East C-in-C for a year, yet had done nothing to galvanise the slothful British war machine in Egypt. The Americans finally acceded to British wishes for Alexander to take over in the Mediterranean, precisely because they attached much less importance to Italy than to *Overlord*.

On 22 December the British chiefs of staff signalled from London that they supported Churchill's proposal for a new amphibious assault in Italy. Initial planning assumed that there was only enough shipping to move a single division, while both Churchill and the chiefs wanted to land two. On Christmas Day, Eisenhower, Maitland-Wilson, Alexander, Tedder and Cunningham converged by air upon Carthage from all over the Mediterranean to discuss plans for Operation *Shingle*, a descent on Anzio, just south of Rome, provisionally scheduled for 20 January. The meeting endorsed a two-division initial assault, subject to the proviso that it should not threaten the May date for *Overlord*.

On 27 December Churchill flew to Marrakesh for a prolonged spell of recuperation. 'I propose to stay here in the sunshine,' he wrote to Roosevelt, 'till I am quite strong again.' On his second day at the Villa Taylor, to his surprise and delight he learned that the president had approved *Shingle*, subject only to renewed emphasis upon the sanctity of the French invasion date. This, however, was now to be put back a month, until June, at the insistence of

Eisenhower and Montgomery. Having studied the D-Day plan for the first time, they were convinced that additional preparation, as well as a reinforced initial landing, were essential. The new date would fall in the first week of June. Churchill was hostile to the use of the word 'invasion' in the context of D-Day: 'Our object is the liberation of Europe from German tyranny . . . we "enter" the oppressed countries rather than "invade" them and . . . the word "invasion" must be reserved for the time when we cross the German frontier. There is no need for us to make a present to Hitler of the idea that he is the defender of a Europe we are seeking to invade.' This was, of course, one semantic dispute which he lost.

On 4 January 1944 he wrote to Eden: 'I am getting stronger every day . . . All my thoughts are on "*Shingle*", which as you may well imagine I am watching intensely.' His convalescence in Marrakesh ended on 14 January. He flew to Gibraltar, where Maitland-Wilson and Cunningham gave him a final briefing on the Anzio plan. Then he boarded the battleship *King George V* to sail home. On the night of 17 January he landed at Plymouth, where he joined the royal train which had been sent to fetch him. Next morning, after an absence from England of nine weeks, he reached Downing Street. He cabled Roosevelt: 'Am all right except for being rather shaky on my pins.' Arriving at Buckingham Palace for lunch with the King, a private secretary asked if he would like the lift. 'Lift?' demanded the indignant prime minister. He ran up the stairs two at a time, then turned and thumbed his nose at the courtier.

The House of Commons knew nothing of his return until MPs looked up in astonishment in the middle of Questions, leapt to their feet and began shouting, applauding and waving order papers. Harold Nicolson described how cheer after cheer greeted him, 'while Winston, very pink, rather shy, beaming with mischief, crept along the front bench and flung himself into his accustomed seat. He was flushed with pleasure and emotion, and hardly had he sat down when two large tears began to trickle down his cheeks. He mopped clumsily at himself with a huge white handkerchief. A few minutes later he got up to answer questions. Most men would have been unable, on such an occasion, not to throw a flash of drama into their replies. But Winston answered them as if he were the young Under-Secretary, putting on his glasses, turning over his papers, responding tactfully to supplementaries, and taking the whole thing as conscientiously as could be. I should like to say that he seemed completely restored to health. But he looked pale when the first flush of pleasure had subsided, and his voice was not quite as vigorous as it had been.' Churchill retained his extraordinary ability to hold the attention of the House through long, discursive assessments of the war. After one such, he suddenly leaned across to the opposition and demanded casually: 'That all right?' MPs grinned back affectionately. His mastery of the Commons, wrote Nicolson, derived from 'the combination of great flights of oratory with sudden swoops into the intimate and conversational'.

On the afternoon of 19 January, Churchill presided at a chiefs of staff meeting, during which he urged commando landings on the Dalmatian coast, progressively to clear of Germans the islands off Yugoslavia. His hopes for Anzio were soaring. He spoke of forcing the Germans to withdraw into northern Italy, or even behind the Alps. Then Alexander's armies would be free to pursue towards Vienna, to strike into the Balkans, or swing left into France. Two days later, as the American Maj.Gen. John Lucas's corps prepared to hit the beaches in Italy, the US Fifth Army staged crossings of the Rapido river south of Rome. Churchill cabled to Stalin: 'We have launched the big attack against the German armies defending Rome which I told you about at Tehran.' By midnight on the 22nd, 36,000 British and American troops and 3,000 vehicles were ashore at Anzio, having achieved complete surprise.

Yet through the days that followed, news from Italy turned sour. The Rapido crossings proved a disaster. The Germans snuffed out each precarious American bridgehead in turn. Kesselring acted with extraordinary energy, recovering from his astonishment about Anzio to concentrate troops and isolate the invaders. Four Allied divisions were soon ashore, yet going nowhere. As the Germans poured fire into the shallow beachhead, British and American soldiers manning their foxholes and gun positions found themselves trapped in one of the most painful predicaments of the war. 'We did become like animals in the end,' said a soldier of the Sherwood Foresters. 'You were stuck in the same place. You had nowhere to go. You didn't get no rest . . . No sleep . . . You never expected to see the end of it. You just forgot why you were there.'

Casualties mounted rapidly, and so too did desertions. Nowhere from the beach to the front line offered safety from bombardment. The Luftwaffe attacked offshore shipping with new and deadly glider bombs. 'It will be unpleasant if you get sealed off there and cannot advance from the south,' Churchill wrote to Alexander on 27 January. On 8 February he signalled to Dill in Washington: 'All this has been a disappointment to me.' It was true that German forces were tied down in Italy which would otherwise be fighting elsewhere. 'Even a battle of attrition is better than standing by and watching the Russians fight. We should also learn a good many lessons about how not to do it which will be valuable in "*Overlord*".' But these were poor consolations for what was, indubitably, one of the big Allied failures of the war.

Anzio was the last important operation which sprang from the personal inspiration of the prime minister. Without his support, neither Eisenhower nor Alexander could have persuaded the American chiefs of staff to provide means for such a venture. It reflected his passion for what Liddell Hart called 'the strategy of indirect approach', the exploitation of Allied command of the sea to sidestep the difficulties of frontal assault amid some of the most difficult terrain in the world. In principle, *Shingle* was valid. But to an extraordinary degree commanders failed to think through a plan for what was to happen once the troops got ashore. In this, the weakness of the Anzio operation closely resembled that of Churchill's other notorious amphibious failure, in the Dardanelles in 1915 – as American corps commander Maj.Gen. Lucas suggested before it began. Alexander, as commander-in-chief, must bear responsibility for the inadequacy of strategic planning for *Shingle*. He and his staff grossly underestimated the speed and strength of the German response, believing that the mere threat to Kesselring's rear would cause him to abandon the defence of his line at Monte Cassino. They never identified the importance of quick seizure of the hills beyond the Anzio beaches, a far more plausible objective than a dash for Rome. The Americans, always deeply sceptical, displayed better judgement about the landing's prospects than the British.

Moreover, all operations of war must be judged in the context of the forces available to carry them out. The Allies had insufficient shipping in the Mediterranean to put ashore an army large enough to risk a decisive thrust inland. Lucas has often been criticised for failure to strike towards Rome in the wake of his corps' successful landing. He was certainly a poor general. But had he done as the fire-eaters wished and pushed hard for the capital, he would have exposed a long, thin salient to counter-attack. The Germans always punished excessive boldness, as they would do a year later at Arnhem. The likeliest outcome of a dash for Rome from Anzio would have been the destruction of Lucas's corps. As it was, despite the four months of misery which the defenders of the Anzio perimeter now resigned themselves to endure, they were rewarded with belated success.

So bitter was the struggle on the coast, matched by the battle further south for the heights of Monte Cassino, that the Allies experienced little joy in the belated capture of Rome when it came in June 1944. But what took place was preferable to what might have been, had a more daring commander led the Anzio assault. *Shingle* confirmed the US chiefs of staff in their conviction that Italy offered only poisoned fruits. 'The more one sees of this peninsula, the less suited it seems for modern military operations,' wrote Harold Macmillan. The campaign could not be abandoned, but henceforward the Americans viewed it as a liability. They would support no more of Churchill's adventures, in the Mediterranean or anywhere else.

Events in Italy in the winter of 1943–44 once more highlighted the gulf between the prime minister's heroic aspirations and the limitations of Allied armies fighting the Germans. 'I gather we are still stronger than the enemy,' he signalled to Alexander on 10 February, 'and naturally one wonders why over 70,000 British and Americans should be hemmed in on the defensive by what are thought to be at most 60,000 Germans.' He wrote to Smuts on 27 February that his confidence in Alexander was 'undiminished', adding sadly: 'though if I had been well enough to be at his side as I had hoped at the critical moment, I believe I could have given the necessary stimulus. Alas for time, distance, illness and advancing years.' If the generals of Britain and America had been Marlboroughs or Lees, if their citizen soldiers had displayed the mettle of Spartans, they might have accomplished in the Mediterranean such great deeds as Churchill's imagination conceived for them. But they were not and did not. They were mortal clay, doing their best against an outstanding commander, Kesselring, and one of the greatest armies the world has ever seen.

Churchill had been right, in 1942 and 1943, to force upon the Americans campaigns in the Mediterranean, when there was nowhere else they could credibly fight. He told the House of Commons on 22 February: 'On broad grounds of strategy, Hitler's decision to send into the south of Italy as many as eighteen divisions, involving, with their maintenance troops, probably something like half a million Germans, and to make a large secondary front in Italy, is not unwelcome to the Allies . . . We must fight the Germans somewhere, unless we are to stand still and watch the Russians.' But by now there was a lameness about such an explanation. In 1944 Churchill's Italian vision was overtaken by that of *Overlord*, a huge and indispensable American conception. After Anzio, even the prime minister himself implicitly acknowledged this, and embraced the prospect of D-Day with increasing excitement. Though his enthusiasm for Mediterranean operations never subsided, he was obliged to recognise that the major battles in the west would be fought in France, not Italy.

In the spring of 1944, Churchill was full of apprehension not only about *Overlord*, but also about the mood of the British people. Several lost by-elections exposed voters' lack of enthusiasm for the coalition government, and weariness with the war. After an Independent Labour candidate in West Derbyshire on 18 February defeated the Tory Lord Hartington, who campaigned with the prime minister's conspicuous endorsement, Jock Colville wrote: 'Sitting in a chair in his study at the Annexe, the PM looked old, tired and very depressed and was even muttering about a General Election. Now, he said, with great events pending, was the time when national unity was essential, the question of annihilating great states had to be faced; it began to look as if democracy had not the persistence necessary to go through with it, however well it might have shewn its capacity of defence.' In Churchill's Commons speech of 22 February he delivered a contemptuous jab at his critics, 'little folk who frolic alongside the juggernaut of war to see what fun or notoriety they can extract from the proceedings'. Five days later, writing to Smuts, he alluded to such people again: 'their chirpings will presently be stilled by the thunder of the cannonade'. On 25 March, to Roosevelt, he wrote ruefully: 'We certainly do have plenty to worry us, now that our respective democracies feel so sure that the whole war is as good as won.' Tory MP Cuthbert Headlam wrote in April 1944: 'In the H of C smoking room a new leader is decided upon almost every other day.'

There was much to vex Churchill, the burden made heavier because so few of the difficulties and hazards could be publicly avowed. Countless hours were devoted to Poland. The Polish exile government in London was obdurately opposed to changes in its frontiers – the shift of the entire country a step westward – which Churchill had reluctantly accepted. Its representatives persisted in proclaiming their anger towards Moscow about the Katyn massacres. What adherent of freedom and democracy could blame them? Yet so astonishing was the popularity of Russia in Britain, that polls showed a decline in public enthusiasm for the Poles, because of their declared hostility to Moscow. Again and again the prime minister urged the exiles to mute their protests. Since Russia would soon possess physical mastery of their country, Soviet goodwill was indispensable to any possibility that they might share in its post-war governance. Stalin lied flatly to Churchill, asserting that he had no intention of influencing Poland's internal politics, and that the Poles would be free to choose their own post-war rulers. But in a stream of cables and letters the Soviet warlord vented his own anger, as real as it was base, about the London Poles' declarations of hostility to the Soviet Union.

It was plain to Churchill that the prospects of a free Poland were slender, and shrinking. Amid the exiles' rejections of his pleas for realism, his lonely battle to restore the nation to freedom was being lost. In all probability, nothing the Western Allies could have done would have saved Poland from Stalin's maw. There was one dominant, intractable reality: the Soviet Union's insistence upon exacting its price for the twenty-eight million Russians who died in the struggle to destroy Nazism. On 3 March, Eden asked Churchill to cable Moscow personally about the case of two Royal Navy seamen, seized in Murmansk after a drunken brawl and sentenced to penal servitude in Siberia. The prime minister wrote to the Foreign Secretary: 'I cannot send such a telegram which would embroil me with Bruin on a small point when so many large ones are looming up.' Instead, he suggested to Eden that questions in Parliament might generate useful publicity about the case: 'A little anti-Russian feeling in the House of Commons would be salutary at the present time.' When Sir John Anderson wrote to Churchill urging that the Russians should be told of the Allies' 'Tube Alloys' project – creation of the atomic bomb – Churchill scrawled in the margin of Anderson's minute: 'On no account.'

Eden wrote in his diary about Poland: 'Soviet attitude on this business raises most disquieting thoughts. Is Soviet regime one which will ever co-operate with the West?' A few days later he added: 'I confess to growing apprehension that Russia has vast aims and that these may include the domination of Eastern Europe and even the Mediterranean and the "communising" of much that remains.' In Italy, the Soviets refused to deal with the Allied Control Commission, and instead appointed their own ambassador with a mandate to embarrass the Anglo-Americans. It was painful for Churchill, who knew the truth about Stalin's tyranny and the perils posed by his ambitions, to be obliged to indulge the British people's romantic delusions, and to echo their gratitude for Russian sacrifices. Even as he was participating in an exceptionally harsh exchange of cables with Moscow on a range of issues, in a BBC broadcast on 26 March he nonetheless paid generous tribute to the Red Army. Its 1943 offensive, he said, 'constitutes the greatest cause of Hitler's undoing'. The Russian people had been extraordinarily fortunate to find, 'in their supreme ordeal and agony a warrior leader, Marshal Stalin, whose authority enables him to combine and control the movements of armies numbered by many millions upon a front of nearly 2,000 miles, and to impart a unity and a concert to the war direction in the East which has been very good for Russia and for all her Allies'. All this was true, but represented only a portion of reality.

Meanwhile, elsewhere, difficulties persisted with the French. Harold Macmillan wrote from Algiers: 'I would much rather get what we want – if we can – through the French rather than by imposing it on the French. But it is a difficult hand for me to play . . . the trouble is that neither the President nor the PM has any confidence in De Gaulle.' Churchill had adopted a jaundiced view ever since, at Brazzaville in the Congo in July 1941, the intransigent general gave an interview to the *Chicago Daily News* in which he suggested that Britain was 'doing a wartime deal with Hitler'. Churchill and Eden several times discussed the possibility that De Gaulle was mentally unhinged. The prime minister had become sick to death of his petulance and studied discourtesy. It seemed intolerable that Britain should struggle with Washington on behalf of Free France, which the Americans despised, and be rewarded only with ingratitude from its leader.

During Churchill's time in North Africa he spent many hours with Macmillan, De Gaulle and other prominent Frenchmen, seeking to sustain a veneer of unity. His efforts were sabotaged by De Gaulle's unilateralism. At one moment the general ordered the arrest of three prominent Vichyites in Algiers, which provoked an explosion of Churchillian exasperation. British politicians and diplomats exhausted themselves pleading before the prime minister the case for De Gaulle, a habitual offender facing a judge minded to don the black cap. After one exchange, Macmillan wrote: 'Much as I love Winston, I cannot stand much more.' Yet two days later, like almost every other close associate of the prime minister, he relented: 'He is really a remarkable man. Although he can be so tiresome and pig-headed, there is no one like him. His devotion to work and duty is quite extraordinary.'

Churchill's commitment to restoring France to its rightful position as a great nation never wavered. For this, and for fighting the Americans so staunchly in support of its interests, the British government merited, though never received, its Gallic neighbour's enduring gratitude. In Quebec the previous year, Eden argued fiercely with Cordell Hull about the virtues of French resurrection: 'We both got quite heated at one time when I told him we had to live twenty miles from France and I wanted to rebuild her as far as I could.' Macmillan observed that while Roosevelt hated De Gaulle, Churchill's sentiments were more complex: 'He feels about De Gaulle like a man who has quarrelled with his son. He will cut him off with a shilling. But (in his heart) he would kill the fatted calf if only the prodigal would confess his faults and take his orders obediently in future.' Since this would never happen, however, there were many moments in 1943–44 when, but for Eden's loyalty to De Gaulle, Churchill would have cut the Frenchman adrift.

Even now, with two million men training and arming in Britain for the invasion, Churchill chose to sustain the dangerous fiction – dangerous, because of the mistrust of himself which it fed among Americans – that *Overlord* still represented an option rather than an absolute commitment. In February he invited the chiefs of staff to review plans for *Jupiter* – an assault on north Norway – if the French landings failed. He convened a committee to report to him weekly on the progress of D-Day preparations, and wrote to Marshall on 15 February: 'I am hardening very much on this operation as the time approaches in the sense of wishing to strike if humanly possible, even if the limiting conditions we laid down at Tehran are not exactly fulfilled.' The conditional was still there, as it was in a message to Roosevelt which he drafted on 25 March: 'What is the latest date on which a decision can be taken as to whether "*Overlord*" is or is not to be launched on the prescribed date? . . . If . . . 20 or 25 mobile German divisions are already in France on the date in question, what are we going to do?' This cable, which would have roused the most acute American dismay, was withheld after prudent second thoughts. But it reflected Churchill's continuing uncertainty, ten weeks before D-Day.

In the Mediterranean, Harold Macmillan wrote: 'I am much distressed to see a worsening of Anglo–American relations generally since Eisenhower left and I am also not very hopeful of getting any new idea into the PM's mind at present.' There was much debate and many changes of heart about *Anvil*, a prospective landing in the south of France originally scheduled to coincide with the descent on Normandy. The British, having favoured the scheme, now turned sour because of its inevitable impact on Allied strength in Italy. On 21 March Maitland-Wilson signalled, recommending *Anvil*'s cancellation. After protracted exchanges with Washington, most about landing craft, it was agreed to postpone the operation. Churchill became increasingly sceptical, and finally absolutely hostile. He favoured diversionary landings by commandos on the Atlantic coast of France. He also remained resolute in his enthusiasm for an invasion of Sumatra, exasperating his own chiefs of staff and especially Brooke. They opposed the scheme on its merits, and also knew that the Americans would never provide the necessary shipping. Washington was interested only in an offensive into upper Burma, to open a China passage. This, with deep reluctance, the British finally agreed to undertake.

Churchill's closest wartime colleagues, above all the chiefs of staff, emerged from the Second World War asserting the prime minister's greatness as a statesman, while deploring his shortcomings as a strategist. Yet no Allied leader displayed unbroken wisdom. Churchill's grand vision of the war was superb. Even acknowledging his delusions about the future of the British Empire, he articulated the hopes and ambitions of the Grand Alliance as no other man, including

Roosevelt, was capable of doing. His record as a warlord should be judged by what was done rather than by what was said. He indulged many flights of fancy, but insisted upon realisation of very few. The 1943 Aegean adventure was an exception rather than a commonplace. The operation of the British war machine should not be assessed in isolation, but rather by comparison with those of Britain's allies and enemies, and for that matter against the experience of every other conflict in history. By that measure, Churchill presided over a system of military planning and political governance which was a model for all time.

If, as those who worked with him believed, in 1944–45 he was no longer what he had been in 1940–41, this is not to be wondered at. Smuts told Eden after a lunch of the prime minister's: 'He may be mentally the man he was, he may be, but he certainly is not physically. I fear he overestimates his strength and he will wear himself out if he is not careful.' The wise old South African took care to say this within earshot of the prime minister. Ismay was wryly amused by the sternness with which Smuts often urged on Churchill the care of his health, admonishing him for overstaying his bedtime. The prime minister responded 'rather like a small boy being sent off by his mother'.

For all Churchill's exhaustion and ill health, his personal fearlessness persisted. He loved to watch the Luftwaffe's occasional night attacks from a Whitehall roof. 'The raids are very fine to look at now,' he wrote to Randolph, who was in Yugoslavia, on 4 April, 'because of the brilliant red flares which hang seemingly motionless in the air, and the bright showers of incendiaries . . . sometimes I go to Maria's battery [Mary Churchill's anti-aircraft position] and hear the child ordering the guns to fire.' This was a lovely line. On 4 March, Jock Colville described the prime minister on a Saturday at Chequers:

Late at night, after the inevitable film, the PM took his station in the Great Hall and began to smoke Turkish cigarettes – the first time I have ever seen him smoke one – saying that they were the only thing he got out of the Turks. He keeps on referring to the point that he has not long to live and tonight, while the gramophone played the Marseillaise and Sambre et Meuse, he told Coningham, Harold Macmillan, Pug, Tommy and me that this was his political testament for after the war: 'Far more important than India or the Colonies or solvency is the Air. We live in a world of wolves – and bears.' Then we had to listen to most of Gilbert and Sullivan on the gramophone, before retiring at 3.0am.

A mooted Easter meeting with Roosevelt on Bermuda was aborted because the president was ill – indeed, his health never recovered from the strains of the Tehran conference. Brooke, Moran and others anyway opposed any further long flights by the prime minister. His desire to see Roosevelt was driven more by restlessness and exaggerated faith in his own persuasive powers than by any real need for a summit. On 4 April 1944, Churchill told the House of Commons that 197,005 of the United Kingdom's people had perished since the war began in September 1939. This figure omitted many others who were posted merely as missing, but would never come home. The public, and even some of those closest to power, perceived the war as entering its final phase. Churchill himself never succumbed to such a delusion, above all in the shadow of *Overlord*. Another hundred thousand Britons had yet to die before victory would be won. He must rouse himself, and his people, for new exertions.

SEVENTEEN

Setting Europe Ablaze

The spring and summer of 1944 witnessed a flowering, albeit imperfect in the prime minister's eyes, of one of his most cherished inspirations: Resistance in occupied Europe and the Balkans. Back in 1940, Churchill famously ordered the Minister of Economic Warfare, Hugh Dalton: 'Set Europe ablaze.' This instruction prompted the creation of Special Operations Executive, a secret organisation charged with promoting resistance – explicitly terrorism, armed action by non-uniformed civilians – everywhere that the Axis held sway. By submarine and small boat, plane and parachute, British-trained agents descended on Europe, and later South-East Asia, to establish contact with those willing to raise the banner of opposition to tyranny, albeit by means unsanctioned in the Geneva Convention. Events in France have received most attention from post-war chroniclers, though Resistance in Yugoslavia achieved much greater strategic significance, as Churchill perceived from 1943 onwards.

The men and women of SOE helped to create one of the enduring legends of World War II. It seemed then, as it still does today, especially heroic to risk torture and death alone, far behind enemy lines. Support for domestic insurrection represented a personal act of faith by the prime minister, which ran contrary to the views of many of his service advisers. He cherished a belief that the peoples of Europe could play an important part in their own liberation, declaring on 10 June 1941: 'We shall aid and stir the people of every conquered country to resistance and revolt. We shall break up and derange every effort which Hitler makes to systematize and consolidate his subjugation.' At the prime minister's behest, a War Office planning document the same month addressed the promotion of Resistance: 'Subjugated peoples must be caused to rise against their oppressors, but not until the stage is set. The "attack from within" is the basic concept of such operations – and we should be able to do it in a bigger way than did the Germans. They had but a few Quislings to help them, and we have whole populations. The Patriots must be secretly organised and armed with personal weapons to be delivered to them by air if necessary.'

Churchill anticipated that indigenous peoples would play a major part in their own liberation. If the US entered the war, he wrote in a minute to Portal, the chief of air staff, on 7 October 1941, there would be 'simultaneous attacks by armoured forces in many of the conquered countries which were ripe for revolt'. In a paper of 15 June 1942 he cited 'rousing the populations' among the first objectives of Allied landings on the Continent. The mission of SOE was to hasten such ripening and 'rousing'. In many books published even in the twenty-first century, accounts of what took place in the attempt to fulfil his vision are heavily coloured by romance. Reality was at least as inter-esting, but much more complex.

In June 1940, expressing to Canadian premier Mackenzie King his uncertainty about whether France would stay in the war, Churchill wrote: 'I hope they will, even at the worst, maintain a gigantic guerrilla.' In the event, through the first years of occupa-tion, France and the rest of Western Europe remained passive. Acts of violent opposition were sporadic. It took time for the trauma of defeat to be overcome, for like-minded defiant spirits to meet and coalesce into groups. The British were in no condition to offer assist-ance. Most important, only a tiny minority of people were willing actively to oppose the Germans. In the matter of Resistance, as in so much else, Churchill's heroic enthusiasm struck little resonance with the mood of Europe's citizens, preoccupied with more humdrum concerns. They needed to feed their families, earn wages, preserve roofs above their heads. All these simple human purposes were put at risk – mortal risk – by any defiance of the occupiers.

Violent demonstrations flew in the face of national consensuses. It was not that people liked the Germans, but that acquiescence in their hegemony appeared to represent the only rational course. Such prominent figures as the French writer André Gide, who utterly rejected collaboration with the occupiers, nonetheless dismissed the notion of violent opposition. Until the Soviet Union and United States entered the war, Hitler's grasp upon his empire was beyond military challenge. Britain's prime minister uttered stirring words, echoed by broadcasters speaking from London in many languages to oppressed peoples, but no British army was capable of re-entering the Continent. This made most people in Hitler's new dominions unwilling to threaten the welfare of their own societies by actions which promised retribution.

Even for those who wanted to fight, Churchill underestimated the difficulties of conducting guerrilla operations against an efficient and ruthless occupier in heavily urbanised regions of Europe. In Denmark, Holland, Belgium and large parts of France, there were few hiding places for armed bands. The Germans adopted policies designed to promote passivity. Any action against their forces brought down punishment upon entire communities. On 27 May 1941, Churchill sent a note to Lord Selborne, Dalton's successor at the Ministry of Economic Warfare, suggesting providing oppressed people with simple weapons and sticks of dynamite. Yet the use of 'simple weapons' by such 'oppressed people' provoked determinedly disproportionate German responses. On 20 October that year, an Alsatian communist shot dead the German military commandant of Nantes, and made good his escape. Historian Robert Gildea has written: 'Far from welcoming this assassination as the first step towards their liberation, the population of Nantes was horrified,' not least because the dead German seemed to local bourgeois an unusually sympathetic personality, though a ruthless anti-Semite. Ninety-eight civilian hostages were executed. This caused Maurice Schumann to broadcast from London on the BBC French Service, urging that such terrorist action should not be repeated. De Gaulle delivered the same message on 23 October: 'In war there are tactics. The war of the

French must be carried out by those in charge, that is, by myself and the National Committee.'

Churchill, however, dissented. He believed that it was essential to impose maximum pain and inconvenience upon the enemy. He deemed the deaths of hostages a necessary sacrifice for enabling the French people to show that they would not bow to tyranny, as most had indeed bowed since June 1940. He once told a meeting of the cabinet defence committee that while acts of resistance prompted bloody reprisals, 'the blood of the Martyrs was the seed of the Church'. The behaviour of Hitler's minions in occupied Europe had made the Germans hated as no other race had been hated, he said, and this sentiment must be exploited. He deplored any attempt to stifle resistance in the interests of innocent bystanders: 'Nothing must be done which would result in the falling off of this most valuable means of harassing the enemy.' This was an extension of the view he adopted when Britain was threatened with invasion. In 1940, Generals Paget and Auchinleck urged that the civil population should be told to stay at home, rather than risk their lives offering ineffectual resistance to the Germans with scythes and brickbats. The prime minister strongly disagreed. In war, he said, quarter is given not on grounds of compassion, but to deter the enemy from fighting to the end: 'Here, we want every citizen to fight desperately and they will do so the more if they know that the alternative is massacre.' What he expected from British civilians in 1940, he sought thereafter from those of occupied Europe.

Here was Churchill at his most ruthless. He was constantly fearful that, left to itself, Europe would lapse into subservience to Hitler's hegemony. It provoked his chagrin that few French people rallied to De Gaulle's standard not only in 1940, but through the years which followed. Usefully for Churchill's aspirations, Germany adopted towards most of its European empire policies so shamelessly selfish, as well as brutal, that even the rulers of Vichy France came progressively to understand that they could forge no partnership with their occupiers. Berlin wanted only economic plunder. Hitler's policies thus assisted those of Churchill.

Yet, at least until after D-Day in 1944, reprisals convinced most people in the occupied countries that the cost of violent acts outweighed their value. The Norwegians, though strongly anti-German, conducted resistance with notable prudence. Norwegian special forces dispatched from Britain attacked occasional important targets, such as the Rjukan heavy water plant, but local people avoided open combat. In Czechoslovakia, the killing of Reinhard Heydrich, 'Protector' of Bohemia and Moravia, on 27 May 1942 by Czechs parachuted from Britain, prompted shocking reprisals, most notoriously the slaughter of the 198 men of the village of Lidice, whose women were dispatched to concentration camps. Local Resistance groups were smashed. Many Czechs believe to this day that the assassination was mistaken, because it was purchased so dearly in innocent lives.

In France, the detonation of a roadside bomb in Marseilles prompted the Germans to demolish the entire *vieux quartier* of the city, making 40,000 people homeless. Terrasson, a pretty little town in south-central France, suffered heavily both from Resistance activism and German reprisals. 'The cycle is simple,' its mayor Georges Labarthe wrote wretchedly to his mother in Paris in June 1944: 'The *maquis* conduct an operation, the Germans arrive, the civil population pay the tariff, the Germans go away and the *maquis* reappear. Where there are casualties among the Germans, the retribution is terrible. I must confess that in these circumstances it is hard to be the representative and defender of the people.'

In Western Europe Resistance achieved its greatest strength in wildernesses which mattered least to Hitler strategically – those most remote from potential invasion coasts. An overwhelming majority of people with large possessions – the aristocracy and the business community – collaborated with the occupiers, because they had most to lose. Many SOE agents captured by the Germans were betrayed by local inhabitants. British officers relied for assistance and shelter chiefly upon the little people of their societies – schoolteachers, trades unionists, peasant farmers. Only 20 per cent of letters opened by French censors even late in the war, in the first six months of 1944, expressed approval of 'terrorism'. A typical comment was: 'The *maquis* act in the name of patriotism, but fortunately the police are getting tough and I hope with all my heart that these youths are soon destroyed, for they commit all kinds of atrocities on innocent people.' Julian Jackson writes: 'Other evidence exists that *maquis* violence was widely condemned.' In the Jura, where terrible German acts of savagery took place in 1944, some local doctors refused to tend Resistance wounded. Many people refused fugitives shelter. Priests declined to say prayers for the dying. In Haute-Saône, the Vichyite prefect noted: 'Less and less do the terrorists enjoy the complicity of the rural population.' Extreme repression, unbridled brutality, fuelled hatred but also fear. German policy was notably effective in suppressing dissent.

Churchill envisaged the peoples of Europe causing such trouble for the Germans that occupation became costly, even unviable. Yet untrained and ill-organised civilians could never aspire to defeat regular troops. 'What is an army without artillery, tanks and air force?' demanded Stalin contemptuously about the Polish Resistance. 'In modern warfare such an army is of little use.' He was by no means wrong. The objection of many decent and patriotic Europeans to Resistance was that its sluggishly mounting tempo of violence sufficed to annoy the Germans, but imposed no crisis upon them. With brave and notable exceptions, it may be suggested that Resistance was most enthusiastically supported by those, both British and people of the occupied nations, who had no personal stake in local communities vulnerable to reprisals.

Some senior British officers opposed SOE's mandate on both pragmatic and ethical grounds. They perceived the unlikelihood of stimulating successful mass revolt, such as Churchill wanted, and were uncomfortable about promoting terrorism by armed civilians. The Chief of Air Staff, Portal, in February 1941 attempted to insist that one of the first SOE parties parachuted into France should wear uniform: 'I think the dropping of men dressed in civilian clothes for the purpose of attempting to kill members of the opposing forces is not an operation with which the Royal Air Force should be associated,' he told Gladwyn Jebb of the Foreign Office. 'I think you will agree that there is a vast difference, in ethics, between the time-honoured operation of the dropping of a spy from the air, and this entirely new scheme for dropping what one can only call assassins.' Such fastidiousness may seem ironic when displayed by one of the architects of area bombing. But it illustrates the sentiments of many senior service officers. Others, such as Sir Arthur Harris of Bomber Command, became fanatical foes of SOE, because they resented the diversion of aircraft to supporting its networks.

Sir Stewart Menzies and his subordinates of the Secret Intelligence Service hated their amateur rivals first on Whitehall territorial grounds, and second because in the field ambushes and acts of sabotage excited the Germans and made more difficult discreet intelligence-gathering by SIS's agents. An early SOE hand in the Middle East, Bickham Sweet-Escott, wrote of his own introduction to cloak and daggery: 'Nobody who did not experience it can possibly imagine the atmosphere of jealousy, suspicion, and intrigue which embittered relations between the various secret and semi-secret departments in Cairo during that summer of 1941.' Matters were not much better a year later, when Oliver Lyttelton was dispatched to the Mediterranean as minister resident. He recorded: 'I was disturbed . . . by the lack of security, waste and ineffectiveness of SOE.' The same strictures were often voiced in London.

Between 1940 and 1943, the highest achievement of SOE in most occupied countries was to keep agents alive and wireless transmitters functioning, with most success in rural areas. The Soviet Union's entry into the war prompted a dramatic accession of strength to Resistance, from Europe's communists. A second critical development in France was Germany's 1943 introduction of massed forced labour, known as the *Service de Travail Obligatoire*, STO. Tens of thousands of young men fled into hiding in the countryside, to the *maquis*, to escape deportation to Germany. They formed bands under leaders of differing and often mutually hostile political hues. Most were preoccupied with feeding themselves through banditry, which enraged its bourgeois victims, rather than with fighting the Germans. Many French people asserted bitterly after the war, in private at least, that the Germans behaved better than did communist *maquisards*. There is a widespread delusion that Resistance groups were commanded by SOE officers, but this was rarely so. Most British agents fulfilled a liaison role, exercising varying degrees of influence upon French group leaders through their control of cash and supply drops.

Above all, until the spring of 1944 Resistance was poorly armed. Only then did the Allies possess sufficient aircraft and weapons to begin equipping *maquisards* wholesale. A whimsical November 1941 proposal from Lord Cherwell, to drop containers of arms randomly across occupied Europe to encourage spontaneous acts of violence, was rejected as a waste of scarce air resources. Until the last months before liberation, sabotage and guerrilla operations in most European countries – with the notable exception of Yugoslavia, of which more below – were on a relatively tiny scale. The so-called *Armée Secrète*, which recognised the authority of De Gaulle, generally respected instructions from London to remain passive until the approach of D-Day. Communist bands of the FTP – *Franc-Tireurs et Partisans* – adopted more activist tactics, with ruthless disregard for the interests of local people.

Churchill loved to meet British agents and Frenchmen returned from their hazardous missions. He entertained at Downing Street Wing Commander Edmund Yeo-Thomas – 'the White Rabbit' – Jean Moulin and Emmanuel d'Astier de la Vigerie. Such encounters invariably prompted him to urge the RAF to divert more aircraft to aid their struggle. His personal enthusiasm for Resistance was critical in overcoming the scepticism of conventional warriors. It was sometimes said of the 'Baker Street Irregulars' that Britain was tipped on its side, and everything loose fell into SOE. Many of its personnel, unsurprisingly, were individualists and eccentrics. Their perspicacity often failed to match their enthusiasm. They cherished extravagant faith in their unseen protégés in occupied Europe. A sceptic remarked of Col. Maurice Buckmaster, chief of SOE's French Section: 'He believed that all his geese were swans.'

SOE's most conspicuous security lapse was its failure, despite many warnings, to perceive that the Germans had so deeply penetrated its Dutch operations that almost every agent parachuted into Holland in 1942–43 landed into enemy hands. The revelation of this disaster, at the end of 1943, precipitated a crisis in the organisation's affairs. Its Whitehall foes, of whom there were many, crowded forward to demand curtailment of its operations and calls on resources. Menzies and his colleagues at SIS argued that the débâcle reflected the chronic amateurishness and lack of tradecraft prevailing at SOE's Baker Street headquarters and pervading its operations in the field. They were by no means wrong. SOE since 1940 had indeed been learning on the job, at severe cost in life and wasted effort. Meanwhile in September 1943, the army's exasperation with SOE's Balkan operations, which it claimed were out of control, caused the C-in-C Middle East to demand that the organisation should be brought under his orders. This issue was still unresolved when the Dutch scandal broke.

On Churchill's return from Marrakesh in January 1944, he found the row appealed to himself. He renewed SOE's mandate (though rejecting its presumptuous demand for a seat on the chiefs of staff committee), confirmed its independence, and ordered the RAF to release more aircraft for arms-dropping. The organisation's internal historian wrote later: 'There is no doubt that, in this critical phase of its development, SOE and the Resistance movements which it led were sustained very largely by the personal influence of Mr Churchill.' The prime minister took the view that SOE's enthusiasm and activism outweighed its deficiencies. It was too late in the war to undertake wholesale restructuring. Much of the criticism of SOE, he believed, derived from Whitehall jealousies. It was impossible to conduct a secret war of such an unprecedented kind without misfortunes which cost lives, as do all mistakes in conflict.

Thus, in the last months before liberation, relatively large quantities of arms – though pathetically small quantities of ammunition – began to reach resisters. The British estimated that some 35,000 active *maquisards* were in the field, though De Gaulle claimed a strength of 175,000 for France's secret army. SOE believed that its *parachutages* provided weapons for 50,000. The intoxicating confidence thus created persuaded some groups to conduct disastrous pitched battles with the Germans. At Montmouchet on 20 May 1944 the regional *Armée Secrète* commander, Emile Coulaudon, ordered a mass concentration of his groups, 6,000 strong. On 10 June the Germans attacked them. At least 350 *maquisards* perished, while the remainder dispersed and fled. Local communities suffered devastating reprisals.

Another act of folly, the brief liberation of the town of Tulle in the Corrèze by the communist FTP for a few hours on 9 June, caused SS Panzergrenadiers to hang ninety-nine innocent hostages from the lampposts in reprisal for the alleged Resistance massacre of the elderly Wehrmacht reservists who had garrisoned the town. At Oradour-sur-Glane next day 642 men, women and children were slaughtered, in reprisal for the abduction by *maquisards* of a popular SS battalion commander. That day from London General Pierre Koenig, commander of the *Forces Françaises de l'Intérieur*, ordered a 'maximum brake on guerrilla activities'. Such a demand was at odds both with the mood of the moment and all previous briefing. It created confusion in the ranks of Resistance. On 17 June, Koenig issued a new order: 'continue elusive guerrilla activity to the maximum', while avoiding concentrations. This did not prevent the madness of the Vercors on 21 July, where 640 *maquisards* and 201 local civilians were killed as the Germans assaulted another ill-judged gathering of resistance forces.

Around 24,000 FFI fighters died during the struggle for France. Thousands more, most of them civilians, perished in reprisals and executions of prisoners, for instance 11,000 in and around Paris, 3,673 in Lyons, 2,863 in the Limoges area, 1,113 in Lille, and similar proportions in lesser cities, together with thousands of others deported to German concentration camps, from which most never returned. It seems doubtful whether it was useful or prudent to arm the French Resistance on a large scale. Churchill's enthusiasm caused the *maquis* to become dangerous enough to enrage the Germans, but insufficiently powerful to defend themselves or their communities. Most *maquisards* had only pistols or Sten sub-machine guns, with two or three magazines apiece. They lacked heavy weapons, ammunition and radio communications for sustained or large-scale engagements.

The courage and sacrifice of those who supported the Resistance, or even withheld support from Vichy, deserve the profound respect of posterity. But the moral achievement must be detached from cool analysis of the military balance. Post-war claims for the damage inflicted on the enemy by the French Resistance and its SOE sponsors were grossly exaggerated, as German war diaries make plain. Resistance historians, for instance, have claimed that the *maquis* inflicted hundreds of casualties upon the 2nd SS Das Reich armoured division on its march from southern France to Normandy in June 1944. German records, by contrast, reveal only thirty-five killed. The impact of *maquis* attacks on German communications that summer was infinitesimally smaller than that of Allied air attacks. Resistance fulfilled a striking moral function, especially important in resurrecting the post-war self-respect of occupied nations. But one of the best historians of the period, Julian Jackson, has written: 'In the history of France, Resistance is more important as a social and political phenomenon than a military one.'

The Balkans, however, were different. There, the terrain was much more favourable to guerrilla warfare. In Albania, Greece, Yugoslavia and also Italy, the prime minister perceived political circumstances and military opportunities which might yield dramatic benefits. New Zealand premier Peter Fraser urged caution on Churchill, sensibly observing that the Balkans was a region 'of seething factions, who would turn to whoever would give them most support'. But the prime minister believed that local passions could be harnessed to Allied purposes. It was often remarked by critics that the enthusiasm of the prime minister and SOE's agents reflected a 'T.E. Lawrence complex', wild delusions about the prospect that a few personable British officers might influence the behaviour of entire Balkan societies in support of British foreign policy objectives. American suspicions that imperialistic motives underpinned SOE caused Roosevelt in October 1943 to advance to Churchill a clumsy request, swiftly dismissed by the prime minister, for Colonel Donovan of the American OSS to assume authority for all Allied special operations in the Balkans.

From 1943 onwards, SOE lavished much effort upon Mediterranean countries, with mixed results. Some of its most flamboyant British officers, men such as Billy Maclean and David Smiley, were dropped into the mountains of Albania to work with local partisans. Almost without exception they loathed the country and its people. They found the Albanians far more eager to accept weapons and to steal equipment and supplies than to fight the Germans. 'How pleased I shall be to return to civilisation again,' a British officer confided to his diary, 'to be among people one can trust and not to be surrounded by dirt, filth and bad manners . . . It is not as if one was doing anything useful here or could do so. There is so little charity among these people that they cannot believe anyone would come all this way just to help them . . . They are boastful and vain with nothing to be boastful or vain about. They have no courage, no consistency and no sense of honour.'

Enver Hoxha, the Albanian communist leader who dominated guerrilla operations, was chiefly concerned to secure his own power base for a post-war takeover. It is easy to see why the Albanians, mired in poverty and a struggle for existence, showed so little enthusiasm for supporting the activist purposes of British missions. Guerrilla operations provoked the Germans to reprisals which SOE's teams were quite incapable of deflecting. Young British officers in Albania hazarded their own lives with considerable insouciance. Local peasants, however, saw their homes, crops and families imperilled, for no discernible advantage save to pursue a misty vision of 'freedom'. Beyond a few useful acts of sabotage, in Albania the military achievements of Resistance were slight.

Throughout the Balkans, internal political rivalries dogged British efforts to mobilise societies against their occupiers. In Greece and Crete, the population was overwhelmingly hostile to the Germans. The country had a long tradition of opposition to authority. Unfortunately, however, Greek society was racked by dissensions, the ferocity of which bewildered British officers thrust into their midst. There was no love for the king, nor for the Greek exile government backed by Churchill. Each guerrilla band cherished its own loyalties. Col. Monty Woodhouse, one of the most celebrated SOE officers who served among the Greeks, reported to Cairo: 'No one is ever free from the struggle for existence; everything else is secondary to it. That is why no one outside Greece can speak for the Greeks.' The British, on instructions from Cairo and ultimately from Churchill, were predisposed to support royalists. When Napoleon Zervas, leader of the relatively small republican group EDES, told SOE in 1943 that he backed the restoration of King George, he was rewarded by receiving twice the arms drops provided to the communists of EAM/ELAS, even though the communists were six times more numerous, and were doing all the fighting. Zervas repaid British largesse by establishing a tacit truce with the Germans, and biding his time to pursue his own purposes. As so often in occupied Europe, political and military objectives pulled British policy in different directions.

In 1944, realities on the ground seemed to make it essential to provide arms to the communists of ELAS, only some of which were employed against the Germans. Monty Woodhouse was recalled to Britain during the summer, and visited Churchill at Chequers to make the case for sustaining aid to ELAS. Woodhouse told the prime minister that if supplies to the communists were cut off, 'I very much doubt whether any of my officers will get out of Greece alive.' Churchill brooded for a moment, then took Woodhouse by the arm and said, 'Yes, young man, I quite understand.' As the British officer left Chequers, the prime minister said at parting: 'I am very impressed, and oppressed and depressed.' Albeit hesitantly, Churchill directed that aid to the communists should be maintained. British agents strove to persuade the Greeks to make common cause, but mutual hatreds were too strong. Moreover, every Resistance attack on the Germans provoked reprisals on a scale as dreadful as those in Russia and Yugoslavia, overlaid upon widespread starvation.

Nevertheless, Resistance in Greece became a more widespread popular movement than in Western Europe. Some spectacular acts of sabotage were carried out by SOE teams, notably the 1942 destruction of the Gorgopotamos viaduct. But 'pundits overestimated what guerrillas could achieve', in the words of Noel Annan, who served on the joint intelligence staff of the Cabinet Office. He asserts that such successes as the destruction of the Gorgopotamos came too late to be strategically useful, and made the planners in London over-optimistic. 'It took months for our liaison officers to persuade ELAS to blow up the bridge. Had it been destroyed earlier it would have cut one of Rommel's supply lines when he stood at El Alamein. But it was not ... The difficulties with ELAS should have warned the Foreign Office that ELAS's first objective was less to harass the Germans than to eliminate other guerrilla forces and their leaders.' Nick Hammond, a British officer with the Greeks, wrote afterwards: 'Armed resistance in the open countryside is something rarely undertaken. Only men of extreme, even fanatical enthusiasm will undertake the initiation and leadership of such a resistance, because it invites terrible reprisals on one's family, friends and fellow-countrymen.'

In Greece and other occupied countries, the Germans economised on their own manpower by recruiting local collaborators for security duties. In France there were several brutal Pétainist militias, which until the summer of 1944 were notably more numerous than the *maquis*. The Croat Ustashi in Yugoslavia became a byword for savagery. Cossacks in German uniform, later the objects of much sympathy in the West for their enforced repatriation to Russia, played a prominent role in suppressing Resistance in northern Italy and Yugoslavia, where their brutality was notorious. The Athens puppet government deployed its own 'security battalions' against the guerrillas. A million Greeks lost their homes in consequence of German repression, and a thousand villages were razed. More than 400,000 Greek civilians died in the war, albeit most by mere starvation.

Bloodshed became relentless. Hitler's OKW headquarters ordered that fifty to a hundred hostages should be killed to avenge each German victim. At the end of October 1943, guerrillas in the northern Peloponnese achieved a notable coup, capturing and then killing seventy-eight men of 117 Jaeger Division. In consequence, 696 Greeks were executed, twenty-five villages burned. On 1 May 1944, 200 hostages were shot in Athens after an attack on a German general.

On the 5th, 216 villagers were massacred in Klisura. On the 17th, a hundred more hostages were executed in Khalkis. The tempo of such atrocities rose until the last day of the German presence in Greece. As the Wehrmacht withdrew, British officers sought with limited success to persuade the rival armed factions to harass the retreat. 'We didn't inflict as much serious damage as we might have done,' wrote Monty Woodhouse of SOE. 'But by that time, certainly in the case of EAM and ELAS, their sights were set on the future and not on the immediate future.' It can convincingly be argued that much of what did and did not take place reflected domestic strife between Greeks, together with spontaneous acts of opposition to the occupiers, over which the British could exercise negligible influence.

In Italy, partisan warfare began to gather momentum after the Rome government's surrender of September 1943. Again, there were deep divisions between communist and non-communist bands. In June 1944, amid the euphoria of the breakthrough to Rome, broadcasts from Alexander's headquarters urged guerrilla bands, by now reckoned to be over 100,000 strong, to attack the Germans in their rear. The consequence was a surge of local assaults, followed by ghastly reprisals. As the armies' offensive in Italy bogged down in the autumn rains, on 13 November a new broadcast was made in Alexander's name, this time urging discretion. It was perceived at Allied headquarters that the call to arms had been delivered prematurely.

In the early spring of 1945, partisans resumed their harassment of the Germans, and played a noisy part in the last phase of the Italian campaign. They sabotaged bridges, power and phone lines, and attacked German lines of communications. Alexander nonetheless felt obliged to issue a directive on 4 February, formally abandoning any aspiration to create a mass partisan army, and substituting a commitment to selective sabotage. The problem was that Resistance groups proved chronically resistant to direction from SOE missions: 'self-organised bands . . . are already getting out of hand'. It was decreed that weapons should thereafter only be provided to those who could be trusted to use them against the Germans, rather than to promote their own local political ambitions. HQ 15th Army

Group noted ruefully: 'A Resistance movement may suddenly transfer itself from the credit to the debit side of the Allied ledger.' Here was the nemesis of Churchillian hopes, though in the last weeks of the war Italian partisans seized many towns and villages on their own initiative.

Russia and Yugoslavia were the only countries where partisan warfare significantly influenced Hitler's deployments. In Russia, the Red Army sponsored large irregular forces to harass German lines of communication. Such Soviet operations were assisted by Stalin's indifference to casualties or victims of reprisals. In Yugoslavia, almost from the moment of their conquest in April 1941 the Germans faced local opposition. Field Marshal von Weichs ordered that German troops should shoot male civilians in any area of armed resistance, regardless of whether there was evidence of individual complicity. That October, after suffering a dozen casualties in a clash with partisans, the Germans massacred the entire 2,000-strong male population of the town of Kragujevac in Serbia. Men and boys were shot in batches of a hundred, through a single day. Even wholesale brutality failed to suppress the communist guerrillas, however, which grew to a strength of some 200,000. Hitler was determined both to secure the right flank of his eastern front, and to maintain his hold on Yugoslavia's mineral resources. To achieve this, by 1944 twenty-one Axis divisions were deployed.

Michael Howard, historian of British wartime strategic deception, believes that this commitment was far more influenced by fears of an Allied amphibious landing in Greece or Yugoslavia than by partisan activity, which could have been contained by much smaller forces. He argues that the German high command was importantly misled by a deception operation, codenamed *Zeppelin*, which suggested an Allied army group in Egypt poised to move against the Balkans. As late as the spring of 1944, OKW in Berlin estimated that there were fourteen Allied divisions in Egypt and Libya, instead of the real three. At the time, however, it was the guerrillas' alleged successes which captured Churchill's imagination. News of Tito's doings, considerably exaggerated in the telling, excited him. Back in January 1943, when he was first briefed about Yugoslavia by his old researcher Bill Deakin, he had perceived possibilities which now seemed to be maturing. Here, at last, was the sort of popular revolt from which he hoped much.

In the autumn of 1943 the British, who had hitherto been supporting General Draza Mihailovic's royalist Cetnik forces, concluded that Tito's partisans were conducting much more effective operations against the Germans, notably in Bosnia and Herzegovina. With persistent naïveté at best – and possibly deceit aforethought, since one of SOE's Cairo officers, James Klugmann, was an NKVD agent and others held strongly left-wing views – they convinced themselves that Tito's people were 'not real communists'. At the Tehran conference, the 'Big Three' agreed that maximum support would be given to the Yugoslav partisans. It suited Stalin's interests to soft-pedal the ideological allegiance to Moscow of 'the Jugs', as British soldiers called Tito's people. The Soviet warlord urged a partisan delegation – unsuccessfully – to forgo the red stars on their caps 'to avoid frightening the English'.

Churchill, in Cairo on his way back from Tehran, reasserted his enthusiasm for the Yugoslav commitment. Ignoring protests that it was inconsistent to support royalists in Greece and 'reds' in Yugoslavia, he embraced the simple view that Tito's army would kill more Germans than Mihailovic, and in this he was surely right. The axis of British effort shifted ruthlessly and dramatically. Beyond air drops and Dakota landings, in 1944 it became possible to ship arms by sea to the Dalmatian coast. Tito's forces began to receive supplies in large quantities, transforming their capabilities. Between 1943 and 1945, 16,470 tons of Allied arms were provided to Yugoslavia, against 5,907 tons dropped into Italy, and 2,878 tons sent to southern France.

A high-powered British mission, led by Brigadier Fitzroy Maclean MP, took over Bill Deakin's liaison role at Tito's headquarters in September 1943, and was soon joined by Major Randolph Churchill MP. The partisans, while implacably ideologically hostile, recognised that the prime minister had sent his brightest and best to represent him in their camp. Partisan leader Milovan Djilas wrote: 'Deakin was outstandingly intelligent . . . We found out that he was a secretary of a sort to Churchill and this impressed us, as much for the consideration shown to us as for the lack of favouritism among the British top circles when it came to the dangers of war.' As for the dissolute Major Churchill, 'we of course felt honoured, though it did occur to us that Randolph might be the grey eminence of the mission. But he himself convinced us by his behaviour that he was a secondary figure, and that his father had decided on this gesture out of his aristocratic sense of sacrifice and to lend his son stature. Randolph soon enchanted our commanders and commissars with his wit and unconventional manner, but he revealed through his drinking and lack of interest that he had inherited neither political imagination nor dynamism with his surname.'

Djilas's perception of British behaviour, after almost three years in which the partisans had conducted an unaided struggle, was unsurprising and not unjust: 'The British had no choice but either to carry out a landing in order to fight the Partisans, or else to come to an agreement with them on a rational, mutually profitable basis. They chose the latter, cautiously and without enthusiasm . . . Our own dogmatic ideological distrust kept us from understanding them, though it also preserved us from any hasty enthusiasm.' The Americans never shared British warmth towards Tito. In April 1944 they angered Churchill by dispatching a mission to Mihailovic, which he ordered to be delayed in transit for as long as possible: 'The greatest courtesy being used to our friends and Allies in every case,' he wrote on 6 April, 'but no transportation.' The US team eventually reached the Cetniks, but the British were successful in deflecting Washington from dispatching supplies to them.

Tito's partisans never had the training, organisation or weapons and equipment to defeat German forces in head-to-head combat. They were unable to evict the occupiers from any substantial towns. Nonetheless, they achieved control of large rural areas of Yugoslavia. Repeated German offensives, supported by the Luftwaffe, inflicted heavy casualties, above all on the civilian population, but failed to destroy Tito's army. More British officers were dropped to local headquarters, so that there were soon eleven missions and wireless transmitters on the ground. The SOE teams found themselves frustrated, because the partisans were indifferent to their proposals and advice, save about the mechanics of supply. SOE's internal historian observed laconically: 'It is a little doubtful whether the Missions served any purpose save to give adventurous occupation to a number of very tough young men . . . half a ton of ammunition and explosives would have been more effective than half a ton of British Liaison Officers.' The allegiance of Tito's people was unequivocally to their own communist movement. From 1942 to 1945, paralleling the struggle against the Germans a bloody civil war was waged between partisans and Cetniks, in which the balance of atrocities was about even.

The British were unable to influence this, though Churchill made repeated efforts to reconcile Tito to the exiled King Peter. Even in June 1944, when the partisan leader had to flee from a German surprise attack and accept airborne evacuation to sanctuary at the Allied headquarters in Bari, Tito became no more biddable. The obliging British thereafter dispatched him to the offshore island of Vis, where he was secure from German assault, and could prepare for a renewed partisan advance. Yet Tito's forces were unable to deliver a decisive blow against their occupiers, and were obliged to enlist the aid of the Red Army to dispossess the Cetniks of Serbia late in 1944. Unlike any guerrilla movement in Western Europe, Yugoslav resistance diverted significant enemy forces from the war's main battlefields – though considerably less, if Michael Howard's interpretation of OKW documents is correct, than legend has suggested.

The political complexities of aiding Resistance prompted exasperation among British ministers and field officers charged with reaching local accommodations. Harold Macmillan wrote in May 1944 that it was all very well for the prime minister to urge support for anti-German factions of widely varying political hues, but in an age of rapid communications, 'the difficulty is that with . . . the universal listening to the radio, it is difficult [for the British] to be a Communist in Yugoslavia and a Royalist in Greece'. Though the Greek communists wanted British weapons they hated Churchill, because they knew that he wished to restore their king. Almost all the arms shipped to the Balkans in the course of the war, and likewise those provided to nationalists in South-East Asia, were used later to advance anti-Western, anti-capitalist interests. Churchill told Eden, 'I have come to the conclusion that in Tito we have nursed a viper . . . he has started biting us.'

Sir William Deakin has written: 'Paradoxically, British influence on Resistance in Europe was at its strongest at the lowest point of our military strength and resources, and during the period of our own isolation.' As Resistance groups gained in confidence and the Germans began to withdraw, any gratitude they felt towards the British for supplying them with arms was outweighed by alienation from perceived British political objectives. The French historian of resistance, Henri Michel, has written: 'Great Britain promised to the Resistance the return to a pre-war Europe, which the Resistance had rejected.' This was an overstated generalisation, but reflected widespread sentiment.

By May 1944, during the approach to D-Day, 120 British and American heavy aircraft were committed to dropping arms to European Resistance movements. SOE had grown into an organisation staffed by more than 11,000 soldiers and civilians, operating a network of training schools in Britain, the Mediterranean and India, and communicating with agents in some twenty countries. Its postwar internal history argued that no other force of its size contributed so much to the Allied war effort. Its agents and activities have stimulated a flood of books and films, historical and fictional, which continues to this day. The romance of the story is indisputable, though service with SOE in the field – again, contrary to popular myth – was actuarially less hazardous than fighting with an infantry battalion, never mind flying with Bomber Command. For instance, of 215 SOE personnel dropped into Yugoslavia, only twenty-five died. 'F' Section lost a quarter of the 400 agents dispatched to France, but even this percentage compares favourably with the casualties of rifle companies in many campaigns.

It was unquestionably vital for the Allies to sustain contact between the free world and the occupied countries. The BBC's broadcasts in many languages kept alight candles of hope which played a moving and critical role in the lives of millions of people enduring tyranny. There remains no doubt of the merits of dispatching agents to gather intelligence, contact anti-German groups, establish networks and assist escaping Allied personnel. In 1944–45, partisans were often useful as guides and intelligence sources for the advancing Allied forces, though this was a marginal activity.

The important question about SOE concerns the wisdom of its military policies. To the end of the war, while the chiefs of staff were eager for Resistance to 'make a mess', as one SOE officer in occupied France interpreted his orders, no coherent strategy was promulgated, based on a realistic assessment of what guerrillas might hope to achieve. Though useful work was done in France after D-Day, attacks on communications and German garrisons almost invariably hurt local populations more than the enemy. What else could have been expected?

The British chiefs of staff in 1944 urged that local resisters should be warned against provoking pitched battles with the Germans. Maj. Gen. Colin Gubbins, military head of SOE, was formally rebuked when a bloody uprising took place in Slovakia, because his organisation appeared to have defied its orders and promoted it.

But the high command was thus attempting belatedly to reverse the policy pursued by SOE, strongly encouraged by the prime minister, since 1940. Nor did Churchill share the generals' scruples. For instance, at a 27 January 1944 meeting with the air chiefs, the Minister of Economic Warfare, Ismay and others, he expressed the desire to promote large-scale clashes between the French Resistance and the Germans. 'He wished and believed it possible to bring about a situation in the whole area between the Rhone and the Italian frontier comparable to the situation in Yugoslavia. Brave and desperate men could cause the most acute embarrassment to the enemy and it was right that we should do all in our power to foster so valuable an aid to Allied strategy.' On 22 April, Churchill was urging on the chiefs of staff Operation *Caliph*, a scheme to land some thousands of British troops on the coast near Bordeaux simultaneously with D-Day. There was, he wrote, 'a chance of a surprise descent into a population eager to revolt'.

Though *Caliph* was never executed, Churchill was still eager to incite guerrillas to strike wholesale at the Germans. A million Yugoslavs died in strife which he explicitly sought to replicate in southern France. Popular revolts, of which the last took place in Prague in May 1945, cost many lives to little useful purpose. Mark Mazower has written: 'Only in the USSR did German counter-terror fail.' Churchill's grand vision for revolt by the oppressed peoples of Europe was heroic, but could play no rightful part in industrialised war against a ruthless occupier. Deliverance relied upon great armies.

Any judgement on Resistance must weigh the balance between moral benefit and human cost, acknowledging that the military achievement was small. Colonel Dick Barry, chief of staff to Gubbins, admitted afterwards: 'It was only just worth it.' The French people, for instance, took pride in the FFI's flamboyant demonstration when they took to the streets of Paris as the Germans retreated in August 1944. But the German decision to quit the capital was quite un-influenced by Resistance. In Crete in July 1944, against the orders of SOE, local guerrillas embarked upon open attacks which provoked the Germans to execute a thousand innocent civilians, and burn thirty villages. SOE's own historian wrote ruefully: 'The game was not worth pursuing on these terms.'

The most disastrous Resistance epic of all was, of course, the Warsaw rising which began in August 1944. There, Churchill's 1940 vision of an oppressed people breaking forth in revolt against their occupiers was dramatically fulfilled, though SOE did not directly encourage the Polish initiative. But, in the absence of Allied regular forces, the Home Army was comprehensively defeated. The British made much of their attempts, thwarted by Russian intransigence, to parachute arms to the Warsaw Poles. Gubbins was even rash enough to urge the chiefs of staff to accede to the urging of the Home Army's leaders that a Polish parachute brigade then in Britain should be dropped to aid the rebels. Even beyond the practical difficulties, it reflected lamentably on Gubbins's professional judgement that he endorsed such a romantic and futile notion. Parachute-dropped aid from Britain might have assuaged the frustration of Churchill and his people, but could not conceivably have altered the tragic outcome in Warsaw. Large-scale popular uprisings were doomed, unless conducted in concert with the advances of armies, which rendered them strategically irrelevant. The incitement of violent opposition in occupied countries made sense between 1940 and 1942, when every ruthless expedient had to be tried, to avert Allied defeat. But it became irresponsible in 1944–45, when Allied victory was assured.

Among the occupied nations, post-war gratitude to Britain for the promotion of Resistance was often equivocal. De Gaulle, with characteristic gracelessness, expelled SOE personnel from France as soon as he had power to do so. Georgios Papandreou, the Greek exile prime minister, told Harold Macmillan shortly before his country's liberation that the British should not disguise from themselves the fact that their prestige in the Balkans had fallen, while that of the Russians had risen, despite Allied victories in France and Italy: 'Moreover, in our desire to attack the Germans we had roused and armed most dangerous Communist forces in Greece itself.' Churchill's wartime enthusiasm for Resistance was soured in 1944 and thereafter by the triumphs of several communist and nationalist movements in their own countries. They seized power, or in some cases merely attempted to do so, throwing themselves into domestic struggles with greater determination than they had displayed against the Germans.

Towards the end of the war, Jock Colville describes how the controller of BBC European services, former diplomat Ivone Kirkpatrick, 'gave a damning account of the inefficacy of both SOE and PWE [Political Warfare Executive], both of which have been loud in self-advertisement'. Kirkpatrick observed that their failures confirmed his own beliefs in the importance of parliamentary scrutiny. Secret mandates rendered SOE and PWE immune from the sceptical oversight their activities would otherwise have received. This is a criticism applicable to most secret intelligence organisations in war or peace, but Kirkpatrick saw enough of SOE to render his view significant. 'Special ops' recruited some remarkable men and women, and could claim useful sabotage achievements. But its essential purpose was misconceived. 'The occupied nations believed with passion,' in the words of Sir William Deakin, 'and fought to construct their secret armies in the interior and exterior Resistance which would play a leading part in the last stage of liberation of their countries. But this was an obsessive dream.'

The educator and historian Thomas Arnold declared sternly in 1842: 'If war, carried out by regular armies under the strictest discipline, is yet a great evil, an irregular partisan warfare is an evil ten times as intolerable . . . letting loose a multitude of armed men, with none of the obedience and none of the honourable feelings of the soldier.' It may be argued that Arnold's idealised view of warfare was rendered anachronistic by Hitler's tyranny, and by the need to mobilise every possible means of undoing it. Arnold, indeed, qualified his own assertion by saying that if an invader breached the laws of conflict, 'a guerrilla war against such an invader becomes justifiable'. But nowhere, even in Yugoslavia, did Resistance operations avert the need for regular forces to defeat those of the Nazis. France would not have been liberated one day later had the *maquis* never existed. The case for Resistance, though by no means a negligible one, rests upon its contribution to the historic self-respect of occupied societies, to national legend.

The most baleful consequence of Resistance was that it represented the legitimisation of violent civilian activity in opposition to local regimes, of a kind which has remained a focus of controversy throughout the world ever since. Not only the Germans, but also many citizens of occupied countries, endorsed the view that 'One man's freedom-fighter is another man's terrorist.' It is useful to recall that such a man as Portal perceived SOE's personnel as terrorists. Though British agents were seldom directly concerned in the more ruthless actions of local groups, it was endemic to the nature of the struggle that partisans armed by London shot prisoners, sometimes wholesale; murdered real or supposed collaborators, and members of rival factions; and often supported themselves through institutionalised banditry. A precedent was set by the wartime democracies' support for irregular warfare which could never be undone.

It would be an exaggeration to say that SOE enabled dissident elements of several societies to overthrow their traditional social orders. The collapse of the Balkan monarchies was inevitable, cause for lament only to a Victorian sentimentalist such as the prime minister. In Western Europe anti-communist governments, decisively assisted by the presence of Anglo-American armies, were able to prevail in 1944–45. But the impact of SOE's aid to Resistance movements was significantly greater upon post-war societies than on military outcomes in the struggle against the Germans. Churchill came to recognise this. David Reynolds notes the remarkable fact that, in the six volumes of his war memoirs, SOE is mentioned only once, in an appendix. ' "Setting Europe ablaze" had proved a damp squib,' says the historian. It was fortunate for the peoples of many occupied countries that this was so.

EIGHTEEN

Overlord

In the fifth year of Britain's war, all those concerned with its direction were desperately tired: 'It's not the hard work, it's the hard worry,' said Robert Bruce Lockhart, head of the Political Warfare Executive. After a ministerial meeting presided over by Churchill, Dalton wrote: 'I sense that Woolton and a number of the rest are almost completely exhausted.' To the British public the wait for D-Day, decisive milestone in the war in the west, seemed interminable. The Ministry of Information, in one of its regular opinion surveys, described domestic morale in the spring of 1944 as 'poor', not least because of public apprehension about invasion casualties. 'Spirits remain at a low level,' reported the ministry's monitors on 14 April.

More and more workers flaunted disaffection. Industrial stoppages soared. February found 120,000 miners on unofficial strike in Yorkshire, 100,000 in Wales, and several hundred thousand more elsewhere. Even the president of the miners' union suggested that Trotskyite agitation was playing a part. Miners' strikes abated in April after a reconstruction of wages, but there were also stoppages among gas workers and engineering apprentices. Some 730,000 man-hours were lost in one Scottish aircraft factory. At another firm in August 1944, 419,000 hours were lost when workers rejected a management proposal that women should manufacture textile machinery – the firm's normal business – while men continued to make aircraft components. On 8 April 1944, the British embassy in Washington reported to London about American public opinion: 'Considerable disquiet is being evidenced over general political situation in England.

This has centred mainly round Churchill's demand for a [parliamentary] vote of confidence, through continuing coal and shipyard strikes, alleged evidence of failures of party truce . . . are being taken as indications that all is by no means well. Press reports give impression that there is deep dissatisfaction over domestic policy and that British public no less than American is apprehensive over apparent lack of Allied unity.'

The British and American peoples would have been even more alarmed had they known of the acrimony which overtook relations between Churchill and his chiefs of staff in the spring of 1944. Ironically, given that the prime minister's interest in the Japanese war was desultory, this was provoked by argument about operations in the Far East. Churchill had become obsessed with the desire to commit all available British forces, including the powerful fleet earmarked to join the Americans in the Pacific, to a 'Bay of Bengal' strategy for the recapture of Burma and Malaya. He was especially enthusiastic about a prospective landing on Sumatra, to provide a stepping stone. He threatened to impose this plan on the chiefs of staff, against their implacable opposition, by exercising his prerogative as Minister of Defence. On 21 March, Brooke wrote of a meeting with Cunningham and Portal: 'We discussed . . . how best to deal with Winston's last impossible document. It is full of false statements, false deductions and defective strategy. We cannot accept it as it stands and it would be better if we all three resigned sooner than accept his solution.'

It was a measure of the extravagance of Churchill's behaviour, and of the exhaustion of the chiefs at this time, that they should have discussed resignation in the shadow of D-Day. The prime minister had never visited the Far East, knew nothing of conditions there, and seldom acted wisely in his occasional interventions in a hemisphere where Allied operations were overwhelmingly dominated by the US. In the event, a compromise was fudged. The British projected a campaign against the Japanese, launched from Australia through Borneo. A minor-key version of this was executed by Australian forces in the summer of 1945. Relations between the chiefs of staff and the prime minister steadied in the weeks following the awful March 1944 meetings as the minds of these strained and weary men focused on the overpowering reality of impending invasion of the Continent.

Churchill's misgivings about *Overlord* persisted until D-Day. Sir Frederick Morgan, the D-Day planner whose rancour was increased by being denied an operational role in the landings, said later: 'Until the invasion of NW Europe was actually demonstrated to be successful, I believe [the prime minister] had the conviction it could not succeed.' This is an overstatement and oversimplification, but there is no doubt of Churchill's unhappiness about Allied deployments. All through the spring of 1944 he chafed at the inadequate resources, as he perceived it, committed to Italy, and about continuing American insistence upon *Anvil*, the planned Franco-American landing in southern France. Ironically, after so many clashes between Churchill and his chiefs of staff, they were now brought together by opposition to US European strategy. 'Difficulties again with our American friends,' Brooke wrote on 5 April, 'who still persist in wanting to close down operations in Italy and open new ones in the south of France, just at the most critical moment.' The same day, Churchill minuted the chiefs: 'The campaign in the Aegean was ruined by stories of decisive battles in Italy. The decisive battles in Italy were ruined by pulling out seven of the best divisions at the critical time for *Overlord*.'

On 19 April he talked of the invasion to Cadogan: 'This battle has been forced upon us by the Russians and the United States military authorities.' The diplomat, who spent some hours that day in meetings with the prime minister, was dismayed by his rambling: 'I really am fussed about the PM,' he wrote in his diary. 'He is not the man he was twelve months ago, and I really don't know whether he can carry on.' When the Dominion prime ministers met in London on 1 May to begin a nine-day conference, Canadian premier Mackenzie King joined South Africa's Jan Smuts in paying tribute to Churchill's achievement in having deflected the Americans from a D-Day in 1942 or 1943. Churchill freely avowed to the Dominion leaders that he himself would have 'preferred to roll up Europe from the south-east, joining hands with the Russians. However, it had proved impossible to persuade the United States to this view. They had been determined at every stage upon the invasion in North-West Europe, and had consistently wanted us to break off the Mediterranean operations.'

The range of problems besetting the prime minister was as daunting as ever, especially when others saw in him the same exhaustion as did Cadogan. 'Struck by how very tired and worn out the prime minister looks now,' wrote Colville on 12 April. Churchill was full of fears about the likely cost of *Overlord*, though he wrote cheerfully to Roosevelt that day, asserting that he did not think losses would be as high as the pessimists predicted: 'In my view, it is the Germans who will suffer very heavy casualties when our band of brothers gets among them.' The prime minister had never liked Montgomery, whose egoism and crassness grated on him. Now he told the War Office that the general must abandon his noisy round of public receptions and civic visits. In particular, Churchill recoiled from Monty's proposal to hold a 'day of prayer' and to 'hallow' Britain's armed forces in advance of D-Day at a grand religious service during which the king's coronation regalia would be paraded. Such an occasion, thought Churchill, would be more likely to demoralise the invasion forces than inspire them.

Intelligence warned that Hitler's secret weapons, flying bombs and rockets, would soon start to fall upon Britain. There was continuing difficulty with the Americans about the Free French: Washington refused to concede authority in France to De Gaulle following the invasion. Churchill agreed that it would be prudent to keep the intractable general in Algiers until the last moment before D-Day. He chafed unceasingly abut the stalemate in Italy, both at Anzio and around Monte Cassino. Again and again, Allied forces suffered heavy casualties in assaults frustrated by Kesselring's stubborn defenders. Greek troops and sailors in Egypt mutinied, calling for communist participation in their own leadership. An ugly armed confrontation took place. Churchill insisted on rejection of the mutineers' demands. The revolt was suppressed after a British officer was killed.

The Foreign Office and service chiefs urged the prime minister to curb his telegraphic bombardment of Roosevelt about strategic issues. Churchill now favoured additional landings on the Atlantic coast simultaneous with *Overlord*. Dill cautioned him on 24 April: 'The president, as you know, is not military-minded.' Appeals to Roosevelt were simply referred to Marshall, who must be irked by attempts to circumvent him. The British lost an important battle with Washington about pre-invasion bombing of French rail links. Churchill and the war cabinet opposed extensive attacks, which were bound to kill many French civilians. Eisenhower and his staff insisted that a sustained interdiction campaign was essential, to slow the German post-D-Day build-up. Roosevelt and Marshall agreed, and were surely right. The RAF joined the USAAF to mount raids by night and day in the weeks before 6 June, which inflicted damage of critical value to the Allied armies, at the cost of around 15,000 French lives. In the course of the whole war, Allied bombing killed 70,000 French people, against 50,000 British who died at the hands of the Luftwaffe.

Relations with the Russians had grown icy. Moscow accused the British of intriguing against them in Romania. Churchill wrote bleakly to Eden on 8 May: 'The Russians are drunk with victory, and there is no length they may not go.' In the preceding six months, 191 British ships had carried more than a million tons of weapons and supplies to Russia, at last matching the scale of deliveries to the need. But there was no gratitude from Stalin. Wrangles about Poland persisted. Churchill again urged the London Poles to show themselves less intractable. He perceived how little leverage they possessed, with the Russians on the brink of overrunning their country, and Washington apparently indifferent.

The British won a notable victory that spring by repulsing a Japanese offensive in north-east India, against Imphal and Kohima. This, however, increased tensions with the Americans. They intensified demands for a major offensive into north Burma, to open the land route to China. Churchill deplored the prospect of a campaign in steaming, fever-ridden jungles, to no purpose that he valued. But, in the absence of US shipping for amphibious landings in South-East Asia, Slim's Fourteenth Army was indeed committed to invade north Burma.

On 14 May there was good news from Italy. Alexander's *Diadem* offensive broke through the German line, a notable contribution being made by General Alphonse Juin's French colonial forces. On the 23rd, the Anglo-Americans launched their breakout from the Anzio perimeter. Churchill urged on Alexander the importance of cutting off Kesselring's retreat, a much more important objective than the seizure of Rome. General Mark Clark disagreed, however. His US Fifth Army drove hard for the Italian capital, diverting only a single division to impede the enemy's withdrawal. So skilful were German disengagements, in Italy as later in north-west Europe, that it is unlikely Clark could have stopped Kesselring even had he committed himself wholeheartedly to do so. But he did not. The liberation of Rome on 4 June prompted celebration among the Allied nations for a symbolic victory, but its strategic significance was small. As everybody concerned from the prime minister downwards should have perceived, the Italian capital was a mere geographical location. Kesselring was once more able to establish a defensive line. The Italian campaign continued as it had begun, in frustration and disappointment for its commanders and above all for its principal sponsor, Winston Churchill.

The prime minister seems quite wrong to have supposed that the Allied cause would have profited from an increased Italian commitment in 1944. For all Churchill's personal enthusiasm for Alexander, the Guardsman was an inadequate commander whose chief virtue was that he worked amicably with the Americans, as Montgomery did not. He seldom pressed a point, because he rarely had one to make. The terrain of Italy favoured the defence, which Kesselring conducted brilliantly. It was right for the Allies to take Sicily in July 1943, right to land and fight in Italy two months later. It was essential, once committed, to sustain a limited campaign there until 1945.

But the Americans were correct, first to insist upon *Overlord*, then to accord its interests overwhelming priority. It is hard to believe that the forces later diverted to Operation *Anvil* would have achieved commensurate results if they had been retained in Italy. The Germans were too good, the battlefield unsuited to Allied purposes. Moreover, with the northern French rail net wrecked by bombing, Marseilles later proved a vital logistics hub for all of Eisenhower's armies, a channel for 40 per cent of their supplies up to December 1944.

The prime minister thus expended capital in a struggle with Washington that he was bound to lose, and deserved to. He might have fared better in some of his trials of strength with the US in 1944 had he not chosen to challenge his ally on so many fronts. On 4 June, following the news of Rome's fall, he cabled Roosevelt: 'How magnificently your troops have fought. I hear that relations are admirable between our own armies in every rank there, and here certainly it is an absolute brotherhood.' It is necessary for great men at great moments to say such things to each other, but Churchill's rhetoric stretched truth to its limits. The American journalist John Gunther put the matter more realistically when he wrote in a con-temporary book about *Overlord*: 'Lots of Americans and British have an atavistic dislike of one another.'

The best that can be said about Anglo–American relations in 1944 – and it is a very important best – is that at operational level, the two nations' armed forces worked adequately together. The men on the spot knew it was vital that it should be so. The Americans liked some senior British officers – Portal, Tedder, Morgan, Montgomery's chief of staff De Guingand – even if they found it hard to relate to others such as Brooke. Cunningham, for the Royal Navy, observed that he found it easier to get along with America's soldiers than with her sailors, above all the glowering chief of naval operations, King. The US admiral never forgave the British for rejecting a request for the loan of an aircraft-carrier for Pacific operations at a desperate moment in 1942, after the Americans had several times made their own 'flat-tops' available to support British purposes in the west. But if it is acknowledged that all alliance relationships are profoundly difficult, there remains much cause for admiration and gratitude for the manner in which US and British armed forces made common cause between 1942 and 1945. Eisenhower, who privately liked the British a good deal less than his geniality caused them to suppose, deserved much of the credit.

The troubles of the alliance were most conspicuous at its summit. Churchill, speaking of Allied deception plans, famously observed that truth is so precious that it must be protected by a bodyguard of lies. He might have said the same about his relationship with the US. Benign deceits were indispensable. In May 1942, when criticism of his leadership was at its height, a letter-writer to *The Times* suggested that instead of being prime minister, Churchill should fill 'a place that has long been vacant in our body politic; it is the post of Public Orator'. The proposal was mischievous, but this was a role which Churchill indeed filled to supreme effect in conducting Britain's dealings with the US. In his speeches between 1940 and 1945 he created a glorious fiction of shared British and American purposes. He never hinted to his own public, still less the transatlantic one, his frustrations and disappointments about the policies of Roosevelt, any more than he did about those of Stalin. Roosevelt, in his turn, largely reciprocated. The key to understanding the wartime Anglo–American relationship is to strip aside the rhetoric of the two leaders and acknowledge that it rested, as relations between states always do, upon perceptions of national interest. There was some genuine sentiment on Churchill's side, but none on Roosevelt's.

As D-Day approached, Churchill's attitude was bewilderingly complex, perhaps even to himself. He thrilled to a historic military operation, the success of which would go far to fulfil every hope he had cherished since 1940. He emphasised to his own people, as well as to the Americans, that Britain was wholeheartedly committed. He took the keenest interest in every detail of the invasion plans, and personally originated the *Mulberry* artificial harbours which were to be deployed off the Normandy coast. But he never ceased to lament the consequences of the huge commitment to Eisenhower's campaign for that of Alexander in Italy. He knew that the United States would dominate operations in north-west Europe once the Allies were ashore. The British war effort would attain its apogee on 6 June. Thereafter, it must shrink before the sad gaze of its chieftain. At the British Army's peak strength in Normandy, Montgomery commanded fourteen British, one Polish and three Canadian divisions in contact with the enemy. The US Army in north-west Europe grew to sixty divisions, while the Red Army in mid-1944 deployed 480, albeit smaller, formations. Seldom was less than two-thirds of the German army deployed on the eastern front. Throughout the last year of the war, Churchill was labouring to compensate by sheer force of will and personality for the waning significance of Britain's contribution.

For all his declarations of optimism to Roosevelt and Marshall, and at the 15 May final briefing before the King and senior Allied commanders at Montgomery's headquarters, St Paul's School in West London, he nursed terrible fears of failure, or of catastrophic casualties. Every rational calculation suggested that the Allies, aided by surprise, air power and massive resources, should get ashore successfully. But no one knew better than Churchill the extraordinary fighting power of Hitler's army, and the limitations of the citizen soldiers of Britain and the United States, most recently displayed at Anzio. His imagination often soared to heights unattained by lesser mortals, but also plunged to corresponding depths. So often – in France and the Mediterranean, at Singapore, in Crete, Libya, Tunisia, Italy – his heroic expectations had been dashed, or at least limply fulfilled.

If, for whatever reason, D-Day failed, the consequences for the Grand Alliance would be vast and terrible. Hitler's defeat would still be assured, but no new invasion could be launched until 1945. The peoples of Britain and the United States, already tired of war, would suffer a crippling blow to their morale, and to confidence in their leader. Eisenhower and Montgomery would have to be sacked, and replacements identified from a meagre list of candidates. This was a US presidential election year. Disaster in Normandy might precipitate defeat for Roosevelt. At Westminster and in Whitehall there were already plenty of mutterings that Churchill himself was no longer physically fit to lead the country. 'I'm fed up to the back teeth with work,' he growled to his secretary Marion Holmes on the night of 14 May, 'so I'll let you off lightly.' Though his fears about *Overlord* were unlikely to be fulfilled, and his apprehensions were magnified by his burdens and exhaustion, who could blame him for allowing them to fill his mind? What seems most remarkable is the buoyancy and good cheer with which, in the last weeks before D-Day, he concealed black thoughts from all but his intimates.

Alan Brooke invoked the authority of the King to dissuade Churchill from viewing the D-Day assault from a cruiser in the Channel. The prime minister felt that he had earned the right to witness this greatest event of the western war: 'A man who has to play an effective part, with the highest responsibility, in taking grave and terrible decisions of war may need the refreshment of adventure,' he wrote aggrievedly. Yet, beyond the risk to his safety, Brooke surely feared that, should there be a crisis on the day, Churchill would find it irresistible to meddle. It was for this reason that, since 1942, the CIGS had always sought to ensure that the prime minister was absent from any theatre where a battle was imminent. On the morning of 6 June, had Churchill been aboard a warship in the Channel, he would have found it intolerable to stand mute and idle while – for instance – the Americans struggled on Omaha beach. Commanders striving to direct the battle deserved to be spared from Churchillian advice and imprecations.

Thus he was obliged to content himself with a round of visits to the invasion forces as they prepared for their moment of destiny. 'Winston . . . has taken his train and is touring the Portsmouth area and making a thorough pest of himself!' wrote Brooke ungenerously. The day of 4 June found the prime minister aboard his railway carriage, parked a few miles from the coast in a siding at Droxford in Hampshire, amid a revolving cast of visitors. Eden was irritated by the inconveniences of the accommodation, which had only one bath and one telephone: 'Mr Churchill seemed to be always in the bath and General Ismay always on the telephone. So that, though we were physically nearer the battle, it was almost impossible to conduct any business.' Out of earshot of the prime minister, Bevin and the Foreign Secretary chatted amiably, though disloyally, about the possibility of sustaining the coalition government if 'the old man' was obliged to retire. Bevin said he could work with Eden as prime minister, so long as the Tory committed himself to nationalising the coal mines, which the unions would insist upon. Smuts joined them, and asked what they had been discussing. When told Bevin's terms, 'Socrates' said crisply: 'Cheap at the price.' It was a curiously tasteless discussion for the three men to hold, as half a million young men prepared to hurl themselves at Hitler's Atlantic Wall. But it reflected the new mood among Britain's politicians, looking to a future beyond Winston Churchill.

De Gaulle came, belatedly summoned from Algiers. The prime minister walked down the rail tracks to meet him, arms outstretched in welcome. De Gaulle ignored the offered embrace, and vented his bitterness that he himself was denied a role in the Allied return to his country. Churchill told him that the Americans insisted that his committee should not be granted the governance of liberated French territory. The British must respect US wishes. He urged De Gaulle to seek a personal meeting with Roosevelt, in the hope that this might resolve their differences. The Frenchman later claimed that it was at Droxford Churchill told him that if forced to choose between America and France, Britain would always side with the United States. This was almost certainly false, or at least a wilful exaggeration. But De Gaulle's bitterness about being denied authority in France, a claim he had striven for four years to justify, confirmed an animosity towards Britain which persisted for the rest of his life. Churchill exchanged cables with Roosevelt about the possibility of sending the Free French leader back to Algiers. In the event, he was allowed to remain. But Anglo–French relations were poisoned to a degree unassuaged by De Gaulle's subsequent elevation to power.

The Yugoslav partisan leader Milovan Djilas was with Stalin at his *dacha* outside Moscow when word came that the Allies would land in France next day. The Soviet warlord responded with unbridled cynicism: 'Yes, there'll be a landing, if there is no fog. Until now there was always something that interfered. I suspect tomorrow it will be something else. Maybe they'll meet up with some Germans! What if they meet up with some Germans? Maybe there won't be a landing then, but just promises as usual.' Molotov hastily explained to the Yugoslav that Stalin did not really doubt that there would be an invasion, but enjoyed mocking the Allies. On this matter, after the prevarications and deceits of the previous two years, the Soviet leader had perhaps earned his jibe.

By the evening of 5 June, Churchill was back in London. As Clementine departed for bed, she bade goodnight to her husband in his map room below Whitehall. He said: 'Do you realise that by the time you wake up in the morning, twenty thousand young men may have been killed?' Unlike the Americans with their unshakeable optimism, Churchill had borne the consequences of so many failures since 1940. It would be the crowning misery if British arms now failed to acquit themselves in a manner worthy of this crowning hour.

The D-Day landings of 6 June represented the greatest feat of military organisation in history, a triumph of planning, logistics and above all human endeavour. The massed airborne assault on the flanks which began in darkness, the air and naval bombardment followed by the dawn dash up the fire-swept shoreline by more than 100,000 British, American and Canadian engineers, infantrymen, armoured crews and gunners, achieved brilliant success. In a spirit that would have warmed the prime minister's heart, as one landing craft of the East Yorkshire Regiment approached the beach at La Brèche, company commander Major 'Banger' King read *Henry V* aloud to his men:

> On, on you noblest English!
> Whose blood is fet from fathers of war-proof

At Colleville, the local mayor appeared on the sands to welcome the invaders, his person adorned by a gleaming brass fireman's helmet. At Omaha beach, the US 29th Division landed to meet the most savage resistance of the day. 'As our boat touched sand and the ramp went down,' an infantryman recalled later, 'I became a visitor to hell.' To Ernest Hemingway, serving as a war correspondent, the guns of the supporting battleships 'sounded as though they were throwing whole railway trains across the sky'. The invaders fought doggedly through flame and smoke, wire entanglements, pillboxes, minefields and gun positions, to stake out the claims of the Allied armies inside Hitler's Europe.

Hitler's Atlantic Wall was breached. Churchill spent the morning of D-Day in his map room, following the progress of the landings hour by hour. To few men in the world did the battle mean so much. At noon, he told the House of Commons: 'This vast operation is undoubtedly the most complex and difficult that has ever taken place.' He lunched with the King, returned for the afternoon to Downing Street, then at 6.15 felt able to tell the Commons that the battle was proceeding 'in a highly satisfactory manner'. Instead of the carnage which Churchill feared, just 3,000 American, British and Canadian troops died on D-Day, together with about the same number of French civilians. By nightfall, in places the invaders had advanced several miles inland, securing perimeters which would soon be linked. A long and terrible struggle lay ahead, as invaders and defenders raced to reinforce their rival armies in Normandy. There were days when more Allied soldiers perished than on 6 June. But the triumph of *Overlord* was assured.

Critically aided both by Anglo-American deception plans, which kept Hitler in expectation of further landings, and by pre-invasion bombing, the German build-up proved much slower than had been feared. By nightfall on 7 June, 250,000 of Eisenhower's men were ashore. Three evenings later there were 400,000. Churchill warned MPs of the need to avoid exaggerated optimism. Though 'great dangers lie behind us, enormous exertions lie before us'. On 10 June, in a cable to Stalin he expressed extravagant hopes about Italy. Alexander, he proclaimed, was 'chasing the beaten remnants of Kesselring's army swiftly northwards. He is on their tracks while mopping up the others.' In truth, such a display of energy, so comprehensive a victory, was entirely beyond Alexander and his armies.

Two days later, on 12 June, Churchill was at last allowed to visit the invasion beachhead in Normandy, an expedition which, of course, he adored. On the way to Portsmouth he sought to tease a companion, Admiral Ernest King, a venture akin to striking a match on an iceberg: 'Don't look so glum. I'm not trying to take anything away from the United States Navy just now.' He was enchanted by the spectacle of the invasion coast, cabling again to Stalin: 'It is a wonderful sight to see this city of ships stretching along the coast for nearly fifty miles and apparently safe from the air and the U-boats which are so near.' Lunching with Montgomery, he expressed surprise that the Norman countryside seemed relatively unscathed: 'We are surrounded by fat cattle lying in luscious pastures with their paws crossed.' Before returning to England, the destroyer which carried him fired a few rounds towards German shore positions, at a range of 6,000 yards. He declared his delight at sailing for the first time aboard a ship of the Royal Navy in action.

Back home, a grim welcome awaited. That night, German V1 flying bombs began to fall on London. Churchill stood outside Downing Street, scanning the sky and listening to the growling motors of the 'doodlebugs' overhead, whose sudden silence presaged their descent and detonation. They were soon landing close by him. On Sunday, 18 June, a V1 killed sixty people during a service in the Guards' Chapel, 300 yards from his study. During one noisy night of explosions and anti-aircraft fire, at 2 a.m. he was dictating to his secretary, Marion Holmes. 'The PM asked if I were frightened. I said "No." How can one feel frightened in his company?' The First Sea Lord, Cunningham, was often a critic of the prime minister, but wrote in his diary after a meeting of the anti-flying bomb 'Crossbow' Committee on 19 June: '[Churchill] was at his best, and said the matter had to be put robustly to the populace, that their tribulations were part of the battle in France, and that they should be very glad to share in the soldiers' dangers.'

In truth, however, the British people were much shaken by the

V1 offensive. They were almost four years older, and incomparably more tired, than they had been during the blitz of 1940. The monstrous impersonality of the doodlebugs, striking at all hours of day and night, seemed a refinement of cruelty. Mrs Lylie Eldergill, an East Londoner, wrote to a friend in America: 'I do hope it will soon be ended. My nerves can't take much more.' Brooke was disgusted by the emotionalism of Herbert Morrison, the Home Secretary: 'He kept on repeating that the population of London could not be asked to stand this strain after 5 years of war . . . It was a pathetic performance.' The bombardment severely affected industrial production in target areas. In the first week, 526 civilians were killed, and thereafter the toll mounted. It was a godsend to morale that Rome's fall and D-Day had taken place before the V1 offensive began. Hitler made an important mistake by wasting massive resources on his secret weapons programme. The V1s and subsequent V2 rockets were marvels of technology by the standards of the day, but their guidance was too imprecise, their warheads too small, to alter strategic outcomes. The V-weapons empowered the Nazis merely to cause distress in Britain. They might have inflicted more serious damage by targeting the Allied beachhead in Normandy.

Macmillan described Churchill one evening at Chequers, around this time: 'Sitting in the drawing-room about six o'clock [he] said: "I am an old and weary man. I feel exhausted." Mrs Churchill said, "But think what Hitler and Mussolini feel like!" To which Winston replied, "Ah, but at least Mussolini has had the satisfaction of murdering his son-in-law [Count Ciano]." This repartee so pleased him that he went for a walk and appeared to revive.' One of Brooke's most notorious diary entries about the prime minister was written on 15 August:

> We have now reached the stage that for the good of the nation and for the good of his own reputation it would be a godsend if he could disappear out of public life. He has probably done more for this country than any other human being has ever done, his reputation has reached its climax, it would be a tragedy to blemish such a past

by foolish actions during an inevitable decline which has set in during the past year. Personally I have found him almost impossible to work with of late, and I am filled with apprehension as to where he may lead us next.

Yet if Churchill was indeed old, exhausted and often wrong-headed, he was unchallengeable as Britain's war leader, and Brooke diminished himself by revealing such impatience with him. The prime minister possessed a stature which lifted the global prestige of his country far beyond that conferred by its shrinking military contribution. Jock Colville wrote: 'Whatever the PM's shortcomings may be, there is no doubt that he does provide guidance and purpose for the Chiefs of Staff and the F.O. on matters which, without him, would often be lost in the maze of inter-departmentalism or frittered away by caution and compromise. Moreover he has two qualities, imagination and resolution, which are conspicuously lacking among other Ministers and among the Chiefs of Staff. I hear him much criticised, often by people in close contact with him, but I think much of the criticism is due to the inability to see people and their actions in the right perspective when one examines them at quarters too close.' All this was profoundly true.

Even in the last phase of the war, when American dominance became painfully explicit, Churchill fulfilled a critical role in sustaining the momentum of his nation. After D-Day, but for the prime minister's personal contribution, Britain would have become a backwater, a supply centre and aircraft-carrier for the American-led armies in Europe. On the battlefield there was considerable evidence that the British Army was once more displaying its limitations. The war correspondent Alan Moorehead, who served through the desert, Italy and into Normandy, enjoyed a close relationship with Montgomery. His view was noted after the war in terse notes made by Forrest Pogue: 'By July, the American soldier better than the British soldier. Original English . . . came from divisions which had been much bled. In first few days [I] went with Br. tanks. They stopped at every bridge because there might be an 88 around.' These strictures might be a little harsh, but the Americans were not wrong in thinking the British, after five years of war, more casualty-averse than themselves.

In 1944–45 Churchill exercised much less influence upon events than in 1940–43. But without him, his country would have seemed a mere exhausted victim of the conflict, rather than the protagonist which he was determined that Britain should be seen to remain, until the end. 'So far as it has gone,' Churchill told the Commons, 'this is certainly a glorious story, not only liberating the fields of France after atrocious enslavement but also uniting in bonds of true comradeship the great democracies of the West and the English-speaking peoples of the world . . . Let us go on, then, to battle on every front . . . Drive on through the storm, now that it reaches its fury, with the same singleness of purpose and inflexibility of resolve as we showed to the world when we were alone.' And so he himself sought to do.

NINETEEN

Bargaining with an Empty Wallet

For Churchill, the weeks that followed D-Day were dominated by further fruitless wrangles with the Americans. Roosevelt sent him a headmasterly rebuke, drafted by Cordell Hull, for appearing to concede to the Russians a lead role in Romanian affairs, in return for Soviet acquiescence in British dominance of Greece. To the Americans, this attitude reflected the deplorable British enthusiasm for bilaterally agreed spheres of influence. Churchill replied irritably next day: 'It would be quite easy for me, on the general principle of slithering to the left, which is so popular in foreign policy, to let things rip, when the King of Greece would probably be forced to abdicate and [the communists of] EAM would work a reign of terror . . . I cannot admit that I have done anything wrong in this matter.' If Roosevelt proposed to take umbrage about British failure to inform the White House about every cable to Stalin about Greece and Romania, then what of US messages to Moscow concerning Poland, which the British were not made party to? Churchill ended sadly: 'I cannot think of any moment when the burden of the war has lain more heavily upon me or when I have felt so unequal to its ever-more entangled problems.'

The prime minister still favoured landings on the Atlantic coast of France instead of *Anvil* and, even more dramatically, a major assault on Istria, the north-east Italian coast beyond Trieste, to take place in September. Brooke was cautious about this, warning that the terrain might favour the defence, and could precipitate a winter campaign in the Alps. But the chiefs and their master were

493

galvanised by an intercepted 17 June German signal. In this Hitler declared his determination to hold Apennine positions as 'the final blocking line' to prevent the Allies from breaking into the north Italian plain of the Po. Here, in British eyes, was compelling evidence of the German commitment to Italy, and thus of the value of contesting mastery there. The Americans – both Eisenhower and the US chiefs – were unimpressed. There followed one of the most acrimonious Anglo–American exchanges of the war.

The British chiefs insisted that it was 'unacceptable' for more Allied forces to be withdrawn from Italy. Eisenhower, as supreme commander, reasserted his commitment to the landings in southern France, and even more strongly rejected British notions, propounded in a plan drawn up by Maitland-Wilson as Mediterranean C-in-C, for a drive from north-east Italy to the so-called 'Ljubljana gap'. On 20 June, Ike wrote to Marshall that Maitland-Wilson's plan 'seems to discount the fact that Combined Chiefs of Staff have long ago decided to make Western Europe the base from which to conduct decisive operations against Germany. To authorise any departure from this sound decision seems to me ill-advised and potentially dangerous . . . In my opinion to contemplate wandering off overland via Trieste to Ljubljana repeat Ljubljana is to indulge in conjecture to an unwarrantable degree . . . I am unable to repeat unable to see how over-riding necessity for exploiting the early success of *Overlord* is thereby assisted.' The American chiefs signalled on 24 June that Maitland-Wilson's Trieste plan was 'unacceptable'. They confirmed their insistence that the planned three US and seven French divisions earmarked for *Anvil* should be withdrawn from Italian operations.

Ill-advisedly, Churchill appealed against this decision to Roosevelt, while on 26 June the British chiefs of staff reaffirmed in a signal to their counterparts in Washington the 'unacceptability' of the re-deployment. Marshall remained immovable. On the 28th, Churchill dispatched a note to the president in which he wrote: 'Whether we should ruin all hopes of a major victory in Italy and all its fronts and condemn ourselves to a passive role in that theatre, after having broken up the fine Allied army which is advancing so rapidly through the peninsula, for the sake of "*Anvil*" with all its limitations, is indeed a grave question for His Majesty's Government and the President, with the Combined Chiefs of Staff, to decide.' He himself, he said, was entirely hostile to *Anvil*. Next day, Roosevelt rejected Churchill's message: 'My interests and hopes,' he said, 'centre on defeating the Germans in front of Eisenhower and driving on into Germany, rather than on limiting this action for the purpose of staging a full major effort in Italy.' Roosevelt added, in the midst of his own re-election campaign, that there were also political implications: 'I should never survive even a slight setback in "*Overlord*" if it were known that fairly large forces had been diverted to the Balkans.'

Amazingly, Churchill returned to the charge. In a message to Roosevelt on 1 July, after a long exposition of the futility of *Anvil* – 'The splitting up of the campaign in the Mediterranean into two operations neither of which can do anything decisive, is, in my humble and respectful opinion, the first major strategic and polit-ical error for which we two have to be responsible' – he concluded: 'What can I do Mr President, when your Chiefs of Staff insist on casting aside our Italian offensive campaign, with all its dazzling possibilities . . . when we are to see the integral life of this campaign drained off into the Rhone Valley? . . . I am sure that if we could have met, as I so frequently proposed, we should have reached a happy agreement.' This was woeful stuff. It was supremely tactless for the prime minister to suggest to the president that, if he had been able to browbeat him face to face, he might have persuaded him to override his own chiefs of staff. To the British chiefs he expressed contempt for their American counterparts: 'The Arnold-King-Marshall combination is one of the stupidest strategic teams ever seen. They are good fellows and there is no need to tell them this.'

The Americans were unmoved by the barrage of cables from London. The British, with icy formality, acceded to the launch of *Anvil* – now renamed *Dragoon* – on 15 August. This was the moment at which

Overlord and *Anvil*

Churchill perceived his own flagging influence upon the US president, and thus upon his country. 'Up till *Overlord*,' wrote Jock Colville later, 'he saw himself as the supreme authority to whom all military decisions were referred.' Thereafter, he became, 'by force of circumstances, little more than a spectator'. The prime minister afterwards told Moran: 'Up to July 1944 England had a considerable say in things; after that I was conscious that it was America who made the big decisions.'

The British adopted a stubbornly proprietorial attitude to the Italian campaign long after it had turned sour, and even after the dazzling success of *Overlord*. Marshall had made his share of mistakes in the course of the war – but so had Brooke and Churchill. Nothing in the summer exchanges between London and Washington justified the prime minister's condescension towards the US chiefs. Though Eisenhower is often, and sometimes justly, criticised for lack of strategic imagination, he and Marshall were assuredly right to insist upon the concentration of force in France.

Yet it was hard for Churchill to bow to the relegation of himself and his country from the big decisions. An American political scientist, William Fox, coined the word 'superpower' in 1944. He took it for granted that Britain could be counted as one. The true measure of superpowerdom, however, is a capability to act unilaterally. This, Churchill's nation had lost. Dismay and frustration showed in his temper. Eden wrote on 6 July: 'After dinner a really ghastly defence committee nominally on Far Eastern strategy. We opened with a reference from W. to American criticism of Monty for over-caution, which W. appeared to endorse. This brought explosion from CIGS.' Brooke wrote in his own diary:

A frightful meeting with Winston which lasted until 2am!! It was quite the worst we have had with him. He was very tired as a result of his speech in the House concerning the flying bombs, he had tried to recuperate with drink. As a result he was in a maudlin, bad-tempered, drunken mood, ready to take offence at anything, suspicious of everybody, and in a highly vindictive mood against the Americans. In fact so vindictive that his whole outlook on strategy was warped. I began by having a bad row with him. He began to abuse Monty because operations were not going faster . . . I flared up and asked him if he could not trust his generals for 5 minutes instead of continuously abusing them and belittling them . . . He then put forward a series of puerile proposals, such as raising a Home Guard in Egypt to provide a force to deal with disturbances in the Middle East. It was not until midnight that we got onto the subject we had to come to discuss, the war in the Far East! . . . He finished by falling out with Attlee and having a real good row with him concerning the future of India! We withdrew under cover of this smokescreen just on 2am, having accomplished nothing beyond losing our tempers and valuable sleep!!

Eden commented later: 'I called this "a deplorable evening", which it certainly was. Nor could it have happened a year earlier; we were all marked by the iron of five years of war.' Accounts like that of Brooke, describing such passages of arms with Churchill, dismayed those who loved the prime minister, both his personal staff and family, when they were published in the next decade. The prime minister's former intimates took special exception to criticisms that his conduct of office was adversely affected by alcohol. The CIGS was coupled with Lord Moran, whose diary appeared in 1966, not only as a betrayer of the Churchillian legend, but also as a false witness about his conduct. Yet the two men's views were widely shared. After listening to the prime minister for a time at a committee meeting, Woolton leaned over and whispered to Dalton like a naughty schoolboy: 'He is very tight.' Exhaustion and frustration probably influenced Churchill's outbursts more than brandy. But the evidence is plain that in 1944–45 he suffered increasingly from loss of intellectual discipline, sometimes even of coherence.

The pugnacity that had served his country so wonderfully well in earlier years became distressing when directed against his own colleagues, men of ability and dedication who knew that they did not deserve to be so brutally handled. Churchill could rouse his extraordinary powers on great occasions, of which some still lay ahead. There would be many more flashes of wit and brilliance. But key figures in Britain's war leadership, instead of looking directly to him as the fount of all decisions, were now peering over his shoulder towards a future from which they assumed that he would be absent. Eden, craving the succession, chafed terribly when the prime minister seemed unwilling to acknowledge his own political mortality. 'Lunched alone with W,' he wrote on 17 July. 'He was in pretty good spirits. My face fell when he said that when coalition broke up we should have two or three years of opposition and then come back together to clear up the mess!'

Yet there were still many moments when Churchill won hearts, including that of the Foreign Secretary, by displays of whimsy and sweetness. On 4 August, when Eden called in at Downing Street with his son Nicholas, on holiday from Harrow school, the prime minister surreptitiously slipped into the boy's hand two pound notes, more than a fortnight's pay for an army private, with a muttered and of course vain injunction not to tell '*him*'. Churchill's companions became bored when he recited long extracts from *Marmion* and *The Lays of Ancient Rome* across the dinner table at Chequers, but how many other national leaders in history could have matched such performances? He was moved to ecstasies by a screening of Laurence Olivier's new film of *Henry V*, not least because he was in no doubt about who was playing the king's part in England's comparable mid-twentieth-century epic. His impatience remained undiminished. Driving with Brooke from Downing Street to Northolt, their convoy encountered a diversion for road repairs. Churchill insisted on lifting the barriers and urging the cars along a footpath. The King himself would never do such a thing, the miscreant declared gleefully, for 'he was *far* more law-abiding'.

As for the war, by late summer 1944 the apprehension which dogged Churchill and his service chiefs through the spring was now supplanted by assurance that Germany's doom was approaching. But when? On this, the prime minister displayed better judgement than the generals. Until the end of September, they envisaged a final Nazi collapse by the turn of the year. Churchill, by contrast, told a staff conference on 14 July: 'Of course it was true that the Germans were now faced with grave difficulties and they might give up the struggle. On the other hand, such evidence as there was seemed to show that they intended to continue that struggle, and he believed that if they tried to do so, they should be able to carry on well into next year.' His view remained unchanged even after the drama of the failed bomb plot against Hitler on 20 July. This highlighted German internal opposition to Hitler – and its weakness.

Some illusions persist that the wartime Allies missed opportunities to promote the cause of 'good Germans' who opposed Hitler, rejecting approaches from such men as Adam von Trott. Yet the British seemed right, first, to assume that any dalliance of this kind must leak, fuelling Soviet paranoia about a negotiated peace; and second, in believing that the anti-Hitler faction was both weak and flawed. Michael Howard has written: 'We know that such "right-minded people" did exist; but the remarkable thing is that . . . there should have been so few of them, and that their influence should have been so slight.' Howard notes that most of the July 1944 bomb plotters were fervent nationalists, who cherished grotesquely extravagant ambitions for their country's post-war polity.

If Hitler could be deposed, his domestic foes hoped to persuade the Allies to recognise Germany's 1914 frontiers, and even to deny France the return of Alsace-Lorraine, annexed from her in 1870 and again in 1940. Most of the bomb plotters shared stubbornly right-wing notions about Germany's future governance. Claus von Stauffenberg in May 1944 explicitly embraced a vision based on preserving Germany's union with Austria, retaining the Czech Sudetenland and offering 'autonomy' to Alsace-Lorraine. The principal objective of most of those who joined the conspiracy against Hitler, as the Foreign Office perceived at the time, was to enlist Anglo-American aid against the Russians. It is easy to understand why post-war Germans sought to canonise the July bomb plotters. But it would have represented folly for Churchill's government to dally with them, and there is no cause for historians to concede them exaggerated respect. A large majority of the 20 July conspirators turned against Hitler not because he was indescribably wicked, but because they perceived that he was leading Germany to defeat.

The historian John Wheeler-Bennett, a friend of Eden who knew Germany intimately, compiled a memorandum for the Foreign Office about the plot. He wrote on 25 July, suggesting that its failure was a blessing. He believed that if Hitler had been killed and 'Old Army' German generals had then approached the Western Allies seeking to negotiate terms short of unconditional surrender, major embarrassments would have ensued. Oliver Harvey went further, writing in his diary: 'I despise the generals even more than Hitler who deserves better treatment from them.' This surely carried British notions about soldierly duty to perverse extremes. Harvey claimed, after a conversation with Sir Frederick Morgan, that the general agreed 'about the necessity of rooting out the German General Staff and thankful Hitler wasn't bumped off the other day'. Wheeler-Bennett wrote likewise, that 'The present purge is presumably removing from the scene numerous individuals who might have caused us difficulty, not only had the plot succeeded, but also after the defeat of a Nazi Germany.'

This was an extravagantly brutal verdict. But it is certainly true that British and American public opinion might have been plunged into confusion, and Western relations with the Soviets into crisis, if an opportunity had been suddenly presented to end the carnage in Europe through a negotiation with allegedly 'good' Germans.

That July, in the face of new intelligence reports about the operations of the death camp at Auschwitz-Birkenau, Churchill wrote to Eden in the most explicit terms he used during the war about the nature of Nazi action against the Jews: 'There is no doubt that this is probably the greatest and most horrible crime ever committed in the whole history of the world . . . It is clear that all concerned in this crime who may fall into our hands, including the people who only obeyed orders by carrying out the butcheries, should be put to death.' Yet once again the British dismissed the notion of bombing the death camp's facilities or transport links, partly on the grounds of inefficacy – that any damage could be readily repaired – and partly on the spurious grounds that deportations of Jews from Hungary, reports of which prompted Churchill's note, appeared to have ceased.

Even at this stage, the scale of Nazi killings eluded British policy-makers. An intelligence officer privy to Ultra decrypts who lectured to senior soldiers in 1944 about Germany's machinery of repression spoke in his briefings of killings in thousands, not millions, and did not explicitly mention Jews. Likewise the November 1943 joint Allied Moscow Declaration, warning of retribution against Germans who participated in 'wholesale shooting of Italian officers or in the execution of French, Dutch, Belgian or Norwegian hostages or of Cretan peasants, or who have shared in the slaughter inflicted on the people of Poland or in territories of the Soviet Union', omitted Jews.

There seems little doubt that British and American intelligence possessed enough information by late 1944, from Ultra and escaped Auschwitz prisoners, to deduce that something uniquely terrible was being done to the Jews in Nazi-occupied Europe, if the evidence had been appropriately highlighted. The failure of either government to act has incurred brutal strictures from post-war critics. Yet Churchill,

Roosevelt and their principal subordinates seem to deserve some sympathy for their inadequate responses. First, an instinctive reluctance persisted, both in London and Washington, to conceive a European society, even one ruled by the Nazis, capable of killings on the titanic scale exposed in 1945–46. Second, evidence about the massacre of Jews was still perceived in the context of other known mass killings of Russians, Poles, Greeks, Yugoslavs, Italians and other subject races. The British, especially, were wary of repeating the mistakes of the First World War, when reports of German atrocities were wilfully exaggerated for propaganda purposes. Such exploitation roused post-war anger and cynicism among British people towards their own government.

Finally, given the known limitations of precision bombing even where good target intelligence was available, the case for specific action against the Nazi death machine seemed overborne by the overarching argument for hastening military victory to end the sufferings of all Europe's oppressed peoples. The airmen could be sure that any bombing of the camps would kill many prisoners. It is the privilege of posterity to recognise that this would have been a price worth paying. In the full tilt of war, to borrow Churchill's phrase from a different context, it is possible to understand why the British and Americans failed to act with the energy and commitment which hindsight shows to have been appropriate. Most measured historians of the period recognise a real doubt about whether any plausible air force action would substantially have impeded the operations of the Nazi death machine.

Again and again that summer, Churchill found his aspirations thwarted. He was eager that Britain should have the honour of hosting a summit, after he himself had travelled so far and often to dance attendance on Roosevelt and Stalin. He now proposed as a venue Invergordon in Scotland, arguing that each leader could arrive there by battleship. The King would be able to entertain the 'Big Three' at Balmoral. Stalin flatly refused to leave Russia. Even when Roosevelt agreed to a bilateral meeting, and after briefly professing enthusiasm for Invergordon, to Churchill's chagrin he finally decided that the conference should not take place in Britain. The president was unwilling, especially in a US election year, to be seen as the guest of his nation's subordinate partner. A second visit to Quebec was scheduled for September.

Churchill's lonely struggle to save fragments of Polish freedom became ever less rewarding. He allowed himself a surge of hope when Stalin cabled on 23 July, endorsing a 'unification of Poles friendly disposed towards Great Britain, the USSR and the United States'. Interpreting this – which Eden did not – as a sign that Stalin was willing to accommodate the 'London Poles' in a new regime, Churchill told Roosevelt: 'This seems to be the best ever received from Uncle Joe.' But the significance soon became clear of Stalin's recognition of Moscow's puppet Polish National Committee, dubbed in London 'the Lublin Poles'. Stalin was bent on a communist-dominant Polish government, with only token representation of other interests. Under extreme pressure from Churchill, the Polish exile prime minister in London, Stanislaw Mikolajczyk, agreed to fly to Moscow. But Mikolajczyk rightly anticipated that obeisance to Stalin would serve no purpose either for himself or for his country's freedom.

On 31 July, with Soviet forces only fifteen miles away across the Vistula, the Polish 'Home Army' in Warsaw launched its uprising. Through the agonising weeks that followed, Churchill strove to gain access to Russian landing grounds, to dispatch arms to the Poles. The most earnest and humble pleas to Stalin – and in some of Churchill's cables he was indeed reduced to begging – failed to move Moscow. The Russian leader believed that Churchill had deliberately provoked the Warsaw Uprising to secure for the 'London Poles' the governance of their country. Moscow was determined to prevent any such outcome. The prime minister had certainly since 1940 promoted an ideal of popular revolt, and some SOE officers had encouraged Polish delusions. But he was in no way complicit in the launch of the Warsaw Rising, an explicitly local initiative. Though he sustained his campaign on behalf of Polish freedom for many months to come, he knew how great were the odds against success. If the Americans were not indifferent, they seemed so both in London and in Moscow. The Red Army stood deep inside Poland, while Eisenhower's forces were far, far away.

Even more serious, from Churchill's viewpoint, was the frustration of his strategic wishes. He made a last, vain attempt to persuade the Americans against a campaign in Burma. Throughout the war, while Churchill was eager that British forces should be seen to regain Britain's colonies in the Far East, his interest in the military means by which this should be accomplished was sporadic and unconvincing. Most of his attention, and almost all his heart, focused upon the German war, even as Slim's imperial army prepared to advance towards the Chindwin frontier of Burma.

Until almost the last day before the landing in southern France on 15 August, Churchill argued doggedly against 'the *Anvil* abortion', pleading for alternative assaults on the Atlantic coast of France, or in north-east Italy. 'I am grieved to find that even splendid victories and widening opportunities do not bring us together on strategy,' he wrote to Hopkins in Washington on 6 August. The British failed to perceive that the arguments for getting into southern France were less persuasive in rousing US determination than those for getting every possible man out of Italy.

As Churchill railed in the face of so many difficulties and disappointments, he adopted a familiar panacea: personal activity. In a fashion imbued with pathos, because it marked his transition from prime mover to spectator, he became for some weeks a battlefield tourist. During his travels he conducted some business. But his journeys represented a substitute for implementing policy, rather than a means of doing so. On 20 July he flew to Normandy, where 1.4 million Allied troops were now deployed. On 5 August he again toured the battle zone and met commanders. Both trips delighted him, for he savoured proximity to the music of gunfire as much as ever. He underrated the scale and speed of the developing German collapse in France, and the new strategic opportunities which would follow. He expected months more fighting before Allied troops reached the borders of Germany. Had he understood that dramatic

'Setting Europe ablaze'.
(*Above*) Instructing French *maquisards* on the use of the sten sub-machine gun, supplied in large quantities to the Resistance by SOE in 1944.
(*Below*) An SOE mission looking suitably flamboyant in occupied Yugoslavia.

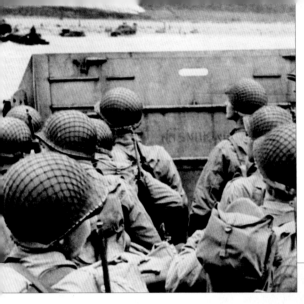

Images of D-Day: Operation *Overlord*, 6 June 1944, climactic moment of World War II in the west.

With his unworthy favourite Alexander in Italy, 26 August 1944.

In Paris on Armistice Day, 11 November 1944, an unusually affable moment with De Gaulle.

In Athens on 26 December 1944, meeting the warring Greek factions in conference with Eden, Archbishop Damaskinos, Alexander and Macmillan, while gunfire raged in the streets outside.

t Yalta in February 1945
ne USN's Admiral King
ngages in sober conver-
ation with Brooke, Ismay
nd Marshall.

One of the Valentine tanks supplied by Britain to the Red Army enjoys a moment of triumph as it carries victorious Russian soldiers through the streets of Sofia, the Bulgarian capital.

Last set-piece of the western campaign: Churchill stands at a vantage point overlooking the Rhine with Brooke and Montgomery before the British crossing in March 1945.

The sublime consumma-
tion of Churchill's war
leadership of Britain:
(*above*) on the balcony of
Buckingham Palace with
the royal family on VE-day,
8 May 1945. (*Below*) He
addresses his nation, and
the world, from Downing
Street.

With Truman and Stalin at Potsdam on 17 July 1945.
Though he did not know it, Winston Churchill had only
nine more days to serve as Britain's wartime prime minister

change in the circumstances of Eisenhower's armies was imminent, with the collapse of German resistance in France, he would probably have remained at hand, to dispatch a flood of imprecatory messages to Roosevelt, Marshall, Eisenhower and Brooke. As it was, however, he departed for the Mediterranean.

On 11 August he landed in Algiers. Summoning De Gaulle for a meeting, he was infuriated when the Frenchman, seething with indignation about the Allies' refusal to grant him authority in his own country, declined to attend. Randolph Churchill, recuperating after a plane crash in Yugoslavia, met his father and heard a stormy denunciation of De Gaulle. Afterwards, in an unusually statesman-like intervention, Randolph urged pity: 'After all, he is a frustrated man representing a defeated country. You as the unchallenged leader of England and the main architect of victory could well afford to be magnanimous.' Churchill wrote to Clementine: 'I feel that de Gaulle's France will be a France more hostile to England than any since Fashoda [in 1898].'

Nonetheless, under relentless pressure from Eden, Churchill supported De Gaulle's cause against the Americans. Before D-Day, Admiral Leahy, Roosevelt's chief of staff who had served as US ambassador to Vichy, told the president that the Allies would find Marshal Pétain their most appropriate French negotiating partner, because of his popularity with his own people. In the weeks following the invasion this delusion was confounded by Resistance fighters who seized power in liberated areas, and displayed overwhelming support for De Gaulle. The men of Vichy were consigned by their countrymen to prison or oblivion. Late in August the general was allowed to return to France, where he became the country's *de facto* ruler. Two months later, albeit with the deepest reluctance, Washington recognised his leadership of a French provisional government.

On 12 August Churchill flew to Italy, where he installed himself in Maitland-Wilson's residence, the Villa Rivalta overlooking the Bay of Naples. He remained in Italy for more than two weeks, bathing several times in the sea, much to his pleasure, and conducting meetings. He continued to fume about the diversion of forces to

France. In those days of mid-August, 100,000 men were being transferred in landing ships from Italy. Offshore in a launch one sunny morning, Churchill found himself hailed by thousands of troops lining the rails of vessels on passage to the Côte d'Azur. He acknowledged their cheers, but wrote in his memoirs: 'They did not know that if I had had my way, they would have been sailing in a different direction.' As for the Italian people, after years of proclaiming the need for firmness, if not harshness, towards Mussolini's nation, the sight of smiling Italian faces now softened his heart, rekindling his lifelong instinct towards mercy.

He met Tito, flown in from Yugoslavia, and fêted him considerably. The communist leader returned to his headquarters so enchanted by the prime minister that some of his partisan comrades were alarmed. Dismissing their warnings of the British leader's duplicity, the Yugoslav enthused: 'It isn't as simple as you think! Yes, Churchill is an imperialist, an anti-Communist! But you won't believe it, his eyes were filled with tears when he met me. He almost sobbed, "You're the first person from enslaved Europe I have met!" Churchill even told me that he had wanted to parachute into Yugoslavia, but he was too old!' One partisan shook his head and muttered to another: 'The English are clever: an escort of warships and naval manoeuvres in honour of the Old Man [Tito], and I see that it's had its effect on him!'

On 16 August, Churchill watched the *Dragoon* landing from an assault vessel a few miles offshore. In a letter to Clementine he portrayed the splendour of the armada 'all spread along twenty miles of coast with poor St. Tropez in the centre'. The invaders met little opposition, and were soon racing north-eastward to a linkage with Eisenhower's armies on 12 September. The prime minister spent hours in talks about Mediterranean policy with Macmillan, Maitland-Wilson and others. British handling of Italian affairs was unimpressive, and perceived as such by the Americans. Churchill and Eden acquiesced in the return from Moscow of exiled communist leader Palmiro Togliatti, and his inclusion in the Italian government in exchange for its recognition by the Russians. Dogged British resistance to the participation of Count Carlo Sforza, a former foreign minister who had been living in the US and was esteemed by the Americans, annoyed Washington intensely. London was taken unawares when Marshal Badoglio was ejected from the Italian leadership in June 1944. Thereafter, British struggles to create and sustain a Rome government acceptable to Churchill and his colleagues incurred constant criticism from the US State Department and media. The Americans' own ideas were naïve, but founded in a commitment to Italian rights of self-determination, which they perceived the British as flouting in their old imperialistic way.

Increasingly Churchill's attention focused upon Greece, where he perceived a serious danger of communist takeover. The guerrillas of EAM-ELAS, armed by SOE, were the best-organised force in the country. As the Germans began to withdraw from southern Greece, Churchill ordered that British troops should be readied to fly into Athens the moment the enemy abandoned the city, to forestall a communist coup. It was hard to find men, when the Allied armies in Italy had been so much depleted for *Dragoon*, but forces for Greece the prime minister insisted that there must be. Some airborne units were earmarked.

Then he advanced towards the front, dressed in army summer rig with medal ribbons and a sola topee that would have looked absurd on any other man. Alexander drove him to a hilltop from which he could hear small-arms fire, watch machine-gunners flail the enemy amid showers of empty cases spinning away into the dust, see tanks grinding into action. The outing provided him with as much happiness as any experience in the last months of the war. He was in the midst of a British army which, if not immediately triumphant, was indisputably predominant, in the company of a general whom he deemed a paladin. Alexander received far fewer reproaches for slow progress than did Montgomery. Churchill blamed the misfortunes of the joyless, bloody Italian theatre exclusively upon the Americans. They, he believed, had stripped Alex's army of the means with which it might have changed the fate of Europe and spared the Balkans from Soviet domination. Many of those engaged in the struggle,

507

and bearing its sacrifices, shared his opinion. A humble Eighth Army signaller wrote in his diary on 27 August 1944: 'I feel sure this is a secondary front and therefore being denied the vital necessities of war.'

On 29 August, Churchill landed back in Britain with a temperature of 103° and a patch on his lung which caused his doctors to prescribe another course of M & B drugs. He had achieved nothing of substance in the Mediterranean, nor in Normandy, save to assuage a growing sense of his own impotence, and to indulge his passion for witnessing great events. Foreign Office official Oliver Harvey muttered scornfully about the prime minister 'fooling about in Italy'. Amid the miseries and slaughter inflicted on London by the flying-bomb offensive, Churchill faced greater personal risk at home than in Normandy or the Mediterranean. Though his government had much to do, most of the tasks were uncongenial to him. More and more of ministers' time was occupied with preparing for peace. At worst, victory could not be more than a year or two away. The British people looked with eagerness mingled with uncertainty towards a future without war. Yet the prime minister's interest in domestic matters was spasmodic and perfunctory. David Reynolds notes that in Churchill's memoirs he makes no mention of the 1944 Butler Education Act, the most important piece of domestic legislation during his wartime premiership. Ismay once observed: 'The PM can be counted on to score a hundred in a Test Match, but is no good at village cricket.' The issues of post-war reconstruction, the mundane concerns of the careworn British people, required ministers to take the field in many village cricket matches.

Winning the war, and securing the place of the British Empire in the new world, were Churchill's unalterable preoccupations. For those obliged to work with him, difficulties mounted. His flagging health, rambling monologues and refusal to address mundane matters which did not stimulate his interest, posed great difficulties. Leo Amery complained: 'Our Cabinet meetings certainly get more and more incoherent, though I notice that there is much more talking by everybody, often simultaneously, than there used to be when Winston held the field entirely by himself . . . What makes me so tired at Cabinets is the same feeling that one has in a taxi wishing to catch a train with a driver who dawdles and misses every green light.'

The philosopher and historian Isaiah Berlin wrote: 'Churchill is preoccupied by his own vivid world, and it is doubtful how far he has ever been aware of what actually goes on in the heads and hearts of others. He does not react, he acts; he does not mirror, he affects others and alters them to his own powerful measure . . . His conduct stems from great depth and constancy of feeling – in particular, feeling for and fidelity to the great tradition for which he assumes a personal responsibility, a tradition which he bears upon his shoulders and must deliver, not only sound and undamaged but strengthened and embellished, to successors worthy of accepting the sacred burden.' This seems profoundly true of Churchill's behaviour in the last months of the war. Two or three years earlier, he had power to shape events as well as popular perceptions of them. Now, the world was going on its way with ever less heed for his grandiose antique vision, though it could still be moved by his words.

Through the autumn, the miseries of Poland provided a running theme, as the Nazis suppressed the Warsaw Rising with familiar savagery. Not only Stalin, but also Roosevelt, resisted Churchill's impassioned pleas to press Moscow about the Warsaw Home Army. The Americans wanted Siberian bases for their B-29 bomber operations against Japan, and were unwilling to provoke the Russians about what they perceived as lesser matters. On 26 August the president rejected an appeal from Churchill that the US and Britain should dispatch a strongly-worded joint protest to Moscow about Poland. Roosevelt wrote: 'I do not consider it advantageous to the long-range general war prospects for me to join with you in the proposed message to Uncle J.' On 4 September the prime minister, still unwell, felt obliged to rise from his sickbed to calm a cabinet whose members were really angered by events in Warsaw. While he welcomed spontaneous media expressions of dismay, he urged that ministers should remain temperate about Russian behaviour.

Churchill was still ailing when he boarded the *Queen Mary* at Greenock on 6 September, bound for Quebec. Brooke remarked that he seemed 'old, unwell and depressed. Evidently found it hard to concentrate and kept holding his head between his hands.' Conditions below decks for most of the crossing were oppressively hot. After the austerities of British diet, on the liner the customary sybaritic fare was provided for the prime minister's party. Jock Colville described their meals as 'gargantuan in scale and epicurean in quality; rather shamingly so'. There was the usual glittering table talk, faithfully recorded by the three notable diarists aboard – Colville, Brooke and Moran. The prime minister said that he would not regret the loss of any Labour colleague from his government save Bevin, the only one whose character and capacity he esteemed. He lamented the fact that he no longer felt that he had a message to deliver to the British people: 'all he could now do was to finish the war, to get the soldiers home and to see that they had houses to which to return. But materially and financially the prospects were black.'

He found time to read, first Trollope's *Phineas Finn*, then *The Duke's Children*, which describes a Victorian political grandee's embarrassments with his offspring. The latter novel can scarcely have failed to prick Churchill, at a time when his own son's marriage to his wife Pamela was breaking up. She had conducted a notable affair with Averell Harriman, a future husband, and was later unkindly described as having become 'a world expert on rich men's bedroom ceilings'. Earlier that year, Churchill achieved one of his few moments of intimacy with Brooke, when the two men discussed *tête-à-tête* over supper their difficulties with their respective grown-up children.

But, while the prime minister struggled to recruit his strength, as usual he spent many hours on the *Queen Mary* preparing for the summit. He minuted the chiefs of staff during their passage that Britain should 'not yield central and southern Europe entirely to Soviet ascendancy or domination'. This was, he said, an issue of 'high political consequences, but also has serious military potentialities'. He expressed distress that the British and imperial armies were nowhere advancing the nation's standard as he would have wished. One-third of their strength, in north-west Europe, was deployed under US command; one-third in India was about to launch an offensive in Burma, 'the most unhealthy country in the world under the worst possible conditions', merely to appease America's China ambitions; and the remaining one-third in Italy had been emasculated for *Dragoon*. Had he known, he said, that the Americans would use their monopoly of landing ships unilaterally to enforce strategy, he would have ensured that Britain built her own. He was appalled to hear that Mountbatten was demanding 370,000 men and 24,000 vehicles from Europe before launching an assault against Rangoon. He still craved an amphibious landing on the Istrian peninsula, 'in the armpit of the Adriatic'.

Churchill arrived in Quebec by overnight train on the morning of 11 September, within a few minutes of the president. They drove together from the station to the Citadel. Next day, Colville heard the prime minister say that he would that evening discuss post-war occupation zones in Germany with Roosevelt. The private secretary, knowing his master had not studied the relevant papers, offered to read them aloud to him in his bath. This procedure proved only partially successful, because of Churchill's tendency to submerge himself from time to time, missing key passages of the brief. The prime minister cabled to the war cabinet in London that the conference had opened 'in a blaze of friendship'. There was indeed a blaze of courtesies, but not of agreed policies. In Churchill's opening exposition of events, he sought to flatter the Americans by saying that the results of the detested *Dragoon* were 'most gratifying'. Roosevelt interrupted him, observing mischievously – even maliciously – that 'some of the credit for the conception was due to Marshal Stalin'. Churchill then talked much about Italy, and the merits of striking for Vienna. He seemed oblivious of American boredom and indifference. Cunningham, the First Sea Lord, thought Roosevelt 'looked very frail, and hardly to be taking in what was going on'.

The two leaders wasted considerable time discussing the plan of Henry Morgenthau, the Treasury Secretary, for pastoralising post-war Germany. The president, knowing that Churchill was increasingly fearful about how Britain could pay its bills when Lend-Lease ended, said that de-industrialising the Ruhr would remove Britain's principal competitor in Europe. Great economic opportunities could thus shine upon the British people. This notion prompted a spasm of enthusiasm in Churchill. Cherwell, in one of his baleful interventions, urged the scheme's merits. On 15 September both leaders formally endorsed the Morgenthau Plan, to the horror of both Cordell Hull and Anthony Eden, who said the British cabinet would never accept it. Roosevelt quickly recognised that he had made a mistake. The Morgenthau Plan was forgotten – except by Nazi propagandists, when the story leaked. In the last months of the war, many Germans believed Goebbels when he told them that if they bowed to defeat they would be condemned to become slave labourers in a peasant economy. The Treasury Secretary's foolish initiative at Quebec motivated some enemies to fight even more desperately than they might otherwise have done, in the last ditch.

The final formal session of the conference took place on 16 September. Churchill proclaimed his commitment to dispatch a major fleet to join the Pacific campaign, as soon as the European war allowed. He made much of this, heedless of the fact that the Royal Navy's ships were as worn and battered as their crews. They lacked ventilation systems appropriate to Pacific conditions. And carrier operations, dominant feature of the campaign, were the least impressive British naval combat skill. At the closing press conference of the summit, appearing as usual beside the president, the prime minister trumpeted Britain's commitment to the eastern theatre. He prompted laughter among the assembled American correspondents when he said: 'You can't have all the good things to yourselves. You must share.' He then waxed lyrical about the virtues of summitry: 'When I have the rare and fortunate chance to meet the President of the United States, we are not limited in our discussions by any sphere ... The fact that we have worked so long together, and the fact that we have got to know each other so well under the hard stresses of war, makes the solution of problems so much simpler, so swift and so easy it is.'

This was flummery. In truth, even after two days with Roosevelt at Hyde Park before boarding the *Queen Mary* in New York on 20 September for the voyage home, Churchill knew how little he had achieved. 'What is this conference?' he rumbled to Moran. 'Two talks with the Chiefs of Staff; the rest was waiting to put in a word with the President.' The British had been dismayed to note the absence of Harry Hopkins from Quebec. Even when their favourite American sage appeared at Hyde Park, it was plain that Hopkins no longer enjoyed his old intimacy with Roosevelt. Especially in a US election year, he represented baggage which the president did not wish to be seen on board, not least because Hopkins was perceived by his countrymen as too susceptible to British special pleading. Now the British saw that his influence was gone, their old affection ebbed shamelessly. Brendan Bracken dismissed him as 'weak' and 'useless'. Yet there is no reason to suppose that Hopkins was moved by pique when he warned Halifax, in Washington, that a Republican victory in the imminent presidential election might serve British interests better than the return of Franklin Roosevelt. To this the 'historic partnership' had descended.

Churchill was in mellow mood on the voyage home, but saw nothing in which to rejoice. The Warsaw Rising was all but over, despite a belated and almost entirely unsuccessful arms drop to the defeated Home Army by 110 USAAF Flying Fortresses, which were grudgingly permitted to refuel in Russia. Eden had failed to persuade the Quebec conference to recognise the French National Committee as the nation's government. Churchill told Colville that following the events of recent years, 'my illusions about the French have been greatly corroded'. It was another month before De Gaulle's obvious primacy among his countrymen obliged Washington to relent.

On 28 September, back in London, Churchill reported to the Commons. With barely permissible nationalistic hyperbole, he described Normandy as 'the greatest and most decisive single battle of the whole war'. He hailed Burma as 'the campaign of Admiral Mountbatten', a slight upon General Bill Slim, the fine commander conducting the British offensive. He sought to make the best of defeat at Arnhem, seeing cause for celebration in an unaccustomed display of boldness by the Allies, even though the airborne assault had failed to secure a Rhine crossing. At the beginning of October, British troops began to move into southern Greece behind the retreating Germans. Churchill made a renewed plea to Roosevelt, for the transfer of three American divisions from France to Italy – and received the inevitable refusal.

It was against the background of repeated American snubs that Churchill now embarked upon one of his most controversial wartime journeys. He determined to fly to Moscow, for bilateral talks with Stalin. It is impossible to perceive this mission as other than a gesture of desperation. Having failed to enlist American support for any of the purposes which now mattered most to him, instead he sought to achieve them by going head-to-head with the Russians. Yet Stalin bargained only for advantage. Britain could offer nothing of interest to him. He well understood that the Americans had distanced themselves from Churchill's nation. The prime minister's behaviour can only be explained by acknowledging that he still nursed an exaggerated self-belief about his ability to reach personal understandings with Stalin. There was a pathos about his flight to Moscow in October 1944, well understood by those who worked most closely with the tired old prime minister.

He paused briefly in Italy, hearing from his commanders a tale of inadequate resources and sluggish progress. He saw Georgios Papandreou, and embarrassed the Greek prime minister by subjecting him to a long lecture on the virtues of monarchy. On 9 October he arrived in Moscow and was driven to Molotov's *dacha*, his residence for the visit. At the first meeting with Stalin, he plunged immediately into a demand that Britain should have the principal voice in determining the future of Greece. He soon made it plain to the Soviet warlord that he spoke for himself, for Britain, and not for its transatlantic partner. Stalin observed silkily that Roosevelt 'demanded too many rights for the United States of America, leaving too little for the Soviet Union and Great Britain'. Churchill produced what he called a 'naughty document'. This was the draft of what became known as the 'percentages agreement', in American eyes the most notorious piece of chicanery in Churchill's premiership. In Romania, Russia was to be recognised as having a 90 per cent interest, while 'the others' had 10 per cent. In Greece, these figures were to be reversed. In Yugoslavia and Hungary, interests would be shared 50–50. In Bulgaria, Russia would have a 75 per cent interest, 'the others' 25 per cent. Churchill pushed this half-sheet of paper across the table to Stalin, who glanced at it, added a large blue tick, and passed it back across the table.

During the hours and days that followed, there was much general talk between the two men: about Greece and Yugoslavia, where Stalin agreed with Churchill that they should seek to prevent civil war between rival ideologies; about Italy, where the prime minister requested that Moscow should not 'stir up Italian communists'; and about monarchs – Churchill said that nowhere would Britain seek to re-enthrone a ruler against the will of the people. He made it plain that Britain would not support mass executions of defeated Nazis, though he hoped that as many as possible would be killed on the battlefield. He asserted his belief that no ideology should be imposed on small states, which must be free to decide their own destinies. Meanwhile, Eden haggled with Molotov about details of the percentages agreement, with the Russian foreign minister demanding, for instance, 90–10 influence in Bulgaria.

On 11 October Churchill sought to resolve such matters in a long missive to Stalin which he drafted, then showed to Averell Harriman, now US ambassador in Moscow. Harriman said that Roosevelt and Cordell Hull would certainly repudiate the letter, if it was sent. Instead, the prime minister telegraphed to the president urging the importance of acting swiftly to prevent an eruption of civil wars in the Balkans. Already, communist partisans in Albania had rejected the return of King Zog, exiled from the country since 1941.

Then Churchill's delegation set forth for the British embassy, to host a dinner for Stalin and Molotov. Stalin told his host that it had not been policy, but military realities, which had prevented the Red Army from succouring the Warsaw Poles. The prime minister asked Lazar Kaganovich, commissar for railways, how he made his nation's transport trains run on time. When an engine driver failed in his duty, said Kaganovich with a wolfish grin . . . then he drew his hand across his throat. Churchill rarely displayed anxiety about his own safety, but in Moscow he was furious to discover that his plane was left overnight in the hands of Russian guards. He insisted that thereafter a member of its RAF crew must remain aboard the aircraft around the clock. It is hard to suggest that this represented paranoia.

As always at these meetings, talking continued into the small hours. The Russian mood seemed unreservedly benign. Churchill cabled to Roosevelt about 'an extraordinary atmosphere of goodwill'. To Clementine, he wrote on the 13th: 'The affairs go well. We have settled a lot of things about the Balkans & prevented hosts of squabbles that were maturing. The two sets of Poles have arrived & are being kept for the night in separate cages . . . I have had v[er]y nice talks with the Old Bear. I like him the more I see him. Now they respect us here & I am sure they wish to work with us. I have to keep the President in constant touch & this is the delicate side.'

In almost all of this Churchill was mistaken. Unaccustomed Russian civility, even warmth, was inspired by a new self-confidence, born of battlefield triumph. Virtually none of the assurances Stalin offered had substance. He had no intention of honouring them. What he wanted in the Balkans, he would take. Stalin could always raise a laugh from his obeisant courtiers by saying, as he often did: 'We fucked this England!' The prime minister could claim only one success which proved enduring: Greece. Stalin recognised the strength of British sentiment about the country, together with the reality of Western Allied dominance of its air space and surrounding seas. All the rest of the Balkans lay within the Soviets' grasp. Though strife lay ahead in Greece, the Russians made no attempt to promote communist victory. Thus far, and thus far only, Churchill may have accomplished something useful in Moscow.

His most notable failure was the attempt to save Poland. He

summoned from London a Polish exile delegation, led by prime minister Mikolajczyk, who attended under threat from Churchill. Days of icy round-table discussion followed, with the Russians half-amused, half-embarrassed, by the slavish puppet show put on by their own 'Lublin Poles'. Churchill wrote to the King from Moscow: 'Our lot from London are, as your majesty knows, a decent but feeble lot of fools, but the delegates from Lublin seem to be the greatest villains imaginable.' Between sessions, Churchill made desperate efforts to induce the London Poles to accept the proposed new frontiers for their country, which would cede territory to Russia in exchange for land carved from eastern Germany. Blandishments and threats alike failed to move Mikolajczyk and his colleagues. They remained obdurate. Stalin dismissed a compromise proposal advanced by the British. When the Polish leader returned to London and put the final Soviet offer to his colleagues, it was decisively rejected. He then resigned as prime minister. Churchill found himself accepting commiserations from Stalin, that 'his' Poles rejected a deal. It was apparent that, in these circumstances, Moscow's appointees would rule the country.

It would have suited Stalin to gain Mikolajczyk's acquiescence both in the new borders and in accepting a marginal role in the new government. But since there was no possibility that non-communists would be granted real influence, far less power, the London Poles lost nothing and preserved their honour by rejecting Stalin's proposals. Churchill, however, was left to nurse despondency and failure. He thought the Poles almost demented in their refusal to make terms with Moscow. When General Anders, Polish corps commander in Italy, expressed hopes that the Allies would free Poland by force once Germany was beaten, Churchill said despairingly: 'This is crazy. You cannot defeat the Russians.' In his perception, Mikolajczyk's stubbornness had handed his country to Stalin. 'The Poles' game is up,' he said tersely to Moran. Better, he thought, to accept a Russian mess of pottage than nothing at all.

Posterity should surely be moved that Churchill cared so much about Poland, where Britain had no selfish interest whatever. He waged a long, thankless struggle on behalf of the nation which had become the victim of Nazi aggression at the outbreak of the Second World War. It seemed to him unbearably tragic that impending Allied victory should merely offer a new servitude to the people on whose behalf Britain had declared war on Germany. Yet this was the case, and would have been so even had Roosevelt entered the lists in support of Churchill. The Russians were on the Vistula, while the Anglo-Americans were not yet at the Rhine. 'Far quicker than the British and also the Americans,' Sir William Deakin has written, 'the Russians grasped the inner logic of the situation, namely that at the final victory the fate of the occupied countries of Europe . . . would be decided neither by the Resistance leaders themselves on the spot nor their representatives . . . in London and Moscow, but along a frontier between the armies of the Western Allies on the one hand and the Russians on the other.'

The Moscow visit ended with the usual round of banquets. Churchill told Stalin that he favoured some grouping of Poland, Hungary and Czechoslovakia after the war, which the Russian leader cared for not at all. Stalin surprised Churchill by expressing a passionate hatred for Switzerland. But the Russians displayed no hostility to the British, as they had so often done in the past. On the contrary, Churchill and Stalin talked with freedom and, on the Russian side, unembarrassed mendacity. On the 18th, Churchill addressed a press conference at the British embassy. Next morning, Stalin not only came to the airfield in the rain to see the prime minister off, but condescended to inspect the interior of his York aircraft. The two men parted with every evidence of cordiality. On the afternoon of 22 October, Churchill landed back in Britain.

The world was allowed to suppose that his Moscow visit was merely a routine meeting of allies. It inspired in Churchill a brief surge of illusion, that he had forged an understanding with Stalin which might yield fruits such as he had failed to harvest from Roosevelt. The US president, by contrast, was irked. He was in no doubt about Churchill's purpose. Britain's prime minister was attempting to achieve what the US was absolutely committed to resist: the creation of spheres of influence in post-war Europe and the Balkans. The divide between

British and American policy had never been greater since December 1941.

For all their public expressions of mutual regard, it is hard to suppose that by this time Churchill or Roosevelt cherished much private affection for each other. Their objectives were too far apart. The president's world vision was more enlightened than that of the prime minister, yet even less realistic. He pinned his faith for the future upon the new United Nations organisation, the rise of Chiang Kai-shek's China, and a working partnership between America and the Soviet Union. His motives were exalted. Churchill's impassioned commitment to freedom excluded the world's black and brown races, as that of the president did not. But while Churchill had a quixotic strand of personal humility intermixed with his vanity, Roosevelt had none. His faith in his own power, as well as that of his nation, was unbounded. His unwillingness to acknowledge his own mortality, which was even more pressing than that of men threatened by death on the war's battlefields, was a grievous omission in the last months of his presidency. He might at least have ensured, as he did not, that vice-president Harry Truman was admitted to the secrets of the Grand Alliance.

It seems mistaken to be surprised, however, by Washington's cavalier treatment of both Britain and its prime minister. Beyond the new hubris of the United States, on many matters of strategy and policy the British had displayed poor judgement in 1944. They were wrong about *Overlord*, about Italy both militarily and politically, and were dilatory and confused about the Japanese war. On the battlefield their soldiers performed adequately rather than impressively. Churchill allowed himself to be distracted into pursuit of self-indulgent whims, such as a proposal that some aged British naval guns mounted at Dover should be shipped to the Continent to aid Eisenhower's campaign. British attempts to ignore their own impoverishment and retain a giant's role in the world inspired pity among their American friends, contempt among their American enemies. Churchill told Smuts: 'You must remember . . . that our armies are only about one-half the size of the Americans and will soon be little more than one third . . . It is not as easy as it used to be for me to get things done.' Churchill often asserted that, far from owing a huge cash debt to the US when the war was over, Britain should be recognised as a creditor, for its lone defence of freedom in 1940–41. This was never plausible. When the war ended, the world would assess Britain's rightful place merely by reading its bank statement. Informed British people recognised this, and feared accordingly.

On 27 October, Churchill reported to the Commons on his visit to Moscow. He now commanded an affection among MPs which transcended partisan loyalties. 'How much depends on this man nowadays,' wrote Tory MP Cuthbert Headlam, for so long a sceptic. 'Without Winston's prestige and personality, where should we be with Roosevelt and Stalin? They are tiresome enough as things are – but how could Anthony Eden, or Attlee, stand up to them? No – I have never been a Winstonian, but I do realize that today if a man ever be indispensable, Winston is that man.'

When Attlee told MPs that Churchill was again in Moscow, Labour MPs were seen shaking their heads in mingled admiration and sympathy, saying: 'He oughtn't to do it. Poor old boy, he really oughtn't to do it.' There was a readiness to indulge him, almost unique in parliamentary experience: 'He is not of course as vigorous or pugnacious as in 1940,' wrote Harold Nicolson. 'But he has no need to be. He is right to take the more sober tone of the elder statesman.' Conservatives who had spurned Churchill in 1940 recognised him in 1944 as offering the only political hope for their party, which was profoundly unpopular in the country. The old ruling class perceived that the electorate yearned for its dispossession as soon as ballot papers were offered to them at a general election. In Nicolson's words: 'The upper classes feel that all this sacrifice and suffering will only mean that the proletariat will deprive them of all their comforts and influence, and then proceed to render this country and Empire a third-class State.' The prime minister himself was far from immune from the effects of public alienation. Nicolson was shocked one day to notice graffiti scrawled in a station lavatory: 'Winston Churchill is a bastard.' When he remarked upon it to an RAF officer standing beside him, the airman shrugged:

'Yes. The tide has turned. We find it everywhere.'
'But how foul. How bloody foul!'
'Well, you see, if I may say so, the men hate politicians.'
'Winston a politician! Good God!'

On 27 October, the prime minister delivered a brilliant speech about his experiences in Moscow. Then he adjourned to the smoking room, and addressed the barman: 'Collins, I should like a whisky and soda – single.' After sitting down for a moment, he struggled out of his armchair and returned to the bar. 'Collins, delete the word "single" and insert the word "double".' 'Then,' in the words of an MP, 'grinning at us like a schoolboy, he resumed his seat.' Here was another of those impish miniatures which help to explain why love for Churchill ran so deep among most of those who worked with him. For all Alan Brooke's exasperation with his master at this time, he wrote fondly of a scene that winter, as the two men visited the snow-bound French front in the Vosges. The prime minister arrived for lunch with De Gaulle 'completely frozen, and almost rolled up on himself like a hedgehog. He was placed in a chair with a hot water bottle at his feet and one in the back of his chair. At the same time good brandy was poured down his throat to warm him internally. The results were wonderful, he thawed out rapidly and when the time came produced one of those indescribably funny French speeches which brought the house down.'

But the British people had by now hardened their hearts towards their rulers, even the greatest. Many felt less gratitude to those presiding over victory in the most terrible conflict in history, than implacable resentment against the politicians whom they held responsible for getting them into it in the first place. Even if Churchill had not himself been among the Guilty Men of the thirties, he was now their political standard-bearer. And for all his giant stature as Britain's war leader, millions of voters sensed that his interest in the humdrum domestic troubles of peace was perfunctory. An anonymous officer of Second Army, fighting in Holland, wrote in *The Spectator* about the mood of the British soldier under his command: '[He] is fighting for the future of the world and does not believe in that future... He asks a lot of the future, but he doesn't expect to get any of it.' The writer perceived his men as chronically mistrustful of all authority, institutions and politicians, but Tories most of all: 'It is, perhaps, encouraging that Tommy, 1944, will not be foozled by facile talk of a land fit for heroes. He wants deeds, not words.' Few among such men perceived Winston Churchill as the national leader likely to fulfil such hopes once victory came, and his great duty was done.

TWENTY

Athens: 'Wounded in the House of Our Friends'

German withdrawal from the Balkans precipitated a crisis for Churchill which severely damaged his standing in America, engaged him in bitter political dispute at home, and provided the last perilous military adventure of his life. Experience at the end of World War II demonstrated that it is much more difficult to order the affairs of liberated nations than of defeated ones. This is because it is undesirable, if not impossible, to arbitrate their affairs with the same ruthlessness. If Washington's twenty-first-century neo-conservatives had possessed a less muddled understanding of the experience of 1944–45, had studied more closely Allied difficulties managing liberated territories in the Roosevelt–Churchill era, they might not have inflicted such grief upon the world in our own times by their blunders in Iraq and Afghanistan.

In almost every European country freed from German domination, former Resistance groups armed by SOE sought to assert themselves in governance. In France, only De Gaulle's extraordinary personal authority and the presence of the Anglo-American armies – together with Stalin's abstention from mobilisation of his followers in a country where political instability might damage Soviet interests – made it possible to contain the communists of the FTP. In neighbouring Belgium, the exiled government which returned from London in September found itself facing a strong challenge from left-wingers, including communist resisters. Having played a modest role in Belgian liberation they now, to the alarm of the authorities, refused to be disarmed. There was anger about the Belgian government's alleged reluctance to impose retribution upon those who had served the German occupation regime. On 25 November, leftist trades unionists staged a big demonstration in Brussels and appeared bent upon forcing entry to government buildings. Police overreacted, firing on the demonstrators and wounding forty. In the weeks that followed, tensions ran high. The British Army, strongly backed by Churchill, was determined to tolerate neither a threat to its lines of communications to the battlefront, nor any attempted communist takeover. British troops deployed in Brussels in large numbers.

This action restored a resentful peace, but prompted hostile press comment. American correspondents, especially, deplored the use of force to suppress 'heroic Resistance fighters', of whatever political persuasion. Churchill displayed insensitivity in his support for the restoration of long-exiled governments to societies traumatised and radicalised by the experience of occupation. However, American enthusiasm for self-determination underrated both the malevolence of the communists and the danger of anarchy overtaking the liberated nations.

Meanwhile in the Balkans, as the Germans fell back, in Albania and Yugoslavia communist partisan movements set about seizing control. No other political element was strong enough to stop them, and in Serbia Tito enjoyed direct assistance from the Red Army. 'Tito is turning very nasty,' Churchill told Smuts on 3 December. The Yugoslav partisans demanded the expulsion of the British from the Dubrovnik coastal area. At the same time in Eastern Europe, the 'Lublin Poles' proclaimed themselves the provisional government of their country, with no offer of participation for the exiled administration in London. All this made Churchill acutely anxious about the future of Greece. In the first days following German withdrawal, arriving British troops were greeted with unbridled enthusiasm. When Eden visited Athens on 26 October, his car was mobbed by cheering crowds. Lord Moyne, accompanying him, said brightly: 'It is good that there is one country where we are so popular.'

The Greek honeymoon ended abruptly. Armed factions roamed city streets, amid well-founded reports that communists were slaughtering alleged 'reactionaries'. The Papandreou government strug-gled to assert its control of the country while the communists of EAM/ELAS refused to demobilise, and guerrilla bands converged on Athens. The British strove to reinforce their weak forces in the capital, scouring the Mediterranean for men. 'Everything is degenerating in the Greek government,' the prime minister wrote to Eden on 28 November, 'and we must make up our minds whether we will assert our will by armed force, or clear out altogether.' Two days later, he reached a predictable decision: 'It is important to let it be known that if there is a civil war in Greece we shall be on the side of the Government we have set up in Athens, and that above all we shall not hesitate to shoot.'

Next day, 1 December, the six communist and socialist ministers in the Athens regime resigned *en bloc*, and called a general strike. On the 3rd, frightened and ill-disciplined police fired on a demon-stration. One policeman and eleven demonstrators were killed. Furious crowds besieged Athens police stations. The police, like other elements of the Papandreou government's makeshift security forces, were widely perceived by Greeks as having collaborated with the German occupiers. The historian Mark Mazower has written: 'Despite Churchill's belief that he had forestalled a communist attempt to seize power, there is no sign that the uprising in Athens was anything other than a spontaneous popular movement which took the [communist] party leadership by surprise.' At first, the guerrillas of EAM/ELAS concentrated their fire on Greek government forces. But when they perceived British troops furthering the cause of their right-wing foes, they started shooting at the 'liberators'.

The nuances of this situation escaped British commanders on the spot. They merely perceived their authority violently challenged. It should also be noticed, as it was not by most American observers at the time, that all over Greece the communists were conducting murderous purges of bourgeois opponents, often along with their families. Churchill was bitterly angry. He assessed the Greek situ-ation, and communist intentions, through the prism of developments in Poland, Albania, Yugoslavia, Belgium.

The Greek crisis broke while the Belgian one was still making headlines. Churchill was harshly misjudged by Americans, who supposed that he sought an undemocratic outcome in Greece. His mistake was that, for two turbulent months, he conceded to Greek King George II, exiled in London, a veto on constitutional arrangements. So intemperate were Churchill's expressions of hostility to the communists of EAM/ELAS that Clementine felt moved to write him a note of warning:

> My darling Winston,
>
> Please do not before ascertaining full facts repeat to anyone you meet what you said to me this morning i.e. that the Communists in Athens had shown their usual cowardice in putting the women & children in front to be shot at. Because altho' Communists are dangerous, indeed perhaps sinister people, they seem in this War on the Continent to have shown personal courage . . .
>
> Your loving & devoted Clemmie

Clementine's words were significant, because they reflected widespread public sentiment in Britain as well as America. Allied propaganda throughout the Nazi occupation had made much of the communist role in resistance, portraying EAM/ELAS, like Tito's partisans in Yugoslavia, as heroic freedom fighters. Not only was their contribution to the anti-Nazi struggle exaggerated, but reports of their atrocities, well-known to SOE officers on the ground, were suppressed. Many people on both sides of the Atlantic thus viewed the Greek left in roseate hues.

Worse, Churchill's lingering desire to salvage the Greek monarchy, despite overwhelming evidence of its unpopularity, compromised his own authority. Almost all his ministers, including Eden and Macmillan, were unwilling to offer even vestigial support to George II. They were also conscious of the rickety character of the Papandreou regime, an unconvincing foundation for the restoration of democracy. Churchill's instinct was probably right, that if the Allies had done nothing the communists would have seized Greece with the same ruthlessness they were displaying everywhere else in Eastern Europe and the Balkans. But clumsy diplomacy caused the British to be seen, above all in Washington, as would-be imperialist oppressors of a liberated people. Lincoln McVeagh, the US minister in Athens, criticised the British for 'handling this fanatically freedom-loving country as if it were composed of natives under the British raj'.

On 5 December Edward Stettinius, who had just replaced Cordell Hull as US Secretary of State, raised the stakes by publicly criticising British policy in Greece and also in Italy, where the British were at loggerheads with the Americans about whether Count Sforza should be permitted a role in the new Rome government. Stettinius said: 'We expect the Italians to work out their own problems of government along democratic lines without influence from outside. This policy would apply to an even more pronounced degree with regard to governments of the United Nations* in their liberated territories.' Whatever the merits of the argument, it was deeply unhelpful of Stettinius, and damaging to Churchill, thus publicly to have distanced the United States from Britain.

A marked shift in American media sentiment was taking place. Conservative commentators, hitherto bitterly sceptical about British foreign policy, now showed themselves sympathetic to Churchill's efforts to check the onset of European communism. The liberal press, however, deplored what it perceived as new manifestations of British imperialism. It is a striking reflection upon the mood of those days, that perceived British misconduct in Greece and Italy provoked much more comment and protest in the US than did Russia's ruthless handling of its newly-occupied East European territories.

Many American papers asserted the right of Resistance movements, whatever their political complexion, to a voice in the governance of their countries. A State Department opinion survey stated: '"Liberal" papers, pleading for a greater representation for Resistance forces, were critical of Churchill's alleged attempt to maintain a reactionary regime against the wishes of the Greek people.' William Shirer of CBS urged that the US back up its words by taking action in opposition to British 'toryism'. The State Department said:

* Meaning the Allies.

'Substantially universal approval has greeted the proposition that the composition of governments in Italy and in "liberated territories" is an internal affair . . . Representatives of Greek-American organizations visited the State Department to protest British intervention in Greece . . . The Department also received numerous letters from organizations and individuals protesting British policy and applauding the United States's [5 December] declaration.'

Many American newspapers perceived the Soviets and British as tarred with the same brush, both seeking to impose their selfish wills on free peoples. Isolationists blamed Britain, and explicitly Churchill, for 'seeking to bury the Atlantic Charter' with its declared right to self-determination. The North Carolina *Raleigh News & Observer*, for instance, cited 'the shooting of Greeks for no greater crime than opposing a Government which seeks to bring back a discredited King' as being 'not only a mistake but a tragedy'. There were increasing demands, echoed in Congress, for a revision of Lend-Lease legislation, to link US aid to Britain and Russia with less high-handed foreign policies. The *Chicago Sun*, urging Lend-Lease revision, observed that 'Washington has both the right and obligation to let the British government know that we do not propose to aid the enemies of democracy in Italy, Greece, or elsewhere through Lend-Lease or any other means.'

A Princeton poll in December found that Americans thought Britain likely to be a much less trustworthy post-war ally than China. On 13 December 1944, the US press reported anti-British student protests and marches at Harvard, Radcliffe, Wellesley and Northeastern. In Boston, students waved placards proclaiming: 'AMERICANS SUPPORT CHURCHILL AS WAR LEADER, NOT TORY'. The protesters issued a statement: 'We are not against Churchill as a war leader, but against his reactionary policy in Belgium, Italy, and Greece.' US trades unionists also demonstrated against British policy.

An attack on the prime minister by H.G. Wells was widely reported. 'Churchill must go,' the aged British literary sage wrote in *Tribune*: 'Winston Churchill, the present would-be British Fuhrer, is a person with a range of ideas limited to the adventures and opportunities of British political life . . . Now he seems to have lost his head completely . . . When the British people were blistered with humiliation by the currish policy of the old Conservative gang in power, the pugnacity of Winston brought him to the fore. The country liked fighting and he delighted in fighting. For want of a better reason he became the symbol of our national will for conflict, a role he has now outlived.' Thomas Stokes wrote in the *Los Angeles Times* on 12 December: 'What we are seeing is the opening of the big battle between the right and the left for the control of post-war Europe. There's Great Britain on one side and Russia on the other, with the United States as a sort of arbiter or umpire trying to establish some middle course, and being in the difficult position of the harassed liberal who is caught in the crossfire from each side.'

For Churchill, the only positive news coming out of Greece was that the Russians appeared to be holding back. 'This is good,' he wrote to Eden, 'and shows how Stalin is playing the game.' For once, the prime minister's optimism was justified. Throughout the unfolding imbroglio in Greece, there was no sign that Moscow sought to meddle. Churchill, indeed, was moved to assert that on this issue he found the Russians much more biddable than the Americans. Stalin acknowledged spheres of influence, however broadly he sought to draw his own. Roosevelt did not.

On 8 December 1944 there was a stormy Commons debate about Greece, in which Emanuel Shinwell and Aneurin Bevan, men of the left, led the attack on the government. Churchill, who once more chose to remind the House that it could dismiss him if it so wished, won a vote of confidence by 279 votes to thirty. But many MPs remained dissatisfied. Harold Nicolson thought the prime minister misread the mood of the House, which 'at its best was one of distressed perplexity, and at its worst of sheer red fury'. Harold Macmillan, who attended the debate, saw the prime minister afterwards in the Downing Street Annexe. He found him tired and petulant: 'He rambled on in rather a sad and depressed way. The debate had obviously tired him very much, and I think he realised the dangers inherent in the Greek policy on which we are now embarked. He has won the debate, but not the battle of Athens.'

Churchill seemed to have dug in his heels. He cabled Rex Leeper, British ambassador in Greece, on 10 December: 'In Athens as everywhere else our maxim is "no peace without victory".' Yet Lt.Gen. Ronald Scobie, commanding British troops, signalled that he lacked sufficient men to hold the capital, never mind to enforce the prime minister's desired disarmament of the guerrillas. Alexander was now Mediterranean C-in-C, having replaced 'Jumbo' Maitland-Wilson, who was dispatched to become British military representative in Washington following the sudden death of Sir John Dill. Churchill urged Alexander to find more troops for Greece.

Relations with the Americans took a sharp turn for the worse. On 5 December, Churchill had signalled to Scobie, urging him to adopt a ruthless policy towards the communist guerrillas: 'Do not hesitate to fire at any armed male in Athens who assails the British authority or Greek authority . . . act as if you were in a conquered city where a local rebellion is in progress.' Jock Colville dispatched this message at 5 a.m., when amid exhaustion he forgot to mark it 'GUARD' – not to be shown to Americans. Admiral Ernest King, on his own initiative and even before hearing of Churchill's draconian signal, ordered that US shipping should not be used to supply or reinforce the British in Greece. Churchill cabled Harry Hopkins on 9 December: 'It grieves me very much to see signs of our drifting part at a time when unity becomes even more important, as dangers recede and faction arises.' Hopkins persuaded King to rescind his order, apparently without reference to Roosevelt. But a *Washington Post* editorial declared on 9 December: 'the American people simply do not relish the spectacle of Sherman tanks going into action against the men who held the pass in war-stricken Hellas'. Correspondent Barnet Nover attacked Churchill for his harsh words about the Greek communist guerrillas: 'What suddenly transformed those patriots into "bandits"?'

A malevolent hand in Washington leaked Churchill's draconian directive to Scobie to columnist Drew Pearson, who published it in the *Post* on 11 December. The ensuing anti-British tirade caused Churchill to draw unfavourable contrasts with Moscow's useful silence. 'I think we have had pretty good treatment from Stalin in

Greece,' he wrote to Eden, 'much better in fact than we have had from the Americans.' The *Post* editorialised on 6 December: 'The use of force carries within it the seeds of its destruction.' On the 8th, a *Post* article by Marquis Childs argued: 'Winston Churchill and the clique around him want to believe that you can put a little paint and a little varnish on the old order and prop it up in place again. It won't prop. That's the meaning of the news out of Brussels and Athens . . . the course that is being followed in Greece and Belgium is the best way to ensure communism in the end.'

Walter Lippmann wrote in the *Washington Post* of 14 December that problems had arisen in Greece 'because Mr Churchill is trying to apply the great principle of legitimacy in government without a correct appreciation of the unprecedented condition of affairs which the Nazi conquest and occupation have created'. The problem facing those trying to reconstruct Europe is 'how to fuse the legitimacy acquired by Resistance movements with the legitimacy inherited by the old governments'. This was an accurate analysis of Churchill's dilemma, lacking only an answer to it. Events in Greece, and else-where, were critically influenced by the outcome of policies promoted by the prime minister himself through SOE. It was only possible for ELAS to mount a challenge to the Greek government and its British sponsors because London had provided the communists with arms.

Halifax cabled gloomily from the Washington embassy: 'Our version of the facts is largely disbelieved.' On the ground in Athens, Scobie's units faced increasingly violent pressure from ELAS guer-rillas. Open insurgency was breaking out. Alexander signalled: 'British forces are in fact beleaguered in the heart of the city.' Both Macmillan and Leeper, at the British embassy, believed that Churchill failed to grasp the complexities of the situation. However distasteful were the communists, the Greek right was at least as much so. Macmillan urged the prime minister to accept that the king – 'the real villain of the piece' – must remain exiled in London, while the primate of Athens, Archbishop Damaskinos, should be appointed regent in Athens, to reconcile the warring factions. Damaskinos, fifty-three years old, born Dimitrios Papandreou, had become famous during the Occupation for his public defiance of the Germans, and especially for his denunciations of the persecution of the Jews. Macmillan had little time for the Greek prime minister: 'We do not wish to start the Third World War against Russia until we have finished the Second World War against Germany – and certainly not to please M. Papandreou.' The British in Athens, who perceived a regency as offering by far the best chance of a settlement acceptable to the Greek people, were enraged by the perceived duplicity of the Greek prime minister, who urged George II to reject a regency.

Men of the British Army who found themselves seeking to sustain by force the Athens regime were as divided as the rest of the world about the merits of their cause. Captain Phillip Zorab, for instance, hated the communists and everything that he saw and heard of their doings: 'These ELAS guerrillas don't care who they hit,' he wrote in a letter home, 'and I have four first-hand reports of atrocities committed by them on other Greeks . . . Greeks now know that when we said that political differences would not be settled by use of arms, we meant it.' Other British soldiers, however, were deeply troubled by the role in which they found themselves cast. Major A.P. Greene, like Zorab a gunner, told his family:

> I thought a good deal before writing this letter, because it contains some pretty definite views. But they must be aired or ten years of principles go for naught. Briefly I think our country is being misled on the subject of Greece. I have just finished reading Churchill's speech, and I disagreed with it vehemently. Greece is a country with no background of real democracy in its modern history . . . We, the preachers of non-intervention, are forcing on Greece the government we want, and think it wants . . . Churchill's speech was, to me, a political falsehood . . . People at home should know that it is the *Manchester Guardian* and not Churchill that represents the opinion of 80% of the army here. Whether they be regulars or volunteers, high ranking officers or privates, the vast majority want no part in what, to them, is a face-saving war of Churchill's own making.

Greene acknowledged that all the local factions were guilty of atrocities, 'but I think the bulk of Greek youth wants socialism . . . I shall stay until I'm so heartily sick of assisting in the installation of a fascist regime in Greece that I summon up enough courage to resign.' He was right in believing that the wartime experience had radicalised Greek youth, as it appears to have radicalised him. Yet if Churchill's support for restoring the monarchy was mistaken, he was surely justified in his revulsion against allowing power to fall by default into communist hands, as would have been most likely to happen in the absence of British military intervention.

On 17 December, Alexander signalled that another infantry division might be needed to hold Athens, a shocking prospect since the formation would have to be withdrawn from the Italian front. Two days later, 563 RAF personnel at the British air headquarters at Kifissia, outside Athens, surrendered to ELAS after a battle in which fifty-seven airmen had been killed or wounded. During the month's fighting in Athens, the British Army lost 169 killed, 699 wounded and 640 missing – mostly prisoners – an appalling scale of casualties for what began as a post-liberation security operation. Macmillan wrote in his diary on 21 December: 'Poor Winston! What with Greece, Poland and the German breakthrough on the Western Front, this is going to be a grim Christmas.' By the 22nd, with strife intensifying, Churchill was at last becoming persuadable about the possibility of a regency, keeping the king out of Greece pending a referendum on his future. But he said crossly to Cadogan: 'I won't install a Dictator.' In truth, the prime minister was dithering. An almost daily barrage of hostile questions in the Commons sustained pressure on the government. He cabled to Smuts: 'I have had endless trouble about Greece where we have indeed been wounded in the house of our friends. Communist and Left-wing forces all over the world have stirred in sympathy with this new chance and the American Press reporting back has to some extent undermined our prestige and authority in Greece. There would be no chance of our basing a British policy upon the return of the King. We must at all costs avoid appearing to be forcing him on them by our bayonets.'

Much grief – even perhaps the bloody strife in Greece – might have been averted if Churchill had reached this conclusion months earlier, and explicitly proclaimed it to the Greek people. But it was hard to resolve the affairs of half a world emerging from the horrors of occupation, amid the new reality of Soviet expansionism. If British policy was sometimes misjudged, so too was American. The British embassy in Washington reported to London about US media opinion: 'Indignation with Britain has given way to a kind of disgruntled and disenchanted cynicism which says that it was foolish ever to have supposed that the European, and in particular Russian and British, leopards could really have been expected to change their spots as the result of a few idealistic words from America.'

What now was to be done? On the afternoon of Saturday, 23 December, Churchill drove to Chequers, where a large family party was assembled for Christmas. He had scarcely arrived before he declared his determination to abandon the celebration, and travel to Athens. His decision caused consternation, above all to Clementine. This was one of the very rare moments of the war at which she broke down, fleeing upstairs in floods of tears. Her husband was just seventy, and in poor health. Private secretary John Martin wrote in his diary: 'Glad I am not going on an expedition of which I disapprove, the prize not being worth the risks.' Late on Christmas Eve Churchill and his entourage, including Anthony Eden, drove to Northolt and took off for Italy in a new American C-54 Skymaster. 'Make it look British,' Churchill urged when the plane was delivered, and the aircraft had been refitted to an extraordinary standard of comfort for the times. Its principal passenger complained only that the clock in his private compartment ticked too loudly, and insisted upon disconnection of an electrically heated lavatory seat.

What did Churchill hope to achieve in Athens? It seemed to him, rightly, essential to Britain's global prestige, and above all to relations with the US, that he should succeed in stabilising Greece. It was implausible that this could be achieved under Papandreou. Some broadly-based coalition government was needed. His advisers believed that Archbishop Damaskinos might provide the necessary sheet anchor, and supervise the creation of such a regime. Yet Churchill was mistrustful of surrendering the country to some wily local prelate. As ever, he wanted to see, and then to be seen to act, for himself. Early in the afternoon of Christmas Day, his Skymaster landed at Kalamaki airfield.

One of the welcoming party observed cynically that the visitors 'had the air of men to whom a brilliant idea had been vouchsafed after the third glass of port upon which they had immediately decided to act but which they could now no longer very clearly recall'. Macmillan found the prime minister 'in a most mellow, not to say chastened mood'. A two-hour conference took place in the plane, the interior of which became icy cold. Churchill's shivering typist, Elizabeth Layton, was increasingly fearful for 'Master's' health. The security situation was much worse than had been recognised in London, with snipers active in many parts of the Greek capital. Towards evening, a convoy of armoured cars took the party on a long, tense, uncomfortable journey to Phaleron, where they were transferred by launch to the light cruiser *Ajax*, a veteran of the 1939 River Plate battle, which was anchored offshore, safely beyond small-arms range.

Her captain warned the exalted visitor that it might be necessary to disturb his tranquillity by firing the ship's main armament in support of British ground forces. Churchill, of course, enthused at the prospect: 'Pray remember, Captain, that I come here as a cooing dove of peace, bearing a sprig of mistletoe in my beak – but far be it from me to stand in the way of military necessity.' Shortly afterwards Macmillan, Leeper, Papandreou and Damaskinos boarded the ship. The spectacle of the prelate in full canonical dress, complete with black silver-knobbed staff, brushing past sailors in the ship's companionways who were celebrating Christmas in fancy dress, impressed the British as irresistibly droll.

Churchill was captivated by the jolly archbishop, who made plain his revulsion towards the communists and the atrocities which they had committed. The prelate, the prime minister told MPs later, 'struck me as a very remarkable man, with his headgear, towering up, morally as well as physically, above the chaotic scene'. Colville wrote: 'We are now in the curious topsy-turvy position of the prime minister feeling strongly pro-Damaskinos . . . while [Eden] is inclined the other way.' Next morning, the visitors rose to survey the battlefield – what Churchill called 'the pink and ochre panorama of Athens and the Piraeus, scintillating with delicious life and plumed by the classic glories and endless miseries and triumphs of its history'. The shore was bathed in bright sunshine. 'One can see the smoke of battle in the streets west of the Piraeus,' wrote Colville, 'and there is a constant noise of shellfire and machine-guns. We had a splendid view of Beaufighters strafing an ELAS stronghold.'

Osbert Lancaster, the artist then serving as press attaché at the British embassy, described the arrival next afternoon of Churchill, once more borne by armoured car from the harbour through the drab, dusty, bullet-scarred streets. The prime minister wore the uniform of an RAF air commodore: 'The change in his appearance since I had last seen him at close quarters some three years previously was marked. His face seems to have been moulded in lard lightly veined with cochineal and he badly needed a haircut. But the sound of mortaring and rifle-fire, combined with the historic associations of the countryside through which he had just passed, were clearly already having a tonic effect and he was distinguished from all his companions by an obvious and unswerving sense of purpose none the less impressive for being at the moment indeterminate.' The latter intimation of confusion was unwarranted. The British had already convened a conference of all the warring parties, to meet under Churchill's auspices, but Damaskinos's chairmanship.

The embassy resembled a besieged outpost during the Indian Mutiny. Power was cut off, while gunfire provided orchestration. Some fifty staff, many of them women, had been subsisting for nine days on army rations in conditions of acute discomfort. The ambassador's wife, whom Harold Macmillan found more impressive than her husband, directed domestic operations with a courage and energy likewise worthy of a Victorian imperial drama. Fortunately for the inmates, ELAS guerrillas had only small arms, so the British remained safe if they avoided exposing themselves at doors and windows. Between meetings with commanders, Churchill met and applauded the embassy staff, for whom he afterwards arranged an immediate issue of decorations.

At 4 p.m., representatives of the Greek factions assembled around a long table in the freezing, otherwise barren conference room of the Foreign Office. The rattle of musketry punctuated the proceedings, with voices sometimes drowned out by rocket and mortar concussions. Churchill seated himself in the centre, flanked by Archbishop Damaskinos, Eden and Macmillan. At one end were American, Russian and French representatives. The Greeks filled in around them, leaving space at a vacant end for the communists, who were late. Churchill and the prelate spoke brilliantly and at length, with long pauses for interpretation, before news arrived of the absentees, 'three shabby desperados'. The communists had been delayed arguing with British security guards about their demand to bring weapons into the conference chamber. On their appearance, Churchill wrote to Clementine later, 'after some consideration I shook the ELAS delegates' hand[s] and it was clear from their response that they were gratified'. He repeated much of his opening harangue: 'Mr Eden and I have come all this way, though great battles are raging in Belgium and on the German frontier, to make this effort to rescue Greece from a miserable fate and raise her to a point of great fame and repute . . . Whether Greece is a monarchy or a republic is a matter for Greeks and Greeks alone to decide. I wish you all that is good, and good for all.'

Alexander said: 'Instead of me putting my brigades into Greece, I should like to see Greek brigades coming to help me in Italy in the war against our common enemy.' Macmillan was disgusted by the oily platitudes offered by the communists, who extolled their own desire for peace: 'I thought it all very disingenuous, especially remembering the frightful atrocities these men are committing both on our troops and on harmless fellow-countrymen throughout Greece. Winston was much moved, however.' Then the foreigners rose and left the table, to enable the Greeks to negotiate with each other.

Once they were outside, their exchanges provided several notable vignettes. The prime minister engaged the head of the Russian military mission in conversation: 'What's your name? Popov? Well, Popov,

I saw your master the other day, Popov! Very good friends your master and I, Popov! Don't forget that, POPOV!' Even the colonel's limited English enabled him to grasp Churchill's attempt to brandish his relationship with Stalin. Then it was explained that the delay to proceedings had been caused by the need to disarm the communist delegates. The prime minister looked thoughtful and withdrew a pistol from his own pocket, growling complacently: 'I cannot tell you the feeling of security one enjoys, knowing that one is the only armed man in such an assembly as that!' He replaced the weapon in his overcoat before retreating with his entourage by armoured car to the embassy, and thence to Phaleron. When his typist Elizabeth Layton seated herself at the opposite end of the naval barge's cabin to the prime minister, Churchill said, 'No, come and sit by me.' To Alexander's wry amusement, the two travelled back across the water to *Ajax* cosily enfolded together in a huge rug.

Next day, the archbishop came to the British embassy to report on progress of the noisy, bitter talks at the Foreign Office. At one point, apparently, General Plastiras – whom Churchill insistently addressed as 'Plaster-Arse' – shouted at a communist: 'Sit down, butcher!' The prime minister was in high spirits, having been taken by Alexander to a vantage point from which the general explained the Athens battlefield. Macmillan saw this as a reprise of Churchill's famous appearance at a London shoot-out with terrorists during his 1911 incarnation as Home Secretary: 'Of course this affair is a sort of "super Sidney Street", and he quite enjoyed having the whole problem explained to him by a master of the military art.' When the ELAS delegates asked to see Churchill privately, he was eager to accept. But Macmillan and Damaskinos persuaded him that it was essential now to leave the Greeks to sort out their own affairs. That evening, the archbishop announced Papandreou's resignation as prime minister. His last act in office was to cable to King George II in London, declaring the united endorsement of Greece's politicians for a regency. Churchill wrote to Clementine: 'This Wednesday has been an exciting and not altogether fruitless day. The hatreds between these Greeks are terrible. When one side have all the weapons which we gave them to fight the

Germans and the other, though many times as numerous, have none, it is evident that a frightful massacre would take place if we withdrew.'

Lack of both electricity and camera flashbulbs made it necessary to hold the prime minister's parting photocall in the embassy garden, much to the dismay of those responsible for his safety. Access was possible only by traversing a short walkway from the drawing room, on which he was visible to the world from Constitution Avenue. Attempts to hustle him behind the safety of the garden wall were frustrated by an onrush of photographers which caused the prime minister to halt on the walkway. To the dismay of the press attaché behind him, 'a short crack followed by a shower of plaster announced that a bullet had hit the wall two feet above our heads. Summoning all my courage, I . . . gave the infuriated Prime Minister a sharp shove in the back, precipitating him smartly down the steps into the comparative safety of the garden.' On 28 December, Churchill flew out of Athens for Naples. He had yearned to linger, and again to meet the Greeks. Macmillan, however, persuaded him that his duty was to return to London and reconcile King George of the Hellenes to the regency. Churchill allowed himself to be buckled into his seatbelt on the Skymaster, acknowledging that 'Even the most eminent persons are subject to the laws of gravity.' As the plane taxied, he suddenly ordered it to halt. He insisted on passing down to the ground party an amendment to the British final communiqué. Then he took off for Italy, and home.

Back in London next afternoon, the prime minister twice met the King of the Hellenes, at 10.30 p.m. and 1.30 a.m. At 4 a.m., George II at last agreed to the regency. Churchill retired to bed after a working and travelling day that had lasted twenty-two hours. General Nikolaus Plastiras became prime minister, though he was obliged to resign soon afterwards, following the leak of a letter revealing that in 1941 he had offered himself to the Nazis as leader of a collaborationist Greek government. On the night of 4 January 1945, the firepower of the British Army and diminished confidence in their own prospects persuaded the communist guerrillas to retire to the countryside. An uneasy armistice was agreed between the factions. Violence in Athens subsided, though it required the deployment of 90,000 British troops to secure the country. Greece remained in a state of civil war between 1946 and 1949, but a non-communist – indeed, bitterly anti-communist – government survived until the Americans relieved the British of responsibility for Greek security.

Churchill's visit was significant chiefly because it reconciled him to a course of action which all the other British players had already endorsed. The decisive factor in Greece was Stalin's abstention. It suited Moscow to acknowledge the principle that whichever ally liberated an occupied country should determine its subsequent governance. The ELAS guerrilla leaders were vastly more impressed by the silence of Colonel Popov, Stalin's man in Athens, than by the eloquence of Britain's prime minister. In Greece, Churchill received his sole reward for the Moscow 'percentages agreement' which Americans so much disliked. So tormented and riven was Greek society in the wake of the occupation that it is hard to imagine any course of action which might have brought about the peaceful establishment of a democratic government. What emerged was probably the least bad outcome, in which no one could take just pride.

Churchill's dramatic venture into personal diplomacy commanded less world attention than it might otherwise have done, because it coincided with the Battle of the Bulge in Belgium and Luxembourg. According to a State Department survey, the overriding US media impression of British action remained unfavourable: 'Anglo–American differences and British military action in Greece during early December received more than twice as much front page space as Churchill's mission to Athens . . . Predominant editorial opinion throughout the crisis was never categorically opposed to British leadership in Greece and the Mediterranean, but strongly objected to the possible imposition of an unrepresentative and unpopular government on the Greek people, and to the possible creation of a closed British sphere of interest.' Drew Pearson's final column of 1944 unfavourably compared Churchill's 'outgrown imperialism' with more enlightened attitudes elsewhere in the British body politic. Criticism of British shortcomings at home and abroad was now a running theme in the US press. Virginius Dabney wrote in the *New York Times* on

31 December that opinion in the American South, traditionally friendly to Britain, was turning hostile: 'The development which has provoked most adverse comment is Winston Churchill's policy in Greece and Italy. Even in this strongly pro-British region criticism is being heard, not only of Churchill but of the British people.'

The British did not receive this bombardment in silence. On 30 December, after a surge of American comment which added allegations of 'slacking' to other charges against America's ally, the *Economist* delivered a counterblast:

> What makes the American criticisms so intolerable is not merely that they are unjust, but that they come from a source which has done so little to earn the right to postures of superiority. To be told by anyone that the British people are slacking in their war effort would be insufferable enough to a people struggling through their sixth winter of black-out and rations and coldness – but when the criticism comes from a nation that was practising Cash-and-Carry during the Battle of Britain, whose consumption has risen during the war years, which is still without a national service act – then it is not to be borne.
>
> There is still a great deal of wishful thinking in Britain, even in the highest quarters, to the effect that good behaviour on our part will procure some great prize, such as an Anglo–American alliance . . . It is as well to be brutally frank: there is no more possibility of any of these things than of an American petition to rejoin the British Empire . . . What, then, is the conclusion for British policy towards America? Clearly it is not that any quarrels should be picked . . . But let an end be put to the policy of appeasement which, at Mr Churchill's personal bidding, has been followed, with all the humiliations and abasements it has brought in its train.

Following the *Economist*'s outburst, the State Department recorded 'an orgy of recrimination between the American and British presses'. The Washington embassy reported to London the following week on US attitudes: 'The general reaction is that although the British attack was not unprovoked and the British cannot have been expected to take the flood of criticism poured by the United States press and radio lying down, yet the British are surely much too touchy and the tone of their retort is much too harsh.' Though a 14 January *Life* magazine editorial described the *Economist*'s criticisms as well-merited, many American publications remained hostile. OWI and State Department surveys in the early months of 1945 found that Americans consistently rated the British more blameworthy than the Russians for the difficulties of the Grand Alliance.

The State Department study noted: 'Despite recent press comment sympathetic to the British, a confidential opinion poll indicates that dissatisfaction with the British has increased among the public at large. The tabulation shows that mass opinion, dissatisfied with the way in which Russia, Britain and the United States are cooperating, blames chiefly Britain . . . The "nationalist" press, even in comment praising Field-Marshal Montgomery and the British people, continued to charge that the "British and Russians are playing power politics against each other in the middle of this war, while we, at least at this moment, do most of the fighting".'

Churchill found little to celebrate in what he called the 'new, disgusting year' of 1945. Russian intransigence was familiar, but overbearing American behaviour filled a bitter cup. Tempers were sorely frayed, in government and among the British people. Eden wrote on 12 January: 'Terrible Cabinet, first on Greece . . . Whole thing lasted four and a half hours. Really quite intolerable. I was in a pretty bloody temper . . . for everyone started taking a hand in drafting messages for me.' Churchill found it much harder to sustain relative inactivity in Downing Street than to undertake initiatives abroad, even if these were ill-rewarded. One morning he told his typist Marion Holmes: 'You know I cannot give you the excitement of Athens every day.'

There seemed no limit to the troubles sent to vex him. Montgomery gave an outrageously hubristic press conference following his modest personal contribution to the Bulge battle. This excited new American hostility, and correspondingly exasperated the prime minister. Churchill was obliged to recognise that there was no more chance of restoring King Peter of Yugoslavia to his throne than King Zog of Albania or King Carol of Romania to theirs. Roosevelt agreed to Stalin's proposal for a February summit at Yalta in the Crimea, causing Churchill to cable: 'I shall be waiting on the quay. No more let us falter! From Malta to Yalta! Let nobody alter!' In reality, however, the British complained bitterly about the inconvenient venue. They remained resentful that Roosevelt was unwilling to visit their own country, or to accept Churchill's alternative suggestion of a meeting in Iceland. The prime minister sent congratulations to Stalin on the Russian Vistula offensive, all the more fulsome because of his anxiety for Soviet goodwill in Greece and Poland. Brooke expressed relief that Churchill seemed finally reconciled to the fact that there could be no Adriatic amphibious landing, nor a drive on Vienna. Churchill brusquely dismissed De Gaulle's demand that he should attend the Yalta conference in the name of his country. 'France cannot masquerade as a Great Power for the purposes of war,' he told Eden.

The prime minister said to Marion Holmes: 'You wouldn't like my job – so many different things come up which have to be settled in two or three minutes.' At a time when many of his own ministers were wearying of Churchill, Holmes paid a tribute which reflected the passionate affection and loyalty he retained among his personal staff: 'In all his moods – totally absorbed in the serious matter of the moment, agonized over some piece of wartime bad news, suffused with compassion, sentimental and in tears, truculent, bitingly sarcastic, mischievous or hilariously funny – he was splendidly entertaining, humane and lovable.' While ministers and commanders complained with increasing impatience about the prime minister's failing concentration and outbursts of irrationality, he remained a unique repository of wisdom. Consider, for instance, his words to Eden, who had been pressing him about arrangements for post-war Germany:

It is a mistake to try to write out on some little pieces of papers what the vast emotions of an outraged and quivering world will be either immediately after the struggle is over or when the inevitable cold fit follows the hot. These awe-inspiring tides of feeling dominate most people's minds . . . Guidance in these mundane matters is granted to us only step by step, or at the utmost a step or two ahead. There is therefore wisdom in reserving one's decisions as long as possible and until all the facts and forces that will be potent at the moment are revealed.

Likewise, on 18 January he delivered to the House of Commons a report on the war situation which some thought as glittering a display of oratory as he had produced since 1940. In a two-hour speech, he said of Greece:

> The House must not suppose that, in these foreign lands, matters are settled as they would be here in England. Even here it is hard enough to keep a Coalition together, even between men who, although divided by party, have a supreme object and so much else in common. But imagine what the difficulties are in countries racked by civil war, past or impending, and where clusters of petty parties have each their own set of appetites, misdeeds and revenges. If I had driven the wife of the Deputy Prime Minister out to die in the snow, if the Minister of Labour had kept the Foreign Secretary in exile for a great many years, if the Chancellor of the Exchequer had shot at and wounded the Secretary of State for War . . . if we, who sit here together, had back-bitten and double-crossed each other while pretending to work together, and had all put our own group or party first and the country nowhere, and had all set ideologies, slogans or labels in front of comprehension, comradeship and duty, we should certainly, to put it at the mildest, have come to a General Election much sooner than is now likely. When men have wished very much to kill each other, and have feared very much that they will be killed quite soon, it is not possible for them next day to work together as friends with colleagues against whom they have nursed such intentions or from whom they have derived such fears.

Churchill said to Colville in those days, speaking of the South African prime minister, 'Smuts and I are like two old love-birds moulting together on a perch, but still able to peck.' He 'pecked' to incomparable effect. After his difficult passages with MPs about Greece in December, he had now restored his position. Yet he told one considerable untruth to the Commons on 18 January, denying that events in the Mediterranean were in any way influenced by rival notions about 'spheres of influences'. In reality, in his gratitude for Stalin's forbearance on Greece, he was desperate to be seen to keep his own side of the Moscow bargain. He was exasperated to hear that British diplomats in Romania had been protesting about Soviet actions there, and wrote angrily to Eden: 'Why are we making a fuss about the Russian deportations in Roumania of Saxons and others? It is understood that the Russians were to work their will in this sphere. Anyhow, we cannot prevent them.' He told Colville on 23 January: 'Make no mistake, all the Balkans, except Greece, are going to be bolshevized; and there is nothing I can do to prevent it. There is nothing I can do for poor Poland either.'

If Churchill often displayed greatness on great matters, his ministers and commanders were increasingly sensitive to 'the old man's' limitations. His rambling dissertations at cabinets, often about papers which he had not troubled to read, exasperated colleagues. So too did his willingness to invite and accept ill-informed opinions across the table from Brendan Bracken and Beaverbrook, in preference to the considered views of cabinet committees. Clement Attlee wrote him a note of protest about his behaviour, which fired the prime minister's wrath, but which his own staff and Clementine agreed to be both courageous and just. Attlee had typed the note with his own fumbling fingers, to ensure that no other eye saw it. Yet Churchill vented his spleen by reading it aloud down the telephone to Beaverbrook. Private secretary John Martin said: 'That is the part of the prime minister which I do not like.' Jock Colville agreed. The prime minister was eventually persuaded to reconsider his first thought, of an angry riposte to Attlee. He responded temperately. Then he said: 'Let us think no more of Hitlee or of Attler: let us go and see a film.' If he was sometimes roused to stand high upon his dignity, he seldom retained the posture for long. If he sometimes behaved unworthily, he had earned the right to be readily forgiven.

TWENTY-ONE

Yalta

Almost every day of the war that he was not travelling, Churchill visited his map room. Captain Richard Pim RN, the lanky Welshman who presided there, was a key figure in the Downing Street entourage, often accompanying the prime minister on his journeys to maintain the flow of battlefield news he craved. Churchill still intervened constantly in matters of detail concerning the armed forces. Britain's falling troop strength was a preoccupation. He deplored the dissolution of some units to fill the depleted ranks of others. There were wearisome wrangles about the respective manpower claims of the army, RAF and coal mines. Churchill was anxious that soldiers dispatched to the Far East at the end of the German war should receive additional pay. He followed with the keenest interest the commitment of Germany's new advanced U-boats to the Atlantic, British progress towards producing jet fighters to match those of Hitler, and efforts to counter the V2 rocket bombardment which continued to inflict distress on southern England.

But these were all minor matters, by comparison with the great strategy decisions of earlier years. The Allied armies were advancing across Europe with little opportunity for the prime minister to influence their courses. He hailed successes, chafed in familiar fashion at setbacks and delays, but knew that power resided at Eisenhower's headquarters and in Washington. Oliver Harvey wrote, somewhat patronisingly: 'As the purely military problems simplify themselves, the old boy's tireless energy leads to ever closer attention to foreign affairs.' Almost all Churchill's thoughts were now fixed upon the post-war settlement of Europe, which might be critically influenced by the Yalta summit. 'I have great hopes of this conference,' he told the House of Commons, 'because it comes at a moment when a good many moulds can be set out to receive a great deal of molten metal.' Nonetheless, he complained to Harry Hopkins, who was in London, that if the Allies had spent ten years researching a possible rendezvous, they could not have devised a less convenient one than the Crimea. It was farcical that a desperately sick US president should be obliged to travel 6,000 miles to suit the whims of Soviet doctors who had allegedly told Stalin not to venture abroad. As for the prime minister himself, on 29 January he arrived at Malta, Anglo-American staging point for Yalta, with a temperature of 102°.

The combined chiefs of staff held an unpleasant preliminary meeting, its atmosphere poisoned by personality clashes entwined with the north-west Europe campaign. Montgomery's boorish behaviour towards Eisenhower sustained friction. Brooke was distressed to find that Marshall refused even to enter into argument with the British about strategy. America's course was set, for a measured advance to the Elbe. Franklin Roosevelt arrived aboard the cruiser *Quincy* on 2 February. If Churchill was feverish, the British were shocked to perceive in the leader of the United States the wreck of a man. It was a grim prospect to set off for a summit with an American president unfit for important business. After the delegations' first dinner together at Malta, Eden fumed about lack of serious discussion: 'Impossible even to get near basics. I spoke pretty sharply to Harry [Hopkins] about it . . . pointing out that we were going into a decisive conference and had so far neither agreed about what we would discuss nor how to handle matters with a Bear who would certainly know his mind.' Human sympathy for Roosevelt was eclipsed by dismay about the implications of his incapacity to defend the interests of the West.

The Allied leaders' arrival in the Crimea on 3 February was inauspicious. After the planes carrying the great men landed, Roosevelt had to be assisted into a jeep to inspect a Russian guard of honour, with Churchill walking beside him. There followed a nightmare six-hour trip to Yalta, along terrible roads. The prime minister looked around him without enthusiasm. 'What a hole I've brought you to!' he said to Marion Holmes. Later, he described the resort bleakly as 'the Riviera of Hades'. Generals found themselves billeted four to a room, colonels in dormitories of eleven. From national leaders downwards, all complained about the shortage of bathrooms. On 4 February there was a pre-conference dinner of the principals. Eden wrote: 'A terrible party, I thought. President vague and loose and ineffective. W., understanding that business was flagging, made desperate efforts and too long speeches to get things going again. Stalin's attitude to small countries struck me as grim, not to say sinister.' Security around the Soviet leader was so tight that he arrived for a photocall almost invisible amidst a phalanx of armed guards.

Despite all the criticism of Churchill in the US during past months, few Americans at Yalta doubted the power of his personality. C.L. Sulzberger wrote in the *New York Times* that among the 'Big Three', Roosevelt was 'certainly blander than either of his colleagues', while Churchill 'with his romantic conceptions, his touch of mysticism, his imperialism, his love of uniforms and color, is something of a Renaissance figure. He combines more talents than either Stalin or Roosevelt – more than almost any political figure who has ever attained his stature.'

Polls in America continued to report widespread personal respect for the prime minister, and a renewed faith that Britain would prove a reliable post-war ally. But enthusiasm for Churchill's country was importantly qualified. Most Americans – 70 per cent – were implacable in their belief that at the end of the war the British should repay the billions they had received in Lend-Lease supplies. Even when told that their ally lacked means to do this, 43 per cent of respondents said that they must do so anyway. It was a perverse and unhelpful compliment to Britain that the United States, its leaders and people alike, still overestimated the wealth of Churchill's nation. Few grasped the extent of its moral, strategic and financial exhaustion. Finally, of course, the war had done nothing to diminish US anti-imperialism. A March OWI survey reported: 'During the past year, Britain . . . has been under severe attack by an active minority for its alleged failure to play its proper role in the "Big Three Team" . . . During December and January dissatisfaction with Big Three cooperation was . . . directed chiefly at Britain . . . [which was] chiefly blamed for "not living up to the Atlantic Charter". The attitude of the unusually large anti-British minority . . . found striking expression in a widely-publicized article in the *Army and Navy Journal*. In a stinging passage, equally critical of Russian and British policy, the *Journal* accused Britain of "showing greater pre-occupation in Italy, Greece and Albania to protect her life-line through the Mediterranean to India than in achievement of the prime object-ive of our American armies – prompt defeat of Germany".' The survey concluded: 'A shift in the allocation of chief blame from Russia to Britain is revealed by recent polls.'

All this should be considered in the context of the miracle that, thanks to the statesmanship of George Marshall, Dwight Eisenhower, Alan Brooke, Winston Churchill and Franklin Roosevelt, the Western Allies preserved to the end of the war a façade of unity. Given the shortcomings of every alliance in history, the Anglo–American working relationship remains remarkable. But Roosevelt made policy during the last months of his life in the knowledge that the American people supported his own post-war vision, and felt scant sympathy for that of Churchill. Britain could draw upon only a meagre credit balance of sentiment in the United States.

The Western leaders' first meeting with Stalin, at the Livadia Palace, briefly revived Churchill's spirits. Stalin, the affable host, deployed some of his limited repertoire of English phrases: 'You said it!', 'So what?', 'What the hell goes on around here?' and 'The toilet is over there' – all except the last presumably garnered from American movies. Churchill wrote later, describing the sensation of finding himself among the three most powerful men on earth, now gathered together: 'We had the world at our feet, twenty-five million men marching at our orders by land and sea. We seemed to be friends.' Such romantic illusions were soon banished. For the British at least, the Yalta experience became progressively more distressing.

Churchill opened on an entirely false note, by expounding to the first plenary session his hopes for an Allied drive from north-east Italy through the 'Llubjanja Gap'. This idea had been dead for months in the minds of everyone save the prime minister. It seemed otiose now to revive it. With Eisenhower's armies approaching the Rhine, Churchill sought to flatter the Russians by inviting their advice on large-scale river crossings. Stalin, in his turn, asked Roosevelt and Churchill what they would like the Red Army to do – for all the world as if their answer might cause him to alter his deployments. He declared sanctimoniously that he had considered the launching of Russia's vast January offensive 'a moral duty', after the Anglo-Americans requested action to relieve pressure from the German offensive in the Ardennes. In reality, it is unlikely that the timing of the Soviet assault was advanced by a single day in deference to Western wishes.

Churchill told Stalin that Eisenhower's forces wanted the Red Army to do only one thing: keep going. The Soviets always knew, however, that British dollops of flattery masked a fundamental hostility to their objectives, while the US president was much less intractable. 'Our guards compared Churchill to a poodle wagging its tail to please Stalin,' wrote Sergo Beria. 'We shared friendly feelings towards Roosevelt which did not extend to Churchill.' Yet Soviet cynicism was evenly apportioned between the two. Molotov quoted an unnamed colleague who said of Roosevelt: 'What a crook that man must be, to have wormed his way to three terms as president while being paralyzed!' Soviet eavesdroppers laughed heartily when they heard Churchill complain that he could not sleep at night because of the bedbugs.

Each day, the principals met at 4 p.m. for sessions which lasted four or five hours. In between, there were lunches, dinners and tense national consultations among the delegations. Stalin was astonishingly amiable, as well he might be, as the most conspicuous profiteer from the war. Roosevelt drifted in and out of consciousness of the proceedings. When he engaged, it was most frequently to press for delay – for instance, in settling German occupation zones – or to accede to Soviet views. Again and again, the British found themselves isolated. Churchill opposed the 'dismemberment' of Germany, to which Stalin was committed, and also argued against imposing extravagant reparations on the vanquished. He reminded the conference of the failure of such a policy in 1919: 'If you want your horse to pull your cart, you had to give him some hay.' But the Americans and Russians had already settled on a provisional figure of $20 billion, of which the Soviet Union was to receive half.

The Americans joined with the Russians in resisting Churchill's proposal to give France a seat on the Allied Control Commission in Germany. At British insistence, however, France was grudgingly conceded a zone of occupation. Churchill's bilateral meetings with Roosevelt were fruitless. At lunches and dinners, platitudes were exchanged, but no business was done. The combination of Roosevelt's mortal languor and disinclination to indulge Britain was fatal to Churchill's hopes. There is little doubt that, at Yalta as at Tehran, the president deliberately sought to reach out to Stalin by distancing himself from the prime minister. It is hard to suggest that this tactic did Western interests substantial harm, for Stalin's course was set. But it certainly conferred no discernible advantage.

Churchill, returning to his villa on the night of 5 February, was irked to find that no intelligence brief had arrived from London. John Martin wrote: 'It has gone to my heart to hear "Colonel Kent" calling again and again for news and being offered only caviar.' That night, before he went to sleep, Churchill said to his daughter Sarah, 'I do not suppose that at any moment in history has the agony of the world been so great or widespread. To-night the sun goes down on more suffering than ever before in the World.' Churchill's fund of compassion towards the enemy, incomparably greater than that of his peers at Yalta, was among his most notable qualities. 'I am free to confess to you,' he wrote to Clementine, 'that my heart is saddened by the tales of the masses of German women and children flying along the roads everywhere in 40-mile long columns to the West before the advancing Armies. I am clearly convinced that they deserve it; but that does not remove it from one's gaze. The misery of the whole world appals me and I fear increasingly that new struggles may rise out of those we are successfully ending.' Amid such phrases, allegations crumble against Churchill 'the war-lover'.

The US president and British prime minister have often been criticised for agreeing at Yalta to transfer to Stalin all Soviet subjects detained in Europe. Of those who returned, even from German captivity, some were shot and most were dispatched to labour camps. Almost all who had served in enemy uniform were liquidated. Yet, on the repatriation issue, it is impossible to see how the Anglo-Americans could have acted otherwise. The Soviet Union had borne the overwhelming burden of the land war against Hitler. The Western Allies were still soliciting the assistance of the Red Army to complete the defeat of Japan. The price of Soviet military aid, of so much Russian blood spilt while so much American and British blood was saved, was acquiescence in a large measure of Soviet imperialism. Churchill expressed to the Soviet warlord his anxiety for the return of British PoWs, whom the Russians were liberating in increasing numbers. In a world which, as Churchill so vividly described, was consumed by suffering, it was hard for the Anglo-Americans to demand much priority of sympathy for Soviet subjects who had served the Nazi cause. The integrity of Allied purposes in the Second World War was inescapably compromised by association with the tyranny of Stalin to defeat that of Hitler. Once this evil was conceded, lesser ones remorselessly followed. Among these was the surrender of hundreds of thousands of perceived Soviet renegades.

The foremost business of Yalta, above all in Churchill's eyes, was the future of Poland. Stalin wanted recognition of its new frontiers – the so-called 'Curzon line' in the east, the Oder-Niesse in the west. Churchill made plain that he was now less concerned with territory than with the democratic character of the new Polish government. He sought to exchange Western recognition of the frontiers Moscow wanted for some shreds of domestic freedom for the Poles. He could not, he said, accept that Moscow's 'Lublin Poles' represented the will of the nation. Stalin riposted that the new Warsaw regime was as representative of the Polish people as was De Gaulle's new government of France. Roosevelt sought to adjourn the session, but Churchill insisted that the Polish issue must be resolved. The president observed impatiently that 'Poland had been a source of trouble for over 500 years'. The prime minister said: 'We must do what we can to put an end to the trouble.' Here was another exchange sorely damaging to British purposes. Roosevelt's apparent indifference was once more flaunted before Russian eyes.

Overnight, however, some reinforcement was secured for the Polish cause. Roosevelt signed a letter to Stalin saying that the US – like Britain – could not recognise the Polish government as then composed. At the conference's third plenary session on 7 February, the president described the Polish issue as of 'very great importance'. There was more talk of occupation zones in Germany. Agreement was reached about respective states' voting rights at the proposed new United Nations. On 8 February, Churchill reasserted the urgency of settling Poland. Molotov said that the new communist government had been 'enthusiastically acclaimed by the majority of the Polish people'. Churchill pressed for immediate free elections, which prompted Stalin again to raise comparisons with France, where no poll was scheduled. Then, however, the Russian leader conceded that an election might be held in Poland within a month. There was still no visible anger in the conference chamber. There followed, indeed, more exchanges of compliments between the principals. But that night Churchill said bleakly: 'The only bond of the victors is their common hate' towards Hitler.

Anglo-American leverage with Stalin derived solely from Lend-Lease supplies. Even had Roosevelt threatened to suspend shipments unless the Western powers gained satisfaction about Poland, the Russians would not have bowed. Stalin had shown himself implacable in imposing his territorial demands since 1941, when Western aid was much more important than in 1945. From start to finish he grasped the fact that the Anglo-Americans needed Russia's vast human sacrifice even more than Russia needed Western supplies. Even had the president himself been willing to exercise such pressure – as, of course, he was not – neither the American nor the British people would have supported sanctions. Popular enthusiasm for a common front against the Axis still ran high. Attempts to impose

Western wishes upon the heroic Russians would have commanded sympathy only with a small minority of people who grasped the reality of looming East European servitude.

At the fifth plenary session on 9 February, Churchill said that diplomatic observers must monitor the Polish election. The Russians responded smoothly that this was perfectly acceptable to them, but the Warsaw government must be consulted: the presence of such observers might wound the Poles by implying that they were not trusted. Likewise, when Churchill said that a British ambassador should be sent to Warsaw, the Russians deferred the matter to Polish arbitration. With his usual serpentine skill, Stalin reminded the prime minister of his debt to Moscow by asserting that he had 'complete confidence' in British policy in Greece.

Next day, the 10th, Roosevelt caused consternation to the British by announcing that he would leave Yalta on the following morning. When the president had cabled the prime minister back in January, asserting his intention to spend only five days at Yalta, Churchill expostulated to his staff that even the Almighty had allowed himself seven to make the world. Now, in British eyes, the summit had yet to achieve decisive conclusions. But the president was thus far right, that even had he lingered it was unlikely anything further would have been accomplished. The chasm was unbridgeable between Russian intentions and Western aspirations in Eastern Europe. Nonetheless, an agreement had been reached about Poland which, if Stalin kept his word, might sustain some figleaf of democracy. Churchill professed satisfaction. He could do little else. He spent 12 February as a tourist, visiting British battlefields of the Crimean War and gazing on the ruins of Sebastopol. Next day, he rested aboard the British liner *Franconia*, anchored off the coast at his pleasure, then flew to Athens.

The contrast could not have been greater between his previous visit, amid gunfire, and the hysterical applause with which he was received on the afternoon of 14 February. Vast crowds thronged the streets of the Greek capital, offering a vindication that was sweet to him. He elected to make a further brief stop in Cairo. 'A wandering minstrel

I,' he sang to himself, a ditty from his beloved Gilbert and Sullivan, 'a thing of threads and patches.' He landed back in Britain on 20 February. Beaverbrook was among those who offered extravagant congratulations on his alleged 'success' at Yalta, which 'followed so swiftly on the heels of the Greek triumph, that you now appear to your countrymen to be the greatest statesman as well as the greatest warrior'.

Even by Beaverbrook's standards, this was a travesty. In the House of Commons there was profound anxiety about the outcome of Yalta, and its implications for the Poles. The concluding communiqué by the 'Big Three' had asserted that Poland's provisional government should be 'reorganized on a broader democratic basis with the inclusion of democratic leaders from Poland itself and from Poles abroad'. The new government 'shall be pledged to the holding of free and unfettered elections as soon as possible . . . In these elections all democratic and anti-Nazi parties shall have the right to take part.' The cession of eastern Poland to Russia was acknowledged, in return for indeterminate territorial compensation in the west, which should 'thereafter be determined at the peace conference'.

Churchill told the war cabinet that he was 'quite sure' Stalin 'meant well to the world and to Poland'. Likewise, facing fierce criticism in the House on 27 February, he cited the fact that 'most solemn declarations have been made by Marshal Stalin and the Soviet State' about Polish elections. 'I repudiate and repulse any suggestion that we are making a questionable compromise or yielding to force or fear . . . The Poles will have their future in their own hands, with the single limitation that they must honestly follow . . . a policy friendly to Russia. That is surely reasonable.' Fortified by the fulfilment of Stalin's promise of non-interference in Greece, he clung to the hope that the Soviet warlord would keep his word about Poland: 'I know of no government which stands to its obligations, even in its own despite, more solidly than the Russian Soviet Government. I decline absolutely to embark here on a discussion about Russian good faith.'

Over a drink in the smoking room afterwards with Harold Nicolson and Lord de la Warr, he said that he did not see what else he could have done at Yalta, save accept Stalin's assurances. On the night of the 28th he told Jock Colville that he would refuse to be cheated over Poland, 'even if we go to the verge of war with Russia'. He voiced aloud his fear that he might be deceived by Stalin, as Neville Chamberlain had been deceived by Hitler – then dismissed it. He was exultant when an amendment on Poland moved by Tory right-wingers in the Commons was defeated by 396 votes to twenty-five. But eleven ministers abstained, and one resigned. Eden, lacking confidence in Russian good faith, remained deeply depressed. General Anders, for the Poles, told Brooke that 'he had never been more distressed since the war started . . . He could see no hope anywhere.'

Back in Moscow, Stalin expressed satisfaction about the outcome of Yalta. Unsurprisingly, he spoke more warmly of Roosevelt than of Britain's prime minister. 'Churchill wants a bourgeois Poland to be the USSR's neighbour,' he told Zhukov, 'a Poland that would be hostile to us. We cannot allow this. We want to ensure a friendly Poland once and for all, and that is what the Polish people want, too.' *Pravda*'s political columnist told Russian readers with satisfaction: 'We see unprecedented unanimity in the United States and England in welcoming the resolutions of the Crimea Conference.' The paper asserted that American and British commentators treated the protests of Polish émigrés with the contempt which these deserved.

No course short of war with Russia could have saved Polish democracy in 1945, and by February only a compound of vanity and despair could have caused Churchill to pretend otherwise. The Soviet Union believed that, having paid overwhelmingly the heaviest price to achieve the defeat of Hitler, it had thus purchased the right to determine the polity of Eastern Europe in accordance with its own security interests. To this day, Roosevelt's admirers declare that he displayed greater realism than Britain's prime minister by recognising this. The Western Allies lacked power to contrive any different outcome. Churchill, who had fought as nobly as any man in the world to deliver Europe, was now obliged to witness not the liberation of the East, but the mere replacement there of one murderous tyranny by another.

TWENTY-TWO

The Final Act

In the last months of Churchill's war premiership, his satisfaction about the Nazis' imminent downfall was almost entirely overshadowed by dismay at the triumph of Soviet hegemony in Eastern Europe. He wrote to a Tory MP on 6 March: 'We are now labouring to make sure that the Yalta Agreement about Poland and free elections is carried out in the spirit as well as in the letter.' In reality, of course, Yalta was flouted in both. Almost daily, news reached Downing Street of savage Soviet oppression in Poland, including the imprisonment of sixteen prominent Poles who attended a meeting under safe-conduct from the Red Army, and the deportation to labour camps of thousands of non-communists. Beria's NKVD conducted a war of repression against Polish democrats which persisted until the end of the German war, and after. Churchill drafted a fierce cable to Stalin, for which he invited American approval: 'All parties were exercised,' he wrote, 'about the reports that deportations, liquidations and other oppressive measures were being put into practice on a wide scale by the Warsaw administration against those likely to disagree with them.'

The dying Roosevelt vetoed this message, and thereafter repeatedly rejected Churchill's imprecations for the US to adopt a harsher policy towards Moscow. The president proposed a 'political truce' in Poland, which the British believed would merely strengthen the Soviet puppet regime. 'I cannot agree that we are confronted with a breakdown of the Yalta Agreement,' Roosevelt wrote on 15 March. '. . . We must be careful not to give the impression that we are proposing a halt to the land reforms [collectivisation] imposed by the new Polish government.' A stream of messages followed from Churchill to Roosevelt, emphasising the prime minister's perception of the urgency and gravity of the Polish situation. Most went unanswered. The British persisted with their efforts, but received scant comfort from Washington, and none from Moscow.

Events on the battlefield had a momentum of their own, which Churchill could not influence. At this very late hour he made a brief attempt to assert British influence, by exchanging Tedder with Alexander. He wrote to his field marshal on 1 March, as if this was a done deal: 'I have written privately to Eisenhower to tell him that you will be replacing Tedder as Deputy Supreme Commander about the middle of this month and that I propose Tedder shall replace you in the Mediterranean.' The purported justification was that Alexander's presence in north-west Europe would ease tensions between Eisenhower and Montgomery. In reality, Churchill wanted his favourite to assume control of the entire Allied ground battle for the last phase of the German campaign. The proposal was mistaken from every possible standpoint, not least Alexander's unfitness for the role. The Americans swiftly quashed it. Churchill received no more satisfaction from Washington when he remonstrated about Eisenhower's signal to Stalin, assuring him that the Western armies would stay away from Berlin. The Americans were not listening. If their manner towards Churchill was increasingly brusque, on the points of military substance it is impossible to doubt that they were right.

Churchill made one further intervention on strategic bombing policy, which has cast a baleful shadow over the historiography of the Second World War. On 28 March he minuted Portal, Chief of Air Staff, and the chiefs of staff committee:

> It seems to me that the moment has come when the question of bombing of German cities simply for the sake of increasing the terror, though under other pretexts, should be reviewed. Otherwise we shall come into control of an utterly ruined land . . . The destruction of Dresden remains a serious query against the conduct of Allied

bombing . . . I feel the need for more precise concentration upon military objectives, such as oil and communications behind the immediate battle-zone, rather than on mere acts of terror and wanton destruction, however impressive.

Portal, standard-bearer of the Royal Air Force, was affronted by these remarks, as well he might have been. He persuaded Churchill to withdraw them, substituting a fresh document which omitted such phrases as 'acts of terror'. The new minute began in more pedestrian terms: 'It seems to me that the moment has come when the question of the so-called "area bombing" of German cities should be reviewed from the point of view of our own interests . . .' This sanitised version was signed on 1 April. Churchill was anyway in no doubt that he had ordered a halt to area attacks on cities. He was thus dismayed, soon afterwards, to learn that 500 Lancasters of Bomber Command had devastated Potsdam. Some 5,000 civilians were alleged to have perished because the population had neglected air-raid precautions, supposing that the city's architectural treasures granted it immunity from bombardment. Churchill wrote crossly to Sinclair, the Secretary for Air, and Portal: 'What's the point of going and blowing down Potsdam?' Portal replied that the Luftwaffe's operational headquarters had been transferred there, and that the attack was 'calculated to hasten the disintegration of enemy resistance'.

The truthful answer to Churchill's question was that a huge force of British heavy bombers existed, and there was deep reluctance to stand this down as long as German resistance continued. The Red Army had begun to fight the last great battle of the European war for Berlin, a few miles from Potsdam. Churchill's attitude, displayed in his draft note to Portal of 28 March, was characteristic in its impulsiveness, even irrationality. Earlier in the war he had been a committed supporter of area bombing, though once delivered from the desperate predicament of 1940–41, he never shared the exaggerated faith of the airmen that this could win the war. When the great land campaigns began in Italy and France, he lost interest in Bomber Command. Its contribution might be useful, but was plainly not decisive. It may sound flippant to suggest that Britain's prime minister was oblivious of the operations of hundreds of heavy aircraft, dealing nightly death and destruction to some of the greatest cities in Europe. Yet amid the huge issues crowding in upon him each day, the air offensive receded into the background – as also, it must be said, did the issue of the Nazi death camps and possible RAF operations to impede their activities. In Churchill's mind, the fate of the Jews was entwined with that of millions of other European captives of Hitler. The best means of securing their delivery was to win the war as swiftly as possible.

So vast was the scale of the war by 1944–45, so diverse its manifestations, that no human being, even Winston Churchill, could address every aspect with the commitment which some modern critics believe should have been expected of him. How could it have been otherwise? He interested himself in a wider range of affairs than any national leader in history. But many things, including air policy in the last year of the war, were neglected. Commanders were left to do as they thought best. The only important bombing controversy to which Churchill seriously addressed himself from 1942 onwards was that concerning the 1944 assault on the French road and rail network before D-Day, which he was persuaded reluctantly to endorse.

Throughout the war, the direction of strategic bombing was impeded by the fact that its achievements were shrouded in mystery. The progress of armies was readily measured by advances or retreats, that of rival fleets by sinkings. But the airmen's extravagant claims could be assessed only through problematic interpretation of aerial photography, with limited assistance from Ultra signal decrypts. In December 1941, Mr Butt's Cabinet Office report caused the prime minister to accept that the RAF's campaign against Germany, prodigious in its demands on national resources, was not achieving commensurate results. Thus the decision was made to change policy, to conduct 'area bombing' of cities, in place of discredited precision attacks on military and industrial targets. 'In the full tilt of war,' observed Churchill in old age, 'it was the only means of hitting back. I was of course ultimately responsible . . .

But later I was not so sure of the effectiveness of the bludgeon.' Until June 1944, however, when great Allied armies became committed to the battlefield, the prime minister found it convenient to promote the view that strategic bombing was making an important contribution to the defeat of the enemy. If it was not, then many people – among whom Stalin was the most important – would have asked whether Britain was playing anything like a large enough part in fighting the war.

In attempting to distance himself from the bombing of Dresden, as Churchill did on 28 March 1945, he ignored his own request to Sinclair at the Air Ministry, just before Yalta, to launch major air attacks in eastern Germany, to assist and impress the Russians, who expressed an eagerness for such support. Dresden had featured for years on Bomber Command target lists. It had been left unscathed only because it was a low priority, and a long haul from British airfields. Throughout the war, none of Britain's senior airmen showed much aesthetic sensitivity. Portal had advocated heavy bombing of Rome when the city still belonged to Mussolini. Harris had assured the chief of air staff that he had 'no false sentiments' about dispatching his bombers against one of the greatest cultural centres in the world. Only American opposition deflected attacks on the centre of Rome. Churchill's personal intervention was responsible for causing Dresden, together with Chemnitz and Leipzig, to be pushed up the February target schedule, and largely destroyed on the night of 13–14. It is unsurprising that no one at Bomber Command headquarters voiced concern about the fate of baroque churches before unleashing the Lancasters.

The prime minister, however, had not thought much before making his own, almost casual request to Sinclair. Throughout the war a host of matters briefly engaged his attention, then receded. It is implausible, but just possible, that by 28 March he had genuinely forgotten that he had urged the RAF to attack east German cities. The key to understanding the destruction of Dresden, so often misinterpreted as a unique atrocity, is that amid daily global carnage, the attack order had much less significance to those responsible than it seems to posterity to have deserved.

In the aftermath of Dresden, however, the raid was the subject of widespread comment – and some criticism. Following a SHAEF* press conference about bombing policy on 16 February, an AP correspondent named Howard Cowan filed a dispatch stating: 'The Allied air commanders have made the long-awaited decision to adopt deliberate terror bombing of German population centres as a ruthless expedient to hastening Hitler's doom.' This story received prominent play in American newspapers, though it was censored in British ones. US Secretary for War Henry Stimson demanded an inquiry into Dresden, which prompted Gen. 'Hap' Arnold of the USAAF to respond: 'We must not get soft. War must be destructive and to a certain extent inhuman and ruthless.' In Britain, though there was no widespread outcry, questions were asked in the Commons by the government's inveterate critic, Labour MP Richard Stokes. For the first time in many months Churchill addressed himself seriously to the issue of area bombing. He perceived that it was indeed wanton to continue the destruction of great cities when the Germans were so close to collapse. With his usual instinct for mercy towards the vanquished, he wished to halt the process. This was both right and humane. The prime minister injured himself, however, by attempting in his draft minute to Portal to make this judgement retrospective, to condemn the Dresden decision to which he had been an implicit, if not absolutely explicit, party.

He also gave a formidable hostage to history by declaring that Bomber Command's campaign was terroristic. No one in the upper reaches of Britain's war machine had ever privately doubted that this was so, but ministers and airmen took elaborate pains to avoid acknowledging it. This was not Churchill's first mention of terror, in the context of bombing. He had used a similar word much earlier, in a memorandum to the war cabinet in November 1942, about policy towards Italy. 'All the industrial centres should be attacked in an intense fashion,' he wrote, 'every effort being made to terrorise and paralyse the population.' In war as in peace, there is unlikely to

* Supreme Headquarters Allied Expeditionary Force.

be much cause for pride in a policy about which it is deemed necessary to deceive one's own people. The reputations of Churchill, Portal and Bomber Command were damaged by the exchanges of March–April 1945. The prime minister, who of all men should know, had put his signature to a document, albeit subsequently withdrawn, declaring Britain's strategic air offensive to have been terroristic. He had then been privy to an administrative sleight of hand, designed to suppress this admission of the truth.

Churchill's writings, dating back to World War I, make plain that he thought air bombardment of civilians barbaric. In the early part of World War II, when Germany had already ravaged half the cities of Europe and Britain had no other plausible means of attacking Hitler's Reich, he suppressed his instincts, and endorsed the bomber offensive. That decision seems both inevitable and justifiable. It is a gross abuse of language to identify area bombing as a 'war crime', as do some modern critics. The policy was designed to hasten the defeat of Germany by destroying its industrial base, not wantonly to slaughter innocents. Yet it remains a blot on the Allied conduct of the war that city attacks were allowed to continue into 1945, when huge forces of aircraft employed sophisticated technology against negligible defences, and German industrial output could no longer influence outcomes. Both the operational necessity to attack cities – because the RAF could do nothing else – and the strategic purpose of such operations were gone. Yet the assault was maintained because, until Churchill's belated intervention, nobody thought to tell the air forces to stop, or rather to restrict themselves to residual military targets.

Here was a classic example of technological determinism. The weapons existed, and thus they continued to be used. The pity of Churchill's 28 March memorandum, not least from the viewpoint of some 200,000 German civilians who perished in 1945, was that it had not been written several months earlier. Yet it is hard not to sympathise with the exhausted old prime minister, bearing the troubles of the world upon his shoulders, for being slow to act. The record of his conduct towards Hitler's people shows an overarching instinct towards mercy, remarkable in the leader of a nation which had suffered so much at German hands since 1939. Churchill's 1945 papers contain many charitable reflections and directions about the treatment of Germans. These should be set in the balance against the undoubted excesses of the bomber offensive, and his own responsibility for them.

In the last weeks of the European war, Churchill undertook two more battlefield joyrides. Much to his own satisfaction, he relieved himself in the Siegfried Line on 3 March, with an aside to photographers: 'This is one of the operations connected with this great war which must not be reproduced graphically.' He performed the same ceremony in the Rhine three weeks later, on a visit to watch Montgomery's great river crossing with Alan Brooke. As he gazed down upon the vast panorama from a chair set out for him on Xanten hilltop, he said: 'I should have liked to have deployed my men in red coats on the plain down there and ordered them to charge.' Then he added, not without satisfaction: 'But now my armies are too vast.' At the sound of aircraft, he sprang to his feet: 'They're coming! They're coming!' He watched fascinated as the great airborne armada passed overhead, thousands of multi-coloured parachutes blossoming forth above the German bank. He was hurried unwillingly to the rear by the generals when desultory German shells began to fall. Brooke wrote: 'It was a relief to get Winston home safely . . . I honestly believe that he would really have liked to be killed on the front at this moment of success. He had often told me that the way to die is to pass out fighting when your blood is up and you feel nothing.'

At a lunch at Chequers a few days later, Churchill told his cousin Anita Leslie how much he had enjoyed his outing: 'I'm an old man and I work hard. Why shouldn't I have a little fun? At least, I thought it was fun but one has to hate seeing brave men die.' Leslie was driving an ambulance for the Free French. 'With childish longing in his voice Winston asked what the French thought of him. "They do like me? They are fond of me?" Give them my love.' If these were the words of a sentimental old man, his flagging interest in daily business reflected the condition of an exhausted one. 'The PM is now becoming an administrative bottleneck,' wrote Colville.

There was a last spasm of frustration about his inability to influence military operations. When he learned that Eisenhower had signalled to Stalin that the Anglo-American armies would make no attempt to close upon Berlin, he expressed strong displeasure that such a communication should have been made without reference to the British or US governments. As Russian behaviour rapidly worsened, he urged that the Anglo-American armies should advance as far eastwards as possible and stay there, heedless of agreed occupation zones, until Moscow showed some willingness to keep its side of the Yalta bargain. Meanwhile, Russian paranoia intensified, that the West would make its own peace deal with the Germans. Zhukov visited the Kremlin on 29 March. Stalin walked to his desk, leafed through some papers, picked one out and handed it to his marshal. 'Read this,' he said. It was a report based upon information from 'foreign sympathisers' who claimed that representatives of the Western Allies were conducting secret talks with emissaries of Hitler about a separate peace. Berlin's overtures had been rejected, said the letter, but it remained possible that the German army would open its western front to give the Allies passage to Berlin. 'What do you think?' asked Stalin, continuing without waiting for Zhukov's answer: 'I do not believe Roosevelt will violate the Yalta agreement. But as for Churchill – that man is capable of anything.'

The Americans indeed showed no interest in diplomatic brinkmanship with the Kremlin. Though Roosevelt was persuaded to send a last challenging missive to Stalin about Poland, Washington would precipitate no confrontation. When Himmler sought to parley with the Western Allies, Churchill reported the fact to Stalin, who had dispatched a stream of angry and indeed insulting cables to London and Washington about US negotiations in Switzerland with SS General Karl Wolff concerning a German surrender in Italy. Now the Russian leader sent a notably emollient message to Churchill: 'Knowing you, I had no doubt that you would act just in this way.' The prime minister found the cable waiting in Downing Street on returning from dinner with the French ambassador on the night of 25 April. It prompted a spasm of maudlin goodwill towards Stalin. Jock Colville noted in dismay that Churchill, not entirely sober, sat for ninety minutes in the Annexe, talking enthusiastically to Brendan Bracken about the cable, and then spent a further ninety minutes doing the same before the young private secretary: 'His vanity was astonishing and I am glad U[ncle] J[oe] does not know what effect a few kind words, after so many harsh ones, might well have on our policy towards Russia . . . No work was done and I felt both irritated and slightly disgusted by this exhibition of susceptibility to flattery. It was nearly 5am when I got to bed.' Three days later, Churchill cabled Stalin, offering a further olive branch: 'I have been much disturbed at the misunderstanding that has grown up between us on the Crimea agreement about Poland.' There was no misunderstanding, of course. Stalin was bent upon asserting Soviet hegemony over Poland, and that was an end of the matter.

Back in December 1941, when Eden cabled Churchill from Moscow urging the necessity for acceptance of Russia's demands for recognition of its pre-*Barbarossa* frontiers, the prime minister replied: 'When you say that "nothing we and the US can do or say will affect the situation at the end of the war", you are making a very large assumption about the conditions which will then prevail. No one can foresee how the balance of power will lie, or where the winning armies will stand. It seems probable however that the US and the British Empire, far from being exhausted, will be the most powerful armed and economic bloc the world has ever seen, and that the Soviet Union will need our aid for reconstruction far more than we shall need theirs.' By 1945, the frustration of such hopes was plain. The Soviets were vastly stronger, the British much weaker, than Churchill had anticipated. The US commitment to perceived common Anglo–American interests, in Europe or anywhere else, was more tenuous than it had ever been.

In the cold light of day, the prime minister understood this. On 4 May he wrote to Eden, then in San Francisco for the inaugural meeting of the United Nations, about the evolving situation in Eastern Europe as he saw it:

I fear terrible things have happened during the Russian advance through Germany to the Elbe. The proposed withdrawal of the United States Army to the occupational lines which were arranged . . . would mean a tide of Russian domination sweeping forward 120 miles on a front of 200 or 400 miles. This would be an event which, if it occurred, would be one of the most melancholy in history. After it was over and the territory occupied by the Russians, Poland would be completely engulfed and buried deep in Russian-occupied lands . . . The Russian frontier would run from the North Cape in Norway . . . across the Baltic to a point just east of Lubeck . . . half-way across [Austria] to the Izonzo river behind which Tito and Russia will claim everything to the east. Thus the territories under Russian control would include the Baltic Provinces, all of Germany to the occupational line, all Czechoslovakia, a large part of Austria, the whole of Yugoslavia, Hungary, Roumania, Bulgaria, until Greece in her present tottering condition is reached . . . This constitutes an event in the history of Europe to which there has been no parallel . . . All these matters can only be settled before the United States Armies in Europe are weakened . . . It is to this early and speedy showdown and settlement with Russia that we must now turn our hopes. Meanwhile I am against weakening our claim against Russia on behalf of Poland in any way.

The Allies now found themselves in a bewildering and uncharted new world: Roosevelt was gone. Following the vast shock of his death on 12 April, Churchill briefly entertained the notion of flying to Washington for the funeral. Finally, he decided that he was needed in London, an outcome that was also probably influenced by personal disinclination. The prime minister's enthusiasm for the president had waned dramatically. There had been so many slights. Some were relatively trivial, such as a March decision by Washington to halt meat exports to Britain. Some were more serious, such as the imposition of draconian curbs on post-war British civil aviation in accordance with the terms of Lend-Lease. Above all, of course, there was American unilateralism on Eastern European issues. Roosevelt's greatness was not in doubt, least of all in the mind of Churchill. But it had been deployed in the service of the USA, and only incidentally and reluctantly in the interests of the British Empire or even of Europe. 'We have moved a long way,' wrote Moran in February, 'since Winston, speaking of Roosevelt, said to me in the garden at Marrakesh "I love that man."'

Now, Churchill had to deal with the wholly unknown figure of Harry Truman. In the first weeks of the new president's tenure, though his inexperience was manifest, there were welcome indications that he was ready to deal much more toughly with the Russians than had Roosevelt in his last months. But no more than his predecessor was the newcomer at the White House willing to risk an armed clash with the Soviet Union for the sake of Poland, or indeed any other European nation. At this stage, Washington believed, there was no virtue in empty posturing, when the Red Army stood on the Elbe. Nor did Churchill's combativeness towards Moscow find much resonance among his own people. For four years the British had embraced the Russians as heroes and comrades-in-arms, ignorant of the absence of reciprocal enthusiasm. Beyond a few score men and women at the summit of the British war machine, little was known of Soviet perfidy and savagery. No more in Britain than in the US was there any stomach for a Churchillian crusade against a new enemy.

VE-Day was proclaimed on 8 May 1945. On the afternoon of the 7th, the chiefs of staff gathered at Downing Street for a moment of celebration. Churchill himself set out a tray and glasses, then toasted Brooke, Portal and Cunningham as 'the architects of victory'. Ismay wrote in his memoirs: 'I hoped that they would raise their glasses to the chief who had been the master-planner; but perhaps they were too moved to trust their voices.' This was disingenuous. Brooke and Cunningham, if not Portal, nursed complex emotions towards the prime minister. Others, including Ismay and the Downing Street staff, forgave rough handling amid their love and admiration for Churchill. The field marshal and the admiral found this more difficult. Brooke wrote on 7 May: 'I can't feel thrilled, my main sensation is one of infinite mental weariness! A sort of brain lethargy which refuses to register highlights, and remains on an even dull flat tone.' Next day he added, with some bitterness: 'There is no doubt that the public has never understood what the Chiefs of Staff have been doing in the running of this war. On the whole the PM has never enlightened them much, and has never once in all his speeches referred to the Chiefs of Staff . . . Without him England was lost for a certainty, with him England has been on the verge of disaster again and again. And with it all no recognition hardly at all for those who help him except the occasional crumb intended to prevent the dog straying too far from the table.'

Brooke was envious of the greater power and fame enjoyed by Marshall, his American counterpart. A man of notable vanity, which suffused his diaries, he overrated his own talents, and was ungenerous in his estimate of Churchill's. But a significant part of his achievement as CIGS – and it was a remarkable achievement – lay in his willingness to fight Churchill day or night when he believed him wrong. If Brooke was a cautious soldier, who might not have prospered as a field commander, he had provided a superb foil for the prime minister, preserving him from many misfortunes. His contribution to Britain's war effort had been substantial. Like the hedgehog, he had understood one big thing: that the Allies must not prematurely engage the full weight of the Wehrmacht. He was unable, however, to accept that the price of serving a towering historical figure was to be obscured by his shadow.

Clementine was visiting Russia on behalf of the Red Cross on VE-Day, much to the sorrow of both Churchills. At 3 p.m. the prime minister broadcast to the British people: 'Yesterday morning at 2.41 a.m. at Headquarters, General Jodl, the representative of the German High Command, and Grand Admiral Doenitz, the designated head of the German State, signed the act of unconditional surrender of all German land, sea and air forces in Europe to the Allied Expeditionary Force, and simultaneously to the Soviet High Command . . . The German war is therefore at an end.' He recalled Britain's lonely struggle, and the gradual accession of great allies:

'Finally almost the whole world was combined against the evil-doers, who are now prostrate before us. We may allow ourselves a brief period of rejoicing; but let us not forget for a moment the toil and efforts that lie ahead. Japan, with all her treachery and greed, remains unsubdued . . . We must now devote all our strength and resources to the completion of our task, both at home and abroad. Advance, Britannia! Long live the cause of freedom! God save the King.' His secretaries and staff lined the garden of Downing Street to clap him to his car. He grinned back: 'Thank you so much, thank you so much.' Then he drove to the House of Commons, to repeat to MPs the speech which he had made to the nation.

A few grumblers muttered that they would have liked to hear from him some expression of gratitude to the Deity, and it is interesting to speculate whether Churchill offered any private expression of indebtedness to a higher power at that afternoon's Commons Service of Thanksgiving at St Margaret's, Westminster. Jock Colville believed that the events of the war, especially the Battle of Britain, moved Churchill a considerable distance from defiant atheism towards faith. The prime minister once remarked to the private secretary that he could not help wondering whether the government above might be a constitutional monarchy, 'in which case there was always a possibility that the Almighty might have occasion to send for him'.

From a balcony in Whitehall that evening, Churchill addressed the vast, cheering crowd: 'My dear friends, this is your hour. This is not victory of a party or of any class. It's a victory of the great British nation as a whole. We were the first, in this ancient island, to draw the sword against tyranny . . . .' The crowd sang 'Land of Hope and Glory' and 'For He's a Jolly Good Fellow' as Churchill returned to the Downing Street Annexe, to spend the rest of the evening with Lord Camrose, proprietor of the *Daily Telegraph*. In his company, the prime minister cast aside the exuberance of the afternoon, once more rehearsing his dismay about Soviet barbarism in the east. At 1.15 a.m., when Camrose left, Churchill returned to his secretaries and papers.

Pravda asserted triumphantly that 'the significance of the link-up of the Red Army and the Allied Anglo-American forces is as great politically as militarily. It offers further proof that provocations by Hitler's people designed to destroy the solidarity and brotherhood-in-arms between ourselves and our allies . . . have failed.' Yet Churchill spent the first days of peace plunged in deepest gloom about the fate of Poland. On 13 May he cabled Truman:

> Our armed power on the continent is in rapid decline. Meanwhile what is to happen about Russia[?] I have always worked for friendship with Russia but, like you, I feel deep anxiety because of their misinterpretation of the Yalta decisions, their attitude towards Poland, their overwhelming influence in the Balkans excepting Greece, the difficulties they make about Vienna . . . and above all their power to maintain very large armies in the field for a long time. What will be the position in a year or two, when the British and American armies have melted . . . and when Russia may choose to keep two or three hundred [divisions] on active service? An iron curtain is drawn down upon their front . . . Surely it is vital now to come to an understanding with Russia, or see where we are with her before we weaken our armies mortally, or retire to the zones of occupation. I should be most grateful for your opinion or advice . . . To sum up, this issue of a settlement with Russia before our strength has gone seems to me to dwarf all others.

Truman answered: 'From the present point of view, it is impossible to make a conjecture as to what the Soviets may do when Germany is under the small forces of occupation and the great part of such armies as we can maintain are fighting in the Orient against Japan.' The president agreed with Churchill that a tripartite meeting with Stalin had become urgently necessary.

Yet what if talking to Stalin got nowhere, as was highly likely? Within days of Germany's surrender, Britain's prime minister astounded his chiefs of staff by enquiring whether Anglo-American forces might launch an offensive to drive back the Soviets by force of arms. Churchill was enthused by the robust attitude of Truman, whose tone suggested a new willingness to respond ruthlessly to communist flouting of the Yalta terms. Brooke wrote after a war cabinet meeting on 13 May: 'Winston delighted, he gives me the feeling of already longing for another war! Even if it entailed fighting the Russians!' On the 24th, the prime minister instructed the chiefs of staff that, with the 'Russian bear sprawled over Europe', they should consider the military possibilities of pushing the Red Army back eastwards before the Anglo-American armies were demobilised. He requested the planners to consider means to 'impose upon Russia the will of the United States and British Empire' to secure 'a square deal for Poland'. They were told to assume the full support of British and American public opinion, and were invited to assume that they could 'count on the use of German manpower and what remains of German industrial capacity'. The target date for launching such an assault would be 1 July 1945.

The Foreign Office – though not Eden himself – recoiled in horror from Churchill's bellicosity. One of Moscow's Whitehall informants swiftly conveyed tidings to Stalin of an instruction from London to Montgomery, urging him to stockpile captured German weapons for possible future use. Zhukov wrote in his memoirs:

> We received reliable information that while the final campaign was still in progress Churchill sent a secret telegram to Marshal Montgomery instructing him carefully to collect German weapons and material and store it in such a way that would permit retrieving it easily in order to distribute among German units with which they would have to cooperate if the Soviet advance had continued. We had to make a harsh statement at the next session of the Allied Control Commission. We stressed that history knew few examples of such perfidy and betrayal of allies' obligations and duty. We declared that we thought that British government and army leadership deserved the most serious condemnation. Montgomery attempted to refute the Soviet statement. His colleague American General [Lucius] Clay was silent. Apparently, he was familiar with this instruction by the British Prime Minister.

Though Zhukov's version was sensationalist, it was founded in a reality unacknowledged in detail in Britain until the relevant papers were released by the National Archive in 1998. Alan Brooke and his colleagues faithfully executed the prime minister's wishes, to examine scenarios for initiating military action against the Russians. The report prepared by the war cabinet joint planning staff required feats of imagination from its creators unprecedented in Churchill's premiership. In the preamble, the drafters stated their assumption that, in the event of hostilities between the Russians and the Western Allies, Russia would ally itself with Japan. 'The overall or political object is to impose upon Russia the will of the United States and British Empire.' Yet the planners immediately pointed out that the scope of any new conflict initiated by the Western powers would not thereafter be for them to determine: 'Even though "the will" of these two countries may be defined as no more than a square deal for Poland, that does not necessarily limit the military commitment. A quick success might induce the Russians to submit to our will . . . but it might not. That is for the Russians to decide. If they want total war, they are in a position to have it.'

The planners observed that even if an initial Western offensive was successful, the Russians could then adopt the same tactics they had employed with such success against the Germans, giving ground amid the infinite spaces of the Soviet Union: 'There is virtually no limit to the distance to which it would be necessary for the Allies to penetrate into Russia in order to render further resistance impossible . . . To achieve the decisive defeat of Russia . . . would require . . . (a) the deployment in Europe of a large proportion of the vast resources of the United States (b) the re-equipment and re-organisation of German manpower and of all the Western European allies.'

The planners concluded that Western air power could be used effectively against Soviet communications, but that 'Russian industry is so dispersed that it is unlikely to be a profitable air target.' They proposed that forty-seven Allied divisions might credibly be deployed in a Western offensive, fourteen of these armoured. More than forty divisions would have to be held back for defensive or occupation tasks. The Russians could meet an Allied thrust with 170 divisions of equivalent strength, thirty of them armoured. 'It is difficult to assess to what extent our tactical air superiority and the superior handling of our forces will redress the balance, but the above odds would clearly render the launching of an offensive a hazardous undertaking.' The planners proposed two main thrusts, one on a northern axis, Stettin–Schneidemuhl–Bydgoszcz, the second in the south, on an axis Leipzig–Poznan–Breslau. They concluded: 'If we are to embark on war with Russia, we must be prepared to be committed to a total war, which will be both long and costly.'

They warned in an annexe that Moscow could probably call upon the aid of local communists in France, Belgium and Holland to conduct an extensive campaign of sabotage against Western lines of communications. The word 'hazardous' is used eight times in the planning document to describe the proposed Anglo-American operations. Annexe IV addressed likely German attitudes to an invitation to participate in hostilities between Russia and the West: 'The German General Staff and Officer Corps are likely to decide that their interests will be best served by siding with the Western Allies, although the extent to which they will be able to produce effective and active co-operation will probably be limited at first by the war-weariness of the German Army and of the civil population.' It was dryly suggested that German veterans who had fought on the eastern front might be reluctant to repeat the experience. However, addressing the issue of morale among Allied soldiers invited to fight the Russians, the planners displayed astonishing optimism. They claimed that their men might be expected to fight with little diminution of the spirit they had displayed against the Germans – this, though Alexander in Italy had already annoyed the prime minister by reporting that his troops were reluctant to engage Tito's communists.

The chiefs of staff were never under any delusions about the military, never mind political, impracticability of launching an offensive against the Russians to liberate Poland. The CIGS wrote on 24 May:

'The idea is of course fantastic and the chances of success quite impossible. There is no doubt that from now onwards Russia is all-powerful in Europe.' On the 31st, the chiefs 'again discussed the "unthinkable war" against Russia . . . and became more convinced than ever than it is "unthinkable"!' The debate cannot have failed to rouse, in the minds of those privy to the secret, echoes of 1918–19, when Churchill insisted upon committing to Russia a British military expedition designed to reverse the verdict of the 1917 Bolshevik revolution.

Passing the planners' report to the prime minister on 8 June, Ismay wrote: 'In the attached report on Operation "UNTHINKABLE", the Chiefs of Staff have set out the bare facts, which they can elaborate in discussion with you, if you so desire. They felt that the less was put on paper on this subject the better.' The chiefs themselves appended a comment to the report: 'Our view is . . . that once hostilities began, it would be beyond our power to win a quick but limited success and we should be committed to a protracted war against heavy odds. These odds, moreover, would become fanciful if the Americans grew weary and indifferent and began to be drawn away by the magnet of the Pacific war.'

Churchill responded on 10 June:

If the Americans withdraw to their zone and move the bulk of their forces back to the United States and to the Pacific, the Russians have the power to advance to the North Sea and the Atlantic. Pray have a study made of how then we could defend our Island, assuming that France and the Low Countries were powerless to resist the Russian advance to the sea. What naval forces should we need and where would they be based? What would be the strength of the Army required, and how should it be disposed? How much Air Force would be needed and where would the main airfields be located? . . . By retaining the codeword 'UNTHINKABLE', the Staffs will realize that this remains a precautionary study of what, I hope, is still a purely hypothetical contingency.

In the original draft of this note, Churchill's final words were 'a highly improbable event'. He altered these in his familiar red ink, to make implementation of *Unthinkable* seem remoter still.

On 11 July, the chiefs' joint planning committee responded to the prime minister's enquiries about the implications of a possible Soviet advance to the Channel following demobilisation of Eisenhower's armies. Russian naval strength, they concluded, was too limited to render an early amphibious invasion of Britain likely. They ruled out a Soviet airborne assault. It seemed more likely, they suggested, that Moscow would resort to intensive rocket bombardment, on a scale more destructive than that of the German V1s and V2s. To provide effective defence against a long-term Russian threat, they estimated that 230 squadrons of fighters, 100 of tactical bombers and 200 of heavy bombers would be necessary.

The *Unthinkable* file was closed a few days later, when another cable arrived from Truman. He rejected the arguments for renouncing or even delaying Allied withdrawal to the occupation zones agreed at Yalta. Washington had decided there was no case. The prime minister was obliged to recognise that there was not the slightest possibility that the Americans would lead an attempt to drive the Russians from Poland by force, nor even threaten Moscow that they might do so. It was also unimaginable that Churchill's own government and fellow countrymen would have supported such action. In June 1945 his perception of the Soviet Union was light years apart from that of his nation. Most British people were much less impressed by the perils facing Poland than by the wartime achievement of their Russian comrades-in-arms, whom they had learned to regard with enthusiasm. Churchill was hereafter obliged to undertake a dramatic reversal of view. If the Western Allies could not liberate Poland, then a new attempt must be made to persuade Stalin to compromise about its future. Turning aside from his brief dalliance with *Unthinkable*, the prime minister committed himself to renewed diplomatic efforts, to exploit his supposed relationship with Stalin in pursuit of Polish interests.

It was fortunate for Churchill's reputation that his speculation about confronting Russia in arms was not revealed in detail for another half-century. In the years following the end of the war, it became progressively apparent to the chiefs of staff, and to the Western world, that it was necessary for the Western Allies to adopt the strongest possible defensive measures against further Soviet aggression in Europe. On 30 August 1946, Field Marshal 'Jumbo' Maitland-Wilson reported from Washington that the US chiefs of staff had become sufficiently fearful of possible conflict with the Russians to favour commencing military planning for such a contingency. In London, the *Unthinkable* file was taken out and dusted down. Military preparations for a conflict with the Soviet Union became a staple of the Cold War, though at no time was it ever deemed politically acceptable or militarily practicable to attempt to free Eastern Europe by force of arms. In May and June 1945, Churchill's warrior instincts were still astonishingly powerful. But the society in which he lived had only just sufficient ardour to finish the Japanese war. There was none whatsoever for engaging new enemies, whatever the principled merits of the cause.

Labour leader Clement Attlee at first favoured sustaining the coalition government and delaying a general election until the defeat of Japan. His party, however, was minded otherwise. On 23 May the coalition was dissolved, after five years and thirteen days of office. There was an emotional farewell gathering of ministers at Downing Street. Then Churchill set about forming a new ministry, without Labour and Liberal members. An election was called for 6 July, which almost every pundit anticipated that the Tories would win. The nation's gratitude to Winston Churchill, it was assumed, outweighed its alienation from the Conservative Party and its pre-war failure.

Yet for those who sought straws in the wind about the mood of the British people, there were many to be found. On 3 July 1940, American General Raymond Lee had lunched in London with an unnamed Tory MP who asserted his conviction that even if Britain won the war, Labour would govern afterwards. By 1945, roosting time had come for many old chickens. Anthony Eden, widely perceived as the brightest star of his Tory generation, disliked his own party even more than did Churchill. He wrote during a visit to Greece about his sense of remoteness from British soldiers he met, and his doubts about how to reach them on the hustings: 'It would be the highest honour to serve and lead such men. But how is one to do it through party politics? Most of these men have none, as I believe that I have none. And how is this General Election to express any of this, for they could not be farther from the men of Munich in their most extreme form, for whom I have to ask the electors to vote. It is hell. Curiously enough W[inston] doesn't seem to feel any of this and is full of the lust for electoral battle, and apparently content to work with men afterwards, with many, probably most, of whom he doesn't agree. No doubt he is confident that he can dominate them, but I feel a responsibility to ask the electorate to vote for them.'

British soldier Edward Stebbing had written back in November 1940: 'There are . . . many who think that this war will only be worth fighting if there is a new order of things to follow.' Everything that had happened since strengthened this belief in the minds of many British people. In December 1944 the *Wall Street Journal* displayed notable prescience, identifying popular anger in Britain towards Churchill's Greek policy with a deeper rejection of old Tory imperialism: 'It is clear that the Churchill government will last out the war in Europe, but the chances of its return to office when the election after victory is held are more doubtful. It is not very likely that Mr Lloyd George's [1919] "khaki election" [victory] will be repeated.'

The Mayhews were an upper-middle-class Norfolk family, of whom in 1945 one younger scion, Christopher, was standing as a Labour candidate in the county against a Tory who was a former member of a notorious right-wing movement, The Link. Mayhew's uncle, Bertram Howarth, secretary of the British Association for the Advancement of Science, wrote in a family newsletter: '[I am] in the throes of a mental political upheaval. I believe I have voted Conservative all my life, but unless something epoch-making happens between now and the General Election, I can't do it again.' His wife Ellie, district commandant of the local Women's Voluntary Service, felt likewise: 'Personally I cannot vote for our sitting [Tory] member; he is stupid, elderly and reactionary ... He was the sole MP to vote against the Beveridge Report. So I shall have to be a Liberal.' When Churchill spoke optimistically about his election prospects to General Bill Slim, home on leave from Burma, Slim responded with character- istic bluntness: 'Well, Prime Minister, I know one thing. My Army won't be voting for you.'

A tide of sentiment was sweeping British people of all classes, driven by preoccupation with building a new future rather than cher- ishing pride in the past. Churchill himself said back in 1941, of the state-school boys who occupied most of the RAF's cockpits: 'They have saved this country; they have the right to rule it.' Labour's Aneurin Bevan told one of his many election audiences: 'We have been the dreamers, we have been the sufferers, now we are the builders.' Churchill was applauded everywhere he went during his June 1945 election tours, and public admiration for him was very real. But with the wisdom sometimes displayed by democracies, few people allowed this to influence their votes. Churchill's election broadcasts were harshly combative. He deployed against the threat of socialism all the impassioned verbiage which he had mobilised for so long against the nation's enemies. But even many supporters thought these tirades ill-judged, and there were moments when he himself seemed to recognise this.

Clementine wrote to her daughter Mary on 20 June: 'Papa broad- casts tonight. He is very low, poor Darling. He thinks he has lost his "touch" and he grieves about it.' Londoner Jennifer McIntosh wrote to her sister in California on 4 July: 'One of the most extraordinary things has been the terrific slump in the Churchill prestige ... I wish you could have heard his election broadcasts – they were deplorable, the last one pitifully cheap.' Likewise, more surprisingly, Oliver Harvey at the Foreign Office perceived Churchill as conducting 'a jingo election which is terrifying in its inappropriateness'. Churchill was much more a social conservative than he was a political Conservative. He lacked real sympathy for or interest in the party which he nominally led at the hustings. He anticipated that the election outcome would represent a vote of confidence in his own war leadership, rather than a verdict on the Tories' fitness to rule. But the war was almost ended.

While the rival candidates campaigned, most of the complexities of occupying Germany and sustaining the struggle against Japan were addressed without interventions from the prime minister. Addicted to tidings from battlefields, he often stumped into the secretaries' room at Downing Street to demand: 'Any news come in?' Told, perhaps for the sixth time in a day, that there was none, he said irritably: 'I won't have it . . . I must have more regular reports. It's your business to keep me informed.' Yet opportunities were now few to order the movements of armies, fleets or air forces. He directed Alexander to act vigorously to expel Tito's partisans from Trieste and north-east Italy, to which they laid claim. When the C-in-C warned that British troops were much less enthusiastic about fighting Yugoslavs than Germans, Churchill dismissed his fears – and ordered a display of force. Faced with this, the Yugoslavs withdrew behind the Izonzo river. The prime minister again used British troops to force the French to withdraw from Syria, which was handed over to an indigenous Arab government. France occupied an area of northwest Italy to which it laid claim. Here too Churchill acted ruthlessly and successfully, insisting upon removal of De Gaulle's forces.

In South-East Asia, Slim's Fourteenth Army was mopping up the last of the Japanese in Burma, and preparing for an amphibious assault on Malaya, scheduled for September. Captain Pim diligently moved the relevant pins and arrows on the walls of the Map Room at Downing Street, but the prime minister's heart was never deeply engaged. He remained preoccupied with the fate of Europe, and with urging upon the new US president the need to adopt firm policies towards the Russians.

On 18 May the Churchills entertained to lunch at Downing Street the Russian ambassador, Feodor Gusev. When Clementine and other guests left the table, the prime minister unburdened himself to the

Soviet emissary. It seems worth rehearsing at length Gusev's account of the meeting, both as evidence of Churchill's sentiments, and of the manner in which these were reported to Moscow. The prime minister began by describing the importance he attached to a new summit meeting at which 'either we shall achieve an agreement on future cooperation between our three nations, or the Anglo-American community will become united in opposition to the Soviet Union. It is difficult to anticipate the possible consequences of this second scenario.' Gusev wrote:

> Here Churchill raised his voice, saying 'We are full of grievances.' I asked him what he had in mind. Irritably and in heightened tones, he began to catalogue the issues: 1) Trieste. Tito has 'sneaked up to Trieste and wants to seize it.' Churchill laid his hands on the table and showed how Tito was sneaking up to Trieste. We will not allow', – Churchill roared, – 'the resolution of territorial disputes by seizure . . . We and the Americans are united in our resolution that all territorial issues should be resolved through a peace confer- ence.' I remarked that as far as I knew Tito did not intend to resolve any territorial issues. Churchill ignored me and continued: 'Armies are confronting each other. Grave trouble can break out at any time unless goodwill is displayed.' 2) Prague. Churchill declared that we did not allow British representatives into Prague. 'Our accredited ambas- sador has been prevented from entering Czechoslovakia,' he said. I remarked that only the previous day Czech government representa- tives had travelled from London to Prague on a British aircraft. Churchill continued: 'You wish to claim exclusive rights for yourselves in every capital occupied by your troops. The British government cannot understand such a Soviet attitude and cannot justify it to the British people, mindful that we are under mutual obligations to display friendship and cooperation . . . We, the British, are a proud nation and cannot allow anyone to treat us in this way.'

'Churchill would not listen to my comment on this and continued: 3) Vienna. "You do not allow us to enter Vienna. The war is over,

but our representatives cannot inspect quarters for our soldiers."'
Gusev launched into an exposition of the Soviet position which the
prime minister cut short: 'Why will you not allow our representatives
to enter Vienna? Now the war is over, what possible consideration
can justify the refusal of the Soviet government to admit our
representatives to Vienna?' There were more brusque exchanges about
the Soviet establishment of a puppet regime in Austria, then Churchill
turned to the German capital: 'You do not allow us into Berlin. You
want to make Berlin your exclusive zone.'

> I declared that Churchill's statement was groundless as we have an
> agreement on occupation zones and control of greater Berlin.
> Churchill again repeated that he is willing to allow any number of
> Soviet representatives to go anywhere. Churchill moved on to Poland
> and spoke with even greater anger. Things were going from bad to
> worse where the Polish issue was concerned, he said. He saw no hope
> of a satisfactory resolution of it: 'We have endorsed Polish delegates,
> and you have imprisoned them. Parliament and the public are deeply
> concerned' . . . Churchill thinks that forthcoming debates in
> Parliament will demonstrate the great indignation of the British
> nation, and he will find himself at a loss about how to satisfy public
> opinion. Churchill then vaguely hinted that a satisfactory outcome
> of the Polish issue might lead to a resolution of the issue of the Baltic
> States.
>
> Churchill did not want to hear my comments and moved on to
> characterize the gravity of the general situation. 'Your front stretches
> from Lubeck to Trieste. You allow no one to enter the capitals which
> you control. The situation in Trieste is alarming. Polish affairs have
> reached a dead end. The general climate is at boiling point.' I told
> Churchill that he was familiar with the Soviet government's position –
> that it makes no claims on territory or on the European capitals. Our
> front does not stretch as far as Trieste. Marshal Tito's troops may be
> there, but we are not responsible for Marshal Tito. He and the Yugoslav
> people have won themselves a place of honour among the United
> Nations by their struggle.

Churchill said: 'I know that you are a great nation. By your struggle you have won an equal status among the great powers. But we, the British, are also a proud nation and we will not allow anyone to abuse us and trample upon our interests. I want you to understand that we are profoundly concerned by the current situation. I have ordered that demobilization of the Royal Air Force should be delayed.' He then abruptly terminated the conversation, apologized for his frankness and departed to discuss with Attlee the forthcoming parliamentary elections.

The Soviet ambassador appended to this dispatch a personal commentary on the meeting:

Churchill was extraordinarily angry, and seemed to be making an effort to keep himself under control. His remarks were full of threats and blackmail, but it was not just blackmail. Following his radio broadcast of 13 May, the English press has adopted a stronger anti-Soviet line in reporting European events. It seeks to interpret all the emerging problems in terms of the USSR's attitude. Churchill's speech was an instruction to the press. Polish agents are conducting a bold anti-Soviet campaign in parliamentary circles and demand new debates on the Polish issue. Eden had already announced in the House of Commons that a foreign affairs debate will take place after the holidays. We may expect this to develop into a big anti-Soviet demonstration intended to pressure and threaten the USSR. So far we have no precise information on the purpose of Eisenhower's and Montgomery's forthcoming visit to London, but we have reason to think that they have been summoned to discuss and evaluate the Allies' military position. We should recognise that we are dealing with an adventurer who is in his element at war, who feels much more at ease in the circumstances of war than those of peace.

Gusev's account of this meeting is unlikely to have been shown to Stalin, because Churchill's bluntness would have displeased him. In any event, it could have exercised not the smallest influence upon

Moscow's policies. The Russians knew that the Americans shared little of the prime minister's passion about Eastern Europe. For all Churchill's bluster, his mutterings to the chiefs of staff about the possibility of launching 'Operation *Unthinkable*', neither Western nation was ready to challenge the Russians by force. The old statesman's diatribe merely vented his personal bitterness and frustration. He knew in his heart that the tyranny established by the Red Army could not be undone either through diplomacy or by force of arms.

After polling day on 6 July, there was a three-week pause before the election result was announced, to allow the overseas service vote to be counted. Churchill flew to south-west France for his first holiday since 1939, at a château owned by a Canadian well-wisher. Then, on 15 July, he took a plane onward to Berlin for the last great Allied conference, the closing episode of his own war.

Churchill professed confidence about the election outcome. This was shared by Stalin who believed he would be returned to power with a parliamentary majority of at least eighty. Nonetheless, in a most honourable display of his respect for democracy, Churchill invited Clement Attlee, the possible prime minister-in-waiting, to join the British delegation at Potsdam. The Labour leader was waiting to greet him at his appointed villa, 23 Ringstrasse, along with Montgomery, Alexander and Eden. On the 16th, Churchill held his first two-hour meeting with Harry Truman. He emerged much encouraged by what he saw and heard. Truman spoke much more toughly than had Roosevelt in his last months. Later, the prime minister toured the ruins of Berlin, and gazed without animosity upon the Germans foraging amid the rubble. 'My hate had died with their surrender,' he wrote later. 'I was much moved by their desolation, and also by their thin haggard looks and threadbare clothes.' Gazing on the remains of Hitler's bunker, he reflected that this was how Downing Street would have looked, had matters turned out differently in 1940. But he quickly wearied of tourism. Now as ever, what seized his imagination was the opportunity to discuss great issues with the most powerful men on earth, if not as their equal in national might, as their acknowledged peer in personal stature.

The Potsdam conference, of which the first formal session took place on 17 July, achieved no meaningful decisions or conclusions. Churchill said of himself: 'I shall be only half a man until the result of the poll.' Diplomat John Peck noted with some foreboding that when the prime minister and Attlee inspected a parade of British troops in Berlin, Attlee received the louder cheers. Opening a soldiers' club, Churchill said: 'May the memory of this glorious pilgrimage of war never die!' Yet many of his audience, men of Montgomery's armies, viewed both their recent past and future prospects in much more pragmatic terms.

Churchill's first responsibility was to take the measure of Harry Truman, and to lay before the new president his fears for Britain and the world. Truman, in his turn, felt a certain apprehension about the encounter. Harry Hopkins, in Moscow late in May, told Zhukov as he bade farewell before flying to London to see Churchill: 'I respect the old man, but he is difficult. The only person who found talking to him easy was Franklin Roosevelt.' Now, in Potsdam, Churchill described to Truman his fears for British solvency, when the country owed £3 billion of external debt. He expressed his hopes of American support. They talked much of Eastern Europe, from which the news daily grew worse. Churchill was much excited by news which reached the president at Potsdam, of the successful atomic bomb test at Alamogordo. He encouraged the president to disclose to Stalin 'the simple fact that we have this weapon' – a significant and optimistic use of the plural possessive.

Churchill agreed, without consulting his cabinet colleagues, that the Americans would employ the atomic bomb against Japan without further reference to London. He urged that Britain and the US should maintain the closest post-war military links, with reciprocal basing rights around the world. When Truman took refuge in bromides, and declined an explicit commitment, Churchill sallied in disappointment: 'A man might make a proposal of marriage to a young lady, but it was not much use if he was told that she would always be a sister to him.' He was rash enough to indulge a tirade against China and its pretensions, which of course irked the Americans. Brooke was indignant that the US chiefs of staff discussed strategy for the final phase of the Pacific war in the absence of the British. What else could he have expected? The most significant British role was to endorse, and marginally to modify, the so-called Potsdam Declaration to Japan, warning of dire consequences if she failed forthwith to surrender to the Allies.

Brooke was exasperated by Churchill's exuberant display of enthusiasm about the news of 'Tube Alloys' – the atomic bomb project, and displayed an extraordinary failure of understanding when the prime minister discussed the issue with his chiefs of staff over lunch on 23 July. 'I was completely shattered by the PM's outlook!' wrote the CIGS.

He had absorbed all the minor American exaggerations, and as a result was completely carried away. It was now no longer necessary for the Russians to come into the Japanese war, the new explosive alone was sufficient to settle the matter. Furthermore we now had something in our hands which would redress the balance with the Russians! The secret of this explosive, and the power to use it, would completely alter the diplomatic equilibrium! Now we had a new value which redressed our position (pushing his chin out and scowling), now we could say if you insist on doing this or that, well we can just blot out Moscow, then Stalingrad, then Kiev, then Kuibyshev, Karkhov [sic], Stalingrad, Sebastopol etc. etc. And now where are the Russians!!! I tried to crush his over-optimism based on the results of one experiment, and was asked with contempt what reason I had for minimizing the results of these discoveries. I was trying to dispel his dreams and as usual he did not like it. But I shudder to feel that he is allowing the half-baked results of one experiment to warp the whole of his diplomatic perspective!

If the prime minister failed to perceive the strategic limitations of nuclear weapons, his senior military adviser displayed in this encounter an extraordinary ignorance about the greatest scientific undertaking of the war, indeed the most momentous in history. Here was a manifestation of the manner in which even exalted Allied directors of strategy were slow to grasp the significance of the Bomb. Back in 1940–41, British scientists' theoretical nuclear research was well ahead of American. Following the joint commitment to build an atomic bomb, and the transfer of all relevant British material and personnel to the US, the Americans adopted an increasingly ruthless proprietorial policy towards 'Tube Alloys'. It had been agreed that the project should be a partnership. But Sir John Anderson, the responsible minister, soon reported to Churchill that the Americans were concealing information from the British in a 'quite intolerable' fashion. At Quebec in May 1943 a new agreement was reached between Britain's prime minister and the US president, subsequently confirmed in writing at Hyde Park in August. At Hyde Park again in September 1944 Churchill persuaded Roosevelt belatedly to sign a document agreeing that Anglo–American nuclear cooperation and exchange of information should continue after the war. But the Americans nonetheless displayed little inclination to regard atomic research as a shared venture – and impoverished Britain was in no condition to build a bomb of its own. After the war, successive British governments were reduced to pleading with Washington for the honouring of the nuclear agreements struck between Roosevelt and Churchill.

The social nuances of Potsdam were endless. During an Allied reception at Churchill's villa, the host offered a toast to Marshal Zhukov. The Russian, caught by surprise, responded by addressing the prime minister as 'comrade'. Then, alarmed by the perils of being heard to use such fraternal language to an arch-capitalist, he hastily amended this to 'comrade-in-arms'. Next day in Stalin's office, the soldier was indeed taunted about the readiness with which he had made a comrade of Churchill. Only Stalin, among the Russians, allowed himself freedom to take personal liberties with the Western Allies.

Churchill spent much time – there was one session of five hours – alone with the Soviet warlord. Stalin was in the highest humour. He perceived himself as the foremost victor of World War II. Not for decades would it become apparent that the Soviet Union's devastation, and the economic consequences of subordinating all other interests to Russia's vast military machine, had sown the seeds of the communist system's eventual collapse. In July 1945 the world, like the Soviet leader himself, perceived only that he presided over the greatest power on the European Continent, militarily unassailable. Stalin professed to confide in Churchill as if he was an old friend, apologising for Russia's failure publicly to display its gratitude for British wartime supplies, and promising that he would make amends at some suitable moment. At a banquet given by Churchill, the tyrant amazed guests by circling the table, collecting autographs on the menu: 'his eyes twinkled with mirth and goodwill'. He flattered the prime minister shamelessly – and was rewarded with Churchill's beaming benevolence. Eden wrote in dismay: 'He is again under Stalin's spell. He kept repeating "I like that man."' Yet the Soviet warlord, inevitably, conceded nothing. The puppet Polish leadership was brought to Potsdam at Churchill's urging, and listened stonily to his urgings that non-communists should be included in the Warsaw government, and that Poland should moderate its western frontier expectations.

Churchill never doubted the malevolence of Soviet intentions in Eastern Europe, and indeed around the world. But he sustained residual delusions that he himself might influence Stalin, and thus fulfil purposes from which the full commitment of the US was withheld. Sergo Beria, son of the NKVD chief, wrote: 'Of all the western leaders Churchill had the best understanding of Stalin and succeeded in seeing through almost all of his manoeuvres. But when he is quoted as suggesting that he gained an influence over Stalin I cannot help smiling. It seems amazing that a person of such stature could so delude himself.'

Stalin could be dispossessed of his vast trove of booty only by force of arms. He knew that the Western Allies lacked stomach or means for such a trial. Thus he felt at liberty to divert himself in the company of the old imperialist, who indeed perhaps amused him, as he amused the world. Britain lost nothing by Churchill's dalliance with Stalin at Potsdam and elsewhere, because nothing could have been said or done to change outcomes. But it was a sad end to so much magnificent wartime statesmanship by the prime minister, that the lion should lie down with the bear, roll on his back and allow his chest to be tickled. Far back in October 1940, Churchill had observed that 'A lot of people talked a lot of nonsense when they said wars never settled anything; nothing in history was ever settled except by wars.' In July 1945 it was impossible to pretend that the affairs of Europe had been satisfactorily 'settled' by Allied victory in the Second World War.

On the 25th, the British delegation left the Americans and Russians to confer, and returned to Britain to discover the election outcome. Churchill landed back at Northolt that afternoon, expecting to return to Potsdam two days later. Even the Russians assumed this: 'No one in our conference delegation had the slightest doubt that he would be re-elected,' recalled Admiral Kuznetsov. At Downing Street, Captain Pim had reorganised the Map Room to display poll results as they came in – a somewhat generous inter-pretation of his naval duties, on behalf of a political party leader. On the morning of the 26th, Churchill settled himself in front of Pim's boards, remaining there through the day with the companion-ship of Beaverbrook and Brendan Bracken. It was soon plain that the Conservatives had suffered a disaster. In the new House of Commons, Labour would hold 393 seats. The Tories' numbers fell from 585 to 213. The Conservative government was at an end. Churchill had lost his parliamentary majority. He could no longer serve as prime minister. At 7 p.m. he said quaintly to Pim: 'Fetch me my carriage, and I shall go to the Palace.' He resigned his office. Clement Attlee assumed the mantle, formed his own government, and returned to Potsdam in Churchill's stead. The Russians were bewildered by Churchill's defeat. 'I still cannot comprehend how this could happen that he lost the election!' said Molotov later. 'Apparently one needs to understand the English way of life better . . . In Potsdam . . . he was so active.'

The fallen leader strove to act manfully. On his return to Downing Street from Buckingham Palace he said to his private secretary Leslie Rowan: 'You must not think of me any more; your duty is now to serve Attlee, if he wishes you to do so. You must therefore go to him, for you must think also of your future.' Rowan broke down and cried. When Moran said something about voters' ingratitude, Churchill responded: 'Oh no, I wouldn't call it that, they have had a very bad time.' Yet the misery of his predicament cut to his heart. For almost six years he had inhabited a universe of fevered action. An almost unbroken stream of reports, minutes, cables and issues for decision flowed through his study, map room, cabinet room, bedroom and even bathroom day and night. Now, instead, with devastating abruptness, there was nothing. The vacancy seemed almost unendurable. 'The rest of my life will be holidays,' he said to Moran. 'It is a strange feeling, all power gone.'

Churchill moved from Downing Street into Claridge's Hotel. He was confronted with all manner of domestic problems, such as he had been allowed to ignore for six years, not least the need to pay bills. His personal finances during the war years remain somewhat opaque. He received a monthly salary of £449 from the Treasury for his services as prime minister. In addition, his books generated substantial income. There was some post-war political controversy about the fact that throughout the war he gained handsome royalties from sales of collections of his prime ministerial speeches. For instance *Into Battle*, the first volume, generated £11,172, of which sum the prime minister instructed his bank to divert half to the account of his son Randolph. He received a huge amount of money, £50,000, in October 1943 for the film rights of his biography of Marlborough, and a further £50,000 in April 1945 from Alexander Korda for film rights to his *History of the English-Speaking Peoples*. He was able to adopt a lofty attitude about book contracts and delivery dates with his publishers, Macmillan, because one of its most influential directors was a member of his government. An old friend, Sir Henry Strakosch, who died in 1943, bequeathed the prime minister £20,000 in his will. Yet punitive wartime taxation, more than 80 per cent, absorbed a large part of these sums. Even on a care-and-maintenance basis Chartwell, his home in Kent, incurred costs. Randolph, the monstrous pelican in the family, represented a major drain on his purse. As prime minister Churchill contributed about £35 a month for his personal share of the costs of Chequers. What is undisputed is that he emerged almost penniless from his experience as the saviour of his nation.

Smuts said, more than two years earlier: 'Winston's mind has a stop in it at the end of the war.' Churchill grumbled: 'I do not believe in this brave new world . . . Tell me any good in any new thing.' Even had he won the election, the great conflict with which he would be inseparably identified for the rest of human history had barely three weeks to run. The nugatory military decisions still at the discretion of a British national leader could exercise little influence upon the manner in which its final operations were conducted. Thereafter, while Churchill might have enjoyed retaining the trappings of power, as all prime ministers do, he was quite unsuited to address the challenges of peace. Isaiah Berlin wrote: 'Churchill sees history – and life – as a great Renaissance pageant: when he thinks of France or Italy, Germany or the Low Countries, Russia, India, Africa, the Arab lands, he sees vivid historical images – something between Victorian illustrations in a child's book of history and the great procession painted by Benozzo Gozzoli in the Riccardi Palace . . . No man has ever loved life more vehemently and infused so much of it into everyone and everything that he has touched.'

Yet by July 1945 the British people hungered for simpler and more immediate things. They had played their parts in the most terrible global drama in history. Now they were eager to quit the stage, to address themselves to their own private and social purposes, which Churchill only dimly understood, and was unsuited to assist them to fulfil. Alexandre Dumas wrote: '*Il existe des services si grands par qu'ils peuvent se payer que l'ingratitude.*' The electorate had performed a service to Churchill, as well as to itself, by parting company with its great war leader when there was no more war for him to lead. He was profoundly glad for his nation that its struggle was approaching a conclusion, but deeply grieved for himself. At noon on 27 July he held his final cabinet – 'a pretty grim affair', in Eden's words:

After it was over I was on my way to the front door when W. called me back and we had half an hour alone. He was pretty wretched, poor old boy. Said he didn't feel any more reconciled this morning, on the contrary it hurt more, like a wound which becomes more painful after the first shock. He couldn't help feeling his treatment had been scurvy. 'Thirty years of my life have been passed in this room. I shall never sit in it again. You will, but I shall not,' with more to the same effect.

As he left Chequers after a final weekend with his family and intimates, he wrote in its visitors' book: 'FINIS'. Three weeks later, on 15 August, Japan's surrender brought an end to the Second World War.

Churchill had wielded more power than any other British prime minister had known, or would know again. In 1938 he seemed a man out of his time, a patrician imperialist whose vision was rooted in Britain's Victorian past. By 1945, while this remained true, and goes far to explain his own disappointments, it had not prevented him from becoming the greatest war leader his country had ever known, a statesman whose name rang across the world like that of no other Englishman in history. Himself believing Britain great, for one last brief season he was able to make her so. To an extraordinary degree, what he did between 1940 and 1945 defines the nation's self-image even into the twenty-first century.

His achievement was to exercise the privileges of a dictator without casting off the mantle of a democrat. Ismay once found him bemoaning the bother of preparing a speech for the House of Commons, and obviously apprehensive about its reception. The soldier said emolliently: 'Why don't you tell them to go to hell?' Churchill turned in a flash: 'You should not say those things: I am the servant of the House.' General Sikorski remarked at Chequers that the prime minister was a dictator chosen by the people. Churchill corrected him: 'No, I am a privileged domestic, a *valet de chambre*, the servant of the House of Commons.' It should be a source of wonder and pride, that such a man led Britain through the war, more than half-believing this. It was entirely appropriate that he led a coalition government, for he was never a party man. He existed, *sui generis*, outside the framework of conventional politics, and never seemed any more comfortable with the Conservative Party than was it with him. A.G. Gardiner wrote of Churchill back in 1914: 'He would no more think of consulting a party than the chauffeur would of consulting the motor car.' The same was true in 1945.

As for Churchill's war direction, it is not difficult to identify his strategic errors and misplaced enthusiasms. Anatole France wrote, '*Après la bataille, c'est là que triomphent les tacticiens.*' Yet the outcome justified all. The defining fact of Churchill's leadership was Britain's emergence from the Second World War among the victors. This, most of his own people acknowledged. No warlord, no commander, in history has failed to make mistakes: as Tedder observed, 'War is organised confusion.' It is as easy to catalogue the mistakes of Alexander the Great, Caesar, Napoleon as those of Churchill. Both Britain's most distinguished earlier war leaders, Pitt the Elder and Younger, were responsible for graver strategic follies than himself.

Historians and biographers have a duty to present evidence for the prosecution, to identify blunders and shortcomings. But before the jury retires, it is necessary to strip away nugatory matter, and focus upon essentials. Churchill towers over the war, standing higher than any other single human being at the head of the forces of light, as many Americans recognised. Mark Sullivan wrote in the *New York Herald Tribune* on 11 May 1945: 'Churchill's greatness is unexcelled ... Churchill's part in this world war reduces the classic figures of Rome and Greece to the relatively inconsequent stature of actors in dramas of minor scope ... Churchill was the fighting leader, and his own poet.' Anyone who attempts the difficult feat of imagining British wartime history deprived of his presence will find it sadly shrunken in stature. Even Brooke was once moved to complain: 'dull cabinet without PM'. To an extraordinary degree, one man raised his nation far above the place in the Grand Alliance which its contribution in troops, tanks, ships, planes could have justified from 1943 onwards.

It must be mistaken to assess Churchill's war leadership in isolation. When it is measured against that of Roosevelt or Stalin, not to mention Hitler, Mussolini or Tojo, his failures and shortcomings shrink dramatically. No honourable course of action existed which could have averted his nation's bankruptcy and exhaustion in 1945, nor its eclipse from world power amid the new primacy of the United States and Russia.

Churchill possessed the ability, through his oratory, to invest with majesty the deeds and even failures of mortal men. More than any other national leader in history, and aided by the power of broadcast communications, he caused words to become not mere assertions of fact or expressions of intent, but acts of governance. 'His countrymen have come to feel that he is saying what they would like to say for themselves if they knew how,' wrote Moran. '. . . Perhaps for the first time in his life, he seems to see things through the eyes of the average man. He still says what he is feeling at the moment, but now it turns out that he is speaking for the nation.'

In reality, as this book has sought to show, Churchill did not command the respect and trust of all the British people all of the time. But he empowered millions to look beyond the havoc of the battlefield, the squalor of their domestic circumstances amid privation and bombardment, and to perceive a higher purpose in their struggles and sacrifices. This was, of course, of greater importance in averting defeat in 1940–41 than later, when the Allies were able to commit superior masses of men and material to securing victory. Churchill's rhetoric has played a significant part in causing the struggle against Hitler to be perceived by posterity as 'the good war'. He explained the struggle as no one else could, in terms mankind could comprehend and relate to, now as then. Even most American historians, when chronicling the wartime era, are more generous in their use of quotations from the words of Winston Churchill than from those of their own president, Franklin Roosevelt.

He cherished aspirations which often proved greater than his nation was capable of fulfilling. This, too, has been among the principal themes of this narrative. But it seems inconsistent to applaud his defiance of reason in insisting that Britain must fight on in June 1940, and then to denounce the extravagance of his later demands upon the nation and its armed forces. The service chiefs often deplored his misjudgements and intemperance. Yet his instinct for war was far more highly developed than their own. If they were often right in pleading that the time was not ripe to fight, left to their own devices they would have been intolerably slow to fight at all. While Brooke was an officer of remarkable qualities, like many soldiers he was a limited human being. He deluded himself in claiming, as he did after the conflict, that Western strategy had evolved in accordance with his own conception. While this may have been so in 1942–43, thereafter the European war was brought to a conclusion in consequence of Soviet exertions aided by American supplies, with significant assistance from the strategic air offensive and Eisenhower's armies. In the west, major military operations – which means the north-west Europe campaign – conformed to an American design, to which the foremost British contribution was to delay the invasion of the Continent until conditions were overwhelmingly favourable.

Britain produced few outstanding military commanders in the Second World War, a reflection of the institutional debility of the British Army which also afflicted its tactics, choice of weapons, and battlefield performance. The Royal Navy was Britain's finest fighting service, its performance tarnished only by the limitations of the Fleet Air Arm. The Royal Air Force also made an outstanding contribution, but like the USAAF it suffered from the obsessive reluctance of its higher commanders to subordinate their independent strategic ambitions to the interests of naval and ground operations.

It is often and justly remarked that Churchill enjoyed war. He revered heroes. Yet away from the battlefield, he seldom found such men congenial companions. Few generals are highly cultured men or notable conversationalists, capable of illuminating a conference room or dinner table to Churchill's standard. In his peacetime life, even after the two world wars, old warhorses played little part. Many people supposed that he himself would have coveted a Victoria Cross.

This was surely true in his youth. But when his daughter Mary asked in his old age whether he felt that anything was missing from his wondrous array of laurels, he said nothing of medals, but instead answered slowly: 'I should have liked my father to have lived long enough to see that I made something of my life.'

During the war years, his commanders far more often disappointed his hopes than fulfilled them. He was forever searching for great captains, Marlboroughs and Wellingtons, yet towards the end he grew impatient even with Alexander, his unworthy favourite. He valued both Brooke and Montgomery, but never warmed to them, save as instruments of his will. Neither the British Army nor its chieftains fulfilled his soaring warrior ideal, and it was never plausible that they should. Much of the story of Churchill and the Second World War is of Britain's leader seeking from his nation's torpid military culture greater things than it was capable of achieving. He inspired it to accomplish more than it dreamed possible in June 1940, but never as much as he wanted. Such is the nature of the relationship between many great leaders and their peoples, who know themselves mortal clay. Had Britain – or America – produced legions of warriors such as those of wartime Germany and Japan, they would have ceased to be the kind of liberal democracies the war was fought to preserve.

If Churchill's rhetoric and personality had been less remarkable, if he himself had not been so lovable, some of his military decisions might have been more harshly judged both by his contemporaries and by posterity. As it was, he was able to weave spells in the House of Commons and in his writings, which deflected even the best-merited criticisms. The only charge against him which stuck with the public, and lost him the general election of 1945, derived from his indifference to forging a new society. Moran wrote in 1943: 'With Winston war is an end in itself rather than a means to an end.' The British people understood his indifference to humdrum domestic issues, and thus acted as sensibly in evicting Churchill from Downing Street in 1945 as they had done by supporting his installation there in 1940.

Macmillan was at least half right in asserting that only Churchill could have secured the commitment of American power to the

Mediterranean and Europe in the year following Pearl Harbor. Without his personal influence, the lure of the Pacific might have proved irresistible to Roosevelt and his chiefs of staff. If the Americans in 1944–45 came to regret their engagement in the Mediterranean, in 1942–43 it is impossible to perceive how else the Western Allied armies could have played their part in fighting Hitler's armies.

There is an inescapable pathos about Churchill's predicament in the last year of the war, because almost all his ambitions were frustrated, save for victory over the Axis. His engagement with armies became almost exclusively that of a tourist, because he could no longer much influence their movements. For such a mighty warrior, this was a source of unhappiness. The limits to his powers of negotiation with Roosevelt and Stalin were set by economic and strategic realities. But he accomplished the little that a British leader could.

Churchill's view of the British Empire and its peoples was unenlightened by comparison with that of America's president, or even by the standards of his time. This must be set in the balance against his huge virtues. He excluded brown and black peoples from his personal vision of freedom. Yet almost all of us are discriminatory, not necessarily racially, in the manner and degree in which we focus our finite stores of compassion. In this as in many other things, Churchill displayed mortal fallibility. Most great national leaders are cold men, as Roosevelt ultimately was, for all his capacity to simulate warmth. Churchill, despite monumental egoism, displayed a human sympathy that was none the less impressive because he often neglected intimates and servants, and failed to extend his charity to imperial subject races.

Any assessment of Churchill's wartime contribution must include words of homage to his wife. Clementine provided a service to the world by her manifold services to her husband, foremost among which was to tell him truths about himself. He was a domestic and parental failure, as most great men are. It would be disruptive to any family to accommodate a lion in the drawing room. Without ever taming Winston, Clementine managed and tempered him as far as any mortal could, while sustaining her husband's love in a fashion which moves posterity. Whatever he might have been without his indomitable wife, it would surely have been something less than he was.

History must take Churchill as a whole, as his wartime country-men were obliged to do, rather than employ a spokeshave to strip away the blemishes created by his lunges into excess and folly. If the governance of nations in peace is best conducted by reasonable men, in war there is a powerful argument for leadership by those some-times willing to adopt courses beyond the boundaries of reason, as Churchill did in 1940–41. His foremost quality was strength of will. This was so fundamental to his triumph in the early war years that it seems absurd to suggest that he should have become more biddable, merely because in 1943–45 his stubbornness was sometimes deployed in support of misjudged purposes.

He was probably the greatest actor upon the stage of affairs whom the world has ever known. Familiarity with his speeches, conversation and the fabulous anecdotage about his wartime doings does nothing to diminish our capacity to be moved to awe, tears, laughter by the sustained magnificence of his performance. He was the largest human being ever to occupy his office. If his leadership through the Second World War was imperfect, it is certain that no other British ruler in history has matched his direction of the nation in peril, nor, please God, is ever likely to find himself in circumstances to surpass it.

ACKNOWLEDGEMENTS

My first debt is to Richard Johnson of HarperCollins in London and Ash Green at Knopf in New York, for showing the confidence to commission this work, when less optimistic souls might have judged that there was no more usefully to be said about Winston Churchill. Robert Lacey of HarperCollins is a superb editor, who contributes immeasurably to the coherence of all my books, likewise Andrew Miller at Knopf. Michael Sissons and Peter Matson have been my agents for longer than they care to remember, and have always been wonderfully supportive.

Dr Lyuba Vinogradova has been responsible for research and translation in Moscow on this book, as for my earlier *Armageddon* and *Nemesis*. It has today become much more difficult to access Soviet archives than it was a decade ago, but Lyuba achieved a remarkable amount by scouring published document collections. I am especially grateful to her for translating hundreds of pages of material concerning Churchill and the Allies from the wartime Soviet press.

Edward Young, who I met when he was assisting Douglas Hurd with his biography of Peel, has done important and extraordinarily energetic research for me in US archives. He is on the threshold of becoming a distinguished historian in his own right. As usual, I owe thanks to the peerless staff of the London Library, whose patience and goodwill are invaluable. Allen Packwood and his team at the Churchill Archive Centre in Cambridge have been tirelessly helpful, a great tribute when they contend with a column of Churchill scholars threading daily through their doors. Beyond generosity with his time while I was visiting Churchill College, Allen was generous enough to read my draft MS and make helpful comments and corrections.

William Spencer and his colleagues at the British National Archive, together with their American counterparts at the National Archive in Washington, Tim Nenninger most conspicuous among them, show how magnificently great collections function when staffed by men and women who really care. The Imperial War Museum's library and manuscript archive become ever more important, now that most 1939–45 eye-witnesses are dead. The Liddell Hart Archive at King's College, London holds many important papers, and I am especially grateful for access to Sir John Kennedy's diary. I am indebted to copyright holders who have given permission for extracts from their material to be quoted in my text, including Antonia Yates for the papers of Captain Andrew Yates. Extracts from the writings and speeches of Winston Churchill are reproduced with permission of Curtis Brown Ltd, London, on behalf of The Estate of Winston Churchill, copyright © Winston S. Churchill.

Anyone who writes about Winston Churchill must pay tribute to Sir Martin Gilbert, his official biographer, whose work laid the foundations for all who follow. Gilbert's massive *Life*, accompanied by the equally fascinating companion document collections, represents one of the great scholarly achievements of our time. Future writers and biographers will owe Sir Martin a further debt, when he completes his forthcoming volumes of War Papers for 1942–45.

Professor Sir Michael Howard OM, CH, MC and two other old friends, Godfrey Hodgson and Don Berry, have read my draft manuscript. Both made immensely helpful suggestions and proposed amendments, most of which I have acted upon. I am indebted to Antony Beevor for focusing my attention on Operation *Unthinkable*, and for the time and wisdom of Professor David Reynolds, Professor Robert Gildea, Professor Christopher Andrew and Chris Bellamy. Douglas Matthews's index is a work of art, for which I am warmly grateful. In the United States, Dr Williamson Murray made many helpful suggestions about the text, based upon his own exhaustive knowledge of the period. Dr Tami Biddle of the US Army War College is extraordinarily generous with her own material, in this case pointing me to Harris's and Slessor's 1941 reports from Washington. The contribution of my secretary, Rachel Lawrence, is always indispensable, not least in collating notes and references. So too is that of my infinitely long-suffering wife, Penny, who feels doomed forever to share my spirit existence, focused upon 1939–45. She deserves to believe that some day we shall progress towards a real life in our own times.

NOTES AND SOURCES

Abbreviations

BNA   British National Archive
CAC   Churchill Archive Centre
IWM   Imperial War Museum
LHA   Liddell Hart Archive at King's College London
USNA   US National Archive

After much vacillation, I have omitted references to some documents which have been for many years in the public domain, and which are clearly identified and dated in the text. All direct quotations from Churchill not otherwise sourced are to be found in Martin Gilbert's volumes.

Introduction

xv   'He had once conceived' James Boswell *The Life of Samuel Johnson* Everyman 2004 p.1100

xvi 'Andrew Roberts has painted' Andrew Roberts *Masters and Commanders* Penguin 2008

xvi 'The most vivid wartime memory' author interview 1992

xvi 'he told his staff' John Colville *The Fringes of Power: Downing Street Diaries 1939–1955* Hodder & Stoughton 1985 10.12.40

xviii 'Everything depended upon him' *Action this Day* ed. Sir John Wheeler-Bennett Macmillan 1968 p.236

xviii 'He was not mad' Nigel Knight *Churchill Unmasked* David & Charles 2008 p.366

xviii 'may overstate his indispensability' Chris Wrigley *Churchill* Haus 2006 p.85

xx   'It would be easy by a cunning' LHA MS diary of Maj. Gen. Sir John Kennedy 26.1.41

xxii 'Churchill so evidently' *The Diaries of James Lees-Milne* John Murray 2007 p.69 19.8.72

xxiii 'I wish I were twenty' *The Diaries of Harold Nicolson 1939–45* ed. Nigel Nicolson Weidenfeld & Nicolson 1967 9.9.39

Chapter 1: The Battle of France

2 'It was a marvel' David Reynolds *In Command of History* Penguin 2004 p.126

3 'If there is going to be a war' SB to Lord Davidson – Kenneth Young *Stanley Baldwin* Weidenfeld & Nicolson 1976 p.112

3 'several fishing rods' IWM Sir C. Nicholson Papers p.9

3 'I don't think WSC will be' quoted Roberts op. cit. p.199, undisclosed source 13.5.40

3 'It's all a great pity' Butler Papers G11 quoted Roberts op. cit. p.209

3 'If I had to spend' *Nella Last's War* ed. Richard Broad and Suzie Fleming Sphere 1983 p.51

4 'Events are moving so fast' *New Yorker* 12.5.40

4 'Elizabethan zest for life' Harold Nicolson *Spectator* 17.5.40

4 'How Winston thinks' *The Empire at Bay: The Leo Amery Diaries 1929–1945* ed. John Barnes and David Nicholson Hutchinson 1988 p.615 11.5.40

4 'conscious of a profound' WSC *Second World War* vol. i Cassell 1948 p.526

5 'David, sir, David!' Hugh Sebag-Montefiore *Dunkirk* Penguin 2006 p.59

7 'British troops have landed' Sir Michael Howard personal recollection to the author 28.12.08

8 'Perhaps the darkest day' *Chips: The Diaries of Sir Henry Channon* ed. Robert Rhodes-James Weidenfeld & Nicolson 1965 p.248

9 'In May 1940, while few' Robert Rhodes-James *Churchill: A Study in Failure 1900–39* London 1970

9 '"Keep your eye on Churchill"' A.G. Gardiner *The Pillars of Society* Dent popular edn 1916 p.77

9 'additional complication' *Collier's* January 1939

9 'the poor tank' *News of the World* 14.4.38

9 'the submarine will be mastered' WSC to Neville Chamberlain 25.3.39

9 'I feel we may compare' *The Churchill War Papers* ed. Martin Gilbert Heinemann 1993 vol. i p.568

10 'It may well be' speech to the St George's Association 24.4.33

10 'I am beginning to come round' Amery op. cit. p.584 14.3.40

10 'Winston has not been' ibid. p.617 11.5.40

11 'So at last that man' *Parliament and Politics in the Age of Churchill and Attlee: The Headlam Diaries 1935–51* ed. Stuart Ball Cambridge 1999 p.197 10.5.40

11 'The new War Cabinet' Brian Bond *Liddell Hart: A Study of His Military Thought* Cassell 1977 p.131

11 'perfectly futile for war' Stephen Roskill *Hankey: Man of Secrets* Collins 1974 vol. iii p.464

11 'May I wish you every possible' *Action this Day* op. cit. p.219

12 'seemed well satisfied' *The Eden Memoirs: The Reckoning* Cassell 1965 p.98

12 'In Winston's eyes' Lord Moran *Winston Churchill: The Struggle for Survival 1940–1965* London 1966 p.275

13 'He proved in this' *Philadelphia Inquirer* 14.5.40

13 'That smart, tough, dumpy little man' *Time* 27.5.40

14 'We have for twenty years' Charles Richardson *From Churchill's Secret Circle to the BBC* Brassey's 1991 p.77

14 'purely physical soldiers' Raymond Lee *The London Observer* ed. James Leutze Hutchinson 1972 p.216 9.1.41

15 'not too happy about' Colville op. cit. p.131

15 'I think myself that the battle' *Churchill and Roosevelt: The Complete Correspondence* ed. Warren Kimball Princeton 1984 vol. i p.37 15.5.40

15 'The summer landscape' quoted Alastair Horne *To Lose a Battle* Macmillan 1969 pp.286–7

16 'Harold, I think it would be' Harold Nicolson *Diaries and Letters 1939–45* Weidenfeld & Nicolson 1967 p.86 17.5.40

17 'superb confidence' *Action this Day* op. cit. p.219

17 'What a beautiful handwriting' Colville op.cit. p.184 3.7.40

17 'Embracing his staff as' *Action this Day* op. cit. p.219

18 'I went up to my father's bedroom' quoted Martin Gilbert *Finest Hour: Winston S. Churchill 1940–41* Heinemann 1983 p.358

18 'News no worse' Eden op. cit. p.106

18 'It must be remembered' BNA INF1/264 19.5.40

19 'Militarily, I did not see' Eden op. cit. p.107

19 'About time number 17' ibid.

21 'sole remaining bargaining counter' Kimball op. cit. vol. i p.40 20.5.40

22 'the government should at once' *New Statesman* 25.5.40

22 'Nobody minds going down' *The Diaries of Sir Henry Pownall* ed. Brian Bond Leo Cooper 1972 vol. i. p.327

22 'Can nobody prevent him' ibid. p.333 23.5.40

24 'Everything is complete' *The Diaries of Sir Alexander Cadogan* ed. David Dilks Cassell 1971 p.189 25.5.40

25 'A Gallup poll showed' Gallup 29.5.40

26 'too rambling and romantic' Cadogan op. cit. p.190 26.5.40

26 'He is still thinking of his books' Colville op. cit. p.132 16.5.40

27 'he would be addressing' ibid. p.118 7.5.40

27 'so great ... it is madness' quoted Sheila Lawlor *Churchill and the Politics of War 1940–41* Cambridge 1994 p.96

27 'It is not the descendants' Harold Nicolson *Spectator* 17.5.40

27 'I think they're going to beat us' *Wartime Women* ed. Dorothy Sheridan Heinemann 1990 p.91

28 'We're finished' David Howarth *Pursued by a Bear* Collins 1986 p.93

30 'The decision affected us all' *The Memoirs of Lord Ismay* Heinemann 1960 p.131

31 'It is a drop in the bucket' Morgenthau diary Morgenthau Papers Franklin D. Roosevelt Library Hyde Park

32 'The least costly solution' *New York Herald Tribune* 24.5.40

33 'I thought Winston talked' Halifax diary 27.5.40 Borthwick Institute York

34 'His world is built upon' Isaiah Berlin *Personal Impressions* Hogarth Press 1980 p.6

35 'Some of Mr Churchill's broadcasts' Evelyn Waugh *Men at Arms* Chapman & Hall 1952 pp.222–3

Chapter 2: The Two Dunkirks

36 'And so here we are back' Pownall op. cit. vol. i pp.351–2

37 'on reasonable conditions' Reynolds op. cit. p.170

37 'Andrew Roberts' Roberts op. cit. p.232

37 'He was quite magnificent' *The War Diaries of Hugh Dalton* ed. Ben Pimlott Cape 1986 28.5.40

38 'I hope you realise' John Horsfall *Say Not the Struggle* Roundwood 1977 p.142

38 'There was a limit to what' private information to the author 2001

39 'We were told' Antony Hichens *Gunboat Command* Pen & Sword 2007 p.81

39 'No one in the room' Jacob 'His Finest Hour' *The Atlantic* March 1965

40 'The Luftwaffe, badly weakened' *Germany and the Second World War* vol. ii Oxford 1991 p.291

41 'A dejected-looking old man' Ismay op. cit. p.133

43 'he could count on no artillery' Basil Karslake *The Last Act* Leo Cooper 1979 p.124

45 'The political object' C.P. Stacey *The Canadian Army 1939–45* Ottawa 1955 p.278

45 'the Breton redoubt' L.F. Ellis *The War in France and Flanders* HMSO 1953 p.298

45 'People who go to Italy' Colville op. cit. p.152 10.4.40

46 'Reynaud was inscrutable' Eden op. cit. p.116

46 'Mr Churchill appeared imperturbable' De Gaulle *L'Appel* p.54

47 'That woman . . . will undo' Ismay reported conversation in Kennedy MS op. cit. 4.3.41

47 'M. Reynaud felt that' FRUS 1940–41 pp. 4–115

48 'Normally I wake up' Eden op. cit. p.182 19.12.40

48 'All this on the assumption' Amery op. cit. p.624 11.6.40

50 'Churchill, who objected' Colville op. cit. p.232

51 'If the French will go on' ibid. pp.155–6

51 'it was impossible to make' Lord Alanbrooke *War Diaries 1939–1945* ed. Alex Danchev and Daniel Todman Weidenfeld & Nicolson 2001 p.81 14.6.40

52 'It is a desperate job' Brooke op. cit. p.83 15.6.40

53 'Much equipment had been' Stacey op. cit. p.284

53 'The lack of previous training' quoted Karslake op. cit. p.262

53 'Their behaviour was terrible!' ibid.

54 'repeating poetry' Colville op. cit. pp.157–8 15.6.40

54 'told one or two dirty stories' ibid.

54 'less violent, less wild' ibid. p.170 25.6.40

55 'The French will never forgive' MH interview with George Starr 3.3.80

56 'Mr Churchill finds that there are' *Le Matin* 24.6.40

57 'When a flood comes' Brooke op. cit. p.69 25.5.40

57 'My reason tells me' Nicolson op. cit. p.96 15.6.40

57 'This period was one of' Peter Fleming *Invasion 1940* Hart-Davis 1957 pp.88 & 92

58 'Here lies the material' Potsdam Research Institute for Military History Bock diary 2.6.40

58 'An American correspondent' *New Yorker* 17.6.40

Chapter 3: Invasion Fever

60 'Thank heavens they have' Horsfall op. cit. p.153

60 'Winston Churchill has told us' IWM G.W. King 85/49/1 16.6.40

60 'Now we know that we have got to' Hichens op. cit. p.90

61 'Now I suppose it's our turn' *One Family's War* ed. Patrick Mayhew Hutchinson 1985 p.77

62 '[Captain] Bill Tennant came in' CAC Edwards diary REDW1/2

63 'A government must never assume' Carl von Clausewitz *On War* ed. Michael Howard and Peter Paret Princeton 1976

64 'one thing that strikes me' Lee op. cit. p.5 17.6.40

64 'It is no secret that Great Britain' quoted Joseph Lash *Roosevelt and Churchill: The Partnership that Saved the West* Norton 1976 p.197

64 'The great majority of Americans' *Philadelphia Inquirer* 23.5.40

65 'Richard E. Taylor of Apponaugh' IWM Misc 200/3160

65 'I have a feeling' Somerset Maugham *Time* 21.10.40

65 'Propaganda is all very well' Colville op. cit. p.175 28.6.40

65 'One queer thing' Lee op. cit. p.23 25.5.40

66 'I don't know what we'll fight' Kennedy MS op. cit. 12.11.42 story recounted by Walter Elliott

66 'when so many interesting things' CAC Martin diary MART1 p.12

67 'You ought to have cried' Colville op. cit. p.135 19.5.40

67 'We should have had an enormous' Kennedy MS op. cit. 27.5.41

67 'I went on my knees' Halifax diary op. cit. 8.2.41

69 'It was a terrible decision' Moran op. cit. p.316 9.7.45

70 'Oran, a painful necessity' see for instance Stanley G. Payne *Franco and Hitler* Yale 2007 passim

71 'But all contingent upon' BNA PREM3/131/1 27.6.40

71 'You will observe that the document' BNA PREM3/131/2

71 'Am profoundly shocked and disgusted' ibid.

71 'Please remember the serious nature' ibid.

71 'This declaration would' ibid.

72 'There are difficulties' CAC Bevin Papers Ernest Bevin to Professor W.K. Hancock 13.11.40 BEVNII/4/1

73 'if the Government of Eire' Kimball op. cit. p.106 7.12.40

73 'Winston was in great form' *The Ironside Diaries* ed. R. Macleod and D. Kelly Constable 1962 6.7.40

74 'strikes me as tired' Gilbert *The Churchill War Papers* op. cit. vol. ii 10.7.40

74 'They paid lip-service' Fleming op. cit. p.80

74 'The menace of invasion' ibid. p.307

75 'Hitler must invade or fail' Colville op. cit. p.195 14.7.40

75 'Not until March 1941' F.H. Hinsley et al. *British Intelligence in the Second World War* HMSO 1979 vol. i pp.429 & 451

75 'in wonderful spirits' Brooke op. cit. p.92 17.7.40

76 'Radio sets were not then' Henry Fairlie 'The Voice of Hope' *New Republic* 27.1.82 p.16

76 'Gradually we came under' *Few Eggs and No Oranges: The Diaries of Vere Hodgson* Persephone 1999 p.5

76 'sent shivers (not of fear)' Nicolson op. cit. p.93 5.6.40

76 'Mr Churchill is the only man' *New Yorker* 25.8.40

76 'Like a great actor' Berlin op. cit. p.22

77 'It is certainly his hour' Headlam op. cit. p.213

77 'I won't go on about the war' IWM Papers of Mrs E. Elkus

77 'she had saved her wages' CAC Eade Papers 2/2 11.9.42

77 'Romans in Rome's quarrel' CAC Martin diary op. cit. p.7

Chapter 4: The Battle of Britain

80 '*Il y a beaucoup*' Boswell op. cit. p.876

80 'I shall always associate' Colville op. cit. p.505 24.8.44

80 'Winston wept' CAC Martin diary op. cit. p.29

81 'The odds today' George Barclay *Fighter Pilot* William Kimber 1976 pp.51–2

81 'This sounds very peculiar' IWM Alec Bishop MS 98/18/1

83 'a farrago of operational' Colville op. cit. p.288 7.11.40

83 'It is the sneaks' BNA PREM3/220/48

84 'Jones spent twenty minutes' R.V. Jones *Most Secret War* Hamish Hamilton 1978 p.101

84 'Here was strength' ibid. p.107

86 'a little ruffled' Colville op. cit. p.211 7.8.40

86 'Don't speak to me' Ismay op. cit. pp.179–80

87 'He paweth in the valley' John Kennedy *The Direction of War* Hutchinson 1957 p.62

87 'I try myself by court martial' Colville op. cit. p.231 27.8.40

88 'glaucous, vigilant, angry' Nicolson op. cit. p.127 20.11.40

89 'There goes the bloody' Colville op. cit. p.340 24.1.41

89 'Gimme "Pug"!' Elizabeth Nel *Mr Churchill's Secretary* Hodder & Stoughton 1958 p.74

89 'whether very great men' Colville op. cit. p.389 20.5.41

89 'an unscrupulously rough-and-tumble' Lee op. cit. p.77 3.10.40

90 'You know, I may seem' CAC Martin diary op. cit. p.4

90 'Ll[oyd] G[eorge] was purely' Amery op. cit. p.1034 26.3.45

90 'It's very naughty' Moran op. cit. p.287

90 'the formidable ramparts' ibid. p.324

90 'Darling Winston' quoted *Speaking for Themselves: The Personal Letters of Winston and Clementine Churchill* ed. Mary Soames Doubleday 1998 p.454

91 'to find himself subjected' *Action this Day* op. cit. p.53

92 'He has more wit' Moran op. cit. p.226

92 'collapsed between the chair' Colville op. cit. p.319 15.12.40

92 'Winston feasts on the sound' Moran op. cit. p.8 12.12.41

92 'No one could predict' *Action this Day* op. cit. p.177

93 'the ferment of ideas' ibid. p.150

95 'almost certain invasion' Channon op. cit. p.266 16.9.40

96 'like all the other soldiers' Neville Chamberlain diary 1.7.40

96 'the nakedness of our defences' Brooke op. cit. p.90 2.7.40

96 'not satisfied that ... the co-operation' BNA CAB69/1

97 'I feel an immense joy' Hichens op. cit. p.99

97 'On 25 August ...' Sir Thomas Elmhirst *Recollections* p.51

98 'Thank God ... the defeatist opinions' Lee op. cit. p.108 15.9.40

98 'usual vigorous rhetorical' Dalton op. cit. p.80

99 'I am on top of' Elmhirst op. cit. p.53

101 'Publicity is anathema' A.B. Cunningham *A Sailor's Odyssey* Hutchinson 1951 p.410

102 'Do you like Bovril?' Gen. Sir Frederick Pile *Ack-Ack: Britain's Defence Against Air Attack* Harrap 1949 p.171

102 'That man's effort' Colville op. cit. p.261 11.10.40

103 'The club is burning' CAC Martin diary op. cit. p.32

104 'a farmer driving pigs' Colville op. cit. 10.8.41

104 'For something like a year' R.W. Thompson *Churchill and Morton* Hodder & Stoughton 1976 p.41

104 'One can now say' *Dokumenty Vneshnei Politiki 1940 – 22.12.41* Moscow 1999 pp.361 & 387

105 'Thus fades the last hope' Channon op. cit. p.263

105 'Lothian's "wild" appeal' Nicolson op. cit. p.104 22.7.40

105 '[He] was very interesting about' Lee op. cit. 8.12.40

105 'David Kynaston' David Kynaston *A History of the City of London* vol. iii Chatto & Windus 1999 p.472

105 'come back into his own' ibid. p.479

106 'Feeling in the Carlton Club' Channon op. cit. p.268

107 'I think it's a good thing' IWM Green Papers 99/9/1 Letter of 4.9.40

107 'this was the sort of war' Colville op. cit. p.262 12.10.40

108 'We . . . soon adapt ourselves' Anthony Trollope *Autobiography* Trollope Society edn 1999 p.102

108 'If one looked on all this' Colville op. cit. 16.9.40

108 'Malaya, the Australian government's' Eden op. cit. 21.1.41

108 'We [have] got to admit' Colville op. cit. p.312 13.12.40

108 '*Mon général, devant*' ibid. p.289 9.11.40

109 'the narrowest, most ignorant' ibid. p.406 22.6.41

Chapter 5: Greek Fire

111 'saw no prospect beyond' see Bond *Liddell Hart* op. cit. pp.119–59

111 'sit tight and defend ourselves' Dalton op. cit. p.87

111 'They say no one knows' Lee op. cit. p.54 12.9.40

112 'in a month's time' ibid. p.10 3.7.40

112 'If Hitler were to postpone' Nicolson op. cit. p.103 20.7.40

112 'I have heard' diary 14.11.40 quoted Simon Garfield *Private Battles: How the War Almost Defeated Us* Ebury 2006 p.18

112 'At our weekly meeting' CAC Bevin Papers letter from F. Price BEVN6/59 22.9.40

113 'Winston, why don't we land' 6.3.41 CAC Eade Papers 2/2

113 'We will go easy' Andrew Gibb *With Winston Churchill at the Front* Gowans & Gray 1924 pp.40–1

113 'the discharge of bombs' BNA PREM3/21/1

113 'No more than anyone else' Pownall op. cit. vol. ii p.8 2.11.40

114 'As the PM said goodnight' Colville op. cit. p.266 13.10.40

114 'He was always, in effect' Attlee to NYC press conference 1.2.46

114 'These military men v[er]y often' *Speaking for Themselves* ed. Mary Soames Doubleday 1998 p.23 30.5.1909

115 'The book is full of' ibid. p.357 19.2.32

115 'A series of absurd' Winston Churchill *The World Crisis 1911–1918* Odhams 1927 pt iii chap X pp.1131 & 1134–5

116 'I am so glad' Churchill to Tovey 7.4.41

116 'by 300 determined men' Colville op. cit. p.186 3.11.40

119 'He lay there in his' ibid. p.285 3.11.40

120 'as if it were the only source' Nicolson op. cit. p.121 17.10.40

120 'You should not telegraph' Gilbert *Finest Hour* op. cit. pp.905–6

120 'I purred like six cats' WSC *The Second World War* vol. ii p.480

121 'At long last we are' Ismay op. cit. p.195

121 'If, with the situation as it is' BNA PREM3/288/1

121 'He advanced a mad notion' Eden op. cit. p.180 5.12.40

122 'Off we went across' Correlli Barnett *The Desert Generals* Allen & Unwin 1983 pp.37–65

123 'For the first time' Harvey diary 22 February 1941

124 'Mr Churchill's speech' Hodgson op. cit. 11.2.41

124 'Here is the hand' Colville op. cit. 16.2.41

124 'We cannot, from Middle East' Eden op. cit. p.168

125 'The weakness of our policy' ibid. p.170 3.11.40

125 'We were near the edge' Kennedy MS op. cit. 26.1.41 & 11.2.41

125 'He thinks Greece' *The White House Papers of Harry L. Hopkins* ed. Robert Sherwood Eyre & Spottiswoode 1948 vol. i pp.239–40

127 'Found Wavell waiting' Eden op. cit. p.131 13.8.40

127 'a good average colonel' ibid. p.133

128 'Wavell, I think' Tedder diary 18.4.41 quoted Lord Tedder *With Prejudice* Cassell 1966 p.74

129 'Churchill and his generals' Hinsley op. cit. vol. i p.260

130 'I hope, Jack' Eden op. cit. p.240

130 'General Wavell should regain' BNA CAB120/10 14.4.41

131 'I think it is desperate' Kennedy MS op. cit. 10.4.41

131 'CIGS is miserable' ibid. 11.4.41

131 'Chiefs of staff overawed' ibid.

132 'I am afraid of a disaster' Robert Menzies diary *Dark Days* ed. A.W. Martin and Patsy Hardy National Library of Australia 1993 p.120

132 'Aren't you going to listen' Nella Last op. cit. 27.4.41

132 'All that the country' Nicolson op. cit. 13.4.41

133 'He himself took' Hankey op. cit. p. 506 13.5.41

134 'We hold our breath' Hodgson op. cit. 25.5.41

135 'The difference between' IWM 92/12/1 Belsey Papers

136 'Churchill a few months later' Colville op. cit. p.443 28.9.41

136 'Once more Germany' Mikhail Sebastian *Journal 1935–44* Heinemann 2001 9.4.41

136 'You've lost the game' Kurt Pauli *Von Serbien Bis Kreta* Steirische Verlagsanstalt 1942 p.137

136 'the utter darkness' Brooke op. cit. p.379 4.2.43

136 'The PM in conversation' Menzies op. cit. 1.3.41

137 'Churchill observed crossly' CAC Eade Papers 2/2 op. cit. 24.7.41

138 'was right when he asserted' *Germany and the Second World War* Oxford 1995 vol. iii p.555

138 'As far as I can make out' BNA PREM4/17/2 20.3.41

138 'He said some very' Colville op. cit. 3.6.41

139 'that fine commander' BBC broadcast 27.4.41

139 'I understand he has' *Speaking for Themselves* op. cit. p.480 13.5.43

139 'Wavell's best biographer' Ronald Lewin *The Chief* Hutchinson 1980

139 'My trouble is that' Pownall op. cit. vol. ii p.95

139 'Now I'm going to waste' Kennedy MS op. cit. 14.9.39

140 'They are a pretty fair' Pownall op. cit. vol. ii p.19 3.6.41

140 'It is a bad feature' Kennedy MS op. cit. 9.7.42

140 'When he is in' Kennedy MS op. cit. 9.2.41

141 'It is a strange thing' Brooke op. cit. p.647 20.1.45

141 'At times you could kiss' CAC A.V. Alexander Papers AVAR6/1 diary 10.6.42

141 'Captain Stephen Roskill' see Stephen Roskill *Churchill and the Admirals* Collins 1977

142 'I . . . have to confess' Cunningham op. cit. pp.578 & 580

142 'I never saw him' Denis Richards *Portal of Hungerford* Heinemann 1977 pp.202–3

143 'I am thankful I have' Kennedy MS op. cit. 5.12.41

143 'Ismay is such a devotee' ibid. 10.4.41

144 'Is there any evil' IWM Alec Bishop unpublished MS 98/18/1

144 'The chief difficulty' Martin diary op. cit. p.10

145 'In truth it is only' Michael Davie and Anne Chisholm *Beaverbrook* Hutchinson 1992 p.664 14.5.41

146 'If you see that' Thomas Wilson *Churchill and the Prof* Cassell 1995 p.16 & passim

147 'Moran was seldom' *Action this Day* op. cit. p.110

147 'He always retained unswerving' Colville op. cit. p.125

148 'The people strike me' Lee op. cit. p.243 16.4.41

148 'Young man' Kennedy *The Business of War* op. cit. p.236

149 'War consists of fighting' quoted Reynolds op. cit. p.244

149 'I suppose you realise' Kennedy MS op. cit. 21.6.41

Chapter 6: Comrades

150 'There is nothing straightforward' Garfield op. cit. p.129

152 'None of this conflicts' 17.9.39. On this issue see for instance David Carlton *Churchill and the Soviet Union* Manchester 2000 passim.

152 'That the Russian armies' BBC broadcast 1.10.39

154 'a sentiment widely felt' Colville op. cit. p.436 3.9.41

154 'They think they are dealing' Pownall op. cit. vol. ii p.36 17.7.41

154 'I don't suppose' Headlam op. cit. p.157 22.6.41

154 'One feels that God' ibid. p.258

155 'I glory in all this' IWM 85/49/1 G.W. King MS 30.7.41

155 'The Russians have not' Hodgson op. cit. p.185 22.6.41

155 'Somehow I think Stalin' ibid. p.190 2.7.41

155 'I was agreeably surprised' IWM 92/12/1 Belsey letters 25.6.41

156 'It's impossible to say' Pownall op. cit. vol. ii p.30 29.6.41

156 'I don't believe Winston' ibid. p.31 30.6.41

157 'Why the authorities' Cunningham op. cit. p.350

159 'It was quite evident' Lee op. cit. p.416

159 'Britain's radio spies' *Daily Mirror* 14.2.41

159 'The danger of enemy' Hinsley op. cit. vol. ii p.671

160 'almost a pariah' Lee op. cit. p.317 23.6.41

161 'an obstinate, high-minded man' quoted Reynolds op. cit. p.256

162 'The British government, by its passive' Chris Bellamy *Absolute War* Macmillan 2007 p.415

163 'We would like to inform you' *Ocherki Istorii Rossiikoi Vneshney Razvedki* Studies on the History of the Soviet Foreign Intelligence Service Moscow 2007

164 'In order to enable Russia' Hansard 30.9.41

164 'Hitler is throwing' IWM 85/49/1 G.W. King MS

166 'I can still remember' G.A. Kumanyov 'Close to Stalin' [*Ryadom so Stalinym*] Moscow 1999 p.300

166 'Now I have to bring' Hankey op. cit. vol. iii p.533

167 'Chris Bellamy' Bellamy op. cit. p.446

168 'The effect upon us' *Observer* 17.8.41

168 'My main feeling is' quoted Garfield op. cit. p.172 9.10.41

168 'the rising temper' *The Churchill War Papers* ed. Gilbert op. cit. vol. iii p.1372 25.10.41

168 'Things are pretty hard' Churchill Archive CHAR1/362

168 'The fundamental difficulty' Kennedy MS op. cit. 7.9.41

168 'Would that the two loathsome' Pownall op. cit. p.50 29.10.41

168 'After his first enthusiasm' Harvey op. cit. 27.10.41

169 'In two years struggle' *Churchill War Papers* op. cit. vol. iii p.1204 12.9.41

169 'Winston's attitude to war' Menzies op. cit. p.99 31.3.41

169 'The Army must do something' Kennedy MS op. cit. 9.10.41

169 'Winston is in a difficult position' ibid. 13.10.41

169 'Yes, I am afraid' ibid. 11.10.41

Chapter 7: The Battle of America

171 'I wonder if the Americans' Kennedy MS op. cit. 25.5.41

171 'rushing vast quantities' *The Memoirs of Cordell Hull* Hodder & Stoughton 1948 vol. ii p.967

172 'The United States Administration' Eden op. cit. p.176

172 'after the victory was won' Kimball op. cit. vol. i. p.102

173 'I have never realised' quoted Kynaston op. cit. vol. iii p.472

174 'Our desperate straits' Eden op. cit. p.135

174 'I have never liked Americans' quoted Roberts *The Holy Fox* op. cit. p.280

174 'the heavy labour of toadying' ibid p.278

174 'I only said' Eden op. cit. p.182

174 'During a trip to Detroit' *Christian Science Monitor* 12.5.41 p.15 & 4.11.41 p.8

174 'pretty hopeless' Harvey op. cit. p.20 15.7.41

174 'because he couldn't' Dalton op. cit. p.272 25.8.41

175 'They really are' Headlam op. cit. p.270 15.8.41

175 'no great enthusiasm' BNA FO371/34114

175 'it wouldn't really pay' LHA Slessor Papers Box XIIC

175 'when one is dealing with' RAF Museum Hendon Harris Papers folder H98 15.9.41

176 'It is just a little humiliating' Dalton op. cit. p.247 10.7.41

176 'the average man's' Planning Committee minutes 4.6.41 BNA INF1/249

176 'Donovan . . . is extremely friendly' Kennedy MS op. cit. 7.3.41

177 'a possible America' D.C. Watt *Succeeding John Bull* Cambridge 1980 p.161

177 'he quite understood' Colville op. cit. 1.11.40

177 'I was . . . only a Second Lieutenant' Robert H. Pilipel *Churchill in America* NEL 1977 p.16

178 'Had he been pure English aristocracy' Hodgson op. cit. pp.189–90 2.7.41

178 'Here's a telegram' Colville op. cit. p.136 19.5.40

178 'By late 1941' Report by Richard L. Coe *Washington Post* 11.1.42

180 'I believe that we really can' Sherwood op. cit. vol. i p.125

180 'He can work only seven' *Time* 10.3.41

180 'of the exact state' Sherwood op. cit. vol. i p.239

181 'I suppose you could say' ibid. p.237

181 'We seek no treasure' *Memoirs of Lord Chandos* Bodley Head 1962 pp.165–6

182 'Hopkins was, I think' quoted Gilbert *Finest Hour* op. cit. pp.997 & 999

182 I have never had such' Lee op. cit. p.220

182 'Apparently the first thing' *The Secret Diary of Harold L. Ickes* Simon & Schuster 1953–54

183 'He finished with really' Hodgson op. cit. 27.7.41

183 'Winston is completely certain' Menzies op. cit. p.64 22.2.41

184 'It is never very easy' *Books & Bookmen* October 1977 review of Joseph Lash's *Roosevelt and Churchill 1939–41* André Deutsch 1977

185 'Personally I am very sorry' IWM MP Troy Papers 95/25/1 1.1.41

185 'As soon as the Lend-Spend' Averell Harriman and Elie Abel *Special Envoy to Churchill and Stalin* Random House NY 1975 p.5

186 'We can't take seriously' ibid. p.15

186 'He resented this so much' Lee op. cit. p.307 9.6.41

186 'By contrast Colonel' Forrest Pogue *George C. Marshall: Ordeal and Hope 1939–42* Viking 1965 pp.133–4

186 'If rather than when' ibid. p.139

187 'I was deeply worried' Harriman op. cit. p.18

187 'I must attempt to convince' ibid. p.18

187 'The PM is much smaller' ibid. p.61

188 'the PM bluntly stated' ibid. p.28

188 'believing that we shall get' Amery op. cit. p.689 19.5.41

188 'The great difficulty is' Harriman op. cit. p.57

188 'The idea of being our armoury' Headlam op. cit. p.234 31.12.40

189 'The great thing is not to' Nicolson op. cit. 21.3.41

189 'Well, yes' Lee op. cit. p.357 26.7.41

189 'frightened of nothing' Cadogan op. cit. p.393 21.7.41

190 'A wonderful story' quoted *Churchill War Papers* op. cit. vol. iii p.810

191 'a disorderly day's rabbit-shooting' BNA PREM4/27/9 13.3.41

191 'I must say I do not think' BNA PREM3/485/6 fo.16

191 'with a retinue which' Colville op. cit. 3.8.41

192 'Working in H[arry] H[opkins]'s cabin' CAC Geoffrey Green GREE1

193 'really incapable of' quoted Kenneth S. Davis *FDR: The War President* Random House 2000 p.212

195 'Not a single American officer' CAC Jacob diary 11.8.41 JACB1/10

196 'It would be an exaggeration' Sherwood op. cit. vol. i p.364

197 'My God, this is history!' CAC Green op. cit. GREE1 10.8.41

197 'the occasion must fulfil' CAC Jacob diary op. cit. 10.8.41

197 'That afternoon, Churchill took' CAC Martin diary op. cit. p.60

197 'Am I going to like it?' ibid. p.62

198 'It was hard to tell' *Action this Day* op. cit. p.206

198 'a very interesting and by no means' Churchill Papers 29.8.41 CHAR1/362/28–32

198 'Roosevelt is all for coming' Pownall op. cit. vol. i

199 'nothing dressed up' Kennedy MS op. cit. 24.8.41

199 'There was a statement' Hodgson op. cit. p.201 15.8.41

199 'I ought to tell you' Gilbert *Churchill War Papers* op. cit. vol. iii p.1125 28.8.41

200 'The PM said that after' Colville op. cit. p.434 30.8.41

200 'He even questioned' Harvey op. cit. p.39 31.8.41

200 'The attitude of the people' quoted Lee op. cit. p.376 24.8.41

201 'It will not be possible' Gilbert *War Papers* op. cit. vol. iii p.1202

201 'plans were worked out' V.G. Trukhanovsky *Winston Churchill* Progress Publishers Moscow 1978 p.273

203 'the Food Account was' CAC Churchill Papers CHAR1/379/12–20

204 'Oh, Miss, you'll never guess' Nel op. cit. pp.43–5

204 'Now run inside' ibid. p.67

204 'Winston was depressed' Eden op. cit. 22.9.41

204 'in the event of a collision' BNA HWI/25

204 'Make sure they have' Hinsley op. cit. vol. ii appendix 3 p.655

205 'Another Prayer' CAC Edwards diary REDW2/3 24–25.8.41

206 'There is nothing like' Kimball op. cit. vol. i p.165 2.11.41

206 'People are wondering' Harriman op. cit. p.109 20.10.41

207 'Whatever may happen' Pownall op. cit. vol. ii p.41

207 'Camrose was sufficiently' quoted Lord Hartwell *William Camrose: Giant of Fleet Street* Weidenfeld & Nicolson 1992 p.316

207 'On the 19th' CAC Eade Papers 19.11.41

208 'A.E. is much perplexed' Harvey op. cit. p.48 3.10.41

208 'He said he had no use' Hankey op. cit. vol. iii 15.10.41

210 'Winston's methods were frequently' Brooke op. cit. p.192 20.10.41

210 'too much impressed' Kennedy *The Business of War* op. cit. p.78

211 'his ability to shake himself' Kennedy MS op. cit. 19.3.42

212 'If they declare war on us' John G. Winant *A Letter from Grosvenor Square* London 1947 pp.196–7

212 'tired and depressed' Harriman op. cit. p.111

213 'saturated and satiated' quoted Reynolds op. cit. p.264

Chapter 8: A Glimpse of Arcadia

214 'Well then, this war is over' Pierre Billotte *Le Temps des armes* Plon Paris 1972 p.187

214 'We simply can't be beaten' Nicolson op. cit. p.197 11.12.41

214 'Though I do not wish' Hodgson op. cit. p.232 9.12.41

214 'While the public are prepared' BNA INF1/292

218 'I do not know when' *Speaking for Themselves* op. cit. p.460 21.12.41

220 'All is very good indeed' ibid. p.461 24.12.41

221 'No one but he' Harold Macmillan *War Diaries* 16.11.43

222 'Senators' . . . office telephones' *Washington Post* 27.12.41

223 'the greatest orator in the world' Ickes diary op. cit. 26.12.41

223 'It is a great weight' Moran op. cit. p.23

224 'to put it on its throne' Lash op. cit. p.15

224 '"Tommy" clapped her hands' ibid. p.16

224 'the aura of the office' Charles Bohlen *Witness to History* Norton 1973 p.210

224 'a patrician democrat whose every' Amery op. cit. p.882 15.4.43

225 'The difference between' William Hassett *Off the Record with FDR* Allen & Unwin 1960 p.171

225 'one of the most untidy rooms' CAC Jacob diary op. cit. JACB1/12

225 'How *do* these people' Cadogan op. cit. p.586

225 'By the side of the Prime Minister' CAC Jacob diary op. cit. JACB1/14

225 'They will have first to' ibid. p.90

227 'They tell me I have' Ickes diary op. cit. 1.2.42

227 'The time had now come' WSC *The Second World War* vol. iii p.625

228 'Amery noted wryly' Amery op. cit. 17.1.42

228 'He wanted to show' Moran op. cit. p.21

228 'There is bound to be' Eden op. cit. p.319 28.1.42

229 'There is one lesson' *Denver Post* 6.2.42

229 'It is unfortunate that' *Chicago Tribune* 20.2.42

229 'Who writes Churchill's' *Time* Book Review section 17.3.41 p.94

230 'Even those closest' Lash op. cit. p.195

230 'proposed to reshape' Michael Howard *Books & Bookmen* October 1977

230 'The academic yet sweeping' Eden op. cit. p.374

231 'My whole system' ibid. Nov. 1942

231 'The British are evidently' Stimson diary Sterling Memorial Library Yale 11.1.42

232 'as if these had been swept' Pogue op. cit. vol. ii p.265

232 'It is odd' quoted Alex Danchev *Very Special Relationship* Brassey's 1986 p.10

Chapter 9: 'The Valley of Humiliation'

234 'There seems to be plenty' Moran op. cit. p.28

235 'with the mentality of' Brooke op. cit. p.212 19.12.41

235 'We should thank God' Kennedy *Business of War* op. cit. p.318

235 'The PM is not really interested' Moran op. cit. p.20

236 'Mr Churchill has been unwilling' *New Statesman* 31.1.42

236 'When Amery wished' Christopher Bayly and Tim Harper *Forgotten Armies* Penguin 2004 p.234

236 'I think he is' Harvey op. cit. 9.2.42

236 'The whole reputation' 9.2.42

237 'Lots of people want' *Champion Redoubtable: The Diaries of Violet Bonham-Carter* ed. Mark Pottle Weidenfeld & Nicolson 1998 Feb. 1942

237 'Sometimes . . . the PM is just like a child' Dalton op. cit. p.368

237 'striding up and down' Layton Papers quoted Gilbert *The Road to Victory* Heinemann 1986 p.56

238 'Defeatism is in the air' Garfield op. cit. p.223

238 'I think it is time' MO report quoted Leonard Mosley *Backs to the Wall* Weidenfeld
& Nicolson 1971 p.241

238 'I'm fed up' Bonham-Carter op. cit. 11.2.42

238 'The nature of his words' CAC Colville MS diary 16.2.42

239 'We have so many men' Nicolson op. cit. p.211 12.2.42

239 'But my God, sir' Pim Papers quoted Gilbert *Road to Victory* op. cit. p.62

239 'If the army cannot fight' Brooke op. cit. p.231 18.2.42

240 'At the back of his mind' Harvey op. cit. p.91 5.2.42

240 'We have masses of' Kennedy MS op. cit. 3.2.42

241 'These simple rules' Dill to Brooke 5.3.42

242 'This process does not' Arthur Bryant *The Turn of the Tide* Collins 1957 vol. i p.375

242 'We are indeed walking' Hopkins Papers Georgetown University Washington
DC Box 4 Folder 1 Accession 1 Series 1 correspondence

242 'always been as distant' Eden op. cit. p.539

243 'fighting to keep their country free' Cripps BBC broadcast 6.2.42

243 'The talk was very much' Kennedy MS op. cit. 5.3.42

244 'Although the British are' Harriman op. cit. p.126

244 'he is always careful' Moran op. cit. p.32

244 'saddened – appalled by events' quoted Gilbert *Road to Victory* op. cit. p.69

244 'Poor old P.M.' Cadogan op. cit. p.440 4.3.42

246 'a pregnant fact' Roskill op. cit. p.232

247 'I believe that if' Hansard 16.11.37

248 'I hope you were' Kimball op. cit. vol. i p.504 1.6.42

248 'As I lay in bed' Hodgson op. cit. p.407 15.8.43

248 'a considerable commander' Anthony Montague Browne *Long Sunset* Cassell
1995 p.201

249 'perverse to heap praise' *New Statesman* 28.2.42

249 'The disaster of this policy' Hansard 24.2.42

249 'can be implemented only' Kennedy MS op. cit. 31.5.42

250 'a stubborn and obstinate man' Roskill op. cit. p.130

251 'I find it very difficult' Kimball op. cit. vol. i p.438

252 'CIGS says WSC is' Kennedy MS op. cit. 7.4.42

252 'hypothetical post-war problems' Amery p.785 8.3.42

252 'He does not seem to see' *New Statesman* 11.4.41

252 'It is difficult to find' *New Statesman* 17.1.41

252 'This nation has become' Kennedy MS op. cit. 23.2.42

253 'lack enthusiasm and interest' BNA WO163/52 Quarterly Morale Report

253 'that America will emerge' BNA FO371/30656

253 'When has the Prime Minister' *Economist* 19.12.42

254 'the Britain we hope to build' *Picture Post* 17.1.41

254 'unsatisfactory attitude of the workers' Amery op. cit. 7.4.42

255 'a strange combination of' ibid. pp.746 & 750 19.11.41 & 25.11.41

255 'the humiliation of being' ibid. p.822 27.7.42

255 'lay down arms and accept' D.G. Tendulkar *Mahatma* vol. v p.291

256 'Anything like a serious difference' Kimball op. cit. vol. i p.449

256 'We must remember that' Cadogan op. cit. p.450 7.5.42

257 'The depression following Singapore' CAC Churchill Papers CHAR1/369/5–8 2.5.42

257 'Everyone feels safer now' ibid. pp.107–8

258 'there are many people in the USA' Nicolson op. cit. p.222 15.4.41

258 'One trouble is that' BNA CAB122/96 7.4.42

258 'It must be accepted that' Arthur Salter *Slave of the Lamp* Weidenfeld & Nicolson 1967 pp.185–6

Chapter 10: Soldiers, Bosses and 'Slackers'

259 'I don't know what' Kennedy MS op. cit. 11.6.42

259 'Our soldiers are the most' Cadogan op. cit. pp.374 & 389 29.4.41 & 18.6.41

259 'What will happen if' ibid. p.433 9.2.42

261 'He presents to me' WSC *Great Contemporaries* Leo Cooper 1990 p.144

261 'We manage by terrific efforts' Kennedy MS op. cit. 31.7.42

262 'Rommel was an abler general' Alan Moorehead *African Trilogy* Cassell 1998 p.418

262 'There is a general feeling' Garfield op. cit. p.260

263 'The feeling is growing that' ibid. p.212 10.2.42

263 'Maisky, the Russian ambassador' Dalton op. cit. 18.11.41

263 'Our [career officers] regard [war]' Pownall op. cit. vol. ii p.98

264 'Petrol, food, NAAFI supplies' J.K. Stanford *Tail of an Army* Phoenix 1966 p.110 and passim

264 'The Augean stables' Macmillan op. cit. p.322 8.12.43

265 'All this has a devastating' Kennedy MS op. cit. 5.3.42

266 'We are going to lose' Brooke op. cit. p.243 31.3.42

266 'too stupid to be employed' Harold Macmillan *War Diaries* Macmillan 1984 p.313 2.12.43

266 'These British administrative generals' ibid. p.347 1.1.44

267 'Following Byng's shooting' see N.A.M. Rodger *The History of the Royal Navy* vol. ii Penguin 2005

267 'Churchill muttered to Dill' Kennedy MS op. cit. 5.12.41

267 'I am devoted to Neil' Brooke op. cit. p.270 22.6.42

267 'Fundamental to many defeats' David French *Raising Churchill's Army* Oxford 2000 passim

268 'Arm yourself therefore' quoted Gilbert *Churchill* op. cit. vol. iv p.63

269 'a mere handmaid' BNA PREM3/499/9 WSC to Attlee 29.7.42

269 'the tendency to bridge over' M.M. Postan *British War Production* HMSO 1952 p.325

270 'In all its branches' Moorehead op. cit. p.409

270 'Father, the trouble is' Eden op. cit. 6.10.42

270 'I love Randolph' Montague Browne op. cit. p.148

271 'a very daring and skilful' Hansard 29.1.42

271 'These beastly Huns' Ian McLaine *Ministry of Morale* Allen & Unwin 1979 p. 139

272 'because they did not feel' Amery op. cit. p.754 18.12.43

273 'by far the best' Dalton op. cit. p.677

273 'he didn't know why' ibid. p.736

273 'He never really understood' John Wheeler-Bennett *John Anderson Viscount Waverley* Macmillan 1962 p.224

274 'There is no better warhorse' ibid. p.256

275 'He has had no political training' Dalton op. cit. p.729

275 'I am in exceptionally good form' ibid. 20.3.42

275 'the three profs' Amery op. cit. p.707

276 'that the work people' Headlam op. cit. p.231 5.12.40

277 'I was disgusted to hear' Colville op. cit. 2.9.41

277 'Of eight serious strikes' BNA AVIA10/269

277 'a marked absence of discipline' BNA CAB102/406

277 'had failed to improve' BNA CAB70/6

277 'Strikes continue to cause' BNA INFI/282 October 1943

277 'Byrd complained to' BNA FO371/34115

278 'I do not see why' Kennedy MS op. cit. 12.3.42

278 'Of all wartime industrial disputes' P. Inman *Labour in the Munitions Industries* HMSO and Longmans 1957

278 'The Cost of Living Index' Inman op. cit. p.365 passim

279 'it became necessary to' W.H.B. Court *Coal* Longman 1951 p.158

279 'The mining community' quoted ibid. p.452

279 'One can hardly overstress' Inman op. cit. p.325

279 'The center of the problem' BNA CAB123/21

280 'many of the people' Min of Health report Cmd.6468

280 'children in rags' Richard Titmuss *History of the Second World War: Problems of Social Policy* HMSO 1950 p.115

280 'From the way men like' Headlam op. cit. p.243 9.3.41

280 'Labour MPs, in turn' Colville op. cit. p.401 19.6.41

281 'Except for our Fighting Services' Hansard 29.7.41

282 'We [Chamberlain's ministers in early 1940]' quoted McLaine op. cit. p.104

Chapter 11: 'Second Front Now!'

283 'I was fortunate' Brooke op. cit. p.247 10.4.42

283 'no very great contribution' ibid. p.246 9.4.42

284 'In many respects he is' ibid. p.249 11.4.42

284 'The CIGS told his staff' Kennedy MS op. cit. 5.4.42

284 'The extraordinary thing' ibid.

284 'I am in entire agreement' 12.4.42 Kimball op. cit. vol. i p.448

286 'we are proceeding' Kimball ibid. p.459

286 'Arrangements are being made' ibid. p.515

287 'This universal cry' Brooke op. cit. p.243 30.3.42

288 'I might be the best' Halifax diary op. cit. 31.3.42

288 'Concerning the second front' O.A. Rzheshevsky *Stalin and Churchill: Meetings, Conversations, Discussions* Moscow 2004 pp.113 & 190

289 'We do not consider this' ibid. p.157

290 'It is the irony' Joan Beaumont *Comrades in Arms* Davis-Poynter 1980 p.99

290 'Considerable though these' ibid. p.142

290 'sending very few aircraft' ibid. p.147

291 'They offered no definite' Rzheshevsky op. cit. p.231

291 'preparations for the second front' ibid. p.222

291 'Finally, we think it' ibid. p.250

291 'First, and as the Russian leader' F. Chuev *140 Conversations with Molotov* Moscow 1991 p.258

292 'Here Churchill interrupted' ibid. p.319

292 'Roosevelt had calmly told' Harvey op. cit. 10.6.42

292 'We had to squeeze' Chuev op. cit. p.66

292 'the High Contracting Parties' *Pravda* 14.6.42

293 'found Churchill "smarter"' Chuev op. cit. p.26

293 'I knew them all' ibid. p.65

293 'As for Roosevelt' ibid. p.67

294 'Two-thirds of weapons' French op. cit. passim

295 'This vicious rag should' BNA PREM4/26/8 7.6.42

295 'Advocacy of a second front' *Washington Despatches* ed. H.G. Nicholas Weidenfeld & Nicolson 1981 25.7.42

295 'A US officer at dinner' Kennedy MS op. cit. 5.4.42

295 'No Englishman here' BNA CAB109/47 Birley to Jacob

296 'We simply hold no cards' Dykes diary 12.10.42 quoted Danchev op. cit. p.20

296 'Private secretary John Martin' Hassett op. cit. p.68

296 'No responsible British' Churchill Archive JACB1/14

297 'It was Britain's beleaguered' Douglas Porch *Hitler's Mediterranean Gamble* Weidenfeld & Nicolson 2004 p.208

297 'Anti-British feeling is still' *Washington Despatches* op. cit. 14.5.42

297 'there was little point in supplying' ibid. 26.6.42

297 'These English are too aggressive' Hassett op. cit. 20 & 24.6.42

297 'a delightful companion' ibid. 20.6.42

298 'I knew when I saw' BNA FO371/30656

299 'All the old animosities' USNA RG84 Box 5

299 'Phrases such as' ibid. OWI Survey No. 113 10.6.42

299 'The OWI's July survey' USNA OWI Survey No. 114 1.7.42

299 'Some 65 per cent said' USNA OWI No.117 29.8.42

300 'The dominant underlying feeling' BNA FO371/30656

300 'The Asiatic war has revived' Yale Lippmann Papers 18.4.42

300 'old-fashioned imperialism' BNA FO371/30656 Clark Kerr Despatch 28.9.42

300 'The Embassy . . . has a quite fantastically' BNA FO371/30656 6.7.42

301 'were about as friendly' BNA FO371/30656 5.10.42

302 'We must have a victory!' Harvey op. cit. 22.6.42

302 'I told him what Winston' Kennedy MS op. cit. 18.7.42

302 'The people do not like' IWM Cons Shelf P Yates letters 22.6.42

302 'I myself felt' quoted Mosley op. cit. p.254

303 'The enemy did not seem' Hodgson diary op. cit. p.293

303 'Mr Churchill's speech did not' ibid. 5.7.42

303 'We heard yesterday' IWM G.W. King 85/49/1 22.6.42

303 'Russian successes continue' BNA INF1/292 26.1.42–1.2.42

304 'We received nothing' Brooke op. cit. p.223 27.1.42

304 'There is an extraordinary' Kennedy MS op. cit. 23.3.42

304 'Little as I formerly liked him' IWM Cons Shelf P 2.1.42

304 'That danger will never come' McLaine op. cit. p.210

304 'Reactionary attitudes are spreading' IWM Belsey 92/12/1 6.8.42

305 'When the Anglo–Soviet Alliance' IWM Papers of Mrs E. Elkus

305 'English people are willing' Pravda 5.8.42

306 'Every week of successful' BNA INF1/284

306 'Ismay said that he admired' Nicolson op. cit. 7.8.42

308 'The trouble . . . is that' Macmillan op. cit. p.46 20.3.43

308 'I suppose that, with the exception' Sir Alan Lascelles King's Counsellor Weidenfeld & Nicolson 2006 p.41 24.7.42

309 'The fact that, during one of' Los Angeles Times 28.6.42

309 'Winston is I think' Amery op. cit. p.818 6.7.42

310 'His speech sounds very good to us' Mrs Millburn's Diaries Harrap 1979 1.7.42

310 'He is a giant among pygmies' Headlam op. cit. p.322

310 'It is to be hoped that the PM' Millburn op. cit. p.145 2.7.42

310 'The simple question' The Times 1.7.42

311 'a most objectionable young pup' Brooke op. cit. 3.7.42

311 '"discreditable" and "deplorable"' Reynolds op. cit. p.303

311 'The cheek of the young brute' Brooke op. cit. 3.7.42

311 'May I suggest with all respect' BNA AIR8/1074 Dill JSM 300 Aide Memoire on Future Operations 16.7.42

312 'Churchill, however, believes' Wallace diary 25.5.43 quoted J.M. Blum (ed.) *The Price of Vision* Houghton Mifflin 1977

312 'Well, how are we' Kennedy MS op. cit. 18.7.42

313 'We failed to see' Pogue op. cit. vol. iii p.330

Chapter 12: Camels and the Bear

315 'What energy and gallantry' Harvey op. cit. 30.7.42

315 'He felt the need' Eden op. cit. p.338

316 'looked exactly as though' Ronald Winfield *The Sky Belongs to Them* William Kimber 1976 p.69

316 'Often had I seen' WSC *The Second World War* op. cit. vol. iii p.412

316 'Old Miles' Harvey op. cit. p.307 14.10.43

316 'There seem to me' IWM 4/27/1 8.7.42 Papers of Lt.Gen. Sir Charles Gairdner

317 'far too many cases' Charles Richardson op. cit. p.119

317 'In the Middle East there was' Moorehead op. cit. p.412

318 'I intend to see every' *Speaking for Themselves* op. cit. p.467 9.8.42

318 'The general received his dismissal' Kennedy MS op. cit. 23.8.42

319 'All right. You can have' Roskill *Churchill and the Admirals* op. cit. pp.236–7

321 'Our NKVD resident' *Studies on the History of Russia's Foreign Intelligence Service* Moscow 2007 op. cit. 4.8.42

322 'Churchill departed for the USSR' ibid. 12.8.42

322 'We know from a reliable source' ibid.

325 'I am downhearted and dispirited' Moran op. cit. p.68 13.8.42

326 'You know, I was not' Harriman op. cit. p.161

326 'May God prosper' Moran op. cit. p.138

327 'Don't be afraid' Golovanov *Memoirs* Moscow 2007 p.345

328 'No one but the Prime Minister' Richardson op. cit. p.144

328 'Churchill was decidedly' *Action this Day* op. cit. pp. 215–16

329 'He appealed to sentiments' Brooke op. cit. p.300 13.8.42

329 'Stalin told me the British Navy' Harriman op. cit. p.161

330 'When Harriman reported' ibid. p.169

331 'The deliveries were curtailed' Trukhanovsky op. cit. pp.283–4

332 'savages' Harriman op. cit. p.352

332 'He commissioned the ambassador's wife' CAC Churchill Papers CHAR1/379/12–20

Chapter 13: The Turn of Fortune

334 'have changed so frequently' *The Times* 19.8.42

334 'While I grumble' Garfield op. cit. p.280

334 'When looking back' Brooke op. cit. p.314 24.8.42

335 'was the only one trying' ibid. p.324 24.9.42

335 'super-chief of staff . . . Dill agreed' Amery op. cit. p.830 25.8.42

336 'Churchill later described' Moran op. cit. p.85

336 'It is an awful thing' Amery op. cit. p.838 24.9.42

336 ' a "bent" man, and couldn't' Harvey op. cit. 9.10.42

336 'The dominance of Churchill' Hume Wrong diary 4.11.42

336 'He sat down' Kennedy MS op. cit. 17.10.42

337 'If we are beaten' Moran op. cit. p.91

337 'the unnecessary battle' Porch op. cit. p.290

337 'Winston was like' Lascelles op. cit. pp.66–7 23.10.42

339 'I am terribly anxious' Amery op. cit. p.840 26.10.42

339 'How minute and fragile' Norman Craig *The Broken Plume* IWM 1982 p.79

339 'There is more jam' Nicolson op. cit. 2.11.42

339 'If *Torch* succeeds' Brooke op. cit. p.338 4.11.42

340 'A sense of exaltation' *The Times* 11.11.42

341 'The self-respect of the British Army' Dalton op. cit. p.519

343 'Pity our 1st victorious general' Bonham-Carter diary op. cit. 7.11.42

343 'It was nice Monty' Kennedy MS op. cit. 1.8.43

343 'We are winning victories!' Hodgson op. cit. p.331

344 'the only occasion on which' Brooke op. cit. p.340 9.11.42

345 'Is it really to be supposed' Harvey op. cit. 10.11.42

345 'I never meant the Anglo-American' Gilbert *Road to Victory* op. cit. p.260

346 'The Russian army having played' Harvey op. cit. 14.11.42

347 'La France ne marchera pas' Colville op. cit. p.311 13.12.40

347 'Although the French' Kennedy MS op. cit. 18.11.42

348 ' "In war," he said' Gilbert *Road to Victory* op. cit. p.277

348 'I have always deemed it' Harriman op. cit. p.173

349 'It shows how wrong' Harvey op. cit. 26.12.42

349 'The historian David Reynolds' Reynolds op. cit. p.330

349 'One comes away' Macmillan op. cit. p.101 1.6.43

350 'I do not want any of your' Brooke op. cit. p.376 31.1.43

351 'not much good' ibid. p.364 20.1.43

351 'Conversations with the British' Eisenhower *War Papers* Johns Hopkins 1970 vol. i p.98

351 'Getting on with Americans' Dalton op. cit. p.722

354 'still something of an enigma' Pogue op. cit. vol. iii p.5

355 'a general atmosphere' Macmillan op. cit. p.8 26.1.43

355 'At present they are' *Speaking for Themselves* op. cit. p.473 15.1.43

355 'I think CIGS's extremely' CAC Jacob diary op. cit. JACB1/19

356 'throwing down his facts' Moran op. cit. 1.1.42

356 'Then you will have to' Pogue op. cit. vol. iii p.7

356 'with consummate skill' Macmillan op. cit. p.9 26.1.43

356 'The PM stood in the hall' Moran op. cit. 22.1.43

357 'Being naturally extremely gullible' CAC Jacob diary op. cit. JACB1/19

357 'We feel that the Americans' Kennedy MS op. cit. 14.1.43

357 'Many American officers' Stephen Ambrose *Eisenhower the Soldier* Allen & Unwin 1984 p.146

357 'a pointer pup' Orlando Ward Papers USAMHI Carlisle diary Jan. 1943

357 'They viewed the Mediterranean' CAC Jacob diary op. cit. JACB1/19

358 'You know what a mess' Brooke op. cit. p.362

359 'My object is to serve my country' Roosevelt Papers Hyde Park PPF 8832

359 'The better I get to know that man' LHA Alanbrooke Papers 14/39/B 9.2.44

359 'Mr Churchill . . . takes his place' *The Times* 27.1.43

359 'He was offended' Harriman op. cit. p.188

360 'we had made a public statement' BNA CAB65/24 27.11.41

360 'He always enjoyed' Harriman op. cit. p.191

362 'Whatever we decided' CAC Jacob diary op. cit. JACB1/19

362 'Hundreds of thousands of Soviet people' G.K. Zhukov *Vospominaniya i Razmyshleniya* (Memories and Reflections) Moscow 1992 vol. ii p.314

363 '"Ah! that is good"' Brooke op. cit. p.370 26.1.43

364 'I told him that' ibid. p.374 30.1.43

365 'if they marched with us' WSC *The Second World War* op. cit. vol. iv pp.647–8

365 'It would be a pity to have to' CAC Jacob diary op. cit. JACB1/19

366 'they are now warrior nations' Hansard 11.2.43

Chapter 14: Out of the Desert

369 'In absolute terms' French op. cit. p.284

370 'Americans require experience' quoted Gilbert *Road to Victory* op. cit. p.360

371 'Good news today' Bonham-Carter op. cit. 9.3.43

371 *'How Green is My Ally'* Dalton op. cit. p. 557

371 'The enemy make a great mistake' Reynolds op. cit. p.207

371 '50 per cent "Russia" 43 per cent "Britain"' Gallup Poll 1.6.43

371 'They all look exactly alike' Macmillan op. cit. p.256 14.10.43

371 'I am told that our efforts' Headlam op. cit. p.410 26.6.44

373 'It is rather strange' Brooke op. cit. p.464 28.10.43

373 'He says he would not' Dalton op. cit. p.551 8.2.43

373 'The less said about that' Nicolson op. cit. 20.4.43

374 'Sawyers brings the breakfast' CAC Jacob diary op. cit. JACB1/19

374 'There is nothing in the world' quoted Gilbert *Road to Victory* op. cit. p.356 letter of 17.3.43

374 'He is so funny' Layton letter 7.4.43 quoted ibid. p.375

374 'so the boss was in a good temper' ibid. pp.374–5

374 'sharing his secret thoughts' Moran op. cit. p.198

375 'He is always so reassuring' ibid. p.209 20.8.44

375 'I had never seen him' Kennedy MS op. cit. 6.4.43

377 'Oh, I shall like that' quoted Lord Birkenhead *Life of Halifax* Hamish Hamilton 1965 p.537

377 'Have you noticed' Moran op. cit. p.116 25.5.43

378 'unless almost the entire bulk' BNA CAB120/83

378 'It was quite evident' Brooke op. cit. p.406 18.5.43

379 'the most exhausting entertainments' Brooke op. cit. pp 409–11 24/25.5.43

380 'I had always wondered' WSC *The Second World War* op. cit. vol. iv p.727

380 'very human & lovable side' Kennedy MS op. cit. 8.12.43

380 'I was speaking from where' Brooke op. cit. p.416 1.6.43

382 'Experience has taught me' BNA CAB120/683 25.7.43

382 'I am the last to plead' CAC CHUR4/301/187 fs272–4 276

382 'In my view there is' Library of Congress MS Div H.R. Luce Papers Box 1 Folder 7

382 'When Mr Churchill received' IWM 85/49/1 King Papers

382 'To some of the Government' Harvey op. cit. 10.2.43

383 'All these instructions' Macmillan op. cit. p.1767 29.7.43

385 'On this, I'm thankful' Harvey op. cit. 24.7.43

385 'Agreement after agreement' Brooke op. cit. p.398 4.5.43

385 'I firmly believe' USMH Carlisle OCMH Forrest Pogue notes of 1947 interview with Morgan for *The Supreme Command*

387 'The guests take hardly' Moran op. cit. p.130

388 'stir the imagination' Pogue op. cit. vol. iii p.241

388 'As usual, he was' ibid. p.244

388 'Yet there is no period' Harvey op. cit. 24.10.43

389 'The full implications of this' BNA WO205/33

389 'If we once set foot' Kennedy MS op. cit. 13.8.43

391 'The Quebec conference has' Brooke op. cit. p.450 30.8.43

391 'He subsequently acknowledged' ibid. p.466 1.11.43

391 'It was like fighting tanks' quoted Rick Atkinson *The Day of Battle* Henry Holt 2007 p.207

392 'He did not believe' BNA CAB120/83

393 'Must be a relief to the Boss' Hassett op. cit. pp.169 & 315

393 'loves W as a man for the war' Harvey op. cit. p.238 11.3.43 & p.239 29.3.43

394 'The chief of the army indulged' see Pogue op. cit. vol. iii p.318

394 'mercurial inconstancy' ibid. p.320

395 'But we cannot dictate' Kennedy MS op. cit. 3.9.43

395 'In the end I suppose' ibid. 26.9.43

395 'Beaverbrook had tabled' Hansard 23.9.43

395 'I need him' A.J.P. Taylor *Beaverbrook* p.500

395 'He says we must not' Dalton op. cit. p.660 29.10.43

396 'he says a Second Front is in existence' IWM G.W. King 85/49/1 22.8.43

396 'will save a piece of rope' IWM 92/12/1 Belsey letters 23.9.41 and 12.9.43

397 'no loss . . . I never did like' ibid. letters of 1.5.43 and 23.9.43

397 'It would be wrong to belittle' *Pravda* 6.8.43

398 'Even such help' Chuev op. cit. p.39

398 'had made himself' Vladimir Sokolov and Pyotr Stegny *Eagles and Lions* Moscow 1998 p.261

399 'I think I may claim' BNA INF1/220

Chapter 15: Sunk in the Aegean

403 'his jumbonic majesty' Macmillan op. cit. p.425 19.4.44

403 'Good. This is a time' WSC *The Second World War* op. cit. vol. v p.182 et seq.

404 'He believed, probably rightly' Brooke op. cit. p.185 25.9.41

405 'was clearly affected' Wilson Despatches 1946 quoted Jeffrey Holland *The Aegean Mission* Greenwood Press 1988 p.33

410 'It is pretty clear' Brooke op. cit. p.458 6.10.43

410 'He is excited about Kos' Cadogan op. cit. p.565 7.10.43

410 'I have never wished' Kimball op. cit. vol. ii p.498

410 'worth at least up to a first-class' BNA FO954/32

411 'I am slowly becoming' Brooke op. cit. p.459 8.10.43

411 'I propose . . . to tell Gen. Wilson' BNA FO954/32

411 'It does seem amazing' Kennedy MS op. cit. 13.10.43

413 'the price we were paying' ibid. 28.10.43

414 'a very nasty problem' Brooke op. cit. p.464 28.10.43

415 'The enemy had boldly' Stephen Roskill *The War at Sea* HMSO 1960 vol. iii pt 1 p.202

415 'Lack of RAF support' IWM LRDG 2/3

415 'As the battle progressed' Holland op. cit. p.135

415 'We were amazed to see' Anthony Rogers *Churchill's Folly* Cassell 2003 p.203

416 'The Germans moved quickly' Holland op. cit. p.148

416 'At midnight on 14 November' Ralph Bennett *Ultra and Mediterranean Strategy* Hamish Hamilton 1989 appendix xiii p.398

416 'I much regret' quoted Tedder op. cit. p.485

416 'One would have thought' ibid. p.486

417 'I am still strongly of' Cunningham op. cit. p. 582

418 'Bad news of Leros' Cadogan op. cit. p.576 16.11.43

419 'The fall of Leros should be' *The Times* 24.11.43

419 'CIGS feels that the war' Kennedy MS op. cit. 7.11.43

420 'Likewise, the British' C.J.C. Molony *The Mediterranean and Middle East* HMSO 1973 vol. v p.541

420 'Am still grieving' *Speaking for Themselves* op. cit. p.485 21.11.43

420 'the most acute difference' WSC *The Second World War* op. cit. vol. v p.199

421 'and if they were disregarded' ibid. pp.198–9

421 'All the British were' Pogue op. cit. vol. iii p.307

421 'I cannot pretend to have' *Speaking for Themselves* op. cit. p.487 26.11.43

Chapter 16: Tehran

422 'that he is often deaf' Michael Foot *Bevan* McGibbon & Kee 1962 p.326

422 'Mr Churchill did not like' Eden op. cit. p.441

422 'Winston handled the debate' Amery op. cit. p.1016 2.10.44

423 'The red and gold dressing gown' Brooke op. cit. p.223 27.1.42

423 'and that it was really too much' Dalton op. cit. p.676

424 'remind the Turkey' Brooke op. cit. p.467 3.11.43

424 'Why break off the handle' ibid. p.468 8.11.43

424 'Trying to maintain' ibid. p.516 24.1.44

424 'Adam Tooze' Adam Tooze *The Making and Breaking of the Nazi Economy* Allen Lane 2006

426 'In an expansive moment' Dalton op. cit. p.947 18.10.43

427 'We were greeted by' Macmillan op. cit. p.293 15.11.43

427 'From the street below' Moran op. cit. pp.156–7 18.11.43

427 'We have now crystallised' Kennedy MS op. cit. 7.11.43

427 'the PM's stock is not high' Pownall op. cit. vol. ii p.119

427 'The pattern of battle' Fred Majdalany *Cassino: Portrait of a Battle* Cassell 1999 p.33

428 'Winston is getting' Macmillan op. cit. p.304 25.11.43

429 'This caused Eden to observe' Sherwood op. cit. vol. ii p.717

429 'We are inclined to forget' Kennedy *The Business of War* p.317 at lunch 19.11.43

430 'W. had to play the role' Eden op. cit. pp.424 & 426

431 'PM and President ought' Cadogan op. cit. p.579 28.11.43

431 'bloody Italian war' Moran op. cit. p.159

431 'We are preparing for a battle' ibid. p.160

431 'They are far more sceptical' ibid.

431 'Poor Harry' Hassett op. cit. p.161 9.3.43

431 'the reported recalcitrance' *Washington Post* 13.1.44 Selden Menefee

432 'quite enthralling' Brooke op. cit. p.483 28.11.43

432 'Of course the man' Eden op. cit. p.514

433 'Do you think' Sergo Beria *My Father Beria* Moscow 2002 p.124

433 'He was turning his hose' GCM interview 15.11.56 cited Pogue op. cit. p.313

434 'Cadogan recorded the distress' Cadogan op. cit. p.580 29.11.43

434 'Soviet eavesdroppers reported' Beria op. cit. p.126

434 'That the President should deal' *Action this Day* p.210

435 'Roosevelt has given' Zhukov op. cit. vol. iii p.94

435 'Cunningham and Portal declared' Moran op. cit. p.168

436 'Every morning' Coote Papers 27.1.44 quoted Gilbert *Road to Victory* op. cit. p.646

436 'The Americans have been' 9.12.43

436 'sitting on his suitcase' Bryant op. cit. vol. ii p.114

437 'If I die' quoted Gilbert op. cit. p.606

437 'We all hope and pray' IWM diary of WA Charlotte 93/19/1

437 'Papa much better' quoted Gilbert *Road to Victory* op. cit. p.613

438 'Macmillan strongly urged' Macmillan op. cit. p.322 8.12.43

439 'Our object is the liberation' WSC to CoS 2.1.44

439 'while Winston, very pink' Nicolson op. cit. pp.344–5 18.1.44

440 'That all right?' ibid. p.321 21.9.43

441 'We did become like animals' quoted Carlo d'Este *Fatal Decision: Anzio and the Battle for Rome* HarperCollins 1991 p.316

441 'as American corps commander John Lucas' see Atkinson *The Day of Battle* op. cit. p.354

442 'The more one sees' Macmillan op. cit. p.429 23.4.44

444 'Sitting in a chair in his study' Colville op. cit. p.474 18.2.44

444 'their chirpings will presently' Hansard 27.2.44

444 'In the H of C smoking room' Headlam op. cit. p.403 25.4.44

445 'On no account' Gilbert *Road to Victory* op. cit. p.715 21.3.44

445 'Soviet attitude on this business' Eden op. cit. p.439 4.3.44

445 'I confess to growing apprehension' ibid.

446 'I would much rather' Macmillan op. cit. pp. 124 & 126 15.6.43 & 18.6.43

447 'Much as I love Winston' ibid. p.335 23.12.43 & p.338 25.12.43

447 'We both got quite heated' Eden op. cit. 20.8.43

447 'He feels about De Gaulle' Macmillan op. cit. p.335 23.12.43

448 'I am much distressed' ibid. p.389 4.3.44

449 'He may be mentally' Eden op. cit. p.442 1.5.44

449 'rather like a small boy' Kennedy MS op. cit. 24.9.42

449 'The raids are very fine' CAC Churchill Papers CHAR1/381/11–18

450 'Far more important than India' Colville op. cit. p.476 4.3.44

Chapter 17: Setting Europe Ablaze

452 'Subjugated peoples must' Pownall op. cit. vol. ii p.21

452 'simultaneous attacks by armoured forces' *Churchill War Papers* op. cit. vol. iii p.1313

452 'I hope they will' ibid. vol. ii p.254

453 'On 27 May 1941, Churchill sent' BNA CAB120/827

453 'Far from welcoming' Robert Gildea *Resistance, Reprisals and Community in Occupied France* in Transactions of the RHS 2003 p.165

454 'Nothing must be done' cabinet defence committee 2.8.43

454 'Here, we want every' Colville op. cit. pp.192–3 12.7.40

454 'Berlin wanted only' see for instance Mark Mazower *Hitler's Empire* Penguin 2008

455 'The cycle is simple' quoted Max Hastings *Das Reich* Michael Joseph 1981 pp.148–9

456 'Other evidence exists' Julian Jackson *France: The Dark Years* Oxford 2001 p.534 and passim

456 'I think you will agree' AHB/1D3/1588 quoted MRD Foot *SOE in France* HMSO 1966 p.153

457 'Nobody who did not' Bickham Sweet-Escott *Baker Street Irregular* Methuen 1965 p.73

457 'I was disturbed' *Memoirs of Lord Chandos* op. cit. p.239

457 'Many French people' Hastings *Das Reich* op. cit. interviews by the author passim

458 'A whimsical November' Peter Wilkinson and Joan Bright Astley *Gubbins and SOE* Leo Cooper 1993 p.117

458 'He believed that all his geese' Hastings *Das Reich* op. cit. p.35

459 'There is no doubt that' William Mackenzie *The Secret History of SOE* St Ermins Press 2000 p.415

461 'German records, by contrast' Hastings *Das Reich* op. cit.

461 'In the history of France' Jackson op. cit. p.387

461 'of seething factions' BNA CAB99/28

462 'How pleased I shall be' quoted Roderick Bailey *The Wildest Province* Cape 2008 p.134

463 'No one is ever free' quoted Mackenzie op. cit. p.486 26.5.44

463 'As so often in occupied Europe' Mark Mazower *Inside Hitler's Greece* Yale 1993 passim

463 'I am very impressed' IWM audio archive quoted *Forgotten Voices of the Secret War* ed. Roderick Bailey Ebury Press 208 p.250

463 'pundits overestimated' Noel Annan *Changing Enemies* HarperCollins 1995 p.75

464 'Armed resistance in the open' *Venture into Greece* William Kimber 1983 p.180

465 'But by that time' Roderick Bailey op. cit. p.251

465 'self-organised bands' quoted Molony op. cit. vol. vi pt iii p.210

466 'a Resistance movement may' ibid.

466 'Michael Howard' see Michael Howard *British Intelligence in the Second World War* vol. v *Strategic Deception* HMSO 1990 pp.135–55

467 'Deakin was outstandingly intelligent' Milovan Djilas *Wartime* Secker & Warburg 1980 p.253

468 'we of course felt honoured' ibid. p.368

468 'The British had no choice' ibid. p.348

469 'It is a little doubtful' Mackenzie op. cit. p.434

469 'the difficulty is that' Macmillan op. cit. p.445 1–23.5.44

470 'I have come to the conclusion' BNA PREM4/381C/341 and 4/369/438 19.12.44

470 'Paradoxically, British influence' CAC Deakin Papers *A Note on Resistance* MS DEAK16 p.25

471 'He wished and believed' war cabinet paper quoted Mackenzie op. cit. p.612

472 'Only in the USSR' Mark Mazower *Hitler's Empire* op. cit. p.485

472 'It was only just worth it' author interview 4.3.80

472 'The game was not worth' Mackenzie op. cit. p.483

472 'Gubbins was even' Wilkinson and Astley *Gubbins and SOE* op. cit. p.202

473 'Moreover, in our desire' Macmillan op. cit. p.545 9.10.44

473 'gave a damning account' Colville op. cit. p.581 3.4.35

474 'The occupied nations believed' CAC Deakin Papers op. cit. DEAK16 p.24

474 'If war, carried out' Thomas Arnold *Lectures on Modern History* Longman 1874 pp.160–1

475 'David Reynolds' Reynolds op. cit. p.175

475 ' "Setting Europe ablaze" had proved' ibid. p.176

Chapter 18: Overlord

476 'It's not the hard work' Dalton op. cit. p.714 29.4.44

476 'Spirits remain at a low level' BNA INF1/293

476 'Considerable disquiet' *Washington Despatches* op. cit. p.345

477 'We discussed . . . how best' Brooke op. cit. p.533 21.3.44

478 'Difficulties again with' ibid. p.537 5.4.44

478 'This battle has been forced' Cadogan op. cit. p.621 19.4.44

478 'preferred to roll up' BNA CAB99/28

479 'Struck by how very tired' Colville op. cit. p.484 12.4.44

479 'In my view, it is' Kimball op. cit. vol. iii p.87 12.4.44

481 'So skilful were German' see for instance Atkinson op. cit. passim

482 'How magnificently' Kimball op. cit. vol. iii p.163

482 'Lots of Americans and British' John Gunther *D-Day* Hamish Hamilton 1944 p.59

483 'a place that has long been' Mr T. Bowman *The Times* 30.5.42

485 'A man who has to play' WSC *The Second World War* op. cit. vol. v p.551

485 'Winston . . . has taken his train' Brooke op. cit. p.553 4.6.44

485 'Mr Churchill seemed to be' Eden op. cit. p.452

486 'Cheap at the price' ibid. p.454

489 'Don't look so glum' Pogue op. cit. vol. iii p.394

489 'We are surrounded by' Brooke op. cit. p.557 12.6.44

489 'The PM asked if I were' Holmes diary quoted Gilbert *Road to Victory* op. cit. p.813

489 '[Churchill] was at his best' Cunningham diary quoted Gilbert

490 'I do hope it will soon' IWM Papers of Mrs E. Elkus letter of 2.9.44

490 'He kept on repeating' Brooke op. cit. p.563 27.6.44

490 '"I feel exhausted"' Macmillan op. cit. p.474 25.6.44

490 'We have now reached' Brooke op. cit. p.581 15.8.44

491 'Whatever the PM's shortcomings' Colville op. cit. p.489 13.5.44

Chapter 19: Bargaining with an Empty Wallet

493 'Roosevelt sent him' Kimball op. cit. vol. iii p.201 22.6.44

493 'I cannot think of' ibid. p.202 23.6.44

494 'Whether we should ruin' ibid. p.219

495 'I should never survive' ibid. pp.222–3

495 'What can I do' ibid. pp.229

495 'The Arnold–King–Marshall combination' PM's personal minute to CoS 6.7.44 D.218/4 quoted Gilbert *Road to Victory* op. cit. p.843

496 'Up till *Overlord*' Colville op. cit. p.574 20.3.45

496 'Up to July 1944 England' Moran op. cit. 5.7.54

497 'After dinner a really ghastly' Eden op. cit. p.461

497 'A frightful meeting' Brooke op. cit. p.566

497 'I called this "a deplorable evening"' Eden op. cit. p.462

498 'He is very tight' Dalton op. cit. 29.4.44

498 'Lunched alone with W' Eden op. cit. p.463

498 'On 4 August, when Eden' Eden op. cit. p.467

499 'he was *far* more law-abiding' Brooke op. cit. p.673 23.3.45

499 'Of course it was true' BNA CAB79/77

499 'We know that such' Michael Howard *Liberation or Catastrophe* p.75

500 'I despise the generals' Harvey op. cit. p.349 5.8.44

500 'about the necessity of' ibid. p.351 18.8.44

500 'The present purge is' BNA FO371/39062

503 'This seems to be the best' Kimball op. cit. vol. iii p.261 29.7.44

505 'After all, he is a' CAC Randolph Churchill to WSC Churchill Papers CHAR1/381/42–44 11.8.44

505 'I feel that de Gaulle's France' *Speaking for Themselves* op. cit. p.501 17.8.43

506 'They did not know' WSC *The Second World War* op. cit. vol. vi p.84

506 'The English are clever' Milovan Djilas *Wartime* op. cit. p.401
506 'all spread along twenty miles' *Speaking for Themselves* op. cit. p.500 17.8.44
508 'I feel sure this is' IWM diary of WA Charlotte 93/19/1
508 'fooling about in Italy' Harvey op. cit. p.355 26.8.44
508 'David Reynolds notes' Reynolds op. cit. p.395
508 'the PM can be counted on' Colville op. cit. p.595 1.5.45
508 'Our Cabinet meetings certainly' Amery op. cit. pp.994 & 1020 9.8.44 & 23.11.44
509 'Churchill is preoccupied' Berlin op. cit. pp.13 & 15
509 'I do not consider it advantageous' Kimball op. cit. vol. iii p.296
510 'old, unwell and depressed' Brooke op. cit. p.589 8.9.44
510 'gargantuan in scale' Colville op. cit. p.509 6.9.44
510 'The prime minister said' ibid.
510 'all he could now do' Colville op. cit. p.510 7.9.44
510 'Earlier that year' Brooke op. cit. p.525 25.2.44
510 'high political consequences' WSC to chiefs of staff 9.9.44
513 'Brendan Bracken dismissed him' Colville op. cit. p.555 23.1.45
513 'Yet there is no reason' BNA FO371/38550/AN4451
513 'my illusions about the French' Colville op. cit. 20.9.44
516 'The affairs go well' *Speaking for Themselves* op. cit. p.306 13.10.44
516 'We fucked this England!' Chuev op. cit. p.75
517 'Our lot from London' BNA CAB120/165
517 'The Poles' game is up' Moran op. cit. p.249 17.10.43
518 'Far quicker than the British' CAC Deakin Papers op. cit. DEAL16 p.14
519 'You must remember' BNA PREM4/337/23 3.12.44
520 'How much depends on this man' Headlam op. cit. p.435 13.12.44
520 'He oughtn't to do it' Nicolson op. cit. p.406 9.10.44
520 'But he has no need' ibid. p.352 22.2.44
520 'The upper classes feel' ibid. p.356 27.3.44
520 'Winston Churchill is a bastard' ibid. p.347 7.2.44
521 'Collins, I should like' ibid. pp.408–9 27.10.44
521 'completely frozen' Brooke op. cit. p.625 13.11.44
522 '[He] is fighting for the future' *Spectator* 24.11.44

Chapter 20: Athens: 'Wounded in the House of Our Friends'

524 'It is good that there is' Eden op. cit. 26.10.44
525 'Despite Churchill's belief' Mazower *Inside Hitler's Greece* op. cit. p.352
526 'My darling Winston' *Speaking for Themselves* op. cit. p.507 4.12.44
527 'We expect the Italians' Foreign Relations of the United States 1944 vol. iii p.1162

527 '"Liberal" papers' USNA RG59 Box 11 State Department Surveys of public opinion on international affairs 1943–1975

528 'Substantially universal approval' USNA RG59 Box 11 Survey No. 17 23.12.44

528 'A Princeton poll' USNA RG59 Box 11 Princeton Poll 23.12.44

528 'Winston Churchill, the present' *Tribune* December 1944

529 'This is good' WSC to Eden 23.11.44

529 'at its best was one' Nicolson op. cit. p.416 8.12.44

529 'He rambled on' Macmillan op. cit. p.600 8.12.44

530 'I think we have had' *Post* 11.12.44

531 'Our version of the facts' BNA CAB121/559

532 'We do not wish to start' Macmillan op. cit. p.612 19.12.44

532 'These ELAS guerillas' IWM 06/110/1 letter of 7.1.45

533 'but I think the bulk' IWM 86/61/1 letters of 5.12.44, 12.12.44 & 5.2.45

533 'Poor Winston!' Macmillan op. cit. p.613

533 'I won't install a Dictator' Cadogan op. cit. p.689 21.12.44

534 'Indignation with Britain' *Washington Despatches* op. cit. p.481 24.12.44

534 'Glad I am not going' CAC Martin Papers op. cit. MART/2 24.12.44

535 'had the air of men' Osbert Lancaster *Spectator* 12.11.65

535 'in a most mellow' Macmillan op. cit. p.616 25.12.44

535 'struck me as a very remarkable' Hansard 18.1.45

535 'We are now in the curious' Colville op. cit. p.540 26.12.44

536 'the pink and ochre' Hansard 18.1.45

536 'One can see the smoke' Colville op. cit. p.540

536 'The change in his appearance' Lancaster *Spectator* op. cit.

537 'three shabby desperados' Colville op. cit. p.541 26.12.44

537 'after some consideration' *Speaking for Themselves* op. cit. p.509 26–27.12.44

537 'I thought it all very disingenuous' Macmillan op. cit. p.619 26.12.44

538 'I cannot tell you the feeling' Lancaster op. cit.

538 'Sit down, butcher!' Macmillan op. cit. p.619 27.12.44

538 'Of course this affair is' ibid.

538 'This Wednesday has been' *Speaking for Themselves* p.509 28.12.44

539 'a short crack followed by' Lancaster *Spectator* op. cit.

540 'Anglo–American differences' USNA RG59 State Department Surveys of public opinion on international affairs 1943–1975 Box 11

541 'an orgy of recrimination' USNA RG59 Box 11 p.500 21.1.45

542 'The general reaction' *Washington Despatches* op. cit. p.494 7.1.45

542 'OWI and State Department surveys' USNA RG59 Box 11 Survey No. 22

542 'Despite recent press comment' USNA RG59 Box 11 State Department Surveys of public opinion on international affairs 1943–1975 No. 19

542 'Terrible Cabinet' Eden op. cit. p.506

543 'You know I cannot' quoted Gilbert *Road to Victory* op. cit. p.1138

543 'France cannot masquerade' WSC to Eden 19.1.45

543 'You wouldn't like my job' Holmes diary 14.1.45 quoted Gilbert *Road to Victory* op. cit. p.1148

543 'In all his moods' Holmes letter to Gilbert 12.2.85 quoted ibid.

543 'It is a mistake to try' WSC to Eden 4.1.45

544 'Smuts and I are like' Colville op. cit. p.553 17.1.45

545 'Why are we making a fuss' BNA FO954/26/382

545 'Make no mistake' Colville op. cit. p.555 23.1.45

545 'Let us think no more' ibid. p.554 20.1.45

Chapter 21: Yalta

546 'As the purely military problems' Harvey op. cit. p.365 11.11.44

547 'I have great hopes' Hansard 18.1.45

547 'Impossible even to get' Eden op. cit. p.511 2.2.45

548 'What a hole' Holmes diary 3.2.45 quoted Gilbert *Road to Victory* op. cit. p.1172

548 'A terrible party' Eden op. cit. p.512

548 'Big Three' *New York Times* 4.2.45

548 'During the past year' USNA RG59 Box 1 Opinion Studies special poll 22.3.45

549 'We had the world' quoted Gilbert *Road to Victory* op. cit. p.1174

550 'Our guards compared Churchill' Beria op. cit. p.137

550 'What a crook' Chuev op. cit. p.76

550 'Soviet eavesdroppers' Beria op. cit. p.138

551 'It has gone to my heart' CAC Martin Papers op. cit. MART2

551 'I do not suppose' Sarah Churchill *Keep on Dancing* pp.75–6

551 'I am free to confess' *Speaking for Themselves* op. cit. p.512 1.2.45

553 'We must do what we can' BNA CAB120/170

555 'followed so swiftly' BNA PREM4/77/1B/359

556 'even if we go to the verge' Colville op. cit. 28.2.45

556 'He voiced aloud his fear' ibid. p.562 23.2.45

556 'he had never been more distressed' Brooke op. cit. p.665 22.2.45

556 'Churchill wants a bourgeois Poland' Zhukov memoirs op. cit. vol. iii p.216

556 'We see unprecedented unanimity' *Pravda* 18.2.45

Chapter 22: The Final Act

557 'I cannot agree' Kimball op. cit. vol. iii p.568

559 'calculated to hasten' BNA PREM3/12/2 20.4.45

560 'In the full tilt of war' Montague Browne *Long Sunset* op. cit. p.248

561 'Portal had advocated' BNA AIR8/436

564 'It was a relief' Brooke op. cit. p.678 26.3.45

564 'I'm an old man' Anita Leslie *A Story Half Told* Hutchinson 1983 pp.142–3

565 'The PM is now becoming' Colville op. cit. 24.4.45

565 'What do you think?' Zhukov op. cit. vol. iii p.224

566 'His vanity was astonishing' Colville op. cit. 26.4.45

566 'I have been much disturbed' 29.4.45

567 'I fear terrible things' BNA FO954/20

568 'We have moved a long way' Moran op. cit. p.277

568 'I hoped that they would' Ismay op. cit. p.394

568 'I can't feel thrilled' Brooke op. cit. p.688

569 'There is no doubt' ibid. p.689

569 'Without him England' ibid. p.590 10.9.44

570 'in which case there was' Colville op. cit. p.128

570 'the significance of the link-up' *Pravda* 29.4.45

571 'From the present point of view' BNA FO954/26c

572 'Winston delighted' Brooke op. cit. p.690 13.5.45

572 'Russian bear sprawled' ibid. p.693 24.5.45

572 'We received reliable information' Zhukov op. cit. vol. iii p.322

573 'The overall or political object' CAB120/691

575 'The idea is of course' Brooke op. cit. p.693 24.5.45

575 '"the unthinkable war"' ibid. p.695 31.5.45

577 'In London, the *Unthinkable* file' BNA FO954/26c

577 'On 3 July 1940, American General' Lee op. cit. p.10 3.7.40

578 'It would be the highest honour' Eden op. cit. p.522 16.2.45

578 'There are . . . many who think' Stebbing 27.11.40 quoted Garfield op. cit. p.24

578 'It is clear that' *Wall Street Journal* 13.12.44

578 '[I am] in the throes' Mayhew op. cit. pp.234–5

579 'Well, Prime Minister' quoted Ronald Lewin *Slim: The Standard Bearer* Leo Cooper 1977 p.246

579 'They have saved this country' Colville op. cit. p.433 30.8.41

579 'We have been the dreamers' Foot op. cit. p.505

579 'One of the most extraordinary' IWM Papers of Mrs E. Elkus

579 'a jingo election' Harvey op. cit. p.383 10.6.45

580 'I won't have it' Moran op. cit. p.319

583 'Churchill was extraordinarily' Rzheshevsky op. cit. pp.519–24

584 'My hate had died' WSC *The Second World War* op. cit. vol. vi p.545

585 'I shall be only half a man' Moran op. cit. p.313 8.7.45

585 'I respect the old man' Zhukov op. cit. vol. iii p.325

586 'He had absorbed' Brooke op. cit. p.709 23.7.45

587 'During an Allied reception' Zhukov op. cit. vol. iii p.336

588 'He is again under Stalin's spell' Eden op. cit. 17.7.45

588 'Of all the Western leaders' Beria op. cit. p.135

589 'A lot of people talked' Colville op. cit. p.273 22.10.40

589 'No one in our conference delegation' Kumanyov op. cit. p.303

589 'I still cannot comprehend' Chuev op. cit. p.85

589 'You must not think of me' *Action this Day* op. cit. p.262

590 'The rest of my life' Moran op. cit. p.353

591 'Churchill contributed about' CAC Churchill Papers CHAR1/379/12–20

591 'Winston's mind has a stop' Eden op. cit. p.350 9.11.42

591 'I do not believe in this' Moran op. cit. p.224 20.9.43

591 'Churchill sees history' Berlin op. cit. pp.4 & 12

592 'After it was over' Eden op. cit. p.551 27.7.45

592 'Why don't you tell them' Nicolson op. cit. 7.8.42

592 'No, I am a privileged' Kennedy MS op. cit. 16.2.41

593 'He would no more think' A.G. Gardiner *Prophets, Priests and Kings* London
    1914 p.234

593 'dull cabinet without PM' Brooke op. cit. p.388 8.3.43

594 'His countrymen have come' Moran op. cit. p.13 23.12.41

596 'I should have liked' Mary Soames to the author 23.5.2004

SELECT BIBLIOGRAPHY

The published literature on Winston Churchill is enormous. My own library includes more than a hundred titles by or about him, and over a thousand books on World War II, many of which have been marginally useful in writing this book. It seems meaningless, however, to catalogue them all. The list below details only works extensively consulted, or explicitly quoted in my own text.

Addison, Paul, *Churchill on the Home Front 1900–1955* Jonathan Cape 1992

Aglan, André, *La Résistance sacrifice: Le Mouvement Libération-Sud 1940–1944* Paris 1999

Alanbrooke, Field Marshal Lord *War Diaries 1939–1945* ed. Alex Danchev and Daniel Todman Weidenfeld & Nicolson 2001

Ambrose, Stephen, *Eisenhower the Soldier* Allen & Unwin 1984

Amery, Leo, *The Empire at Bay: The Leo Amery Diaries 1929–1945* ed. John Barnes and David Nicholson Hutchinson 1988

Andrew, Christopher and Gordievsky, Oleg, *KGB* Hodder & Stoughton 1990

Annan, Noel, *Changing Enemies* HarperCollins 1995

Astley, Joan Bright, *The Inner Circle: A View of War at the Top* Hutchinson 1971

— and Wilkinson, Peter, *Gubbins and SOE* Leo Cooper 1993

Atkinson, Rick, *An Army at Dawn* Henry Holt 2004

— *The Day of Battle* Henry Holt 2007

Attlee, Clement, *As it Happened* Heinemann 1954

Bailey, Roderick, *The Wildest Province* Jonathan Cape 2008

— *Forgotten Voices of the Secret War* Ebury Press 208

Barclay, George, *Fighter Pilot* William Kimber 1976

Barker, Elisabeth, *Churchill and Eden at War* Macmillan 1978

Barnett, Correlli, *The Desert Generals* Allen & Unwin 1983

— *The Audit of War* Macmillan 1986

Bayly, Christopher and Harper, Tim, *Forgotten Armies: The Fall of British Asia 1940–45* Penguin 2004

Beaumont, Joan, *Comrades in Arms* Davis-Poynter 1980

Bellamy, Chris, *Absolute War* Macmillan 2007

Bennett, Ralph, *Ultra and Mediterranean Strategy* Hamish Hamilton 1989

Beria, Sergo, *My Father Beria: In the Corridors of Stalin's* Regime (Moi oets Beriya: V koridorakh stalinskoi vlasti) Moscow 2002

Berlin, Isaiah, *Personal Impressions* Hogarth Press 1980

Best, Geoffrey, *Churchill: A Study in Greatness* Hambledon & London 2001

— *Churchill and War* Hambledon & London 2005

Billotte, Pierre, *Le Temps des armes* Plon 1972

Birkenhead, The Earl of, *Halifax: The Life of Lord Halifax* Hamish Hamilton 1965

Blum, John Morton, *Years of War 1941–1945: From the Morgenthau Diaries* Houghton Mifflin 1977

Bohlen, Charles E., *Witness to History 1929–1969* Norton 1973

Bond, Brian, *Liddell Hart: A Study of His Military Thought* Cassell 1977

Bonham-Carter, Violet, *Champion Redoubtable: The Diaries of Violet Bonham-Carter* ed. Mark Pottle Weidenfeld & Nicolson 1998

Boswell, James, *The Life of Samuel Johnson* Everyman 2004

Brendon, Piers, *Winston Churchill: An Authentic Hero* Methuen 1984

Broad, Richard and Fleming, Suzie eds, *Nella Last's War* Sphere 1983

Browne, Anthony Montague, *Long Sunset: Memoirs of Winston Churchill's Last Private Secretary* Cassell 1995

Bryant, Arthur, *The Turn of the Tide* Collins 1957

Butcher, Harry C., *My Three Years with Eisenhower* Simon & Schuster 1946

Butler, J.R.M., *Grand Strategy* vol. ii HMSO 1957

— *Grand Strategy* vol. iii Parts I and II HMSO 1964

Cadogan, Alexander, *The Diaries* Jonathan Cape 1986

Carlton, David, *Churchill and the Soviet Union* Manchester 2000

Chandos, Lord (Oliver Lyttelton), *Memoirs of Lord Chandos* Bodley Head 1962

Channon, Henry, *Chips: The Diaries of Sir Henry Channon* ed. Robert Rhodes-James Weidenfeld & Nicolson 1967

Charmley, John, *Churchill: The End of Glory* Hodder & Stoughton 1993

— *Churchill's Grand Alliance: The Anglo–American Special Relationship 1940–1957* Hodder & Stoughton 1995

Chuev, F., *Conversations with Molotov* (Sto sorok besed s Molotovym) Moscow 1991

Churchill, Sarah, *Keep on Dancing* Weidenfeld & Nicolson 1981

Churchill, Winston S., *The World Crisis* two vols Odhams 1927

— *My Early Life* Thornton Butterworth 1930

— *The Second World War* six vols Cassell 1948–54

— *Great Contemporaries* Leo Cooper 1990

— *Speeches 1938–45* five vols vol. i ed. Randolph Churchill; vols ii–v ed. Charles Eade Cassell 1941–45

— *The Secret Session Speeches* ed. Charles Eade Cassell 1946

Clarke, Peter, *The Cripps Version* Allen Lane 2002

Clausewitz, Carl von, *On War* ed. Michael Howard and Peter Paret Princeton 1976

Colville, John, *Fringes of Power: Downing Street Diaries 1939–1955* Hodder & Stoughton 1985

Court, W.H.B., *Coal* Longman 1951

Craig, Norman, *The Broken Plume* IWM 1982

Cunningham, Andrew Browne, *A Sailor's Odyssey* Hutchinson 1951

Dalton, Hugh, *The War Diaries of Hugh Dalton* ed. Ben Pimlott Jonathan Cape 1986

Danchev, Alex, *Very Special Relationship: Field Marshal Sir John Dill and the Anglo–American Alliance*, Brassey's 1986

Davie, Michael and Chisholm, Anne, *Beaverbrook* Hutchinson 1992

Davis, Kenneth S., *FDR: The War President* Random House 2000

De Gaulle, Charles, *War Memoirs* vol. i *Call to Honour 1940–42* Collins 1955; vol. ii *Unity 1942–44* Weidenfeld & Nicolson 1959

D'Este, Carlo, *Warlord: Winston Churchill at War 1878–1945* Harper 2008

— *Eisenhower: A Soldier's Life* Henry Holt 2002

— *Fatal Decision: Anzio and the Battle for Rome* HarperCollins 1991

Djilas, Milovan, *Wartime* Secker & Warburg 1980

Dokumenty Vneshnei Politiki 1940 – 22.12.41 Moscow 1999

Dykes, Vivian, *Establishing the Anglo–American Alliance: The Second World War Diaries of Brigadier Vivian Dykes* ed. Alex Danchev Brassey's 1990

Eden, Anthony, *The Eden Memoirs: The Reckoning* Cassell 1965

Ehrman, John, *Grand Strategy* vols v and vi HMSO 1956

Eisenhower War Papers vol. i Johns Hopkins 1970

Ellis, L.F., *The War in France and Flanders* HMSO 1953

Elmhirst, Sir Thomas, *Recollections* privately published 1991

Fisk, Robert, *In Time of War* André Deutsch 1983

Fleming, Peter, *Invasion 1940* Hart-Davis 1957

Foot, Michael, *Bevan* McGibbon & Kee 1962

Foreign Relations of the United States, *The Conferences at Washington, 1941–1942 and Casablanca, 1943* Washington DC 1968

— *The Conferences at Washington, 1942* vol. iii Washington DC 1961

— *The Conferences at Washington and Quebec, 1943* Washington DC 1970

— *The Conferences at Cairo and Tehran, 1943* Washington DC 1961

— *The Conference at Quebec, 1944* Washington DC 1972

— *The Conferences at Malta and Yalta, 1945* Washington DC 1955

Fraser, David, *Alanbrooke* HarperCollins 1997

French, David, *Raising Churchill's Army* Oxford 2000

Gardiner, A.G., *The Pillars of Society* Dent popular edn 1916

— *Prophets, Priests and Kings* Dent 1914

Garfield, Simon, *Private Battles: How the War Almost Defeated Us* Ebury 2006

Gibb, Andrew, *With Winston Churchill at the Front* Gowans & Gray 1924

Gilbert, Martin, *Churchill: A Life* Macmillan 1991

— *The Churchill War Papers* three vols Heinemann 1993–2000

— *In Search of Churchill* HarperCollins 1994

— *Finest Hour: Winston S. Churchill 1940–41* Heinemann 1983

— *Road to Victory: Winston S. Churchill 1942–45* Heinemann 1986

— *Never Despair: Winston S. Churchill 1945–1965* Heinemann 1988

Gildea, Robert, *Resistance, Reprisals and Community in Occupied France* Transactions of the Royal Historical Society 6th series 2003 pp.163–85

Golovanov, Alexander, *The Long-Range Bomber Force: Memoirs of the Chief Marshal of Aviation* Moscow 2007

Gunther, John, *D-Day* Hamish Hamilton 1944

Haffner, Sebastian, *Churchill* Haus 2003

Hammond, Nicholas, *Venture into Greece* William Kimber 1983

Harriman, W. Averell and Abel, Elie, *Special Envoy to Churchill and Stalin 1941–46* Random House NY 1975

Harris, Sir Arthur, *Bomber Offensive* Collins 1947

Harrison, Mark ed., *The Economics of World War II* Cambridge 1998

Hartwell, Lord, *William Camrose: Giant of Fleet Street* Weidenfeld & Nicolson 1992

Harvey, Oliver, *The War Diaries of Oliver Harvey 1941–1945* ed. John Harvey Collins 1978

Hassett, William, *Off the Record with FDR* Allen & Unwin 1960

Hastings, Max, *Bomber Command* Michael Joseph 1979

— *The Battle of Britain* (with Len Deighton) Rainbird 1980

— *Das Reich: The 2nd SS Panzer Division's March to Normandy: June 1944* Michael Joseph 1981

— *Overlord: D-Day and the Battle for Normandy* Michael Joseph 1984

— *Armageddon: The Battle for Germany 1944–45* Macmillan 2004

— *Nemesis: The Battle for Japan 1944–45* HarperCollins 2006

Headlam, Cuthbert, *Parliament and Politics in the Age of Churchill and Attlee: The Headlam Diaries 1935–51* ed. Stuart Ball Cambridge 1999

Hichens, Antony, *Gunboat Command* Pen & Sword 2007

Higgins, Trumbull, *Winston Churchill and the Second Front 1940–1943* Oxford 1957

Hinsley, F.H et al., *British Intelligence in the Second World War* four vols HMSO 1979–90

Hodgson, Vere, *Few Eggs and No Oranges: The Diaries of Vere Hodgson* Persephone 1999

Holland, Jeffrey, *The Aegean Mission* Greenwood Press 1988

Holmes, Richard, *In the Footsteps of Churchill* BBC 2006

Horne, Alastair, *To Lose a Battle* Macmillan 1969

Horsfall, John, *Say Not the Struggle* Roundwood 1977

Howard, Michael, *Grand Strategy* vol. iv *1942–43* HMSO 1972

— *British Intelligence in the Second World War* Hambledon & London 2007

Hull, Cordell, *Memoirs of Cordell Hull* Hodder & Stoughton 1948

Inman, P., *Labour in the Munitions Industries* HMSO and Longmans 1957

Ironside, Lord, *The Ironside Diaries* ed. R. Macleod and D. Kelly Constable 1962

Ismay, Lord, *The Memoirs of General the Lord Ismay* Heinemann 1960

Jackson, Julian, *France: The Dark Years* Oxford 2001

Jackson, Sir William and Bramall, Lord, *The Chiefs: The Story of the United Kingdom Chiefs of Staff* Brassey's 1992

Jeffreys, Kevin, *The Churchill Coalition and Wartime Politics* Palgrave Macmillan 1993

Jenkins, Roy, *Churchill* Macmillan 2001

— *Franklin Delano Roosevelt* Macmillan 2004

Jones, R.V., *Most Secret War: British Scientific Intelligence 1939–1945* Hamish Hamilton 1978

Karslake, Basil, *The Last Act* Leo Cooper 1979

Keegan, John, *Churchill* Weidenfeld & Nicolson 2002

Kennedy, David, *Freedom from Fear: The American People in Depression and War 1929–45* Oxford 1999

Kennedy, Sir John, *The Business of War* Hutchinson 1957

Kersaudy, François, *Churchill and De Gaulle* Collins 1981

— *Norway 1940* Collins 1990

Kershaw, Ian, *Fateful Choices: Ten Decisions that Changed the World 1940–41* Allen Lane 2007

— *Making Friends with Hitler* Allen Lane 2004

— *Hitler: Hubris 1889–1936* Allen Lane 1998

— *Hitler: Nemesis 1936–45* Allen Lane 2000

Kimball, Warren ed., *Churchill and Roosevelt: The Complete Correspondence* three vols Princeton 1984

Knight, Nigel, *Churchill Unmasked* David & Charles 2008

Kumanyov, G.A., 'Close to Stalin' (*Ryadom so Stalinym*) Moscow 1999

Kynaston, David, *A History of the City of London* vol. iii Chatto & Windus 1999

Lacouture, Jean, *De Gaulle: The Rebel 1890–1944* Collins Harvill 1984

Langworth, Richard M. ed., *Churchill by Himself* Ebury 2008

Lascelles, Sir Alan, *King's Counsellor: The Diaries of Sir Alan Lascelles* ed. Duff Hart-Davis Weidenfeld & Nicolson 2006

Lash, Joseph P., *Roosevelt and Churchill 1939–1941: The Partnership that Saved the West* Norton 1976

Lavery, Brian, *Churchill Goes to War: Winston's Wartime Journeys* Conway 2007

Lawlor, Sheila, *Churchill and the Politics of War 1940–41* Cambridge 1994

Lee, Raymond, *The London Observer: The Diaries of General Raymond Lee 1939–41* ed. James Leutze Hutchinson 1972

Lees-Milne, James, *The Diaries of James Lees-Milne* John Murray 2007

Leslie, Anita, *A Story Half Told* Hutchinson 1983

Lewin, Ronald, *Churchill as Warlord* Scarborough 1982

— *The Chief* Hutchinson 1980

— *Slim: The Standard Bearer* Leo Cooper 1977

Lukacs, John, *The Duel: Hitler versus Churchill* Oxford 1990

— *Five Days in London, May 1940* Yale 2001

Lysaght, Charles Edward, *Brendan Bracken* Allen Lane 1979

Mackenzie, William, *The Secret History of SOE* St Ermins Press 2000

McLaine, Ian, *Ministry of Morale* Allen & Unwin 1979

Macmillan, Harold, *War Diaries* Macmillan 1984

Martin, Sir John, *Downing Street: The War Years* Bloomsbury 1991

Mayhew, Patrick ed., *One Family's War* Hutchinson 1985

Mazower, Mark, *Hitler's Empire* Penguin 2008

— *Inside Hitler's Greece* Yale 1993

Meacham, Jon, *Franklin and Winston: Portrait of a Friendship* Granta 2004

Menzies, Robert, *Dark Days: The Diaries of Robert Menzies* ed. A.W. Martin and
   Patsy Hardy National Library of Australia 1993

Millburn, Clara, *Mrs Millburn's Diaries* Harrap 1979

Molony, C.J.C., *The Mediterranean and Middle East* vol. v HMSO 1973

Moorehead, Alan, *African Trilogy* Cassell 1998

Moran, Lord, *Winston Churchill: The Struggle for Survival 1940–1965* Constable 1966

Morgan, Sir Frederick E., *Overture to Overlord* Hodder & Stoughton 1950

Morgan, Ted, *Churchill 1874–1915* Jonathan Cape 1982

— *Franklin Roosevelt* Simon & Schuster 1992

Mosley, Leonard, *Backs to the Wall: London Under Fire 1939–45* Weidenfeld &
   Nicolson 1971

Nel, Elizabeth, *Mr Churchill's Secretary* Hodder & Stoughton 1958

Nicholas, H.G. ed., *Washington Despatches* Weidenfeld & Nicolson 1981

Nicolson, Harold, *The Diaries of Harold Nicolson 1939–45* ed. Nigel Nicolson
   Weidenfeld & Nicolson 1967

Ocherki Istorii Rossiikoi Vneshney Razvedki (Studies on the History of the Soviet
   Foreign Intelligence Service) Moscow 2007

Overy, Richard, *War and Economy in the Third Reich* Oxford 1995

— *Why the Allies Won* Jonathan Cape 1997

— *Russia's War* Allen Lane 1998

— *The Dictators: Hitler's Germany and Stalin's Russia* Allen Lane 2004

Pauli, Kurt, *Von Serbien Bis Kreta* Steirische Verlagsanstatt 1942

Payne, Stanley G., *Franco and Hitler* Yale 2007

Pickersgill, J.W. and Forster, D.F., *The Mackenzie King Record* vols i & ii University
   of Toronto 1968

Pile, Gen. Sir Frederick, *Ack-Ack: Britain's Defence Against Air Attack* Harrap 1949

Pilipel, Robert H., *Churchill in America* NEL 1977

Pogue, Forrest C., *The Supreme Command* Washington DC 1954

— *George C. Marshall: Education of a General 1880–1939* Viking 1964

— *George C. Marshall: Ordeal and Hope 1939–42* Viking 1965

— *George C. Marshall: Organizer of Victory 1943–45* Viking 1973

Porch, Douglas, *Hitler's Mediterranean Gamble* Weidenfeld & Nicolson 2004

Portelli, Alessandro, 'The Massacre of Civitella Val Di Chianti: Myth and Politics, Mourning and Common Sense' in *The Battle of Valle Giulia: Oral History and the Art of Dialogue* Wisconsin 1997

Postan, M.M., *British War Production* HMSO 1952

Potsdam Institute for the Study of Military History *Germany and the Second World War* nine vols published in translation by Oxford University Press 1990–2008

Pownall, Henry, *Chief of Staff: The Diaries of Lieutenant-General Sir Henry Pownall* ed. Brian Bond two vols Leo Cooper 1972 & 1974

Ramsden, John, *Man of the Century: Winston Churchill and His Legend Since 1945* HarperCollins 2002

Ray, John, *The Battle of Britain: New Perspectives* Arms & Armour Press 1994

Reynolds, David, *In Command of History: Churchill Fighting and Writing the Second World War* Penguin 2004

— *The Creation of the Anglo–American Alliance 1937–1941* Chapel Hill 1982

— ed. with Warren Kimball and A.O. Chubarian *Allies at War: The Soviet, American and British Experience 1942–45* Palgrave Macmillan 1994

— *From World War to Cold War* Oxford 2002

Rhodes-James, Robert, *Churchill: A Study in Failure 1900–39* Weidenfeld & Nicolson 1970

Richards, Denis, *Portal of Hungerford* Heinemann 1977

Richardson, Charles, *From Churchill's Secret Circle to the BBC: The Biography of Lieutenant General Sir Ian Jacob* Brassey's 1991

Roberts, Andrew, *The Holy Fox: A Life of Lord Halifax* Weidenfeld & Nicolson 1991

— *Masters and Commanders* Penguin 2008

Robinson, Derek, *Invasion 1940* Constable 2005

Rodger, N.A.M., *The History of the Royal Navy* vol. ii Penguin 2005

Rogers, Anthony, *Churchill's Folly* Cassell 2003

Roosevelt, Elliott, *As He Saw It* Duell, Sloan & Pearce 1946

Rose, Norman, *Churchill: An Unruly Life* Simon & Schuster 1995

Roskill, Stephen, *Churchill and the Admirals* Collins 1977

— *Hankey: Man of Secrets* three vols Collins 1974

— *The War at Sea* HMSO 1960

Royal Historical Society Proceedings, *Record of the Churchill Conference at the Institute for Historical Research Jan 2001* Cambridge 2001

Rzheshevsky, O.A., *Stalin and Churchill: Meetings, Conversations, Discussions* (Stalin i Cherchil: Vstrechi, besedy, diskussi) Moscow 2004

Salter, Arthur, *Slave of the Lamp* Weidenfeld & Nicolson 1967

Sayers, R.S., *Financial Policy 1939–45* HMSO 1956

Sebag-Montefiore, Hugh, *Dunkirk* Penguin 2006

Sebastian, Mikhail, *Journal 1935–44* Heinemann 2001

Sheridan, Dorothy ed., *Wartime Women* Heinemann 1990

Sherwood, Robert, *The White House Papers of Harry L. Hopkins* vols i & ii Eyre & Spottiswoode 1948

— *Roosevelt and Hopkins: An Intimate History* Harper 1948

Slessor, Sir John, *The Central Blue* Cassell 1956

Slim, Field Marshal Viscount, *Defeat into Victory* Cassell 1956

Soames, Mary, *Clementine Churchill* Doubleday 2002

— ed. *Speaking for Themselves: The Personal Letters of Winston and Clementine Churchill* Doubleday 1998

Sokolov, Vladimir and Stegny, Pyotr, *Bridges and Barriers II Rodina No. 5* Moscow 2003

Stacey, C.P., *The Canadian Army 1939–45* Ottawa 1955

Stafford, David, *Roosevelt and Churchill* Little, Brown 1999

Stanford, J. K., *Tail of an Army* Phoenix 1966

Strong, Kenneth, *Intelligence at the Top* Cassell 1968

Sweet-Escott, Bickham, *Baker Street Irregular* Methuen 1965

Taylor, A.J.P., *Beaverbrook* Hamish Hamilton 1972

Tedder, Lord, *With Prejudice* Cassell 1966

Tendulkar, D.G., *Mahatma* New Delhi 1969

Thompson, R.W., *Churchill and Morton* Hodder & Stoughton 1976

Thorne, Christopher, *Allies of a Kind* Hamish Hamilton 1978

Thurlow, Richard, *Fascism in Britain: A History 1918–1985* Oxford 1987

Titmuss, Richard, *History of the Second World War: Problems of Social Policy* HMSO 1950

Tooze, Adam, *Wages of Destruction: The Making and Breaking of the German War Economy* Allen Lane 2006

Trollope, Anthony, *Autobiography* Trollope Society 1999

Trukhanovsky, V.G., *Winston Churchill* (Uinston Cherchil. Politicheskaya Biograpiya) Progress Publishers Moscow 1978

Wallace, Henry, *The Price of Vision: The Diary of Henry A. Wallace 1942–1946* ed. John Morton Blum Boston 1973

Watt, D.C., *Succeeding John Bull* Cambridge 1980

Waugh, Evelyn, *Men at Arms* Chapman & Hall 1952

Wheeler-Bennett, Sir John, ed., *Action this Day* Macmillan 1968

— *John Anderson Viscount Waverley* Macmillan 1962

Wievorka, Olivier, *Une Certaine idée de la Résistance: Défense de la France 1940–1949* Paris 1995

Wilmot, Chester, *The Struggle for Europe* Collins 1952

Wilson, Thomas, *Churchill and the Prof* Cassell 1995

Winant, G., *A Letter from Grosvenor Square* London 1947

Winfield, Ronald, *The Sky Belongs to Them* William Kimber 1976

Wrigley, Chris, *Churchill* Haus 2006

Young, Kenneth, *Stanley Baldwin* Weidenfeld & Nicolson 1976

Zhukov, G.K., *Vospominaniya i Razmyshlenita* (Memories and Reflections) vol. ii
Moscow 1992

INDEX

Abyssinia: campaign in, 123, 138
Accolade, Operation, 402–3
Adam, Gen. Sir Ronald, 208, 427
Admiralty: submarine tracking room, 337; cancels March convoy to Archangel, 372; *see also* Royal Navy
Aegean *see* Dodecanese
Afrika Korps *see* German army
airborne forces: WSC urges expansion, 245
Alam Halfa: Afrika Korps repulsed, 335, 337
Alamein, battle of (1942), 337–42, 344, 351, 353
Alanbrooke, 1st Viscount *see* Brooke, Gen. Sir Alan
Albania: Italians withdraw to from Greece, 118; Resistance movement, 462; rejects return of King Zog, 515; communist partisans seize control after liberation, 524
Albery, Sir Irving, 13
Alexander, Albert Victor (*later* Earl), 10, 19, 105
Alexander, Gen. Sir Harold (*later* 1st Earl, of Tunis: on reasons for weak army leadership, 265; public knowledge of, 307; reluctance to express view of course of war, 308; appointed C.in C. Middle East, 320; and prospective North African offensive, 332; signals from WSC on impending Eighth Army offensive, 337; reputation after Alamein, 341; on US incompetence in North Africa, 351; on Allied North African campaign, 370; relations with WSC, 375; commands in Sicily campaign, 382, 389; given command in Mediterranean, 438, 530; proposed for British commander on D-Day, 438; and campaign in Italy, 440, 481, 489; and Anzio stalemate, 441, 443; WSC maintains confidence in, 443; urges restraint on Italian partisans, 465; entertains WSC in Italy, 507; on British forces in post-liberation Greece, 531, 533, 537; at Athens conference with WSC, 537–8; WSC proposes to replace Tedder as Deputy Supreme Commander, 558; on troops' reluctance to engage Tito's communists, 573; instructed to expel Yugoslav partisans from Trieste, 580; at Potsdam conference, 584; WSC grows impatient with, 596
Algeria: WSC visits, 380
Allied Control Commission in Germany, 551
Alsace-Lorraine, 500
Amery, Julian, 311
Amery, Leo: diary, xx; scepticism over WSC's powers and roles, 4; accepts WSC's leadership qualities, 10; serves under WSC, 11; on prospective French defeat, 48; contrasts WSC and Lloyd George, 90; and campaign in Greece, 119; revulsion towards Russia as ally, 154; and WSC's not mentioning visiting Canada, 228; and WSC's apathy towards Bengal famine, 236; on WSC's hostility to Indian independence, 255; 1922 Committee member complains to, 272; and WSC's reaction to criticism, 309; on dealing with WSC, 335; favours Wavell as super-chief of staff, 335; on Alamein, 339; on WSC's handling of debate on Town and Country Planning Bill, 422; complains of disorganised cabinet meetings, 508
Anders, Gen. Wladyslaw, 328, 517, 556
Anderson, Sir John: in war cabinet, 140; qualities, 273–4; on recall of Beaverbrook, 395; and development of atom bomb, 445, 587
Anderson, Gen. Sir Kenneth, 351
Annan, Noel, Baron, 463–4
Anvil, Operation *see* Dragoon, Operation
Anzio: landings and stalemate, 438, 440–3, 479; Allied breakout, 481
Arcadia (US-British summit, December 1941), 219, 226, 229
Archangel, 331, 372
Arctic (PQ) convoys, 251, 323, 325, 330, 337
Ardennes: German advance in (1940), 5, 13
Army & Navy Club, London, 260
Army Bureau of Current Affairs (ABCA), 208
Army and Navy Journal (USA), 549
Arnhem, battle of, 442, 514
Arnold, Gen. Henry ('Hap'): at Placentia Bay meeting, 194–5; WSC criticises, 495; on bombing of Dresden, 562
Arnold, Thomas, 474
Ashford, Pam, 238, 262
Astier de la Vigerie, Emmanuel d', 458
Athens: WSC visits (December 1944), xxii, 534–40; WSC revisits (February 1945), 554–5
Atlantic, Battle of the: conduct of, 113, 119, 171, 199, 206, 367; shipping losses in, 138, 188, 202, 244, 337, 372; RAF denies use of heavy aircraft for, 149; US escorts in, 197, 199, 220; merchant ship crossing times, 241; and air cover, 250
Atlantic Charter, 197–9, 253
Atlantic Committee (British cabinet), 187

IRELAND

Dublin

*NORTH
SEA*

DENMAR

*ATLANTIC
OCEAN*

**GREAT
BRITAIN**

London

G

Brest

G F

Paris

F R A N C E

*Bay
of
Biscay*

Vichy

I T A L Y

PORTUGAL

Madrid

Menton

La Spezia

Marseilles

Toulon

S P A I N

Barcelona

Corsica

Lisbon

Ro

Anzio

Sardinia

Na

Gibraltar

Palermo

Rabat

**SPANISH
MOROCCO**

Oran

Algiers

Bizerta

Casablanca

Bône

Tunis

Safi

TUNISIA

Sousse

M O R O C C O

Hajjerat M'Guil

Sfax

Gabès

A L G E R I A

Médenine

Tripoli

TRIPOLITANIA

| 0 | | 200 miles |
| 0 | | 300 km |

L

Knots in My Yo-yo String

The
Autobiography
of a Kid

by
Jerry Spinelli

Alfred A. Knopf 🐎 New York

RO1278 11457

Copyright © 1998 by Jerry Spinelli
Cover photograph copyright © 1998 by Penny Gentieu
Map copyright © 1998 by Jennifer Pavlovitz

All rights reserved under International and Pan-American Copyright
Conventions. Published in the United States by Alfred A. Knopf, Inc., New York, and
simultaneously in Canada by Random House of Canada Limited, Toronto. Distributed by
Random House, Inc., New York.

Grateful acknowledgment is made to Sidney Lippman for permission
to reprint excerpts from "Too Young," copyright © 1951 by Aria Music,
Sylvia Dee, and Sidney Lippman.

Photographic acknowledgments: page 22: *Norristown Herald*, copyright © 1947; page 151
(right): Chuck Cully.

www.randomhouse.com/kids/

Library of Congress Cataloging-in-Publication Data
Spinelli, Jerry.
Knots in my yo-yo string : the autobiography of a kid / by Jerry Spinelli.
p.   cm.
Summary: This Italian-American Newbery Medalist presents a humorous
account of his childhood and youth in Norristown, Pennsylvania.
1. Spinelli, Jerry—Childhood and youth—Juvenile literature. 2. Authors,
American—20th century—Biography—Juvenile literature. 3. Norristown (Pa.)—Social
life and customs—Juvenile literature. 4. Italian Americans—Pennsylvania—Norristown—
Biography—Juvenile literature.
[1. Spinelli, Jerry—Childhood and youth. 2. Authors, American.
3. Italian Americans.] I. Title.

PS3569.P546Z47   1998
813'.54—dc21   97-30827

ISBN   0-679-88791-1 (pbk.)
            0-679-98791-6 (lib. bdg.)

Printed in the United States of America
10 9 8 7 6 5 4 3 2 1

This book is dedicated to
Kathrine Kressmann Taylor

and to
my Gregory's Running Team mates:
Roger Adelman
Bill Glazier
Bob Hopple

and to
Louis Darden
wherever you are

Acknowledgments

To write this book about myself I needed more help than for any other. Considering the clarity of his memory, I think my old friend Roger Adelman ought to try his own hand at this. Contributions from my brother, Bill, and my mother were invaluable. What the three of us could not personally recall, I usually found in my father's meticulously compiled scrapbooks. Of great assistance also were Pete and Tina Pennock, Joe Mesi, Bill Steinberg, Millie Vircsik, Regina Simmonds, Ruth Riley, Bernice Foley, Carl Francis, Sandi Robinson, Judy Bitto, Larry Walker, Ellen Adams, my first editor John Keller, my agent and friend Ray Lincoln, and, as always, my wife, Eileen.

And Bill Hemsing, rifle-armed outfielder who stopped the ground balls that I missed and who hits the curve ball today better than ever.

For any inaccuracies contained in this account, I apologize. Where history could not be confirmed, it trembled at the mercy of my imperfect if well-meaning memory.

Contents

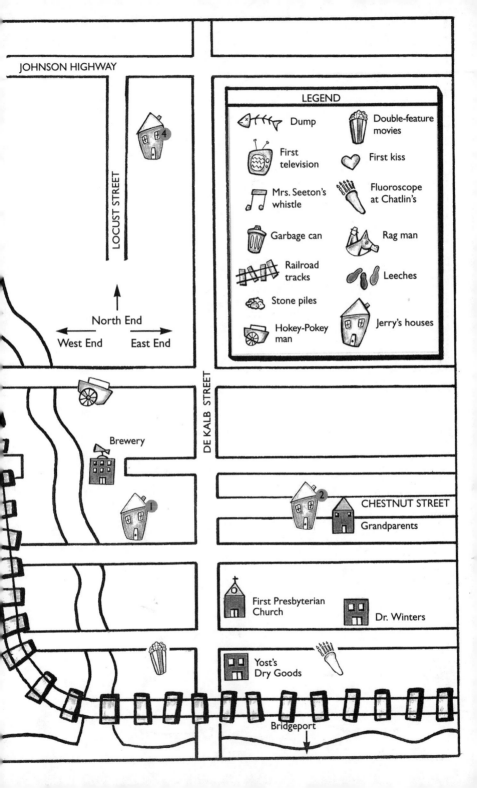

Johnson Highway

Like much of my life until that sixteenth year, it was a sunny day. A Sunday afternoon. I was in Carol Eckert's house on Pine Street. We were in the living room. Carol was telling me about her new boyfriend, and I, as always, was the good listener.

The doorbell rang. It was my younger brother, Bill, panting. "Lucky was hit by a car!"

Lucky was our dog.

I didn't know what to say except, "Where?"

"Johnson Highway."

I apologized to Carol and left with Bill. We ran. We ran down Pine to Roberts, down Roberts to Locust, and up Locust toward Johnson Highway. As we came near, I wanted to say to Bill, "You look. I'm not stopping." I wanted to cross Johnson Highway and not look down but run on, run out of town, out of time, out of myself, because I was having a bad year, and it was too few hours ago that I was king.

East End

I am outside in the yard. There is the smell—sour, vaguely rotten. And then the sound. It is high-pitched, but that is not the problem. The radio makes high-pitched sounds, too, and so does my mother when she sings to me. The problem is the loudness, a force as feelable as a blizzard. Every morsel of me shrivels and shakes. And even so, maybe I could stand it if only it would stop. But it does not and does not—and I cannot hear my own scream. My mother is running out to get me...

This is my first memory of my first house. It was on Marshall Street in the so-called East End of Norristown, Pennsylvania. Behind the house was a brewery—the Adam Scheidt Brewing Company—and that, I later learned, was where the smell and the sound came from.

The smell was hops, used in the beer-brewing process. Forming a constant cloud about us, the odor was especially strong once a day when a horse-drawn wagon hauled spent mash down the alley that led from the brewery past our side yard. Then the alley became a sour, steaming stream from the drippings of the wagon's sopping cargo.

The source of the sound was an air-raid siren. It was propped on the roof of the brewery, hardly a stone's throw from our house. This was during the early 1940s. World War II was raging in Europe, Africa, and Asia, and air-raid drills were a common practice in towns and cities throughout the land.

While the siren's frightful wail seemed to come from everywhere, another frequent sound—a long, low drone—came from directly overhead. Many a day I looked up to see planes or airships—dozens, sometimes hundreds of them—moving in neat geometric shapes across the sky.

Our house was red brick, flanking a block-long row of red-brick houses that ended at the brewer's alley. The sidewalk was brick also. We lived in an apartment on the second floor. The Printzes—Mickey, Big Leroy, and Little Leroy—lived on the first floor. And on the third. Each night they trooped through our quarters to go up to bed.

The landlady lived in the adjoining house. Neighborhood kids said she was mean. Stray balls that landed in her yard never came out. Luckily for my father's baseball budget, she was nice to us. My father lobbed underhand pitches to me, and I regularly whacked them over the back fence into the landlady's yard. My father, according to Marshall Street lore, was the only person ever to return alive from her yard, ball in hand.

Unable to find a bat for a four-year-old, my father bought a standard-size Louisville Slugger, then put the saw to it. He presented me with seventeen inches of hickory handle—perfect. That stunted, clubbish "bat" stands in a corner of my office today. It reminds me of how small I once was, and that the landlady's fence was both the first and last fence that I ever hit a baseball over.

A budding ballplayer (age 4, 1945).

Over the fence out front, I sent something else. The gate facing the sidewalk was metal, and I used to grip those bars with my tiny hands and plant my feet and belt out "Jesus Loves Me" to the turning, smiling passersby.

At some point during my brief singing phase, I acquired a baby brother, Billy. My mother tells me that because I then had to compete for her attention, I brought my performances inside to the living room and kitchen.

The next house we lived in we had all to ourselves. It was also a row house, but it had a front porch. It was deeper into the East End, on Chestnut Street. I always remember the number—224 Chestnut—because my grandparents lived at 226, the house next door.

I wasn't allowed to cross the street. But I did roam up and down the sidewalk, and that led me to the vacant lot at the end of our row of houses. When I think of that lot, I think of weeds and of brown and blue broken glass. It became my first playground, my first ballfield. Many of my days were spent there, until I began school.

I did not go to kindergarten, so my first taste of school was first grade at Gotwals Elementary. We learned to write the letters of the alphabet, then our names. I recall laboring over each pencil-printed letter, and the miracle of completing my name on the blue-lined paper: my first written work.

I was destined to learn little else at Gotwals. We rented our house on Chestnut Street, but my parents had been searching for a place to buy. When they got the chance, they took it, even though it meant transferring me to a new first grade in a new school.

We were moving to the West End.

West End

The West End became more than my home and neighborhood. It became my New World. No coonskin pathfinder ever explored his patch of earth more thoroughly than I explored mine.

The address was 802 George Street, second house in from Elm. Another brick row house, another brick sidewalk. For ten years I would live there, from ages six to sixteen.

The 800 block was the last block on George Street. It was a dead end. Beyond the last house the asphalt stopped. A three-foot-high wooden barrier made it official. I learned that "dead end" meant two different things. To a grownup it meant Stop—Turn the Car Around. To me, a kid, it meant Go—Your Territory Starts Here. Before the wooden barrier was the structured, orderly world of grownups, the neat grid of streets and houses that gave shape to their lives. Civilization.

Past the barrier was frontier. Climb over the fence or simply walk around it, as a car could not, and you found yourself in knee-high weeds. Then came the railroad tracks, then the woods, then the creek (pronounced "crick" in Norristown). This swatch of undeveloped land featured not one but two dumps, plus a swamp, Red Hill, the spear field, the stone piles, and a black and white pony. Who needed playgrounds? And lucky me, the portal to this kid-size continent was the dead end of my new street named George.

I spent much of the next ten years in this houseless, streetless wilderness and in the park on the other side of the creek. Sometimes I was with others, sometimes alone. By the time the ten years were up, I had caught a handful of salamanders, hit a home run, raced against my stopwatch, searched for the Devil, kissed a girl, and bled from an attack of leeches.

But I did not go to sleep on the frontier side of the dead-end fence, or wake up there, or go to school there. And that was okay, because the civilized side also had something that seemed expressly made for me and my playmates, geographic features that appeared on no map, had no names, yet were intimately familiar to all kids in the neighborhood. Seen from above, they would appear as a second, nameless grid overlaid on the public one. I speak of alleyways.

To me and the neighborhood kids, the back of a house was more important than the front, and we happily roamed the alleyways that bordered our backyards. Alleys were sized to make us comfortable—with a running start, you could practically broad-jump across some of them. In an alley it was the car, not the kid, that was the intruder. Alleys were for sneakers and bikes and trikes and wagons.

Alleys had no rules, no signs. Danger and parental interference were minimal. You could lie on your back in the middle of an alley (if you wanted to) and close your eyes for five minutes and not be run over. You could hang the frame of an old wooden chair from a telephone pole spike and use it as a basketball rim. In an alley you could practice riding your new bike in peace, then ram it into potholes and get yourself thrown, like a bronco buster. You could check out other people's garbage cans. If you wanted.

If you ran away from home, or planned to, you would go by alleyway. The network of nameless alleys mimicked the town's official layout. You could go any-where—for all I knew, clear across the country.

With the frontier and the park and the alleys avail-able to us, you might think we would stay off the streets. We did not, of course. If it pleased us to get up a foot-ball game in the middle of the street or hide from seek-ers under parked cars, that's what we did. Because, in truth, our territory was wherever we happened to be. Whichever side of the dead end we were on, whichever side of the door, we confiscated the turf and made it our own.

And so, if we felt like resting, we would alight like a small flock of birds onto the nearest front steps. Except for those at the house directly across the street from

802. For reasons too vague for words, we were afraid of the man who lived there. His front steps were never sat on, his sidewalk never hopscotched, his doorbell never rung, his backyard fence never climbed. The truth was, he was simply a widowed barber who preferred to keep his shades down all the time, but try telling that to us.

Ten years, from six to sixteen. Ten years in the West End. Ten years of twin Popsicles and Bonomo's Turkish taffy, hightop Keds and a plaid cummerbund, Howdy Doody and Willie the Worm and Uncle Miltie on TV Tuesday nights, salamanders and snakes and candy cigarettes, coal dust on the clothesline, baseball cleats swinging from my handlebars, Ovaltine in my milk, knots in my yo-yo string.

War

I hate war. But when I was little, I loved it. War was a game, guns were toys, death an amusement ride. The first card game I ever played was called war.

I also played with little green soldiers, maybe two inches high. I loved their perfect, tiny helmets that reminded me of cereal bowls. Even the faces of the soldiers were perfect and green. Their tiny mouths and eyes were forever locked into a battlefield moment that I could only imagine.

I read G.I. Joe and Combat Kelly comic books. Then, down at the creek, I would poke a stick into the powdery bottom silt, pop it upward, and go "Boom!" I pretended the resulting brown underwater cloud was an atomic bomb explosion.

And of course, I played war with my friends. Beyond the dead end, there were two major arsenals: the stone piles and the spear field. The stone piles were on the other side of the tracks, between the main dump and the creek. There were five of them, each about ten feet high. The piles no doubt belonged to a construction company, but as far as we dead-end kids were concerned, they were there strictly in answer to our instinct to fling a stone.

Yet the one real stone battle I recall happened not there but at the creek (another inexhaustible source of stones; it wasn't called Stony Creek for nothing). We divided ourselves into two platoons and took up positions on either side of the creek. We loaded up and fired away.

The creek at that point was hardly wider than an alleyway. Across the water Johnny Seeton was firing from behind a tree. I waited till he poked his head out. He was looking right at me. I fired. I was aiming to hit him in the eyebrow. This is not as malicious as it sounds, for we were only playing at war—we were pretending, and everybody knew you didn't get hurt pretending. Besides, Johnny Seeton was one of my two best friends. And double-besides, who ever actually hit what they were aiming at?

The stone hit him in the eyebrow.

He screamed. He wouldn't stop screaming. Blood streamed down his face. He galloped across the water, ignoring stepping stones, screamed up the creek bank, and screamed all the way home. As for me, pretend did not give way to horror instantly. For several seconds of fanciful confusion, as Johnny Seeton thrashed wildly past me, I felt surprised that our relationship as best friends did not seem to count in this matter, as if a stone thrown by me should hurt him less.

Neither Johnny nor his parents ever said anything to me about the incident. They didn't have to. The two-week patch on Johnny's eye punished me every day.

Spears were safer.

Go to the dead end, turn left, walk up the tracks past Red Hill and the other, smaller dump, climb the trackside bluff, and you were in the spear field—so named for the plants growing there. Strip one of them of its leaves, and you were left with a sturdy four-foot-high stalk straight as a pool cue. Pluck it from the ground, shake off the root dirt, and bring on the enemy.

As I passed through the grade-school years, war became less about machine-gun chatter and spectacular explosions and more about people.

I read about war, about the bodies of soldiers, even enemy soldiers, whose lifeless hands clutched photographs of loved ones back home.

I read of the torture of captive troops. I especially cringed over the fingernail torture, in which a pair of pliers pulled out the victim's fingernails, slowly, one by one. Such things happened to spies and to people who knew too many secrets. I resolved that if I was ever in a war, I would be a dumb nonspy.

But I could not resolve not to be a soldier. Every passing day, every February 1—the date of my birth—prodded me closer to the ominous cloud that hung over my future. It was called the draft, and it meant that when I (and all other boys deemed healthy enough) got out of high school or college, I would have to join the armed forces whether I wanted to or not.

As if to prepare me, my daydreams placed me in grim

wartime situations. I saw myself, apparently a failure at avoiding secrets, in the hands of enemy interrogators.

"Tell us," they growl.

"Never," I say firmly, for I am a good American soldier.

Then I feel the pliers grip the end of the nail on my right index finger, and cold sweat pours from me, and I feel the tug of the pliers and then the pain begins—and I sing. I sing like the Vienna Boys' Choir. I empty my head like a box of cornflakes. I tell them everything from our deepest military secrets to my shoe size.

And I anguish. Because, though I realize this is only a daydream, I am afraid that if such a thing ever really happens, I will play my part poorly. I am afraid that I will crack during torture. I am ashamed that I cannot measure up to a captive spy I once read about, whose lips were still sealed after losing all ten fingernails.

Sometimes in my fearful fantasies my captors by-passed torture and simply marched me out to the firing squad. But I never got shot. Even as six rifle sights met at my trembling heart—"Ready! Aim!"—I call out to the commanding officer, "Wait a minute!"

The commanding officer pauses.

"There's something you don't know. If you shoot me you'll never find out."

The officer calls off the guns. He expects me to divulge vital military secrets, but the information I offer is purely personal. I tell him something about his wife, his family back home, something he could never have known without me. He is overcome with gratitude. He dismisses the firing squad. And I have discovered something: Words can save me.

Despite all the attention I paid to warfare, I was never in a real fight. Around sixth grade this began to bother me. I saw other kids flailing and clubbing, tearing each other's shirts to shreds, trading bloody noses, and I said to myself, "Hey, why not me?" I began to feel deprived because my right hand had never known the feel of fist on chin. I felt a growing need to hit somebody.

But who? I could think of no one I wanted to hit. And apparently nobody wanted to hit me. Every day I walked to and from school unchallenged. I was a bur in no one's saddle. A likable bloke.

However, the prospect of going through life punchless was too strong to ignore. I looked around my classroom. Who was as small as I, or better yet, even smaller? Who was unlikely to hit me back? Who needed hitting?

There was only one answer: Joey Stackhouse.

Joey Stackhouse was skinny. Mash down his blond pompadour and he was maybe half an inch shorter than I. He had a narrow, foxy face. But his main feature was teeth. He was a walking warning against not brushing. When he smiled, you found yourself looking at all the colors in your crayon box. Plus his clothes were shabby.

For several days I hung close to Joey, alert for an offending remark or gesture. He remained obstinately harmless, as friendly as ever. It became clear that I myself would have to manufacture the momentum for the punch.

I worked myself into a snit. I convinced myself that anybody with teeth like that was asking for it. One day he walked home with me after school. We were on the 700 block of George Street, close to my house. I picked a fight with him, accused him of something, I don't remember what. Then I hit him. I balled my fist and swung, and when my knuckles landed—*thock*—against his chin bone, I was as surprised as when my stone hit Johnny Seeton.

As punches go, it was dainty, more tap than wallop, my intention being to match a punch's form, not force. I'm sure that, physically, he barely felt it. But a punch has a double impact, as I was about to learn, and only the first lands on the chin. Joey's eyes widened. He stood there staring at me with such wild astonishment that I knew at once he had not, not in a million years, been asking for it. He started to cry. He blurted out, "Why'd you do that?" and ran back down George Street.

If ever I had notions of becoming a warrior, they died that day as I turned the other way and walked home alone. It has been more than forty years since I hit Joey Stackhouse—the first and last person I ever punched—and it remains the only taste of war I ever needed.

Lash La Rue

Early on I learned, without anyone actually telling me, that in this world it is not enough just to *be*. You have to *be something*.

So around the age of five I decided to be a cowboy.

Cowboys rode three trails into my life: (1) The Garrick Movie Theater downtown, which showed Western double features on Saturday afternoons, (2) comic books, and (3) *Frontier Playhouse*.

Frontier Playhouse came on TV every weeknight at six, right after *Howdy Doody* and right in the middle of dinnertime. I was not allowed to eat in the living room, where the TV was, but I was allowed to move my chair to the doorway between the kitchen and dining room. I placed my dinner on the seat, knelt down, and watched the nightly cowboy movie while eating on my knees. It's a wonder I could see the platter-size screen at the far end of the house.

From TV and movies and comics I knew lots of cowboys: Roy Rogers, Gene Autry, Hopalong Cassidy, Lash La Rue, Red Ryder, Tom Mix, the Lone Ranger, Tex Ritter, Ranger Joe, Tim McCoy, Hoot Gibson. And horses: Trigger, Topper, Silver, Champion, Tony, Buttermilk.

When my friends and I played cowboys, almost everyone wanted to be Roy Rogers. With his fringed shirts and silky neckerchief and white hat and golden horse, how could you not want to be Roy? I was usually the first to call out, "I'll be Roy Rogers!"

But when I was alone and my secrets came peeping out from their hiding places, I knew there was a cowboy I wanted to be even more than Roy Rogers. I wanted to be Lash La Rue. From hat to boots, Lash La Rue dressed all in black. But that wasn't what made Lash La Rue special—it was the whip. He carried it coiled at his belt, and with it he did most everything the others did with their six-shooters. Was a bad guy reaching for his gun? Lash was quicker with his whip. A flick of the wrist, the whip uncoils—leather lightning!—darts ten, twenty, thirty feet across the dust to snatch the gun, barely clear of its holster, from the bad guy's hand. Is the bad guy running away? The whip catches him at the ankles, trips and hogties him, ready for the sheriff. The rawhide tongue could lick the spit from a horse's lips or kiss it on the ear.

Lash La Rue. I recognized him as "cool" before I ever knew the word.

I loved the West. The songs: "Home on the Range," "Tumbling Tumbleweeds," "Red River Valley." Cattle drives. Sarsaparilla. (The movies made sarsaparilla seem like liquid fire. Imagine my surprise, years later, when I drank my first glass—and discovered it was root beer.)

Stagecoach holdups. Box canyons. Harmonicas and campfires and coyotes howling in the night.

I had an armament Roy Rogers himself would have been proud to own: twin golden pistols in twin white leather holsters. My white leather gun belt had a dozen little leather loops to hold a dozen red wooden bullets. Of course, the bullets were just for show. The real ammo was caps, five rolls to a box. They could be bought at one of two grocery stores, Freilich's next door or Teufel's across the street.

I drew pictures of good guys and bad guys shooting it out. I considered myself an expert at drawing horses, but my favorite part I always saved for last: the orange, red, and yellow streaks that indicated gunfire crisscrossing the picture.

My early cowboy artwork.

I practiced my draw until it was as fast as Tim McCoy's. I twirled my golden guns on my fingers. I drank my Ovaltine from a Ranger Joe mug. I played the harmonica. I yodeled.

And then one day in third grade I went all the way. When I woke up, instead of getting dressed as usual, I put on my cowboy outfit: ten-gallon hat, studded shirt, jodhpurs, golden guns, boots and spurs. My mother must have thought, *Oh, no!* as she heard my spurs clanking toward the breakfast table. I drew plenty of stares on my three-block walk to school.

Such was the class facing our teacher, Miss Davis, that morning: twenty-five pupils and one cowboy. She probably checked her calendar to see if this was Halloween. I remember her looking down at me in the first row, smiling gently, and saying, "Jerry, would you like to do something for us?" Apparently I did, for I stood, faced the class, and serenaded them with "I Got Spurs That Jingle Jangle Jingle." And I shook my boots.

A couple of summers later I had a chance to really live the cowboy life. I had gotten a pup tent for Christmas. Now I could camp out, pretend I was on a cattle drive, pretend our backyard was a tumbleweed range somewhere in Texas or Wyoming.

I invited my other best friend, Roger Adelman, to join me. We laid out our blankets in the tent. We talked and played card games, and as the sun went down we turned on a battery-powered lantern and played some more. Eventually it was time to go to bed. We crawled under our covers and turned off the lantern.

An hour later I was still awake. I had never known it got so dark on the range. And so quiet. No cows mooing, no coyotes calling, only Roger's breathing. And the ground—even with a blanket it was so hard. How did cattle stand it? In vain I kept trying to sleep. I felt immense and bristling, the only soul awake on the planet. I longed for a night-light.

When I couldn't stand it any longer, I shook Roger awake. Five minutes later he was trudging homeward while I climbed into my bed, in my bedroom. Alas, I was not at home on the range after all. I was strictly a living-room cowboy.

Ashes in the Grass

Two years after wearing my cowboy getup to school, I donned an outfit of a different sort. It was a Saturday morning in September, and I was getting ready for my first organized athletic event: a grade-school football league game. First I pulled shoulder pads over my undershirt; then I put on my number 15 blue and white football shirt; then my football pants with knee pads; then my sneakers; then my football helmet. Looking in the mirror, I could hardly find myself in all that armor.

I was a nervous fifth grader. Most of the players would be sixth graders, so I did not protest when my mother offered to go with me. We walked down George to the dead end and along the dirt path to the park. The field was swarming with kids from the six public grade schools in town, and none of them looked like me. No helmets, no shoulder pads—just T-shirts and jeans (which we called dungarees). The only thing we had in common was sneakers.

What had I expected? I had known this was two-hand touch football.

I was mortified. I dared not approach my team, Hartranft Elementary. My mother and I stood at a distance, watching the game in awkward silence. I prayed no one would recognize me.

Officially, then, my athletic career began a week later, when I arrived dressed like everybody else, and without a mother in tow.

My cowboy boots, spurs still attached, grew dusty on the floor of my bedroom closet. The twin white holsters and golden guns hung over one of the maple posts at the foot of my bed. As the years went by, the red toy bullets disappeared one by one, until only empty ammo loops were left.

I had given up cowboys for quarterbacks, horses for stitched horsehide. No longer were my seasons summer, fall, winter, and spring but baseball, football, and basketball. I was a sports nut.

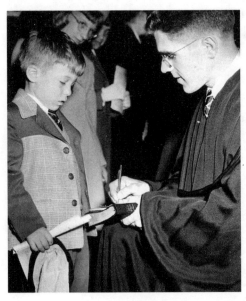

Sports had taken their hold on me, even at age 6. I'm getting the autograph of Gil Dodds, a mile-run champion (and minister).

Perhaps it was inevitable. Not long after I belted my last ball over the landlady's fence on Marshall Street, my father had begun taking me to Norristown High School games, basketball at first, then football and track and field. He was a ticket collector for football games, scorekeeper for basketball, and would hold those jobs for over fifty years. The world of sports had simply been waiting for me to grow into it.

We took our sports seriously, my friends and I, getting up games to fill every spare moment. Lunchtime at school, for example. We had an hour and a half, as I recall, since Hartranft had no cafeteria and all students went home to eat. I ran the three blocks to my house, wolfed down my lunch, and ran back, leaving me with an hour and fifteen minutes to play basketball on the playground. It's a wonder the teacher didn't pass out deodorant when afternoon lessons began.

We played wherever we could: alleys, streets, playgrounds, the park, even living rooms. But there was one special place. My old friend Roger Adelman, in a letter to me, describes it perfectly:

"This field was unique. We played baseball there, but it really wasn't set up for baseball. There wasn't a right field, since what would have been right field was occupied by the stand of spear weeds which, for some mystic reason, no one would (or could) cut down (although it was burned down several times by Bill Zollers, the neighborhood firebug). So all players had to bat right-handed—or promise not to pull the ball to right field. The outfield—left and center—was full of weeds and rough spots but was playable. The infield was in good shape because Johnny Rizzuto and I mowed the grass regularly. We also marked the foul lines with white ashes from the coal-burning furnaces in our houses.

"Left field was a special place. The boundary of deep left field was the dump. If you hit one into the dump in the air, you got a home run. If the ball took one bounce into the dump, you got a double. If it rolled in, you got a single. Only qualified players were assigned to left field: fast enough to stop those bouncers and rollers from going into the dump, brave enough to run right up to the edge of the dump and snag a liner headed into it (I have a memory of Pickles Noblett taking a header into the dump after a valiant try to stop a home run), and daring enough to go down into the dump to dig out a ball that ended up there. The dump had its own mystique—not to mention rats—and I am sure that, to this day, there are still a few hardballs there."

I envied my playmates their nicknames. Besides Pickles Noblett, there were Boogie Batson, Yock Doyle, Booper O'Hara, and Buffalo Morris. My own nickname was Spit—their choice, not mine.

For my money, the best player of all was Jerry Fox. He was several years older than I, and a dead-end legend. He was not very fast, but he did not have to be, for he was magically elusive. This talent came most prominently into play in street football. Sometimes he would just stand there, the ball cradled in his arm, one foot on the bumper of a parked car, daring us to tag him. We reached for his arm—it was gone; for his stomach—gone. Each body part was under separate control, free to move in all directions. It was like trying to tag an eel. If Jerry Fox were a letter of the alphabet, he would have been an S. He was untouchable. His nickname said it all: "The Pro."

Summers gave us time to gorge on sports. On a typical summer day I dropped my baseball glove into the chrome-plated basket of my bicycle and pedaled out the dirt path to the Little League field at the park. Other guys came from other directions. The rest of the day went like this: Play baseball until lunch, pedal home to eat, pedal back to the park (this time with basketball in bike basket), play basketball at park court until dinner, pedal home to eat, return for more basketball until dark.

Next day: Do it again.

I'm in the back row (with a cap), a finalist in a foul-shooting contest in the park (age 12, 1953). On my right is Dennis Magee, whose last name I gave to a character called Maniac.

Never the Monkey

In a green metal box in a bedroom closet, tucked into a fuzzy gray cotton pouch, lies the most cherished memento of my grade-school days. It is a gold-plated medal no bigger than a postage stamp. Inscribed on the back are the words "50-YARD DASH—CHAMPION."

The medal came from the only official race I ever participated in. There were many unofficial ones...

"Race you to the store!"

"Last one in's a monkey!"

"Ready...Set...Go!"

Like kids the world over, we raced to determine the fastest. In the early 1950s on the 800 block of George Street in the West End of Norristown, Pennsylvania, that was me. I was usually the winner, and never the monkey.

I reached my peak at the age of twelve. That summer I led the Norristown Little League in stolen bases. In an all-star playoff game I did something practically unheard of: I was safe at first base on a ground ball to the pitcher.

Some days I pulled my sneaker laces extra tight and went down to the railroad tracks. The cinders there had the feel of a running track. I measured off fifty or a hundred yards and sprinted the distance, timing myself with my father's stopwatch. Sometimes, heading back to the starting line, I tried to see how fast I could run on the railroad ties. Sometimes I ran on the rail.

It was during that year that I won my medal. I represented Hartranft in the fifty-yard dash at the annual track-and-field meet for the Norristown grade schools. The meet was held at Roosevelt Field, where the high school track and football teams played.

Favored to win the race was Laverne Dixon of Gotwals Elementary. "Froggy," as he was known to everyone but his teachers, had won the fifty-yard dash the year before as a mere fifth grader. Surely he would win again. My goal was to place second.

When the starter barked, "Ready!" I got into position: one knee and ten fingertips on the cinder track. I knew what to do from the many meets I had attended with my father. I glanced to my left and right and saw nothing but shins—everyone else was standing. I could not have known it then, but the race was already mine.

I was off with the gun. My memory of those fifty yards has nothing to do with sprinting but rather with two sensations. The first was surprise that I could not see any other runners. This led to a startling conclusion: *I must be ahead!* Which led to the second sensation: an anxious expectation, a waiting to be overtaken.

I never was. I won.

Froggy Dixon didn't even come in second. That went to Billy Steinberg, a stranger then, who would become my best friend in junior high school. He would also grow to be faster than I, as would many of my schoolmates. But that was yet to come. For the moment, as I slowed down and trotted into a sun the color and dazzle of the medal I was about to receive, I knew only the wonder of seven astounding seconds when no one was ahead of me.

The fifty-yard-dash champion for Hartranft Elementary (age 12, 1953).

Shortstop

From ages eleven to sixteen, if someone asked me what I wanted to be when I grew up, I gave one of two answers: "A baseball player" or "A shortstop."

Major league baseball—that was the life for me. And I wanted to live it only as a shortstop. When I trotted onto a diamond, I instinctively headed for the dusty plain between second and third. I never wanted to play any other position. When we got up sandlot games, no one else occupied shortstop. They knew it was mine.

I was eleven when I first played Little League baseball. To give as many kids as possible a chance to participate, the Little League declared that some of us would share uniforms with others. And so the season was exactly half over when I pedaled my bike up to Albert Pascavage's house to pick up his uniform: green socks, green cap, gray woolen shirt, and pants with green trim. I packed my precious cargo into my bike basket and drove it carefully home. I was a member of the Green Sox.

During one game in that half season I played second base—apparently no one told the manager I was going to be a major league shortstop. Our opponent was the Red Sox. The batter hit a ground ball right at me. I crouched, feet spread, glove ready, as I had been taught in the *Times Herald* baseball school. I could hear the ball crunching along the sandy ground. It hit my glove—but not the pocket. Instead it glanced off the fat leather thumb and rolled on behind me.

Shortshop, Green Sox
(age 12, 1953).

My first error!

I was heartbroken. I stomped my foot. I pounded my fist into the stupid glove.

When the inning was over and I slunk to the Green Sox bench, the manager was waiting for me. I thought he was going to console me. I thought he would say, "Tough luck, Jerry. Nice try," and then tousle my hair.

That's not what happened.

What he really did was glare angrily at me, and what he really said was, "Don't you ever do that again." He pointed out that while I was standing there pounding my glove, two Red Sox runs had scored. "Next time you miss the ball, you turn around and chase it down. You don't just stand there feeling sorry for yourself. Understand?"

I nodded. And I never forgot.

Like most of the kids in my class, I got better at sports simply by growing older. I went from being one of the worst players in Little League as an eleven-year-old to making the all-star team as a twelve-year-old. The following year I was the only seventh grader to start on the Stewart Junior High School team—at shortstop, of course. It mattered little that I was not very good at hitting a curve ball, since most pitchers threw only fastballs.

During the summer of junior high school I played in a baseball league called Connie Mack Knee-Hi, for thirteen- to fifteen-year-olds. Before each game, one team would line up along the first-base line, the other team along third base. The umpire stood on the pitcher's mound, took off his cap, and read aloud the Sportsmanship Pledge, pausing after each line so the rest of us could repeat it in chorus. We pledged ourselves to be loyal to, among other things, "clean living and clean speech." In the final line we promised to be "a generous victor and a gracious loser."

In the Knee-Hi summer of 1955, I had little chance to be a gracious loser. My team, Norristown Brick Company, swept through the local league undefeated, winning our games by an average score of 12–1. One score was 24–0. One team simply refused to show up. Our pitchers threw four no-hitters, three by Lee Holmes. Opposing batters could no more hit Bill Bryzgornia's fastball than spell his name. We were a powerhouse.

We beat Conshohocken two out of three to gain the state playoffs. Three wins there put us into the title game. On a bright Saturday afternoon at War Memorial Field in Doylestown, Norristown Brick Company defeated Ellwood City, 4–2, to become Connie Mack Knee-Hi champions of Pennsylvania.

In the awards ceremony after the game, we were given jackets saying STATE CHAMPIONS. Ellwood City players got trophies. A jacket would eventually wear out and be thrown away, leaving me with nothing to show for our great triumph. But a trophy was immune to frayed cuffs and moth holes. A trophy would be forever. I watched as each Ellwood City player walked up for his trophy and half-wished I had been on the losing side.

A week later, during a banquet at the Valley Forge Hotel in downtown Norristown, to my relief, we were each given a magnificent trophy.

Two buddies (Anthony Greco and Bob Hopple) and me (left), heading off to dance at Grace Lutheran Church, 1955. I'm wearing my Knee-Hi State Champions jacket.

Chucking dust on a four-base diamond was only part of the baseball life. There was the long list of major league batting averages to pore over each Sunday in *The Philadelphia Inquirer*. There was the baseball encyclopedia, my first history book, to study. Long before I knew the difference between Yorktown and Gettysburg, I knew Ty Cobb's lifetime batting average (.367) and Cy Young's total career pitching victories (511).

There were cards to flip. We bought Fleer's bubblegum just to get the baseball cards, and then we dueled. Slip one corner of the card between forefinger and middle finger and flip outward, Frisbee-like, toward a wall. The kid whose card lands closest to the wall picks up the other kid's card. The stacks of cards I won this way would be worth a fortune today if I had kept them.

There were baseballs to tape. Seldom in our sandlot games did we have a ball with a real stitched horsehide cover still on it. Most often the balls were covered in black utility tape. A white ball was a real treat. It meant that someone had sneaked into the medicine chest at home and used up half a roll of first-aid tape.

There were hours to spend bouncing tennis balls off neighbors' brick walls, any wall but that of the mysterious barber across the street. For hours each week I scooped up the rebounding grounders, practicing to be a great shortstop. Considering the thumping I gave those houses, it's a wonder I was never chased off. Maybe the people behind the walls understood that in my mind I was not really standing on George Street but in the brown dust of Connie Mack Stadium, out at shortstop, fielding hot shots off the bat of Willie Mays.

And there was the glove. My glove bore the signature of Marty Marion, slick-fielding shortstop of the St. Louis Cardinals.

Each year at the end of summer vacation, I rubbed my glove with olive oil from the kitchen cabinet. Then I pressed a baseball deep into the pocket of the glove, curled the leather fingers about the ball, and squeezed the whole thing into a shoebox. Standing on a chair, I set the box high on a closet shelf. Baseball season was officially over.

For the next six months we would hibernate, shortstop and glove, dreaming of the Chiclets-white bases at Connie Mack Stadium, feeling in the palm the hard, round punch of a grounder well caught.

Good Boy

Like cowboys and then sports, grade school was a constant presence in my life, though not an especially interesting one. It seems to me that most interesting stories about grade school are told by kids who got in trouble. I never got in trouble. I was, as they say, a Good Boy.

But what is a Good Boy? From the world's point of view, it is a boy who appears to be good. The key word here is *appears*. For I believe that beneath the appearance of most Good Boys is a Bad Boy waiting to break out. Oh, I don't mean bad in the sense of committing crimes or hurting people. I mean bad in the sense of, say, leaving a wad of chewing gum on the teacher's chair. Or washing the blackboard with spit. Or jumping up from your seat in the middle of silent reading, standing on top of your desk, raising your fists to the ceiling, and roaring with all your might, "Phooey!"

That kind of bad.

Let me tell you something about the Good Boy: Just because he doesn't get into trouble doesn't mean he doesn't appreciate trouble. I know I did. I understood what a boring world this would be without the trouble-makers. And so I was a big fan of Leonard Wilfong, who was always getting into trouble. I didn't exactly stand up and applaud when Leonard did something bad, but I gave him my undivided attention, and if I thought I could get away with it, I laughed.

To the Bad Boy, that's the reward: laughter. It's the payoff of a deal that is never spoken of, never written down, yet is understood perfectly by the kids in class. It's as if back on the first day of first grade, all the boys had a secret meeting and one of them was voted to be Bad Boy. He—in our case, Leonard Wilfong—accepted the job, along with the punishments that would surely fall to him, with the understanding that the rest of us would (1) pay attention and (2) laugh.

And the meeting broke up and Leonard Wilfong went forth and did outrageous things, and we laughed. Neither Leonard nor the rest of us understood this, but in a sense we were laughing at ourselves, for Leonard Wilfong was the embodiment of the Bad Boy in all of us. Leonard did what we did not have the nerve to do. Leonard did not have the same fears we had. He feared spelling tests and long division and report cards. He did not fear trouble. He did not fear rules. And though we did not envy Leonard Wilfong his punishments or his bad grades, we absolutely envied him his recklessness. We respected him as the representative of that which was secret in ourselves. We saluted him with our attention and our laughter.

When the teacher wasn't looking.

At age 6 (1947):
a Good Boy in the making.

So if you want an interesting Hartranft Elementary School autobiography from those days, go see Leonard Wilfong. As for me, I have already mentioned the fifty-yard dash and my spur-song serenade. Only four other interesting things happened to me in grade school:

1. Second grade. This did not happen directly to me but to a calf. Mrs. Care, our teacher, lived on a farm. One spring day she took the whole class there for a visit. While jumping into the hay in the barn, Roger Adelman landed on a pitchfork and had to go to the

hospital. Ordinarily, that would have been the high-light of the day, but out in the barnyard something even more interesting was happening.

A mother cow and her calf were hanging around just inside the fence, close enough for some of us to reach out and touch. Then, as we watched in amazement, the mother—who, you must understand, was a lot taller than her offspring—backed up to the calf and pooped on its head. Until Mrs. Care finally wiped it off, the plop just stayed there, like a brown beret. Was it my imagination, or did the calf really have an expression on its face, as if to say, "Hey, Ma—wha'd I do?"

2. Second grade. We had a student teacher from West Chester University. Though she was careful not to give me preferential treatment, I remember feeling proud and special. Why? She was my cousin, Dolly.

3. Third grade. I got sick with a kidney ailment. I was in the hospital for ten days and out of school for two months. My mother tells me that in the hospital I put on a brave front. She says that whenever she and my father visited me, I chatted away happily with them. Then, the second they left the room, I started to cry. My mother found this out from the nurses. Personally, I don't remember. My mother also says they gave me so many needles in the hospital that my rear end looked like a pincushion. I don't remember that either. As a reward for all the needles each night, a smiling nurse in a candy-striped uniform brought me a milkshake. That I remember.

4. Sixth grade. In early spring of that year the two sixth grades were brought together for a series of spelling bees. Since I won more of them than anyone else, I was declared spelling champion of Hartranft Elementary. That honor earned me the chance to compete in the Montgomery County spelling bee, the winner of which would go to Washington, D.C., for the national bee.

As a sixth grader among contestants ranging up to eighth grade, I was one of the youngest on the stage at Norristown High School that night in April 1953. I don't think it ever occurred to me to try to win. My goal was to survive until at least the fourth round, since I had been told that no one from Hartranft had ever gotten that far.

Ninety-six school champions sat in long curved rows of folding chairs. Hanging on a string from everyone's neck was a square of white cardboard with a large black number. Mine was thirteen. Before the competition began, the master of ceremonies announced to the auditorium that we were honored to have last year's county champion with us—Nancy Ann Hammerschmidt of North Wales. He then turned from the audience to the stage and asked Nancy Ann to stand and take a bow, and who should stand up but number twelve, the pretty blond older girl sitting next to me.

The competition got under way. The opening words were easy, and most of us made it through the first two rounds. Then we started dropping like flies. When somebody misspelled a word—*bong!*—the judge hammered a big brassy bell and the kid was gone. No arguing, no whining—wham, bam, next, please.

Meanwhile back in the seats Nancy Ann Hammerschmidt and I were chatting away. Actually, Nancy Ann did most of the chatting. I mostly nodded and smiled in wonder that the famous, glamorous fourteen-year-old champion would be so familiar with the likes of me. When we returned to our seats after nailing our third-round words, Nancy Ann took out her wallet and showed me a picture of her boyfriend.

When in the fourth round Nancy Ann spelled "ecstasy" with a second *c* instead of an *s*, I was sure no bong would dare banish her from the stage. But it did, and off she marched. And so did I a few seconds later, having spelled lacquer "l-a-c-q-u-o-r." Considering how smitten I was with Nancy Ann, I'm surprised I even bothered to take my last turn at the mike before following her off the stage. She must have made a quick exit, though, for she was not among the growing crowd of misspellers behind the curtain, nor did I ever see her again. I guess neither Nancy Ann Hammerschmidt nor the spelling bee bonger cared that I was a Good Boy.

George Street

Baseball is still baseball, and school is school, but George Street is no more. Oh, sure, if you travel to Norristown today and go west on Elm, you'll come to a street sign that says GEORGE. Don't believe it.

A street sign does not make a street. A time makes a street, and a people of that time. The sign will tell you nothing, nor will the people who live there today. Go ahead, ask them. Ask them whose front steps they better not sit on. Challenge them to a game of chew-the-peg. (Flip penknife from shoulder. If it doesn't stick in ground, pull out planted peg with teeth.) Or just stand there on the sidewalk outside 802 and close your eyes and listen for the avalanche of coal. Listen for days. You won't hear it. George Street is as gone as 1950.

I heard it. I heard it on coal day. Nearly every house on the block had a coal-burning furnace. In a front corner of the cellar, beneath the living room, was a plank-walled bin. It held a ton of coal. When the coal truck came, my job was to run to the cellar and open the window above the bin. The truck turned sideways in the street and backed up to the curb. From under the truck bed the coal man pulled the chute, which looked like a sliding board, and fed it through the open cellar window and into our bin. He lifted the hatch and the coal started coming, avalanching down the chute with such a racket that I had to clamp my hands over my ears. I had to tie a hanky around my nose, too, because of the coal dust that made a black, choking blizzard. I would crouch down under the washtub, fold my arms about my head, and wait out the bombardment from the enemy battleship and its sixteen-inch guns. Or if I wasn't pretending that day, I simply ran outside.

Softer sounds came from the Victrola. The Victrola was an early phonograph, a record player. Ours was portable, like a small boxy suitcase. Whenever I lifted the hinged cover I was treated to a special scent, a sweet dustiness that suggested slumbering songs, music's bunkhouse. To get the thing to work I had to crank it, like an old Model T Ford. The crank was a stepped metal rod with a black wooden egg-shaped handle. I placed a record on the turntable, then inserted the rod into a hole in the side of the player and cranked away. I flipped a switch, and the record began to spin. Breathlessly I lowered the needle to the smooth black edge of the disc. The needle slipped into the first groove, and "Too-ra-loo-ra-loo-ral"…Bing Crosby was crooning.

The main sound machine, of course, was the radio. Unlike many people my age, I cannot give a long list of the programs I listened to. What I do recall are three motifs: the Lone Ranger theme song, otherwise known as the *William Tell* Overture, footsteps walking down hallways, and doors creaking open. Beyond that I simply remember listening. And picturing.

For radio was a partnership. The radio furnished the sounds, and the listener supplied the pictures. TV and movie screens have shaded us from the evocative power of sound. Our eyes enslave us. "Seeing is believing." In contrast to TV, which asks us merely to turn it on and become a passive dartboard, radio asked us to meet it halfway, to co-create the moment. The resulting pictures in our heads had a depth of reality possible only when the camera is the person.

Despite my love of radio, I soon gave in to the lure of television.

The first TV set in my corner of the West End belonged to the Beswicks up on Kohn Street, a block west of George. Butchie Beswick's popularity zoomed. Day after day a mob of kids sat on the Beswick living room rug after school, goggle-eyed and gaping like so many guppies at *Willie the Worm* on the ten-inch black and white screen. Mrs. Beswick must have been a saint. Over time the mob diminished, one cross-legged floor-sitter at a time, as new families acquired television sets.

Our family got one in 1950—a twelve-inch Magnavox—when I was in third grade and home with my kidney illness. Doctor's orders confined me to my bed, but I made such a fuss that I was finally allowed to be carried downstairs and plopped in a chair to watch TV for one hour, not a minute more.

Television and I grew up together; meanwhile movies seduced me with Technicolor and 3-D and CinemaScope. By the time I got my driver's license, the only radio in my life was in the family car.

On July 20, 1969, *Apollo 11* astronauts rode the lunar module *Eagle* to the surface of the moon. Like much of the world, I was in front of a TV set watching fuzzy images of the event: *Eagle* launching from the mother spacecraft, *Eagle* orbiting the moon, *Eagle* coming in lower, lower, skimming lunar hills and craters, seeking a spot to land. I strained my eyes watching, and still I wasn't seeing, not well enough...*the pictures in my head*. I rushed outside to my car, I turned on the radio, and that's where I experienced the landing on the moon. I had rediscovered what I knew back on George Street: *listening* is believing.

And so is remembering, remembering George Street:

Cooling myself with a Popsicle stick fan...playing chew-the-peg..."smoking" punk...digging up the grass between the front-walk bricks (my most hated chore after taking out the garbage)...Mr. Freilich's long-handled grocery grippers, allowing him to reach to the highest shelf and pull down a box of cereal...purple ribbons on a door, meaning someone had died in that house...pouring Morton salt on the fat summer slugs that left silver trails across the bricks…Quaker Oats…bathtub-shaped Hudson cars…the bug truck spraying everything, including me, with mosquito poison…cat's-eye marbles in the dirt…Bono's fruit and vegetable bus…on a winter morning, a slow white plug of cream pushing up the cap of the milk bottle on our front step…the bread man…the rag man…the rag man's horse, itself slow and drooping as a sack of rags, as if every *clop* upon the street would be its last…the rag man's mournful warbling bleat: "Raaaaaaags!"…the sad, slow syncopation passing George, heading for Kohn, Noble, Buttonwood, westward…"Raaaaaaags!" *clop-clop*, "Raaaaaags!" *clop-clop*.…

Mrs. Seeton's
Whistle

More than a Victrola crank handle or the blizzard of coal dust, George Street was its people. It is something I understand better now than I did then. I can find old marbles and baseball cards in antique shops and rummage sales. I wish I could find the people there, too. I have so much to ask them.

I have questions for the Freilich family, who operated the grocery store next to us, on the corner of George and Elm. The Freilichs were, I believe, the only Jews on the block, and to live next to them was on some days like living next to another country.

Nothing but a thin wire fence separated our backyards. On most days the Freilichs' backyard was just like ours: trash barrel and garbage can, a flower bed or two, a clothesline, a walkway down the middle to the back gate. But on certain Sundays in summer there suddenly appeared in the Freilichs' backyard people such as I had never seen. The men especially were distinctive, for they dressed all in black and wore black hats and long shaggy beards. Afraid to stare openly at them, I ran upstairs to my bedroom window and stared until my eyeballs ached.

Next day on the way to school I usually saw Nancy Freilich. Nancy was the older of two sisters. She was thin and had long red hair and walked pigeon-toed in her black and white saddle shoes. She was very bright and friendly, and she would have made a terrific friend, but she was a year older and a grade ahead of me, and fifth-grade boys did not mix much with sixth-grade girls, even if they were next-door neighbors. So I did not ask Nancy Freilich about the black-suited shaggy-bearded people in her backyard the day before. And instead of becoming terrific friends, we simply smiled and waved and said hi to each other.

Nancy's older brother Morton was seldom seen on George Street. Unlike most of us, who seemed to have sprouted like grass from the cracks between the side-walk bricks, Morton Freilich occupied a higher plane. He was brilliant. He became a doctor. He made people well. But he could not make himself well. Morton had always had a bad case of asthma. Sometimes it was hard for him to breathe.

So he moved himself and his medical practice to Arizona. I pictured him arriving in that faraway state, smiling to see the palm trees and desert sands and adobe-style houses. I pictured him looking up at the cloudless sky and throwing out his arms and going "Ahhh!" and for the first time in his life taking a long, deep clean breath of air. And maybe he did, but within several years the asthma had tracked him down and killed him, Morton Freilich in Arizona, only in his thirties, brilliant, the grocer's son.

Nancy's little sister was Sharon. From the day she was born, some kids on the street, I don't remember who, seemed to have it in for her. They were always saying unkind things about her. I remember thinking, Why? What did she do? I could understand people getting mad at someone who was always bugging them, but Sharon Freilich had just been *born*. She hadn't had time to bug anyone. I wondered if there was a secret that I had missed.

I began to study little Sharon Freilich as she toddled about the grocery store and the brick sidewalk outside. I tried to detect what it was in her that offended others. I saw her sitting one day on the front step of the store. Her knees were smudged, and I thought, Is *that* it? Dirty knees?

She wasn't just sitting there, she was crying. I looked around to see if someone had said something mean to her, but the block was deserted, and I did not understand that an ugly word, once spoken, once heard, remains in the ear forever. Seeing her cry, alone and dirty-kneed on the front step, as alone as I've ever seen anybody in my life, I tried not to feel bad, because I knew so many others who would not have felt bad, who would have laughed. But I failed.

On the other side of us, at 804, lived the Corys. Virginia, the younger of two sisters, was a year behind me in school. We played together at first, then less and less as we got older.

My enduring memory of Virginia Cory centers on a particular Fourth of July at Elmwood Park. She was about fourteen years old and had entered herself in the annual talent show at the band shell. When she was announced, she walked onstage and sang a romantic ballad called "Too Young":

> "They try to tell us we're too young
> Too young to really be in love…"

Her normally pale cheeks were red as apples as she sang earnestly—and off-key—into the microphone:

> "They say that love's a word,
> A word we've only heard
> And can't begin to know the meaning of…"

Out in the audience I felt uncomfortable, even embarrassed. I wondered if the people sitting around me knew that Virginia Cory was my next-door neighbor. Didn't she know she was off-key? What ever made her think she could win a talent contest? Why doesn't she stop? I wondered. But she went on singing and singing into the microphone until the very last note:

> "And then someday they may recall
> We were not too young at all."

She took a bow and left the stage. People politely clapped. Naturally she did not win, not even the lowest of honorable mentions. But that was it. What had registered as a catastrophe with me left the rest of the world unfazed. They did not cancel the pet show or the fireworks that night, and Virginia herself, to my knowledge, did not spend a single minute under her bed hiding in shame.

If I met her today, I would like to tell her that when I think of my favorite songs of those days, I think of Les Paul and Mary Ford singing "Tennessee Waltz" and the Chordettes singing "Mr. Sandman" and Virginia Cory singing "Too Young." I would tell her that I play it often in the jukebox of my memory. I would ask her to sing it again, and this time to honor her moxie, I would clap long and loud.

Spider Sukoloski lived next to the Corys, at 806. Spider's given name was Eugene, but no one (except maybe his mother) called him that. Spider's hair was long and dark blond and combed back and cemented with Brylcreem. Spider wore his collar up and his sleeves rolled. His pants were pegged so tight at his ankles that they must have threatened the circulation in his feet. On the 800 block of George Street, in the Age of the Cool Cat, in the days of ducktail haircuts and pink shirts and suede shoes, Spider Sukoloski was the coolest cat of all.

If I could go back, I would ask Spider if I could touch his hair. I would ask if he would like to trade nicknames, for who would not rather be called Spider than Spit?

The Freilichs did not run the only grocery store on the block. Across the street from Spider's house was Teufel's. Teufel's was about as small as a store could get, no bigger than a row house living room. In fact, it *was* a row house living room before it was converted to a grocery store.

My family did most of its shopping at Freilich's. I bought only two products at Teufel's: candy and Popsicles.

There were two Teufels. One was a stout black-haired woman who managed the store. The other was assumed to be the manager's mother, or grandmother, or great-grandmother, for she was the oldest-looking person any of us had ever seen. We guessed her age at anywhere from ninety to one hundred fifty. She was thinner than a taffy stick. Her scalp looked as if it had been planted with dandelion fuzzballs. I found myself speaking lightly to her for fear that a loud word might blow her over.

No doubt her skin had once been as solidly pink as mine, but much of its pigment had drained away so that she now seemed skinned in waxed paper. Wherever she was left uncovered, you could follow the humped blue tributaries of her circulation. I imagined that her doctor, examining her, could peer, like a tourist on a glass-bottomed boat, right through to her heart and other organs.

The older Miss Teufel was seldom seen. She lived behind a doorway curtain that separated the store from the living quarters. But on occasion when the younger Miss Teufel was away, the older one came out to wait on customers. She sorely tested a kid's patience: It could take forever just to buy a Mounds bar. But I for one did not mind, for watching the old Miss Teufel behind the counter was a fascinating experience. As I stared at the thin, blue-corded hand that passed me the Mounds bar, I wondered, would that be my hand in eighty years? My common sense said yes, but I couldn't quite believe it. The bell above the green-framed screen door tinkled as I happily rejoined the sunshine and the hard reassuring warmth of the sidewalk bricks. Inside, the old woman disappeared behind the curtain.

Henry Doerner lived in the next-to-the-last house on the block—the end of the dead end. Henry was a burly, rambunctious kid. He got into his share of trouble. He didn't take any guff. He was active, feisty, you might even say pushy. When there were games to be played, he was there, in the middle. When there were sides to be chosen, he was there, up front, staring down the chooser.

Maybe that's why Henry Doerner was seldom chosen last. On the other hand, he was never chosen first, for Henry had disabilities. He had been born with one leg too short and an incomplete hand. The short leg required him to wear a special shoe, the sole of which was a leather platform about six inches thick. It leveled off both feet to the ground and made walking, if not graceful, at least possible. The hand was a hand in name only. The wrist tapered to one finger with, as I recall, an extra finger or thumb projecting from where the palm should have been.

And here is the thing: In my memory Henry Doerner is always running. The good leg moves normally, like mine, while the other swings straight outward from the hip, more like an oar than a leg. But he doesn't seem to know, he doesn't seem to care. He just runs. And the rocking chair on his porch is empty, and nobody says, "You can't do that."

The other day I found Henry in one of my high school yearbooks. It's the group picture of Homeroom 49. He stands in the second row, and you can't see the hand or the foot. But you can see the face, and it's pure Henry Doerner: eyes that pierce the camera as if it's the chooser in a pickup game of street football, and a smirk that says, "Go ahead, I dare you not to pick me."

If I could go back and if I could be chooser, I would pick Henry Doerner first.

Among the dead-end population, I count one soul who had no address on George Street. As far as I knew, he had no address anywhere, though he was at home everywhere. He was the hokey-pokey man.

In the warmer months of the year the hokey-pokey

man roamed the streets of town, pushing before him a white wooden cart. The bed of the cart was occupied by a block of ice covered with a dishtowel. Flanking the ice were two rows of bottles containing flavored liquids in a variety of colors that always reminded me of a barbershop shelf.

The hokey-pokey man knew kids. He knew our ways better than we did. As we got older and our routes about town changed, he was always there, ahead of us, waiting: at the dead-end barrier, outside the school, clattering along a random street. Coming upon him, we crowded around the cart.

He went into action. He flipped off the dishtowel, grabbed the ice shaver, clacked it like a castanet, and scraped ice until the scoop was full. He deposited a white snowball into a paper cone and awaited the first order.

"Lime!"

He snatched the lime bottle, shook it, and—presto—bright green snowball.

"Grape!"

"Orange!"

"Lemon!"

I waited till last, thinking about the flavors. I always decided on root beer.

We took off then, relishing the winter on our tongues, giving no thought to the hokey-pokey man. For he was not someone to think about. He was simply there. Where we were.

And then, in time, he wasn't. Though still, on a summer's day, when heat waves dance above the street, I sometimes imagine I see him in the distance, waiting where I have yet to arrive.

And then there were the Seetons. Officially, the Seetons did not live on George Street. The lived on Elm, with their property running perpendicular to the backyards of the Freilichs, the Spinellis, the Corys, and the Sukoloskis.

During my grade-school years, as I have mentioned, I considered Johnny Seeton one of my two best friends, the other being Roger Adelman.

As the years go by, there is something I remember about the Seetons even more than Johnny. It is his mother's whistle. With it she called in however many of her six children were away from the house at dinnertime. She would come out the kitchen door, stand by the fence, and deliver it once, maybe several times. It was not loud. Not nearly as loud as a hot Chevy revving or a kid yapping or a parent scolding. It was a simple two-note whistle. And yet her kids, all of us kids, no matter where we were—Kohn Street, the tracks, Red Hill—we always seemed to hear it.

Dinnertime upon dinnertime, year after year, Mrs. Seeton's whistle reeled in her kids. Sometimes the rest of us came running, too, to our own homes, for a mother's call somehow touches us all. Those two not-very-loud notes echo down to millennium's end and powerfully recall to me a time and a place. A fantasy I have goes like this: Mrs. Seeton returns to her house on Elm Street. The nineties neighborhood kids in bubble-soled sneakers stare at the gray, slow-moving woman whom they do not know. She goes to the backyard, to the old spot by the fence, and she whistles. It's the old two-noter, sounds exactly the way it did in 1955. She doesn't need to whistle again—one is all it takes, because we're already on our way. The nineties kids gape in amazement as we return from our homes and cemeteries around the world—Henry Doerner and Spider Sukoloski and Virginia Cory and Jerry Fox and the Teufels and even little Sharon Freilich, her knees still dirty but not crying anymore—across the Schuylkill River and along the tracks and the path and down the streets and nameless alleyways, all of us one more time heading home on Mrs. Seeton's whistle.

Night

chh

It always began as a solitary chuffing, a sudden explosive snort as if a night beast rising in the distance, down in Conshohocken maybe, had cleared its snout. So faint and faraway was it, so alien, that I usually persuaded myself that it wasn't there. But sooner or later, again, it was.

chh

It seemed to enter my night room from below, catching on the antenna of my bedsprings, running up the coils, whispering through the mattress, the sheet, making an ear of my entire body.

chh

Then the furious flurry.

chhchhchhchhchhchh

My eyes were wide, groping for light, but I could not even see the pillow. I wished I had the nerve to run for the light switch. I wished my room was not at the back of the house, nearest the tracks.

The sound was still far off, along the Schuylkill (SKOO-kul) River, somewhere in the East End, but it had movement now, direction. It was coming. The breath of the night beast beat faster and louder. It was passing the DeKalb Street station now, turning from the river, behind the empty dark Garrick Theater, under the erector set Airy Street bridge, Marshall Street now, between the black and white striped crossing gate, bell tinkling, red light blinking— louder and louder—past the sand place, where I went with my father to bring home a wagonful; past the shoebox-shaped Orange Car store, where my mother could buy a bagful of Florida in February; crossing Elm, bending with the creek—louder, louder, *chhchh chhchhchhchhchh*—behind the ice plant now, Astor Street, the stone piles, the dump—louder still—the iron beast pouring sooty blackness into all the world, creating night—how loud can something be?—coming around the curve at the dead end of Chain CHHCHHCHHCHHCHHCHHCHHCHHCHH CHHCHHCHHCHHCHHCHHCHHCHHCHH— into my room, the bedsprings under me singing like the fiddle strings of Hell...

✳   ✳   ✳

Did it really happen? In morning's comforting sunshine I could never be sure—until I ran my finger along the clothesline or over the yellow face of a pansy in the backyard, and the tiny black particles of grit confirmed: yes, a train—a coal-fired, smoke-belching locomotive—had passed the night before.

Nighttime lent a horror not only to trains but also to garbage. Garbage had status in those days. Garbage was garbage, and trash was everything else. Garbage had a can of its own, basically an oversize metal pail with a lid. The garbage pail could be found in the back of the backyard. To lift the lid off the garbage can was to confront all the horrors of the creepiest movie: dead, rotting matter; teeming colonies of pale, slimy creeping things; and a stench that could be survived only in the smallest whiffs.

Ironically, the garbage can was never more disgusting than the day *after* garbage collection—for the collection was never quite complete. The garbage man would snatch the can from our curbside and overturn it into the garbage truck's unspeakable trough. He would bang it once, maybe twice, against the trough wall. This would dislodge most of the garbage, including a rain of maggots, but not the worst of it, not the very bottom of it, the most persistent, the oldest, the rottenest, the vilest. I held my breath while putting the lid back on. Sometimes I pushed the can all the way to the backyard with my foot.

When garbage met darkness, the potential for horror doubled.

Emptying the garbage after dinner was a frequent chore of mine, but only one particular instance do I remember. My mother had dumped the leftovers into a cake batter bowl and sent me off. The season was winter; it was already dark outside. The light from the back door petered out halfway down the yard, leaving me to moonlight. At the garbage can I went through my usual ritual: I curled my fingers around the metal handle of the lid, took a deep breath, held it, and with an almost audible winching of willpower, yanked the lid off. Careful not to look directly into the can, I overturned the batter bowl. I tapped it against the can to loosen any stragglers—and discovered I had a problem.

Whatever we had had for dinner that night must have been sticky, because half of it was still clinging to the bowl. I tapped harder. Still the stuff stuck. Risking breakage, I banged the bowl against the can. Nothing came loose. My chest was getting tight, my lungs demanded breath. In the moonlight I caught a glimpse of white worms. I panicked. I dropped the bowl into the garbage can, slammed down the lid, and raced for the house. I waited until I was inside to gasp for air, as I was sure that the garbage can, open so uncommonly long, must have fouled all outdoors. When my mother asked about the missing bowl several days later, I said I knew nothing about it.

Though night at various times conspired with a locomotive or a garbage can or a pup tent to frighten me, at other times night did not scare me at all.

We used to play a game called outs. It was the major leagues of hide-and-seek games. The kid who was It covered his eyes and counted to a hundred while everyone else ran and hid. If the It kid found you, he yelled "You're out!" and then the two of you were It and went seeking the others, and so on, until all were It but one—the winner.

There were no boundaries. You could hide anywhere. Popular hiding places included the stone piles, Red Hill, alleys, assorted backyards. As if the hiding needed to be made any easier, we always played outs after dark.

My favorite hiding place was behind a stone pile near the creek. I would crouch silently for an hour or more in utter darkness. The dark did not scare me when playing outs. What scared me was being found.

One night I heard the Its coming close to my hiding place. I slipped away down the path to the park and trotted up past the state hospital. I didn't stop until I was more than a mile west of town, in Jeffersonville. By the time I got back home my parents were calling my name down the dark alleys and streets. All the other players were home in bed.

*   *   *

Night was at its best once a week: outdoor movies in the park. After dinnertime and baseball games and Popsicles for dessert, kids from all over town headed for the band shell. Little kids sat in the cement-anchored benches that still form the stage's permanent seats. On the hill behind, older kids pulled up wooden benches or just sat on the grass. One night I must have been thinking I was older than I was. As I made myself at home on a wooden bench on the hill, several teenagers decided that was where they wanted to sit. They lifted the bench at one end, and off I slid to the grass.

The movies were usually in black and white. Occasionally we got through the show without the projector breaking down or the film snapping. More often than not the movie was about Francis the talking mule.

Afterward everyone scattered, across the fields to the East End, North End, West End. We George Streeters walked through the American Legion field and over the granite bridge spanning Stony Creek and turned left. Sometimes we took the dirt path, sometimes the tracks.

On moonlit nights the tracks looked like silver ribbons. Behind me, ahead of me, I could hear the voices of other kids. I could see their dark shadows. Atop the ten-foot clay bluff to the right was the spear field, then the dump, then Red Hill. A bald, packed dome of eraser-colored clay, Red Hill was said to be the home of the Devil, the clay's color coming from the infernal fires burning below. I always looked to see if it was true that at night you could see the hill glowing. Once, I thought, it was.

Always glowing, however, was the dead end, the faint "Welcome home" from the last streetlight. From the path, from the tracks we funneled onto George, the after-dark, midsummer band shell park movie kids. You could always bet that someone would face the row house windows and do his best imitation of a talking mule.

And somewhere beyond the East End a locomotive was moving through the night…

chh

A Family Thing

On the night of May 16, 1936, my mother and father got married. This was three years after Lou Spinelli, nicknamed Poppy, had spotted pretty, dark-haired Lorna Bigler on the dance floor at the Orioles Lodge and said to his friend Babe Richards, "See that girl. That's who I'm going to marry." On the night of their wedding, they were on another dance floor, at the Little Ritz, a nightspot on Route 202 north of town. They were broke, so this was all the honeymoon they would have.

At one point during the evening an announcement was made: A contest would determine the prettiest lady in attendance. My mother doesn't recall the contest procedure, only the result. The winner was the new Mrs. Lou Spinelli. Her prize was a gift certificate to have her portrait done at the Davis Photography Studio.

Four and a half years later, on February 1, 1941, I was born. My brother, Bill, came along four and a half years after that, on July 29, 1945. My mother's wedding-day prize, the framed portrait from Davis Studio, stands today on her bedroom dresser, the center of a triptych flanked by photo portraits of toddlers Bill and me.

And Jerry makes three. Here I am at three months (1941).

Mothers can get short-changed by memory. My recollections, for example, begin somewhere in my third year. By then some of my best experiences with my mother, some three years' worth of constant daily interaction, were already over. When my mind's recorder finally turned on, it was moments with my father that made the more memorable impressions: trips to high school ball games, backyard baseball, setting up the Christmas crèche. My mother's attentions continued, of course, but they tended to be less obvious, less noticed. They were the background of my life, the everyday care and support that at last came into full recognition when I acquired a family of my own.

∗   ∗   ∗

The marriage of Louis Anthony Spinelli and Lorna Mae Bigler brought together two heritages: Italian (my father) and Pennsylvania Dutch (my mother).

When I think of my Italian side, I think first of Sundays after church. The four of us would walk—or after 1954, when we got our first car, ride—the four blocks from First Presbyterian to my grandparents' home at 226 Chestnut. It was a row house with porches front and back and a rose arbor and dark polished furniture that made the living and dining rooms feel gloomy to me. The kitchen was where the light and the people and the food were.

Around the kitchen table sat aunts and uncles and cousins and, always at the head, my grandfather, Alessandro "Alex" Spinelli. In front of him was a small glass pitcher of red wine. Before each meal, including a breakfast of cold spaghetti, he drew the wine from his own barrel in the cellar. He was bald and he did not speak English very well and his breath always smelled of garlic and he smoked thin black wicked stogies and his fingers were as thick as sausages. He had labored many years for the Pennsylvania Department of Highways. Later the Borough of Norristown employed him as a street sweeper. Sometimes, riding my bike, I would see him with other old men, pushing a broom along a curb.

That was his job. His love was the "farm," a small patch of vacant land that he rented in the East End.

During the growing months, every day after work, he went to the farm to tend his vegetables. I like to think that, as he put hoe to earth, he sometimes reflected on what to me was the remarkable central fact of his life:

"He came over on a boat all by himself when he was only fourteen years old."

That's how I say it, even now, when describing my grandfather's coming to this country. He was an orphan in Italy. He worked in the olive groves around Naples. An aunt arranged for relatives to meet him in New York, handed him a one-way ticket on a steamship, and off he went, across the Atlantic Ocean, a black-haired teenager, alone, *solo*.

Fifty years later I, a nine-year-old American-born boy, sat at his kitchen table, eating the roast chicken with my fingers because that's how he did it, trying to imagine the bald old man at the head of the table with black hair.

The first course was always salad, as simple as salad gets: lettuce with oil and vinegar. Then came the chicken, then spaghetti and meatballs. My grandmother often made her own spaghetti, rolling out the dough and slicing it into strands with a device that reminded me of a harp. She would spend a whole day nursing the gravy at the stove. (To many Italians, spaghetti sauce is "gravy.") The dessert was often hot chestnuts, roasted on a second stove in the cellar.

As with the Spinellis, a table stands in the center of

my memory of the maternal relatives. In this case the table is not in a kitchen but on a sloping lawn under a huge oak tree. Made of planks laid over sawhorses, the table is very long and is crowded with pickled eggs and cold cuts and potato salad and three-bean salad and lemon meringue pie and dozens of other goodies. The place is my Aunt Isabel and Uncle Ted's home in Phoenixville, Pennsylvania, about ten miles from Norristown. The occasion is the annual family reunion.

In my early years the reunion was, after Christmas, the biggest event on my calendar. It was the only time I got to see Aunt Lizzie and her gang from Highspire, some eighty miles away. Even their names seemed different. There was a Willard and a Juanita and a second cousin exotically named Kendra.

One year there was even more excitement than usual: Uncle Elwood and Aunt Kay drove in from Michigan. I kept staring at my midwestern cousins Bruce, Janey, and Suzie. They might as well have come from Mars. Alas for Aunt Margaret and Uncle Chet and their kids Cindy, George, JoAnne, and Patty, there was no magic of distance. They lived on Chain Street in Norristown, a mere block and a half from 802 George. I barely noticed them.

As a once-a-year event, the reunion became a gauge by which to measure my progress, both physical and social. On the tennis court–size side yard, the uncles always got up a game of softball for the kids. I began as a tiny, grunting fumbler, swinging in vain at the slowest underhand tosses with a bat as big as I was. By the age of ten or eleven, I was clipping the grass with sharp grounders; then line drives to the garage; then, as a seasoned teenage shortstop, long flies into the strawberry patch beyond the trees. But by then the family reunion was no longer number two on my calendar. It had been eclipsed by such happenings as school dances and miniature golf with my friends. The year came when I felt myself too big to participate in the softball game. In college, some years, I did not even attend the reunion.

But home—home is a reunion daily. And I never felt too big for Christmas. Christmas was a Bible thing, of course, and a school-vacation thing and a wrapped-presents thing and a homemade-cookies thing—but most of all, as I look back, it was a family thing.

My parents spent almost nothing on themselves. They bought only the clothes they needed. It was a big deal to treat themselves to a milkshake. They never went to the movies. And yet, for all they gave my brother and me, you'd have thought they were rich. My Christmas gifts came in piles. From Lincoln Logs to the inevitable walnut in the toe of my red felt stocking, I accepted the presents strictly as the objects they appeared to be. Only years later did I realize the truth: the gift was my parents' selfless love.

One Christmas morning it bounced lightly off my

chest as I came down the stairs, and I looked to see my first football wobbling at my feet. Another year it waited for me in the kitchen. I had unwrapped the last present from under the tree, and my father said, "Well, I guess that's it. Looks like you did pretty good this year." And then someone asked me to go to the kitchen for something, and there it was, in front of the sink: a spanking-new cream and green whitewall-tired Road-master bicycle. Love leaning on a kickstand.

My mother and father at the beach in 1940, six months before I was born.

Big Brother

When my younger brother became student council president as a ninth grader at Rittenhouse Junior High, I was proud. In the years that followed Bill and I played golf, flung Frisbees, shared friends and cars. We were pals.

But those days were yet to come. During the George Street years, the four-and-a-half-year difference in our ages ruled out being pals. When I was in fourth grade, Bill was in kindergarten; when I was in tenth, he was in sixth. We had different friends, different involvements. Except for two years, we attended different schools. We shared parents and a house, but that was about all.

Because I wasn't paying much attention to him then, my store of memories today is not nearly as well stocked as I would like it to be. I remember him, when he was very young, eating ashes from the coal furnace.

I remember him pilfering my penny collection to buy an ice cream cone.

I remember him as a toddler, packing our first puppy, Spot, into our father's black-domed lunchpail. When this kept happening, Spot was sent off to a family without toddlers.

A few years later along came Lucky (so named because

after the lunchpail puppy, we were lucky to get another), part terrier, part unknown, a pretty mutt, mostly black, with white chest and paws and tip of tail. She was friendly, eager, barely disciplined, which is to say, she was like my little brother. They got along wonderfully.

Our dog Lucky.

I remember feet-fighting in my bed—lying on our backs and flailing our feet at each other. It was just harmless, boy horseplay, but sometimes I carried it far enough so that Bill wound up crying. I think now that in making him cry, I was fabricating an outlet for tender feelings toward my little brother that found no expression in the natural course of events.

I remember Bill getting into trouble more than I, both at home and in school. I secretly admired him for daring to just do things, regardless of consequences.

And I envied him his animation. Well before I entered junior high, I began cooling out. Gone were the days when I would serenade passersby from the gate in my yard or jingle-jangle off to school in my cowboy outfit. I was still friendly, but in a shyer, quieter way. Meanwhile Bill was just lighting up. He was everything I was not: bold and lively and funny. He was a natural mimic and a clown. He had, as the Lloyd Price song went, "Personality."

And that's about it, the extent of my kidhood relationship with my brother, Bill.

Or so I thought.

For something surprising happened, something nice, when I told him I was working on my autobiography. I invited him to jot down any recollections of me that he might have, in case I missed any. Several weeks later he handed me a list of memorable moments. I read it over. I was stunned: I hardly recalled any of them.

He remembers his own hurt feelings when I wouldn't let him ride my tricycle.

He remembers, as a preschooler, how impressed he was that I could read cereal boxes.

He remembers how angry I got when he raided my closet for shirts and when he tangled the strings of my Howdy Doody puppet.

He remembers fearing for me when Raymond Chillano beaned me with a pitch during a Knee-Hi baseball game. And when the same Raymond Chillano, knowing I could not swim, tipped me in my street clothes into the deep end of the pool at the Valley Forge Swim Club. (Raymond was not always so hard on me. In fact, he was one of my best friends.)

He remembers an episode which, at the time, he considered positively historic. I was in the fifth grade at Hartranft Elementary. Bill was in first. Normally we walked the three blocks home for lunch. But on this particular day our mother had to be somewhere else, so she gave me money and told me to take my brother somewhere to eat. We met at noon. We went to a luncheonette a block away. We ordered our lunch, and for a little while Billy Spinelli felt as big as anyone in that place. He was having lunch in a restaurant, not a parent or teacher in sight, off into the world with his big brother. On the way back to school we were chased by bees.

Bill remembers as clearly as I the dirt path by the railroad tracks. He especially remembers one day when I propped him on the bar of my Roadmaster and gave him a lift from the dead end to the park. He remembers feeling the carnival-ride thrill of it. He remembers feeling proud and special. Most of all he remembers feeling safe, his brother's breath in his ear, his brother's arms joining the handlebars in a protective embrace.

Such are Bill's recollections, and after all these years they bumped me over to a new point of view. I have always tended to see our relationship from a single perspective, from my own eyes; that is, Bill as my little brother. Now I see it from a second perspective: myself as his big brother.

I have decided that I like Bill's memories of us better than my own. I especially like the one about the bike ride on the dirt path. I am picturing it now. I am feeling Bill's feeling of safety, and I am feeling the big brother in myself. Maybe, if I keep picturing this memory of Bill's and feeling it for a long-enough time, it will begin to fool me into thinking it is my own.

My brother (left) and me, clowning around at Christmas, 1957. The cigarettes are candy.

Sixteen Things I Wished I Could Do

1. Spit between my front teeth
2. Blast an earsplitting, two-fingered whistle
3. Braid a lanyard with the colorful plastic cord called gimp
4. Drink a quart of milk, or anything, at one sitting (like Roger Adelman)
5. Rock the cradle with my yo-yo
6. Bless myself like a Catholic
7. Tap the side of my nose and blow out a booger
8. Crack a twin Popsicle perfectly in half every time, never to be left with three quarters in one hand and one quarter in the other
9. Bend my thumb backward until it touches my wrist
10. Like cream soda
11. Play clarinet without practicing
12. Stay on my notes when singing harmony
13. Eat hot peppers
14. Hit the curve ball
15. Swim
16. Understand eternity

A Swooner
in Sneakers

Some kids, when no playmates were around, didn't know what to do. I didn't have this problem. There was always exploring, and exploring was best done alone.

The Red Hills, the spear field, the tracks, the path, the dumps—all were sectors to be investigated time and again. But usually my route of exploration followed Norristown's signature waterway: Stony Creek. My territory ranged from two grassy blanket-size islands near the Elm Street bridge to the far end of Elmwood Park, where the creek forked, one branch turning west into the vast farmland of the state hospital, the other meandering north on toward East Norriton Township.

In some places the going was easy, such as the stony flats under the Steriger Street bridge. In others the banks were so steep and near the water that I had to pull myself along with roots for handholds or hop the rocks midstream. The total length was a mile or more— to me it seemed Mississippian—and not an inch along the way, on either side, was unknown to the rubber soles of my black and white hightop Keds.

The zoo toward the far end of the park was, and still is, one of Norristown's treasures, and I visited it often.

But it was near the western edge of the zoo, along the creek, where I came to know creatures unpenned. Squatting over the shallows, I studied schools of minnows in the finger-deep water. I pulled up a rock, and more often than not a crayfish—we called the tiny lobster look-alikes crawfish—scooted briefly into the sunlight and then under another rock. Water spiders skated over the glaring surface while angel-winged dragonflies and neon blue darning needles shimmered above.

Lurking below was something nasty—leeches. Bloodsuckers. They were everywhere, but unseen, unfelt. The only way to observe them was to leave a hand or foot in the water too long. That's what I did once. It was one of the few times I found myself with others at the creek. I was wading—I don't remember why—with my shoes and socks off and my dungarees rolled up, and when I got out, one of the other kids screeched and pointed. I looked down and saw them—black wormlike bloodsuckers clinging to the snow-white skin of my shins. Frantically I scraped them off. Now I was staring at a half-dozen driblets of blood, where the vampires had been dining. Were leeches poisonous? I didn't know, but rattlesnakes were, and I knew from my cowboy days how to handle a snakebite.

I sat on the bank, hoisted a bare leg into the air, and announced, "Okay, you guys, you gotta get the poison out. Start sucking." Suddenly everyone remembered they had to be somewhere else that instant. As they clambered up the banks, I wiped off the blood with my shirt, picked up my socks and sneaks, and walked home as delicately as I could, afraid that if I came down too hard on my bloodless legs, they might crumple. I took a bath and survived the night.

And there were frogs—heard but almost never seen. Try as I might, I was never silent enough to sneak up on them. I knew them only by the watery plops that preceded me as I walked along the creek bank.

There were snakes. Mostly the common garter. But occasionally I chanced upon a truly special snake. Once, down near the Elm Street bridge, I found a large black one sunning on a flat rock. I pinned it behind the head with my stick, picked it up, and took it home. I put it in a two-handled tin picnic box and covered it with perforated cardboard. The next morning the snake was gone. I looked under everything in the house but couldn't find it. Nor could I understand why my mother was so upset. She must have blabbed to the neighbors, because for the next several days panic held the 800 block in its grip. We never found it.

On another day I looked into the creek and saw a small brown and yellow water snake. It was like a jewel set among the sun diamonds sparkling in the water. It was the most beautiful thing I had ever seen, and at first I didn't believe it. When I did, it was gone with the current. I raced downstream, concentrating on shadow patches, for only there was it visible. I caught sight of it once for a moment, then lost it for good. I kept running the bank, searching, searching. The next day I returned to the spot. I stared so long and hard into the creek that once I imagined I saw it, but it was only the rippling, sun-dappled water itself. For the rest of the summer, and the next, as I visited my frogs and crawfish and minnows, I continued to search. And to this day I cannot walk along a stream without hoping for one more glimpse of the beautiful water snake.

And there was my favorite of all—salamanders. I loved the little critters, two inches of wriggle under a rock. Plain brown was the most common coloring. Sometimes I'd find one with an orange stripe. Yellow stripes were the rarest. I became so good at knowing where they lived that I seldom lifted a rock without finding one.

But I loved them wrongly. I wasn't satisfied with simply finding and watching them. I wanted to collect them, as if they were marbles or baseball cards. I remember walking through the park one day with two fistfuls of them and more in my pockets. Once, I brought several home. I turned the black snake's brief abode, the picnic box, into a terrarium: dirt, rocks, water. In went the salamanders. I forget what I fed them. Whatever it was, they didn't eat. One day I found them dead, dried up like pieces of chewed rawhide. I buried them in the backyard, in the earth they should never have been taken from, and kept the lifeless picnic-box terrarium as a reminder of a lesson learned.

When I got my Christmas bicycle, I roamed far beyond the creek. The whole town was now within reach. I rode without destination, with no intent but to look and look and look. To find myself on an unfamiliar street was all the thrill I needed.

I saw the rooftops of row houses stepping down the hills of the East End, like stairways for giants. I coasted the broader avenues of the more affluent North End, amazed to see unattached homes with backyards *and* side yards *and* front yards. I saw the riverbanks of the great Schuylkill—and learned to spell it. I saw the P&W high-speed trolley wobble across the river trestle from Bridgeport to nest at the terminal platform high above Swede Street. In the shadow of the P&W platform I saw the green newsstand with every magazine in the world (or so I thought) and the line of radio taxis, black boxy little Plymouths, one of which was driven by my neighbor, Mr. Seeton. I saw the domed courthouse and the high stone walls of the county prison and the steeple of my church, First Presbyterian, said to be one of the tallest in the land, poking a hole in the sky. I saw the impossibly long (one block!) city hall, where you could get yourself into or out of trouble at one end and buy penny candy at the other. I saw the sprawling red-roofed building of the *Times Herald*, "Montgomery County's newspaper since 1799." I saw and smelled—again—the Adam Scheidt Brewery and the garlicky tang on East Main that came from Linfante's and Lou's, famous for the zep sandwich (salami, provolone, tomato, Bermuda onion, oil, with or without hot peppers), created in Norristown in 1938. I saw the bustling commercial districts of Main Street and West Marshall, with movie theaters—four of them—and restaurants and shops of all sorts and Chatlin's department store, home of the famous fluoroscope.

When you needed new shoes, you went to Chatlin's with your mother. The salesman helped you try them on until you found a pair your mother liked. Then came the best part. The salesman stood up from his fitting stool and said, "Well, why don't we have a look," and off went the three of you to the fluoroscope. It looked something like the big floor console radio in your living room. Six inches up was a step leading to an opening into the interior of the scope. Since you knew the procedure, you didn't even wait for the salesman to say, "Step up." You slid your feet into the opening, and then you had to fight impatience. First the salesman bent over and pressed his face to the goggle-shaped viewer. "Wiggle your toes," he said. You wiggled your toes. He straightened up, nodding. "Plenty of room." Then your mother looked. At last it was your turn. You bent down and scrunched your face to the viewer and there they were—your feet—or rather the skeleton of your feet, your bones, your toe bones wiggling in an eerie green glow. "We'll take them," said your mother, and already you were eager to wear them out so you could come back to Chatlin's and do this again.

Other favorite stops were Block's and Yost's. Block's department store had the only Santa Claus I would talk to at Christmastime. For a long while, I was convinced that Block's was home to the *real* Santa. And though I never bought anything at Yost's, a dry-goods store on the corner of DeKalb and Main, I stopped in occasionally because of a feature I had never seen anywhere else. The selling floor had no cash registers. When someone made a purchase, the salesclerk took the customer's money and stuffed it into a small canister hanging above her head. The canister was threaded onto a heavy string that swooped from the sales counter up through a portal on the second floor. Exactly how and why it all happened was a mystery to me. I only knew that the customer's money was soon zipping up to the second floor, and a minute later down came the canister like a chair on a ski lift with change and receipt. Every counter had its own string to the second-floor portal, so canisters were forever zipping back and forth just out of my reach—and all of this accompanied by tinkling bells. It was a show!

My bike was more than wheels for aimless wandering. It helped me answer many needs.

Did I want to cool off? I coasted through the alley between Kohn Street and Haws Avenue, past the Flavorite ice cream plant.

Was I hungry? I pedaled to a mulberry tree. I knew every one in town. My favorite was in Roger Adelman's backyard. I climbed it often and snacked off the branches, staining my fingers purple.

Did I want a thrill? I rode out to the park zoo, to the top of Monkey Hill. I waited until the road was clear of cars and took off, pedaling hard all the way, down past the monkey cages. My record, according to my speedometer, was forty-five miles per hour, not bad for a single-gear, fat-tired Roadmaster.

Or another kind of thrill? Some days I must have pedaled past Dovie Wilmoth's house on Haws Avenue ten times, hoping that the beautiful platinum blonde would be on the front porch. If she was, I waved and called "Hi, Dovie!" and kept circling the block. Every three minutes: "Hi, Dovie!" She always smiled and waved back.

When I was thirteen, I was old enough to leave town. My Roadmaster took me as far as Valley Forge National Historical Park, about five miles away. I crossed the Schuylkill on the singing bridge, so called for the sound of tires on the steel grate deck. You could see through the deck to the river below. For hours I rode the winding hills past cannon muzzles and monuments and replicated log cabins. Once, I parked my bike and walked into a hillside meadow to lie back and get some sun. When I opened my eyes, hawks were circling overhead. Not trusting them to know I wasn't dead, I got out of there fast.

Sometimes if my planned route for the day took me across the tracks at the dead end, I had to wait for a freight train to pass. I never felt thwarted or impatient about this. In fact, the longer the train the better, and if there were three or four engines, I knew it would be a very long one. By the end of junior high the steam locomotives had given way to diesels. The diesels were neither as terrifying at night nor as exciting in daylight, nor did they leave me with a headful of coal grit.

As the train went by, I counted the cars: boxcars, tankers, flatcars, coal hoppers. By the time the caboose came clicking by, the engines were out of sight and earshot, out beyond the park band shell. I loved the caboose. I was surprised that no one was ever standing at the back rail, coffee mug in hand, watching the world go by.

In those days I was many whats. A kid can be that. Grownups have gone ahead and answered the question: "*What* shall I be?" They have tossed out all the whats that don't fit and have become just one. Teacher. Truckdriver. Businessperson. But a kid is still becoming. And I, as a kid alone, was free to be just about anything.

So many careers came and went through me: salamander finder, crawfish annoyer, flat-stone creek skipper, cedar chest smeller, railroad car counter, tin can stomper, milkweed blower, mulberry picker, snowball smoother, paper bag popper, steel rail walker, box turtle toucher, dark-sky watcher, best-part saver. They didn't last long, these careers of mine, but flashed into and out of existence like mayflies. But while they employed me, I gave them an honest minute's work and was paid in the satisfactions of curiosity met and a job well done.

When I went roaming by myself on foot or bike, I discovered more than water spiders and foreign neighborhoods. I discovered myself. By myself, not boxed in by rules of play, I was free to think, to wonder, to swoon.

That's what I did sometimes: I swooned, just thinking about things. Like time. Like space. I tried to imagine, tried to grasp the speed of light. One hundred eighty-six thousand miles per *second!* And how about those stars up there? The ones I saw when the sky turned the color of my dungarees. I had heard that these were only the closest ones, visible from earth. I had heard that there were billions and billions more too far away to see, that they went on and on and on until the end of the universe. I tried to imagine zooming out past the last stars and looking around—at what? What does the end of the universe look like? And what about time? What about *before* time?

Thoughts like these did not come to mind as I flipped baseball cards with Spider Sukoloski or played street football with Jerry Fox or gunslingers with Johnny Seeton. They presented themselves behind closed eyes on hillside meadows and during the long lazy wait for a box turtle to cross the path. The questions were as elusive as the answers, as delicate as a dragonfly's wing. They gave me goosebumps. They made me dizzy. I swooned in my sneakers.

A Little Stiff from Swimming

But I did not read. Not books, anyway. Now, cereal boxes—that was another story. Every morning I pored over boxes of Wheaties and Cheerios at the breakfast table. I looked forward to new cereals as much for a change in reading material as for a change in breakfast fare.

And comics. I read them by the hundreds.

Mostly I read cowboy and war comics. I bought them at corner stores and newsstands. Then when I was twelve, I got serious. I decided the comic should come to me. I got my first subscription: *Bugs Bunny*. Once a month, accompanied by the metallic flapping of the front door mail slot, the postman delivered Bugs's latest adventures to me.

My favorite comic character of all, however, was neither man nor rabbit. In fact, I'm still not sure what it was. All I know is that it was called the Heap, and it looked something like a haystack. The Heap never spoke, and the reader never saw it move, but the Heap appeared on the scene when people were having problems. Somehow or other the Heap managed to solve the problem, though it never got credit. As far as most of the people knew, it was just another haystack in the field.

Of course, I read the newspaper comics too. While I never missed "Dick Tracy," "Little Lulu," and "Mandrake the Magician," my favorite of all was "Alley Oop."

Another part of the newspaper got my attention as well: sports.

Mostly I read the sports pages of the *Times Herald*. I especially liked the clever writing of sports editor Red McCarthy in his daily column. Until then I had thought there was only one English language—the language I spoke and heard in the West End of Norristown. I was happily surprised to discover that there was more than one way to say something, that the words and their arrangement could be as interesting as the thing they said.

From April to September in the Sunday *Philadelphia Inquirer*, I read the major league baseball batting statistics. They were printed in small type in a long box, row after row of numbers and names, hundreds of them—every player in the majors. To the non-baseball fan, they were as boring as a page in a phone book. I loved it. I wallowed in the numbers. What was Ted Williams's batting average this week? Stan Musial's? Richie Ashburn's? Was Ralph Kiner still the leader in home runs? Who had the most RBIs? Did Mantle have a shot at the Triple Crown? Or Mays? It was like peeking at a race once every seven days, watching the lead change places from week to week.

Cereal boxes, comics, baseball stats—that was my reading. As for books, I read maybe ten of them, fifteen tops, from the day I entered first grade until graduation from high school. I remember reading a few Bobbsey Twins adventures, and in junior high, sports stories about Chip Hilton, a fictional high school hotshot athlete. I read *The Adventures of Robin Hood*, a Sherlock Holmes mystery, and *Kon-Tiki*, the true story of a man who crossed the Pacific in a raft. That's about it.

Why didn't I read more?

I could blame it on my grade school, which had no library. I could blame it on the curriculum, which limited my classroom reading to "See Dick run. See Jane run. See Spot do something on the rug." I could blame it on history, for enrolling me in life and school before the time of book fairs and author visits. I could blame it on my friends, because like me, the only books they read were comic books.

But I can't do that.

It's always handy to blame things on one's parents, but I can't do that either. My father had his books on display in the dining room. Thirty times a day I passed his collection of histories and Ellery Queen mysteries. Some of my earliest memories are of my mother reading to me, stories like *Babar* and *The Little Engine That Could*. My parents steered me in the right direction.

And the fact is, on those few occasions when I actually did read a book, I enjoyed it. Yet for some reason I would not admit this to myself. Instead of saying, Hey, that was good, that was fun, I think I'll read another— I would dump my baseball glove into my bike basket and head out the path to the Little League field, and months would go by before I picked up a book again. Reading a book was for times when I was totally bored and lacking anything else to do.

And what about words, which, packed together, made up a book as cells made up my body? I liked them. Yet this was such a naturally occurring, unachieved sort of thing that if someone had asked me in those days, "Do you like words?" I probably would have shrugged and blithely answered, "No."

Still, whether I knew it or not, words were claiming me. When I visited Hartenstine Printing, where my father worked as a typesetter, I saw words being created letter by letter, one thin slug of lead at a time.

Once, in a comic book, someone with a bad heart was described as having a bum ticker. That tickled me to no end. I kept whispering "bum ticker" to myself for days.

Except for the Heap, my favorite comic book characters were Bugs Bunny and Daffy Duck. I liked them as much for their words as their ways. For me, the highlight of a scene was not what happened, but what Bugs or Daffy said about what happened. This is probably why Mickey Mouse never much appealed to me. His speech was too bland for my taste.

When I was eleven or twelve, my mother and I laughed for months over a corny old vaudeville joke that I kept asking her to repeat. She gave the joke a local twist. It went like this:

Man goes to the beach for a vacation. Goes into the water. When he comes out, he sees a lady sitting next to his blanket.

He says, "Hi, I'm a little stiff from swimming."

She says, "Hello, I'm a secretary from Norristown."

(I'm laughing again.)

Occasionally I had to look up a word in the dictionary. Sometimes my eye would stray to the surrounding words. Invariably it stopped at an interesting one, and I read the definition. In one such instance I discovered that I was a gossoon. I clearly remember two feelings attached to these moments: (1) surprise that a dictionary could be so interesting, and (2) a notion to sit down and look through more pages. I never did.

And then of course there was my success in spelling.

All of these items were indicators of an early leaning toward language, but I failed to see them as such. The tickle of a rabbit's wit, the rattle of alphabet in a compositor's drawer—they simply took their place among the Popsicles and penknives and bike tires of my days.

With one exception.

In sixth grade our teacher assigned us a project: Make a scrapbook of Mexico. I found pictures of Mexico in *National Geographic* and other magazines and pasted them in my scrapbook, for which my father made a professional-looking cover at the print shop. Then I did something extra. It wasn't part of the assignment. I just did it.

I wrote a poem.

Three stanzas about Mexico, ending with a touristy come-on: "Now, isn't that where you would like to be?" I wrote it in pencil, longhand, my best penmanship, on a piece of lined classroom paper. I pasted it neatly on the last page of my scrapbook and turned in my project.

Several days later my mother walked the three blocks to my school. She met with my teacher, who told her she did not believe that my poem about Mexico was my own work. She thought I copied it from a book. (Hah! If she only knew how few books I read, and never one with poetry.) I was suspected of plagiarism.

I don't know what my mother said to her, but by the time she walked out I was in the clear, legally at least. Five years would pass before I wrote another poem.

Staying in the Lines

I was neat.

How neat was I? Say I had to cut a rectangle out of a piece of paper. First I would measure a perfect shape with my ruler, then draw it with a sharp pencil. Then with my scissors I would cut it out. But not *just* cut it out. I would cut precisely along the right edge of the pencil line, or precisely along the left edge, or I would split the line in half and cut precisely right down the middle. Consistently, all the way around the rectangle.

In seventh grade at Stewart Junior High, I astonished my shop teacher, Mr. Rohn, with the precision of my mechanical drawings and the perfection of my hand-lettering.

That same year I won numerous Palmer Method penmanship certificates and was declared the outstanding boy penmeister.

Every Eastertime the merchants of the West End shopping district—three blocks on Marshall Street—sponsored a coloring contest. Every day for two weeks line drawings—coloring-book-type pictures—were printed in the *Times Herald*. Each business had its own picture. Kids were invited to cut out the pictures, color them, and deposit their entries in boxes in the stores.

Unlike most kids, I did not use crayons. I used colored pencils. My frequently sharpened points never—*never*—strayed outside the lines. And my colors were right, too. No green sky or red grass for me.

For me, staying inside the lines was more than a color-the-picture matter.

Give me a direction, I followed it. Put a rule in front of me, I obeyed it. In twelve years I never stayed after school for detention. Once, though, I came close. It happened in the spring of ninth grade. Our homeroom teacher, Miss Busch, announced that our lockers would be reviewed for neatness. Since I kept my locker neat at all times, there was nothing for me to tidy up.

The next morning as the students entered Homeroom 213, we looked to the blackboard for the names of those whose lockers failed to pass muster. Shockingly, my name was among them. The punishment, besides cleaning up the offending locker, was detention.

I told Miss Busch there must be a mistake. She said there wasn't. I said I wouldn't be there for detention. It was the only time I ever talked back to a teacher. She said I'd be sorry.

After school that day, as usual, I went to baseball practice. When I arrived at school the next morning, I discovered I was no longer on the team. Nor was I homeroom president. I was stripped of every office and association.

My locker may have been tidy, but suddenly my life was a mess. One day of watching my backup shortstop was enough. I couldn't stand it. I apologized to Miss Busch, and the picture of my life fell back into place.

I loved routine, repeatedness. To do the same thing twice was to establish a personal tradition. In other words, where there were no lines, I drew my own. I stepped inside and stayed there—cozy, safe.

Summer Saturdays, for example. In the morning I walked a mile from George Street to the YMCA. There I played Ping-Pong in the game room with Lee Holmes, Ralph Cottman, and others. Then a screen and projector were brought out, the lights turned off, and we all settled in to watch a black and white movie, usually a Tarzan adventure.

After the movie I walked down to Main Street, past Block's department store, past the Norris Theater, to Texas Hot Wieners. The best hot dogs in town were sizzling right there in the front window, daring each passerby not to come in. I sat at the counter and placed my order, always the same: hot dog with mustard and chopped onions, and chocolate milk. I've had a lot of wimpy hot dogs since then, hot dogs so soft you can't feel your teeth go through them, so mushy with fat and cereal you could almost drink them with a straw. Not Texas Hot Wieners. They had spunk. They fought back.

By now it was one o'clock. Across the street I went to the Garrick Theater and the Saturday matinee double feature—cowboy movies plus a Flash Gordon or Captain Midnight serial.

Hours later I emerged blinking in the late-afternoon sun. I walked home along Markley Street, past the sweet-smelling Wonder Bread plant, the sidewalk dusty with flour, past the *Times Herald*, over the Markley Street bridge that spanned Stony Creek. I always stopped at the bridge railing to look for sunfish in the sparkling water below. Only when I spotted one would I continue my journey homeward.

Every summer Saturday. The same thing.

Needless to say, I was well acquainted with perfect attendance in school. Most years went by without my missing a day.

When I walked, I trained myself to keep my feet pointed straight ahead, not pigeon-toed or splayed outward.

I even fantasized about neatness. I imagined our house had been selected for a visit by President Eisenhower. I saw myself going from room to room putting everything precisely in its place. On the racks in the bathroom the corners of the towels came together perfectly.

In another fantasy I set out to tidy up the world. Anything I couldn't fix with hedge trimmers and lawn mower I paved over with asphalt. By the time I was finished, the

Amazon jungle looked like the flower beds and crewcut lawns of the North End of Norristown.

I spread my peanut butter evenly over my bread.

I never said bad words (unless you count "poop").

I hardly ever laughed out loud.

As I said, I was neat. And though I did not think of it this way, I believe that what I was actually trying to do was to become perfect.

Funny thing: For all my neatness, my sharp pencil points, my devotion to the right side of the line, I never won the West End shopping district coloring contest. Every year I tried harder than before, tried to be even neater, and still I lost. I couldn't figure out why.

Wasn't neatness enough? Wasn't perfection possible?

No, said my yo-yo. Often I had what seemed to be a perfect day—100 on a spelling test, winning touchdown in a pickup game, a new haircut—only to come home and find knots in my yo-yo string. I began to think the string had a mind of its own. I imagined it waiting until I wasn't looking, then rising up like a cobra and looping itself into knots. My paranoia seemed confirmed one morning when I awoke to find knots that I could have sworn were not there when I went to bed.

When I was eleven and twelve, I played Biddy basketball, the equivalent of Little League baseball. In my final year I made the all-star team, but not because I was a great scorer. The most points I ever scored in a game was twelve, and usually it was half that. I think I made the all-stars as much for what I did not do as for what I did. That is to say, I did not make mistakes.

Playing the guard position, I dribbled a lot and passed a lot. But these were relatively risk-free ventures. Shooting was where the risk was, and I rarely took more than five shots in a game. I wasn't a bad shooter, but each shot I missed discouraged me from taking more. At home after each game, I neatly entered into a notebook my statistics: assists, shots taken, shots made, fouls. Of course I hardly ever committed a foul. And because I played the game so carefully, I never found out how good a basketball player I might have become. Too late I learned that neatness does not serve all endeavors equally well, that what is good for penmanship is not necessarily good for basketball.

A willingness to take risks, to color outside the lines, was slow in coming to me. Some stubborn idea of perfection deterred me from fully extending myself in simple, pure participation. I was too afraid to fail. I did not appreciate the value of a mess.

Not that I wasn't given the chance. Looking back, I can see now that that's what the school-locker incident was: an opportunity to grow beyond my own self-imposed limits. And for one day, I did. Falsely accused of having a disorderly locker, I was properly outraged. I defied my teacher. I refused to submit to injustice. I turned my back on detention. I charged across the line. I became a new me.

Then came the consequences—banishment from the baseball team, from all offices. Did I rise up and cry, "Punish me if you will! I don't care! I will never capitulate to this injustice"? Did I finish out the year in noble exile, stripped of all honors? Did I stand up for what I knew was right?

No.

I caved in. I apologized for protesting an unjust verdict. My life was reinstated. Order was restored, the mess was cleaned up. I was back inside the lines. Once again I was the old familiar me.

Yet even as I publicly conformed in word and deed, a contrary tendency was forming within me. It showed briefly in sixth grade when I wrote the unassigned poem on Mexico. It showed in my neatness fantasies—not in the subject matter but in the mere act of fantasizing. It showed in my swooning wonderment over the endlessness of the sky at night.

And it showed most commonly in my own version of the Garrick Theater's double features. When an event in my life—say, a baseball game—was over, it was not really over. For that night in bed I would relive it in my head. I would again see the vivid colors and hear the voices and feel the feelings, and the reliving would be, in its own way, as real to me as the first time around. Sometimes it was even better. Sometimes I couldn't wait for the event to be over and bedtime to arrive so that I could play it back.

As I have said, if you had asked me what I would grow up to be, I would have answered, "A baseball player." But even as I oiled the deep, fragrant pocket of my Marty Marion glove and taped the hickory handle of my thirty-three-ounce bat, I was unknowingly developing the tool of another trade. The urge to write a poem, to daydream, to ruminate, to wonder, even my tolerance of solitude—all became components of a bearing that I would never have guessed would fit me so well, an aptitude that thrives on disorder, that welcomes green sky and red grass, that serves neither master nor homeroom teacher, that respects no line or limit. I speak, of course, of imagination—a gift that, like my Roadmaster on that Christmas morning, waited in another room for my discovery.

Dr. Winters'
Finger

There was one line in my life that I did cross freely, frequently, and deliberately. This line ran from one end of town to the other and it had a name.

DeKalb Street.

That is its name in Norristown. Elsewhere it is known as U.S. Route 202, running from Delaware up to Maine. DeKalb Street came off the bridge across the Schuylkill and ran south to north past the Reading Railroad station, past Hartenstine Printing where my father worked, past Yost's Dry Goods and Sames Book Store and First Presbyterian and city hall and the YWCA and St. Patrick's Church and on past the large stone homes of the North End and across Johnson Highway and out of town.

But DeKalb Street divided more than east from west in Norristown. It also divided black from white. With few exceptions, African Americans lived to the east of DeKalb Street. So did many Italian Americans, including my grandparents and, for a while—at 224 Chestnut—me.

My first memory of a black person dates to that time, when I was three or four. My mother took me with her to the dentist one day. The dentist was Dr. Winters. Dr. Winters was black. His office was in the East End.

The story as I have sometimes told it goes like this: My mother has her dental work done while I sit off to the side. When Dr. Winters is finished, I decide I'm jealous of all the attention my mother has been getting. I want some, too. So the dentist hoists me into the chair, tells me to open wide, and checks me over.

In truth, my mother and I have no specific recollection of why I wound up in the dentist's chair. My memory is clear, however, on one thing: Dr. Winters' finger in my mouth. I can feel it, I can see its dark brownness. I notice that it is a color different from my own, but that's all there is to it, a flat, casual observation. What I feel is the rightness of that thick and hard and smooth and gentle and expert finger. My mouth yields naturally to it, seems to recognize that this is the way of things.

Dr. Winters never actually worked on my teeth, but to this day the sense and touch of that "examination" is inscribed vividly in my memory.

Though I lived in the East End for several years, I had no black friends or playmates. Halfway through first grade we moved to George Street, where everyone was white. In my class at Hartranft Elementary there was only one black student, a girl, Viola Fisher. For six years Viola Fisher barely said a word, barely moved. Though her color made her conspicuous at Hartranft, her demeanor rendered her all but invisible. Socially speaking, we white students did not see Viola Fisher.

Looking back today, I can easily imagine Viola Fisher's discomfort. I imagine she often wished she could attend Washington School, deep in the East End, where almost all the students were black. I imagine she was afraid of us. And that's ironic, because in grade school, in my experience, fear went the other way: *we* were afraid of *them*. At least I was.

One day when I was nine, a black boy about my age walked up to me on a school playground, made a fist, and clipped me on the tip of my chin. *Thock*. That was all. The punch did not hurt me, at least not my chin. Nor did the boy seem interested in continuing. Perhaps he simply wanted to make some point. Perhaps it was something he needed to do, as several years later I "needed" to clip Joey Stackhouse on the chin. Whatever, at that moment my fear of black kids felt confirmed. I turned from the boy, trotted over to a nearby tree, knelt in the surrounding dirt, dumped out my bag of marbles, and began shooting mibs.

The fear that steered me through streets and playgrounds came from a perception for which I had no words, a perception I did not question. It said that black people were different from me in ways that went beyond skin color. It did not tell me how they were different, just that they *were* different. It is not clear how I acquired this information. I don't believe it came from home, yet somehow, from the world around me, I absorbed it.

There were signs everywhere. I saw, I heard, but that was all. I did not much think. I did not question.

Crayola crayons came in small and large boxes. The large box contained a pale pink-orange color called flesh. I did not often use it. After all, the pages of the coloring book were white, so it was easier to simply leave faces untouched. I never asked, "*Whose* flesh?"

The most popular private trash collector in town was a black man. He worked hard. In the summer especially he became thirsty. Sometimes he would ask a business client if he could get a drink of water from their faucet, and he would show the glass that he always carried with him. He was widely commended for this. I never asked him, "What do you think would happen if you didn't bring your own glass?"

I once attended a picnic of mixed races. Things were going along normally when, with the picnic only half over, I suddenly noticed that all the black people were gone. I did not run after them and call out, "Wait! Why are you leaving early?"

When my father took me to high school basketball games, I noticed that most of the black people sat in one section of the bleachers. I never asked, "Why do they always sit together?" Or, "Why do *we* always sit together?"

I saw these little separations in a hundred places and a hundred ways, and never once did I say, "Why?"

Though I had neither wit nor grit to ask such questions, sometime in grade school my point of view began to change. It happened when I gave up cowboys and soldiers and turned to sports.

Sports, especially Little League baseball and Biddy basketball, brought me into a new kind of contact with African-American kids. Within the structure of organized games they ceased to be black and I ceased to be white. Instead we were teammates or opponents, identified by the color of our uniforms, not of our skin. The Red Sox. The Green Sox. The Colts. The Wolves. The fear in the streets did not follow me onto sandlots and hardwood courts.

On summer mornings we came from the East End and the West End to play on the Little League field by Stony Creek. In the afternoon the scene switched to the park basketball court. It was during those long hot days that I began to question everything I'd been taught by the countless separations between black and white in Norristown. And I came to see that color was the only difference, as people, between us. And that's all it was: merely a difference, not an exclusion.

One of my best friends was Louis Darden, who was black. At one time or another Louis and I played on football, basketball, and track teams for Hartranft Elementary and Stewart Junior High. Louis was a happy-go-lucky guy. He was truly a player, not a worker, of games.

As the fastest boy at Hartranft, Louis was entered in the hundred-yard dash at the Norristown grade-school track-and-field meet. Something happened in that race which, even more than my own winning of the fifty-yard dash, remains as my most vivid memory of that day. The starter's gun went off and the six runners bolted down the cinder track. At the halfway mark it was clear that Louis was not going to win. The runner from Gotwals, Robert Lee, was well ahead of the pack. But Louis was still in the hunt for a second- or third-place medal, and in the grandstand I stood and cheered him on. About twenty yards from the tape, Louis looked to his left and right at his cinder-churning competitors, and suddenly he eased up, he slowed to a kind of whimsical prance, he threw his arms into the air and as the others raced over the finish line, he laughed.

I was stunned. I was outraged. Not that he lost, not even that he gave up. It was his attitude that bothered me most, lah-di-dahing twenty yards from the finish line. How dare he race and not care! How dare he lose and laugh! Didn't he know this was serious business? The championships of all the grade schools in Norristown, Pennsylvania! I—who took my sports, my baseball cards, my spelling, my life so seriously—could neither understand nor swallow it. Before all the world Louis Darden had disgraced himself. And what was he doing about it? He was laughing.

Two years later it was I who backed off and Louis who cared.

After school one day a group of us were playing basketball under a telephone-pole hoop outside Roger Adelman's backyard. In addition to Roger and me, Louis Darden, Joe Portano, and a few others were there. It fell to Joe Portano to guard me, and that was a mismatch, for Joe was not much of a basketball player. Big and burly, he was more at home in the trenches of a football game. A mouse by comparison, I scooted around him and scored at will. I didn't much note his increasing frustration until suddenly he kicked the ball into the weeds and came after me. He shoved me in the chest with the open palms of both hands. I went reeling backward. I regained my balance, and he slammed into me again, growling and scowling. And then Louis was between us, shoving Joe Portano in the chest, sending him backward, sending him away. There was no laughing this time, no lah-di-dahing, no messing around. For once Louis Darden was all business. Louis Darden, who hadn't cared about winning for himself, made sure that I didn't lose.

The boy who beat Louis in that hundred-yard dash, Robert Lee, was the same boy who'd clipped me on the chin when I was nine. I'm sure he had forgotten the incident long before we met in high school and became friends. By then my views were quite different. I was beginning to ask questions, though not yet out loud. And as was my habit, I fantasized.

I imagined Robert Lee and me back on that playground, and I imagined him again coming up to me and socking me. Only this time I don't turn away. This time I do not fear his color. This time I know that we are the same, and fear is replaced by respect, and because I respect him as I respect myself, I sock him back. And the two of us stare wide-eyed at each other, and then we nod and shake hands and go off together to shoot some marbles.

Louis Darden, 1954.

God and Garfield
Shainline

In 1994 I received a letter from an elementary school reader that ended with this:

"I got my whole life planned out. First I'm gonna grow up. Then I'm going to college. Then off to the air force we go. Then I retire to Hawaii. Then I die. Does that sound good to you?"

What it sounded like was something I myself might have written once upon a time. Except that I would probably have closed with "And then I go to heaven."

Heaven as I saw it would be the logical extension of my perfect attendance in Sunday school. As a military career can be deciphered from parade ribbons on a uniform, so my attendance record could be read on the lapel of my best sport coat. It started with a round blue pin, my reward for attending Sunday school thirteen weeks in a row—one fourth of a year. After twenty-six Sundays in a row, I turned in the blue pin for a red one. Another pin change occurred at week thirty-nine, and then after fifty-two straight Sundays—one year—I received a white pin, mine to keep forever.

A second year of perfect attendance ("perfect" in this case meaning at least forty-eight out of fifty-two

Sundays) earned me a gold wreath to go around my white pin. Then came the bars—red, white, blue—one per year, hanging from the wreathed pin like a little ladder. In time the proof of my perfection was nearly as long as my lapel.

Sometime in junior high, probably at a school dance, I became self-conscious of my Sunday school decorations, and from then on they stayed home.

By then, too, my image of God was changing. Earlier I had pictured God as an old fellow, bearded, abiding somewhere beyond the whipped cream fluffiness of that cumulus cloud out over Elmwood Park. Except for God's magical abilities, I would have been hard put to tell you the difference between him and the last surviving Civil War veteran.

As I got older, that view began to break up, to warp and fuzz over like a TV picture assaulted by interference. I waited and waited for the picture to clear, I fiddled with the dials, but I could not restore God's image to the clarity of my early years. They had taken God out of the coloring book and told me he was not an old man after all but a spirit, that he was not *there* or *there* but everywhere, not *then* or *then* but beyond all whenevers.

Like most kids, I did not take readily to abstraction. Whether tin cans or gods, I felt most comfortable with presences that I could see, could touch, could kick if need be, could hear skittering along a sidewalk. I still spoke to God every night in my prayers, but my sense of a listener had dissipated. How do you speak to both the other side of your pillow and the other side of the Milky Way? I blew my prayers like bubbles into the air and trusted them to winds I could not feel. Hiding by the stone piles during the nighttime games of outs, I gazed into the starry sky and searched the constellations for my Sunday school lessons, and perhaps when I was swooning over time and galaxies, I was swooning over God as well.

If I ever came close to meeting God, I think it was not in the stars but in Garfield Shainline.

For a man with such a big name, Garfield Shainline was quite little, not as short as a dwarf, but almost. As a thirteen-year-old, I was already taller than he. It was said that he shopped for clothes in children's departments. His white hair was crewcut. Tufts of black hair sprouted from his ears and from around a pea-size mole on his chin.

He worked at the YMCA in a wire mesh–enclosed compartment in the locker room. If you were taking a shower, you stopped at the cage and he handed you a small bar of white soap. I'm sure he had other duties, but to most of the boys in town, who never knew his name, that was the sum of who he was: the tiny old man at the Y who hands you soap.

But he was something else, too. When I was a teenager, he was my Sunday school teacher. Every Sunday morning we sat around a heavy round table in the

Christian Education Room of First Presbyterian: Garfield Shainline, Teddy Barrett, David Allen, Jay John, Douglas Nagy, me. We barely listened to him as we snickered and whispered and generally behaved like the immature adolescents that we were. We invented silly questions for him. We dared one another to yank out one of his mole hairs. Our favorite pastime was to pretend to drop something so that we had to bend under the table to retrieve it, there to behold the sight that brought us unending mirth: Garfield's tiny feet, shod in tiny brown leather hightop shoes, dangling in the air like a five-year-old's.

Each session concluded with an around-the-table prayer. Sometimes after the usual petitions for world peace and food for the hungry, someone would say, "And God bless Garfield and give him vitamins so he can grow and touch the floor."

Occasionally Garfield gave us a mild scolding, but mostly he smiled good-naturedly or ignored our nonsense and went on with the important thing, the lesson. No matter how we treated him one Sunday, he was glad to see us the next. Undeserving as we were, we received only the highest recommendations in his prayer.

Upon reaching high school age, we left Garfield behind for another teacher. One day someone told us he was ill and in the hospital and would love to have a visit from his boys, as he called us.

I thought about going to see him, but there were too

many other things to deal with: sports, grades, girls, friends. When I heard that he had died, I did not think much about it. I did not attend his funeral. Nor, I believe, did the others. But deep inside, even as I pretended to ignore my feelings, I sensed that something had changed forever. I pictured him in that hospital bed, waiting day after day for a visit that never came, and I knew—I *knew*—that in his final conscious hours, despite it all, he posted to heaven not a bitter thought about his boys.

Garfield Shainline has been long forgotten by most. Even my mother does not remember him. But I do. Oh, yes, I do. In these many years I have wished many times for him a second death, for myself a second chance. And still today he grows and grows inside of me, Garfield Shainline, the little man who hands you soap, and I have come at last to learn what he never knew he taught, that Garfield Shainline was not the teacher but the lesson.

Girls

The instant my mother saw my face, she gasped. It flashed through her mind that I had suddenly contracted measles or scarlet fever or some such red and rashy affliction. She pulled me farther into the light of the living room. It wasn't a disease—it was lipstick, red lippy patches of it all over my face. I had just come home from a birthday party at Nona Norris's. I explained that we had played some sort of game—the exact nature of which I don't recall—that resulted in all the girls mobbing one boy and smooching him dead with their red, oh-so-grownup lipsticky lips. My mother told me to go upstairs and wash it off. She remembers almost wishing it *had* been measles. I was seven years old. And I already had a girlfriend.

Judy Brooks.

Judy Brooks lived in a yellow-brick front-porch twin house half a block up the street, at 718 George. She wore her brown hair in pigtails. She could tie a dress bow behind her back. She jump-roped double Dutch. She could scream high enough to make dogs howl. She played jacks and handclap games. She whispered and giggled a lot.

We began our relationship in first grade, after I entered Hartranft Elementary partway through the year. I don't remember how I determined that she was my girlfriend, only that I thought of her that way, and that if someone said to me, as adults do, "Do you have a girlfriend?" I would say, "Yes." And the adult would say, "Who?" And I would say, "Judy Brooks."

There wasn't much more to it than that. As a romance, it could be better described by what did not happen as by what did. We did not hold hands, we did not kiss, we did not walk to school together, we did not even talk much to each other. I did, however, accompany her parents to a dance recital that she participated in. And one Saturday morning I went with her to her dentist, Dr. Wenof on Marshall Street. I remained behind in the waiting room while she bravely followed the nurse out of sight. Minutes later I heard her scream. I tensed. I fretted. Was she screaming for me? What were they doing to her? Was it...The Needle? Should I charge in and rescue her? I stewed for another minute or two, then returned to my comic book.

When I say we did not kiss, I mean there was no *we* kissing. Never did she kiss me while I, at the same time, kissed her back. But once, *I* kissed *her*. Whether I wanted to or not.

One day when we were ten, Judy Brooks and I were on the other side of the tracks, near the creek. I was showing her the best kind of rocks to find salamanders under when Eddie Carcarey showed up. This was not good news. Eddie Carcarey and I had been having our problems. They had begun about a year before when I decided to organize a gang and invited Eddie to join. Eddie was one tough hombre, and I figured he would give the gang some muscle. He joined but then refused to abide by the gang's only rule: to call me Captain. So I kicked him out. He retaliated by marching into our backyard in broad daylight and knocking over my mother's basket of clothespins.

And now Eddie Carcarey was coming toward Judy and me with mischief in his eyes.

"Pick her up," he said.

"Huh?" I said.

"Pick her up. Pick her up." His red hair and freckles flared with menace.

Judy was terrified. I imagine I looked terrified to Eddie as well, but in fact I wasn't. I had never picked up a girl before. I had never even *thought* about picking up a girl, but now that I was being ordered to do so, it didn't seem like such a bad idea. In fact, considering that the girl to be picked up was Judy Brooks, it seemed like a darn good idea.

I had seen plenty of pickups on television and in the movies, mostly cowboys hoisting ladies in long dresses who had fainted or sprained their ankle. So I figured I knew the basic move.

"Okay," I said, trying to sound scared.

While Judy stood rigid as a tree trunk, I positioned myself behind her and went through my pre-pickup sequence: spread and plant the feet, crouch, right arm behind her knee, left arm across her back, and—lift. In the movies the lady always came up smartly from the ground, as if she were on a swing, as if she were light as a balloon. It didn't go quite that way for me.

When I lifted, Judy's feet came up all right, as high as my shoulder, but the rest of her went down. Her head was around my knees, and now she was sliding toward the ground, her hand groping for my belt. I quickly dropped to one knee and propped her back against the other.

Eddie Carcarey sneered, "You're weak as an ant."

Maybe so, but I wasn't through yet. Driven not by Eddie Carcarey's sneer but by visions of Lash La Rue and Tex Ritter and how they would have done it, I pulled Judy into my butter pickle biceps, I squatted like a weightlifter, I took a deep breath, I heaved and grunted, and I picked her up. It wasn't a classic—her head and knees were high while her rear end sagged in the middle, giving her a V-shape. My arms turned to stone, my knees buckled under me. But I thought hard of Lash and Tex, and I held it for a good five seconds before I let her down.

"Now kiss her," Eddie said.

Good thing that's what he said, because the only part of my body not in muscular shock was my lips. I gave her a quick peck on the cheek, and that, to my recollection, was the first time I ever kissed a girl.

Eddie Carcarey trotted off, no doubt pleased with himself for forcing me to perform two distasteful acts.

That was the year Judy Brooks broke up with me. Well, strictly speaking, she didn't break up with *me*, she broke up with everyone. She announced that she was through with boys, she hated them all—"you all," I believe, is how she put it. I tried to find a loophole, but no matter how I looked at it, I was a boy, I was one of "you all." For the first time since first grade, I was single.

With a grim, gritting vengeance, I decided to retaliate by hating all girls, which I did successfully for three or four weeks—or was it three or four minutes? In any case, by sixth grade I had another girlfriend.

Bobbi Garber.

Like Judy Brooks, Bobbi Garber lived in the 700 block of George Street. She was one of three beautiful sisters, probably the most famous female threesome in town. The oldest sister, Randy, was Miss Montgomery County. Ruby was a cheerleader at Stewart Junior High. And the youngest, Roberta, called Bobbi, was in fifth grade, a year behind me, at Hartranft.

The Garber girls' father, Bill, was a car salesman on Markley Street, by the brewery. When I was in eighth grade, he sold us our first car, a turtle-green 1952 Pontiac.

Bobbi was a spitfire tomboy. We rode bikes around

the West End. We played in the street. And each school day at noon when classes let out for lunch, Bobbi waited with me at an alley that fed onto Chain Street half a block from school, next to Susan Davis's father's fish market. I was a lieutenant in the safety patrol, and it was my duty to stand at the alley and insure that the kids going home for lunch crossed it safely. I wore a white military-looking strap that circled my waist and looped up diagonally over one shoulder. Pinned to it was my badge, fancy silvered tin with an oval insert painted bright red. I guess I'll never know which dazzled Bobbi more, me or the badge.

I never gave Bobbi Garber a kiss, but I did give her something much more serious, as meaningful a token of my affection as I could manage, and frankly, a fairly painful sacrifice. I gave her my yo-yo. I have since wondered if I truly gave it as a token of affection, or was I finally getting rid of those infernal knots? Whatever, the romance dissolved when I went off to junior high. I never got my yo-yo back.

In seventh grade I moved on to the next level of kissing: lip to lip (or to be precise, teeth to teeth). Until then I had never kissed a female, not even my mother, on the lips, unless you count a few times when our dog Lucky surprised me with a wet one.

This innocent era came to a close on a spring evening in my thirteenth year. I was riding my bike after dinner. There were several hours of daylight left. I was cruising Haws Avenue. I had just made my daily pass of Dovie Wilmoth's house and had crossed Oak into the next block of Haws when I saw several classmates on the sidewalk in front of Kathy Heller's house. They called. I stopped.

Someone said, "Want to play?"

"What?" I said.

"Truth or consequences."

"Okay," I said.

Kathy was there. And Judy Pierson. And Kenny Hengen. And another girl. Apparently they were short on boys.

However the truth part of the game went, the consequence was always the same: You had to kiss a girl. I saw Kenny Hengen do it and thought, *Uh-oh.* He really got into it. Lip to lip, arms around the girl, eyes closed. The smooch seemed to go on for hours, right there on the sidewalk, broad daylight. I had stumbled into the big time. Was I ready for it? Why hadn't I just waved and kept on pedaling? I wished I were still a cowboy. Nearby waited my Roadmaster like a patient, faithful horse.

And then it was my turn. And there was blond-haired Kathy Heller, to whom I hardly ever spoke, with whom I had absolutely nothing in common, standing in front of me, taking off her glasses, awaiting her consequence. Had I time to practice, I might have rehearsed with a pillow or teddy bear. As it was, my lip-eye coordination was a trifle off. I did not so much kiss her as smash my face into hers. Our teeth met with an audible *clack*. But I stayed with it, and so did she. We disengaged teeth and backed off to lip depth and resumed blotting each other. I forgot to close my eyes, however, and to this day I have never had a better view of two eyebrows. When it seemed a respectable amount of time had elapsed, we stopped.

The kiss itself could not have lasted more than three or four seconds, but in my ruminations later it went on for weeks. I soon began to imagine that I had been as bold, smooth, and masterful as Kenny Hengen. Once or twice I heard my Roadmaster whinny, but it was only in my dreams.

When I Was King

It was January. Snow lay heaped outside Stewart Junior High School in the far West End of Norristown. Homerooms had dismissed an hour before, but dozens of ninth graders still milled about in the gym. Earlier that day we had voted for class officers, and we were waiting for the results.

I had run for class president, along with Bill Steinberg, Susan Lane, and Bob Peterson. A teacher came in and made the announcement. I had won. My old pal Roger Adelman had won, too; he was vice president.

I'm the second from the left, the newly elected class president of Stewart Junior High School. In the center is Roger Adelman, my friend and vice president.

I was happy, but I was also uncomfortable. The three other presidential contenders were my friends. In sixth grade Bill Steinberg had finished second to me in the grade-school fifty-yard dash. Now he was my best friend, and here he was trailing me to the finish line again. I apologized to him, he congratulated me, and I think we both took solace in knowing that he was already student council president and that he had gotten faster than I and that if we were to race right then, he would win.

Susan Lane and I had a close, nonkissing kind of relationship. We told each other things we told no one else. We appointed ourselves honorary brother and sister. We trusted each other. Once when a boy asked Susan for a date, she excused herself, hurried to a phone, and called me to ask if she should accept. When I won the election, I apologized to her, too.

I would have apologized to Bob Peterson as well, but I couldn't find him in the gym.

Once I got the apologies out of the way, I was free to feel good—and not just about winning the election. It seems I had won something else, too.

For several years I had admired Judy Pierson, mostly from afar. She had been in my grade at Hartranft, but she was always in the other class. She was at Kathy Heller's house on the Day of the Clacking Teeth, but I don't recall if I ever served as her consequence. In the early months of ninth grade, she had been Nick Salvatore's girlfriend.

But Nick Salvatore was not a basketball player—
and I was—and that led to an interesting coincidence
involving the "He's Our Man" cheer. In this cheer,
each of five cheerleaders was assigned the name of a
starting player—in this case Roger Adelman, Louis
Darden, Bob Hopple, Bruce Lindeman, or me. And so
it went:

"Roger! Roger!
He's our man!
If he can't do it!
Louis can!"

"Louis! Louis!..." and so on to:

"Team! Team!
They're our men!
If they can't do it!
Nobody can!"

To my delight, it was Judy Pierson who had my
name. Often the cheer was performed while we were
gathered around the coach during a time-out. To anyone looking at the huddling team, I must have appeared to be listening intently to the coach. As a
matter of fact, I was listening to Judy Pierson, her
lone girl voice echoing through the gym, calling my
name:

"Jerry! Jerry!"

I'm here, I wanted to say. And then I was listening to the bleachers pick it up and roar back at her:

"He's our man!"

And then I was peeking at her, at the arms churning, the orange and blue sweater:

"If he can't do it!"

And I was wondering, was it just dumb luck that she got my name, or had she made sure?

I had been hearing reports that since Christmas she had been less than happy with Nick Salvatore. And now I was in the gym not to play basketball but to accept congratulations for winning the election, and Nick Salvatore was nowhere in sight, and Judy Pierson was.

I walked her home that day, down snow-flanked sidewalks. She wore red mittens. Somewhere along Marshall Street I asked if I could hold her hand. She said yes.

There are few times in a life of which it can be said: Nothing is wrong. The twenty minutes that it took for Judy Pierson and me to walk from school to her house on Kohn Street was one such time. It was as if a train I had been riding had dropped me off at a solitary station, and the next train would not be along for twenty minutes. Gone were the shakes and sways and rattles of the old train, yet to come were the distant rumbling mysteries of the next. In the meantime there was only silence and stillness and a brisk cold white world and a girl who had taken off her mitten so that our hands could touch.

I left her at her house on Kohn Street and walked on. As I approached 718 George Street, I saw that my old girlfriend Judy Brooks was making out on the porch with Bob Peterson. I hoped to get by unnoticed, but they took a breath and saw me.

Bob, knowing that I had stayed after school for the election results, called, "Who won?"

I didn't have the heart to tell him. "I don't know," I said. "I left early."

At home that day, no one but Lucky was there to greet me. She yelped and jumped. Her white-tipped tail wagged so violently that it took her entire hindquarters along with it. Lucky, then, became the first in the family to hear that I had been elected class president—and the only one to hear whom I had walked home with.

Judy Pierson and I were now a couple. Each weekday morning one of us—whoever got there first (usually me)—waited for the other in front of Care's Drug Store, on the corner of Kohn and Marshall, and we walked to school together.

We went to school dances together. The dances were held on Friday nights, about one per month. We slow-danced and jitterbugged to 45-rpm records of Elvis Presley, Bill Haley and the Comets, and Ivory Joe Hunter singing "Since I Met You Baby." Once, my parents were chaperons. I danced with my mother while Judy danced with my father. It was now these dances, not Sunday school, that I saved my best outfits for.

On other Friday nights we walked downtown to the Norris movie theater, where we paid more attention to each other than to the screen. Across the street at the Garrick, Roy Rogers and Gene Autry still rode and yodeled through Saturday matinees, but I was no longer there.

On Saturday nights we walked up to Grace Lutheran Church on Haws Avenue. The church welcomed teenagers into a basement room for Ping-Pong, dancing, and refreshments. We danced to "Love Me Tender" by Elvis, "Gone" by Ferlin Husky, "Boppin' the Blues" by Carl Perkins and "The Great Pretender" by the Platters. The latter was "our song." If it came on while I was playing Ping-Pong with one of the guys, I put down my paddle and met Judy on the dance floor.

As the months went by, Judy Pierson and I took our place with such other high-profile couples as Kenny Hengen and Honey Magen, Judy Brooks and Bob Peterson, Marianne Stagliano and Bobby Ruth. We were "serious." We were "going steady." To prove it, Judy wanted a ring.

In Norristown in 1956, if you were going steady with a girl, you gave her a friendship ring. It was tradition. It was custom. Everybody did it. I balked. I told Judy that just because everybody else did it was no reason why we had to. In fact, I said, maybe it was a reason not to. Let's be uniquely us, I said, not like the crowd.

She didn't pester, she didn't pout. She didn't have to. Little by little the mice of conformity nibbled away at my resolve, until one Saturday morning I visited the jewelry shop on Marshall Street and forked over two dollars for a silvery circle of tiny hearts. Judy was thrilled, and before long I forgot why I had balked in the first place.

Hardly a day went by when Judy did not pass a note to me by way of a mutual friend. I've kept the notes in a large envelope all these years. They are written in pencil on low-grade classroom paper, sometimes lined. Most are folded repeatedly into small cubes. The most interesting exception unrolls like a narrow scroll and it measures exactly fifty-two and three-quarter inches long. Outer wrappings are addressed to JERRY SPINELLI ONLY or MR. SHORTSTOP. Warnings to would-be snoopers range from PRIVATE to DO NOT TOUCH UNLESS YOU ARE JERRY S. to HANDS OFF—THIS MEANS YOU!!!

The letters close with stacks of P.S.'s and parades of exclamation points and flocks of X's.

If I ever wrote a note to Judy, I don't remember. But

I did write notes to myself. Each morning on a small piece of paper I jotted words to remind me of things to talk about as we walked to school. I slipped the paper into my left—or street-side—pocket. If the conversation dragged as we walked up Marshall, I would pull out my crib sheet and take a quick, well-disguised peek.

As I reread Judy's letters, I discover they are an excellent reminder of who and where I was those many years ago. Phrases, sentences stand out:

> *Good luck this afternoon at the game.*

Almost every note says this or something like it. Games were serious business to me. I seldom got home before five o'clock, as I was always practicing after school. I shared quarterback duties with Bob Peterson on the football team, played guard in basketball, and, of course, shortstop in baseball. Ninth grade was my third year as a varsity starter, and though the curve ball still fooled me, I was as determined as ever to become a major leaguer.

> *I hope you win so you are in a good mood at the movies tonight…If a bad mood is good for your hitting, I hope you have a bad mood, but please get out of it by tomorrow.*

As I said, games were serious business—but not as serious as I led Judy to believe. It is true that I felt that putting on a grim "game face" ennobled me and signified my participation in boy stuff that Judy could only cheer about. God forbid I should play at sports as playfully as Louis Darden. It is also true that whenever we lost a game, I turned sullen and sulky. The hidden truth, however, is that this behavior was largely a show—a show for the benefit of the anti-Louis forces within myself and a show to elicit sympathy and admiration from my girlfriend.

I hope you are not still mad at me.

At first I was surprised at how many of the letters contain this sentence. But now that I think back, I do recall at times being possessive and picky and unreasonable and immature. Which is to say, I remember being fifteen.

Remember when you said you probably spoiled my plans about wearing high heels?

Forty years later I don't remember what I said, but I do remember my problems with high heels. Namely, they made her taller than I. How I envied six-foot two-inch Bobby Ruth, whose girlfriend Marianne Stagliano barely came up to his armpits. Happily for me, Judy was understanding, and if she owned a pair of high heels, she must have worn them only to church or in front of her mirror.

But there was nothing she could do about a sidewalk. Each morning on our trek up Marshall Street we came to a half-block stretch where the sidewalk sloped down toward the street, so that Judy, walking on the inside, suddenly became taller than I. I hated that stretch, and until we got through it I tended to drift toward the curb and pick up the pace.

Good luck in writing your speech!

After forty years, I fished it out of an old cardboard box: the valedictory speech I wrote, memorized, and delivered at our graduation from Stewart Junior High School on June 19, 1956. I read it aloud with an eye on the clock. It took less than three minutes. I was pleased to note that the speech was not embarrassingly pompous or stiff and that it even contained a stab at humor.

If people who were there remember anything at all about me that day, I am sure it is not my speech but my outfit: pink shirt with gold cuff links; jacket whose light brown speckled pattern has always made me think of the eggshell of a wild bird, perhaps quail or pheasant; white hanky peeking out of the upper pocket; cream-white linen pants; snow-white suede shoes—called bucks—with eraser-pink gum soles and heels. And the *pièce de résistance*, the tie: knit, square bottom, the perfect triangle of a double Windsor knot. The color was lemon yellow.

I hope you like me in my green gown.

Though it came last, graduation was not the climactic highlight of the year for me. That distinction belonged to the ninth-grade prom, which took place on a Saturday evening in May in the school gym.

After much deliberation Judy had chosen green—the color of her eyes—for her gown. She looked like a bridesmaid, as did all the girls. The skirt of the gown featured layers of stiff crinoline which, when she sat down, spread out like the wings of a brooding swan. No one could sit within three feet of her.

Judy's note about plans for wearing high heels referred to her prom footwear. She was in a quandary. On the one hand, for this occasion of all occasions, she wanted to wear heels. A girl just did not go to a prom in flats. On the other hand, she did not want to violate the Spinelli Ceiling.

One day she happily announced that she had solved the problem. She had bought a new pair of heels for the prom, but they were not high heels. They were low heels. I had not known there was such a thing. She assured me there was and that she would be wearing them and they would not make her too tall and I should just go and win whatever games I was playing and not worry about it. I worried anyway, and when the big night arrived and I in my white jacket and pink carnation went to call for her and nervously stood beside her in the vestibule of her home on 668 Kohn Street and saw that her green eyes were looking straight into mine, I discovered to my enormous relief that she was right.

But neither the color of the gown nor the height of the heels was the thorniest problem that night. Straps were. Perhaps recalling some unpleasantness from a previous prom, the school administration had decreed that gowns could not be strapless. The totally bare shoulder was forbidden. The month of May crackled with the fury of ninth-grade girls. They protested and pleaded. They enlisted Miss Bosler, our class sponsor, in their cause. They petitioned the office. The office would not back down.

Neither did the girls.

In the golden balmy twilight of May 25, the girls and their dates paraded down a corridor of cheering parents and flashing light bulbs to the main entrance of the school, the only time students ever entered that door. Revealed were not only the girls in their finery but also the extent to which they had stretched the definition of the word "strap." There were the merest strings and strands, filaments a spider would envy. One girl's strap was, literally, a thread from a spool. Another girl used eyeliner to paint straps on herself. There were dreamy wisps invisible from ten feet away, sugary confections that hovered above the bodice like a mist.

Some girls, to be sure, Judy Pierson among them, wore conventional straps. But they did so willingly, for hidden in their purses were scissors. Long before Bill March's band played "Goodnight, Sweetheart" for the last dance, every boy on the floor had a bare shoulder to nuzzle.

> *I'm so happy you're King, I always knew you would be. I'm glad I'm Queen with you.*

Judy Pierson and I did not merely go to the prom—we reigned. An hour into the evening all dancing came to a halt as the band struck up "Pomp and Circumstance." The royal couple and the court gathered on the sideline and began doing the hesitation walk (step right foot, pause, step left foot, pause...) along the midcourt line. The girls did it smoothly and naturally; the boys had had to practice, and still we kept messing up.

Me and Judy Pierson on our thrones, reigning over the ninth-grade prom (1956). Judy Brooks, my girlfriend from grades 1 to 4, is second from the right.

We marched to a raised platform that the prom committee had erected in the space between bleacher sections. Judy and I sat on our thrones while the court fanned out before us. Someone placed a wreath of flowers on Judy's head and a cardboard crown on mine. Raymond Morris, who was in my homeroom, had made it. The ends of the crown were stapled in back to make a circle. The color was sky blue, with glitter sprinkled like stars throughout. While the gym resounded with applause and whistles, a photographer from the *Times Herald* planted himself before us. He did not bow to the king and queen, but he did take a picture, which appeared in the paper the following week.

You will always be my King!!!

Johnson Highway

Lucky was dead.

As my brother and I stood over her, breathing hard from our dash to Johnson Highway, I wished I could believe otherwise. She lay in the street near the sidewalk. There was no blood. Her chest and paws were snowy white in the Sunday-afternoon light. But her eyes were open, she did not move, and I could not bring myself to touch her.

Lucky had been a house dog. She did not know about streets and cars.

I could feel Bill's eyes pleading. "Is she?"

I nodded.

We turned away and walked home. Bill cried. I held back. A neighbor called city hall about the body.

Lucky and me in better days (1953).

My life, once so tidy, so perfect, was coming apart. In those first two years at Norristown High, it seemed I lost everything I once had.

I was no longer the big-shot ninth grader in junior high. I was a nobody tenth grader in high school.

I lost my girlfriend not long after she lost the ring of tiny hearts. Her final note said: "Everyone should get away from each other for awhile."

I lost my leadership in the classroom. Whereas I had been a ninth-grade whiz at algebra, geometry in tenth grade befuddled me.

I lost the election for class president.

I lost Louis Darden, my friend and defender. I looked around one day and he was gone.

I lost my dream of becoming a major league baseball player. Though I played a pretty good shortstop for the junior varsity in tenth grade, the following year found me still on the JV's and still unable to hit the curve ball.

I lost my speed. In gym class and team practice races I found myself in the middle of the pack. Once I was even the monkey.

I lost my dog.

And most of all I lost George Street. Halfway through tenth grade we moved to Locust in the North End, where the cellars were called basements, where the furnace was fueled by gas, not coal. Our new home was a brick single-story twin with a driveway beside it for parking the car. It had a yard in front as well as in back. The sidewalk was gleaming concrete.

I lost George Street not only as a location in town but also as a neighborhood in time, a placid side pool of spear fields and black-taped baseballs, of Lash La Rue and grandstand cheers and Roadmaster roamings, a ten-year-long moment that gave me my sense of myself and the world around me. And then the rush of minutes was upon me and I was swept downstream. Instinctively I listened for Mrs. Seeton's whistle, but it did not reach the North End.

Bleak. Dismal. Dreary. Gray. These are the words that come to mind when I think of that time. In fact, the only sunny day I recall was the one on which Lucky died. I do not mean to say that I gave up. I went out for sports, did my homework, went to school dances with the guys. I got my driver's license. I was still just as friendly as I had been a year before, just as neat, just as earnest. But whereas life had once responded by making me king and valedictorian and president, now I was getting election condolences and C's in geometry. Life, like my girlfriend, had dumped me. My string was nothing but knots.

I visited George Street, trying to feel again how it had been. I rode past Dovie Wilmoth's house on Haws Avenue, this time in the family's turtle-green Pontiac. I walked along the railroad tracks humming "Pomp and Circumstance," doing the hesitation step. In my bedroom I touched the cardboard prom crown, now hanging from a corner of my dresser mirror.

When I looked up at night, I discovered that the stars over Locust Street were in the same places as they had been over George, only now they seemed even farther away. They did not inspire me to think of endlessnesses of time and space, they did not make me swoon. They simply made me feel little and lost. Late one night, still awake, I saw tiny sparkles in the dark, as if the starry sky had fallen into my bedroom. It took a minute to realize that I was seeing glitter fallen from the prom crown, a sprinkling on the floor by my dresser, invisible during daylight, caught now in the moonbeam streaming through the window.

On Friday evening, October 11, 1957, at Roosevelt Field, site of my fifty-yard-dash triumph five years before, Norristown High School played Lower Merion in a football game under the lights. Lower Merion was a powerhouse. Over the preceding three years they had won thirty-two games in a row. But Norristown was good, too. It figured to be a close, fiercely contested game, and it was. I was a junior now, sixteen years old, and my autumn sport had become soccer, but I still loved football. I was one of thousands in the grandstand.

As the teams changed field direction for the start

of the fourth quarter, Norristown was leading, 7–6. Each team had scored a touchdown, but the Aces of Lower Merion had missed the extra point. But now a Lower Merion halfback was breaking free and racing downfield, blue-and-white-shirted Norristown Eagles in pursuit. The Eagles stopped him on the one-yard line, and the stage was set for one of the great moments in Norristown's scholastic sports history.

First down and goal to go on the one. One little yard. Thirty-six little inches. Lower Merion. Thirty-two straight victories. Who could stop them? In the bleachers across the field the Lower Merion fans celebrated. Norristown fans grimly awaited the inevitable.

The first Ace ball carrier plunged ahead helmet-first, the Lower Merion side erupted in a touchdown roar—but, strangely, no touchdown sign came from the referee. The ball carrier was crumpled in the rude arms of Eagle defender Mike Branca. The ball had advanced nary an inch.

Twice more the Aces ran the ball, attacking different points in the Eagle defense. The results were the same. The sound from the Lower Merion side was rising and falling as if directed by a choirmaster. But now, as the Ace quarterback bent over the center for the fourth time and barked out the count, Roosevelt Field fell silent. For the fourth time the Ace quarterback handed the ball to a running back—they refused to believe anyone could stop them from ramrodding the ball thirty-six little inches—and for the fourth time the ball failed to penetrate the end zone.

The impossible had been done.

Now it was the Norristown side that erupted, with a roar and a celebration that continued through the end of the game and burst from the stadium and spread out across the town and late into the night. I rode the tide. Lower Merion! We had beaten *Lower Merion!* I couldn't believe it. At home in my room I could hear the blaring horns, the shrieks of victory.

Again and again, following my old habit, I replayed the miraculous Eagle goal-line defense in my head. I went to sleep re-experiencing the event, re-feeling the thrill. In the morning I woke up and daydreamed on—and began to realize that I had a problem. For no matter how many times I replayed the goal-line stand in my head, I kept falling short of satisfaction. The scoreboard had said the game was over, but for me it wasn't, for me it was somehow frustratingly incomplete. I discovered that Roosevelt Field was not the only field that the game had been played on; the other was inside myself. The game kept happening and happening within me. I could not come to the end of it.

And then for no reason that I can recall, I sat down at my study desk and reached for a pencil and paper and wrote down a title. Then I began to write rhyming verses. And the verses became a poem:

Goal to Go

The score stood 7–6
With but five minutes left to go.
The Ace attack employed all tricks
To settle down its stubborn foe.

It looked as though the game was done
When an Ace stepped wide 'round right.
An Eagle stopped him on the one
And tumult filled the night.

Thirty-two had come their way
And thirty-two had died.
Would number thirty-three this day
For one yard be denied?

Roy Kent, the Eagle mentor, said,
"I've waited for this game,
And now, defense, go, stop 'em dead,
And crash the Hall of Fame!"

The first Ace bolted for the goal
And nothing did he see
But Branca, swearing on his soul,
"You shall not pass by me."

The next two plays convinced all
The ref would make the touchdown sign,
But when the light shone on the ball
It still lay inches from the line.

Said Captain Eastwood to his gents,
"It's up to us to stop this drive."
Said Duckworth, Avery, Knerr, and Spence,
"Will do, as long as we're alive."

The halfback drove with all his might,
His legs were jet-propelled,
But when the dust had cleared the fight,
The Eagle line had held.

At last, for me, the game was over.

Fargo, North Dakota

On a September day in 1992, thirty-five years after Norristown High's historic goal-line stand, I stood before an audience of children and adults in Fargo, North Dakota. I was there in connection with my novel *Maniac Magee*, which had recently won the Newbery Medal for children's literature. The important award on this day, however, was the Flicker Tale, which had been voted to *Maniac Magee* as a favorite of North Dakota's young readers. A hundred elementary-school kids sat crosslegged on the floor as I accepted the plaque.

After giving a little talk, I invited the audience to ask questions. There were many. One of them stays with me still. It came from a boy, who said, "Do you think being a kid helped you to become a writer?"

Good question.

After writing "Goal to Go," I gave it to my father and forgot about it. Several days later I opened the *Times Herald* to the sports section, and there was my poem, printed in a box with the headline "Student Waxes Poetic." At school the next day everyone—kids, teachers, football coaches—told me how much they liked it.

That, I believe, was the beginning. By the time I went off to Gettysburg College two years later, I knew I wanted to be a writer.

I graduated from Gettysburg, attended the Writing Seminars at the Johns Hopkins University, spent six months on active duty with the Naval Air Reserve, got a job as a menswear editor for a department store magazine, and in my spare time began to write my first novel.

Three years later I finished it, but no one wanted to publish it. So I wrote another.

And another.

And another.

Wrote them on my lunch hours, after work, weekends. Four novels over thirteen years.

Nobody wanted them.

In the meantime I gained a wife, Eileen, also a writer, and six kids. One day for dinner we had fried chicken. There were leftovers. I packed the unclaimed pieces into a paper bag and put it in the refrigerator, intending to take it to work for lunch the following day. But when I opened the bag early the next morning, I found only chicken bones. The meat had been eaten away.

No doubt this was the work of one of the six little angels sleeping upstairs. Knowing no one would confess (I'm still waiting), I went to work that day lunchless and began to imagine how it might have gone had I known who the culprit was and confronted him or her in the kitchen. By noon I decided to write down my imaginings. I was about to do so, intending to describe the scene from the point of view of the chicken-deprived father, when it suddenly occurred to me that there was a more interesting point of view here—namely, the kid's.

And so with ballpoint pen and yellow copy paper in a tiny windowless office on the fifth floor of the Chilton Company in Radnor, Pennsylvania, I wrote these words:

> One by one my stepfather took the chicken bones out of the bag and laid them on the kitchen table. He laid them down real neat. In a row. Five of them. Two leg bones, two wing bones, one thigh bone.
>
> And bones is all they were. There wasn't a speck of meat on them.
>
> Was this really happening? Did my stepfather really drag me out of bed at seven o'clock in the morning on my summer vacation so I could stand in the kitchen in my underpants and stare down at a row of chicken bones?

That night at home I kept writing. I gave the chicken snatcher a name, Jason, and an age, twelve. And I started remembering. Remembering when I was twelve, when I lived in the West End, when I went to Stewart Junior High School, when I wanted to be a shortstop, when I rode a bike, when I marveled at the nighttime sky. In my head I replayed moments from my kidhood. I mixed my memories with imagination to make stories, to make fiction, and when I finished writing, I had a book, my fifth novel, my first about kids. I called it *Space Station Seventh Grade*.

It became my first published book.

In the years that followed, I continued to write stories about kids and to rummage through the attic of my memories. Norristown became Two Mills in my fiction, George Street became Oriole. There is a prom in one book and a girlfriend named Judy in another. There is a beautiful blonde who lives on an avenue called Haws and a mysterious man on whose front steps no kid dares sit. There is a zep and a mulberry tree, a Little League field, a park, a zoo, a band shell, a red hill, and a mother who whistles her kids home to dinner. There is a river called Schuylkill and a creek called Stony and a grocery store on a corner next to a house whose address is 802. And a brown finger in a white mouth. And a boy who is a wizard at untying knots in yo-yo strings.

Do you think being a kid helped you to become a writer?

I could have taken days to answer the boy's question, but neither he nor Fargo had that much time. So I simply nodded and smiled and said, "Yes, I believe it did."

Books by Jerry Spinelli

About the Author

Jerry Spinelli is the author of more than a dozen books for young readers, including *Maniac Magee*, winner of the 1991 Newbery Medal, *Wringer*, winner of a 1998 Newbery Honor Award, and *Crash*. A graduate of Gettysburg College, Jerry lives with his wife, Eileen, not far from where he grew up.

Jerry Spinelli, age 11

Jerry Spinelli, today